TOTAL WAR

PETER CALVOCORESSI,
GUY WINT AND JOHN PRITCHARD

TOTAL WAR

THE CAUSES AND COURSES OF
THE SECOND WORLD WAR

Volume One:
The Western Hemisphere

REVISED SECOND EDITION

PANTHEON BOOKS · NEW YORK

Copyright © 1989 by John Pritchard and Peter Calvocoressi
1972 by Peter Calvocoressi and Ben Wint

Grateful acknowledgment is made to George Weidenfeld & Nicolson Limited, Marboro Books, Macmillan Publishing Company, and Martin Gilbert for permission to use maps on pages 116, 122, 135, 175, 187, 194, 202, 241, 245, 247, 256, 258, 360, 469, 471, 483, 496, 502, and 546, which have been adapted from the following previously published works:

Russian History Atlas edited by Martin Gilbert. Cartography by
Arthur Banks. Copyright © 1972 by Martin Gilbert.

Recent History Atlas edited by Martin Gilbert. Cartography by John
Flower. Copyright © 1966 by Martin Gilbert.

Jewish History Atlas edited by Martin Gilbert. Cartography by Arthur
Banks. Copyright © 1969, 1976 by Martin Gilbert.

American History Atlas edited by Martin Gilbert. Cartography by
Peter Kingsland. Copyright © 1969 by Martin Gilbert.

Library of Congress Cataloging-in-Publication Data
Calvocoressi, Peter.
Total war : causes and courses of the Second World War / Peter
Calvocoressi, Guy Wint, John Pritchard.—2nd rev. ed.
p. cm.
Includes bibliographical references and index.
Contents: v. 1. The Western Hemisphere—v. 2. The Greater East
Asia and Pacific conflict.
ISBN 0-679-73091-5 (v. 1).—ISBN 0-679-73099-0 (v. 2)
1. World War, 1939–1945.   I. Wint, Guy, 1910–1969.
II. Pritchard, R. John.   III. Title.
D743.C24 1990   90-52557

Manufactured in the United States of America

Pantheon Paperback Edition

Contents

The Western Hemisphere

Part I
THE SOURCES OF WAR IN EUROPE

Part II
HITLER'S WARS: 1939–41

Contents

Part III
EUROPE UNDER THE NAZIS

Part IV
THE MIDDLE GAME

Part V
THE DEFEAT OF GERMANY: 1942–5

List of Illustrations

List of Maps

List of Maps

Acknowledgements

Acknowledgement is due to Martin Gilbert of Merton College, Oxford, to
  Weidenfeld & Nicolson Limited, and to the Macmillan Company for their
  kind permission to use the maps on pages 116, 122, 135, 175, 187, 194, 202,
  241, 245, 247, 256, 258, 360, 469, 471, 483, 496, 502 and 546, which have been
  adapted from the following: *American History Atlas*, edited by Martin Gilbert,
  cartography by Peter Kingsland, copyright © Martin Gilbert, 1969; *Jewish
  History Atlas*, edited by Martin Gilbert, cartography by Peter Kingsland,
  copyright © Martin Gilbert, 1969; *Recent History Atlas*, edited by Martin
  Gilbert, cartography by John Flower, copyright © Martin Gilbert, 1966;
  Russian History Atlas, edited by Martin Gilbert, cartography by Arthur Banks,
  copyright © Martin Gilbert, 1972.

Foreword to the Second Edition

WHEN this book was being written early in the seventies no governmental archives were generally open to the public. Now many are. This is the first of two important differences between the book's first edition and that which is now presented. The second is the death of Guy Wint – he died in fact before completing his work – and the new partnership of John Pritchard and myself in the preparation of this new edition.

It has frequently been observed that the opening of official archives reveals little or nothing. This sweeping judgement is a useful corrective to the view that history is enshrined, often entombed, in official papers, and it is true enough in so far as it asserts that official disclosure rarely produces revelations of major significance. But such disclosure has two important historical consequences. It exposes a mass of detail, and even if the details are in themselves mostly trivial the accumulation of them is not. In particular, the historian's ability to wallow in these details helps him to enter into the minds of those who guided, or tried to guide, or thought they were guiding, the march of events; to understand – whether sympathetically or not – why they thought as they did and acted as they did, and to readjust the impact upon them of the kaleidoscope of circumstances. Within the ambit of this book the opening of the archives compels and facilitates a reassessment of the politics of appeasement in the 1930s – to which I shall revert.

The second important consequence of the opening of the archives is that it loosens tongues and sharpens pens. It stimulates the memoir industry. This is partly a mere matter of time as men and women who have taken part in memorable events find the leisure in advancing age to recollect and write. But many hesitate to do so and they may be encouraged to put pen to paper, or to face the microphone or the camera, when the past is stirred up by official publications, whether raw materials exposed in public record offices or official histories made out of the storehouses of public papers. There is what may be called the secondary scope of disclosure: the memoirs of the people, mostly in high places, who write of themselves and their immediate experience, and also the testimony of humbler men and women who would normally remain silent but whose stories are elicited, and whose diaries are dug out, by historians anxious to put the flesh of ordinary humanity on to the skeleton of history. The non-official literature generated by official disclosure is voluminous and varied. Alongside the books by or about leading statesmen and commanders are the equally pertinent down-to-earth accounts garnered by, for example, John Keegan in his *Six Armies in Normandy* or Studs Terkel in his *The Good War*.

In reading this mass of secondary material I have gleaned suggestions and found facts which have caused me to correct or helped me to sharpen a number of episodes in this book and so, I hope, to increase its veracity and readability: for example, on the loss of Crete, the battle of the Mareth, the bombing of Monte Cassino. Other episodes have been rewritten owing to a special circumstance – the revelations about Ultra intelligence – of which I shall have more to say later in this Foreword. But I have not found myself induced to alter the principal judgements about the course of the war which were contained in the original edition.

I revert to the official archives. Their main impact – and here I refer to the British archives – is on the prewar years and appeasement. In short, the perusal of British Cabinet papers leads me to a somewhat more charitable assessment of British policy-makers but not to the belief that they were right to shirk war in 1938.

The charges against the appeasers have fallen into two main categories: that they were benighted by their ideological prejudices and therefore soft on Fascism and Nazism, and secondly that their consequent feebleness (particularly at the time of Munich) did more to endanger than to succour Great Britain, France and Hitler's other European victims. What the official records show is that the British cabinet was genuinely concerned about a factor which has not received its due prominence – the danger to British interests and British obligations from Japan. Neville Chamberlain and his colleagues may have been blinkered rightists but this was not the only or main source of their attempts to appease Mussolini and Hitler or of their shameful (and it remains shameful) betrayal of Czechoslovakia. They had worries in the Far East to which they rightly attached major importance and which to a significant extent tied their hands. Yet this is not to say that they steered a sensible course.

There is a clear distinction to be drawn between trying to detach Mussolini from Hitler (which was not only highly desirable but also well worth the effort in spite of the eventual failure) and trying to stop Hitler's expansion by throwing him chunks of Europe. If, as I still believe, the latter policy was never likely to succeed (read *Mein Kampf* and Hitler's speeches *passim*), the question that arose was how to weigh the loss of Czechoslovakia's armoury, armed forces and morale against the risk that

Japan would, in 1938, use war in Europe as an opportunity to make war against British and French possessions in South East Asia and the Pacific and against the British dominions of Australia and New Zealand. This question is not one that can be answered but it has to be put because the repute of British and French leaders of that time depends on whether they are judged in retrospect to have weighed the imponderables well or badly. Japan did go to war but not in 1938 or 1939 or even 1940 when Great Britain and France became actively engaged in war. Hitler was not deterred from war by appeasement, although his attacks on Czechoslovakia and Poland were postponed until 1939 and his attacks in the west until 1940. I still believe, as will be evident in the body of this book, that a war in 1938 would have been more easily won than the awful and chancy conflict of 1939–45, and that it would have been saner in 1938 to gamble with the Japanese threat than to eliminate Czechoslovakia from the anti-German alliance.

The principal addition to Part I of this book concerns Ultra intelligence – the decipherment, sufficiently promptly for operational use, of German high-grade Enigma ciphers used by the three armed services, the SS and certain other agencies. When I was writing the first edition of this book, which was published in 1972, I knew all about Ultra because I had worked on it at Bletchley Park during the war. The Ultra secret was about to be broken but I did not know that and I was personally bound to keep it. I made some discreet inquiries about the possibility of being released, perhaps partially, from my obligations. I was given to understand that if I broke my promise there was not much that anybody could do without looking silly, but I decided that my proper course was to observe my promise. I suspected that the continuing secrecy had become unnecessary but I could not be sure of it at that date. Later, I became convinced that the secrecy was pointless and after some discussion with persons better placed to know I tried to persuade a British Prime Minister that there was much to be said for allowing it to be known that the British Secret Service, even more renowned for its treasonable inmates than for its achievements, had in fact made an exciting and decisive contribution to winning the war. My efforts were rebuffed shortly before the secret was allowed to poke its nose out of the bag.

Part I of this book was therefore written in the full knowledge of certain things which I might neither mention nor explain. I recall in particular how my friend and editor at Penguin, Dieter Pevsner, upon reading my first version of the Battle of the Atlantic, told me that he thought it was splendid but made no sense. He was of course right since I had left out the determining factor. This was the most blatant case but there were other passages where the balance of my presentation was distorted by the suppression of the Ultra ingredient. I still, incidentally, do not know whether the Russians read Enigma ciphers. There are many reasons for supposing that they did not. Yet it remains difficult to account for the completeness of their post-Stalingrad tank victories without suspecting some element – Enigma or something else – which has not yet come to light.

In this new edition I have introduced the story of the breaking of the Enigma ciphers and its effect on the war at various times and places. As I was at pains to point out in my book *Top Secret Ultra*, this effect varied greatly: Ultra could be crucial but it never provided complete and prompt coverage of all German military activities. Besides its contribution to the defeat of the U-boats in the Atlantic it was massively useful in North Africa and copious before and after the landings in Normandy in 1944 – I have rewritten, among other things, my account of the battle of the Ardennes. Ultra shed light on such diverse corners of the war as German scientific developments and who was doing or not doing what in Yugoslavia. Most important was its cumulative and (since it came from the Germans themselves) authoritative revelation of the overall size of the German sea, air and ground forces, their capacities, equipment and dispositions, thereby giving the allied side an unprecedented familiarity with the enemy's strengths and limitations. Like so many things about the war this story is not yet fully told. Not all the relevant British documents have been released and some have been destroyed. In the pre-war story of Enigma the Poles hold pride of place for the brilliant intellectual work which enabled them, and them alone, to read Enigma ciphers before the war. Yet it is also becoming clear that a critical element in this success was presented to the Poles by the French and, furthermore, that the French got it before the Nazi seizure of power from a German working in the German cipher office.

John Pritchard's task in Part II has been the more difficult one, for unlike myself he has had to review another man's work. He has done so with a strong admiration for Guy Wint's scholarship, perceptiveness and literary style. He has also two different starting points: first, as a man of a younger generation and, secondly, as an expert primarily in Japanese matters, whereas Wint's erudition was focused on China and India, which he knew and loved well. To my mind all these points – the basic admiration, the difference in age and the diffraction of viewpoint – are manifest advantages. Much of what Guy Wint wrote is unchanged, notably in relation to China, India and Burma. But in other areas John Pritchard's contribution is decisive. Drawing largely on fourteen years' work on the documents of the Tokyo War Crimes Trial he amplifies and corrects our picture of Japan which, even in those aspects where it remains extremely unattractive, becomes historically intelligible rather than simply demoniacal. Thus he digs deep into the reasons why Japan ran amok in China and exhibited in this century a savagery untypical of Japan in the nineteenth century. He re-examines relevant features of the Japanese constitution, the nature and consequences of the factional fighting between the Japanese army and navy, and the roots of Japanese extremism. While stressing no less than Guy Wint the importance of the Manchurian Incident and the transformation of Manchukuo into an industrial and colonial powerhouse, he portrays this extraordinary achievement in terms of Japanese creativity as well as Japanese power. He brings out the significance for Japan of Russian activities in northern Asia, from the construction of the Trans-Siberian Railway a hundred years ago to the murderous Russian comeback in Manchuria in 1945. He dismisses the notion that the British were taken by surprise by the Japanese onslaught on their possessions in 1941: the British fault was not ignorance but the inability to decide what to do about a menace foreseen, alternating between the itch to dispatch the Royal Navy to teach Japan a lesson and playing it cool and hoping for the best. With the war over, the American régime of General MacArthur emerges as not merely dictatorial, which was not in the circumstances surprising, but also as flouting the terms of the Emperor's surrender.

Passing time changes more than the store of knowledge. Attitudes change too. The first readers of this book were prompted, I surmise, mainly by wonder. They wanted to know how and why this terrible war, which they had experienced and survived, had come about; and how it ran its course, with what shifts and turns, what inventions, skills and pieces of luck. This curiosity was allied with the simple convictions of right and wrong which had ruled during the war; wartime loyalties persisted for a time in post-war exhilaration and relief, equally unquestioning, providing their own scale of values. A later generation has other needs. The curiosity is still there, but an audience further removed from the intensities of war is more critical. It takes less for granted and sees no reason not to query particular reputations or general strategies, ours as much as theirs. War leaders, military and civilian, are subjected to the beady eye of posthumous inquest, which is sometimes justified by the resulting verdicts although it may in some cases smell of a distasteful iconoclasm. Strategies which, during the war, were judged purely in terms of their war-winning efficacy are reviewed and censured in moral terms which the warriors themselves would have dismissed as a luxury rightly banished from the calculation of their wartime exigencies.

War leaders inevitably loom larger than life so long as they are in charge. They become known to, and therefore misunderstood by, thousands of people who have barely heard of them before. This was particularly the case with Churchill and Roosevelt as allied leaders. For the British, Roosevelt was a towering American personality. They were oblivious of the fact that all his life Roosevelt was an object of bitter controversy in his own country. They were oblivious too of the further fact that throughout the period between the wars Anglo-American relations were normally bad. On the American side Churchill was portrayed and accepted with the lineaments of legendary and archetypal heroism, in ignorance of his record as a maverick and inconstant politician whom the electorate would dump as soon as the war was over. Wartime reputations are not made to last. Yet I would argue that these were greater men than their contemporaries and it is a mistake to disinter their evident failings if the object of doing so is to deny them this eminence.

More generally, the conduct of the war has been more critically examined. There was some criticism at the time: for example, British protests against area bombing of civilian targets and criticism in and beyond the United States of the bombing of Hiroshima and Nagasaki without at least some warning. The annihilation of these two cities and so many of their inhabitants shocked by its novelty as much as by its enormity but the first revulsion against this supreme act of destruction was confined to the few. The point is that those few have got no fewer with the passing of time, while the equally frightful bombing of Dresden has evoked, on its fortieth anniversary, passionate recrimination. (This is an instance where official disclosure and the ensuing arguments have not only left my initial judgement unchanged but have reinforced it: I find myself more than ever convinced that this operation lacked the rigorous justification which so fearful a slaughter of undefended civilians requires and – the crucial point – did require even in the press of war.)

The probing of the conduct of the war, alongside the desire to retrace its fortunes, demonstrates that the Second World War now commands attention for two distinct reasons: as a self-contained event in time, and as an example of the species war. This expanded focus of the historical viewpoint prompts two reflections. The first concerns morality and legality in war and the second concerns the status of its opposite – peace – in our post-war scale of values.

The fact that the war was fought against evil Nazis or, to be more guarded, that the war fought to curb German power incidentally entailed the destruction of Nazism – made it for many people a good war. Our side was right. The terrible suffering and devastation had to be. The Middle Ages, trying to justify wars, evolved two sets of tests called *jus ad bellum* and *jus in bello*. The first laid down rules for deciding whether the waging of a particular war was right in the first place. The second set tried to regulate behaviour once war had started. Medieval churchmen and lawyers attached much importance to *jus ad bellum*, which enabled them to distinguish legitimate wars from illicit ones and so to sanctify war on at least some occasions with a clear conscience. To *jus in bello* on the other hand they paid relatively perfunctory attention. That imbalance has been redressed in modern times and nowadays the Hague and Geneva Conventions on permissible and impermissible weaponry and on the treatment of civilians, neutrals, prisoners and others (the descendants of *jus in bello*) are taken no less seriously than restrictions on the right to make war in other international instruments. The conduct of war has become as much a matter of moral concern as its initiation. Hence the concentration in recent years, by a general public as well as lawyers, on the more dubious episodes in the Second World War and what these ready lapses into morally and legally impermissible acts may portend for the future.

Secondly, war itself – as distinct from the ways in which it may be waged – is once more a matter for debate. When the Second World War ended, the prevailing view, which amounted to an unquestioned assumption, was to the effect that nothing like it must be allowed to happen again: peace is paramount. In that spirit the victors took the lead in creating the United Nations (more or less in the image of the League of Nations) and, by Article 2 of the UN Charter, in removing from the state the right to make war except in tightly restricted circumstances. The Japanese went further still and in their post-war constitution explicitly denied the right of the state to belligerency. This novel ban on warfare, in either form, was one of the principal consequences of the Second World War and its horrors. I do not feel confident that this primacy of peace still prevails, least of all among leaders of Superpowers. The antithesis of war and peace is most blatant and compelling in the immediate aftermath of war, but gradually other values reassert themselves and people come to think, as many thought in the 1930s, that there are worse things than war: injustice, for example, or tyranny or systematic and pervasive torture. Just as medieval Christians honestly believed it right to go to war to convert pagans or kill heretics, so today, their modern counterparts have seen virtue in crusading expeditions to impose democracy (the Reagan line) or preserve communist socialism (the Brezhnev doctrine). The trouble with such notions is that they relegate peace to a subordinate place in our scale of values and, furthermore, that they are all too easily, perhaps inevitably, shaped by national self-interest rather than the disinterested virtues which they proclaim. When peace is no longer paramount, when statesmen cast casuistically about for ways of side-stepping the laws of armed conflict or reinterpreting the Charter, then the bestiality of war is that much easier on the mind and that much nearer in practice. Of such attitudes the course of the Second World War is a standing indictment, never to be forgotten.

PETER CALVOCORESSI
BATH, 1988

The Western Hemisphere

Introduction to the Second Edition

THE years 1870 to 1945 were the period in which Europe feared Germany. Before that it was France, afterwards the Soviet Union. In this perspective the Second World War is the end of an era.

In this period much was lost. The European states system disintegrated. One international economic order foundered and was not replaced by another. Concurrently with these two great dislocations Europe's primacy in the world disappeared. Given the centrality of Germany – geographical and dynamic – much retrospective attention has been focused on German responsibility, even (which is not the same thing) culpability, in this tide of events.

The European states system, which evolved and prevailed over the eighteenth and nineteenth centuries, gave priority to the state over the system – it was a system in which the whole was subordinate to the parts – but nevertheless it was a political reality recognized and used by statesmen. It rested on the proposition that where there is a plurality of states there is a community of interests; and that these common interests may be served by constant communication and mutual accommodation, even though the ultimate sovereign right to decide and act unilaterally is retained. The working of such a system required two crucial pre-conditions: that the states which mattered should be few but not too few, and that for most of the time most of them should prefer peace to war and find the system useful in keeping the peace. Its principal feature was balance. It had inherent mobility between its parts, and statesmanship was largely defined by the capacity of statesmen to manage the balancing through alliances and reversals of alliances. It was at risk whenever it became rigid through incompetent management or when any principal statesman had no use for it: that is to say, in the first case, when too many of its possible permutations were blocked or, in the second, when a man like Hitler preferred (to adapt Ludwig Dehio's phrase) *Hegemonie* to *Gleichgewicht*, empire to system. It was also at risk when the sovereign states, which were its components, became too numerous and unequal in power and resources, particularly when (as happened after 1919) the Great Powers were reduced in number and new, lesser states proliferated.

After 1870 Bismarck's new Reich was the greatest industrial and military power in Europe. Bismarck preferred *Gleichgewicht* to *Hegemonie* but he fashioned for his successors a Europe which was not only re-shaped by German victories but also systemically constricted by two fateful acts: the annexation of Alsace and Lorraine in 1871 and his treaty with Austria in 1879. The first eliminated from the system any Franco-German permutation and therefore weakened the system itself; the second tied Germany to Austria's ambitions and apprehensions in the Balkans when the last stage in the slow Ottoman retreat from Europe was setting the Habsburg against the Russian monarchy in south east Europe. Bismarck's successors, often more liberal than he but never as powerful or intelligent, failed to extricate themselves from this unnecessary strait-jacket. That is part of Germany's responsibility for the onset of the First World War. There were other parts, by no means all of them German, although two German factors contributed powerfully to the trend to war: the personality and antics of Kaiser William II, not a bad man but an uneducated one; and the post-Bismarckian attempt to challenge British naval power in the world as well as throw German weight about on the continent. These two factors put paid to another of the system's possible permutations: an Anglo-German condominium.

The two World Wars have obscured the extent to which Great Britain and Germany entertained good feelings for one another throughout most of the period from Bismarck to Hitler. Von Tirpitz and Hitler were potent destroyers of these feelings, but before the First World War there were inklings of an Anglo-German joint power structure, while after that war and the abdication of the Kaiser, British statesmen were keen to re-establish relations with Germany and restore it to the comity of European states – as France had been embraced in the Concert of Europe after the abdication of Napoleon. Great Britain even pursued this endeavour for several years after Hitler became Chancellor and then President in a Third German Reich. One of the main paradoxes of the period under discussion is the tenacity of British hostility in wartime to a country with which, for most of the time, Great Britain had no quarrel.

In the First World War Germany defeated Russia and was then defeated by a western alliance; in the second, Germany was defeated on both fronts. Among the consequences of the first war were the disappearance for ever of the Habsburg and Ottoman empires; the revolution in Russia, which removed the Tsarist monarchy and, with the aftermath of foreign invasions and civil war, removed Russia itself from European affairs for a generation; the emergence in eastern (but not western) Europe of a string of new or revived or enlarged states, all of them economic weaklings and none of them adept performers in a European states system; the reduction therefore of the managers of that system from five or six to two (or three, if Italy be accounted a competent and willing third); and the enfeeblement of Germany, prolonged until the time when it was able by its own exertions to reclaim its place in Europe on its own terms.

The instrument of the curbing of Germany was the treaty of Versailles. In 1919, as during the Second World War, plans for partitioning Germany were abandoned and its French proponents had to be content with a limited occupation of parts of the Rhineland, the emasculation of Germany's armed forces, a swingeing bill of costs and a (broken) promise of an Anglo-American guarantee against renewed German attack. Making the losers pay for a war was nothing new – after the Franco-Prussian war Bismarck imposed heavy payments on France, which paid them more than punctually – but the inclusion in the treaty of the famous 'war guilt' clause in order to justify a big bill rankled unforgettably in Germany; the haggling over the total sum went on for ten years; the American insistence on keeping inter-allied debts, the bulk of them due to the United States, distinct from reparations payments bedevilled post-war international finances, particularly in the case of France, which, owing twice what it was owed, looked to reparations from Germany to enable it to pay its debts to the United States.

The First World War was not only a huge shock. Its cost too was huge. It accelerated, if it did not cause, a breakdown in the international economic order which compounded the breakdown of the European states system. For much of the previous century relations between the (relatively few) sovereign economies were stable. The economic order was dominated by Great Britain, under the signs of free trade and gold. Their balances were measured and settled in gold, and the exchange rates of their currencies were steady. The war greatly devalued all the currencies, even more greatly disrupted the relations between them, exposed Great Britain's inability any longer to combine an international regulatory role with the pursuit of its national economic interests, and provided no alternative leadership since the United States – the world's greatest economic power – abjured any such role. (The United States gave restorative aid to Europe through investment and loans in the 1920s, but the provision of this finance made its withdrawal at the end of the decade all the more painful and disastrous. This withdrawal, beginning in 1928, had mixed causes: the failure to cut back American wartime agricultural production, leading to falling farm prices and rising farmers' indebtedness; enticing opportunities for investment at home instead of in Europe; and maniacal speculation, the stock market crash of 1929 and the consequent rush for liquidity.) So, within the very short space of a decade, the economic consequences of the war and of the Treaty of Versailles combined to create bewildering economic confusion. The Depression of 1929–31 was followed in 1933 by a world Monetary and Economic Conference whose failure – engineered by the United States – deepened the gloom, accelerated nationalist protectionism and promoted revolution.

Revolution was most feared in France but occurred in fact in Germany. Great Britain's was the first major economy to turn a corner, through a policy of substantial spending on new housing which reanimated the construction industry and associated trades. In France, by contrast, governments nailed their colours to deflation, gold and balanced budgets; lent large sums to banks and other undertakings, and lost it; and cut real wages, forced women out of jobs and so added social unrest and political instability to economic disorder. When Leon Blum's Popular Front government tried to go into reverse, it discovered that it could not do so without a coordinated international strategy which did not exist. Frenchmen talked of 1789 and threw Blum out, but although there were violent disturbances there was (as in 1968) no revolution. In Germany, however, there was. There Heinrich Brüning, hagridden by the inflation of 1922 which was ended by decreeing that 1 million million marks made 1 mark, also clung until too late to deflation in a deflating world. The moribund Nazi Party won votes and total power: twelve seats in the 1928 Reichstag elections became 107 in 1930 and the largest party block in 1932. In the next year Hitler was Chancellor.

Hitler knew what he wanted and had written a book saying what he wanted: *Lebensraum* (living space, for Germans). It could not be got without war. Hitler envisaged war and did not at all disapprove of it. Therefore Hitler's contribution to the Second World War was altogether different from any German contribution to the First. One may plausibly conclude that Germany's responsibility for the first war was greater than others, either much greater or only a little greater; but in relation to the second war Germany's responsibility is close to total. This judgement may be challenged only by disjoining a country from its rulers, by considering a term like 'Germany' to be an abstraction incapable of carrying responsibility. That within Germany many people did not want war is self-evident. But in so far as wars are waged by states, and in so far as the responsibility for a war may be apportioned between states, then German responsibility for the Second World War in Europe is in a class of its own.

The responsibility for starting the war resurrected the old charge of Germany's peculiar war guilt in the twentieth century, but in a much altered context, since it is psychologically difficult to separate Hitler's responsibility for the war from related atrocious and guilt-laden policies, particularly the killing – with the machinery of the state and for purely racial reasons – of all attainable Jews and gipsies and the design to reduce the numbers of the Slavs by 30 million. (The fact that until about 1941 Hitler still preferred to export Jews rather than kill them is relevant neither to his racialism nor to the criminality of the subsequent genocide.) Hitler's plans for Europe were not original in as much as they were an expanded version of visions of *Mitteleuropa*, which had allured an earlier generation of thrusting financiers and industrialists. If such visions lead to war the man in the street feels only a limited responsibility (at most) for the outcome. In the sixties Fritz Fischer's *Griff nach der Weltmacht* (1961) reopened the case against Germany in 1914–18 with a scrupulous and scholarly investigation of German aims, before and during the war, to seize for Germany dominion in Europe and the world. The debate which ensued became at times heated but remained essentially academic. But a later debate about German guilt in the thirties and forties went wider and deeper because it went beyond the war-making propensities of governments and ruling classes to the racial and criminal accompaniments of Hitler's conquests, which demanded widespread personal involvement in the bestialities perpetrated in death camps and in territories occupied by the German armies in the east. This later debate, although conducted mainly by historians, was not confined to academics and very many Germans felt a shame akin to guilt. The swell of disgust prompted a counter-attack which tried to explain away conduct so unbecoming a civilized people. A conservative school of writers, more nationalist than scholarly in their inspiration, argued that the mass murders of Jews and Slavs were a secondary crime, secondary because they reflected a mode of thinking and acting with which Europe had already been infected and polluted by the enormities of Stalinist communism. Others have fallen back more modestly on the argument that no man is responsible for another's crime, no generation may be saddled with moral guilt except through its own acts or connivance. But the first post-war generation acknowledged, it would seem, some guilt by association and endorsed the view that the new German state, as the successor in title of the Third Reich, was morally right to accept an obligation to Jewry and offer the sort of reparation (money) which alone can be offered after the event: an acknowledgement and a payment which lie somewhere between expiation and *ex gratia* disbursement.

These debates and their outcome are one indication among others that the Germany which emerged from its second defeat was much more radically altered than was Germany after the first war. The two other principal states of western Europe – Great Britain and France – have changed far less since 1870 than Germany appears to have done: their fundamental political and constitutional assumptions (not to mention their frontiers) have remained the same, their national temper has been, compared with Germany's, subdued, and the trend of their domestic policies has been fairly consistent and equable in a liberal direction. Germany's history in the same years has been episodic. The Second Reich began as a monarchical régime under a Kaiser who was more a military than a civilian figure; its main props, in addition to the army, were a landowning aristocracy (the Junkers of the east) and a new plutocracy (the industrialists and financiers of the west). This was something like the régime envisaged a generation earlier by John C. Calhoun of South Carolina who, before the Civil War, hoped for a partnership between the plantation society of the South and the developing industrial economy of the North, but in a very different constitutional, civilian context. The Second Reich degenerated into a monarcho–military autocracy and then, during the first war, into a military dictatorship which first overrode and then sacrificed the Kaiser. After the war the Weimar Republic, democratic and even socialist in intent, was immediately beset by armed threats from left and right which persisted to 1924 and from which the government was able to save the Republic only with the help of what was left of the army. With the revival of industry in the boom years 1924–9, Weimar governments had either to displease the military and the plutocracy or to lean on them, from which dilemma it had not extricated itself before the advent of the Great Depression and Hitler. Both the military and industry – a nationalist and protectionist combination – welcomed Hitler up to a point, and he in turn was dependent on industry for rearmament and on the army for his aggressive foreign designs. While the Nazis were in many ways repulsive and alarming to these old pillars of the state, there was enough common ground to stifle the Weimar ideals of parliamentary democracy and social responsibility. It took a second war and defeat to bring Germany into line, mentally as well as formally, with the main stream of western political and social attitudes. This alignment of the three main western European states is one of the second war's most significant consequences.

When the second war ended the European states system was left even more jejune than in 1919. In the east the Soviet conquest was a further stage in the division of the continent into east and west, an accentuation of a process already marked by the dissolution in 1919 of its old autocracies (senior members of an overall European system) and by the Treaty of Locarno in 1926 whereby a new order was established for the west from which, on British insistence, the east was excluded. With the Second

World War the Soviet Union erased the three Baltic Republics and took large bites out of Poland and Rumania and a smaller bite out of Slovakia. Otherwise the map looked in the east much the same as before the war, but a map is not the best guide to reality and the states shown on it were states only in name. In the west the map was unaltered: the causes of Hitler's war lay in eastern, not western, Europe. But the states of western Europe, although intact, had lost their confidence in their ability to construct or operate a purely European system; the old European Great Powers were no longer the top powers but were outranked by two Superpowers, and in order to safeguard themselves they prayed the United States, a geographical outsider, to become a political insider. To regulate economic affairs a new international economic order had been devised in 1944 at Bretton Woods but it lasted for less than thirty years and was followed by a fresh bout of economic instability reminiscent of the leaderless inter-war years – widely fluctuating currencies, barely controlled expansion of credit, boom and bust in stock markets, unpayable foreign debts. The new political order, resting on the mutual nuclear deterrence of the Superpower arbiters of the continent, was accepted as a fact of life for about the same span. But the régime in the east, erected by Stalin to protect his western frontiers, was a failure. Subordinate communist parties ruled in the several pre-war states. They were installed by the Soviet armies (except in Yugoslavia, which broke away from the Soviet block almost at once) and were secure so long as Soviet armies might come back in an emergency. This they did in Hungary and Poland in 1956 and in Czechoslovakia in 1968, but in Poland in 1980 the Soviet government deemed it inexpedient to intervene with force even to prevent the overthrow of the party's rule. In western Europe the alliance with the United States remained almost unchallenged. It was an insurance against Soviet hostility and, even when the Kremlin put on a more benign face with Khruschchev or Gorbachev, fear of Soviet might and distrust of Soviet intentions could not be lightly assuaged. Yet the Nato alliance, initially easy and popular, began to become irksome as commercial rivalries developed between Europeans and Americans; world policies, particularly in the Middle East, diverged; and, perhaps temporarily, Europe's assessment of United States leadership lapsed into amazed contempt and ridicule. The terms upon which a European-American alliance might endure needed to be discussed but could not be discussed so long as political leaders on both sides pretended that what was needed was maintenance and not a new model.

As the war ended all the eventual victors abandoned the idea of partitioning Germany. But Germany was partitioned. Partition was a yearning to undo Bismarck's work, a feeling that Europe might cope with pre-Bismarckian Prussia but not with Prussia-writ-large, *alias* Germany. Within a few years of the war's end two entirely new states were born: the Federal Republic of Germany and the Democratic Republic of Germany, both of them as new-fangled as the German Reich had been in 1870. But partition did not have its expected effect. The German impact on events did not evaporate. The (western) Federal Republic quickly became, at first in association with the United States but later by its own exertions, a Great Power – only half armed in as much as it might neither make nor possess nuclear weapons, but an economic giant which by the end of the eighties was the second (after Japan) provider of capital for the rest of the world. This resurgence raised once more an old question whether all, or nearly all, Germans ought not naturally to form one state, and what the power of such a state might be. The war had cut Germany in two and recreated the separate republic of Austria. Before the war and until Hitler's *Anschluss* in 1938 the separation of Austria from Germany had been maintained only because a union had been ruled out by the Geneva Protocol of 1922; but because it was maintained it came to seem proper. By analogy the separation of the two post-war German republics may also come to seem immutable. Yet these two states have long insisted that their relations with one another are not as the relations between other sovereign states, and – unlike Austrians who identify themselves as Austrians – citizens of both German republics identify themselves as Germans. A first post-war generation accepted the separation because it was clearly unable to end it without starting a war, but it will be surprising if a succeeding generation does not mate west with east as surely as the Rumanians once mated Moldavia with Wallachia.

But the future contribution of Germany to Europe's affairs does not depend on reunification. The Federal Republic is by itself strong enough to have and exercise choices, which it is beginning cautiously to consider. It is inhibited by fear of the Soviet Union and a commensurate reluctance to annoy the United States, but within the foreseeable future it may choose one or more of a number of political courses and experiment in combining them: reunion with eastern Germany; a condominium with France; substantially improved relations with the Soviet Union. The code-name for this last option is Rapallo – but with the reminder that the Treaty of Rapallo in 1922 did little for either party except enable it to thumb its nose at everybody else while they were not looking. There is once again a German power. Germany is not a Superpower or likely to become one, but there is no law in politics which says that only Superpowers count nor is there a law which says that no state may deal with a

Superpower except another Superpower. The main thrust of Superpower détente is not confined to arms deals but leads in the longer run to political debate and manoeuvre, and once the United States has given a lead in intercourse with the Soviet Union, others will not be far behind.

The only European state which won in both the World Wars was Great Britain. Except in the obvious sense – it is more agreeable to win than lose – these victories have been a mixed blessing. They have veiled and accelerated Great Britain's industrial decline, for however one may admire the economic management of the British war efforts, the wars were enormously costly and Great Britain stumbled out of them with only partial confidence and independence. A victor's natural inclination to return to what he sees as attainable normality was demonstrated in 1925 by the return to the gold standard with an overvalued pound sterling which could be maintained only by severe and damaging deflation. By reversing such policies Great Britain staged a comparatively early recovery from the Great Depression but the second war was won only at the cost of selling precious overseas assets and incurring large debts. Post-war recovery was gratifyingly swift but without a sufficiently radical transformation of industry, from those which had made fortunes in the past to the materials and methods of a new industrial revolution. With the revival of the French and west German economies Great Britain seemed once more to be flagging. Renewed international instability and inflation in the seventies propelled it, in the eighties, into a fresh bout of extravagant deflation which throttled economic activity and precipitated bankruptcies and unemployment on an unforeseen and unnecessary scale. In spite of remarkable bonanzas (North Sea oil, the collapse of world prices of raw materials, prolific proceeds of denationalization) Great Britain was forced to the bottom of the table of advanced industrial countries and forfeited unrecoverable opportunities. A half-hearted abandonment of the nostrums of the early eighties stimulated recovery, but this sad performance diminished Great Britain's standing in Europe.

The ambiguity of the British position in Europe was enhanced by a different wartime experience: the special relationship between Churchill and Roosevelt. Before the war relations between the two countries had not been close or cordial, and leaders on either side were wont to be derogatory about the other, in private sometimes very derogatory. But the war wrought a big change, not merely through the imperatives of an Anglo-American alliance and the exhilaration of a shared victory but also through the exceptional personal relations which were initiated by Churchill and welcomed by Roosevelt. With other leaders after the war this relationship became something of a fetish, but a fetish grounded in enough reality – a common experience, a common language, shared traditions –

to give substance to the magic. The relationship, however, was special in a more restricted sense than the British imagined. It made for an ease of communication at all levels which neither British nor Americans attained with others, but it could not create a special identity of interests in political or commercial matters and so far from putting American weight behind British ideas it threatened to pull British politicians into a toadying indulgence of American adventures and misadventures. On the British side the belief in this special relationship strengthened hesitations about joining the European Community (whose value and durability the British grievously underrated in the fifties and sixties) and made Great Britain, when it did join, a partner with a difference, less than fully committed to the Community's larger aims. Great Britain muffed its chances of playing a linking role between Europe and America and lapsed into a petulant limbo between the two. Where once in the community Great Britain's absence had been deplored, its presence became a matter of some indifference, even vexation. Germany's obvious European partner was no longer Great Britain but France.

The European Community was a child of war, an experiment for mustering and re-asserting Europe's diminished status and diminished economic clout in the world. Its success is problematic because it has not solved the question how much unity and central authority are necessary to make a community effective. Too much unity goes against the European grain. The Community was established in the first place by Europeans who observed Europe's economic (and therefore political) decline and wished to reverse it by joining forces and resources. The forces and resources to be joined were economic, and the Community in its first phase was an association of advanced industrial and trading states. But it failed to take a leaf out of the book of the German *Zollverein* and, instead of consolidating before expanding, it did the reverse. It did so moreover for non-economic reasons and was to that extent untrue to its first purpose. The original six members welcomed newcomers for, mainly, political reasons. They believed that membership of the Community would deter anti-democratic antics in countries like Greece and in pursuit of this implausible aim attenuated the Community's economic strength by admitting to it economic weaklings which, at this stage, it had difficulty in supporting. The political aspect of the Community has been sharpened by attempts, only half successful, to achieve common policies in extra-European affairs. What the Community most needs is not policies about other continents but a central bank and a common currency: the mobilization of resources before attempts to exert inchoate power. The untimely distension of the Community, in size and in purpose, has jeopardized it.

To argue that the Community is ill-advised to devote its ingenuities to fabricating common external policies is not to deny that some European states have crucial external interests or that these interests are often the same. This is particularly true of the Middle East, a stamping ground for Europeans for centuries, a vital crossroads and an inescapable source of fuels. When the First World War dissolved the Ottoman empire, its Arab subjects hoped for independence but got British and French rule. This rule was eliminated by the second war which, in this area, complemented the first. The second war also gave, in the most horrible manner, a great boost to modern Zionism, which had been a not very successful Jewish minority movement originally founded to find a way to save the persecuted Jews of Russia and Rumania. The founder of this modern Zionist movement, Theodore Herzl, was an attractive but naïve Austrian Jew (Jewish by race but an atheist) who was so appalled by the pogroms of the 1880s that he devoted his life and wealth to finding somewhere – preferably in the Ottoman empire – for oppressed Jews to live a decent life. He grievously misjudged Ottoman readiness to accommodate – as opposed to listen to – his schemes, and after his death and after the First World War his successors were equally unsuccessful in getting British sympathy or support, in spite of the Balfour Declaration (1917) by which the British had promised to look favourably on the creation of a home for Jews in Palestine. (By home, the British understood a refuge for a limited number of Jews without statehood. The Zionists wanted a state.) The second war's horrors created unprecedented sympathy for Europe's surviving Jews, and by allying their own ruthlessness with this sympathy Zionists won their state, evicting all the British and half the Palestinian Arabs. Subsequently financed by the American state and by American Jewish well-wishers (who, however, did not want to go to Israel except as tourists) the new state defeated all Arab attempts to exterminate or contain it but failed to achieve a *modus vivendi* with the Arab world, with the consequence that the Middle East has been almost perpetually at war since the end of the war in Europe. Forty years on the future of the state of Israel appears a great deal less than certain.

In the years 1870–1945 Germany lost whatever chance it may have had to dominate Europe either imperially, as Hitler wanted, or by manipulating the European states system, as Bismarck envisaged. After two catastrophic wars the western German Republic, the more important relic of the Reich, has come to terms with its western foes but is on an uneasy footing with the Soviet Union, a footing which could get better or worse as the one or the other grows richer or stronger. The eastern German Republic lacks formal relations in the one direction and satisfactory ones in the other. The prime question in eastern Europe is the degree of independence which its sovereign states may exact from the Soviet Union, which is perplexed about how to change Stalin's failed post-war settlement without reviving Stalin's fears for the Soviet Union's defences. The prime question in western Europe is whether the exceptional resources and skills of its principal national economies may be integrated to create once more a power in Europe commensurate with other world powers.

Europe's position is a double dilemma. Not only is the deployment of its resources impeded by its fragmentation into sovereign authorities – a luxury which it can hardly now afford. In addition it seems trapped in the ambiguities of power. In the first years after the Second World War power was equated with nuclear weapons. The war in Europe was the last widespread pre-nuclear war, but within a few months of its termination the concomitant war in the Pacific and East Asia saw the use of nuclear bombs. Since then wars have been divided into nuclear and non-nuclear, and states have been sharply categorized in the same way. Yet world powers are not the same as nuclear Superpowers, for the World Powers include, confusingly, Japan which has overwhelming economic power without possessing post-modern nuclear armament. Nor are all the increasingly numerous nuclear states the equals in resources of some non-nuclear ones. Western Europe, epitomized in this respect by western Germany, senses a capacity to graduate to the top level economically but feels unsafe without some kind of nuclear protection, which, however, may so mortgage its resources as to cancel its hopes of emulating Japan. After two mutually destructive wars west Germany and its associates may not do as Japan has done, because Europe's Soviet hinterland is a great deal more menacing than anything that Japan yet perceives in China. Europe therefore is constrained in a way in which Japan is not. A hundred years ago conflict between Russia, China and Japan was already a major element in world affairs, but to most Europeans it was peripheral. Now, by contrast, this continuing power dance on the other side of the globe may condition Europe's future as decisively as the material and psychological ravages of Europe's wars or the loss of Europe's worldwide empires.

Europe's response is not as novel as it looks. Proponents of *Mitteleuropa* in Germany in the early decades of this century were moved by, among other things, the fear that Europe in general and Germany in particular were in danger of being squeezed between Russian and American empires. (They were moved too by greed.) They argued that Europe must be united to meet this eventuality. Being German and nationalist and exuberant they equated unification with German domination. Their visions stretched from France on the one side to Turkey on the other, inclusively.

They were opting for a German Power almost coterminous with continental Europe in place of the German World Power with a European base which Bismarck and his intellectual heirs had hoped to build through manufacturing, commerce and (with hesitations) colonies: Germany would become a World Power by incorporating Europe rather than by expanding beyond Europe. This continental vision, never attractive to non-Germans, was extinguished by the defeat of 1918 but was revived with variations a few years later by Hitler and his early coadjutor, ex-Field Marshal Ludendorff. In Hitler's mind German domination of Europe was required in order to provide living space for the German race – non-Germans might be reduced to serfdom or exterminated, not merely subordinated; but the notion of creating a Great Power by territorial and economic unification was close kin to the *Mitteleuropa* of earlier generations and, subject to one very big qualification, is kin too to the expectations of the European Community. The qualification is the substitution of supranational collaboration for German dominion – a qualitative change that makes the European dream at once more palatable and yet more difficult to attain, since there is no precedent for a World Power created neither by conquest nor nationalism.

The authors of the European Community look beyond the world of Superpower bipolarity to the re-emergence of an international system (similar on a broader scale to the extinct European states system), in which 'Europe', alongside the United States and Japan, the USSR and China, will be the principal actors. In such a world, if it comes to pass, the European Power will need to ponder the experience of Italy in the old European Concert, a member whose credentials were not universally accepted.

Patterns of power change, but power itself remains a prime factor in international affairs. Wars accelerate shifts in power, but their impact on the use or abuse of power is problematic. A great war, by inflicting great suffering and great damage, may be expected greatly to affect attitudes to war, but how deeply or lastingly is again problematic. At the end of every great war people say that such a thing must never happen again, but they say so with more longing than conviction. How, if at all, has the Second World War been different?

It was extraordinarily callous and savage. Half a century afterwards people still shudder at the recollection of the horrors, while those too young to recollect wonder at the atrocities perpetrated and the degree to which they were tolerated: at the deliberate mass bombing of civilians by all sides, the taking and shooting of innocent hostages in droves, the holocaust of the Jews in Europe, the sadistic treatment of prisoners of war at Japanese hands. New weapons, however horrible, are at least a tribute to man's inventiveness; the accompanying inhumanity and acceptance are unrelievedly evil unless they spark a more potent and more effective opposition to the waging of yet more wars in which such things may happen again.

The sources of war include appetites and attitudes. The appetites are easy to identify: greed, envy and the like deadly sins. Of the attitudes which have encouraged the recourse to war and have sanctified its ruthless conduct, two stand out, the one ancient and the other comparatively new. The one is resignation – the feeling that wars are inevitable and that the exhortations of pacifists, the protests of moralists and the arguments of those who point out the futility of war are a waste of breath. The other is the uncomfortable fact that war became at one time popular. Nationalism, nourished by propaganda (much of it false but some of it valid), fashioned a mass approval of war, even a demand for war, which not only propelled governments into war but enabled them, once in, to conduct it with a violence which knew few bounds. It quelled the basic belief that war, although perhaps inevitable, was at bottom a curse. The wars of the mid twentieth century, which coalesced into the Second World War, have posed the question whether this trend has been reversed. Is there a limit to the tolerance of cruelty or does the limit limitlessly recede?

A stouter opposition to war requires the reinvigoration of old ideas about the place of war in human society and the limits which should be imposed on it, together with the application of these ideas to what is new in the war-making of the twentieth century. For centuries war has been widely regarded as an inevitable, even a necessary, evil. Those who glorify it, and those who condemn and hope to eliminate it altogether, are on the fringes. Centrally, the crux has been how to rationalize the conflict between, on the one hand, accepting war as a fact of life and, on the other, condemning it as immoral multiple homicide. The idea of war as a necessary evil has emerged from this dilemma and has dominated all thinking (in Europe) about war since early Christian times. It is what most people felt about war against Hitler. Beginning with St Augustine, Christian and other moralists have tried to resolve the irreconcilable by arguing that war, like the use of other forms of violence, may be justified. By dividing wars into the permissible and the impermissible, they sought to control recourse to war and conduct in war, even though by proscribing some wars they automatically legitimized others. They foreswore the pacifists' simple proposition that all wars are wrong, because this proposition exposed Christianity to the danger of annihilation through a refusal to defend itself or to support the newly Christianized state (the Roman

Empire) whose arms were to be the salvation of Christianity against heathen barbarians. It was better to regulate the evil, since in the rejection of war lay a greater evil.

The regulation began as moral justification but developed by legal definition. The ancestry of the Charter of the United Nations includes lawyers and political thinkers who have devised schemes and mechanisms for keeping the peace, as well as preceptors such as St Augustine and St Thomas Aquinas who laid the basis for the conditional legitimization of war. Whether by divine command or by human contrivance, wars are to be limited, since war cannot be safely eliminated: wars of a kind have a proper place in the world, and the main question is what kind. In every age, including the nuclear age, the problem is to prescribe within the circumstances of that age when a war may justly be started and within what limits it may be waged – and to influence opinion accordingly.

The rules and their interpretation have inevitably varied, but three conditions governing the initiation of war have provided the perennial groundwork. First, a war may be begun only by a sovereign. This category included the Pope and kings and was gradually refined to mean nobody else. In modern times it has meant a duly constituted sovereign state. In very modern times attempts have been made, not so far successfully, to confer legitimacy on wars waged by bodies fighting against states but not themselves invested with the trappings of a state (guerrilla groups, liberation movements within colonial empires, embryonic states – the P L O, the A N C). These attempts seek to widen the laws of war into laws of armed conflict; they face opposition from states, which have arrogated to themselves the sole right to wage war.

The second condition for the initiation of a Just War is that it be righteous. Roman legists regarded a war as justified if the aggressor were bent on recovering stolen territory or property, but Christians had a different point of view. They regarded a Just War as essentially punitive. What made it just was not the aggressor's grievance but the victim's transgression. Therefore a Just War might be undertaken by any sovereign, regardless of his own interest in the matter. If President Nyerere had said that he was attacking Idi Amin's Uganda because its government was evil, he would have been within the Just War tradition, but he preferred to rely (precariously) on the terms of the U N Charter. The right or duty of punitive intervention has fallen into disfavour, partly because the governments of states have successfully contrived to make the state a law unto itself and partly because the claim to be waging war for a righteous cause can so easily be made in bad faith. Thus Hitler could pose as a champion of justice in his aggression against Czechoslovakia, and

Brezhnev and Reagan have come close to doing in their attacks on – again – Czechoslovakia and Nicaragua. So malleable a provision is a reed half broken from the start. Thirdly and finally, a Just War must be pure in the sense that it must not be undertaken by the aggressor for gain or other selfish purpose. This too is a provision more easily judged by God than man.

The rules concerning the initiation of war were radically altered at the end of the Second World War when the signatories of the UN Charter abandoned their sovereign right to make war on other members of the United Nations except in self-defence. Subsequent history suggests that this bold innovation was, to say the least, ahead of its time – as are many bold innovations.

The proponents of Just War sought to regulate behaviour in war as well as the resort to war. The commonest prescriptions of this second aspect of the doctrine were: that fighting must be suspended on special days; that certain classes of person must not be killed or harmed, notably women and children, ambassadors, clergy, sometimes peasants; that new weapons must be eschewed; that warlike acts must be proportionate to the offence which justified the making of war in the first place. The first of these requirements has lost its force long since, although there were attempts as recently as the First World War to suspend killings at Christmas. The second was evaded at an early stage by the counter-argument that it was up to the protected species to keep out of the way of the fighting. The third is a compound of the conservatism of the fighting classes who damned or derided the weapons to which they were not accustomed and, on the other hand, the fear and distress caused by every inventor of crueller and more lethal weapons. Nuclear weapons have given it new force. Most flagrantly breached in the wars of the twentieth century is the requirement of proportionality: that means should bear some acceptable relation to ends. The scale and indiscriminate nature of death and destruction by modern weapons are the most shocking parts of modern war, and both anti-war and anti-nuclear movements have rested much of their case on the impossibility of keeping warfare within just bounds. The logic of the argument is that a Just War is no longer possible if nuclear weapons or other weapons of indiscriminate mass destruction are likely to be used. It unites moral, legal and intellectual traditions with the emotional sentiments evoked by the experience of modern war.

A pessimistic reading of history suggests that mankind has an almost infinite capacity to tolerate horror, particularly in the context of war which suspends prevailing precepts and standards of behaviour. It is therefore rash to suppose that the record of our own times marks the limit of their toleration. There have been dozens of wars since the end of the Second World War and some of them have been at least as frightful and shameful as any which went before. The rules devised to govern the resort to war and the conduct of war have been ignored by governments and individuals with almost complete impunity and with sparse popular outcry. This passivity, or auto-gullibility, has been facilitated by the galloping industrialization of war, which has enabled the instruments of death to function more and more remotely – remote not merely from people hundreds and thousands of miles away from scenes of horror, but also out of sight of the warrior himself up in the dark in his bomber or behind his long-ranging naval gun, endowed by the latest technology with the gift of divorcing the fascination of his doings from their consequences. For a century or so, technology has veiled the facts of war.

Yet here we touch upon one of three developments which point in a more optimistic direction. They are: the new visibility of war through television; the impact of nuclear weaponry; and satellite photographic intelligence. These developments have occurred preponderantly since the Second World War but they have their origins in it.

The reporting of war on television is one of those innovations which may revolt the mind or habituate it. In the case of Vietnam it so sickened the audience that the directors had to cancel the unfinished performance. That the war was brought to an end by the US administration's interpretation of television's effect on American opinion and attitudes is hardly to be gainsaid, however considerable the weight of other matters. This television exposure coincided with a particular turn in the techniques of war. The high-level bomber had been superseded by the low-level helicopter gunship, so that what the cameras showed was not material destruction far away but lifesize figures fleeing helplessly and dying in torment. That, at last, was more than human nature could stomach. Thousands of people knew during the Second World War that Jews were being rounded up, deported and presumably killed, but comparatively few saw these things being done. There is no dodging the evidence of one's own eyes.

Images, it has to be admitted, fade. The holocaust has turned inevitably from a proceeding into a fact of history, and attempts to keep it a present reality cannot in the nature of things succeed; it must lose much of its potency. The same will be true of the atrocities in Vietnam, even as it has been true – to cite a single remoter example – of the once famous genocidal slaughter of Armenians by Turks in 1895 and 1915. What endures is not the event itself but the knowledge that the event took place; and knowledge is a far weaker force than the senses. If wars are to become fewer and behaviour in war less atrocious there will have to be other aids to better conduct. There are two, the one ambivalent but the other more positively hopeful, the one much conversed but the other less frequently remarked. Both impinge upon the incidence of war by affecting, not so much sentiment, as calculation.

The Second World War ended with the dropping of two nuclear bombs on two Japanese cities. These bombs appalled people, even though other bombing operations killed as many people in the space of not much more time. But they were more than just the latest invention in the history of war, for they destroyed the traditional basis for calculating the chances of war. Contrary to popular belief, wars do not happen by mistake; they are initiated by calculation (including miscalculation), and the calculations are made by more or less rational persons reckoning the chances of winning and profiting from war. Hitler, in company with the great majority of warmongers before him, started wars when and where he calculated he would win them. The opposition to him in his own military circles in the thirties derived from the calculation of certain officers that the wars which the Führer planned would lead not to victory but defeat: they too calculated, but otherwise. With the invention and manufacture of nuclear weapons, all these calculations become obsolete and nonsensical if, as was generally supposed, a nuclear war must be suicidal or at least unacceptably costly. So any war likely to involve the use of nuclear weapons must not be started. This axiom has regulated the course of the Cold War (i.e. non-war) between the Superpowers, although its application to wars between the increasing number of other states with nuclear weapons has remained uncertain. Nuclear weapons, in other words, have been treated as unilaterally useless. They can bring death but not victory or gain. Their function, to invert Gibbon, is ostentation, not use – and they have in consequence been accumulated at enormous cost as deterrents in superabundant armouries which would be equally deterrent with a fraction of their contents. In the Superpower conflict these weapons have been a powerful force for peace because of their promise of mutual deterrence. They are what early Christians would have liked the wrath of God and the promise of damnation to provide: a guarantee of peace, albeit in the limited context of nuclear war only. It is an open question whether they will continue to impose this constraint or, with familiarity, will lose their hold over the calculations of impatient or irascible statesmen.

The same caveat applies to the impact of nuclear weapons on the imagination. The special influence of nuclear weapons has been a combination of restraints on both calculation and sentiment, but there was a short space of time when only the latter operated. So long as the United States alone possessed nuclear bombs, their use was inhibited not by the calculations but by awe. American presidents, including Truman who in 1950 authorized the making of the 'Super' or hydrogen bomb, have refused to use nuclear weapons when arguments for doing so were no less seductive than in August 1945 and when neither the USSR nor any other state had retaliatory power. This refusal was not solely due to doubts about whether the use of the bomb might be disadvantageous in a military sense. There was also the sense that to use it would be wrong and the sense too that public opinion would not countenance the incineration of several thousand Russians or Chinese or Koreans in one flash. Since 1945 some 100,000 nuclear warheads have been made and none has been used. Old morality and new public opinion have had a share in this outcome. Those with the power to make nuclear war have apparently recoiled from doing so because of its inhuman consequences as well as its military unprofitability – a powerful combination.

Yet not enough for comfort. Nevertheless, modern technology has produced another peace-keeper, less spectacular and less scaring, but perhaps more effective. In the pre-nuclear age, adversaries accumulated and refined their armouries and kept them secret. They aimed to excel and also to surprise, so that in a crisis they might win. But since nuclear weapons have, for the possessors of these weapons, put deterrence above winning, it has become expedient to let the enemy know how strong you are. (It is also much more difficult to prevent him finding out.) There is little point in assembling an overwhelming deterrent force if the enemy cannot assess it, since the greater his awareness of it the more will he be deterred. Photographic intelligence in the Second World War was incomparably better than in the first, but the deployment of photographic satellites has been an even more striking technological advance and has simultaneously transformed intelligence from the competitive business of keeping and stealing secrets into the spreading of knowledge to mutual benefit. To that extent adversaries are becoming influenced more by what they know than by what, perhaps incorrectly, they fear. Technology, which has done far more for war than for peace, has at last put a substantial weight into the other scale.

Part I

THE SOURCES OF WAR IN EUROPE

CHAPTER 1
The Background

THERE are two extreme views about the European origins of the Second World War. One is that it was all Hitler's fault. The other is that it was a war in which Hitler, along with a lot of other people, and for much the same reasons, got involved. Both views stand condemned by their very simplicity. This book supports neither but it has to start somewhere, and it starts with Hitler and the Nazis.

To begin with Hitler is not to endorse the view that the war was Hitler's war. No great upheaval can plausibly be ascribed to a single individual, however extraordinary. The war that occurred in 1739 is called after a certain Captain Jenkins and his ear, but it was not much of a war and Captain Jenkins may, if a little spuriously, have it. But the conflict of 1939–45 was a World War and not one man's war. It embraced a number of originally distinct wars which merged. Some of these were, in a formal sense, started by Hitler, but the causes of this six-year compendium of fighting in Europe have to be examined in terms of much more than Hitler, or the Nazis, or Germany, or even of Europe. A World War has necessarily complex origins.

But it does not follow that Hitler was a man or a politician like any other. He was not. On the contrary, he was decidedly outside the normal run of men and of statesmen, and the things that made him different contributed to war. He saw human affairs as a conflict; he portrayed this conflict as a moral one in which he had a role which justified every means; yet morally speaking he was, by any ordinary standards, himself a criminal who used murder openly and massively. Such beliefs and such behaviour cannot fail, if allied with power, to promote war.

Hitler, however, was not the demiurge. He could not create or even destroy in a vacuum, and there were, without him, the makings of war in the world and the makings of the sort of wars which were begun like a spreading fire in the years 1939–41.

To see how Hitler and the Nazis came to power in Germany in 1933 it is necessary to understand not only Hitler and the Nazis but also Germany in 1933, and in order to understand the Germany of that time it is necessary to ask questions about the Europe of which Germany had been geographically and culturally a part centuries before Hitler was heard of.

Adolf Hitler was born in April 1889. In January 1933, at the age of forty-three, he became Chancellor of the German Reich. Six years later Germany invaded Poland and so began Europe's part of the Second World War. These are three facts among countless others which belong to the history of the sources in the Second World War. They are cardinal facts. Without them things would have been very different. But by themselves they explain nothing. The war was not the work of one man or one nation but a phenomenon which punctuated the course of Europe's history and the whole world's.

Adolf Hitler's father Alois was the illegitimate son of Maria Schicklgruber. Alois took the name of Hiedler or Hitler after Maria's husband, who may have fathered him before the marriage. Alois was a reasonably well-off minor official, inclined to be self-indulgent and quick-tempered, something of a womanizer. He died in 1903 at the age of sixty-six after having married three times. His third wife bore him six children, of whom only Adolf and a sister Paula survived beyond childhood. Adolf did poorly at school and was difficult at home. From elementary school he went to a *Realschule* and not to a *Gymnasium* which was the goal of the cleverer children or of those with the more ambitious parents. He left school at sixteen and stayed at home, spending his time drawing and making plans for buildings. He dreamed of being asked to design a new municipal theatre for the city of Linz. When he was eighteen he went to Vienna with a competence which was supplemented shortly afterwards when his mother died and he got a small pension. He also sponged on a penurious aunt. He wanted to go to the Academy of Fine Arts but failed the examination. He lived at first quite well but as his money gave out he became not only idle but increasingly lonely, shabby and bitter. He earned a little money by copying pictures; a friend hawked them for him; he was a pavement artist without a pavement. He became a middle-class misfit in a lower-class environment. He was humiliated by this decline and also shocked by what he saw. Years later in *Mein Kampf* he referred to the 'economic misery' of the companions he had at this time and to the 'crudeness of their habits and morals and the low level of their cultural development'. He also noted the fear which grips a social group when it sees itself falling down the social scale and becoming classed with the lowest workers. He looked around for someone to blame.

Vienna, in its last years as an imperial city, a polyglot centre dominated by Germans who were nevertheless fearful of losing their dominant position, was overcrowded and short of housing. The poor and destitute congregated in homes and rest-rooms. Hitler was among them. Here he picked up the common grouse that things would be much better if only Jews and foreigners – especially Czechs – were not allowed to get all the jobs. When things were specially bad this grumbling turned to hatred. Some Austrian politicians played on it and Hitler may have learned in Vienna how potent a weapon racial prejudice can be, for the forerunners of the Austrian Nazis were already at work scaring German Gentiles with the prospect of a flood of undesirable aliens who would overwhelm them economically and besmirch the purity of their race. Statistics were invoked to increase repugnance and envy. Between the middle of the nineteenth century and the outbreak of the First World War the Jewish population of the city rose from 2 per cent to nearly 9 per cent, and in Hitler's time Jews gained more than a quarter of all the places in secondary schools and university. Financial or sexual scandals were exaggerated or invented. Hitler himself swallowed the story that the city's prostitutes were run by a Jewish ring, when it is very unlikely that they were run by a ring at all. Hitler's description of Jewry in *Mein Kampf* as the 'bacillus which destroys humankind', a pestilence like the Black Death, was probably formulated during his years in Vienna, and he specifically wrote of Vienna as the 'ancient nursery of German culture' battened on by 'promiscuous swarms of foreigners'.

In 1913 Hitler left Vienna, probably in order to evade military service. He went to Munich but was traced by the Austrian authorities and summoned back to Austria, where, however, he was pronounced unfit to serve. He returned to Munich. His circumstances were still wretched and he lived the life of an urban beachcomber until war broke out and he joined a Bavarian regiment. The army and the war provided him with activity and a social framework; he became a corporal and won the Iron Cross Second Class and – a rarity for an N C O – First Class. He was in hospital after a gas attack when the Germans collapsed on the western front in 1918. He never served on the eastern front.

After the war Hitler returned once more to Munich. Bavaria had ceased to be a kingdom within the German empire and had become a province within a German republic. This change increased rather than diminished the Bavarians' dislike for Prussia and for centralized government. Moreover, after a brief communist phase, initiated and extinguished by violence, authority in Munich passed to right-wing groups which were at odds with the more left-wing government in Berlin. They were also at odds with one another. There were monarchists who wanted to restore the independent Bavaria which had existed before Bismarck's time; separatists with vaguer but similar aspirations; protagonists of a south German union between Catholic Bavaria and Catholic Austria. Hitler, while sharing the general antipathy to the central government in Berlin, wanted neither the restoration of the Bavarian royal house nor union with the Austria which he despised. He was employed in the Press and News Section of the army headquarters in Munich, was appointed a *Bildungsoffizier* (a cultural instructor or ideological education officer) and was detailed to investigate, among other things, a new political party called the German Workers' Party – DAP. He joined the party, became its star platform performer, provided it with a programme and gave it a new name – the National Socialist German Workers' Party, NSDAP. His military superiors were not only happy to see a member of their staff, still not demobilized, engaging openly in politics in this way; later they also put up some money to enable the party to buy a newspaper, the *Völkischer Beobachter*. Hitler was put on his political feet by the army and when he left the army in April 1920 he was the leader of a party which was similar to a number of other parties except that it had a startling future before it. Post-war Munich saw many parties spring up, wilt and die. They appealed to those who were afraid of Bolshevism, afflicted by defeat in war or crippled by inflation, and they offered an escape into a nationalism which dilated on the glories of the German past and the wickedness of other nations with the implication that the glories could be revived and the wicked put down. Their programmes combined this nationalism with a sort of socialism in so far as they offered the little man protection against the communist commissar on the one hand and the capitalist banker on the other.

Munich provided Hitler with a second political novitiate. Vienna had taught him to hate Jews and had given him glimpses of how to play on popular prejudices and fears. Munich added hatred of Bolshevism, further training in the uses of propaganda, the conviction that the base of political power was mass support, and the further conviction that the way to win this support was not by reasoning but by stirring up emotions. He picked up the idea that Jews and Bolsheviks were equally loathsome and so could be treated as essentially the same thing. His experiences showed him that an audience is better captured by a 'systematically one-sided approach' than by a balanced evaluation of a problem which allows the audience to wonder whether the speaker is himself really convinced of the truth of what he is preaching. This second novitiate closed with a bang and a valuable lesson. In 1923 Hitler staged a putsch. He did so in alliance with General Erich Ludendorff, one of the military heroes of the war, who suffered abnormally from the stings of defeat because his own loss of nerve in 1918 had contributed to it. The putsch was a farcical failure, but the association with Ludendorff gave Hitler the attention of the whole nation. At his trial he announced that he was a man 'born to be a dictator'. He was sentenced to prison for two years, served nine months, did some thinking and wrote *Mein Kampf*. The lesson he learned was that he should try to gain control of the state by constitutional means and not by frontal assault and never against the army.

Mein Kampf, a mixture of autobiography and political manifesto, was an immensely successful book which sold so well that Hitler eventually made a fortune out of it. It is a long book in bad German. Its author remained largely unknown until 1930 and was not taken seriously by many of those who did hear of him. This was a pity because for all its hyperbole *Mein Kampf* proclaimed much of what Hitler wanted to do and how. As a politician Hitler was an unnatural mixture of the normal and the eccentric. After the 1923 putsch he superficially adopted the normal forms of party organization, speech-making and publicity, but he also adapted them up to and beyond the point of distortion. His conformity, so far as it went, reflected his caution and shrewdness, but it was far from being a complete index to his character for his grip on his party was autocratic and intolerant, his speech-making took place in a setting of ostentatiously armed henchmen, party meetings became hierophantic rallies quite unlike the meetings of normal political parties, he was uncommonly uninhibited by scruple and an unrestrained liar (who may have believed what he said while he was saying it but who also believed that lying paid), and he was prepared to use violence whenever and however it served his purpose. In the organization of his party he insisted from the first on his personal ascendancy and refused to allow even his principal colleagues to have views of their own; in his speech-making he was conspicuously violent in what he said and how he said it; and in his propaganda, his mass meetings and the dress and deportment of his followers he deliberately gave his party the appearance, as he himself said, of 'a political fighting force and not a debating society'. If on the one hand he was using the accepted implements of politics, he was also transforming them.

Hitler did not have the mind of a statesman but rather an impresario and improviser. Where a Bismarck imposed himself on events, Hitler imposed himself on people by the fervour of his personality. He was a leader of men first and a framer of policies only a poor second. He was not an original thinker or theorizer but he was adept at picking up ideas which suited him and at taking the opportunities given him by others; he knew how to wait for his chances and how to seize them, and he was guided by certain basic preconceptions. He had a view of history. He was a Manichee, a man who sees the world and its history in terms of black and white, good and evil, god and devil. He saw two powers face to face in 'a world of everlasting conflict where the one creature feeds on the other and the death of the weaker implies the life of the stronger'. For such people the problem is to identify the good and the evil. Hitler saw no difficulty here. He defined the party of the good as the Aryans – a 'race' or biological group which was superior and so had to be tended, preserved and improved by political leaders acting like farm bailiffs.

This definition of good and evil in terms of race stemmed from certain European philosophers and historians who had, during the nineteenth century, evolved the view that races and nations could be graded on a scale of merit and that those lower down the scale would for ever remain below their betters higher up. This way of thinking was fortified by Darwin's contributions to biological science which, taken up by social scientists, were thought to show that social groups, like natural species, evolved to higher stages by a process of conflict involving – and justifying – the extinction of some groups and the survival and expansion of others. Thus backwardness, an inferior culture, was seen as a natural phenomenon rather than as a social challenge, as something to be observed rather than something to be changed. Hitler imbibed these ideas. Conflict, he said, was 'the father of all things'. The German people had to be embattled and purified, preserved from the taint of mixed blood which had caused the downfall of the ancient civilizations; it had also to be trained in devoted obedience to its Leader, to whom had been vouchsafed a vision and a mission to save the world. But to save the world from what?

The party of evil was even more easily identifiable than the party of the good. It consisted of the Jews who, ever since the time of Moses, had been labouring with diabolical ingenuity to destroy nothing less than the human race itself. Hitler's anti-semitism was a genuine and potent hatred. It was sharpened by his ability to equate Jewry with communism. For him Lenin was the latest reincarnation of Moses, Bolshevism the latest device of Jewish malevolence and 'the most radical form of the genocide [plotted] by the Jews'. Through Marx and Lenin and Bolshevism the Jews were repeating what they had done through St Paul and Christianity: European civilization was to be destroyed by the one as Rome had been destroyed by the other. At one time or another Hitler conflated all his adversaries, all those who stood for values which he despised, with the loathed Jews, so that Jewry became a sort of cultural generic term embracing – because it had inseminated and poisoned – not only communism but also social democracy, liberalism, the intellectuals, aristocrats, international finance and Christianity. Either these would be extirpated or they would extirpate humanity. A Jewish triumph would be the 'funeral wreath of the human race' and would leave the planet diving through space 'once again without any human life on its surface'. It was as simple and as terrible as that. The simple view, when wrong, can be the worst because it removes doubt and justifies every means. Hitler did not recoil from slaughter; it was so obviously necessary that it probably never occurred to him to consider whether it was agreeable or disagreeable. Genocide was not a moral issue but the practical application of physical means to social ends. He did not enjoy indiscriminate killing in the way that many simpler Nazis did, although he savoured personal revenge (he revelled over the films of the hangings of the conspirators of July 1944). He enjoyed secondhand descriptions of living and dying in concentration camps but was a strong anti-vivisectionist and could not stomach a demonstration of slaughter when he saw one with his own eyes.

Between the Germans or Aryans on the one hand and the Jews on the other were peoples who were neither. These peoples, of whom the Slavs were the most prominent example, did not have to be exterminated. Their function was to serve the party of the good. Their chief characteristics were their inferiority and their number. These were related terms since it is the destiny of an élite to rule over inferior hordes and use them, as for example the British did in India (Hitler admired the British empire for reasons which would have horrified the Indian Civil Service).

Nazi contempt for the Slavs merged with a far more ancient German-Slav hostility. The conflict between Germans and Slavs is a thousand years old. After the period of the great barbarian invasions and migrations in Europe the Frankish King Charles created in an era of dawning stability an empire in western Europe to match the eastern empire of Byzantium. This empire reached tentatively to the Carpathians and extinguished the alien Avar power in central Europe, but it failed to embrace the rising Slavic state of Moravia; nor did it weld the western Franks of France, still less those in Spain, to its Germanic core. This empire was shortlived. What survived was the idea of a western empire blessed by the papacy – and so essentially Italian as well as German – and distinct from Byzantium. It was revived by Charlemagne's successors in the tenth century, the Saxon emperors. By this time the place of the Avars in central Europe had been taken by the no less alien Magyars or Hungarians, whom the Saxons checked but did not exterminate. The emperors also made war on the Slavs in what is now northern Germany and on the Poles – the first Germano-Polish conflict. They made no attempt to bring the western Franks back into the empire but were even more strongly pulled towards Italy and the papacy than Charlemagne had been. This 'renovation' of the empire was clearly to include Italy but exclude the lands west of the

Rhine and Rhône. About the Slavs, however, there were doubts. Otto III (A.D. 983–1002) conceived a great western Christian empire in which other princes besides himself would have wide autonomous authority as kings. Such an empire could include non-Germans, and the Polish, Czech and Hungarian princes welcomed it and joined it. But Otto died young. His conception of the empire died with him. His successors reverted to fighting the Slavs, and the Slavs, missing an opportunity to create a countervailing empire of their own, quarrelled among themselves: the Czechs remaining in the empire, which the Poles renounced. A pattern evolved which endured, with variations, for centuries and produced in more modern times a strong German power flanked to the east by separate and weaker Polish, Czech and Hungarian ones.

By the twentieth century the opportunities created by this pattern of power were combined with racial theories and economic appetites. In the eyes of German nationalists the Slavs were biologically inferior peoples destined to become a caste of slaves; they also occupied valuable space which was needed by the Germans who, by virtue of their superiority, had every right to take it. The notion of *Lebensraum,* the idea that Germany was too small for the German race, was not invented by Hitler. It was current during the First World War and was one of the pseudo-intellectual props of the policy of *Mitteleuropa*, which aimed to establish a continental empire fit for Germans (and stretching in some versions from France into Asia Minor). Hitler appears to have been genuinely convinced of the need for *Lebensraum*, which, with his racial fantasies, constituted the basis of his foreign political attitudes. In *Mein Kampf* he wrote that National Socialism 'must attempt to remove the disproportion between our population and our living space – the latter regarded both as a source of food and as the basis of political power – between our historic past and the hopelessness of our present impotence'.

Hitler belonged to 'the race of men who dream concretely – a very dangerous breed' (the words come from Ernst Jünger's parable *The Marble Cliffs*). Taken by itself his idea that one being waxes as another declines is neither original nor startling. Goethe wrote:

> *Du musst steigen oder sinken,*
> *Du musst herrschen und gewinnen*
> *Oder dienen und verlieren,*
> *Amboss oder Hammer sein.*

> (Man must rise or fall, He must win and rule
> Or lose and serve, Be the anvil or the hammer.)

But there is a world of difference, in practice and in intent, between the figurative speech of a poet and the concrete programme of a practical politician with a literal mind and power at his command. Hitler's concrete dream envisaged a German nucleus of some hundred million people, flanked by subordinate federations colonized by other Germans. He did not think that this re-ordering of Europe could be effected without war, nor did he think that war was at all agreeable. He said that the next war would be extremely horrible and enormously destructive, but like so many of his contemporaries he believed it would be short. He also believed that too much peace was bad for a people and he took pleasure in the thought that a greater and more beautiful Germany would rise from the devastation, inhabited by survivors welded into a nation by their experiences and guided by a messianic leadership which would last a thousand years: Hitler was a chiliast as well as a Manichee. Some people have been tempted to judge that Hitler did not mean what he said when he indulged in language of this kind, that he got carried away; but it is equally possible to believe that he never spoke truer to his own nature than at these moments. Although cautious, he was not moderate.

Hitler's principal instrument was the Nazi Party, which, exploiting the circumstances of his day and age, he used to win power over the German people and the German state. Through the party he practised the violence, verbal and physical, whose effectiveness became increasingly contrasted with the ineffectiveness of his opponents and of the constitution. The Nazi Party was like the feudal system. In it a man was obligated to an immediate chief and also to the supreme Führer. There were Führers at every level but the supreme Führer was linked with all members of the movement by direct personal allegiance as well as through the hierarchy. The supreme Führer, besides being the apex of a pyramid, was also a unique being, infallible, prophetic, the incarnation of the general (Aryan) will: 'The will of the Führer is law.' His authority was not only absolute but he himself was irreplaceable: he could have no true successor. Successors of a sort – caliphs to Hitler's Mahomet – could be nominated, but this concession to human mortality did not detract from the urgency of fulfilling the Nazi mission in Hitler's own lifetime and while he was still in the prime of life.

This concept of the Führer was reflected in Hitler's relations both with his principal henchmen and with the generality of his followers. After the capture of power in 1933 the machinery of party and the machinery of state coexisted in a kind of semi-merger. The Weimar constitution was never abrogated – it was simply ignored – and the machinery of state was left largely intact, but power passed to numerous party agencies which were given overlapping functions with the result that many decisions could be made only by the Führer; the bureaucracy, reduced to a state of confusion and inefficiency, was eliminated as a barrier between Führer and *Volk*, ruler and ruled. Hitler's principal lieutenants were not men of conspicuous ability and they never constituted a team. Perhaps only Goebbels was more than ordinarily talented and even Goebbels was more marked by the extremity of his devotion to Hitler than by outstanding intellect. There was little trust or friendship in the party's higher reaches and not much cooperation. The Nazi leaders feared and intrigued against each other and, at the end, against Hitler too. Hitler seems to have been neither surprised nor dismayed by this lack of solidarity, so long as it did not affect relations with himself. A suspicious man, he expected others to be suspicious too, and he built their mutual mistrust and malice into his system of government. As a result the principal organs of the party and, after 1933, of the state, were run by feudatories, and government at the top proceeded by a series of clashes. The heads of the government did not govern by talking and working together, and the supreme chief – whether as party Führer or Reich Chancellor – was a dictator conducting a wilfully discordant band which he was not particularly anxious to orchestrate. What mattered to Hitler was the obedience of his lieutenants to himself. They did not have to agree among themselves. The party was held together by the Leader's personal magnetism and not by fellowship or community of ideas. The *Führerprinzip* was hostile to ideas, since an ideologist might find himself in a conflict between his doctrine and his Führer. Alfred Rosenberg, the party's chief racial theorist, never became a figure of the first rank and was increasingly ignored by Hitler, and the Strasser brothers, leaders of the more radical groups of the Nazi Party in northern Germany, were pressed out of the party when the Führer came to have no use for their quasi-socialist ideas.

With his remoter followers the Führer's relations were special in two ways. Without the Führer the followers were nothing, so that the Nazi Party dissolved in 1945 not merely because the Nazi Reich had been defeated but because the Nazi Führer was dead; and secondly, there was an intimacy between Führer and rank and file, a mutual dependence, which gave the movement a democratic force based, not on majorities or voting (a degrading exercise), but on the identification of the leader with the led, expressed by the former's unquestioned authority. The function of the party organization was to 'communicate a definite idea . . . to ensure its conversion from theory to reality' and to do these things with as little intervening 'machinery' as possible. This relationship between party leader and party members was repeated at second remove and transmitted from the movement to the even wider circle of the German people as a whole. While membership of the party was limited and pride (and profit) in membership preserved undiluted, the outer circle of sympathizers was progressively enlarged to create a wider mass movement which, like the party members but less intensively, was attached to Hitler personally and which, because of this emotional attachment, had a stake in his success. Hitler realized the importance of getting the masses to feel but not to think. The Führer divulged his inmost thoughts in a narrow circle whence they percolated to the Nazi élite, thence again into the party in general, beyond the party to the people and beyond the people to the outside world. At each stage they lost something in the telling and so became assimilable by people who would otherwise have rejected them as mad and bad. In such a system the élite and the leader himself could afford to propagate preposterous ideas and even to do so cynically, because the party followers and the people as a whole were blinded by their devotion and their distance from the centre. Hermann Rauschning, with whom Hitler had long and intimate talks until their breach in 1934, relates that Hitler once told him that he was well aware that there was no such thing as race, but that he needed it for his political and salvationist purposes. A saviour of the human race may well permit himself a touch of cynicism. Nor is it incompatible with fanaticism.

The Nazi party served two main purposes. Through its ideology it united the people with their leader and through its techniques it perfected the elimination of opposition. It was not a party in the ordinary sense of the word since it could never be satisfied with partial allegiance or partial dominance. It presented a comprehensive, total way of life, explaining everything, past and future, and regulating everything, public and private. Hitler did not achieve this purpose by catechizing or by arguing. He neither instructed his audiences nor explained things to them. He presented views which, half inarticulately, they were already disposed to welcome, and one reason for his success was his ability to appeal to a variety of different types of people – the disgruntled generation of the First World War, the middle classes downgraded by inflation, the deprived classes which had never played a part in German politics before, youth, the nationalism of the old order and the nationalism of the masses. But although he appealed to these classes, he did not appeal to them as classes. At a meeting addressed by Hitler the message went from Hitler to each listener separately. The audience was a crowd of distinct de-personalized objects. In the aggregate they formed not classes but a mass, 'uniform [as he said once at a marchpast] not only in ideas, but even the facial expression is almost the same . . . a hundred thousand men become a single type'. Each man and woman, whether marching past the Führer or standing in a packed crowd to listen to him, had his eyes and soul focused onto a man who had placed himself in a unique position in German political life: sufficiently remote from the normal political structure which was crumbling (Hitler never got himself elected to the Reichstag and so never operated as a party political leader in that restricted field) and at the same time intensely close to the magnetized individual who wanted a Leader rather than a choice between leaders.

Hitler used fear and persuasion to an unsurpassed degree. Physical terror was one of his principal political weapons. To quote *The Marble Cliffs* again: 'A cloud of fear preceded the Chief Ranger like the mountain mist that presages the storm. Fear enveloped him, and I am convinced that therein far more than in his own person lay his power.' The Nazis thought nothing of assaulting their opponents, torturing them and murdering them – frequently with fanatical brutality. Sadistic thugs were given a licence instead of being shut up, and this licence was accorded to them by Hitler not out of indifference to the finer standards of behaviour but with the positive intention of assuring his hold over Germany in this way. Overt opposition died and even individual thinking was stifled. The dominance of the party was rendered as nearly total as it could humanly be by fear. Education, controlled after 1933 by the certifiable Dr Rust, became a means for destroying the individual's capacity to form opinions and indoctrinating the young with Nazi versions of history and ethics (and even with German, as opposed to inferior, mathematics) through rewritten textbooks and politically reliable teachers. Teachers who did not toe the line were reported by the Hitler Youth, which came virtually to control the schools. Boys and girls spent their leisure hours in uniformed youth associations where the process was continued. Books, plays, the press and broadcasting were brought under Nazi control and censorship. Justice became a farce. It was, said Hitler, 'a means of ruling'. The courts were used to complete the suppression of the individual; the legal profession was regimented, the Führer had the power to quash proceedings, his deputy the power to increase inadequate sentences in cases involving offences against the Führer, the state or the party; illegality was legalized by the invention of the principle of 'hidden right'; an advocate who got his client acquitted would see him being bundled into a police van as he left the court. The whole of life was subordinated to the Nazi purpose with the concentration camps, or the mere knowledge of their existence, in reserve to quell those who felt like protesting openly or, given the perfection of delation within the family, even in private.

This colossal subversion of civilized values was acquiesced in by the

German people and to some extent by Europe too. Only the war put an end to it. What permitted this acquiescence?

Hitler joined an ancient practice with a modern force – ritual with the mass meeting, mumbo-jumbo focused on the microphone. In great squares and open spaces, which he converted into cathedrals of Nazism, he filled ordinary Germans with a sense of destiny, giving them a wonderful vision of unreality as an escape from the chanciness of life and also laying bare to them, with telling candour, how much he had already achieved by violence and how much more he was going to achieve the same way. His performances were brilliantly staged but they would have remained historically inconsequential if they had not fitted the time and place of their presentation.

GERMANY

Germany had been something of an anomaly in Europe for more than a century before Hitler came to power. The Germans did not form a compact group in Europe like the French or the English, nor did they create a nation state; and they failed to find adequate outlets beyond Europe for their power, talents and ambitions. For both these reasons they were the more disposed towards expansion and conquest in Europe.

Modern Europe is a patchwork of conscious nationalisms expressed or seeking expression in statehood. Some of these have been recognizable entities for centuries but the bursting time of European nationalism came with the turn of the eighteenth into the nineteenth century. At this period the dynast, an individual with hereditary right and a personal demesne (his kingdom), came to seem old fashioned. Two changes, the one domestic and the other international, were involved: a shift of political power within the state and a redefinition of the boundaries of the state. The first of these favoured 'the people' at the expense of the dynast; the second was based on the idea of 'the nation', as opposed to history or geography or power, as the criterion for deciding where one state stopped and the next one should begin. The new ideas were most effective in western Europe, where the making of Italy was their outstanding advertisement; they were least effective in eastern Europe, where polyglot autocracies continued until well into the twentieth century. In the centre of Europe Germany looked as though it had developed into a nation state but the appearance was deceptive.

German nationalism was promoted by reaction against French cultural and military hegemony. It asserted that Germans had a separate identity and the right to mind their own affairs instead of being part of Napoleon's empire and of a French-dominated cosmopolitan culture. It aimed not only to liberate Germans but also to unite them and so helped to produce a powerful and efficient state out of an agglomeration of feeble ones. But if German nationalism looked at this stage very much like other European nationalisms, it diverged as the Germans both began to think of themselves as not only distinct but superior and at the same time failed to achieve a nation state to focus and absorb their national energies.

German writers and thinkers made much of the nation state and provided the most famous of the state's champions in the nineteenth century: the Reich created in 1870 was designed by Bismarck and regarded by almost everybody as the German nation's state. But Bismarck's Germany was incomplete. It was a federation of German-speaking states dominated by Prussia and excluding not only Austria, which was only partly German, but also numerous Germans scattered about eastern Europe; the Germans were too dispersed and too intermingled with other peoples to constitute a nation state. Bismarck's Germany was not a national gathering together, like Cavour's Italy. It was an extension of Prussian power, achieved by defeating Austria and France, and a consolidation of class power, achieved by blanketing German liberalism and passing enough social legislation to take the wind out of the German socialists' sails. It was therefore incomplete not only in the sense that many Germans were left outside it but also because whole classes of Germans within the state were excluded from effective political activity and remained subordinated to the socially superior ruling classes: it was a nation state neither in its geographical extent nor in its social cohesion. It was unstable and tense both within and at its borders. Unlike Italy, it was not even a geographical expression. If anything, it was a linguistic aspiration seeking political form and traversed by social rifts. Since it was also the most central of European states and became the most powerful, its malaise dominated European affairs for a century.

German nationalism foiled of what was, in nineteenth-century terms, its natural outcome turned to racialism. Germanism materialized as *Reich* and *Volk*, a pair of politically disruptive and often mystical concepts. A *Reich* is a claim to dominion; a *Volk* is a people linked not by habitat but by race. *Reich* and *Volk* combined imply racial dominion. (When, later, the Nazis chanted: *Ein Reich, ein Volk, ein Führer*, they were acclaiming the political activation of this dual concept.) At the same time the desire to establish a separate identity for Germans was replaced by the idea that Germans were not only distinct but superior. The line between pride and arrogance is a thin one and the assertion of an independent personality passes very easily into a claim to superiority. The Germans were neither alone nor unusual in thinking themselves better than other people, but from early in the nineteenth century Germans began to make extraordinary claims for Germanism as the embodiment of superior virtues deposited by God in people who spoke the German language. Racialists see history as a conflict between races – an alternative to Karl Marx's explanation of history as a conflict between classes – and racialists conscious of their own superiority see a world in which they are bound to do battle with other races and win. Nineteenth-century German racialist ideology postulated an Aryan race of purer, ideal human beings, the founders and custodians of all human culture. History and science were invoked to prove these unhistorical and unscientific postulates, and ancient racial gods were resuscitated to give spiritual support to this denial of the essential equality of man which had been preached for centuries in the tradition of Stoics and Christians. The pseudo-science of phrenology, which enjoyed a curious vogue in an age avid for anything which might be called scientific, measured the differences between Aryan and other skulls and when these outward signs of distinction proved disappointingly trivial, racialists fell back on inner measurements of souls which, though they were more difficult to demonstrate, were also more difficult to deny. Darwin's theories were also used. The world of men (*The Origin of Species* dealt with plants and animals) was divided into the fit and the unfit, and the survival of the fittest was taken to justify and even require the extermination of the unfit. Conflict, in any case inevitable, was the means for the improvement of the race and therefore also noble. There was no such thing as a right to live – let alone a right to liberty or the pursuit of happiness. Human rights were replaced by strife as the path of progress.

German racialism, having evolved from German nationalism, took a further step and became imperialist. Where a race and a state do not coincide the racialist may achieve his aims either by the migration of outlying members of the race into the fatherland or by the extension of the rule of the race to all parts of the world inhabited by the race or needed by it. German minorities in foreign countries were, by definition, superior people living under the rule of their inferiors. Either they must be repatriated or German rule must be extended to cover these areas. The second solution was the more appealing. Hence the notion of a Greater Germany, a German Reich extending to areas well beyond any normally accepted confines of Germany but where Germany ought to rule because some members of the German *Volk* lived there. Towards the end of the nineteenth century various Pan-German groups emerged, both in Vienna with its windows on the east and in Berlin with its consciousness of superabundant power, to advocate what was in effect a German empire in Europe. They were not inspired solely by ideology. Unlike the other great powers of Europe Germany had found no worlds to conquer outside Europe. While the western European nations conquered overseas and the Russians conquered in Asia, the Germans – partly because they were too late – conquered nowhere. Bismarck was indifferent to colonies and Germany's interest in Africa at the end of the nineteenth century was half-hearted as well as belated. So Germany's field of conquest became eastern or middle (*Mittel*) Europe. Bismarck himself preferred that Germany should live in a state of equilibrium with the Russian and Habsburg empires to the east of it, but the German-ness of the Habsburg empire was a standing invitation to call Germans to go east, to regard the Slavs as their Red Indians or 'fuzzy-wuzzies', to embark on one of the great movements of European expansion and colonization – only this time within Europe itself and at the expense of peoples whose systems were neither so alien nor so technically backward as the Asian and African societies which other Europeans subjugated. Like all imperialists the Germans easily convinced themselves that they were benefiting inferior peoples by interfering with them – until eventually the Nazis dispensed with the idea of benefiting anybody but themselves.

These racial and imperial strands in the modern German experience were picked up by the Nazis. Nazism was a product of elements in German history and elements in European history. Its peculiarly evil character was a consequence of amalgamating the worst in German public life with the worst in European public life. It was the German version of European Fascism, combining special German features with the general characteristics of the wider, European genus to which it belonged. Its outstanding special features were the demand for *Lebensraum*, which was a euphemism for imperial conquest, and its anti-semitism. Its special victims therefore were the Jews and the Slavs. These two elements were not unconnected, for the Pan-Germans of the late nineteenth century who pointed Germany towards an imperial destiny not in the sense of Bismarck's compact central European Reich but as a vast overlordship over Slav peoples and lands beyond the strictly German horizon, were also markedly anti-semitic.

During most of the nineteenth century Germans, with some reservations in regard to Austrian Germans, were not pre-eminently anti-semitic. Nor is anti-semitism a necessary ingredient of Fascism, although it has been a common one; the Italian fascists, for example, were comparatively free of anti-semitism until they imported it by a process of reverse Lend-Lease from Germany in the closing phase of the *fascismo*. German anti-semitism seems to have been mainly an indigenous growth coinciding with the growth of German political consciousness. Pan-German anti-semitism was an expression of resentment against people who insisted on being different and who refused to be assimilated to Gentile society and full participation in the German dream. (Hitler's original contribution to anti-semitism was to abandon this demand that Jews become Germans, to insist on the contrary that they could never be Germans and to emphasize the unbridgeable gap by marking each Jew with the star of David.) Although many Jews – not least in Germany in the 1920s – were assimilated into Gentile society when they themselves wished to take this course and when the surrounding circumstances favoured it, they remained liable to be singled out and attacked whenever the Gentile society had a grievance to be vented somewhere. In the latter part of the nineteenth century they were used by conservatives to pin unpopular ideas on: liberal ideas feared by the privileged classes were characterized as Jewish in order to make these classes revile the Jews. This use of racial prejudice for political purposes was begun by Bismarck and adopted and magnified by Alexander III in Russia, where anti-semitism has continued to be exploited in this way ever since. The appearance of the Jews is often markedly recognizable (though it has been embarrassingly discovered that a number of Jews have blue eyes and fair hair). They have a religion and a language which they share with nobody else. In Europe they have performed a function as useful as it is often unpopular – that of the capitalist who provides money for other people's enterprises or follies – but in the nineteenth century they preserved more of their unpopularity than their usefulness as Europe's growing Gentile bourgeoisie began to supplant them as the providers of money. The state found them less useful as it turned to financing its needs more by taxation and less by loans. Moreover, the Jews lacked two characteristics which seemed natural to everybody else: the Jew had no state and, in the state in which he lived, counted as a Jew rather than as a member of an economic or social class. In a society of classes and in a polity of nation states he was a misfit; the fact of his belonging to something which was neither state nor class fostered suspiciousness of exclusive racial loyalties and the myth of machinations behind the scenes; and his exclusion from the class structure helped his defamers to represent him as an enemy of all social structures. In the heyday of his usefulness the Jew had often been close to power and when his usefulness declined his power was thought to have become covert rather than diminished.

Racism endangered the Jews because they were the pre-eminent example of a self-chosen race. Any other self-chosen race was bound to clash with them and hate them. The Germans did so more than most and ascribed to them all the vices which were the counterparts of Aryan

virtues. The German master race arraigned the Jews and the Nazi party
became the principal instrument for destroying them. Again, Hitler did
not invent anti-semitism; he gave it a special twist and he provided the
tools and the opportunities for satisfying it. And the Nazi state did not
protect these people within its borders because in the Nazi scheme of
things the state was not an instrument for preserving public order or
securing the rights of men but an instrument for furthering the destiny of
the German *Volk*. The S A sang:

> *Erst müssen Juden bluten,*
> *Erst dann sind wir befreit.*
> (First must Jewish blood be shed,
> Only then will we be free.)

EUROPE

The ending of the old European order, by the dissolution of its economic
and social foundations and consequently of its political structures, was
effected by a variety of forces which together can be called democratic.
Their general direction was to extend, in the name of freedom, equality
and fraternity, the narrow bases of élitist societies and exclusive policies.
The history of this movement, which is the stuff of the modern world,
cannot be resumed here even in the briefest compass, but it is relevant to
point out that it has been both divided and opposed. The division created
eventually the two broad and increasingly discordant streams called liberal
democracy and totalitarian democracy (that is to say, communism) – both
rooted in the eighteenth-century Enlightenment but diverging over two
fundamental issues, the former regarding politics as a part of human
activity where the latter regards politics as comprehending the totality of
human activity, the former giving a higher value than the latter to individual choice and wellbeing in the inevitable conflict between the individual and the group. The opposition to democracy has been authoritarian, the rejection of the democratic principle of extension and the
reassertion of the right of special men or special groups of men to lay
down the law. Where democracy diffuses power, authoritarianism con-
centrates it once more.

This authoritarian opposition too has been divided. It has conservative
and radical branches. The conservatives have tried to arrest democratic
change, or to minimize and delay it; they have been ambivalent about
democracy, usually accepting for pragmatic reasons a measure of what in
principle they dislike. The radical authoritarians on the other hand have

been frankly anti-democratic and have set out to destroy democracy and revert to a political and social order dominated by a special caste or individual, although not necessarily by the same castes or individuals who were invested with power under the *anciens régimes*. Fascism is the outcome of this active and radical, as opposed to the passive and conservative, opposition to democracy. Mussolini defined Fascism as opposition to the principles of 1789, by which he meant opposition to what others have called the Rights of Man. It was also opposed to the Enlightenment, to reason. It preferred violence: fascists have been bent on destroying an existing democratic order and on doing so by deed and not by argument.

The politics of Europe in the last 200 years have revolved round the ideas summed up in the phrase 'the French Revolution', and the political terms in common use – such as right and left, progressive and reactionary – relate to attitudes towards those ideas. The Bolshevik Revolution of 1917 sharpened the conflict typified by 1789 and, with conservatives often passive or confused about their role, there developed in the twentieth century a triangle of forces and eventually war between the temporarily reunited streams of liberal and totalitarian democracy and their fascist foes who captured the power of the state in various parts of Europe where weak government by conservatives or democrats helped them to do so.

Modern Europe has had to digest industrial, demographic and technical revolutions and at the same time a questioning of accepted values which has amounted to a social and cultural mutation. These changes have been very unsettling. The fundamental change has been the growth of populations and the growth of towns, so that at one and the same time there were quite quickly many more people, many of them living in a completely new way. The change in the demographic and geographical patterns produced social changes. Old ties were loosened and aristocratic and paternalist structures, based mainly on land and caste, were eroded by the motor forces of the Enlightenment (emancipation from dogma and despot) and of the Revolution (power to the people). The new urban classes began to exert pressure and command sympathy. What they wanted was vague – less misery and poverty, more fairness, more self-respect – but it implied upheaval. The traditional givers of laws and *mores* (churches, kings and nobles), and the laws and *mores* themselves, lost authority under rational scrutiny and popular suspicion. It was not immediately clear what the new values were nor where they were to come from. New élites, professing a democratic instead of an aristocratic faith, emerged to take or share the power which was slipping from the exclusive grasp of the old régime and which, owing to technical revolutions in communications and manufacturing, was rapidly becoming much greater than ever before. For the most part power was shared, whether in concert or in a parliamentary system of alternating bouts between nostalgic conservatives and moderate progressives. The result was an orderly but slow development, too slow for those who maintained that no really radical social changes had yet occurred, too decided for the radical forces of the Right which were opposed, not so much to change, but to democracy. There was therefore an ever present possibility of a reversal of alliances in which the conservative opponents of change and the fascist opponents of democracy would join forces against the Left despite the fact that the one group was essentially passive and the other essentially revolutionary. The outstanding example of such a combination was the government in which the aristocratic Papen served as Vice-Chancellor under the fascist Hitler as Chancellor. As early as 1850 Palmerston, in the Don Pacifico debate in the House of Commons, recognized two varieties of radicalism, the reactionary as well as the Jacobin, but it was not until a century later that the fascist combination of reaction with violence was widely recognized as a potent and pernicious threat to European societies.

The fascist leader, like the democrat, had his ideological roots in the eighteenth century, but whereas the democrat put his faith in reason and debate the fascist believed in the power and virtue of the will. Traditionally the high road to right action has been knowledge discovered by reason; the function of reason was to uncover the knowable which, when revealed, was common property. Reason and knowledge assumed therefore universal values. The will, however, was personal. Whereas the individual impelled by reason was moving towards agreement with other individuals, the individual impelled by will was at least as likely to be moving towards a clash with other individuals. The will was subjective rather than communal, aggressive rather than irenic. The will was seen as a creative force in its own right operating in a world in which the objective reality sought by the reasonable man of the Enlightenment was an illusion. There were no external criteria of rightness, only inner promptings. Therefore the strong-willed had right on his side, and the stronger his will the more right he was. What was real was the product of each individual's inner self, and this product was *ipso facto* valid as well as real, so that the individual was entitled and indeed under some compulsion to make his will prevail. His destiny was that of a sovereign creator in a world of his own which impinged upon the personal worlds of other sovereign creators; it was not his lot, nor was it within a man's capability, to discover a single world in which all would participate, because such a world did not exist to be discovered. The world was not a semi-known and orderly system but an unknowable and anarchic non-system.

The consequences of this view were conflict and uncertainty. Both cried out for leadership. What sort of leadership? With knowledge and reason at a discount the emotions were promoted to a dominant role and the intensity of a man's feelings were rated above the soundness of his judgement: there was a deeper, inward truth in the soul by comparison with which the reason was superficial, and the leader was to be distinguished by the qualities of this ill-defined, unlocated, non-rational, even irrational soul. He was above all a doer, an activist, and whatever he wanted to do was right, including crushing weaker beings. He was unpredictable but he was to be trusted and followed none the less, since his unpredictability was only in the eye of the beholder; so long as his acts and commands issued from the dictates of his will they were not to be questioned – and it was as impossible to prove, as it was imprudent to suppose, that they issued from anywhere else. The Italian fascists summed up the position in the slogan: *Credere! Ubbedire! Combattere!* (Believe! Obey! Fight!). The fascist leader was also a saviour and redeemer, more of a superman than a man, half-way between god and man, what the ancients called a hero. By dubbing him Duce and Führer – leader in Italian and German – the fascists usurped a term to which they had no exclusive right, for Churchill and de Gaulle were leaders too. What distinguishes the fascist chief is not leadership, but the role of hero. The hero disdains reason (Homer's heroes never engage in rational debate) and prevails by the weight of authority and by killing. His criteria are quantitative – the bigger the better, whether the subject matter is the length of a speech, the volume of sound at a concert or the number of deaths in a slaughter.

His antithesis is the representative leader who derives his authority from parliaments and elections and depends on a choate body of opinion as opposed to the inchoate mass following on which fascist power is based. In countries like France and Great Britain which have had strong rationalist or parliamentary traditions fascist leaders, although they existed, made little headway. These countries did not go fascist. But their right-wing leaders felt drawn to foreign fascists and praised Mussolini and Hitler and later Franco, who were regarded by conservatives as ready helps against the extreme Left and as performing the salutary task of getting their countries out of messes into which they had fallen. Afraid of rather than familiar with Marxism, they misinterpreted Fascism. Fascist movements and fascist leaders were in truth revolutionary and dynamic, but because they had also certain characteristics which were conventionally dubbed right-wing, they were frequently mistaken for a rather uncouth kind of conservative. The characteristic British and French leaders of this period were capable rather than intelligent, well educated only in terms of an educational system designed to produce mere custodians, suspicious of and so ill equipped to understand new ideas and forces. They could see that communism aimed to subvert the existing order of which they were themselves a part – the communists themselves said so – but they failed to draw the same conclusion about the no less revolutionary fascists, whom they persisted in regarding as respectable. In some degree they were bemused by their own standards and their own democratic precepts. They could not believe that people who said such crazy things as the Nazis meant what they said; the British in particular took little account of theories which they considered to have little bearing on practical politics; they felt that a movement which attracted millions of votes could not be as bad as surface appearances sometimes suggested: thus were they able to turn a deaf ear to the very explicit statements of aims by Nazi and other fascist leaders. (In 1933 Hitler said publicly that the democracies had fortunately not understood what Nazism was about, for otherwise they could have stopped it.) In political circles Neville Chamberlain was a representative figure, hoping that Hitler and the bulk of his party were more sensible than the rowdies of the SA, hoping that they would be tamed by office and responsibility, regarding the Nazis as just another party in the twenties and then from 1930 as a necessary one for the working of government, gradually losing heart and at the end doing his best to avoid war in an impossible situation which had been created partly by his own incomprehension. Outside political circles many leaders, including in particular Roman Catholic hierarchs from the Pope downwards, were over-indulgent – to say the least – to Fascism and to atheistic Nazism because they hated communism more. The propertied classes, underrating the threat of Fascism because they compared it with communism, not expecting to be killed by fascists or even to have to surrender too much of their power and property, had no strong objection to helping fascists with their money. The march of the fascists on Rome in 1922 was a harmless parade compared with the Bolshevik Revolution of five years earlier and life in Mussolini's Italy was disagreeable only for socialists and liberals. Mussolini was appointed Prime Minister by the King in due constitutional form, as Hitler was appointed Chancellor by Hindenburg, and people who read of these appointments in newspapers without seeing for themselves what was going on in streets and prisons were confirmed in their prejudgements that these strange new groups were not revolutionaries in the accepted guillotine sense but champions of order and stability. If King Victor Emanuel of Italy and President von Hindenburg of Germany chose to act thus, what right had any foreigner to object or interfere? It was odd but not outrageous, and if socialists and Jews were having a rough time, they were probably getting no more, or not much more, than they deserved. The ruling classes of western Europe consisted on the whole of cultivated and humane men, but they were men who had also acquired a certain stolidity in the face of misfortune – their own or other people's – which could amount to callousness. They were used to ruling not only their own countries but large empires as well, populated by strange peoples to whom they owed justice and sound administration but over whom it was undesirable for practical reasons to sentimentalize. They were acquainted with 'inferior' races as well as 'inferior' classes, so that the social structure and the imperial experience of Europe combined to establish an order of values and a pragmatic indifference to inequalities which could sometimes be reconciled with ideals of justice and decency only by not inquiring too closely into what was going on. In sum the fascist attitude to socialists and Jews was not utterly different from the imperialist attitude to Blacks. The difference was one of degree, and differences of degree can be minimized or dismissed more easily than most. Hitler, in this respect as in many others, was the supremely disgusting example of something which was not so alien to the European mentality: the tendency to put different kinds of people into different sealed categories and then treat them differently. What his contemporaries, other than his victims, refused to see in time was that the degree of difference in the treatment was so extreme that it amounted to a difference in kind and went in any case far beyond the bounds of what Europe had learnt to call civilized.

CHAPTER 2

From Versailles to the Soldiers' Oath: 1919–34

THE First World War did not destroy German power. As in France after 1870 and Germany once more after 1945 recovery was swift. It was, however, punctuated by economic distress at the beginning and the end of the twenties which had profound political consequences, shaped by Germany's refusal to accept the verdict of 1918 and by resentment against the terms of the peace treaty. Nor did the war destroy much of Germany's pre-war social structure. The departure of the Hohenzollerns and other monarchs gave an appearance of political and social change which masked the fact that the rest of the ruling establishment remained in being and in power. Above all the army remained, until 1934, the arbiter of German politics.

Germany's military traditions were a legacy of its Prussian origins. The Prussian army made Prussia in the seventeenth and eighteenth centuries, and transmitted its traditions to the German Reich in the nineteenth. These traditions included the social exclusiveness of its officers as an aristocratic caste, the military virtues of rectitude and obedience, and a somewhat vague and unspecified position as the guardians of the state's wellbeing as well as its frontiers. The creation of the Reich in the nineteenth century reaffirmed the prestige of the army from the struggle against Napoleon I to the defeat of Napoleon III. The German officer was trained in the exercise of individual judgement on the grounds, elaborated by Clausewitz and other theorists, that the practice of war throws up a great variety of situations which cannot be foreseen and can best be handled by the officer who has learned to take decisions for himself. In addition the German officer had a wider education than his British or French counterpart in the sense that he was expected to concern himself with matters beyond the strictly professional. Yet, because freedom of speculation was not similarly encouraged, his actions in the wider political field were rigidly conditioned, politics were included in his province, but his political equipment was narrow. The German army was therefore significantly different from the British and French armies. The British army, from its beginnings in the time of Cromwell and his rule through Major-Generals, was more suspect as a threat to the civil power than respected as the guardian of the nation (a role reserved for the navy, which had the special advantage of all navies that it guarded the nation from outside without being able to interfere in the streets or take part in politics as easily as armies can). The British army had come to accept its place as subordinate and obedient to the civil government and was therefore denied some of the sources of esteem and self-esteem enjoyed by the German army. In France too the army was regarded since the Revolution as an instrument of civil government and not as properly a power in its own right. There was also a further difference between Great Britain and France on the one hand and Germany on the other. In all these countries the nineteenth century saw the *haute bourgeoisie* trying to get a share in political power. In Great Britain and France it did so by adopting liberal values but in Germany it opted instead for partnership with Bismarck and became a contented adjunct of a conservative oligarchy. The German *bourgeoisie*, having entered upon the political scene later than its French and British counterparts and – more important – at a stage in the evolution of Germany when military power was still actively forming the state, left power to the traditional classes and did not mediate between them and the deprived proletariat. Thus in Germany the power of the military aristocracy in affairs of state was not curbed by civilian, liberal, middle-class opinion. In Bismarck's time it was curbed by Bismarck himself, who opposed and even snubbed the army when he felt so inclined, but he did so not because he incarnated the civil power but because he was Bismarck. After his retirement the army, confronting a series of weak Chancellors, achieved a pre-eminence which culminated in the First World War when Generals von Hindenburg and Ludendorff established a military régime which not only dictated to and dismissed civilian Ministers but also invaded the prerogatives of the Kaiser. In 1918 the Kaiser went too, and the army, contemplating even weaker governments than those of the last thirty years, claimed an autonomy which was not successfully challenged by the civil power until Hitler became Chancellor. Its first post-war chief, Hans von Seeckt, a general endowed with exceptional political acumen, devoted himself to preserving what was left of the German army and its traditions and to rebuilding it. He regarded the Weimar republic as something to be survived and he was prepared to wait and survive it.

The Weimar constitution provided a framework in which Germany might evolve from an oligarchical authoritarianism to a popular democracy, but the evolution was slow to start and then struck by adversity which it was too frail to survive. The middle classes, after being blanketed by the exigencies of war, were torpedoed by the post-war inflation. During the lifetime of the Weimar republic only the Roman Catholic Centre Party maintained its strength (at about 15 per cent of votes cast). Other centre groups declined steadily until they almost vanished. Further to the Left the Social Democrats, who remained to defend the republic with the Centre Party, also lost ground, unused to the political game from which they had been excluded too long, obsessed by the communist threat on their left, and puzzled by the adaptation of Marxism to a vigorous industrial society which falsified some of its premises and drew part of its sting. They ruled Prussia, but whereas Prussia had been the decisive element in Bismarck's and William II's Reich, in Weimar Germany it was only the most important administrative unit.

Weimar Germany enjoyed a number of years of economic prosperity and a remarkable cultural outburst, but politically it remained a promise unfulfilled. It looked as though it might become a parliamentary democracy but it did not look as though it had. After the election of Field Marshal von Beneckendorf und Hindenburg (who had retired from active service in 1911) to succeed Ebert as Chancellor in 1925 it looked more like the pre-war monarchy than anything else and so long as he lived Hindenburg, himself an avowed monarchist, seemed more likely to play General Monk than General Washington. Thus Weimar Germany, besides being smaller and weaker than the old Reich, was uncertain and disunited. At first it was also turbulent. Free Corps, formed out of the disbanded army originally to guard Germany's eastern frontiers, became autonomous units owing shadowy allegiance to senior army officers but acknowledging none to the state. They assumed roving commissions to put down left-wing activities (1919 saw a rash of communist risings in large cities) and where they thought fit they organized murders. They were a throw-back to the medieval Free Knights, freebooters tricked out in romantic trappings. In 1920 the Kapp putsch in Berlin, a right-wing and pro-monarchist attempt by one of these Free Corps to overthrow the government with the open support of a part of the army, demonstrated – the more so because it was a ludicrous failure – the weakness of government and the instability of society. Kapp and his associates failed to take over the government but the government, by failing to punish them or to disband the Free Corps, showed that it was not master in its own house. A similar coup in Munich succeeded and all but withdrew southern Germany from Berlin's authority. There was a continuing struggle for power in Germany in a vacuum in which groups operating outside the law took things into their own hands by virtue only of the fact that they had arms. The atmosphere of violence was aggravated by the murder, by the Free Corps, of the moderate political leaders Matthias Erzberger and Walther Rathenau and also by the fascist march on Rome in 1922 and the Franco-Belgian occupation of the Ruhr in 1923. But the years 1924–9 (from the Dawes settlement to the Great Depression) were much less turbulent: under Stresemann's guidance Germany sought to satisfy its grievances by discussion and by entering into the comity of Europe: it joined the League of Nations in 1926 and saw the withdrawal of the victors' Military Control Commission in 1927; American loans and efficient administration combined to stabilize the currency, modernize communications, re-equip industry and reduce unemployment to (in 1928) 650,000. The army remained in the background. The more extreme parties made less noise. Germany began to look and to behave like the bourgeois politicians who were in charge of its affairs. By the end of this period it had the best roads, the fastest railways and the most modern merchant fleet in Europe. Real wages were back to what they had been before the war; industrial production was more than 20 per cent higher. But the republic was perpetually threatened by a possible alliance between the nationalist ruling classes and the nationalist masses and its governments were inevitably constricted by the aftermath of defeat.

The peace treaty had taken from Germany all its colonies, one eighth of its European territory and one tenth of its European population, and most of its iron and steel and shipping; it had placed the Rhineland and the Saar temporarily under foreign control, eliminated the German navy and air force and reduced the German army to a force of 100,000 men who were required to serve for at least twelve years in order to prevent the creation of reserves; it had extracted from Germany a written admission of war guilt and imposed an obligation to pay extensive but as yet unlimited reparations. These terms were harsh. This, however, was to be expected. They came also to be considered unjust, not only by Germans, on the pleas that the war guilt clause was a vindictive oversimplification of the causes of the war, that the reparations were excessive, that the plebiscitary principle was applied only to Germany's disadvantage and was excluded where it might have worked the other way, and that Germany had surrendered on the terms of Wilson's Fourteen Points which the peace treaty had then contravened. This last plea does not stand up to examination since no such bargain was struck, but the belief was independent of the facts – like the belief, fostered by the ruling classes, that Germany had not been defeated in the field at all but had been forced to surrender by the collapse of civilian morale.

There was nothing unusual about charging the cost of a war to the losers. Most of the war damage had been done to and not by the victors and they felt entitled to get back what they could in order to repair the damage done to their lands and buildings, their disabled soldiers and their widows and children. The obvious way to do this was to present a bill and demand payment in cash; a more sophisticated method, devised by British and French officials and welcomed by the Germans, whereby the damage in north-eastern France would have to be repaired by German labour using German materials, was blocked by French building interests. What was unusual about the bill presented to Germany after the First World War was the refusal of the victors to say how much would satisfy them. For twelve years the Germans did not know how much they might have to pay. In 1921 the Allied Reparations Commission produced the figure of 132 milliard gold marks (£6,850 million) but this amount might be increased later if the Commission decided that Germany could pay more. J. M. Keynes, whose own assessment of Germany's capacity to pay was £2,000 million, stigmatized this arrangement as morally detestable, politically foolish and economically nonsensical. Keynes also argued that all inter-allied war debts should be cancelled, since otherwise they would only be repudiated, in which prophecy only Finland proved him wrong.

This interim reparations settlement was almost immediately destroyed by the collapse of the mark which fell during 1922–3 from a par value of 4.20 to the dollar to 4,200 billion to the dollar. Germany could neither pay nor borrow. It defaulted at the end of 1922, whereupon France and Belgium exercised in January 1923 their right to reoccupy the Ruhr. Great Britain disapprovingly kept apart. A new mark, the Rentenmark, was called into existence by Hjalmar Schacht, President of the *Reichsbank*, to replace the old mark which had become a valueless string of noughts, and in 1924 a fresh attempt was made to quantify reparations. Under the Dawes Plan Germany undertook to resume payments at the rate of 1 billion new marks a year (about £50 million) rising to 2.5 billion in 1928–9. These sums were charged on the product of customs, railways and industry and were to be paid by the *Reichsbank* to Germany's creditors, who provided half the directors of the *Reichsbank* and also exercised control over the German railways. The money for the first payments was lent to Germany by the principal foreign national banks. There was still no limit fixed to Germany's total indebtedness, but Germany's more pressing worries were relieved by its creditors' willingness to lend and go on lending. In the next six years, 1924–30, they lent over 30 billion marks, enough not only to meet the Dawes outgoings but also to replace the capital destroyed by the great inflation of 1922–3, finance post-war reconstruction, pay annual deficits on foreign trade and create a gold reserve. These were good years for Germany. Then in 1929 the Young Plan reduced the Dawes payments, fixed a limit for German reparations, provided Germany with yet another loan of $300 million, removed foreign controls over the *Reichsbank* and the railways, and secured the evacuation of the Rhineland in 1930 instead of partly in 1930 and partly in 1935.

But the Young Plan still kept Germany under a heavy economic sentence. Reparations were to continue for fifty-nine years and, as *The Times* noted, Hitler was able to appeal to millions of Germans who could 'know nothing of the war but that the bill for it will outlast their lifetime'. Moreover the Young Plan, unlike the Dawes Plan, did not turn out to be a fresh start. The depression, which had started in the United States in 1928–9, was already spreading to Europe. Factories were closing, unemployment was growing and American loans were ceasing. Among the casualties was the Weimar republic and among those who gained was Hitler.

During the twenties Germany was put back on its feet by foreign governments, especially the United States, but the mere fact that Germany was once more an active competitor in the world economy revived international strains which had accompanied Germany's first advance to economic power at the end of the nineteenth century. The technically advanced countries were producing more than they themselves and the rest of the world could buy. The obvious remedy for this state of affairs – produce less – was not available since the industrial and technical revolutions which had increased the productivity of the strongest economies had also increased their need for capital accumulation and hence their appetite for higher profits and bigger markets. By the end of the twenties overproduction was creating unemployment, while in various parts of the world surplus stocks were lying unmoved and unconsumed. Germany, with its post-war neuroses and without colonial markets, was particularly vulnerable in this competition for the best slices of the international cake and its business community was looking for a government which would give priority to the requirements of its section of the nation and would secure by any means the revision of a post-war settlement which had cut down Germany's place in the world. Germany was thus predisposed to become increasingly authoritarian and revisionist.

The depression of the late twenties was virtually worldwide. It put twenty to thirty million people out of work, halved the volume of international trade, impoverished national banks and exchequers as well as families, baffled political leaders and helped men like Hitler to take power. It was dramatized, near its beginning, by the sensational collapse of the New York stock exchange in the last hour of business on 23 October 1929. On that day nearly 20 million shares were sold at lower and lower prices and by the end of that month investors were poorer by some $40 billion.

In the United States the late twenties was one of those periods of immense material optimism in which people stop thinking about limits. In a booming economy men of property believed, or acted as if they believed, that an era of richness for all had arrived and that stock prices would continue indefinitely their great leaps forward. As profits and savings satisfied and exceeded the demand for consumer goods and luxuries, they were used to create yet more monetary wealth and were re-consigned to the stock market, where they pushed stock prices up further still. Those who paused to think assumed that higher prices were being matched and justified by higher productivity. In fact, however, the great American boom had shown signs of slackening several months before the stock market's crash in October. Industrial production had taken a downward turn. This had happened before, temporarily, but in 1929 the setback was not followed by a quick recovery; it was not a pause but an about turn.

The effects of the collapse were felt over a vast area because the United States had failed to adjust to the post-war situation in the world at large. During the twenties countries all over the world were importing American goods and borrowing American money. The borrowing had two principal reasons. The first was the high tariffs which the United States maintained and which prevented its customers from selling in the United States enough goods to balance their purchases; they were forced to balance their trade either by payments in gold or by continuous American loans. The second reason was a consequence of the First World War, which created vast intergovernmental debts, partly contracted by the victors in the course of fighting the war and paying for it and partly in the form of reparations. The bulk of the inter-allied debts was owed to the United States, Great Britain and France (although France was only a net creditor if Russian debts were taken at their face value) and the bulk of the reparations payments was owed by Germany to its near neighbours. The debtors borrowed from the United States in order to discharge their obligations. After 1929, however, American loans were no longer forthcoming and at the same time the United States raised its tariffs still further, notably by the inopportune Smoot-Hawley Act of 1930. Since American lending had been financing post-war reconstruction and development in Europe as well as debt settlements and international trade, the turning off of the American tap – first because private investors preferred to play the rising markets in the United States and then because of the collapse of those markets – throttled Europe's economies.

The economic interdependence of different parts of the world was largely a consequence of the industrial and technical revolutions which had begun and flourished in western Europe and northern America. These revolutions created both a demand for primary products in places where they did not exist and speedy means of getting them there. Western Europe, with its higher standards of living and advanced skills, consumed the food and the minerals which other continents produced for its kitchens and factories. But this pattern contained the seeds of its own transformation since international trade enriched the poorer countries as well as the richer and helped the poorer to improve their own standards of living and so eat more of the food they could grow. The First World War also affected the pattern. By concentrating man's needs on munitions it boosted the demand for minerals and their price, and by disrupting communications it boosted food production for local consumption and, likewise, the farmer's profits. In the United States and other prosperous societies agriculture expanded owing to the fear that the war would prevent food from distant countries from reaching its destination. When therefore the war ended, more food was being produced than could be disposed of. Prices began to fall and continued to do so throughout the twenties with only a brief pause in 1925–8. Instead of reducing production, governments, in particular the government of the United States, subsidized the farmer's prices and so encouraged him to keep under cultivation the land which he had worked so successfully under different circumstances. Moreover, since the wartime expansion of American agriculture had been financed by credit, the farmer in the post-war world was not merely an over-producer but an indebted over-producer. From 1929 the system took perforce the violent way to solution by numerous bankruptcies.

The end of the war also brought a drop in the prices of primary products other than food. Initially this change benefited the manufacturing countries at the expense of the producers, but it soon damaged the industrial societies too by contracting their markets; the suppliers of raw materials were also the purchasers of manufactured goods, and when they no longer got good prices for their raw materials they ceased to be able to buy manufactured goods. Less was bought and sold throughout the world. There was less wealth.

By the end of the twenties there were therefore three interlocking problems: agricultural overproduction; the shrinkage of international trade, which was leading nations to protect themselves by tariffs and other barriers; and reparations and inter-allied debts which, like the reconstruction of Germany and deficits on trade between the United States and Europe, were being financed by copious but not inexhaustible American loans. At the end of the twenties the politicians who were grappling with these economic problems became overwhelmed by them.

In Europe the acute phase of the crisis began in Austria in the spring of 1931. Austria, from having been the centre of a great empire, had become a small new state athwart the division between modern industrial western Europe and the relatively backward agricultural hinterlands of south-eastern Europe. It was prohibited by the treaty of St Germain – Austria's counterpart of Versailles – from uniting with Germany and this prohibition had been reinforced by the Geneva Protocol of 1922 when economic aid had been provided for Austria in return for renewed assurances that it would not unite with Germany. Equally Austria was prevented from combining with its other neighbours in a Danubian or central European federation, because these neighbours were determined to have nothing to do with anything which looked like a revival of the Austro-Hungarian empire. Austrian independence was a shibboleth of France as the foremost champion of the post-war settlement, of Czechoslovakia as the most vigorous of the new progeny of the settlement, and of Rumania and Yugoslavia as its beneficiaries, but independence in this case did not mean the defence of Austrian independence against an aggressor but insistence on Austrian independence against, if necessary, the interests of the Austrians themselves. Since Austria was poor as well as small, those who insisted on its independence had to pay to keep it solvent or see it become a dependency of some other power.

Austria's future became an active topic of discussion and negotiation in 1930. Germany was afraid that Austria was looking to Italy for its salvation and regarded an Austro-German union as the only natural solution. Many Austrians would have preferred a wider solution in order not to become a mere province in a new German empire, but this way seemed to be blocked. France and Great Britain were at cross purposes. France was determined to prevent an Austro-German union but Great Britain was less alarmed by this prospect and wanted to patch up Franco-German differences rather than give France unequivocal support. Great Britain preferred the role of mediator to that of ally. In March 1931 Germany and Austria announced that they had agreed to form a customs union. France in particular regarded this projected union as a political scheme rather than an economic expedient. It was referred to the Permanent Court of International Justice at The Hague, which eventually declared it contrary to the Geneva Protocol but not contrary to the treaty of St Germain (in both cases by eight votes to seven). The plan was abandoned.

Meanwhile economic forces were gaining control. In May the principal Austrian bank, the *Credit-Anstalt für Handel und Gewerbe*, closed its doors. It was unable to meet its short term obligations because of the decline of Austrian industry and trade which had impoverished Austrian concerns to which the bank had lent its money. Its difficulties were accentuated when France blocked continued Austrian borrowing in the French money market. Although German banks and the Bank of England lent to the *Credit-Anstalt*, they were unable to save it and succeeded only in weakening themselves. Before the end of the month the German banks were in similar troubles from their own clients. By June the *Reichsbank* had lost over a billion marks and in July one of the leading German banks, the *Darmstadter Nazional*, also closed its doors. American banks which had lent to German banks began to feel alarmed. The Bank of England too was in trouble and borrowed from the Bank of France – France was financially the strongest country in Europe. British industrial and commercial activities were in decline. Unemployment was growing, and in June it became known that under existing arrangements the British government could meet only half of the calls on it for unemployment relief. The Labour government decided that it must balance its budget as a precondition to getting loans from American finance houses, even if part of the cost had to be paid by the unemployed. A special cabinet committee recommended cuts in public expenditure amounting to £78.5 million. The full cabinet decided that cuts of £56 million would do but it then disagreed over one item, a proposal to reduce by one tenth the dole payable to the unemployed. At Invergordon there was a mutiny when it was discovered that cuts in the pay of the lower ranks in the Royal Navy were to exceed the 10 per cent deduction required of all employees of the Crown. The government broke up and the country went off the gold standard.

Some temporary relief, psychological rather than economic, was provided by President Hoover's offer to suspend for one year the payment of debts due to the United States if other inter-governmental debts were likewise suspended. Hoover's offer anticipated an inevitable German default and shortly afterwards Germany declared that it would not resume payments after the end of the Hoover year. The Young Plan was scrapped and a conference at Lausanne in 1932 sanctioned, in camouflaged language, the abandonment of reparations. Another conference at Stresa later in the year tried to find a solution to the economic ailments of Austria and south-eastern Europe but, failing, left the area open to Germany.

The great crash and the great depression shattered more than material things. They destroyed morale. They injected a great amount of fear into ordinary people (including the ordinary people who sat in cabinets) and so turned them to an intent concern for their own affairs, present and future. The sense of community narrowed. Nation protected itself against nation, class turned against class. The millions of victims of the mysterious workings of economics looked for somewhere to lay the blame for their sufferings, and for somebody to lead them out of the mess. And nowhere were the confusion and disruption worse than in Germany, which had relied most completely on foreign loans. There too factories began to close, unemployment grew by leaps and bounds, and the cost of unemployment relief exceeded the capacity of the treasury to pay it. The resulting problem sundered the democratic parties. The Left wanted higher taxes, the Right higher unemployment contributions and lower relief; the Left, in other words, wanted the economy as a whole to subsidize the unemployment fund, while the Right wanted the fund to balance itself at whatever level was dictated by circumstances. Although both sides were prepared to temper their claims, neither would go far enough to meet the other. For two years Heinrich Brüning, who had been appointed Chancellor in March 1930, tussled with diminishing success with these economic and political storms.

Brüning was an intelligent man in his mid-forties, socially of the middle class, politically of the centre-Right, well intentioned and determined to save the republic. It was his fate to preside over the collapse of German credit and German democracy. By 1929 the steady economic expansion of 1925–8 had come to a halt and in the three ensuing years – 1930–32, the worst of the crisis – the national income was almost halved and one in three of the working population was put out of work. The Austrian crisis having triggered off a German crisis and foreigners (to whom half of all German credits were owed) having hurried to demand repayment of their short-term loans, the credit system collapsed. At the same time the problem of how to relieve the unemployed created dissensions among the centre parties of the Reichstag. Brüning, whose instinctive loyalties went not so much to democratic institutions as to the person of the chief of state, once his regimental commander, failed to hold the coalition together, a failure for which the Social Democrats share the blame. His policies were wrong enough to aggravate political dissension among the moderates and then belatedly right enough to give his ultimate successors, the Nazis, a good start. His methods – government by decree in the last resort – accustomed Germany to procedures which the Nazis turned into common form, and so accustomed foreigners to seeing Germany governed that way.

He took office with the determination not to inflate. The post-war inflation was remembered with such horror that any degree of inflation was very difficult to contemplate. A moderate or controlled inflation was not part of the German experience; inflation meant run-away inflation, a situation in which the value of a house falls to that of a box of matches between breakfast and lunch. Any inflation was a national phobia. So Brüning took the traditional, but beyond certain limits socially intolerable, course of deflation. His immediate problem was the flight of capital from Germany. Having decided against devaluation he resorted to import licensing and exchange controls (both of which were later developed by the Nazis) and to deflation, but deflation failed to boost German exports partly because the government deflated too little and partly because Germany's customers had devalued their currencies. The balance of payments grew worse and the reserves went on falling. At home the attempt to balance the budget by cutting social benefits and increasing taxes widened the rift between Right and Left. Brüning's 1930 budget had to be enacted by decree. The Social Democrats moved in the Reichstag to annul the decrees. The President dissolved the Reichstag. No parliamentary majority could be found. If Brüning hoped to gain control of the Reichstag by new elections he was disappointed, for at the elections of September 1930 the Nazis increased their seats from twelve to 107 and the communists from fifty-four to seventy-seven. The anti-parliamentary extremes were carried by the votes of the unemployed to a dominant position in the parliament and even with Social Democrat cooperation Brüning was now dependent on the President and his power to legislate by decree. By the beginning of 1931 unemployment was approaching the 5 million mark (it continued to rise until the latter part of 1932), production had declined by nearly half of what it had been in 1928, and parliament and the constitution were unworkable. Brüning's policy had failed and the failure, a product of the unenlightened economics of the time in government in Washington, Berlin and other political capitals, visited on the German populace economic hardships unparalleled in peacetime in an advanced industrial country. It also alienated an influential segment of the business class which had previously supported Brüning's Centre Party and so, indirectly, the Weimar republic. The economic crisis laid bare weaknesses in the German banking system which the government could not go on ignoring, but Brüning's attempts to correct these weaknesses – by the introduction of state supervision and inspection of banking practices – caused bankers and their associates in industry and commerce to look round for other parties to patronize. The developed world's economic ignorance and incompetence played a large part in making Germany choose Hitler.

Deflation was abandoned in 1932. It had done no good except to prove the need for something different. A new expansionist policy, based on expenditure on public works, was adopted. It was to be greatly expanded by the Nazis and to reduce unemployment – even before the impact of rearmament – from a peak of over 6 million to 2.6 million at the end of 1934. The Nazis, unafraid of state interference with private enterprise and unhampered by the trade unions, which they overpowered, pursued a policy of inflation controlled by tax increases and by wage, price and dividend restrictions. By 1937 Germany was short of labour. But a few years earlier inflation had seemed impossible. Because there had been so much of it in the early twenties, there was too little of it in the early thirties and too late. Deflation reduced Germany to something approaching despair and chaos at a time when powerful forces – the Nazis and the communists – could see that despair and chaos were what they needed.

The Nazi Party had made little impression during the years of prosperity (1924–9). It won only twelve seats in the Reichstag in 1928, but between 1929 and 1933 it grew into a mass party of the discontented. The Nazis attacked in the name of socialism the parties and policies which could produce nothing better than unemployment; they accused the entire political establishment of callousness and unimaginativeness. At the same time and in the name of nationalism they denounced the treaty of Versailles as an affront to Germany and a prime source of its economic ills. In the Reichstag elections of September 1930 they jumped from the category of a splinter party on the lunatic fringe into that of a political force which could be left out of no calculation. Six and a half million Germans voted Nazi and made the party the second biggest in the Reichstag. Newspapers abroad dug into their records to tell their readers something about its Austrian leader, Adolf Hitler, who now became world famous. Less than two years later this popular vote was more than doubled to give the Nazis 230 seats and make it the biggest in the Reichstag. But they never polled half the electorate in a free election. Even after Hitler won the chancellorship the Nazi vote in the election of March 1933 was only 43.9 per cent. But by then figures no longer meant much.

The rapid rise in Hitler's popular support created a problem for the other nationalist and right-wing parties. Either Hitler would come to power in alliance with them or he would be swept into power by the masses, with or without violence. Hitler could see this too and in the declining years of the Weimar republic he played politics in the knowledge that the German Right was in a dilemma. The Right had this much in common with the Nazis, that both were anti-republican. The Right believed, or hoped, that Hitler's wilder strains were the sort of political moonshine which can be ignored by sensible men and which is forgotten by even the worst demagogue when he gets office; Hindenburg among others seemed more put off by Corporal Hitler's social inferiority than by his manic utterances. The Nationalist Party, led by the rich industrialist and newspaper owner Alfred Hugenburg, was the first to make an alliance with the Nazis. Others waited, but when Hitler stood against Hindenburg for the presidency in 1932, the Right voted for Hitler. There were four candidates for the presidency, none of them democrats. Only Hindenburg was strong enough to beat Hitler. So the Field Marshal, receiving substantial support from an unaccustomed quarter, was re-elected, after a second poll, by the votes of the Left – to which he was now useless from senility as well as conviction.

After his re-election Hindenburg discarded Brüning and replaced him with Franz von Papen, the nominee of the anti-parliamentary forces of the Right – the army, the big landowners and big business. Papen was a member of the lesser nobility who was sufficiently insensitive to political reality to imagine that he could outwit Hitler and run a right-wing government without him. Papen fell between two stools. First he destroyed what slight chance of a centre coalition still existed when, in violation of the constitution, he dismissed the Social Democrat government of Prussia and subordinated it to the central government of the Reich. Then he changed his mind about the Nazis and offered Hitler the Vice-Chancellorship. But he was too late. His offer was not good enough for Hitler, who had meanwhile, in the elections of July 1932, become the leader of the biggest parliamentary party. Hitler asked for the Chancellorship. He was refused. Hindenburg declared that he would not give the Nazis full powers because 'they intended to use these powers to further their own ends'. Hitler was both checked and humiliated. Optimists grasped at any sign that somehow somebody was going to prevent Hitler from triumphing. But there was also a growing feeling that the Nazis would and should come to power. The more they spread chaos the more they gave the impression that they alone could allay it. Street violence was an everyday occurrence: public political murders, put at forty-two in 1929 and fifty in 1930, had quadrupled in the first half of 1931 and were still increasing. Terror and brutality, by communists as well as Nazis, sickened public opinion and alarmed the army, which shrank from the prospect of having to fight Nazis and communists at once. Hitler deliberately raised the stakes by sending a telegram of sympathy and support to some Nazis who had broken into the house of a young communist called Hans Potempa and kicked him to death before his mother's eyes. At the same time the Nazis were saying – and demonstrating – that they alone had the energy and the willpower to restore order. The public became inured to the idea that the price of order was a Nazi government.

On the parliamentary front Nazis, communists and socialists combined to defeat Papen in the Reichstag in September and in the ensuing elections in November the Nazi tide receded slightly. But Papen still commanded no majority in the Reichstag and, having failed to contain the Nazis or come to terms with them, he was no longer any use. He had been made Chancellor because the army wanted him and the President commanded him, and his failure forced the army to take the Chancellorship itself in the person of General Kurt von Schleicher. Papen had been a nominee of the army, Schleicher was its embodiment: seconds were out. Schleicher had been in favour of bringing Hitler into the government until he discovered that Hindenburg would not have Hitler. He still thought it necessary to bring Nazis into the cabinet and he proceeded to offer the Vice-Chancellorship to Gregor Strasser, the leader of the northern and more radical section of the party and the representative of what was left of socialism in National Socialism (a by-product of attempts in the twenties to woo the working classes and lesser *bourgeoisie*). Strasser was willing but stipulated that Hitler must first bless the union, which Hitler refused to do. It is difficult to understand how either Schleicher or Strasser ever imagined that he would, and Strasser merely destroyed himself by letting Schleicher use him in this way. Schleicher, who was a political neophyte, next tried an approach to the democratic Left, whereupon the financial and industrial establishment put pressure on Hindenburg to recall Papen and install a Papen–Hitler coalition. The army too failed to stand solid for its own Chancellor. Some officers, led by General von Blomberg, went over to the Nazis. Hitler now had enough backing from the conservatives, the moneyed interests and the army to make his own terms. This was the end of Schleicher, whose short period in office marked the end of the German army's exercise of political power. Out of deference to Hindenburg, who thus performed a last service by easing Hitler into power, Schleicher quietly relinquished his post. On 30 January 1933 Hitler was appointed Chancellor by Hindenburg with Papen as his Vice-Chancellor.

Hitler became Chancellor constitutionally. To say that he became Chancellor legally would be to ignore the activities of his party, which, in the preceding years, had committed countless acts of criminal violence, including murder; but technically Hitler (like Mussolini) did not seize office, it was conferred upon him. There is a difference between seizing office and assuming power. Hitler assumed power between 1929 and 1933 by violent means but he forbore to lay hands on the institutions of the state which he proposed to manipulate. Ever since his abortive putsch in 1923 Hitler had been sagacious enough to sense and insist upon the advantages of observing prescribed constitutional processes. He was a better respecter of pieces of paper than pieces of humanity, because he realized the strength of formalities and the bemusing effect of a show of continuity. He had made no secret of his intentions. In 1931, for example, he had told a German editor, a political opponent, that although he intended to come to power by winning seats in the Reichstag, after he had done so the

Reichstag might as well close its doors and be turned into a museum; and after his appointment as Chancellor it took him only a matter of months to master the whole apparatus of power and propaganda in Germany. The steps which he took were characteristic: legislation and murder.

Between 9 and 10 p.m. on 27 February 1933 the Reichstag was burnt to the ground. Hitler at once blamed the communists. He probably really thought they had done it. Others equally promptly assumed that the Nazis had burnt it with the intention of incriminating the communists and liquidating their party, and at the end of the war General Halder said that Goering had boasted in 1942 that the fire was his doing. The question remains obscure and there is much to be said for the view that the Dutch communist Marinus van der Lubbe did, as he himself claimed, conceive the conflagration and effect it on his own as a one-man protest. It is evident that the three Bulgarian communists tried with van der Lubbe (who was executed) had nothing to do with the deed. They were even acquitted. Whatever the truth the Nazis seized their opportunity with alacrity – proof either of their efficiency or their complicity. Arrests were made within a matter of hours, communist newspapers were suppressed, and an emergency decree was issued the next day overriding basic civil rights such as freedom of expression and assembly, permitting arbitrary searches and seizure of property, empowering the central government to assume the functions of local authorities and imposing severe penalties. This decree was never repealed. In March Hitler supplemented it by an Enabling Act which in effect converted him into a one-man legislature. This act, which required a two-thirds majority in the Reichstag, was passed only because the Centre Party (at the bidding of the Vatican) voted for it. A few Social Democrat voices were raised, for the last time, in courageous but futile protest. With the powers thus conferred upon him Hitler decreed all parties except his own out of existence, subordinated the federal states to the central government, and won 92 per cent of the vote in elections which he staged in November 1933. He abolished free trade unions, intimidated the churches and virtually annexed the judiciary and the educational system, thus moulding a new society in which only Nazi ideas, ethical, social and political, might be expressed and protected.

Hitler also struck down a part of his own movement, the armed SA or *Sturmabteilungen*, led by Ernst Röhm, an even earlier member of the Nazi Party than Hitler himself and one of the few men with whom he used the intimate second person singular *du*. The SA had had a job to do on the streets in the days before the Nazis came to power. They provided the rough and tough arguments for supporting the Nazis or keeping out of their way. But Hitler had had trouble with them from the start. They regarded themselves as an independent force like the Free Corps from which many of them were initially drawn and they wished to be as autonomous *vis-à-vis* the party as the German army traditionally was *vis-à-vis* the state. Hitler had been obliged in 1930 to eliminate their leader Franz Pfeffer von Salomon, an ex-Free Corps man, because he proved too independent and opposed Hitler's policy of achieving power by constitutional means. He also had to suppress an open revolt by the Berlin SA in the same year and had further trouble in the next year. Moreover the SA were growing fast. At the beginning of 1931 they were 100,000 strong, the same size as the army; at the end of that year they were 300,000 strong. By the middle of 1934, their ranks swollen particularly by unemployment and by the march-fever which swept through Germany in these troubled years, they had reached a strength of 4.5 million and were scaring the army as well as Nazi Party chiefs. The SA was the most prominent of various Nazi organizations which duplicated the organizations of the state (like a shadow cabinet duplicates a cabinet) but which had become irrelevant or embarrassing once their party had become the state. Röhm saw the SA as replacing the regular army. Politically naïve and temperamentally unbalanced, he overplayed his hand fantastically. He thoroughly alarmed the officer caste by letting it be known that in his view the armed services should be reduced to being training organizations for the SA, and he failed to see that Hitler needed the army. His ambitions contributed to the alliance which both Hitler and the army desired and provided it with a sacrificial victim. The army began at this period to dismiss its Jewish officers to please Hitler and early in 1934 Hitler forced Röhm to agree, formally and in writing, to moderate his ambitions. But rumours of an SA putsch persisted and in June Blomberg, now Minister for Defence, warned Hitler that the army would turn him out, get Hindenburg to declare martial law, hand over the government to the military and probably restore the Hohenzollerns if the SA were allowed to usurp the functions of the army; if the SA were suppressed, the army would see that Hitler got the Presidency. Hitler thereupon organized a massacre. On 30 June Röhm and about fifty other SA leaders were murdered. The opportunity was taken to murder a great many other people too; they included Schleicher and also Gregor Strasser, although there are doubts whether Hitler wanted the latter's death. But the principal beneficiaries of the destruction of the SA were not the army but Heinrich Himmler and his SS or *Schutzstaffeln*, which flourished on the ashes of the SA and became the rival military force which the army had sought to destroy with the SA.

A month later Hindenburg died. The office of President was merged with that of Chancellor. More important, the death of Hindenburg provided Hitler with the opportunity to annex the officer corps to his revolution. With some exceptions the officer corps disliked the Nazis but it shared some of Hitler's aims and was confident that its power was greater than his. From Hitler's point of view the army differed in two ways from every other institution in the state: it was too powerful to be destroyed and he needed it. Although within Germany it might challenge the power of the Nazis, externally it was essential to Hitler's purposes, especially for the conquest of *Lebensraum*. Therefore it had to be strengthened and at the same time rendered domestically harmless. On the day after Hindenburg's death every member of the armed services swore a new oath of obedience to Adolf Hitler in person as 'the Führer of the German Reich and people and Commander-in-Chief of the armed forces'. This oath was devised by General Walther von Reichenau, one of a group of officers who were at this time keenly pro-Nazi. It gave Hitler a moral authority over the officer corps which endured almost undented until the end of his life. The army, which had virtually ordered the elimination of the SA, had placed itself under the Führer's personal orders by the oath, the mystic force which bound the army together and determined its relation to the state. By this oath the army equated the guardianship of the German state with obedience to the command of Hitler, who was henceforward not only Führer but also President and Supreme War Lord.

CHAPTER 3

The Futile Opposition: 1934–8

IN external affairs Hitler's first aim was to restore German power. He intended to recover for Germany the lands and the peoples lost in Europe after the First World War and to re-establish the armed services which had been destroyed or crippled by the peace settlement. These aims were not novel but they were accompanied by another which, though likewise not novel, was rationalized by Hitler in a new way. Hitler intended that Germany should expand into non-German lands and his reason was his conviction that a people must either wax or die. He did not believe that a people could remain static and survive. So safeguarding the German people meant increasing their number (a biological rather than a military necessity) and securing somewhere for them to live. In *Mein Kampf* he had written, with a mixture of conviction and guff, of securing

... the existence and increase of our race and nation, the sustenance of its children and the purity of its blood, the freedom and independence of the fatherland, and the nation's ability to fulfil the mission appointed to it by the creator of the universe.

The British, so far as they paid any attention to this sort of thing, thought it might be met by offering Hitler colonies, a partial acceptance of the German demand to revise Versailles and a sop to assuage or eliminate his more dangerous aims in Europe; they dangled colonial carrots before Hitler up to the last months of peace. But Hitler was not to be put off in Europe by presents in Africa. He intended to colonize in Europe, not Africa. He made this clear both privately and publicly. A few days after becoming Chancellor he told his service chiefs that the restoration of German power entailed the creation of a unified German nation by converting or breaking all opposing forces and by mastering youth, the struggle against Versailles, the colonization of parts of Europe in order to gain living space, and the reinforcement of the armed services. Publicly he was no less explicit. 'The foreign policy of a nation (*völkisch*) state,' he wrote in *Mein Kampf*, 'must assure the existence on this planet of a race encompassed by the state; it must do this by creating a healthy, life-giving and natural balance between the present and future numbers of the *Volk* on the one hand and, on the other, the quantity and quality of its territory.'

In his next paragraph Hitler made it clear that the prime aim of this foreign policy was to make the *Volk* self-sufficient in food within the boundaries of its state and by extending those boundaries if necessary. This passage comes near the beginning of a chapter entitled Eastern Policy. It left therefore no doubt where Hitler coveted land. It was included in the abbreviated English translation of *Mein Kampf* which was published in 1933 – and reissued in 1935 in a cheap, paperback edition which sold nearly 50,000 copies in three years.

In 1933 he did not know how or when he was going to achieve these aims. In this sense he had no plans, but he had aims and the achievement of his aims for the German people included from the outset measures which other peoples would never willingly accept. He himself was aware of this. He did not expect to win *Lebensraum* – that is to say, other people's territories – without war.

Among the European powers Hitler distinguished between France and the USSR on the one hand and Great Britain and Italy on the other. France he regarded as an irreconcilable foe, the USSR as an inevitable one. Thus the two chief traditional opponents of the extension of German power were opponents still (although the Franco-Russian treaty of 1935 did not create so menacing a combination as the old Dual Alliance). Hitler's attitudes to these two powers were, however, very different. The irreconcilability of Germany and France came from the French side. In his view it was the French who were perpetuating the Franco-German feud; they were unbiddable, nothing could abate their animosity. At the same time Hitler despised them, so that although French hostility was a fact it was not a very serious one. French power was enough to give Hitler pause but not to thwart him – as he showed when he remilitarized the Rhineland in 1936 against the advice of his generals.

Hitler's feelings about the USSR included hatred as well as contempt. Although he despised Russians as Slavs and sub-men and lacked that respect for their tenacity which was felt by many Germans who, unlike himself, had fought on the eastern front in the First World War, the overmastering sentiment in his references to the USSR was a passionate loathing for their communism, which was for him one of the principal contemporary expressions of the age-long Jewish conspiracy against the human race. Ultimately too it was the USSR which Germany would have to fight for *Lebensraum*.

Italy and Great Britain came into a different category. They were potential allies or at least non-objectors. To begin with Hitler thought of Italy as no more than a medium power which could prove useful by engaging and distracting France and Great Britain in the Mediterranean, but the course of international politics in the mid-thirties threw Mussolini into Hitler's arms. The two dictators, though personally loyal to one another, never established a close and confidential alliance between their countries like the wartime Anglo-American alliance. Still less did they coordinate their war efforts, but the Rome-Berlin axis justified Hitler in his judgement that Italy could be brought to serve his purposes by helping to demoralize France with multiple preoccupations in the central and western Mediterranean and to convince British governments that they could not face war with Germany unless Italy were first neutralized.

Hitler's feelings about Great Britain were complex and in the end wrong. The British were Aryan and they were successful imperialists. He could respect them. Hitler must have been aware of the view current in Germany that the challenge to Great Britain in 1914 by the invasion of Belgium had been a mistake, although by the end of 1939 – after war had begun – he said that the violation of Belgian (and Dutch) neutrality was a matter of no importance. *Mein Kampf* assumed no conflict with Great Britain and a decade after he wrote his book Hitler was still pursuing the same policy of appeasement when he sent Ribbentrop to be his Ambassador in London. The Nazis avoided the Kaiser's challenge to British sea power and Hitler never had any intention of rebuilding the German High Seas Fleet. But Hitler's admiration for the British was for what they had done in the past and he thought that they had had their day. He despised Neville Chamberlain when he met him although he admired Lloyd George. The question was whether Great Britain would stand in his way. On the whole he thought not. There was, he believed, a difference between Great Britain and France: whereas France wanted to prevent Germany from becoming powerful at all, Great Britain was only concerned to prevent Germany from becoming the sort of world power which would threaten British world power. But Hitler did not want to threaten this British position. He envisaged two world powers, the one based on dominion in Europe and the other based on dominion of the seas, and he hoped that if he made this plain Great Britain would not object to German hegemony in Europe. Subsequent events seemed to show that Hitler was wrong about Great Britain and failed to gauge its inevitable and implacable opposition to his plans. But his error was pardonable. His view of Anglo-German relations was not confined to Germans. When Halifax was about to visit Hitler in 1937 Sir Nevile Henderson, the British Ambassador in Berlin, urged the Foreign Secretary to 'look facts in the face' and remember that 'the main point is that we are an *island* people and Germans a continental one. On that basis we can be friends and both go along the road of destiny without a clash of vital interests.' Further, as late as 1940, when France fell, some British political leaders gave thought and utterance to coming to terms with Hitler and letting him be. They did not prevail but their hesitations show that Hitler's error about Great Britain was only a marginal one, albeit one of those marginal errors which turn out to be fatal.

Hitler's problem in foreign affairs was to nullify international opposition to his international aims, until he was strong enough to dictate abroad as well as at home. He had to ensure that Germany's strength grew faster than fear of Germany, for if the fear grew faster then the forces which had opposed and beaten the Kaiser's Reich might together destroy the new Reich. Fortunately for Hitler this possibility was largely theoretical, for the victors of 1918 were no longer united. After that war two of them, France and the United States, had put forward entirely different solutions to the German problem and in the upshot neither scheme survived in working order. The twenties therefore had seen the elaboration of substitutes, so that when Hitler came to power the principal formalized constraints upon his freedom of action beyond his borders were, in the west, the Locarno treaties of 1925 and, in the east, a patchwork of alliances designed by France – systems which were scrappily deputizing for the treaty of Versailles and the Covenant of the League of Nations.

After victory Clemenceau's solution to the problem of what to do about a powerful Germany was to put such constraints upon it as to make it harmless for as long as possible. President Wilson's solution was to devise a system which would nullify the excesses of every state. Clemenceau was seeking a specific solution to a specific problem, Wilson a general solution to a universal ill. Clemenceau was by nature a pessimist, Wilson an optimist. Clemenceau was a Frenchman first and a European afterwards, Wilson was not a European at all.

The best that France could hope for at the Peace Conference was to dismember Germany (French policy since Richelieu), extend France and get Great Britain and the United States to promise to go to war as soon as Germany attacked France again. This programme failed completely. Great Britain and the United States offered to guarantee France's territory as part of a bargain which included, in the American case, the acceptance of the Covenant of the League and, in the British case, the formalization of the American guarantee. When the US Senate refused to endorse the Covenant, the American guarantee to France lapsed and with it the British. Nor was France allowed to annex German territory west of the Rhine. It had to be content with the demilitarization of these Rhineland areas together with their occupation by the allies until (in different zones)

1925, 1930 and 1935 and with the possibility of acquiring the small Saar territory, economically rather than strategically valuable, by plebiscite. Germany was also to be and to remain substantially disarmed, and was, as we have already seen, subjected until shortly before Hitler's accession to paying reparations designed to keeping its economy trained upon the discharge of debt instead of the creation of military might.

The collapse of the American and British guarantees was not France's only diplomatic setback. In the east Russia itself had collapsed. To most Europeans the new USSR did not look like a useful (or respectable) ally at any time between 1917 and 1941. This was to be an immensely valuable aid to the revival of Germany as a major power. France tried to replace its eastern ally by new ones – by Poland, which was re-created in 1918 and with which France made a treaty in 1921, and by making friends with Czechoslovakia, Yugoslavia and Rumania, the so-called Little Entente, all of them beneficiaries of the break-up of the Austro-Hungarian empire and so, like France, supporters of the Versailles settlement. The weaknesses of France's eastern policies became clear in the thirties. Poland was no substitute for Russia as an ally against Germany except in the limited sense that it lay at Germany's back door. Poland did not feel committed to an anti-German policy as a first priority but developed a policy of keeping its balance between Germany and the USSR. Its population was only three-quarters Polish and it was on bad terms with its neighbours. It had barely re-emerged as a state when it was launched by Pilsudski on an ambitious attempt to recreate the ancient empire of Poles, Lithuanians, White Russians and Ukrainians. It had invaded the USSR in 1920 and, as a result of securing its old 1792 borders, contained within its frontiers six million Ukrainians and White Russians; it had seized Vilna from Lithuania in 1920 and it coveted Teschen, which had been awarded to Czechoslovakia in the same year at a moment when its invasion of the USSR was going badly; it enjoyed special rights in Danzig, the port of the Vistula but demographically a German city with which it was linked by a corridor cut through Germany; and it gained much – Germans thought too much – of Upper Silesia in 1921 after a dubiously interpreted plebiscite. It was a Slav state at odds with other Slav states, a revived state with more than a touch of the intransigence which goes with the proud reconquest of independence, a new republic which (like Greece at that date) cherished tempting recollections of an ancient empire. Revived in November 1918, at war six months later, it narrowly escaped destruction in 1920 when Lenin was talking of sweeping over it into Germany. It was saved largely because its instability exacerbated European fears of spreading Bolshevism, so that France sent General Weygand to Warsaw to give expert advice on how to stop the Russian counter-attack.

Of the members of the Little Entente Czechoslovakia was the most favoured, partly because its western half lay in the technically more advanced half of Europe and partly because it inherited from Habsburg times an efficient civil service and a high level of education. It was also fortunate in its founders, T. G. Masaryk and Edvard Beneš. But these advantages and its outstanding liberal record obscured weaknesses, for Czechoslovakia was even more a medley of races than its name implied and was also the principal meeting place in Europe of the thrusting industrialism of the west and the more placid conservatism of the agricultural east. In Yugoslavia racial and religious antagonisms made this new state even less homogeneous than Czechoslovakia, while Rumania had received the uncomfortable war prize of a large Hungarian population. And throughout eastern Europe there were significant German minorities.

Furthermore, Great Britain was never happy with the new eastern Europe reorganized on Wilsonian principles. These new states were children of the United States and soon orphaned. They were also allied with France but the alliances were brittle so long as they were disliked by France's greater ally, Great Britain. They were an ingredient in a French policy which was not France's only policy. This policy was to build up a pro-French and anti-German system in the east, while retaining the power to attack Germany directly in the west. The alternative was alliance with Great Britain. This was an alternative and not a complementary policy because Great Britain did not want France to attack Germany and did not want to be entangled in eastern Europe. After the abortive occupation of the Ruhr in 1923 France never did attack Germany, even when Hitler remilitarized the Rhineland in 1936. The price of British support was, first, the surrender of the policy of a direct French threat to Germany and, later, the abandonment of France's eastern system: the first was formalized at Locarno in 1925, the latter consummated at Munich in 1938.

Neither the instability of post-imperial eastern Europe nor France's failure to get territorial safeguards or political guarantees against Germany would have mattered much if the system of collective security embodied in the Covenant of the League of Nations had been made to work. Before 1914 statesmen had tried by various means – diplomacy, conferences, the balance of power, arbitration – to prevent wars within the framework set by a multiplicity of nation states. The First World War not only signalized the failure of these techniques but was regarded as a

EUROPE IN 1914

UNITED KINGDOM

NORWAY

SWEDEN

DENMARK

HOLLAND

BELGIUM

LUXEMBURG

FRANCE

SWITZERLAND

GERMANY

POLAND

AUSTRIA – HUNGARY

ITALY

SPAIN

PORTUGAL

RUSSIA

RUMANIA

SERBIA

BULGARIA

MONTE NEGRO

ALBANIA

GREECE

OTTOMAN EMPIRE

North Sea

Baltic Sea

Black Sea

Adriatic

Aegean Sea

Mediterranean Sea

Bay of Biscay

London

Christiania

Stockholm

St Petersburg

Copenhagen

Berlin

Warsaw

Prague

Vienna

Budapest

Bucharest

Belgrade

Sofia

Constantinople

Athens

Rome

Bern

Paris

Brussels

Madrid

Lisbon

0   250

Miles

– ARTHUR BANKS –

EUROPE IN 1923

0   250

Miles

ARTHUR BANKS~

condemnation of the multi-national system itself. A new comprehensive international system was required. President Wilson, who was among politicians the principal champion of this radical thinking, regarded a collective security system as an alternative to what had gone before, not as a supplement: the old system was bad in itself. He shared the belief that wars were caused by alliances, by armaments and by arms races; he saw the First World War as a logical consequence of the formation of the Triple Alliance and the Triple Entente and Anglo-German naval competition, and he wanted to create an international system which would make such things unnecessary and proscribe them. But the new system embodied in the League of Nations did not work in the Wilsonian way because too many important states remained outside it, because it was too new to be trusted, and ultimately because some of its more important members did not want it to work.

Between the French and American approaches to peace in Europe there emerged a distinctive British attitude which sought security by reconciling Germany with its former enemies and with the terms of the peace settlement, if necessary by modifying the latter. Champions of reconciliation argued that it was a surer safeguard of the peace than anti-German alliances, that the Germans were not after all the horde of savages portrayed by wartime propaganda but a Christian nation which had produced Goethe and Beethoven, that there was in Germany much to admire from standards of public behaviour and public administration to open-air weekends of an unimpeachably healthy nature, that the reparations demanded by the peace treaty were unfairly discriminatory. This was a laudable attempt to bury hatchets, all the more laudable since the British public continued to harbour powerful anti-German emotions. It was also firmly grounded in political calculation. The alternative to reconciliation with Germany was the prospect of a second European war against Germany and the maintenance in peacetime of a military establishment which, however natural to a Frenchman, was anathema to the British: the Dominions too disliked a view of things in which the British empire was a reserve force to be used to redeem the imbalance of power in Europe. Both as an island and as an empire Great Britain was congenitally wedded to a view of the German question which was different from the French view. The principal achievement of the British view was the Locarno treaties of 1925, a local and limited settlement which, however, by-passed the Wilsonian general approach to security and also contradicted the essential bases of French policy.

The Franco-Belgian occupation of the Ruhr in 1923 had been a failure and the tough school in Paris was eclipsed when Raymond Poincaré was succeeded by Édouard Herriot and France accepted the Dawes plan in 1924. A first attempt to reassure France focused on strengthening the League's machinery of collective security. The Covenant provided that a state must not carry a dispute to the point of war without first trying to settle it in one of a number of specified ways and accepting a cooling-off period of three months. If a signatory of the Covenant broke this rule, it was branded as an aggressor and other members would together apply sanctions against it. But the rule was a limited one. It did not apply if the Council of the League was not unanimous about the rights and wrongs of the dispute; it did not apply if the dispute was found to lie within the domestic jurisdiction of the state concerned; and it did not apply if that state observed the cooling-off rule and the dispute was still unresolved at the end of it. These exceptions were called the gaps in the Covenant and in 1924 the so-called Geneva Protocol sought to plug the gaps by providing for the compulsory arbitration of all disputes and the application of sanctions to every resort to war. The protocol was accepted by the British Labour government but the Conservatives, returning to power in 1924, refused to ratify it because Great Britain, strongly reinforced by the independent British Dominions, thought that the scope of the Covenant was already wide enough and ought not to be enlarged in such a way as to cumber members of the League with further commitments. The new British government then proposed something else – a system for keeping the peace in western Europe, based on the acceptance of Germany as a state like any other. This was the genesis of Locarno.

What France feared was a fresh German attack one day across the Rhine and through the Rhineland. Austen Chamberlain, the Foreign Secretary in Stanley Baldwin's new government, proposed that Great Britain and Italy should guarantee the Franco-German and Belgo-German frontiers without discrimination as to an aggressor; that is to say, Germany was guaranteed as much as France and Belgium. For Great Britain this reciprocity was more than a diplomatic nicety, since it ruled out a second Franco-Belgian occupation of the Ruhr, but for France reciprocity meant the end of a special advantage and a fundamental review of French strategy. It was no longer possible to hope that another war would begin beyond France's frontiers instead of with an invasion across them. The best thing now was to take steps to keep the Germans out. A few years later the Maginot Line was begun, a line of fortifications which proved useless when the Germans invaded in 1940 but which meanwhile corroded the French spirit since the obvious thing to do with a fortified line is to sit tight behind it. (The Maginot Line has been chiefly derided for its psychological effects on French military thinking and general

French morale. Tactically it was defective even on the premises of those who believed in it, since it did not cover the whole of France's eastern front – Pétain having pronounced the Ardennes to be impassable. Even had it been completed it was still an anachronism, a defensive line performing essentially the same function as a trench but ineffective in a war of movement in which no line could stop all the enemy's armour or even most of it.)

The Locarno system was also defective from the French point of view because Great Britain refused to extend it to eastern Europe. Germany did not accept its eastern frontiers. It was in fact Stresemann's intention to alter these frontiers, as well as other features of the Versailles treaty which were obnoxious to Germany, and his acceptance of a firm settlement in the west, including the demilitarization of the Rhineland, which was freely reaffirmed at Locarno, was part of the price he was willing to pay in order to separate western from eastern problems and gain a greater freedom of manoeuvre in the east. With Poland and Czechoslovakia he agreed to conclude arbitration treaties but no more. France extended guarantees to these two countries but the British refusal to do so was more significant. In the west Locarno confirmed Versailles, in the east it questioned Versailles and it did so because Great Britain, anxious to conciliate Germany, and Germany, anxious to keep a free hand in the east, prevailed over France, which would have preferred to strengthen the anti-German forces in that area. Locarno was also a principal source of the mistaken notion that Italy was a Great Power.

The Locarno settlement provided the formal basis for western European security for eleven years (1925–36). In 1926 Germany joined the League of Nations. It also took part in the Disarmament Conference which assembled at Geneva in February 1932 in a belated attempt to fix and reduce arms levels as the Covenant of the League had envisaged more than a decade earlier. But to Hitler treaties and conferences represented limitations upon his freedom of action, preventing Germany from getting strong in military muscle and breathing space. As he himself later said he had to extricate Germany from the toils of the League and the Disarmament Conference. He left both in October 1933 and in the next year he concluded a nonaggression pact with Poland, a first stab at the French system in eastern Europe. For some years Hitler managed to persuade foreigners that the sum total of his ambitions was the rectification of legitimate German grievances by negotiation. There was some nervousness about his methods but a strong tendency to credit him with the same aims as Stresemann and Brüning. Hitler achieved this chiefly by alleging it to people who wished to believe it and were in the habit of treating statements as true until they were proved to be untrue: westerners were particularly influenced by his renunciation of claims to Alsace and Lorraine (which he incorporated into Greater Germany in 1940).

Within six months of Hitler's appointment as Chancellor the four principal European Powers concluded a pact among themselves. This Four Power Pact was more important for its signatories than for what it contained, which was vague and platitudinous. It was promoted by Mussolini, who wanted to assert Italy's right to a place above the salt, welcomed by Great Britain because it accorded with the British policy of general reconciliation, accepted by Hitler because it gave him time and recognition, and signed by France because not to sign was to court isolation. It implied that the treaty of Versailles was no longer the basic factor in European affairs and that these would be regulated in future by a concert of the more powerful states, opponents of Versailles as well as its champions. The countries chiefly threatened by this prospect were the medium states of central and eastern Europe which owed their existence to Versailles and were allies of France. One of them, Poland, took the startling step of making a pact with Hitler.

But the lines were not yet drawn. An Anglo-French-Italian front against Germany seemed possible, until it was extinguished by the Ethiopian crisis, which put Italy firmly on Hitler's side. Before that Germany and Italy were at arm's length because of Austria. Austria had a Nazi Party of its own, which was subordinate to the German party. It had also a militaristic right-wing organization, the *Heimwehr* (supported by Italian funds), and a reactionary clerical government under a Chancellor, Engelbert Dollfuss, who had become Chancellor in 1932 and was secretly in league with Mussolini to crush the socialist opposition without having to ally himself either with the *Heimwehr* or, still less, the Austrian Nazis. Soon after Hitler became Chancellor in Germany Dollfuss banned the Austrian Nazi Party. Hitler had been encouraging the Austrian Nazis to make a bid for power, but he realized that he would do himself more harm than good if, with Germany still less than semi-armed and more than semi-isolated, he were to stir up so much trouble in Austria that other states would unite against him. Mussolini was at least as anxious as France to keep Austria from being annexed by Germany and he entered into agreements with Austria and Hungary, whose leaders he received in Rome in March 1934. Hitler decided therefore to hold his hand for the time being, but the Austrian Nazis were less responsive to restraint than to encouragement and in July – with the connivance of some German Nazis but perhaps not Hitler himself – they attempted a coup and assassinated Dollfuss. Mussolini staged an armed display on his frontier with Austria. Hitler did nothing and the coup was a failure. This string of incidents is revealing. Hitler did not lack political courage but he combined courage with caution. He was inclined to attend upon circumstances with the result that the timing of his principal operations was often dictated by circumstance. The later history of Austria confirms the point. At the end of 1937 Hitler was still waiting with a wary eye on France, and although he actually went into Austria in March 1938 the timing was, as we shall see, still not of his own choosing. This readiness of Hitler to bide his time can produce the misleading conclusion that Hitler's aims were never formulated so precisely in his mind as events made them appear; but it was only his timetable and not his programme which was vague. He was like those persons who love to make lists of things to do but without any clear idea when they will get them done. This does not mean that he did not intend to do them.

Austria was one of the two keys to Italian policy. The second was the Balkans. Italy looked nervously at its frontier with Austria on the Brenner and also at Albania where the eastern shore of the Adriatic comes closest to Italy. In the twenties Mussolini's policy was comparatively pacific – to secure Italian interests by treaties of mutual friendship. He wanted a government in Vienna which was neither too left-wing to make and keep bargains with fascist Italy nor too powerful to need to bother about them. In 1925 he was unenthusiastic about the Locarno plan because it created two categories of frontiers, the guaranteed and the unguaranteed, the Brenner frontier being one of the latter, and in 1934 he was alarmed by the prospect of a strong German government in Vienna in place of a more tractable Austrian one. In Albania he had rejected the policy of direct intervention advocated by nationalists like Luigi Federzoni in favour of reducing Albania to puppet status by economic domination and by marrying an Italian princess to King Zog (in the event she married another Balkan monarch, King Boris of Bulgaria, instead). Here Italy's dominant concern was not Germany but France. Albania apart, the eastern shore of the Adriatic belonged to Yugoslavia which was an ally of France and suspected Italy of coveting the Dalmatian coast. Mussolini pursued an irregular policy; Italy was not strong enough to enable him to be anything but opportunistic, especially when his European concerns became linked with ambitions in Africa. He tried to secure his two soft spots in Europe by agreement with France in Laval's time but his attempt to include in the bargain the conquest of Ethiopia caused the collapse of the Franco-Italian rapprochement and propelled him into alliance with Hitler. Then, largely at Ciano's prompting, he reverted to the policy direct intervention in Albania which he proceeded to conquer in April 1939.

Had Mussolini's ambitions been limited to Europe, a Franco-Italian alliance might have come into being, but Mussolini wanted to cut a dash in the world, especially in the Mediterranean which he regarded as an Italian lake and in Africa where, to his chagrin, France and Great Britain had acquired more prestigious empires than Italy. With a sort of Disraelian rapture Mussolini decided to conquer Ethiopia and nominate the King of Italy as emperor. He anticipated no real objections from Paris or London, which, as he correctly judged, were not really interested in Ethiopia. He had had his first encounter with Hitler in June 1934 just before the coup in Austria, but in January 1935 Pierre Laval visited Rome in an attempt to divert Mussolini to a pro-French attitude.

Laval became Foreign Minister in October 1934 in succession to Louis Barthou, who was murdered by a Croat in Marseilles along with King Alexander of Yugoslavia in what was probably an Italo-Hungarian plot to disrupt the Franco-Yugoslav alliance. Laval signed the pact with the USSR which had been negotiated by his predecessor but he did so only because this pact was in any case stillborn. France had a conservative government and the USSR a communist one. Ideological differences were not by themselves a bar to an alliance with a country which Richelieu had allied with Turks against Christians at the noontide of the Ottoman advance into Europe. But Richelieu had never feared what the Turks might do to France, whereas the politicians of the Third Republic feared very much what the USSR might do to France by means of the French Communist Party. Unlike the Sultan, Stalin had a political party inside France which was directed by the Communist International inside the USSR. Although Stalin had abandoned Trotsky's policy of permanent revolution, he had not gainsaid it and as a result an alliance between the USSR and the French Third Republic was all but impossible. For Laval the pact with the USSR which he inherited was distasteful but it was also a possible means to a different end: a rapprochement with Germany.

Laval, like a number of his contemporaries and like even more Frenchmen after the Second World War (including de Gaulle), sincerely desired to put an end to Franco-German hostility. He worked towards a rapprochement by using a Franco-Russian pact as a reserve threat and also by seeking an understanding with Italy which would still further isolate Germany. His Italian policy was dangerous because it disturbed the countries of the Little Entente. These wanted France to make an alliance with the USSR, but they distrusted Italy which was allied with Hungary—an anti-Versailles state which had lost territory to all three members of the Little Entente. So Laval risked losing his Little Entente allies unless he could reconcile them, especially Yugoslavia, with Italy. Moreover Mussolini had his price. It was a free hand for Italy in Africa. During his visit to Rome Laval at least implied that France would pay this price, although it is still open to doubt whether he was signalling to Mussolini that Italy might go ahead and attack Ethiopia or whether he meant no more than to concede to Italy an exclusive economic field in that country. The vagueness was not unintentional. Mussolini interpreted it in the most favourable light to his own ambitions and, at Stresa in April of the next year, he joined France and Great Britain in condemning breaches of the treaty of Versailles and subscribed a series of agreements whose general message was that these three powers were constituting an anti-German front. Again part of the bargain, in Mussolini's mind, was a free hand for Italy in Africa but again the understanding was so tacit that Ethiopia was not even mentioned. The Stresa front was a flimsy affair. In any case the front quickly obeyed its own nature and fell apart. In June the British government, still rather more intent on making friends with Germany than building an opposition to it, made a naval agreement with Germany in contravention not only of the treaty of Versailles but also of the declarations of the Stresa conference. France and Italy were not consulted, although France was informed at a late stage in the negotiations; its protests were ignored. This episode emphasized Great Britain's abandonment of the full letter of Versailles, but by conniving at a breach of Versailles Great Britain undermined its ability to protest against breaches of Locarno, which was its substitute for Versailles and was soon to be equally flouted by Hitler.

Although an Italian conquest of Ethiopia might endanger no vital French or British national interest, it could only be undertaken in breach of the Covenant of the League of Nations. It was therefore bound to weaken international stability by infringing the general principle of *pacta sunt servanda* as well as the precise terms of the Covenant, and a substantial body of opinion in France, Great Britain and elsewhere was not prepared to connive at Italian aggression for fear of encouraging aggression generally and weakening institutions which might be used to stop Hitler. Besides which the butchering of innocent Ethiopians to make a Roman empire was offensive on elementary human grounds. Consequently when war broke out in October, six months after the Stresa meeting, Mussolini discovered that his campaign was running up against more than a scandalized outcry. Laval discovered that his pro-Italian policy would not work so easily and he was forced to take a lead, jointly with Great Britain, in invoking sanctions against Italy.

But Great Britain and France did not persist. Torn between a policy of upholding the Covenant and the rule of law and, on the other hand, securing Italian friendship at the cost of letting Ethiopia down, they found that their zeal for sanctions stopped short of those measures which could have effectively checked Mussolini. Such measures, they feared, would force Mussolini to go to war with them. They were probably right, for Mussolini was too far committed in Africa and too vulnerable at home to refuse the challenge and survive. But by the same tokens he would not only have resorted to war; he would most probably have lost it. London and Paris were, however, not minded to bring the issue to the testing point. The British government was acutely conscious of the risks entailed, not directly from a clash with Italy but at second remove from Japan, which might turn an Anglo-Italian war into an occasion for attacking the British empire in Asia: the British cabinet was repeatedly warned by the Admiralty that the Royal Navy no longer had the capacity to wage war simultaneously in European and Pacific waters. So Great Britain and France both preferred to bluff (a threat of British naval action which had no effect on the Italian government but persuaded the Italian people that Great Britain was an enemy) and they also entered into separate manoeuvres behind the scenes to give Mussolini satisfaction in Africa. In London the Foreign Secretary, Sir Samuel Hoare, resurrected a proposal for partitioning Ethiopia which had been put to Mussolini before the fighting began and took it to Paris where Laval improved on it – from the Italian point of view. The two governments were at this point closer in their foreign policies than at most times between the wars. But this Hoare-Laval plan was then leaked to the press before it was presented to Mussolini. There was a public outcry and the plan (and Hoare) had to be dropped. But Mussolini got what he wanted anyway with the result that France and Great Britain got the worst of both worlds. The failure of sanctions discredited the League and the mechanisms of collective security and created a mood of pessimism. The Stresa front dissolved and the Rome-Berlin Axis was created – although the phrase itself, invented by Mussolini, did not appear until shortly after the outbreak of the Spanish civil war. Mussolini used force with impunity. Hitler converted a potential enemy into an ally and had a free demonstration of how boldness pays. France, estranged from Great Britain by the collapse of the Hoare-Laval plan which confirmed all the worst French suspicions about the British, was left with no entente with Italy, only an empty pact with the USSR, no rapprochement with Germany, and damaged relations with Poland and the Little Entente. The attempt to bring law and order into the international system was manifestly crippled as the League's principal members discovered that their obligations under the Covenant were incompatible with their national interests – particularly in the case of Great Britain which lacked the power to uphold both the Covenant in Europe and British imperial interests and obligations in the East.

In March 1935, just before the Stresa conference, Hitler had introduced compulsory military service in breach of the treaty of Versailles (his first breach of the treaty) and acknowledged the existence of the German air forces. In the same year he recovered the Saar by plebiscite, with nine tenths of the voters choosing reunion with Germany; concluded the Anglo-German naval treaty; promulgated the viciously anti-semitic Nuremberg decrees; recorded a 99 per cent victory in a referendum; and prepared Berlin for the oldest surviving festival of peace, the Olympic Games. In March 1936, he ordered his army to march into the Rhineland which was demilitarized not only by Versailles but also by Locarno which he had reaffirmed twelve months previously. He was copying Mussolini but was still not sure whether he could repeat in Europe the success Mussolini had had in Africa. The French government of the day was a pre-election caretaker team, divided within itself, estranged from Great Britain by the collapse of the Laval-Hoare plan, filled with fear by the gloomy and timorous advice of its own generals, and deceived by a German cover plan which induced it to believe that Hitler was using 265,000 men instead of only a few battalions backed by four divisions. Hitler assured his own generals, who feared war and defeat, that no French soldier would stir and halfway through the operation he refused a request from Blomberg for a partial withdrawal. He had the satisfaction of seeing his generals much more nervous than he was, and the success of the coup redoubled his ascendancy over them, his own self-assurance and his belief in the use of force. This was not Hitler's first challenge to the western powers – his withdrawal from the League and from the Disarmament Conference in October 1933 may be said to be the first and his acknowledgement of German rearmament the second – but it was the first in which he used his army. Yet the risks which he ran were not as great as they seemed, for three months earlier his Ambassador in Paris had passed on to him a strong hint from Laval that the French army would be used only to defend French soil and would not cross France's frontiers. Although the French Foreign Minister, Étienne Flandin, argued that a mere show of force would send the Germans scuttling back, only a minority of his cabinet supported him and it is unlikely that after the first few hours a show of force would have been enough.

By the remilitarization of the Rhineland Hitler challenged with impunity the two strongest powers in Europe, who had been also the principal champions of Versailles and were, since Locarno, Germany's allies in a comprehensive scheme for keeping the peace in western Europe. He broke France's system of alliances in the east no less than the settlement in the west by exposing the feebleness of France's will, and he implicitly asserted that Germany was a greater power in eastern Europe than either France or the USSR; thereafter nobody was prepared to put the assertion to the test. Against these gains there was only one feeble warning signal. The USSR had joined the League of Nations in 1934 and concluded a treaty of mutual assistance with France in May 1935. A similar treaty was made with Czechoslovakia and a British Minister, Anthony Eden, visited Moscow the same year. But the effectiveness of the USSR as an ally was discounted (Germany had beaten Russia in the First World War and seemed well able to do so again), the ratification of the Franco-Soviet pact was tellingly delayed for nine months and Great Britain was even further from considering such a reversal of alliances.

In July 1936 (the month in which sanctions against Italy were abandoned) a revolt broke out against the republican government of Spain. The ensuing civil war cemented the alliance between Hitler and Mussolini who recognized and helped the forces of revolutionary Fascism under General Francisco Franco; it created a new threat to France's back door; it crystallized and embittered the ideological conflict in Europe between Fascism and communism and added to the perplexities of democrats; it raised the level of violence and made it international, for in Spain battle was joined internationally as foreign volunteers and foreign governments took sides in a war which ended only six months before the beginning of the World War in Europe.

The sources and course of the Spanish civil war will not be related here but we have to consider its effects in Europe as a whole. All the principal European powers were faced with the question whether to intervene and, if so, how and how much. The insurgents appealed at once to Italy and Germany for aid. The government appealed to France. Italy and Germany responded promptly but with different motives. Mussolini, and even more so his son-in-law and Foreign Minister Galeazzo Ciano, were comparatively wholehearted in desiring Franco's victory. On the German side such a victory would bring advantages; in a future European war Germany would be entitled to expect Spanish help in the form of submarine bases and iron ore and even possibly co-belligerence, while active participation in the civil war would, as Goering pointed out and as the town of Guernica later discovered, give the Luftwaffe useful training. But Hitler did not want the civil war to turn into a general war for which he felt himself as yet unprepared and he therefore reacted with some caution and limited German aid to the insurgents until he came to feel that this risk was very small. German and Italian help to Franco were decisive on more than one occasion.

The British government was as determined as Hitler to prevent the extension of the war, and this determination overrode all other considerations. In France, Léon Blum wanted at first to help the legitimate Spanish government with arms but changed his mind owing to opposition in his cabinet and parliament: he feared civil war in France too, were he to persist in supporting a Spanish Popular Front which included communists. British opposition added to Blum's constraints. His more right-wing colleagues urged him not to get out of step with Great Britain. Thus the war in Spain intensified French dependence on Great Britain and its right-wing policies at the one moment in the thirties when France, under a socialist Prime Minister, might have been disposed to seek an opening to the Left in its foreign policy and an understanding with the USSR.

There was also a division of opinion in the United States administration where the anti-interventionists, led by the Secretary of State Cordell Hull, won the day, again partly influenced by the British decision. A Non-Intervention Committee, comprising two dozen states, was created and continued to function throughout a war in which intervention was unconcealed. The principal effects were three: first, that the continuance nonetheless of Italian and German help created profound cynicism; secondly, that the persistence of Great Britain and France nonetheless in the policy of non-intervention earned the one a reputation for hypocrisy and the other a reputation for feebleness which were equally deserved; and thirdly, that the Spanish government could get help from nowhere except the USSR which supplied it to the considerable benefit of the Spanish communists who were able greatly to enhance their initially modest position on the government side. Stalin's attitude to aid for Spain was much like Hitler's. He decided to give some aid but not too much. He too feared the extension of the war (if everybody had known of everybody else's fears, each might have been less afraid), but he also feared a Franco victory which, by further distracting and weakening France, might encourage Hitler to press his ambitions in eastern Europe.

In retrospect the Spanish civil war appears as the extreme example of a phenomenon of much wider extent in Europe. It has often been said that one of the most upsetting changes in twentieth-century Europe was the dismemberment of the Habsburg and Ottoman empires, but no less upsetting was the disintegration of apparently more coherent societies like France and Spain. In Spain, as the civil war revealed, the nation dissolved into groups which not only warred among themselves but looked beyond Spain for friends and helpers. Even in countries which did not disintegrate so spectacularly as Spain national bonds were so far enfeebled that ideological chieftains like Mussolini (a successful one) or Charles Maurras (a relatively unsuccessful one) were able to treat whole sections of their fellow-citizens – communists, socialists – as inferior parts of society, as outsiders within the walls. Social conflict was internationalized as these groups looked increasingly to their friends in other countries to help them against their own governments.

The war in Spain had a further consequence for European politics. The tactical and psychological successes of the German dive-bombers, the Stukas, created a false impression of the power of modern air forces, an impression which was immensely to Germany's advantage and played a substantial part in conditioning Anglo-French policies in the year of Munich. The Stukas in Spain spread fear far beyond it.

In November 1936 Germany and Japan signed the Anti-Comintern Pact, a short document by which the signatories undertook to exchange information and consult together about the international activities of communism and to concert counter-activities. Other countries were invited to adhere and Italy did so a year later, but the main point of the published agreement was to worry the USSR about its eastern frontiers and Great Britain about its position as an Asian power. By a secret protocol signed on the same day as the treaty Germany and Japan promised, in the event of an unprovoked attack or threat by the USSR against either of them, to do nothing which would make things easier for the USSR; each of them also promised to enter into no treaty with the USSR without the consent of the other. This secret part of the pact was not all that Hitler desired since Japan had declined to give positive help to Germany in the event of hostilities between Germany and the USSR. Japan was not to be drawn into a European war.

One of the most important pieces of evidence which we have concerning Hitler's intentions at this period is a document known as the Hossbach memorandum. This document was written by Colonel Hossbach five days after a meeting in Berlin on 5 November 1937 which he attended and at which he secretly took notes in spite of instructions by Hitler to the contrary. The meeting was attended by Hitler, his Ministers for War and Foreign Affairs (Blomberg and Neurath) and his three Commanders-in-Chief (Fritsch, Raeder and Goering), and lasted from 4.15 to 10.30 p.m. It consisted of a long statement on foreign affairs by Hitler, introduced with unusual solemnity as the fruit of four and a half years' reflection and as his political testament in the event of his death. Hitler stated, not for the first time, that the object of German policy was the security and multiplication of the German people. He repeated what he had said and written publicly on other occasions about *Lebensraum*. He rejected colonies as a solution; the necessary space had to be found in Europe, although later generations might have other problems which would force them to seek other solutions. There could be no solution without force, and this meant risks. Hitler then got nearer to details. He said that although nobody could tell what the situation would be in the years 1943–5, one thing was certain: Germany could not wait longer than that, partly because he himself would be past the peak of his powers and partly because Germany's advantages would begin to wane as its armament became obsolete and its enemies caught up. At that point he would in any event attack in order to resolve the space problem. Before it he would be guided by circumstances. He would watch his western and south-eastern flanks and he envisaged action against Austria and Czechoslovakia if France were weakened by trouble at home or by embroilments with Italy in the Mediterranean.

This document demonstrates once more Hitler's two main characteristics in external affairs: the fixity of his purpose, which was Germany's forcible territorial expansion in Europe, and the vagueness of his timing. Apart from setting an ultimate date – at least six years in the future and possibly eight – when he would definitely take the initiative, Hitler was leaving everything to opportunity, and in the event he attacked Austria and Czechoslovakia separately and not simultaneously, without the benefit of such a French crisis as he had envisaged or of a diversionary Mediterranean war. When he invaded Austria on 12 March 1938 and annexed it to the German Reich he did so because the Austrian Chancellor, Kurt von Schuschnigg, forced his hand. Schuschnigg decreed a plebiscite in order to strengthen his position in dealing with Austrian Nazi excesses – and Hitler feared Schuschnigg might succeed all too well. There were many stories at the time of the unreadiness of the German forces. Hitler had taken one of the risks which, as he had said in his lecture in the previous November, always attend the use of force. It was not a very big risk. Nobody did anything to stop him. Mussolini acquiesced. He had no choice, but Hitler's effusive thanks reflected his concern about Mussolini's reaction to the flouting of a basic precept of Italian foreign policy. Hitler's relief on this occasion may explain his loyalty to Mussolini through the next seven years.

In the eighteen months following the *Anschluss* Hitler attacked two other states, Czechoslovakia and Poland. The difference between the Austrian case and these other two does not lie in the result: all three states were eliminated. Hitler reckoned that he could have his way with them because greater states than they did not want to fight for their sake. When

THE EXPANSION OF GERMANY 1936 – 1939

Germany in 1936.

The 'Little Entente'.

March 1939, Germany annexes Memel.

September 1939, Germany annexes Danzig.

1 September 1939, Germany invades Poland.

October 1938, Czech borderlands ceded to Germany. Remainder of Czechoslovakia dismembered March 1939.

March 1938, Germany annexes Austria.

March 1936, Germany reoccupies Rhineland.

Shelled by German pocket-battleship DEUTSCHLAND, May 1937.

Germany experiments with its new bomber force in 1936.

MUSSOLINI – HITLER AXIS 1936

~ ARTHUR BANKS ~

an earlier land-grabber, Frederick the Great, had seized neighbouring territory, other European powers took up arms (whether successfully or unsuccessfully is not here the question). They did so, however, in circumstances different from those in which Hitler operated and his enemies agonized over what to do about it. Eighteenth-century monarchs had at their disposal special professional bodies maintained for the express purpose of performing or defeating such acts, but modern cabinets had to consider another kind of war. They could either call a whole nation to arms or do nothing, and so they greatly preferred to do nothing. Calling a nation to arms was a fearful and expensive way to prevent a rearrangement of the map, as Bismarck's enemies had discovered when they were beaten and as the Kaiser's enemies had discovered too, even though they won. But Hitler pressed his adversaries too far. Opposition to him stiffened with a slow desperation until, over Poland as it happened, it overbore their reluctance to go to war.

CHAPTER 4

Munich . . . Prague . . . Warsaw

CZECHOSLOVAKIA was a product of the disruption of the Austro-Hungarian monarchy. It was a sturdy democracy with natural resources, modern skills and – except on its southern or Austrian side – strong frontiers. But this promising offspring of the doctrine of self-determination was also a negation of that doctrine. It was, like Great Britain at the end of the Middle Ages, a mixture of peoples not yet congealed into a nation. It had a population of 14 to 15 million, of whom 10 million were Czechs or Slovaks, 3 million were Germans and the remainder consisted of small but self-conscious Hungarian, Ukrainian and Polish minorities. Most of the 3 million Germans lived scattered along the Bohemian and Moravian borderlands and in the principal cities. They came to be known as Sudeten Germans, but this was a deliberate misnomer. The Sudetenland, properly so called, lay north and east of their homes, but for propaganda purposes it was convenient to attach a name to them and so give the impression that they constituted a compact and detachable ethnic group.

By its nature and origins Czechoslovakia was anchored to the peace settlement which had created it, and was opposed to the reconstitution of a Danubian empire and to the resurgence of German power, especially a German power which would include Austria and so outflank it at its weakest point. Its founder and first president, T. G. Masaryk (resigned 1935, died 1937), and his successor Edvard Beneš based their policies for survival on the military strength and strategic importance of their country. They did not expect to be able to stand alone against a powerful German enemy but they aimed to make Czechoslovakia valuable and perhaps even essential to the vital interests of western states which would see to it that the Czechs and Slovaks were not once more subjected to Germans. They wanted to ensure that an armed attack on Czechoslovakia would never be a local affair; an aggressor would have to reckon with allied powers and so would think twice before beginning what was, if pledges meant anything, bound to become a general war. In 1938 Czechoslovakia had one of Europe's most noted armaments industries and an army which was almost the equal of the German army in men and equipment, though inferior in staying power because of Czechoslovakia's smaller population and human reserves. It had also an alliance with France to counter this weakness: by holding a proportion of the German army in the west the threat of a French attack would prevent a German victory.

But in 1938 the threat did not work. Hitler did not believe it. France no longer gave the Czechoslovak alliance top priority. The chink in Czecho-slovakia's armour was Great Britain.

Great Britain had persistently refused to enter into commitments in eastern Europe, so that Masaryk and Beneš never succeeded in getting a British guarantee as well as a French one – until it was too late. Moreover, as the European situation got more menacing Great Britain began to work to demolish the French guarantee in the belief that it was not, as the French themselves had intended, a way of deterring Germany from going to war but had become a trap whereby a local war in central Europe would be expanded into a general European war. Great Britain hoped that the abrogation of the guarantee would remove this danger and pro-vide a breathing space in which somehow war might be averted. The logic of British policy was to inflict the consequences of war and defeat on Czechoslovakia in the hope of saving everybody else. Czechoslovakia proved vulnerable because the French guarantee was not an Anglo-French guarantee and because, for France, the British alliance was more im-portant than the French security system in central Europe of which the Czechoslovak alliance was a part. Since the evident revival of German power in Europe France had been on the defensive against Germany, and since the collapse of Franco-Italian relations in 1935–6 France had been left with no effective ally in the west except Great Britain. When there-fore Great Britain required France to abandon Czechoslovakia, France did so.

British policy at this period has been summed up in the word ap-peasement. Appeasement describes a range of attitudes stretching from the desire to be fair and decent to a defeated foe to the policy of buying off a resurgent one. It covers the whole of the period between the wars, becoming more disreputable with time. The object of appeasement in the twenties was Weimar Germany, in the thirties Nazi Germany; its aim in the twenties was justice, in the thirties safety; the price in the twenties was the reduction of reparations (primarily to Great Britain) and equal rights for Germans, in the thirties the price was turning a blind eye to German ambitions and what these cost other people (primarily Czechoslovakia). Munich, where Czechoslovakia was sacrificed, became synonymous with betrayal, as Canossa with a similar kind of abasement.

The British ruling class had a propensity for seeing what was least admirable in Frenchmen and what was best in Germans, so that a sub-liminal distrust and dislike of France nourished pro-German sentiments which were often expressed in kith-and-kin terms – though without the excessive racialism of complementary German thinking. (There was also a number of fervent Francophiles who understood the French dilemma, but they were a minority and an increasingly lukewarm one.) This Anglo-Saxon or Anglo-Prussian kinship was reinforced after 1919 by the radical Anglo-French disagreement about the right way to behave towards Germany. Where France felt cheated at not having secured the Rhine frontier, Great Britain felt that Germany was being cheated by the special restrictions imposed on German sovereignty in the Rhineland, by inordinate reparation claims and by the limitations on German armament. Great Britain's vision was of a purged Germany playing its due part in European affairs, and too many British politicians retained this vision even when, with the Nazis, the purging ceased to be a cleansing and became an abomination. They persisted in regarding the change of régime in Germany in 1933 as something like a normal change of government in Great Britain. They were not men who found it easy to recognize abnormality and they persisted in regarding Hitler as a responsible statesman because he occupied the position of one. Even though British Ambassadors (Sir Horace Rumbold and Sir Eric Phipps) and other observers reported what was happening to the German Jews as early as 1933, they clung to a way of thinking and a way of doing business which were tragically inappropriate, to say the least. The efforts of Chamberlain and the language of a later Ambassador, Sir Nevile Henderson, betrayed an inability to understand Hitler which was based on a determination not to: Hitler's ravings were passed over and he was regarded as a man who would make bargains and stick to them because it was difficult to see what to do if he was really a totally different kind of person.

In this way men who were pro-German before Hitler found too little difficulty in going on being pro-German with Hitler. Hence the extreme ludicrousness of their comments about Hitler, when they went to visit him or simply expressed themselves about him without that effort. They believed that there was a point at which Hitler, if given enough territory round his borders and some colonies, would become 'reasonable'. They persuaded themselves that they were giving Hitler pieces of territory which Germany ought to have on the basis of the principle of national self-determination or equal rights and that, having done so, they would have turned Hitler into a man of peace. They had no objection to the absorption of Austria by Germany, and little compunction about bundling a small *parvenu* state like Czechoslovakia into the new German Reich. What they wanted was a version of the Anti-Comintern Pact, an Anglo-German understanding for which they were willing to give Hitler other people's territory in central Europe and (in the mistaken belief that Hitler's quest for living space was a hankering for lost lands overseas), British colonies and even mandated territories entrusted to Great Britain by the League, if these readjustments of real estate would remove the obstacles to a *pax Anglo-Germanica*. In the last years of peace British Ministers discussed among themselves how France might be persuaded to give some of its African territories to Germany in return for British territory in West Africa; or how the whole of tropical Africa might be re-partitioned, a throw-back to the nineteenth century's method of allaying European rivalries by removing them into another continent and buying off the more dangerous and discontented Europeans with African coin.

In May 1937 Neville Chamberlain succeeded Stanley Baldwin as Prime Minister. Chamberlain had been a highly successful provincial politician who, after being Mayor of Birmingham, had moved rather late in life into national politics and had there enhanced his reputation by his work as Minister of Health and Chancellor of the Exchequer. He had the strength, manifested in cabinet before he became Prime Minister as well as afterwards, of the man who sees one side of a case only. He was never the cleverest man in any of the cabinets in which he sat, but it so chanced that his cleverer colleagues were weaker in debate and less effective when it came to taking a decision. As Chancellor he won applause by introducing the lowest defence estimates of the inter-war years. He had the virtues and the limitations of a prosperous middle-class conservative and he had the misfortune – which was also his country's misfortune – to display his virtues in the earlier part of his career and his faults, which included stubbornness, during the last years of his life. He was a man of proven ability and impressive experience who suffered from the peculiarly English notion that there is nothing that a really intelligent man cannot tackle. It was in this spirit that he tackled foreign affairs and Hitler.

He began by getting rid of his Foreign Secretary, Anthony Eden, who was pushed into resignation in February 1938 by the Prime Minister's manners and, to a lesser extent, his policies. Chamberlain was determined to come to terms with Mussolini in spite of the conquest of Ethiopia and Italy's continuing intervention in the Spanish civil war. There was something to be said for recognizing the conquest of Ethiopia once it was an accomplished fact. (Eden himself was in favour of recognizing Franco a year later.) There was also much to be said for repairing Anglo-Italian relations if a European war seemed likely: the Italian navy was a significant factor in world politics, especially before 1939 when Roosevelt, at British request, moved American naval forces from the Atlantic to the Pacific to counter possible Japanese designs against Australia and New Zealand, which the Royal Navy was pledged to protect. Eden, however, was in no hurry to seek Italian friendship so long as Mussolini went on helping Franco. Chamberlain on the other hand regarded the matter as urgent in order to keep Mussolini at least at arm's length from Hitler. This issue – the timing of Anglo-Italian conversations – was the immediate occasion of Eden's resignation. Behind it were both a larger issue and personal pique. Chamberlain was contemptuous of American statesmanship and, like many of his class, basically anti-American. Roosevelt, like Eden but unlike Chamberlain, was opposed to *de jure* recognition of Italy's African conquests without a specific and simultaneous undertaking to take Italian forces out of Spain. Further, Roosevelt ventured to offer his services as a mediator in Europe's affairs. Chamberlain, without telling Eden or consulting the Foreign Office, brushed this offer aside. Unlike Baldwin, Chamberlain was determined to play a leading part in international affairs, as a British Prime Minister has every right to do, but Eden was irked by this incursion into his special fief. Eden's assessment of the forces which shaped European politics included not only the four powers which Chamberlain treated as the only ones that mattered, but also to some degree the USSR, the League and the United States. Yet their policies were at this time so little apart that Eden's resignation was heard by some of his cabinet colleagues with astonished incredulity. In retrospect it seems an early indication of the instability that was to ruin his career after the war.

Chamberlain's attempt to create a concert of four was in any case predoomed to failure. Mussolini privately assured Hitler that Anglo-Italian conversations and agreements would never be allowed to harm the Italo-German accord and when Chamberlain renewed his wooing of Italy after the Munich crisis neither Mussolini nor Ciano took the proceedings seriously. Chamberlain was no less anxious to come to some arrangement with Hitler. During most of 1938 the immediate obstacle to the British policy of appeasement was the so-called Sudeten problem. The Nazi Party had in Czechoslovakia a counterpart called the Sudeten German Party and led by Konrad Henlein, who adopted German Nazi doctrines and behaviour and received funds and instructions from Germany. Henlein was agitating for local autonomy for the German minority. His agitation was echoed by the lesser minorities. It created confusion and disorders calculated to call in question the authority of the central government in Prague at a time when this government was engaged in discussing the rights and status of minorities. At every turn in these discussions Henlein made increasingly unacceptable claims, backed by the undefined but inescapable menace of German military action. In April he demanded not only self-government for Germans in Czechoslovakia but also the subordination of Czechoslovakia's foreign policy to Germany's interests.

In the previous November, a few weeks after the Hossbach meeting in Berlin, British and French Ministers had conferred in London about whether and how to resist German moves in central Europe. They agreed that they should do nothing about a German annexation of Austria but, largely on the insistence of the French Foreign Minister Yvon Delbos, they accepted that a German attack on Czechoslovakia would involve France in a war pursuant to its treaty obligations. Since Great Britain could not risk seeing France engaged in war with Germany and defeated, Great Britain too faced war over Czechoslovakia. The only escape lay in a German-Czech settlement acceptable to, or at any rate accepted by, both Hitler and Beneš, and this became the prime object of British policy. It entailed pressure on Prague rather than Berlin since Czechoslovakia was the weaker state, undoubtedly so if its allies could be eliminated from the equation, which Great Britain thought they could be: after the *Anschluss* France and the USSR had both reaffirmed their obligations to defend Czechoslovakia but the USSR was not judged to be in a position to do much and France was in no position to jeopardize Great Britain's friendship. In the summer of 1938 therefore Chamberlain decided to intensify British pressure on Czechoslovakia which, supplementing German pressures, Great Britain had been exerting since the previous year. After consulting the German government about his proposed intervention but without informing France, Chamberlain sent a special emissary (Lord Runciman) to Czechoslovakia to get Beneš, under the guise of mediation, to accept whatever might be necessary to keep the peace. Runciman arrived in Prague at the end of July. He subsequently reported to the cabinet that Beneš was insincere, stubborn and too clever by half.

Yet it was by this date sufficiently clear that the Sudeten problem was not the real danger to peace and that the excision of this problem would not remove the danger of war. To the accumulating evidence on Hitler's wider intentions there was added in June 1938 a specific warning. In that month Goering's adjutant, General Karl Bodenschatz, officially informed the French assistant air attaché in Berlin that Germany was preparing to build a line of defensive fortifications from the North Sea to the Swiss border, that Germany had no aggressive intentions against France or Great Britain but that, having first secured its southern flank against any threat from Czechoslovakia, it intended to eliminate the 'Soviet threat' and simultaneously secure the living space which was indispensable to Germany. Bodenschatz specifically mentioned the Ukraine and compared Germany's eastward expansion in Europe with the way in which France had secured its own needs by expanding into Africa. This was a clear enough indication of Hitler's intention to overpower Czechoslovakia, make war on the USSR and protect himself in the west by a series of fortifications which could not be completed before the middle of 1939 at the earliest. It presented France and Great Britain with a choice between keeping out of a war in eastern Europe or joining in such a war. It ruled out the possibility of preventing a war in eastern Europe by appeasement.

At the beginning of September Beneš declared himself ready to accept all the demands of the Sudeten Germans for autonomy. On 12 September Chamberlain, under pressure from many sides – the French and American governments, the Vatican, the opposition in the House of Commons, Churchill – and in the hope of inducing Hitler to be less explosive than usual in the speech which he was due to make in Nuremberg on that day, decided to go to the lengths of reminding Hitler that France was bound to fight for Czechoslovakia and that Great Britain would fight with France, but from Berlin Henderson asked the cabinet to excuse him from passing this warning on. Henderson's role in these years negates the view that Ambassadors no longer count. Whereas Chamberlain's dominant aim was to keep Great Britain out of war, Henderson had a more positive policy. He did not want Great Britain to stand in Hitler's way. It is impossible to read his statements and despatches or observe his conduct without concluding that he endorsed Hitler's aims more than he deplored Hitler's character and behaviour. He wanted an Anglo-German entente which would preserve Great Britain's imperial position in the world and license Hitler to lay the USSR low, and he made no secret of his views, either privately or publicly. He even discussed them with Goering, at which point he found that he had gone further than Chamberlain would countenance.

During the summer and autumn of 1938 a violent anti-Czech campaign was in progress in Germany. Press and radio were presenting, with the utmost emotional mendacity, a picture of persecution of Germans in Czechoslovakia and at Nuremberg on 12 September Hitler spoke with such exceptional violence that his words provoked an abortive rising by Sudeten Germans and the imposition of martial law in parts of Czechoslovakia on the 13th. Henlein fled to Germany and with his departure the situation became more manageable. But this improvement at the storm centre was lost on observers further away and two days later Chamberlain unwittingly reversed it. He resolved to put into operation a plan which he had been preparing for some time. He would go and see Hitler. This plan had been discussed only with four Ministers separately (but not in cabinet), with Nevile Henderson and with two or three other close advisers. Like Eden nearly twenty years later in the Suez crisis Chamberlain kept his cabinet very much in the dark about his plans and policies.

As with the Runciman mission France was not informed. Although he had hoped to influence Hitler's tone at Nuremberg, he was also resolved to go and talk with Hitler whatever he said at Nuremberg and however he said it. He flew to Berchtesgaden on 15 September and on the same day he agreed in principle that the Sudetenland, an area still undefined, ought to be detached from Czechoslovakia and given to Germany. At no point does the difference between these two men, now meeting *tête-à-tête* to settle the fate of Europe, appear in retrospect more glaring: Hitler humouring his distinguished guest but keeping up his preparations to use force; Chamberlain returning to London to affirm his belief that Hitler was the sort of man who would be 'rather better than his word'. The nearer the appeasers got to a settlement with Hitler the more they clung to this tattered premise – and the more they needed to still their consciences by working themselves up into a state of hatred against the Czechs as the people who might spoil the whole game.

Besides coercing the Czechs and coming to terms with Hitler, Chamberlain needed to cow France. His policy required him to scare France into dishonouring its treaty with Czechoslovakia. The British Ambassador in Paris, Sir Eric Phipps, had no great difficulty in scaring the French Foreign Minister, Georges Bonnet. He also fortified Chamberlain's views by refraining from reporting to London what Frenchmen of another stamp were saying, until ordered by the Foreign Office to do so. Yet during the September crisis of 1938 the French government and even the pessimistic General Gamelin seemed resigned to going to war for Czechoslovakia and advancing into Germany. After the robber synod at Berchtesgaden however, to which they had not been invited, French Ministers were confronted with an accomplished and perhaps not wholly unwelcome fact. After a conference in London on the 18th they accepted the Anglo-German compact and joined with Great Britain in forcing the Czechs to agree to surrender all territories where half the inhabitants were German. Beneš, who had already conceded all reasonable German demands, at first refused but he had no real choice. He was told that France refused to fight without a promise of British backing and that Great Britain refused to back France in a war begun for Czechoslovakia. All he could get, with French help, was an Anglo-French guarantee of the independence and neutrality of the new Czechoslovakia in place of the discarded French guarantee for the old one. Great Britain reluctantly agreed to give this vulnerable and enfeebled state the promises which it had refused to give to a much more worthwhile ally.

But this was not the end. So far from removing an obstacle to peace the Czechoslovak surrender brought war nearer. Hitler, baulked of the military destruction of Czechoslovakia which he had been talking about, declared that the terms forced on Beneš by Great Britain and France no longer satisfied him. Chamberlain flew back to Germany where, at Godesberg on the 22nd, he discovered that Hitler now demanded even larger stretches of Czechoslovakia, a plebiscite in other areas and the entry of German troops into Czechoslovakia before the lines of partition had been settled. This second meeting was punctuated by a stream of reports of Czech outrages which Hitler caused to be concocted and brought to him while he and Chamberlain were conferring. Chamberlain, returning to London on the 24th, told his cabinet that he believed that he had established some influence over Hitler. He was for accepting Hitler's terms and getting Beneš to accept them but the opposition within the British cabinet was hardening and was temporarily joined by Halifax. Daladier too, once more in London, was firmer; he seemed resigned to war. The Czechs had mobilized on the 23rd. Chamberlain wavered. On the 26th a last attempt by British emissaries to get Hitler to see 'reason' produced a scene of such fury that they fled without saying what they had been told to say. On the 27th Chamberlain, after some hesitation, authorized the mobilization of the British fleet which the First Lord of the Admiralty, Alfred Duff Cooper, had been urging for some days. On the 28th Chamberlain, while speaking in the House of Commons, received an invitation to go to Munich, the outcome of a British appeal to Mussolini to do something.

At Munich on the 29th the substance of the Godesberg demands was conceded – on the basis of proposals which were advanced by Mussolini as a compromise but had been drafted for him by the German Foreign Office. In substance Chamberlain and Daladier let Hitler have practically all he wanted, Mussolini being in attendance. The Russians were treated as irrelevant and neither invited nor consulted. Czechoslovakia, whose representatives came to Munich but were confined to the vestibule, chose acquiescence rather than slaughter. Beneš resigned. On the day after the conference Chamberlain, while taking leave of Hitler, produced a piece of paper on which he had drafted an Anglo-German declaration of friendship and of the determination of the two peoples never to go to war with one another. Hitler, who had no desire to fight the British, was delighted and the two leaders signed then and there. In London Duff Cooper resigned but cabinet colleagues who had talked earlier of doing so too decided not to: Chamberlain's control over his cabinet and his large and still docile majority in the House of Commons was at this time more complete than that of any British Prime Minister since the eighteenth century. In France three Ministers who had resigned before Munich withdrew their resignations after it. In December a Franco-German declaration of friendship, similar to the Chamberlain-Hitler scrap of paper, was signed. Poland took the opportunity to seize in October the area of Teschen, dubiously Polish in character but undeniably a plum.

The Munich agreement was greeted with relief by everybody except the Czechs and Slovaks. So acute had been the fear of war that this relief burst out in scenes of enthusiasm which were particularly galling to the minority whose shame or apprehension overmastered their relief. For most British and French Ministers the surrender had at least staved off war. Chamberlain had enough faith in the piece of paper which he had got Hitler to sign to talk of having secured 'peace for our time'. But some were considerably less sanguine. Soon after Munich Halifax, now Foreign Secretary in place of Eden, wanted to introduce conscription and in the following January – when there was a scare over reports that Hitler was about to invade Holland – he advocated staff talks with France and Belgium, consultation with Washington and soundings about the acceptability of British guarantees to Poland, Rumania, Greece and Turkey. Two months later, in March 1939, all lingering delusions were finally blown away when Hitler, in defiance of the Munich agreement, completed his conquest of Czechoslovakia.

The mutilated Czechoslovakia created in 1938 consisted of three federated provinces: Bohemia-Moravia, Slovakia and Ruthenia. In October Hitler directed his armed services to be ready to deal with the rest of Czechoslovakia and to seize Memel. On 14 March 1939, on orders from Berlin, Slovakia declared itself independent of Prague and asked to become a German protectorate. Hitler had a minor piece of luck over Slovakia. The union of the Slovaks with the much more numerous Czechs had not been a smooth one. When Czechoslovakia was created, Slovakia, formerly a dependency of Hungary, was much less developed than the Czech lands of Bohemia and Moravia which, under Austrian rule, had enjoyed considerable educational as well as industrial advancement. Consequently the Slovak parts of Czechoslovakia were largely administered by Czechs after independence and the Slovaks accused the Czechs with some degree of justice of being slow to remedy this imbalance. Although on nearly every occasion Slovaks gave more votes to Czechoslovak parties than to the specifically Slovak one, there was a significant autonomist movement led by Father Andrew Hlinka. In 1938 Hlinka died and his successor, Monsignor Tiso, abandoned autonomy in favour of separatism. This was a help to Hitler.

Besides turning Slovakia into a distinct German satellite Hitler completed the destruction of Czech independence. Beneš's successor, President Emil Hácha, and his Foreign Minister took the road to Berlin where both were subject to such verbal bludgeoning that Hácha fainted. German troops were already marching on Prague. Under threat of a bombing of their capital the Czech Ministers submitted and Bohemia-Moravia too was declared a German protectorate. Ruthenia was annexed by Hungary in two bites. In November 1938 Hitler, who was not particularly fond of the Hungarians but was pressed by the Italians and Poles, had allowed Hungary to seize part of Ruthenia by what was called the Vienna Award. In March 1939 Hungarian troops occupied the rest of it. Great Britain and France did nothing. Five days before Hitler seized Czechoslovakia Chamberlain told the House of Commons that Europe was settling down and the British Government was turning its attention to disarmament and to more trade with Germany. When the blow fell on Prague both its western guarantors defected on the plea that the severance of Slovakia from Czechoslovakia had nullified their guarantee: the country guaranteed had ceased to exist. A week later Hitler extorted Memel from Lithuania by an ultimatum containing false accusations of Lithuanian brutality. Memel had been renounced by Germany by the treaty of Versailles – like Danzig, which now reached the top of Hitler's agenda.

Danzig stood for different things. It was, in the first place, a largely German city to be recovered for the Reich. Secondly, as a bone of contention between Germany and Poland it was a possible cause of a German-Polish war. In that context it raised, thirdly, the two ultimate issues in Hitler's European policy – the attitude of the western democracies to a German attack on Poland and the attitude of the USSR.

Immediately after the final partition and subjugation of Czechoslovakia Hitler seems to have been in two minds over his next move. If Danzig could have been acquired as easily as Memel Hitler's obvious move was to proceed against Danzig. But Danzig could not safely be isolated in this way. So it was more than ordinarily desirable for Hitler to explore and exploit every possibility of securing Danzig, as he had secured the Sudetenland, by threats and cajolement and without war. He could, and in October 1938 did, push forward his planning for aggression in the west. He needed to be prepared for every contingency. But he also tried in the same month to do a deal with Poland: Danzig and a road across the Polish corridor to be surrendered to Germany, Poland to join the Anti-Comintern Pact. On these terms Poland could be reprieved, but this settlement could hardly be more than an interim one unless Poland were to be persuaded later, as Czechoslovakia had been constrained in its second round, to cede Polish Silesia too (Hitler had already talked of recovering the whole of Silesia) and to remain at least benevolently passive when Hitler decided that the time had come to seize his *Lebensraum* farther east.

Poland rejected the German offer and stood on its rights. It would neither endorse the incorporation of Danzig in the Reich nor would it join the Anti-Comintern Pact and so fatally embroil itself with the USSR and render itself dependent on its other neighbour, Germany.

Danzig, renounced by Germany by the treaty of Versailles but peopled chiefly by Germans, was a Free City with a government of its own under the protection of the League of Nations and with a resident League Commissioner to supervise the maintenance of its status and constitution and adjudicate disputes between the Free City and Poland. It was within the Polish customs area and Poland had rights of access to it along a route or corridor which traversed German territory. In elections in 1933 the local Nazi Party won, partly by force and fraud, just over half the votes. Thereafter it rapidly and illegally strengthened its control, while the League abdicated its responsibilities. The city was to all intents and purposes firmly under German and Nazi control for at least two years before it was forcibly incorporated in the Reich on the eve of war.

Polish foreign policy between the wars was a series of expedients designed to preserve a relatively small country from attack by stronger neighbours. It was based at first on the alliance with France. During the twenties this alliance seemed to serve its purpose but with Germany and Russia both recovering from their defeats in the First World War it was not really tested: Poland's problem was postponed until the revival of German and Russian power. When this took place the French alliance began to look undependable, which it was. Poland then adopted a policy of self-preservation by making defensive treaties with its two big neighbours (the non-aggression pacts of 1932 and 1934 with Stalin and Hitler respectively) and by refusing to be drawn into alliance with the one against the other. This policy too seemed to work for a while but although a number of Polish-German issues were resolved the intractable problem of Danzig remained and Poland was in danger as soon as Germany under Hitler became strong enough to attack the USSR. During the thirties Poland's strategic position was weakened by the declining efficacy of alliance with France and by the destruction of Austrian and Czechoslovak independence. Colonel Jozef Beck, Foreign Minister from 1932, clung to the policy of non-alignment between Germany and the USSR and also secured in 1939 a British alliance. He has been much criticized for failing to opt for the USSR against Germany. This refusal was influenced by his anti-communism, which was pronounced, and also by the fact that Poland had been at war with the USSR as recently as 1920, but alignment with the USSR would also have been a complete reversal of a policy which kept Poland reasonably safe so long as Germany and the USSR neither concluded between themselves any agreement overriding their several non-aggression pacts with Poland nor aimed to fight one another over Poland's dead body. In the end Poland was undone because Germany and the USSR did conclude such an agreement. In running the risk that they might Beck was blinded by his own over-estimate of Poland's importance and power.

According to Rauschning Hitler was thinking of partitioning Poland with the USSR even at the time of the German-Polish treaty of 1934 and regarded a German-Russian agreement as a way of safeguarding his eastern front during a war in the west which would be a necessary preliminary to a war against the USSR. Hitler's anti-communism was no bar to an ephemeral deal with Stalin. He himself said on another occasion that treaties were only meant to be kept so long as they served the purpose for which they had been made in the first place. On this thesis the German-Polish treaty could be succeeded by a German-Russian agreement for the partition of Poland, and a German-Russian agreement could be a prelude to a German attack on the USSR. These were problems in timing and tactics. But in relation to the western democracies Hitler had a problem of a different order: whether to attack them or not. He had no direct interest in doing so; there was no sense in making war on states which showed neither the will nor the capacity to thwart his plans in eastern Europe. The risk of effective French interference was a declining one, and if necessary France could be defeated. Great Britain too would probably not interfere, but if it did it could not so easily be defeated. The Luftwaffe was not suited to an attack on Great Britain and at sea Germany was a secondary power. When Hitler thought about Great Britain he preferred to dwell on the reasons why it should be willing to come to terms with him than on what he would do if it did not. He aspired to appease Great Britain, not to defeat it. *Mein Kampf* presupposed friendship with Great Britain; the dispatch of Ribbentrop to London as Ambassador was a step, however misguided, to this end; the purpose of the Anglo-German naval agreement of 1935 had been not so much to detach Great Britain from France and Italy (although it had that welcome effect) or to sanctify breaches of the naval clauses of the treaty of Versailles (which Hitler had hardly yet begun), but to reassure Great Britain that Hitler intended no threat to Great Britain's naval empire. But by 1939 it was doubtful whether Great Britain could be neutralized. It was also becoming possible that the western democracies might enter into an alliance with the USSR.

The disappearance of Czechoslovakia as an independent state automatically moved Poland and Rumania into the German firing line. Both these states had frontiers with the USSR and so in a sense Hitler's entry into Prague on 15 March 1939 brought Germany and the USSR face to face. For five and a half months between that day and the signing of the Russo-German pact during the night of 23-24 August the pattern of European politics was, on the surface at least, uncertain, as the USSR, moving to escape from an isolation which had become particularly dangerous since Munich, hesitated which side to take. At first the western democracies and the USSR seemed to be trying to overcome their mutual antipathies and draw together. Following a scare in March of imminent German action against Rumania Great Britain made an approach to the USSR. London was at this point more worried about Rumania than Poland, but the Rumanian scare subsided almost at once and when the USSR suggested a conference between itself, the two leading western democracies and the two countries threatened by Hitler, the British took evasive action, being reluctant to rub shoulders so formally with the USSR. Poland was even more reluctant. But it was also the main point of danger. It had partially mobilized on 23 March, three days before rejecting Germany's proposals for a settlement, and Chamberlain, afraid that Danzig was about to create a war at any moment, resolved to cast a British mantle over Poland. He offered it a guarantee and on 6 April, after a visit by Beck to London, the two governments publicly announced their intention to sign a treaty by which Great Britain would go to Poland's aid if it were attacked. France promised to do so too. At the beginning of May Hitler, already enraged by Beck's rejection of his proposals, secretly ordered his army to get ready to attack. Beck publicly proclaimed that peace was less precious than Poland's honour.

Great Britain and France, having committed themselves to succouring Poland, were gambling on a negotiated Danzig settlement which would once more remove a threat to peace, that is to say, give Hitler what he wanted. In default of such an agreement they would almost certainly be called upon to redeem in arms the promises which they had made. But by making these promises Great Britain in particular, which had not before been under any obligation to Poland, had forfeited the power which it had wielded in similar circumstances over Czechoslovakia. Beck was emboldened to continue to refuse to negotiate over Danzig. The guarantee given to him was a guarantee of Poland's national integrity, a guarantee therefore against attack by a dissident minority as well as from external aggression, and most exceptionally the Polish government was itself to judge if and when circumstances had called the guarantee into play. Thus Beck had a weapon which Beneš never had, although in the end it did him no good. The charge that can be made against Beck is that he did not see that the Anglo-French guarantee was worthless. Although aware of the unwillingness of his guarantors to fight for Poland, he did not believe that they would go so far as to dishonour their promises. But Great Britain and France did not mean to implement these promises. For them the guarantee was a means to gain time and to deter Hitler, while they continued to try to lever the Poles into concessions over Danzig: a military promise used as a diplomatic weapon. As such it was inept. The charge against Chamberlain, the principal author of the manoeuvre, is that by giving the guarantee he diminished the pressure that he was trying to exert on Poland over Danzig and at the same time improvidently and inopportunely deprived himself of his chance of an agreement with the USSR. Coupled with Great Britain's known determination on a peaceful settlement of the Danzig question, the guarantee was weak support for Poland and weak deterrence of Hitler.

Similar events with similar consequences occurred in south-east Europe. Ever since the disruption of the Ottoman and Austro-Hungarian empires this area had been contested between the principal land and naval powers of Europe. Most of it became in the 1930s increasingly dominated by Germany but Greece fell within the British sphere of influence and Yugoslavia proved to be a joker in the pack. (This pattern was repeated after the war with the substitution of the USSR and USA for Germany and Britain.)

Greece's principal concerns were Bulgaria and, secondarily, Italy. The Greek government wanted an alliance with Great Britain to counter the threat it perceived from Bulgaria but Great Britain, although more sympathetic to Greece than to Bulgaria, had reasons of its own for equivocation: it did not want to push Bulgaria irrevocably into the German camp. Still less did Great Britain want to offend the Duce whose neutrality in a war with Germany Great Britain hoped to secure. On the other hand Greece was not negligible in British strategic thinking since Greece would be a useful element in a war in which blockade of Germany and German-occupied Europe would play a significant part. This complex was further bedevilled by the fact that Greece had, in theory at least, an alternative policy in a revival of the Greco-Italian friendship treaty of 1928 – which was contrary to British interests since it would take Greece out of the British and into the Axis sphere of influence.

Mussolini's invasion of Albania on 7 April 1939 forced these issues. Great Britain and France gave Greece, and a little later Rumania, guarantees of their integrity and independence, but these undertakings, given in the wake of events, had little power to forestall further events. They were little more than anti-Axis slogans shouted into the wind. They did not deter Mussolini from invading Greece or Hitler from overrunning both Greece and Rumania. Like the guarantee to Poland, they had no impact on the pattern of power in Europe although they may have had some impact on how Hitler played his hand.

Hitler was a man of moods and rage was one of them. He was in a state of rage between the Berchtesgaden and Godesberg meetings in September 1938 and it seems likely that Chamberlain's guarantee to Poland affected him the same way. He riposted by denouncing not only his recently re-affirmed non-aggression pact with Poland but also the Anglo-German naval treaty. He ordered his forces to be ready to attack Poland at the end of August, and he now envisaged – although he still hoped to avoid – a war on two fronts. The essential thing was to keep the USSR out of such a war.

The Russians, like the Germans, feared a war on two fronts. Germany and Japan were allies by the Anti-Comintern Pact and there was already an undeclared war going on in Manchuria between Russian and Japanese forces. Stalin found it difficult to believe that the British and French ruling classes preferred Russian communism to European right-wing fascism. This not implausible judgement had been strengthened by the Anglo-French failure to solicit Russian support for the defence of Czechoslovakia and the transience of the British interest in cooperation for the defence of Poland and Rumania. In any case, what Great Britain and France wanted was not what the USSR needed. Great Britain and France were concerned about the independence and integrity of Poland and Rumania and might in an emergency welcome Russian help to safeguard these states, but Stalin cared nothing for the integrity of Poland or Rumania. He was worrying about the USSR and its vulnerability to German attack. He might welcome British and French aid to avert such an attack but so long as Great Britain and France wanted to strengthen Poland and Rumania and preserve their sovereignty, Stalin saw little chance of turning these states into a defensive glacis which was the only useful function that they could perform for him. Stalin needed help against Hitler and a free hand in the debatable lands between the USSR and Germany; Great Britain and France were looking for help for Poland and Rumania not for the USSR, and were unwilling to blackmail Poland into giving Stalin what he wanted in the way in which they had blackmailed Czechoslovakia into giving way to Hitler.

Stalin had made a mistake about Hitler several years earlier. He had viewed with equanimity the coalition between German conservatives, the German army and the Nazis. The conservatives and the army had a tradition of alliance with Russia, and Stalin believed that these would prove the dominating forces in a post-Weimar Germany. He regarded the

Nazis as no more than ephemeral auxiliaries in the overthrow of Weimar and so instead of impeding Hitler's rise to power by directing the German communists to make common cause with the socialists he incited the communists against the socialists and so played a part in destroying Weimar and making Hitler its heir. Stalin quickly realized his mistake and tried to rectify it. In 1934 he joined the League of Nations and in 1935 he made his ineffective alliance with France. The failure of this alliance and the obvious weaknesses of collective security forced him a couple of years later to seek with Nazi Germany the sort of accord which he would have liked to make with a military-conservative Germany. In 1937 he began the process of appeasing Hitler by dissolving the Polish Communist Party. Poland rekilled would, if necessary, seal the new compact. Stalin knew that Hitler was his enemy as much as Great Britain and France, indeed more so and more menacingly. But he also saw the basis for a business deal with Germany which could give him what he needed – time. Moreover if, like western conservatives, he too saw a world divided into communists and noncommunists, he could nevertheless draw some distinction between fascist anti-communists and democratic anti-communists. He despised and distrusted the latter and concluded in consequence that he would probably have to do a deal with the former, since the countries which had had no stomach to defend Czechoslovakia would be incapable of doing anything useful for the USSR even if they wanted to. But it is doubtful whether he finally made up his mind until August 1939. Until a few days before the signing of the Russo-German treaty he kept open the possibility of an agreement with Great Britain and France.

By their guarantees to Poland and Rumania, Great Britain and France had undertaken to help two countries whose ability to withstand Germany was clearly nil. The British estimate of Poland's capacity to resist, measured in time, was two weeks – and Poland's forty divisions constituted an army twice as large as Rumania's. If Hitler invaded Poland, France and Great Britain could invade Germany, but unless the USSR were added to the alliance the Poles would fight alone and not for long. Thus east–west negotiations were dragged onto the political scene by the logic of events. The French government and, in London, the Foreign Office but not the Prime Minister were driven to seek an alliance with the USSR despite some well-founded doubts about its political value at this date. Political missions proceeded from Paris and London to Moscow in June. They did not give an impression of enthusiasm, but the real cause of their ultimate failure was not their attitude so much as the backlog of distrust between their countries and the impossibility of agreement on the crucial issue of a Russian right of entry into Poland. By the end of July a stalemate

was reached when the western powers refused to give Stalin a free hand in
the Baltic states. They felt that they were being asked to connive at the
suppression of the independence of these countries, which was indeed so,
but was not very different from what they had done at Munich. Stalin then
reanimated the talks by suggesting the dispatch of military missions. These
began discussions in Moscow on 12 August. The fact that they went by
ship instead of by air has been the subject of some ridicule and again there
was a display of an evident lack of enthusiasm (although Daladier at least
wanted an agreement at almost any price), but there was a case for the
chosen method of travel since it was only on board ship that the two
missions got to know each other and were able to concert their plans.

It is impossible to say whether Stalin was by now merely playing with
the western powers or was hoping to do a deal with them. He had been
looking both ways since April when he initiated the first in a series of
moves which eventually produced the Russo-German pact, and the replacement of Maxim Litvinov by Vyacheslav Molotov as Foreign Commissar
on 3 May was regarded by the French Ambassador in Moscow as a step
towards a Russo-German alliance. Hitler responded with further initiatives in June and then appeared to lose interest, but serious exchanges were
renewed before the end of July, at which time the German Ambassador in
Moscow was forecasting a Franco-British-Russian alliance. On 12 August,
the day on which the military talks began in Moscow, Hitler was telling
his Italian allies of his intention to make Stalin his ally; on 20 August he
sent a personal telegram to Stalin to speed things up and on the 22nd, in
an address to military and civilian chiefs, he spoke as though the attack on
Poland were imminent and the Russian pact assured. In the intervening
week the military missions had been pressed by the chief Russian delegate,
Marshal Voroshilov, to answer the question whether Russian troops
would be allowed by Poland to advance into Poland to meet the German
armies. The British and French missions could not give a straight answer,
for although Poland (and Rumania) had withdrawn initial objections to a
Franco-British-Russian alliance, the Polish government still refused to
permit any entry by Russian forces except upon request to be made at the
time and it assumed that the request would be for air support and not for
ground units. At the last moment a member of the French mission was
sent to Warsaw to press the Poles to give way, but the Poles refused and it
is probable that Stalin knew on 19 August of this refusal from intercepted
cipher traffic. On the 21st Daladier cabled the French mission to sign
anything they could get, but on the same day a Russo-German economic
agreement was signed in Berlin. This agreement was regarded as portend-
ing something more spectacular and in Moscow a visit by Ribbentrop was

openly spoken of. Stalin consented to a visit by the Nazi Foreign Minister a week after the signing of the economic agreement but this was too late for Hitler. Ribbentrop arrived in the afternoon of the 23rd and a few hours later, to the amazement of the rest of the world, Germany and the USSR signed a treaty of friendship and non-aggression by which each of them abjured the use of force against the other and undertook not to help any third party in an attack on the other and not to join any group oriented directly or indirectly against the other. The treaty was to endure in the first instance for ten years. It was supplemented by a secret protocol defining spheres of interest: to the USSR, Finland, Estonia, Latvia; to Germany, Lithuania including Vilna; in Poland, the division to run along the line Narev–Vistula–San, the continuance of an independent Polish state to remain an open question; in the south-east the USSR stressed its interest, and Germany its *désinteressement*, in Bessarabia. These arrangements were later altered to give Lithuania to the USSR and the Polish provinces of Lublin and Warsaw to Germany.

One of the unwitting authors of the Hitler-Stalin pact was Neville Chamberlain. His determination to come to terms with Mussolini and secure Italy's neutrality, and his search for ways to avoid an Anglo-German war, are an example of labours which are not only in vain but carry within them the risks of multiplying misfortune. Chamberlain's motives were the reverse of dishonourable. Yet the more he laboured to find common ground with the dictators, the more did he convince Stalin that he must do so too. And Stalin, perhaps because more cynical or perhaps because harder pressed, succeeded, so that Chamberlain's diplomacy recoiled upon him. His overtures to Moscow, however distasteful to him personally, were genuine and by this date forced upon him, as they were too upon the French government.

But the deeper source of the Hitler-Stalin pact lay elsewhere. Whether or not in August 1939 Stalin was still considering an alliance with the western democracies or was merely playing for time, using the Anglo-French missions to needle Hitler into a Russo-German pact and incidentally seeing how much useful intelligence he could worm out of the British and French negotiators, it is in retrospect clear that an Anglo-French-Russian pact was of interest to Stalin only upon terms which Great Britain and France could not fulfil. These powers, having lost Czechoslovakia and a possible Russian alliance, were forced back onto a third and much weaker policy. On 25 August, the day after the Russo-German pact was made known, an Anglo-Polish treaty, implementing the Chamberlain-Beck declaration of April, was signed. It had been delayed by the Anglo-French-Russian conversations but by 22 August the British and French governments knew that the Russo-German entente was imminent. Chamberlain was still determined to avoid any provocation of Hitler and was hoping for a visit from Goering which would somehow prevent war, but he could no longer delay the formalization of his earlier undertaking, empty though it was. The treaty of August, like the declaration of April, was more an attempt to check Hitler than solid comfort for the Poles. The earlier pledge was embodied in a formal pact of mutual assistance against any act of aggression or any direct or indirect threat to the independence of the signatories. An indirect threat meant in fact a German seizure of Danzig. At the same time Great Britain both assured Hitler through diplomatic channels that British promises to Poland meant what they said, and intimated that Germany ought to have Danzig and Great Britain would like to see a peaceful cession of the city. France concluded a similar treaty with Poland, although it was not signed until 5 September, after Hitler's attack.

The only chance of averting war, so it seemed to those who wanted to do so, was to call in Mussolini again and arrange another Munich. Great Britain tried once more to use Mussolini as a lifebelt and a means of appeasing Hitler with Danzig, but the French government, unaware of what Great Britain was doing, was trying to detach Italy from Hitler by emphasizing the dangers ahead without realizing that the Italians knew from their contacts with London that Great Britain was hoping to remove the dangers by giving way to Hitler. Mussolini was unwilling to lose credit with Hitler and with himself by urging a peaceful settlement which Hitler did not want. On the other hand he was not ready for war and knew it, and Ciano was telling him that a German attack on Poland would begin a general war. He told Hitler that Italy could not join in a war which brought Poland's allies into the field unless Germany could supply the materials of war which Italy still lacked. Asked to specify Italy's needs he submitted a huge list. This was tantamount to asking for the impossible. Privately Hitler accepted the conclusion that Italy would not fight. Mussolini resigned himself to the fact that Hitler would make war on Poland.

Hitler's Japanese ally was also proving a disappointment. After Japan joined the Anti-Comintern Pact in November 1936 Hitler tried to get a promise of Japanese military assistance against any enemy of Germany and not merely against the communist USSR. By 1939 the Japanese army was keen on an alliance with Germany and Italy against Great Britain and France but the emperor, his Foreign Minister and the navy opposed such a commitment. Prolonged negotiations during the early months of 1939 ran into the sands and on 22 May Germany and Italy signed the Pact of Steel, which marked the end of hopes for a tripartite alliance against the western democracies. Six months later Japan was the more deeply aggrieved by Hitler's pact with Stalin because Japan was actually engaged in hostilities against the USSR. Japan complained that the Russo-German pact was a breach of the Anti-Comintern Pact. A few days later its government fell and its attitude became more uncertain, but temporarily the Japanese alliance had become irrelevant for Hitler who had just given the order for the war against Poland in which the USSR was his ally.

On 25 August Hitler gave the order for Poland to be attacked before dawn the next morning. At the last moment he revoked his order – so late that one unit could not be reached in time, advanced across the frontier and was destroyed. Hitler's change of plan may have been influenced by the behaviour of his Italian and Japanese allies or by the announcement – also on the 25th – of the Anglo-Polish treaty, but the guarantee to Poland was already an established fact and Hitler was more probably hoping that Chamberlain and Daladier, if given a few extra days to reflect upon the Russo-German pact, would either coerce Poland as they had coerced Czechoslovakia or abandon it. On the 25th he assured the British and French Ambassadors that he had no designs on the British Empire and was not hankering after Alsace-Lorraine, and in the days which followed he tried to get Great Britain and France to force Poland to send a plenipotentiary to Berlin to negotiate the reversion of Danzig to Germany and a plebiscite in the Polish corridor. Given the fate which had attended other plenipotentiaries who had visited Berlin, Beck (who had already agreed in principle to negotiate with Germany) refused and his allies felt unable to press him to accept.

Germany invaded Poland on 1 September. As a prelude a small SS party entered the German radio station at Gleiwitz and announced in poor Polish that it had been seized by Poles. This futile episode, in the course of which a German policeman who was not privy to the escapade was killed, was Germany's attempt to give some colour of justification to the attack which began the Second World War. A few hours after the charade at Gleiwitz, Danzig's Nazi Gauleiter declared the city to be a part of the German Reich; there was some fighting (there is an exciting account of the fight for the Post Office in Günther Grass's novel *The Tin Drum*) but Danzig was not now what mattered. Hitler had taken a risk. He calculated, correctly, that he could dispose of Poland without fear of British or French intervention, and he was happy to know that his generals who feared a war on two fronts would again be proved wrong. But he also calculated, wrongly, that Great Britain and France would either not declare war or not fight if they did. The British and French governments hesitated, but in the House of Commons Chamberlain's reluctance to declare war in response to Great Britain's pledges and Poland's plea for action against Germany in the west, produced tense and angry scenes. Chamberlain's government, it was said, would fall if it did not declare war. On 3 September Chamberlain spoke the necessary words, but it was the Commons of England rather than the government which had taken the plunge. France followed suit.

The outbreak of war in September 1939 marked the failure of policies, for which British and French politicians have been amply criticized. The French recipe for peace and security in Europe had already broken down because it rested on incompatibles – a system of continental alliances plus an alliance with Great Britain to whom the continental alliances were obnoxious. As a result of the failure of the French recipe Great Britain came to be in a position to call the tune. It called it wrong. But why? The obtuseness of British politicians in the face of the fascist phenomenon is only a part of the answer.

It is a commonplace of history that France, denied the British and American guarantees which were its first requirement in 1919, had to fall back on second-best policies which were adequate in the twenties only because France was not then seriously threatened. The significance of Barthou and, in his different fashion, Laval was that these two Ministers tried a second time in the thirties to create an alliance system strong enough to contain Germany and that when this attempt too failed France's isolation was manifest to foe, friend and itself. Thereafter France accepted the consequences of this isolation – inability to conduct an independent foreign policy.

It is no less a commonplace that the United States kept itself aloof from European affairs between the wars. How far the United States was truly isolationist and why will be discussed in a later chapter. American isolationism, unlike the French abnegation, was a matter of choice. But it too involved withdrawal.

What has been little, if at all, noticed is that Great Britain too was isolated. The difference in the British case was that, unlike France and the United States, Great Britain refused to abnegate and continued to try to play an active role. It was, however, reduced to playing the only role possible for a state with commitments but without allies – the role of a man who gives way on one thing after another until he finds he has his back to a wall. At the turn of the century Great Britain had been committed to that search for allies which eventuated in the agreements with

Japan, Russia and France on the basis of which the First World War was fought. After that war the Japanese alliance was abandoned under American pressure, the Russian alliance disappeared with the ancient Russian state itself, and the French alliance became more of a problem than a support because of disagreements over German policy, the growing deficiencies of France as a military partner and the element of contempt and distrust in the British ruling class's attitude to France. In this situation British governments, no less than French, would have liked to believe that the new system of collective security embodied in the League of Nations was the answer to their problems and they consistently gave a high priority to support for the League for this reason, but they also believed that the collective security of their day would not work. They were not unaware of their dilemma but in the first post-war decade it did not seem a pressing one. Then, just as the world came to look more menacing, they were struck by a catastrophe of a different kind which they did not understand and which they consequently greatly exaggerated. The economic crisis of 1931 terrified the governing class, reduced Ministers to a state of helplessness and convinced them that Great Britain had been permanently and irreparably weakened. This misjudgement was a major cause of the refusal to spend money on arms in the thirties, and this failure in turn reinforced the feeling of weakness. By the mid-thirties a combination of diplomatic isolation, economic nightmare and military unpreparedness had produced political and intellectual paralysis. And this paralysis produced wrong decisions. Munich was a wrong decision.

It contained three principal elements. These were: horror of war, unmanageable imperial burdens and miscalculation of the odds in Europe.

The men who sat in British cabinets in the thirties had known the First World War – most of them had fought in it – and felt a compelling responsibility to prevent a second. Their generation had been horrified by the first war and was convinced that a second, in which they themselves would be too old to fight, would be even more frightful. They felt a compelling personal obligation to obviate war at almost any price. This motive does them nothing but credit.

Secondly, they thought in imperial terms and would have held it disgraceful not to do so: their heritage and their office constrained them to give the highest priority to the preservation of an empire whose material riches had placed Great Britain high in the world. Subconsciously too, the preservation of empire was a charge which could not be abandoned without impugning British vitality. This empire seemed to be challenged not so much by changing times as by a specific enemy – Japan – whose evident attempts to dominate China were assumed to entail similar designs in the spheres of influence established in Asia over the centuries by European powers. In 1937 the British government went to the length of giving formal undertakings at the Imperial Conference in that year to send a British fleet to the Pacific to stem or defeat Japanese ambitions. But this promise was incompatible with any policy in Europe that was likely to lead to war with Germany and Italy, since war in Europe could serve as a green light to Japan to despoil the British in Asia while conversely the dispatch of a substantial naval force to the east would negate Great Britain's capacity to make war in Europe. Great Britain's resources no longer matched its commitments as an imperial power which was also critically involved in European affairs. Short of a massive rearmament programme begun at a much earlier date (politically shunned and economically perhaps ruinous) there was no way out of this dilemma except by a retreat from empire or from Europe. The British government came near to the latter but, responding ultimately to Great Britain's inevitable embroilment in Europe, bequeathed to its successors the unenviable and, in the thirties, virtually unthinkable alternative.

The third main factor in the calculations of British foreign policy in the thirties was a misreading of the military situation, beginning with the balance and practicalities of air power. British cabinets believed that on the outbreak of war London would be immediately and catastrophically bombed and Britain forced to capitulate. This belief was absurd. The Air Staff admitted that it could not bomb Germany. This admission should have prompted the question whether the Luftwaffe could bomb England. Yet astonishingly this question seems never to have been put. Had it been the answer must have been no. When the Luftwaffe did bomb England two years later (with much less catastrophic effect than anticipated) it did so from bases in France and Belgium which it did not have in 1938 and could not have conquered so long as Czechoslovakia remained an independent, hostile and well-armed state. The destruction of Czechoslovakia at Munich, completed in April the next year, was an essential precondition for Hitler's air offensive against Great Britain. The betrayal of Czechoslovakia at Munich has been justified on the grounds that the only alternative was to fight Hitler and be defeated. This is a bad plea. In the event France was beaten anyway. Great Britain won the Battle of Britain but the correct conclusion to draw about Munich is not that Chamberlain there gained time to build up the RAF and so save his country but rather that Munich brought upon Great Britain a battle which it would not otherwise have had to fight.

In 1938 Czechoslovakia was the one country among the possible combatants which was ready for battle. Great Britain and France were not ready, nor was the USSR. More significantly, Germany was not ready. Nor of course was Italy. So any alliance with Czechoslovakia in it would have started with a peculiar advantage over its enemy. Czechoslovakia was not only ready but strong, as strong as Germany in all important departments except manpower. The Czechoslovak army of thirty-five divisions faced a German army which was about the same size or slightly larger but which, if the aggressor, needed to be twice as large as its defending antagonist. In 1938 Germany could just about match Czechoslovakia division for division with four or five regular (but imperfectly trained and incompletely officered) divisions over to guard its western front – where Czechoslovakia's ally, France, mustered seventy-six divisions. The Czechs were better equipped than the Germans in a number of ways, notably in artillery and armoured fighting vehicles. The German armoured divisions which scattered and destroyed the French army and its allies in 1940 hardly existed in 1938; even in September 1939 Hitler had only six armoured divisions in place of the ten with which he made war in the west; four of these ten had Czech tanks.

Czechoslovakia was the sixth industrial power in Europe, possessed one of Europe's most famous, extensive and efficient armaments industries and had made plans to remove it from the west to the comparative safety of Slovakia. After 1939 its output, which was roughly equivalent to Great Britain's arms output, was added to Germany's own capacity – not the least of Germany's gains at Munich. Germany also secured the existing equipment of the Czechoslovak armed forces, including 1,500 aircraft. Czechoslovak mobilization plans were excellent. The government was ready to evacuate half the population of Prague. Morale was high. All Czechoslovakia asked in return for these substantial contributions was a declaration of war by France. Confident of its ability to hold the Germans for a matter of months, it did not even depend on an immediate French offensive in strength – unlike the Poles who required, and secured from France in the following year, a promise that the French army would commit the bulk of its forces against Germany within fifteen days of French mobilization.

But there was no equivalent confidence in France or Great Britain. The pessimism of French and British staffs and politicians arose largely out of the view held in the west that, since the *Anschluss*, Czechoslovakia's soft underbelly had been exposed and its capital lay at the mercy of a German pincer attack. In fact Czechoslovakia's southern defences were far from soft and the Germans did not plan a pincer movement. Hitler and his generals had decided that an attack on Prague from the south and the northwest would be held up for too long by the Czechoslovak army and fortifications and they therefore planned a thrust from the west. When, as bloodless victors, they were able to inspect the Czech defences they were awed by the strength and depth of a system which stretched back from the frontiers almost as far as Prague. Addressing 400 journalists a few weeks after Munich Hitler told them of his feelings when he inspected these fortifications and enthused over his success in getting hold of them without firing a shot.

What Stalin would have done in the event of war in 1938 still remains an enigma. The fact that the Russian obligation to act was dependent on French action provides no clue, since this clause in the Russo-Czechoslovak treaty of 1935 was inserted not by the Russians in order to provide a let-out but by the Czechs, on French insistence, in order to discourage the Russians from acting on their own. During 1938 and before Munich the USSR delivered aircraft to the Czechs (who were short of bombers). Moscow also warned Poland not to take action against Czechoslovakia, threatening to denounce the Russo-Polish treaty if Poland attacked Czechoslovakia. Two weeks before the Munich conference Rumania lifted its embargo on Russian aircraft flying over its territory and one Russian aircraft which made a forced landing in Rumania on its way from the USSR to Czechoslovakia was not only given emergency repairs but was allowed to fly on. An airfield in Slovakia was stocked with fuel and spare parts for various types of Russian aircraft. The French Ambassador in Moscow believed that the Russians intended to go to the help of Czechoslovakia. Russian ground and air forces were moved westward in considerable numbers, although for what purpose is uncertain. They could have been used as a contribution to collective action on behalf of Czechoslovakia, or their deployment may have been no more than a defensive precaution, or Stalin may have been keeping both his options open. Furthermore the possibility of Russian action was in itself a factor since it gave Hitler not merely two fronts to worry about but three. He was risking an attack on East Prussia and had no means of meeting it. When war came a year later over Poland this threat had been eliminated. From the Anglo-French point of view Stalin was a far from certain ally in the event of war over Czechoslovakia, but he was an all but certain non-ally in a war begun anywhere else in central Europe.

Hitler's aggression against Czechoslovakia was based on a political calculation, not a military one. On a military calculation it was the lunacy which his generals held it to be. They, seeing only the military equation, were scared out of their wits and even conspired to overthrow him. Hjalmar Schacht too, the coolest of men – the financial genius who served many masters, financed German rearmament, mocked Hitler as he mocked everybody with his merciless drawing-room wit, but who did not leave the Nazi government until he was dismissed from it in January 1938 – bemoaned Chamberlain's visit to Godesberg no less than the generals: Schacht said that Chamberlain could do nothing to prevent war and that Germany was therefore lost. It follows that Czechoslovakia's allies' own calculations were, militarily, wrong. Hitler's political gamble came off not because France and Great Britain were militarily incapable but because they were strategically inept. The French army would have had little more on its hands than a *promenade militaire*, the one military performance which an out-of-date army can execute as well as an up-to-date one. In 1940 the French forces were destroyed in a few weeks by a weight of armour which in 1938 the Germans did not possess. It is moreover implausible to suppose that in 1938, with the Germans engaged in Czechoslovakia, with only five German regular divisions and seven others in the west, with the entire Luftwaffe committed in the east, with incomplete German defences described by General Jodl as a building site, and with the spur of a treaty obligation, the French army would have remained futilely static. However poor its leadership and equipment it could hardly have failed to do better than it did when war came; at least it could not have done worse.

The British case was different. The British army was irrelevant both in 1938 and 1940. Although its role in Europe's wars in the twentieth century was to send troops and not, as in the past, find the money to subsidize the armies of other countries, Great Britain did not in fact equip itself with troops to send. It was therefore unable to contribute much more than a token to continental land warfare until it had raised a wartime army in wartime, fighting meanwhile defensive battles to gain the time to do this. Consequently the crucial issue was the defence of Great Britain itself and the crucial battle was the air battle of 1940.

The British case for Munich has to be tested at two points – in 1939 when war in fact came and in 1940 when the crucial battle was fought. Rearmament was accelerated after Munich, although without much intensity until the fall of France (and Chamberlain) in 1940. Between Munich, when battle was refused, and September 1939, when it was accepted, Great Britain's expenditure on armaments was one fifth of Germany's. British fighter production was about half Germany's. There was therefore no improvement in the British position relative to the German during these twelve months; in these respects the British position actually got worse. At the time of Munich the vital radar screen was incomplete; so it was a year later. The supplementary screen against low-flying aircraft, wholly non-existent in 1938, was still wholly non-existent in 1939.

If the British government feared defeat in 1938 it had even more reason to fear it a year later when the country's defences were still ineffective against air raids and its aircraft, though more numerous and more modern, had declined in proportion to the German air force.

By the spring of 1940, on the eve of the Battle of Britain, British aircraft production had begun to overtake Germany's, so that the gap between the two forces had stopped growing and was beginning to close. In 1938 Great Britain had 600 fighter aircraft, of which 360 were immediately available for operations, but only one in five of these was modern. In 1940 all Fighter Command's forty-three squadrons had Hurricanes or Spitfires (but the squadrons overseas had not). It is therefore plausible to argue that had the Battle of Britain been fought in 1938 the result would have gone the other way. But it is implausible to assume that anything like the Battle of Britain would have been fought in a war begun in 1938 with Czechoslovakia as an ally, for the essential prerequisite to the Luft-waffe's attack on Great Britain was the possession of airfields in France and Belgium – airfields which had first to be captured by the German army which, on the 1938 hypothesis, would have been fully occupied in Czechoslovakia. Great Britain was woefully ill equipped in 1938 but it does not follow that it would have fought Germany at a greater disadvantage in that year than it did when, with Germany also better armed and above all unencumbered to the east, Great Britain was forced into war for Poland in 1939 and so forced to defend its own shores in 1940. On the contrary, there is reason to calculate that the avoidance of war in 1938 was not only a shameful act but an inexpedient and foolish one. The surrender at Munich, by postponing war, shaped its future course, ensured the defeat of France and, so far from buying time for rearmament, committed Great Britain to a battle which it nearly lost.

Munich was an over-optimistic, inadequately analysed, dubiously proper attempt to accommodate Hitler's expansive Germany in the European states system and so stave off war, but the grounds for supposing that Hitler would be satisfied with what he got at Munich were a wilful delusion and the grounds for supposing that war postponed would be more easily won were little more defensible. Chamberlain had become convinced that Czechoslovakia could not be saved. He was intent upon preventing the so-called Sudeten crisis from developing into general war. Hitler's aggressive plans were a threat to the peace, but so too – in Chamberlain's eyes – was the Franco-Czech treaty: Hitler's territorial claims might be satisfied but in order to keep the peace by satisfying them Chamberlain needed to prevent the occurrence of the *casus foederis* embodied in the treaty, or to ensure that it would be dishonoured if it did arise. This was an urgent issue since Daladier (but not all his colleagues) was prepared in the last resort to go to war if Czechoslovakia were attacked. For Chamberlain Munich was a victory because it defused the Franco-Czech treaty, but a defeat because the basis of his policy was unsound. He assumed, wrongly and implausibly, that Hitler could be satisfied by territorial concessions linked to alleged ethnic borders whereas, as the next few months showed, Hitler was determined to annex far more than the territories deemed to be German in character even by him and, ultimately, to fight the USSR for the *Lebensraum* which he had said in *Mein Kampf* Germany must have. At best Chamberlain's policy might hope to disentangle – although it did not disentangle – Great Britain and France from war. It could not prevent the war or even much delay it, and Great Britain and France were quickly involved in the war by Chamberlain's own action in guaranteeing the integrity of Poland, a complete reversal of his policy of engineering the dismemberment of Czechoslovakia in order to keep the peace. For Hitler Munich was no more than a brief, if unwelcome, check which, six months later, had cost him nothing and had incidentally stifled opposition to his expansionist adventures from those, notably in the German army, who were scared by his willingness to risk war with Czechoslovakia.

The policy of appeasement, which culminated at Munich, ensured that Czechoslovakia would be eliminated from a war with Germany. With the effortless elimination of Poland too a year later, war on Germany's eastern front was reduced to war against the USSR alone, so that Stalin, by 1945 sole combatant in the east and sole victor, became the virtually uncontrolled arbiter of the fate of central and eastern Europe.

Part II
HITLER'S WARS: 1939–41

THE European war began when the Germans invaded Poland on 1 September 1939. On 17 September the Russians did so too and Poland ceased once more to exist as an independent state. Successful in the east Hitler paused, but Stalin in November made demands on Finland which led to a war which the Russians at first bungled but eventually won in March 1940. In April Hitler conquered Denmark and Norway and in May–June the Netherlands, Belgium and France. In July–September he failed, in the Battle of Britain, to win the air superiority necessary for an invasion. Great Britain remained at war, not only in the west, but also with naval, ground and air forces in the eastern Mediterranean. Hitler toyed with the idea of a descent into the western Mediterranean through France and Spain, but the war was resumed in the eastern Mediterranean when Mussolini attacked Greece unsuccessfully in October and the British attacked the Italians successfully in North Africa in December. In 1941 Hitler consolidated his control of south-eastern Europe, including Greece, and went to the help of the Italians in Africa. On 22 June he attacked the USSR which, besides strengthening its defences in the north by the peace imposed on Finland, had annexed the three Baltic states of Estonia, Latvia and Lithuania and the Rumanian provinces of Bessarabia and Northern Bukovina. There were therefore at the end of 1941 three separate theatres of war: first, the USSR where Leningrad was invested, German forces had come within sight of Moscow, and the Ukraine had been overrun by German armies on their way into the Crimea and the Caucasus; secondly, the remnant of a war in the west maintained by the Royal Air Force in Great Britain but pushed out into the Atlantic and waged chiefly by German U-boats and their pursuers; and thirdly, the Mediterranean where the Germans and Italians were trying to win North Africa – and thence the Middle East – against the opposition of the British Mediterranean fleet and British land and air forces based in Egypt and Malta. At the end of the year this European war, begun in 1939, ceased to be purely European and merged with the wars begun before and after it by Japan – against China in 1937 and against the United States in 1941.

CHAPTER 5

From Poland to the North Cape

THE German attack on Poland was a combination of a straight punch and a pincer movement. The central German blow was delivered from Pomerania, Silesia and Moravia and was accompanied by simultaneous attacks from eastern Pomerania in the north and Slovakia in the south. All attacks were made with withering material and technical superiority, Hitler having taken the risk of committing the whole of his armoured and mechanized forces in Poland and of denuding his western fronts. The Polish forces fell back rapidly, taking the civilian authorities with them and leaving the German inhabitants exposed to the harsh vengefulness of their Polish neighbours. Fantastic rumours about the activities of a German fifth column – rumours which were to be repeated all over Europe and which were almost totally groundless – produced a panic-struck wave of summary injustice in which as many as 7,000 Germans may have been killed.

No help came to Poland from its guarantors. The French army put a symbolic toe across the German frontier but otherwise France composed itself to await the arrival of the British (that year or the next) and, when pressed by the Polish Ambassador in Paris, hedged over the promise given in May to launch an immediate major offensive. General Gamelin did not disown the promise but said, evasively and incorrectly, that French forces were engaging the enemy on the ground and in the air. Great Britain sent twenty-nine aircraft to attack German shipping (and lost seven of them) but for six months dropped nothing more serious than leaflets on German soil. The cabinet feared massive air reprisals and in Parliament the Secretary of State for Air went so far as to defend this inactivity by reminding his more bellicose critics, who wanted the RAF to attack the Ruhr which was within its bombing range, that the targets proposed were private property. The Germans in the west uneasily oc-cupied the incomplete West Wall. They deployed thirty-three divisions, twenty-five of which were of the second grade or lower. They had no tanks, no aircraft and three days' supply of ammunition. Opposite them was the French army with over seventy divisions on the border, nearly 3,000 tanks and command of the air.

The Poles, whether from misplaced hopes or through temperamental impetuosity or sheer desperation, had placed their forces in forward positions where they were quickly overwhelmed by an enemy who was superior in every way. Their mobilization was slow, their leadership poor, their communications flimsy, their reserves thin, their aircraft obsolete and their tactics – cavalry charging tanks with the aim of dashing into Germany – hopeless. On the ground they were thrown back at all points by the German armour and dive-bombers. In the air the rest of the Luftwaffe, although hampered by fog on the morning and evening of the first day, quickly forced the Poles to battle by attacking Warsaw. The Polish air force was crippled in two days and extinguished in two weeks as a result of air combats and the overrunning of its airfields by the German army. The Polish army scored one noteworthy sucess by night attack southwards across the river Bzura on 9–10 September, but this stroke was held in check by the Luftwaffe and although one German army was temporarily disorganized a second, which was already to the east on its way to Warsaw, turned about and, together with a third army north of the Polish force, encircled the Poles and inflicted fatal casualties on them. On 25 September Warsaw was bombed all day. German command of the air was so complete that even Ju. (Junkers) 52 transports joined in the bombing, and the city surrendered the next day. Hitler arrived to see it on 5 October.

The German victory disconcerted the Russians both for what it was and by its speed, and on 17 September Russian forces moved into what the Russians called Western Belorussia and Western Ukraine on the plea that the Polish state had disintegrated. At the cost of 734 dead the Russians occupied half Poland (admittedly the half where Poles were in a minority). They also, in October, took control of Estonia, Latvia and Lithuania by exacting from their governments treaties of mutual assistance which permitted the entry of Russian troops and meant in effect that the Russians would take over if the Germans looked like doing so. Upon Finland the Russians had even more serious demands to make because of the vulnerability of Leningrad, situated no more than fifteen miles from the Finnish frontier on the Karelian isthmus and close to Lake Ladoga whose shores were partly Finnish territory. The Russians wanted to protect Leningrad against land and sea attack by obtaining Finnish territory in the immediate neighbourhood of the city and control of the Gulf of Finland.

The issue was one between Russian security and Finnish rights. During October and early November Finnish delegations went three times to Moscow. On each occasion the Russians made small concessions but they refused to abate the substance of their demands: a lease of Hangö in south-western Finland at the entrance to the Gulf of Finland, the cession of a number of islands in the Gulf, a slice of territory in the Karelian isthmus

The destruction of Poland was primarily a German action, 1,700,000 German troops soon defeated the 600,000 Polish soldiers. German air attacks destroyed the centres of the main Polish cities. The Poles hoped to make a final stand in the Pripet Marshes, but the USSR advances destroyed all chance of further Polish resistance against either Germany or the USSR

THE GERMAN AND RUSSIAN INVASIONS OF POLAND 1939

Baltic Sea

LATVIA

LITHUANIA

Memel

EAST PRUSSIA

Danzig

"Polish corridor"

Vilna

Minsk

Suvalki

Augustov

Grodno

Poznan

Bialystok

Modlin   WARSAW

Pinsk

Pripet Marshes

Brest–Litovsk

Lodz

P   O   L   A   N   D

Lublin

Lutsk

GREATER

Sokal

Rovno

GERMANY

Tarnov

Cracow

Yaroslav   Lvov

Przemysl

SLOVAKIA

Stanislavov

HUNGARY

U   S   S   R

RUMANIA

Dividing line between the German and USSR zones of occupation, agreed between Germany and the USSR in August 1939.

German advances commencing 1 September 1939.

Russian advances commencing 17 September 1939.

Annexed to the USSR October 1939.

Annexed to Germany.

Annexed to Lithuania.

0   100
Miles

~ ARTHUR BANKS ~

(including the town of Viipuri) to the north-west of Leningrad and – in the far north – the Finnish half of the peninsula guarding the approaches to the Russian port of Murmansk. In exchange the Russians offered a piece of Russian Karelia twice as large as the areas demanded. They also asked for a treaty debarring each signatory from entering into agreements directed at the other. Finnish opinion was overwhelmingly against making any large cessions to an hereditary enemy, although one or two leaders argued that the Russians were not bluffing and could not in the end be denied. When the Russians saw that they could not get what they wanted by negotiation they set up a puppet Finnish government and attacked on the last day of November – for which the USSR was expelled from the League of Nations. Four Russian armies, comprising forty-five divisions, went into action, one on either side of Lake Ladoga, one directed across the waist of Finland and the fourth in the far north. The Finnish armies of 200,000 men offered magnificent resistance. They were much better clad and better shod than the ill-prepared Russians and they operated in small ski groups against inappropriately large Russian formations, but in the long term they lacked practically everything except courage and discipline. Within a short time of the opening of the campaign they were relying on teenagers to fill their fighting ranks.

The Russians began by mismanaging the campaign so thoroughly that their attacks in the south were brought to a standstill before the end of the year and they were decisively defeated in the centre in January. The Russian troops had been led to believe that they would win without serious fighting. They found themselves instead fighting unsuccessfully in a particularly cold winter in which the temperature fell below − 50 degrees C. They suffered commensurately. The Finns on the other hand were so buoyed up by their initial successes that they believed that they had secured the necessary breathing space to allow foreign friends to come to their aid and complete the defeat of their enemy. (The Americans had a special regard for Finland as the only country in Europe which went on paying interest on its foreign debts in spite of the economic collapse of 1931.) But no help came. Hitler stuck to his bargain with Stalin and urged the Finns to come to terms. Sweden, Finland's nearest neighbour, was prepared to offer all aid short of war, but not fighting men. In Great Britain and France there was fervent sympathy and admiration for the Finns. Volunteers scented a cause in which they could worthily engage themselves instead of staying inactively at home watching other weak nations being bullied by Germany.

The British and French governments had more complicated reactions. Going to the help of Finland was part of a scheme for strangling Germany without having to fight it. If Germany's supplies from the USSR and Scandinavia could be stopped, Hitler would be forced to negotiate. So General Weygand, who was in Syria, would march on Baku (the Caucasian oil port) and might even link up with an Anglo-French expeditionary force starting from Finland 2,000 miles away – which would in any case meanwhile get into Scandinavia ahead of the Germans, stop Germany's supply of Swedish iron ore and, even if it could not bring the war to a halt, possibly force Hitler into a war in a northern theatre instead of the threatened attack in the west. This plan, one of the wildest surmises of the war, entailed either the cooperation of Norway and Sweden or the violation of their neutrality. Both countries refused to allow the passage of British and French troops through their territory. Plans were therefore made – or, more correctly, discussed, for nothing like a coherent plan emerged – to send four divisions to fight the Russian armies in Scandinavia. As a first step they were to invade Norway in order to prevent the Germans from getting there first, but while these measures were being discussed by cabinets and staffs in London and Paris (which had however no adequate information about the terrain or the road and rail systems which they hoped to use) the situation at the front changed. The Russians recovered themselves and launched in February a new and overwhelming attack under Marshal Timoshenko in the Karelian isthmus. The Finnish air force was reduced to one hundred aircraft against eight times that number. The Finnish line was broken. The government came to the conclusion that foreign help would be too little and too late. It decided to make peace in spite of Anglo-French – particularly French – attempts to keep Finland in the war and on 12 March Finland capitulated. At a cost of 68,000 dead the Russians secured all their original demands and a few more. Two hundred thousand Finns had to pack up and leave their homes and cross a new frontier in order to remain in their own country. Leningrad was a few degrees safer. The relations between the Soviet Union and Great Britain and France – and the United States – were several degrees colder. But Great Britain and France had been saved by the Finnish collapse from making war on the USSR while they were still at war with Germany. When, a few weeks after the end of the Russo-Finnish war, they entered Scandinavia they did so to fight the Germans and not the Russians. One consequence of this episode was the fall of Daladier. He was succeeded by Paul Reynaud who concluded with Great Britain an agreement that neither country would make a separate peace with Germany.

In February there had occurred one of those incidents which catch the imagination and help perhaps to precipitate events. The German supply ship *Altmark* was threading her way through the Leads along the coast of Norway, homeward bound from the south Atlantic. Aboard were 299 British captives, taken off ships which had been caught by the German battleship *Graf Spee*.

Graf Spee was by this time on the bottom of the sea. Like her sister ships *Scheer* and *Deutschland* (the latter renamed *Lützow* in 1940), *Graf Spee* was a pocket battleship designed to comply with the provisions of the treaty of Versailles which forbade Germany to have warships of more than 10,000 tons. In fact she slightly exceeded that limit. The pocket battleships were faster than anything which could outgun them and out-gunned in range and weight of shell anything which could catch them. On the eve of war *Graf Spee* and *Deutschland* were dispatched into the Atlantic and from October to December they harried the commerce of Germany's enemies in the southern Atlantic and Indian Oceans. Their success was moderate. *Graf Spee* claimed nine victims before the end of her career – roughly one a week. Eight groups from the British and French navies were formed to hunt the German raiders and soon after dawn on 13 December one of these – a British and New Zealand cruiser force consisting of *Exeter*, *Ajax* and *Achilles* under Commodore Henry Harwood – opened battle. *Exeter* was soon very badly damaged and after an hour and a half *Ajax* and *Achilles* were forced to break off the engagement and limit themselves to shadowing. The damage and casualties which they had managed to inflict on *Graf Spee* were slight, but her commander, Captain Hans Langsdorff, decided to make for harbour and shortly after nightfall she dropped anchor in Montevideo Roads in the estuary of the River Plate. The British representatives in the capital of neutral Uruguay used every device of international law to prevent her from sailing again before Commodore Harwood, waiting off shore with *Ajax* and *Achilles*, could be reinforced. During the night of the 14th–15th, the cruiser *Cumberland* joined him. On the 17th *Graf Spee* was seen to be disembarking her crew. In the afternoon she set course for the open sea, accompanied by a German merchant ship. A few miles out the remainder of her crew left her. At sunset she blew up. Captain Langsdorff had been authorized to destroy his ship if he saw no way of bringing her back home. Nevertheless two days later he shot himself.

A sea chase and a sea victory have for centuries given a special delight to the British people. The sinking of *Graf Spee* was a timely tonic during a period of mixed disaster and inactivity. It was an item in the stiffening resolve of Great Britain which was to be put to the test when France fell and the decision to fight on against Hitler rested more upon spirit than reason. More immediately there was the question of *Graf Spee*'s victims whom she had transferred to *Altmark* before being engaged by Commodore Harwood's cruisers. Two months after *Graf Spee* sank, *Altmark* and her prisoners entered Norwegian waters homeward bound. She raised a question of international law. Norway was a neutral and it was argued on the British side that it was a breach of neutrality for Norway to permit the passage of prisoners of war through neutral territorial waters. Moreover the Norwegian authorities, upon being assured by *Altmark*'s captain that she carried no prisoners, had failed to carry out an effective search. A light British force thereupon sailed into Norwegian waters on 17 February, boarded the German vessel and rescued the captives. This dashing episode was another boost to British morale, greatly irritated Hitler and brought an incidental compliment from Ciano who told the British Ambassador that it reminded him of the boldest traditions of the British navy in the time of Francis Drake. (The Italians were already annoyed with Hitler's Scandinavian policies. Hitler had refused to allow Italian aircraft, ordered by Finland before the Russian attack, to be sent via Germany. Pro-Finnish demonstrations in Rome had had a clear anti-German tone.)

The Finnish war and the *Altmark* episode showed that Norway's hopes of keeping out of the Second World War as it had kept out of the First were tenuous. Norway was too important. Its main geographical feature is its coastline of a thousand miles, guarded and punctured by islands and inlets. This coast could provide valuable bases either for a British blockade of Germany or for a German offensive against shipping in the Atlantic. It had also a second importance as an outlet for Swedish iron ore. Northern Sweden is one of Europe's principal sources of iron ore, and early in the war exaggerated hopes were attached to preventing this ore from reaching Germany. The Swedish orefields lie midway between the Swedish port of Luleå in the Gulf of Bothnia, which freezes over in winter, and the Norwegian port of Narvik, which does not. By the beginning of 1940 both sides had their eyes on Norway and when the Finnish war ended in March Churchill wanted nonetheless to proceed to secure a foothold in northern Norway. But he failed to carry the cabinet with him and it was decided instead to mine the Leads and to make preparations to land in Norway if the Germans landed or seemed clearly about to do so.

On the other side Hitler had been pressed for some time by Grand Admiral Raeder to take action against Norway before Great Britain did. By December 1939 he had made up his mind to do this and in that month Raeder introduced to him Vidkun Quisling, the only personage of the Second World War who was destined to give his name to a human type. Quisling, two years older than Hitler, was a well-educated, romantic racialist, who had had the beginnings of a brilliant army career before 1914, had helped his great compatriot Fridtjof Nansen with his humanitarian work for the League of Nations in the twenties, had gone to work and found a wife in the Ukraine, and had then turned to politics as something between a socialist and a communist. Tactless and unpopular, as well as talented, he did not fit into party life and after holding office briefly as Minister of Defence in 1931–3 he founded his own party and newspaper, both of which were complete failures. He was taken up by the Nazi ideologist and eastern specialist, Alfred Rosenberg, and a few years later was passed on to Hitler by Raeder as a useful instrument of German policy. His rewards were the post of Prime Minister during the German occupation and execution by his countrymen after the end of the war.

Hitler issued a formal directive for an invasion of Norway (plus Denmark because it was on the way) on 1 March 1940. Operations were placed under the control of the O K W – *Oberkommando der Wehrmacht*, the inter-service planning headquarters of which Hitler himself was chief with the pliant Keitel to do his bidding. The plan was a daring one. Resistance by Danes and Norwegians could not be a serious obstacle but Great Britain held command of the seas and Germany might therefore be expected – and was expected in Great Britain – to proceed by land (much as the Anglo-American armies proceeded up Italy by land three years later). Hitler chose, however, to confront British naval superiority and to seize points along the Norwegian coast as far north as Narvik, while at the same time seizing airfields by airborne troops – the first such enterprise ever attempted. The attack on Norway, from Oslo to Narvik, was launched on 9 April. In gales and snowstorms it was successful at most points, although a number of ships were lost, including the battleship *Blücher* sunk by gunnery while trying to force the passage up the Oslo fjord, and the admiral and general in command of operations were both captured. So was a Gestapo party on its way to arrest the king. The Norwegian parliament conferred full powers on the king who refused to surrender and, after escaping death in an air attack on a village where he had been located, held out in the hope of British and French help.

In London reports that the Germans had landed as far north as Narvik seemed so incredible that they were for a time believed to be a mistake for Larvik, which is near the Oslo fjord. Although Swedish sources had given warnings of the assembly of the invading forces in north German harbours, it was believed in London that these were being held ready to counter an Anglo-French invasion and not to make the first move. The British cabinet was taken by surprise, the British staffs found themselves equipped with inadequate information about harbours and airfields, plans

THE GERMAN INVASION OF NORWAY 1940

British occupied Narvik 28 May. Withdrew 8 June.

0   100
Miles

German occupied territory.
→ **German advances from 9 April.**
May **Date of German occupation.**
Occupied by British.

British landing 29 April. Withdrew 29 May.

British landing 14 April. Withdrew 3 May.

British landing 17 April. Withdrew 2 May.

16 June

Kirkenes
16 June

Lofoten Is.

Narvik
8 June

Bodö
1 June

Gällivare

Grong 6 May
Namsos 6 May

Lulea

Trondheim 16 April

GULF OF BOTHNIA

SWEDEN

FINLAND

Icebound in winter.

Andalsnes
2 May

Bergen

Lillehammer 22 April

Kongsvinger
16 April

Helsinki

NORWAY

Oslo
9 April

Stockholm

ESTONIA

Stavanger

Kristiansand

Riga

LATVIA

North
Sea

DENMARK

Copenhagen

Baltic Sea

LITHUANIA

Danzig

EAST
PRUSSIA

USSR

Hamburg

HOLLAND

GERMANY

POLAND

~ARTHUR BANKS~

were made and unmade in confused succession even after operations had been set in motion. With the Germans in occupation of all ports and airfields the British and French were faced with the necessity of making hazardous landings from the sea or air. They proposed at first to go ashore near Narvik but then switched to Trondhjem fjord in central Norway, where the Norwegians wanted to concert a combined campaign. Next it was decided to attempt both the northern and the central ventures but later still a direct attack up Trondhjem fjord was abandoned in favour of two separate landings at Namsos and Andalsnes 125 and 190 miles away. In this confusion, made worse by notably inefficient cooperation between the army and the navy, British, French and Polish forces went into action against heavy odds and were worsted. In Scotland troops which had been embarked for Norway were disembarked when news of the German attacks arrived, in order to get the ships to sea as quickly as possible, but were then not used. At Namsos French forces were put ashore but were without even skis or snowshoes, let alone guns and tanks, since the ship carrying their equipment found on arrival that it was too big to enter the harbour. For a week these men were immobile and defenceless against air attacks. Inferior in numbers and ill supported from the air, Anglo-French forces in the centre were withdrawn in the first week of May, giving their Norwegian allies lamentably short notice of the necessity to capitulate. In the north evacuation was delayed until the beginning of June when it was harassed by the German fleet. The Royal Navy lost the aircraft-carrier *Glorious* with two squadrons of aircraft and failed to discover the intentions or the whereabouts of German heavy units which were at sea in the area. The retreating transports nevertheless escaped and reached Great Britain with the survivors of the expedition and also the Norwegian king. The Germans were left in possession of bases from which to operate against Atlantic traffic and, later, convoys bound for the USSR. There would in future be no difficulties about the transport of Swedish iron ore to Germany. Hitler's victory was won by the imaginative use of air transport, skilful handling of naval forces, good inter-service cooperation and a superior meteorological service – helped by the bungling of his adversaries. The cost was borne by the German navy which (like the German glider and parachute arms in the battle for Crete) suffered crippling losses at the hands of the defenders in the first phase of the operation.

The sorry Norwegian campaign was debated in the House of Commons on 7 and 8 May. The Chamberlain government was deserted by one hundred and one of its supporters, and although the Prime Minister still commanded a majority of eighty-one in that solid, stolid House he no longer had the backing needed to carry on the war. He tried to convince himself and others that mounting disaster made it desirable for him to remain at the helm, but this argument did not work. He was deposed by the Commons as a result of disorder within its Conservative ranks. There was also a growing feeling that the country needed an all-party government and the Labour Party would not serve under Chamberlain. The obvious successor in political terms was Halifax. Chamberlain himself, the Conservative Party and the king all wanted Halifax and the Labour leaders were willing to join a Halifax administration. But at a meeting between Chamberlain, Halifax and Churchill on 9 May the lot fell on Churchill. Chamberlain proposed Halifax, expecting Churchill to express his agreement, but Churchill, acting on advice given him by Brendan Bracken, stayed silent. In breaking an awkward pause to say something about the difficulties of leading a government from the House of Lords Halifax threw away his chances, and shortly afterwards Chamberlain was on his way to Buckingham Palace to tell the king that it must be Churchill, who thus assumed office and the responsibility for victory or defeat on 10 May.

When he took office in 1940 Churchill was sixty-five years old. He had been a prominent political figure for forty years and famous for most of that time. He had sat in the House of Commons since 1900 (with only a brief exclusion in 1922–4) and in cabinet on and off since 1908. He had held office as President of the Board of Trade, Home Secretary, First Lord of the Admiralty, Minister of Munitions, Secretary of State for War, Secretary of State for Air, Colonial Secretary and Chancellor of the Exchequer. He was unusually versatile. He had written over a dozen books, including a history of the First World War in five volumes, an excellent biography of his father and another in four volumes of his remoter ancestor the first Duke of Marlborough. He was a competent amateur painter and an addict of English and European history. He had been a war correspondent in Africa and India. In the variety of his aptitudes and his achievements he was matched by two only of his predecessors in the premiership, Disraeli and Balfour; he was closer to the colourful talents of the former than the philosophical intellect of the latter. He had also the vigorous and independent spirit of Palmerston, manifested in longevity and the ability to appeal to the masses. Churchill and Palmerston are the only British Prime Ministers who have been popularly referred to by friendly nicknames. As a war leader Churchill has inevitably been compared with Lloyd George but the similarities between the two men lie in their circumstances rather than their characters or tastes.

Yet in 1940 Churchill had held no office for over ten years. First a

Conservative, then a Liberal and once more a Conservative after the First World War his political career was tinged with an inconstancy which is rare in British politics and is regarded with distrust. Even after the war, when his standing was unique in British political history, he was suffered to become the leader of the Conservative Party because of his enormous popularity and not because he was regarded by Conservative leaders as one of them, and during the thirties he was to all intents and purposes a man without a party, an eccentric without an accepted place in political life. In these years he was chiefly prominent for his opposition to the Conservative government's India Bill and for his campaign in favour of rearmament. He had spent three years of his early life in India and had formed a romantic attachment to the idea of the British-in-India which penetrated his prose style and ever afterwards provided him with some of the most effective embellishments of his oratory. But he was neither much interested in the real India nor well informed about it, so that his opposition to the Bill was romantic rather than sensible and his long but ineffectual crusade against it had no effect on the history of India. It did, however, widen the gap between him and the leaders of his party, and it strengthened the view held by many in political circles that, however great his abilities, his judgement was erratic. He was more liked than listened to. This element in his reputation was not new. As against Baldwin he had been on the side of toughness in dealing with the General Strike in 1926 and he had come in for criticism because as Chancellor of the Exchequer he had accepted, against his better judgement, the arguments for a return to the gold standard in 1925 at the pre-war parity. In 1936 he made no concealment of his sympathies with King Edward VIII during the abdication crisis – a generous attitude which may have been applauded by the people at large but greatly irritated the Baldwin government and the rest of the establishment in state and church. His campaign for rearmament won him few friends: while the left dubbed him a warmonger, Conservatives resented his opposition to their policy of appeasement and feared – especially in the light of the by-election in Fulham in 1933 where the Conservative candidate was defeated by, it was thought, pacifist sentiment – that his agitation was costing them votes.

But when war came there was an almost universal feeling that Churchill must have a big share, perhaps the biggest, in conducting it. It is easier to record this judgement than to identify its sources. There was first of all the fact that Churchill, however often he had been wrong in the past on this issue or that, had been right about Hitler's Germany. His knowledge of history was here crucial, for it was as a historian and not as a moralist that he took his stand. He had not only absorbed European history but had understood it thoroughly and acquired insights which equally well read and more intellectual observers missed. He became certain that war was coming and that Great Britain could not avoid it, for he saw the rise of Nazi Germany in terms of the classic British doctrine that no single power must be allowed to dominate the European continent. He did not suffer from the delusion that Great Britain was not a part of the continent and so could sidestep the catastrophe. Although he sensed the strategic challenge to Great Britain before the moral one to civilized behaviour – he was no quicker than most of his countrymen to react to the moral issue, commended Mussolini's rule on a number of occasions and was for a time ambivalent about Hitler – he developed also a deep and genuine loathing of Nazi brutishness and had the power to express it with peculiar sting.

This was the second source of his special position when war came. The challenge once seen, Churchill was exceptionally well equipped to expose and meet it. He was combative and patriotic in the best sense of these words and he gave the most reassuring appearance of being firm in purpose and unhesitating in action. He was not in fact a man who knew no doubts – only a singularly stupid or vain man could have avoided them and he was often fearfully worried – but he had the courage and the skill to hide his anxieties and to give the impression that he was certain of his course and applying himself undividedly to the business of doing what had to be done. He was able to communicate his attitudes to the British people and to evoke from them their latent determination to resist danger and conquer evil. The essence of his famous oratory was his ability to give voice to elemental sentiments in big words and simple phrases. He was moreover the kind of leader who suited the British people. He was both an aristocrat and a democrat, a combination which the British like and which does not strike them as a paradox. Churchill had the assurance, even something of the arrogance, of the born aristocrat, but he combined this superiority with a capacity for feeling himself a part of the people and not apart from them. For him the people meant all the people and not, as so often in British parlance, the working-class bottom half.

He possessed, finally, an abundant mental energy. This worked both ways. His habits of work sometimes irritated and exhausted his advisers who were required to consider a stream of ideas, some of which were inevitably bad ideas, and to do so at unconventional hours of the day or night. But the gain was great, for with Churchill in command there could never be any doubt about whether things were happening or not. Churchill was a leader who had no intention of allowing anybody inferior to give directions, but he was also a respecter of the people and of their principal institution, the House of Commons. Undoubted head of the executive and of the armed services, master of the bureaucracy and sometimes a rough master, he was at the same time the servant of the legislature and the electorate. He showed, because he believed, that one does not have to be a dictator to be a leader.

On the day that he became Prime Minister Hitler invaded France and the Low Countries. The so-called phoney war had come to an end. The phoney war was a period in which nothing very warlike happened (except locally, sporadically and briefly) and, more than that, in which it was possible for people who were so disposed to go on hoping that nothing very warlike would happen. It was the time in which the era of appeasement and the years of war overlapped. In May 1940 Hitler made war on the western democracies. Less obviously but no less significantly Churchill's government did something which Chamberlain's government had never done: it dropped a bomb on Germany.

CHAPTER 6

The Fall of France

HITLER had won Poland almost as easily as Austria and Czechoslovakia. Although force had to be used instead of being merely brandished and the Russians had to be allowed their share, the operation was swift and was concluded without the intervention of any other power. It might be just the latest in the series of Hitlerian conquests, more expensive and more brutal but essentially not very different. Or it might be the beginning of something much more serious. Hitherto all Hitler's victories had been in central Europe – in Germany itself (the Rhineland) and then in Austria, Czechoslovakia, Danzig, Memel and Poland. Should he now attack France, even though France had acquiesced in the Polish *fait accompli*? Hitler was for action now. In the past he had disagreed with his advisers, especially his military advisers, about the reactions and the capacities of the western powers and he had always proved his advisers wrong.

The Polish collapse could be exploited in different ways. There were those who hoped that the reluctance of the western democracies to help Poland would finally eliminate western opposition to German ambitions in central and eastern Europe without the need for a showdown; that the defeat of Poland would be accepted in the west as a defeat for the west too. On the other hand the glittering successes of the Polish campaign were an incitement to a similar campaign in the west, and so long as there was any doubt whether a war against France would have to be fought one day there was also the argument that from the German point of view the sooner it were fought the better. Before the end of September Hitler, without consulting General von Brauchitsch, the Commander-in-Chief of the army, gave the order to prepare for an attack on France that autumn and a directive was issued by OKW on 9 October. Brauchitsch swallowed this usurpation of his functions and got to work, while continuing to argue that a spring offensive would be more prudent because the army needed to train fresh units and because the autumn weather might bog down the tanks and ground the aircraft. In the event an autumn campaign was washed out by the weather and after several postponements it was cancelled. In addressing his service chiefs at the end of November, Hitler, preferring to lay the blame for his disappointment on the human factor, was so abusive about the army that Brauchitsch offered to resign. He was not allowed to – yet. The postponement of the attack had a most important consequence since it gave army leaders the time to urge changes in the German plan of campaign.

The fundamental factors in German planning were the experiences of their forerunners in 1914 and the Maginot Line. The latter was a string of fortified positions, begun in 1929 and guarding the western approaches to France between its Swiss and Belgian frontiers. This line had an awesome reputation but owing to Belgium's neutrality it stopped short at a geographical point which had little strategic significance. Its existence, however, virtually dictated a German attack through Belgium to the north of it and the question which remained open was the main objective of such an attack. Too much pondering of the campaigns of 1914 had led the German General Staff to plan an attack on a broad front stretching all the way from Luxembourg northwards, with the main weight in the north and the main objective the Channel ports which they had failed to win in the race with which the First World War had opened. This attempt to repeat and improve on the performance of August 1914 reflected a preoccupation with this failure and a special concern with Great Britain rather than France, since the principal value of the ports was their use for submarine warfare against the British Isles. This plan did not aim, primarily at any rate, to knock out the French army as the Polish army had been knocked out and it therefore admitted the prospect of a long and possibly static war. Even if the plan succeeded, the war in France would not be over; and its success was dubious since it involved a direct attack on French and British forces which, if not defeated outright, might stand on prepared lines in northern France and keep themselves supplied through the ports.

General von Manstein, the plan's most effective critic, had other ideas. He proposed that the main weight of an attack in the north should be on its left wing rather than its right and that the prime object should be the annihilation of the French capacity to resist and not the conquest of the Channel coast or any other terrain; the enemy's territory in its entirety would become a prize of war as a consequence of the defeat of his armies. Manstein proposed that German forces attacking through the Ardennes should turn southwards as well as northwards and envelop the French to the west of the Maginot Line. Manstein was Chief of Staff to Field Marshal von Rundstedt, whose Army Group A would win the chief role in the campaign if the Manstein concept were accepted. They together urged Brauchitsch, who agreed with them but did not enjoy arguments with the Führer, to press their views on Hitler; and they had a stroke of luck early in January. An officer taking the plans to a headquarters in the west fell in with some air force friends, celebrated the meeting so well that he missed his train, got his friends to fly him on his way but took a wrong course and crashed in Belgium. With the plans in enemy hands there were special grounds for changing them. (The western staffs, however, concluded that the crash had been a fake and the plans planted on them.)

Hitler was prepared to listen. A serious student of military affairs, he liked discussing military problems with those of his generals whom he respected, and Manstein was one of these for the time being. Hitler was not, as he himself imagined, a military genius, but neither was he the ignoramus and bungler that surviving generals subsequently tried to make out. From the career point of view he was an amateur and not a professional military man, but then so were Stalin and Churchill and, for good or ill, Hitler had studied the science of war at least as carefully as the first and possibly with more application than either. But his talents and inclinations were the reverse of what was needed in a supreme commander. He was strongest on detail. He knew the names of bits and pieces of military equipment and what they were for, just as he was also exceptionally well versed in the details of the architect's craft. He had the mind of a fascinated and perhaps even an inventive quartermaster, but this gift did not make him a strategist and, as a strategist, he was handicapped because his cast of mind was basically political and not military. He put political aims before military sense. His catastrophic fault as a war lord lay even more in attempting the impossible than in his strategy. On this occasion he saw the force of Manstein's arguments (he may have been thinking independently along similar lines) and accepted his plan with some modifications.

Hitler did not begin his attack in the west with any marked material superiority. The battle of France was won by superior skill and not by the crushing weight of numbers. In the vital department of tanks the Germans were numerically the weaker with some 2,700 against nearly 3,000 French and 200 British. The quality of the tanks on the two sides was about the same. But in tactics and leadership the French and British were outclassed. For many French and British officers the tank was a horseless carriage to be used in the role of a horse rather than a carriage, a mechanized charger, more expensive and less lovable than a horse but performing essentially the same function as the cavalry of a bygone age which had fought closely with the infantry arm along a defined front. But defeat in the First World War and the restrictions imposed by the treaty of Versailles had made the German army more receptive to new ideas. Under General von Seeckt, himself somewhat old-fashioned in his views but willing to encourage novel thinking in others, the German army of 100,000 was re-created on the principles, first, that compensation for small numbers lay in mobility; secondly, that armoured vehicles could provide this mobility in place of the horse; thirdly, that the armour of a tank, unlike that of a medieval knight, was even more valuable in offence than for protection; fourthly, that tanks should be used in massed cohorts – divisions, corps and even tank armies – distinct from the other arms of the service; and finally that, with this combination of speed, weight and numbers, their prime purpose was to penetrate the enemy's lines and destroy his communications.

This was the *Blitzkrieg* and it revolutionized not only the handling of armoured forces but also the whole concept of war as a face-to-face contest between rival fronts. The basic ideas were not German. They were developed in the first place by British theorists like Captain B. H. Liddell Hart, Major-General J. F. C. Fuller and Major-General G. le Q. Martel. In Germany the doctrines of these men and later the similar teaching of Charles de Gaulle, published in 1937 and better known in Germany than in France, were studied by Heinz Guderian and other young officers. Before 1933 they were tried out in practice in the USSR under arrangements made clandestinely by Seeckt with the Russian army and government, and although Hitler stopped this collaboration his special interest in armoured warfare encouraged the progressives in the German army and contributed to the formation of the first two Panzer divisions soon after the Nazis took power. In May 1940 the Germans had ten Panzer divisions. (Rather more than half of their tanks were Pkw. Is and IIs, the rest the Pkw. IIIs and IVs which were to become the mainstay of the German armour until the Panther and Tiger began to arrive at the front in 1943. Three divisions with the heaviest punch were equipped with tanks made in Czechoslovakia's captured factories.)

The *Blitzkrieg* had also a special place for airborne troops whose task was to seize key points ahead of the advancing armour. Germany's parachutists so captured the imagination by their novelty that extraordinary steps were taken to defeat them: policemen were armed and trained to deal with them, in Great Britain church bells were to be rung to give warning of their descent and the most fanciful accounts, some of them official, circulated about the guise in which they were likely to do so. But there were far fewer of them than was commonly believed. Hitler had envisaged a war of the future as a 'sky black with bombers and, leaping from them into the smoke, parachute storm troops, each grasping a machine gun', but the Germans never had more than one division of parachutists and in their most notable operation – Crete – most of them jumped with pistols or knives and had to search around afterwards for the machine guns which were dropped separately and sometimes far away.

The German attack in the west opened on 10 May simultaneously against the Netherlands, Belgium, Luxembourg and France. In the Netherlands the weight of the attack was directed against Rotterdam. Its airfield, Waalhaven, was seized by parachute troops who also captured the intervening bridges over the Maas. The main bridge in the centre of the city was seized by units which landed by it in seaplanes. A subsidiary attack on airfields near The Hague was unsuccessful. On the 14th Rotterdam was still holding out. The Germans summoned it to surrender and parleys ensued. At this point the heart of the city was heavily bombed; within a few minutes great destruction was caused and 980 were killed. Nothing like this had been seen in the war so far. Two hours later the city capitulated and on the 15th the Dutch laid down their arms everywhere. The bombing of Rotterdam has been regarded as a piece of unprincipled savagery and vandalism, but there were perhaps extenuating circumstances. The air attack seems to have been made in ignorance of the parleys which were in train and in spite of German attempts to cancel it, and when the bombers appeared German commanders on the spot tried to signal to them to desist and did succeed in making a part of the force sheer off: but doubts have more recently been cast on this attempted explanation.

In Belgium the attack began with one of the most original strokes of the war. The conquest of Belgium involved crossing a series of waterways, notably the Meuse (or Maas) and the Albert Canal which branches off the Meuse just south of Maastricht on a north-westerly course towards Antwerp. Maastricht, which is on the Dutch side of the frontier between Belgium and Holland, is only twelve miles from the German border. Just south of it and in Belgium lay the great fortress of Eben Emael, a wedge-shaped hill unassailable except from the sky and commanding the end of the Albert Canal and three vital bridges over it. In the early hours of 10 May forty-one gliders took off from German airfields with 363 men for an operation which they had rehearsed many times. Two of the gliders came to grief on the way but the rest arrived silently over Eben Emael and in the first glider-borne attack in history captured the fort and its 1,200 defenders and two of the three bridges with the loss (to the attackers) of only five lives.

As soon as the German attack in the west was known, French and British forces began to move forward to make contact with the Belgian army on the line of the River Dyle and so create an unbroken line of resistance to the Germans from the English Channel to the borders of Switzerland. Owing to Belgium's neutrality advance planning had been dangerously meagre, so much so that positions which French forces were to occupy had not been prepared for them. Almost immediately the allied line was punctured farther south. The entire British Expeditionary Force and half the French army, which had moved into Belgium, were cut off. German armour under General Erwin Rommel proved that the Ardennes were not the obstacle to tanks which had been supposed and on 12 May German units, having broken through a sector which was lightly held by second-class divisions, found themselves on French soil north of Sedan. The next day they were across the Meuse at a number of points and after only one more day they had prised open a fateful gap fifty miles wide between two French armies. General Georges, commanding the north-eastern fronts under a cumbrous arrangement as a semi-independent sub-ordinate of the Commander-in-Chief, General Maurice Gamelin, ordered a redisposition on the basis of a false report that French forces were in flight: the general who sent the report shot himself the next day, Georges suffered a nervous collapse (he had been ill for years) and two days later a third general was dismissed for losing his nerve. The Germans advanced 200 miles in a week. One million refugees were footing it along the roads and across country.

In three days the R A F lost half of the 200 bombers which it was oper-ating in France – the highest loss percentage which it ever suffered – and the French air force was extinguished. The French First Army, the British Expeditionary Force to its left and the Seventh French Army further north still were cut off from the rest of the French armies, and French and British reinforcements moving up to the Dyle line were ordered to suspend their advance. On the following day, 16 May, with the Dutch already out of the war, the plan for Belgium having miscarried and the Germans racing into France, Gamelin disclosed to an Anglo-French council of war in Paris that he had no reserves left. His predicament was of his own making. He had neglected to create a reserve before war began, even though one of the main objects of building a defensive position like the Maginot Line was to avoid having to string men out along a long static line and so be able to hold them in a mobile reserve instead. Gamelin had done the opposite, committing his troops to fixed positions from which he could not easily switch them when the need arose. He had compounded this basic mistake by allowing men to go on leave from 7 May in spite of accurate warnings from reliable sources of the date and place of the German attack. Three days later French soldiers hurrying to rejoin their units failed to find them before they were overwhelmed. Yet Gamelin had all the same a small reserve of eight infantry divisions; but it was behind the Lorraine and Rhine fronts.

From the Meuse the German armour pushed on for the coast with powerful and efficient air support. They reached it on 20 May. Instead of a Franco-Anglo-Belgian line containing the Germans there was a German line stretching from Germany to the sea and cutting the allied forces in two. This German line was a thin one, for the German forces which had made it were comparatively small and had advanced far ahead of their supporting formations. The problem for the German high command was to consolidate the line and produce plans for dealing with the two distinct allied forces to the north and the south of it. The problem for the allies was to try to break the line and re-establish contact between their disrupted armies.

Reynaud, who had never had confidence in Gamelin and had been on the point of dismissing him when news of the German invasion arrived, replaced him on 19 May with General Maxime Weygand, a soldier full of honour but also of years (72). Reynaud also appointed another and even older hero, Marshal Philippe Pétain (85), to be Deputy Prime Minister. Weygand's fame and barely diminished sprightliness infused some hope into headquarters staffs but he was powerless to rectify Gamelin's cardinal error. He could not in the midst of a battle create a reserve. He inherited from Gamelin a plan to attack the German corridor simultaneously from north and south but postponed its execution while he made a tour of headquarters. This tour wasted precious days (whether telephone communications were destroyed or overlooked is not clear) and largely failed to achieve its aim, since of the two principal commanders north of the corridor, one, Lord Gort, failed by accident to keep his appointment with Weygand and the other, General Billotte, was killed – also accidentally – immediately after it. But in any case Gort, acting on Gamelin's earlier orders and apparently unaware of Weygand's cancellation of them, shot his bolt prematurely and was checked by the Germans, so that by the time Weygand put the plan in motion again there was no response from the north. The effect therefore of supplanting Gamelin at this late stage was added confusion: an attack from the north at a time when the complementary attack in the south had been stayed, and consequently no possibility of an attack from the north when the new Commander-in-Chief was ready to give the signal for attack in the south. The German line became unpierceable (if it was not so already) and the Germans were able to consider in comparative leisure how they would complete the campaign. If on 20 May, when they reached the sea, there had been some doubt about whether their victories so far had been decisive, the next few days showed that no effective counter-attack could be launched against them and that, whichever way they turned first, they could outnumber the allied divisions on either front by at least two to one.

THE GERMAN INVASION OF FRANCE AND THE LOW COUNTRIES MAY-JUNE 1940

Dunkirk 4 June - Final withdrawal 190,000 British and 140,000 French soldiers evacuated.100,000 Allied soldiers taken prisoner.

KEY TO GERMAN ADVANCE

10 to 14 May	on 29 May
15 to 24 May	on 30 May
25 to 27 May	31 May to 4 June
on 28 May	5 to 12 June
Siegfried Line	Maginot Line

~ARTHUR BANKS~

HOLLAND Surrendered 15 May

BELGIUM Surrendered 28 May

FRANCE

GERMANY

LUXEMBURG

Breached 16 June

Occupied 14 June

Rhine

Rhine

Meuse

Meuse

Dyle

Marne

Aisne

Seine

Seine

Somme

Somme

Cologne

Colmar

Metz

Châlons sur Marne

Sedan

St. Quentin

Rheims

Paris

Namur

Antwerp

Ghent

Brussels

Maastricht

Rotterdam

Ypres

Lille

Arras

Dunkirk

Calais

Boulogne

Abbeville

Amiens

Rouen

Dieppe

Le Havre

50

0   Miles

Yet they were undecided about how to proceed. The allied armies, although disrupted and disjointed, had fought well. The German generals hardly perceived the extent of their triumph. They were anxious to reinforce their forward units and nervous about the large French armies on their southern flank. The first thing to do was to mass their own forces once more. To the south there was need for caution. To the north there was no need for speed since the allied armies were surrounded and the idea that any great number of them could escape by sea entered nobody's head. So after covering 300 miles to reach the Channel in three days the Germans took over three weeks to go another thirty miles up the coast. Rundstedt, although delighted by the dashing successes of his younger subordinates, was taken aback by the speed of his victory, decided not to press his luck too far and ordered his Army Group to halt and regroup.

But Brauchitsch was ready to let the Panzers push on without delay and round up the allied forces to the north, while plans for the subjugation of the rest of France were being worked out. He was angered by Rundstedt's order. On the day of the order, 24 May, Hitler arrived at Rundstedt's headquarters. The plan which, at Manstein's urging, Hitler had adopted early in the year, had emphasized the prior importance of a southward rather than a northward sweep after a break-through. Presumably Hitler still had Manstein's basic reasoning in mind. He endorsed Rundstedt's order and as a result the German armour halted for three days, facing north but motionless. These days were an invaluable respite for the allied armies trapped between the Germans on the Somme and other German armies in Belgium – and the main cause of the salvation of so many men from Dunkirk.

Hitler's motives in blunting his attack on them have been one of the principal enigmas of the war. Among his motives were two different, even contradictory, considerations. Faced with a force which was now mainly British his ambivalence about Great Britain may have reasserted itself. He had no plan for continuing the war against Great Britain and expected it to make peace after France had been beaten. There was nothing to be gained by pounding the British forces on the continent and then incarcerating what was left of them. On the other hand he was under pressure from Goering to leave the rest of this battle to the Luftwaffe. Goering had taken little part in the Battle of France. The Luftwaffe was engaged in close support of the armies; the independent role of Commander-in-Chief of the Luftwaffe had, with the exception of the few days' operations against Holland, been eclipsed. Moreover Goering himself had been suffering from one of his recurrent bouts of drug-taking (to which he had become addicted since drugs had been prescribed for a painful leg wound sustained in the 1923 putsch) and upon emerging from this enforced retreat he was all the more eager for action and distinction. Like Mussolini, he figured that the time was now or never. Although Goering's pleas to leave it to the Luftwaffe and Hitler's political preoccupations with Great Britain could hardly be reconciled, they did have one thing in common: halt the Panzers. That they were stayed by Hitler out of some fellow feeling for the British is implausible and belied by the fact that, although he reined in his tanks, he gave no comparable order to restrain the Luftwaffe from strafing the cornered British.

The allied forces were in a bag round Dunkirk. Boulogne had been lost on 25 May and Calais the next day after a whole day's pounding by artillery, Stukas and tanks. At Dunkirk the evacuation and the Luftwaffe's attacks both began on 27 May. The first results were very discouraging for the beaten troops who, fiercely battered in the town and on the beaches, bitterly reproached the RAF for not protecting them. Then the weather came to their help. With rain half the day on the 29th and fog and rain all day on the 30th the Luftwaffe's onslaughts were restrained and the evacuation rate rose to eight times what it had been on the first day. But on 1 June it turned fine and evacuation by day had to be suspended. By this time the men waiting on the beaches were suffering extreme physical and nervous exhaustion and many of those who got off were sunk in the sea before they reached the other side of the Channel. But in an astonishing rescue operation by large and small craft of every description, by which the British Admiralty had hoped at the outset to save perhaps 100,000 men, more than three times that number – 338,226 – were brought away from Dunkirk.

The Belgian army was forced to lay down its arms soon after the operation began, but many French and other allied combatants escaped with the British (one third of those rescued were not British). The last British troops were taken off on 2 June but the British flotillas returned to collect Frenchmen for two more nights. The Germans were left with 40,000 prisoners. In France a further 190,000, mostly belonging to rear formations, were later evacuated from Normandy and Bordeaux, but an attempt to withdraw the British 51st Division from St Valéry failed, partly because of fog. Altogether over 558,000 (again one third non-British) were evacuated from different parts of the continent into Great Britain. This was a triumph for the British navy and a corresponding defeat for Goering, although the result might have been different if the Luftwaffe had been able to operate at full strength in the Dunkirk area on more days than the weather permitted. Significantly for the future the RAF lost over Dunkirk fewer aircraft than the Luftwaffe. British fighters, flying from bases nearer to the battle area than the German bases, took heavy toll of the Luftwaffe's bombers and Stukas.

On 5 June, the day after the close of the Dunkirk operations, the Germans launched from the Somme–Aisne line a series of attacks to the south which (together with a secondary attack through Alsace) destroyed the French army. They had spent the interval since 20 May debating whether to bring the weight of their armour to the west or east of Paris. The debate serves only to show how unsure the Germans still were about the hard facts of the situation, for in truth it did not much matter which they did. They reached the Seine at various points in three days, entered Paris on 14 June and spread rapidly into the farthest corners of France. The French army fought them – up to the bitter end French units continued to put up tough resistance in spite of the physical and psychological shocks which they had suffered – but was incapable of stopping them. The only conceivable hope of avoiding complete defeat lay with Great Britain. France, defeated and despairing, could no longer rely on itself. It turned to its ally. On the ground the British contribution had always been conceived as ancillary. The British Expeditionary Force might help the French army but could neither be a substitute for it nor rescue it. In the air, however, the British had more to offer. When the campaign opened the RAF committed thirty-nine squadrons to the battle. Ten of these were obsolescent medium bombers which were so badly mauled in daylight operations that they had to be regrouped as six squadrons within a week. The remainder were fighters (including ten Hurricane squadrons) and reconnaissance. The Hurricane force was almost doubled in the next few days but the French government appealed for still more. A first request for ten squadrons was refused. Instead heavy bombers were ordered to attack the Ruhr and then the advancing German armies. On 16 May six more fighter squadrons were detailed to the battle in France, although these aircraft had to operate from bases in Kent. Thenceforward the British squadrons engaged in France were progressively withdrawn to English bases as airfields in France were overrun. By 20 May only a token force remained. On 2 June Reynaud asked for twenty more squadrons, an impossible request. The British government provided a modest reinforcement but as the days passed and it became increasingly clear that Weygand could not turn the tide of battle, the British cabinet had to harden its heart against sending aircraft to France simply to be lost. By 11 June Weygand was himself prophesying the end at any moment. His exhausted divisions were engaged at all points, he had no reserves, and Reynaud's plea for a massive air attack to save the day was painfully unrealistic.

THE FALL OF FRANCE JUNE 1940

North Sea

GREAT BRITAIN

HOLLAND

GERMANY

Dunkirk

Boulogne

BELGIUM

English Channel

Somme

Cherbourg

Le Havre

Rouen

Aisne

Reims

Châlons

MAGINOT LINE

Brest

Seine

PARIS

Belfort

Rennes

Alençon

Orléans

Dijon

SWITZ.

Angers

Loire

Nevers

Nantes

Tours

Cher

Saône

Geneva

14 June German troops enter Paris.

Angoulême

Limoges

VICHY

Lyons

Clermont Ferrand

Grenoble

Isère

ITALY

Bay of Biscay

Bordeaux

New seat of Government.

Rhone

Garonne

Toulouse

Marseilles

Nice

Perpignan

Toulon

SPAIN

Mediterranean Sea

⟵ German advances.

▬ Position of German armies when Armistice was signed on 22 June.

▤ Vichy France.

0   100
Miles

~ARTHUR BANKS~

Churchill had seen for himself the writing on the wall as early as 16 May when he made the first of five visits to France during the campaign. On that first visit he heard Gamelin's gloomy assessment and observed his gloomy mien. Outside the conference room old men with wheelbarrows were burning secret papers. Churchill faced the unexpected horror of the total collapse of his only ally. A week later, on his second visit, Churchill found that the dejected Gamelin had been replaced by Weygand but only a few days later Gort abandoned all thought of an offensive and decided to withdraw the entire British Expeditionary Force to the coast; Churchill's third visit on the last day of May took place during the fighting at Dunkirk. By the time he returned again on 11 June Great Britain had no troops on the continent, Italy had entered the war, the French government had left Paris and the meeting had to take place at Briare on the Loire. Two days later the last of these meetings was held at Tours, where the government was bivouacking on its flight to the south with Ministries and Embassies dispersed in old châteaux round about.

Churchill was throughout fervently anxious to do everything possible for France and keep it in the war. Fighting the Germans without a continental ally would pose huge new problems. In addition, Churchill's generous impulses urged him now, as they urged him later on over convoys to the USSR, to go to the brink of what was wise and practicable in order to help an ally. But other voices counselled otherwise. During May and June the Air Staff became more and more alarmed about losses in France. Scarce and precious Hurricanes were being lost at the rate of twenty-five a day when the factories were delivering new ones at the rate of four a day. At one moment the Commander-in-Chief of Fighter Command, Air Marshal Sir Hugh Dowding, went so far as to say that he could not answer for the defence of Great Britain and would resign if more fighters were committed to the battle in France. By the time of Churchill's last two visits to France the real question was not how to help in that battle but what terms to try to exact before agreeing to France's inevitable surrender.

At Tours Churchill refused to release France from its promise not to make a separate peace. He promised that there would be no recrimination and that Great Britain would, in victory, see that France recovered its full dignity and greatness if it fought on. But Reynaud's cabinet reshuffle of 19 May – a move which he came to regret – had put too many doves among the hawks. Pétain, supported by Weygand and some of the civilian members of the cabinet, was in favour of giving up the fight. They had no hope for themselves and no belief that Great Britain could do anything to help them. On 15 June, with the Germans now in Paris and the French government in Bordeaux, Reynaud proposed that the French army should lay down its arms (as the Dutch had done) but that the government should remain at war and move, with the fleet and air force, to North Africa. The generals and their supporters expressed horror at this idea which would cast the whole odium of defeat on the army. Besides, the losses suffered at the beginning of the campaign made it possible to argue that there was nothing left to carry on with. The Under Secretary for War, Charles de Gaulle, supported Reynaud and those civilian members of the cabinet still anxious to fight on. De Gaulle had earlier urged Reynaud to move his government to Quimper in Brittany rather than Bordeaux in the hope that this could be a first step to a further move overseas and a refusal to surrender. Reynaud's proposal was approved by a majority of the cabinet but the Prime Minister hesitated, unwilling to insist on a course disapproved by the generals. He hoped that by the next day Pétain could be persuaded to talk Weygand round. Instead Pétain resigned.

When the cabinet met again on the 16th Reynaud had received from Churchill Great Britain's consent to Franco-German armistice negotiations on condition that the French fleet should first sail to British ports; Churchill also urged safe passage for Polish and Czechoslovak troops to Africa. But at the last moment de Gaulle telephoned to Reynaud a new proposal from Churchill for the continuation of the war on the basis of a Franco-British political union and common citizenship after the war and a pledge of total British support. This strange plan, which would have revived the abortive union effected by Henry V by the treaty of Troyes in 1420, seems to have been devised by French and British officials, notably Jean Monnet and Arnold Toynbee with the support of Lord Vansittart. It was regarded by most of the French cabinet as irrelevant to France's plight. Perhaps the British cabinet, in endorsing the plan, anticipated the French reaction, for had it been otherwise Great Britain might have found itself committed to military actions which would have lost the war as well as to a political course which would have baffled the British people. Reynaud, upon seeing that the argument among his colleagues was going against the idea, resigned that day (the 16th). Pétain took his place, formed a new government during the ensuing night and immediately sued through Spain for an armistice. But the fighting went on for another six days and so did the talk about moving to Africa. Preparations were made to transport Ministers, members of parliament and others, but nobody actually gave the word to go and so in the end nobody went – except as refugees. The opponents of the idea kept the Germans informed about what was going on and urged them to produce acceptable armistice terms as quickly as possible. After a preliminary meeting between Hitler and Mussolini at Munich terms were presented. They were accepted after what was virtually an ultimatum requiring unconditional French acceptance and on 22 June at Compiègne, surrounded by the memories and even part of the furniture of the armistice scene of 1918, France signed. Two days later a separate agreement was signed with Italy which, in one of the cheapest and least exhilarating conquests of modern times, acquired Nice and part of the Savoy.

Ten days after the signing of the armistice of Compiègne Great Britain took drastic action against the French fleet. The fall of France threatened the naval balance in the Mediterranean. Together the French and British fleets had dominated that sea. Without a French ally, and with other seas to command as well, Great Britain faced a serious Italian challenge. Although marginally superior in battleships (seven against six) and possessing two aircraft carriers against none, the British Mediterranean fleet was significantly outnumbered in cruisers and destroyers. Italy had the largest submarine fleet in the world and ten land-based aircraft for every one which the RAF could spare for the Mediterranean theatre. If, in addition, the French fleet actively joined the war on the Axis side Great Britain might well be swept from the Mediterranean.

The armistice terms originally provided for the recall of all French ships to French metropolitan ports where they were to be demobilized under German or Italian supervision – Germany undertaking not to use them except for coastal defence and mine-sweeping. The French negotiators wished to secure the right to demobilize their vessels in colonial ports and on this issue the Germans proved not unrelenting – presumably because their control over ships in distant ports was in any event limited. The armistice terms were amended to provide for demobilization in any port outside that part of France which the Germans proposed to occupy. But the fate of the French fleet was of such cardinal importance to Great Britain that the British government decided that it must be placed permanently beyond German clutches or be destroyed.

Admiral Darlan had ordered his captains on 24 June to ensure that their vessels should in no circumstances fall into German hands, but the British did not grasp the full significance of this signal, which was made available to them only in abbreviated form. Some French ships were in British ports and these were painlessly disarmed; others were in French waters; but most were in African harbours – Alexandria, Bizerta, Mers-el-Kebir (Oran), Algiers, Casablanca, Dakar. At Alexandria diplomatic interchanges between the British and French admirals resulted in the disarming of the ships by the French themselves, but in the western Mediterranean the issue was decided by gunfire. Admiral Gensoul's force at

Mers-el-Kebir included two of the most powerful capital ships afloat, *Strasbourg* and *Dunquerque*. On 3 July Admiral Somerville delivered to Gensoul an ultimatum giving him four choices: to join Great Britain in the war, to sail with reduced crews and under British control to internment in a British port, to sail under British escort for demilitarization in a French Caribbean port or to United States custody, or to scuttle within six hours. Somerville told Gensoul that if he refused all four courses the British would use whatever force might be necessary to prevent the French ships from falling into German hands. Somerville was empowered to accept a French proposal, if it were made to him, to demilitarize the ships where they were provided this could be done in six hours and under his supervision and in such a way as to keep them out of service for at least a year even at a fully equipped dockyard. This last proposition was not known to Gensoul.

When Gensoul received these terms his fleet was already almost under British fire and, affronted by this manoeuvre, he told the French Admiralty only about the fourth choice put to him. The Admiralty promised to send help. Some hours later Gensoul proposed to Somerville to demilitarize his ships at Mers-el-Kebir and, if threatened by the Germans or Italians, to sail for Martinique or the United States; he said that the disembarkation of crews had already begun. But the day was wearing on and Somerville, who had been instructed to bring matters to a conclusion before nightfall, shortly afterwards opened fire. Action was broken off but then renewed when *Strasbourg* put to sea. *Strasbourg* and twelve other vessels made good their escape to Toulon. *Dunquerque* went aground. Two other battleships were disabled. Nearly 1,300 Frenchmen were killed.

In the Caribbean French ships were damaged and put out of action for the rest of the war. At Dakar in West Africa the battleship *Richelieu* was slightly damaged but played a part in thwarting an expedition by British and Gaullist forces in September. This venture, based on faulty intelligence about the inclinations of the local French authorities who had opted for Vichy, began with an attempt by a few Gaullists who were landed in two light aircraft and one motorboat to talk the authorities into changing sides. When this mission failed the supporting British naval force began a two-day bombardment which was then abandoned because the French did not give in at once. They were, as it happened, about to do so when the attack was stopped and the attackers sailed away.

These episodes, although minor ones in the retrospect of the history of the war, planted a sting in Anglo-French relations which was to endure for a generation. Great Britain, so it seemed to many Frenchmen, acted at the time of France's abasement to take away from France all that the

Germans had left to be taken – its navy and its colonies. But for Great Britain the immobilization of the French fleet was as necessary as the evacuation from Dunkirk to enable the war to be carried on from the British Isles themselves and in the Mediterranean.

The collapse of France in 1940 was first and foremost a military defeat although, as we shall see in a later chapter, there was more to it than that. The French forces were badly equipped, badly trained and badly led. They had not been modernized after the First World War because the military and political chiefs of the Third Republic had based their policies more on hope than on preparation. They had hoped after 1919 that Germany had been as much sickened by war as France and would not start another one, and later they had postponed rearmament and re-equipment because post-depression economics gave them an added reason for doing so. In the vital sectors of tanks and aircraft, industry was producing too many types and too few machines. French tanks were too lightly armoured to survive and their tactics were obsolete. The air force had adopted a modernization plan in 1934 but four years later, when the Czech crisis came, its first line strength was below 1,400 (half the size of the Luftwaffe) and only one in ten of these aircraft belonged to the 1934 programme. Transport, clothing and light weapons were all in short supply, although nobody could say exactly how short. Commanders from Gamelin downwards were paralysed by a well-founded pessimism. In the circumstances the French forces fought surprisingly well.

The defeat of France was the high-water mark of the German army – and something more. The Germans had beaten the French as easily as they had beaten the Poles. From one angle these were two separate examples of the superiority of German arms. But the two events did not strike contemporaries that way. The defeat of Poland was no surprise. Nobody expected the Poles to hold the German army for long. Theirs was a much smaller, much less up to date and much less skilful force. But the French army was one of the great armies of the world and France itself stood – if any single country could be said so to stand – as the embodiment of western civilization. The fall of France was much more than a military decision. It was a portentous distortion of history, all the more shattering because its completeness led nearly everybody to suppose that it was final and irreversible: the post-war resurrection of France and its re-emergence as one of the few countries in the world capable of conducting an independent foreign policy and as a nuclear power were in 1940 all but inconceivable. Whereas the defeat of Poland had been a tragedy which further shifted the balance of power in Europe Hitler's way, the fall of France opened an abyss of uncertainty for the whole continent and shook the imagination as perhaps nothing had shaken it since the victory of the Turks at Mohacs in 1526.

CHAPTER 7

The Battle of Britain

THE defeat of France reduced hostilities in Europe to a single point, the Anglo-German fight. In Great Britain some people felt that the war was over, though not many cared to say so. When a French collapse began to seem inevitable the British cabinet discussed whether to invoke Mussolini as a mediator between Hitler and the two western allies. In the period between Hitler's Polish campaign and his attacks in the west, Churchill had been willing to contemplate a negotiated peace (but with a Prime Minister other than himself). Now he opposed such a move. The cabinet was divided. Chamberlain, Halifax and others favoured an appeal to Mussolini, and Halifax may have threatened to resign if Churchill insisted on obstructing a negotiated return to peace. The issue was resolved by leaving it to the French government to invoke Mussolini on its own, should it so wish. Churchill has been criticized for his obduracy at this point but it is difficult to believe that Hitler would have entertained proposals for peace when he was on the verge of a resounding triumph, or that Mussolini would have invited a snub by trying to interfere. Churchill's character and temperament told against a compromise peace and his gifts infused the British spirit and confirmed a latent feeling that, although the fighting had so far been disastrous, Hitler was so wicked an enemy that peace with him would be dishonourable. Disgust with the barbarities of Nazism kept the British at war under a new leader who was himself pugnacious enough in spirit to shoulder the miseries and scent the triumphs to come.

Hitler more than half hoped that Great Britain would make peace. On 19 July he made a speech which, in his eyes at least, amounted to a peace offer, but its tone and tenor were very ill adapted to any such purpose and it was brushed off by Churchill. As after the defeat of Poland Hitler had ready no precise plan of what to do next. He was half-hearted about attacking Great Britain. He wanted not to conquer it but to ensure that it would let him have his way on the continent. Moreover Great Britain was not only an island fortress but also a Mediterranean power, so that a continuing war could oblige Hitler to campaign against British bases and routes in the Mediterranean, to occupy or at least control the whole of France and Spain, and to put German forces into North Africa. War on this scale would be something very different from the *Blumenkriege* and *Blitzkriege* which he had fought so successfully on the continent. Great Britain was the wrong kind of enemy for the German armed forces, and Hitler, who liked short sharp operations with discernible ends, could not see where such a war might take him. On the other hand Great Britain unsubdued was a thorn in the German side, and so long as the British Isles remained in the war there was a danger that they might become a base for a new war between Germany and the United States. Although the German army could not march into England as it had marched into other countries, the German navy might blockade and starve the British, or the German air force might pound them into submission or destroy their defences and so let the army in.

A naval strategy entailed submarine warfare supplemented by commerce raiding by surface vessels and the mining of coastal waters. But Hitler had neglected his navy, partly because he was not much interested in it and partly because he never wholeheartedly faced up to the possibility of a fight to the finish with Great Britain. At the outbreak of war the German surface fleet consisted of two antiquated and Baltic-bound battleships, three pocket battleships, two battle cruisers, eight cruisers, twenty-two destroyers and as many torpedo-boats and E-boats. In the Norwegian expedition three cruisers and nine destroyers were sunk and two cruisers and one destroyer were damaged. These losses were never made good, although two new battleships and a cruiser – *Bismarck*, *Tirpitz* and *Prinz Eugen* – were commissioned in 1941. The submarine fleet was quite inadequate. On the outbreak of war Admiral Doenitz, the supreme U-boat commander, had only fifty-seven ocean-going boats and, although he made good use of what he had, no prospect whatever of fulfilling his hope of having 300 boats at sea at a time; normally the striking force would consist of one in three – or, at best and for short periods, one in two – of the total force. The British navy, although hardly less antiquated, was much larger.

The alternative to a naval blockade was an air offensive designed either to make Great Britain capitulate under the sheer weight and terror of bombing or to clear the way for an invasion by destroying the air defences of Great Britain, especially its fighter squadrons. This was what Hitler and Goering tried to do and, in the two months from mid-July to mid-September 1940, failed to achieve.

The renown of the Luftwaffe after the campaigns of 1939 and the first half of 1940 was prodigious and its morale was excellent. Officially it was only five years old since the treaty of Versailles had denied Germany an air force and none had been acknowledged until 1935. But the reality was different. The prohibition was evaded in a number of ways. Aircraft designers were sent to work in other countries and German aircraft types were developed in the USSR, Sweden and elsewhere. The commercial airline *Lufthansa* was used to train men, to test machines and above all to keep alive the experience and the spirit of airmanship built up during the First World War.

The principal fashioners of the Luftwaffe were Erhard Milch and Ernst Udet – together with Walther Wever, whose early death in 1936 deprived the Luftwaffe of the heavy bomber force which he alone among the three believed in. Milch was the organization man who created an aircraft industry behind the scenes, supervised the development of new types of aircraft, and used *Lufthansa* (of which he was chairman), weekend flying clubs and foreign factories and bases to make Germany a first-class air power. He became a friend of Goering, who appointed him to take charge of the Air Ministry in March 1935 when the Luftwaffe's existence was officially revealed. It was largely thanks to Milch that the Luftwaffe sprang into existence with over 1,000 aircraft, 20,000 men and the not implausible ambition of achieving parity with the Russians by growing to 4,000 aircraft by 1939–40.

But Milch and Goering fell out; probably Milch became jealous of Goering, while Goering found Milch a bore. The result was a rise in the influence of Udet and a shift in policy. Udet was lively to the point of instability – he committed suicide in 1941 – but he was no organizer and lacked Milch's capacity to get things done. He was interested in fighters and dive-bombers rather than bombers and can claim some of the credit for the appearance in 1938 of the single-seater Messerschmitt (Me.) 109E, an excellent aircraft with good manoeuvrability and an armament of four machine guns or, alternatively, two machine guns and two cannon. Udet also set his faith in the Junkers (Ju.) 87 Stuka or dive-bomber, a fearsome aircraft which dived on its target at 200 m.p.h. in order to drop its two bombs with special precision and with the added psychological effect to be derived from fitting screaming devices and painting sharks' faces on the nose of the aircraft: but it was slow and had a low ceiling and so was better at attacking refugees in open country than at surviving anti-aircraft fire or enemy fighter attacks. It was successful against shipping so long as ships' anti-aircraft guns were poor, as they tended to be at the beginning of the war, but after its successes in the continental land battles the Ju. 87 suffered severely at the hands of British ground and air defences and had to be virtually withdrawn from the battle. Udet, finally, neglected the heavy bomber. Plans for two four-engined bombers like the British Stirlings, Halifaxes and Lancasters were dropped in the mid-thirties and

a third – the Heinkel (He.) 177, originally designed as a long-range reconnaissance aircraft – failed to hold Udet's interest when he discovered that
this huge machine could not be made to dive. Thus Germany entered the
war and fought it with fast, lightly protected medium bombers – the He.
111 and Dornier (Do.) 217, supplemented from 1940 by the Ju. 88 –
which were very vulnerable in daylight unless heavily escorted by fighters.
But the Me. 109E was not right for this work and had not been designed
for it. It was short in range and endurance – its range was 100–125 miles
and its endurance about one and a half hours – and the combination of a
fighter of this kind with medium bombers was the wrong recipe for the
Battle of Britain. The Luftwaffe's long-range fighter, the Me. 110, was
something of a disappointment and had to be relegated to night fighting
and light bombing; its failure meant that German bombers operating
beyond the south-east corner of England had to do so unescorted.

In the Spanish civil war a force of 400 German aircraft – the Kondor
Legion – practised bombing and mobility under war conditions and tested
new types, all with gratifying results. At the time of Munich the Luftwaffe
had a front line strength of 2,800 (it was believed to be stronger) and a
year later, on the outbreak of the World War, its front line strength had
passed the 4,000 mark. Its reserves, however, were low because the war
was expected to be short. The RAF's front line strength in September
1939 was 1,660 but its reserves were proportionately more than twice as
large as the Luftwaffe's and, more significant, British aircraft production
was rising the faster. It did not, however, overtake German production
until it passed the thousand a month mark in the spring of 1940 and so
began at that point to close the gap. The French air force had, on paper, a
first line strength slightly above Great Britain's but poor reserves and an
even more alarming degree of obsolescence.

In the Polish campaign the Luftwaffe committed less than half its front
line strength: 700 long-range bombers, 400 fighters, 150 Stukas and 350
reconnaissance aircraft. Besides bombing Warsaw, they were used chiefly
to attack Polish airfields and army communications and they met little
effective opposition from an enemy who had out-of-date fighters and no
radar or other early warning system. The force used in Norway was less
than half that used in Poland. Its tasks were to attack enemy shipping,
patrol and protect German units at sea, and convey small parachute
detachments to seize Norwegian airfields. These tasks were performed
efficiently and, as in Poland, with very little loss in spite of atrocious
weather. For the Luftwaffe the Norwegian campaign was a cross between
a real war and a training exercise, and an opportunity to introduce the Ju.
88 bomber into active service for the first time. The attack on the Low

Countries and France was much more serious and varied work. Practically the whole of the Luftwaffe's front line strength was involved and for six weeks it averaged 1,500 sorties a day. In Holland parachutists were used in large numbers for the first time, capturing Rotterdam airport in the face of tough Dutch opposition. After the surrender of the Dutch the weight of the German air effort went into the support of the German army against the French army and against the British in Belgium. Airfields and factories were also attacked but the role of the Luftwaffe was first and foremost army cooperation. Only after the disintegration of the French ground forces was certain did the German bombers operate seriously against French railways, harbours and towns. The sole check to the Luftwaffe's easy superiority was in its encounters with the RAF over Dunkirk. This was symptomatic.

There was at this time still no way of measuring the effects of the heavy air bombardment of a defended target. The Germans had wiped out Guernica in Spain and had bombed Warsaw and Rotterdam, but against virtually no opposition. It appeared that the real test would come in Great Britain. In the event German bombing never came near to the point of winning the war by destroying the British economy or morale. The Second World War showed that this could not be done before the development of nuclear weapons. But air forces continued to believe that it might be. So did civilian defenders. In London committees had been set up many years before the war to estimate the probable weight and effects of bombing. They came to the conclusion that Great Britain must expect 3,500 tons of bombs in the first twenty-four hours of war, followed by a further 700 tons a day, each ton causing fifty or more casualties – that is to say, nearly two million casualties in the first two months. The material damage, which commercial insurance companies refused to underwrite on any terms, was put at £550 million in the first three weeks, and this apocalyptic vision of the triumph of Belial included the need to evacuate three quarters of the population of London and bury corpses in their thousands in quick-lime, and to witness the complete collapse of communications and other public services, panic, epidemics and three to four million cases of mental breakdown in six months. These forebodings, so unlike the contents of the usual government paper, were carefully concealed from the public. They were also very wide of the mark, for over the whole course of the war casualties per ton of bombs dropped in Great Britain were under twenty and totalled 60,000 dead and 86,000 seriously and 149,000 slightly injured.

Even had it been technically possible for an air force to inflict in 1940 the sort of damage which the planners of the thirties feared, the German air force had not been designed primarily for that function. Its heavy bombing arm was, as we have seen, the least developed and the Luftwaffe – paradoxically, in view of its status as an independent service – was built up as a partner of the army rather than as an independent force which was going to win wars on its own. The bombing of British military or civilian targets in order to wreck production or break morale was therefore only one way of approaching the problem of how to defeat Great Britain, and not the obvious way. The alternative – assuming that the slow process of blockade and starvation were rejected – was a combined operation in which the Luftwaffe would begin by nullifying the R A F and would then, with the navy, cover the transport of the German army into England. What actually happened was something between the two: a projected invasion in force preceded by an independent onslaught by the Luftwaffe which oscillated between the attempt to destroy Great Britain's Fighter Command and heavy assaults on centres of production and population. Since the Luftwaffe's attack failed, the invasion never took place.

The idea of an invasion was popular in army circles but nowhere else. The navy regarded an invasion as almost impossibly risky. Raeder's conditions were control of the air, the right weather and an attempt no later than the autumnal equinox. The navy regarded the army's requests for naval protection for its vast and lumbering armadas against the Royal Navy as grotesquely unreal, although the naval staff was not very successful in conveying this appreciation to the army staff. The Luftwaffe was not so much hostile as uninterested. Goering and his principal lieutenants hardly troubled to reply to memoranda or attend conferences about it. Hitler himself was half involved, half aloof. He so far responded to the enthusiasm generated by the army staff as to order plans and preparations and he may have hoped that the navy's precondition would be met by the Luftwaffe's separate operations. Men were assigned and trained; barges, tugs and other craft were assembled. There was a great deal of exercising and (often contradictory) paper work. Hitler kept all the options open, including retreat. He was sceptical but also serious. He would have been delighted to finish off the war in the west this way but never confident that he could do so and therefore prepared both to give it a try and to abandon it if it did not work.

The first plan for a landing, produced by the army staff in December 1939, aimed at the east coast. After cutting naval criticism this idea was abandoned in favour of landings at a series of points along almost the entire south coast. The navy consistently argued that the only feasible operation, if any, was one concentrated in the south-east where the waters were narrowest. The first directive to prepare an invasion was issued by Hitler on 17 July 1940. It prescribed that the RAF must first be reduced to insignificance, that all minefields be cleared and that the Royal Navy be kept at a distance in northern waters or the Mediterranean. If these circumstances were met the army proposed to put ashore 260,000 men in three days, assemble a force of eleven divisions in two weeks and bring Great Britain to surrender in a month. Landings would take place along three stretches of coast between Folkestone and Brighton to the accompaniment of feints against Scotland and Iceland to distract the Royal Navy. The SS would follow with a list of 2,700 persons to be incarcerated, and a special booklet was prepared for the use of the six SS commanders and their staffs who were to extinguish opposition (including the Boy Scouts who were thought to be an arm of British Intelligence). The invasion fleets moved from their assembly points to their departure stations in the first days of September, but in these same days the RAF was thwarting the Luftwaffe in what Churchill had already christened the Battle of Britain.

In July 1940 Generals Kesselring and Sperrle, commanding *Luftflotten* 2 and 3 in Belgium and northern France, and General Stumpf, commanding *Luftflotte* 5 in Denmark and Norway, had a front line strength of around 3,000 aircraft, including some 1,400 long-range bombers, 300 dive-bombers, 800 single-engined fighters and 280 twin-engined fighters or fighter bombers. Of this force 2,500 aircraft at most were serviceable and ready for action at the beginning of the battle. In the engagements which followed, Kesselring and Sperrle could on a normal day put up 800 long-range bombers and 820 fighters. On the other side the Royal Air Force had emerged from the Battle of France with less damage than might have been the case if Dowding and Churchill had not hardened their hearts against sending more fighters to help the French. (Half of those sent were lost. The RAF's losses between 10 May and 20 June were 944. They were made good by mid-July but pilot losses were not. Milch wanted to invade Great Britain on the tail of the Dunkirk retreat.) Morale was undented by the fall of France and leadership from Dowding downwards excellent. The RAF's front line strength on the eve of the Battle of Britain was 1,200. It included 800 Hurricane and Spitfire single-seater fighters, of which 660 were operational, and in this sphere the British were roughly equal in numbers to the units opposed to them. Reserves were healthy, production good and expanding but there was only a narrow margin of trained pilots. This weakness was a worrying one, for although one new aircraft was as good as the machine it replaced, a new pilot was not the equal of an experienced one. On the other hand the RAF saved many more of its pilots than did the Luftwaffe since the former could bale out over their own territory and return to the fight, whereas most of the German pilots in the like case became prisoners of war.

The Hurricane and Spitfire, with their eight guns apiece, had the best single-engined fighter armament in the world – thanks largely to Squadron Leader R. S. Sorley and to Dowding. They could destroy an enemy bomber with a two-second burst. Sorley had been so impressed by the mock-up of the Hurricane that he tried, unsuccessfully, to get it put into production before it had flown. The prototype of the Hurricane first flew in 1935 and by the outbreak of war 578 had been made (by the middle of 1940 1,747). The Spitfire, which first flew a year later than the Hurricane, began to reach the service three months before Munich and nine squadrons had been formed by the outbreak of war when 299 had been made (by the middle of 1940 809). At one point during the Battle of Britain reserves of Spitfires fell to thirty-eight but at no time did the Command ask in vain for replacements of this or any other type of aircraft. On the eve of the battle fighter production was verging on 500 a month, which was considerably higher than German fighter production or some German estimates of British production. (Goering thought that British production of all types was only 300.)

Besides this force Great Britain relied for its defence on an early warning system of revolutionary and decisive importance. It was based on radar or, as it was at first called in Great Britain, RDF – Radio Direction Finding – a method for detecting the position of distant objects by the reflection of radio rays. Without radar too many bombers would have got through. After the First World War the problem of how to stop the bomber was acute. Some despaired of solving it. Others examined desperate remedies like the death ray, an attempt to find ways of killing enemy aircrews by (for example) suddenly raising their blood to boiling point, or ways of stopping their engines by radio transmissions. No death ray was ever invented but from 1934 radar was developed by a number of men, including in particular Professors Henry Tizard, A. V. Hill and P. M. S. Blackett; H. E. Wimperis, a civilian engineer who was given a post at the Air Ministry; and Robert Watson-Watt of the Radio Research Laboratory. (Considerable discord was introduced into the research and its application when Professor F. A. Lindemann, later Lord Cherwell, was injected into the work on the insistence of Churchill who, although not in the government, had been made privy to these and other secret matters. Lindemann was neither liked nor highly regarded by many of his fellow scientists. He was wholeheartedly anxious to give of his best for the defence of the country but he tended to treat research as a branch of politics. His day came when Churchill became Prime Minister. He was one of Churchill's closest advisers.) A chain of fifty-one radar stations was built round the coast. Although still incomplete, it was brought into continuous operation in the spring of 1939 and it was later supplemented by a second chain specially designed to detect low-flying aircraft. As early as 1936 Tizard suggested that very small radar sets could be made to go into aircraft and help fighter pilots to find and destroy enemy bombers at night.

Supplementing the radar system was the Observer Corps which, armed with binoculars, manned a network of posts which spotted aircraft as soon as they came within sight or hearing. There were a thousand of these posts. They and the radar stations were connected by telephone with an operations room, to which they transmitted their estimates of the positions, speeds, heights, numbers and directions of all aircraft within their ken, and this information was plotted on large tables by counters which were moved across the table as the information came in. Orders to aircraft, whether waiting on the ground or airborne in search of the enemy, were given by Controllers watching these tables day and night. Radar and the Observer Corps relieved Fighter Command of the need to keep forces on permanent patrol in the air in order to be able to engage the enemy and avoid destruction on the ground. The Controller in the operations room, watching the plots coming in every few seconds and knowing that the aircraft represented were no more than 12–20 miles ahead of the position shown, could order his aircraft off the ground in time and direct them on the right course at the right height until the pilots could see the enemy with their own eyes (or, in later battles, with the radar devices in their cockpits). In the operations room hours of watchful, almost motionless routine would be suddenly broken when a girl in uniform placed a small arrow on the edge of the table which, if it did not turn out to be an atmospheric freak or a flock of geese, was the prelude to action – down below the drama of tenseness combined with the efficiency of techniques mastered by familiarity; up above the more fearful drama of the duel as the pilots cast around them for the enemy and then pitted against him their flying skills and their marksmanship. The Germans knew about radar but underrated its value to the defence of Great Britain.

The preliminary phase of the Battle of Britain was an attempt by the Luftwaffe, beginning on 10 July, to establish local air supremacy over the straits of Dover. Attacks on shipping still using this passage were used as a dress rehearsal to test the tactics and capacities of Fighter Command before proceeding to the main purposes of enticing it into a major battle in order to destroy it. By the end of the month the advantage lay with the RAF which had lost 150 aircraft (promptly replaced) to 286 lost by the Luftwaffe. On the other hand this initial success gave little indication of the ultimate result since the RAF had to husband its strength after its losses in France and could not afford a steady drain of aircraft, whether or not German losses were higher. In the second week of August the Luftwaffe began to attack Fighter Command's airfields and operations rooms with the intention of crippling it on the ground or provoking it into a major battle in which it would be destroyed in the air. Owing to bad weather the Luftwaffe was unable to keep up its attacks on consecutive days and again in this phase the Luftwaffe's losses were the greater – 290 aircraft to 114. In the main battle of this phase, on 15 August, the losses on the German and British sides were 75 and 34. Attacks on shipping continued, chiefly with Ju. 87s which suffered so severely that they virtually disappeared from front line operations. After a pause between 19 and 23 August the attack on Fighter Command was resumed in combination with secondary night attacks on cities. This phase, which lasted until 6 September, opened well for the Luftwaffe but was not decisive. The British suffered heavy damage on the ground. Fighter Command's No. 11 Group, covering London and south-east England, had six of its seven sector (or main control) airfields seriously damaged and five of its forward stations put out of action. One sector headquarters, Biggin Hill, had its operations room and all its communications wrecked. Further blows of this kind would have exposed London to great danger and would have forced upon Fighter Command a change in tactics (owing to the disruption of ground control) which might have overstrained its resources. But except on one day German losses of aircraft of all types exceeded British losses and by the end of this phase German losses were approaching 1,000 while Great Britain's were 550. On the other hand, in fighters alone the RAF's losses were greater and although by the end of the month the RAF was making more sorties per day than the Luftwaffe, fighter losses were beginning to exceed current production and the pilot situation was becoming a grave worry.

Although Great Britain's defences were severely tested during this phase the Luftwaffe failed to take a step which could have strained them even more severely. On direct orders from Goering it gave up attacking radar stations. Goering may have underrated the vital significance of these stations. He certainly underrated the possibility of putting them out of action. Their slim masts were not an ideal target for aircraft and nobody on the German side noticed that one of them – at Ventnor on the Isle of

Wight – had been knocked out by a raid which left delayed-action bombs lying on the site. This was one of the more notable failures of Intelligence during the whole war. The radar screen continued to function almost without interruption throughout the Battle of Britain. German attempts to jam it were too primitive to impair it to any significant degree.

A second major error on the German side occurred at the beginning of September when the mounting attack on Fighter Command was abandoned in favour of attacks on London and other cities. It is impossible to be sure of the chief reason for this switch. Both sides enormously exaggerated enemy losses and on the German side the inflated figures were taken to mean that Fighter Command and fighter production had been virtually eliminated from the battle. Kesselring, though not Sperrle, shared the view of the Air Staff that the battle was won. In addition both Hitler and Goering had been stung by British bombing raids into retaliating against British cities. On 25 August, and thereafter on a number of nights, Bomber Command raided Berlin. The first of these raids was itself a retaliation for the first German raid on London which was itself a mistake – so that the German bomber offensive which began on 7 September was in a sense a consequence of a German error. (The first raid by either side on a town had taken place on 10–11 May when the British attacked München Gladbach, a few miles west of Düsseldorf.) The British raids on Berlin did little material damage but they had enormous psychological effect. They were a great surprise. Neither the Nazi leaders nor the people of Berlin thought that Great Britain was in a position to do anything of the kind, and the former had expressly assured the latter that they could not. The answer was to attack London. An afternoon attack on 7 September was followed by another raid that night. The damage was very heavy and a thousand people were killed. This daylight raid was not repeated and the next night raid did not come until four nights later, but the attack was then renewed.

In Germany hopes rose high. The invasion craft moved to their action stations. On 11 September Churchill broadcast an invasion warning. But the day before Hitler had – for the second time – postponed the day for taking the decision whether to order the invasion or not. He would decide on the 14th. When the 14th came he postponed the date again and on the 15th – the final major engagement of the Battle of Britain took place. In the course of two battles in the morning and afternoon the German bombers suffered heavily (they lost sixty aircraft that day, the RAF lost twenty-six fighters) and the German fighters again failed to win the clear victory that they had been seeking for so many weeks. Two days later, on

17 September, Hitler called off the invasion by postponing the day of decision indefinitely. In October, when the Italians arrived to take part in the air battle, it was over. By the middle of that month the barges and other transports had all melted away. The Luftwaffe turned to night bombing of London and other cities. The famous raid on Coventry took place on 14 November. (Post-war stories to the effect that this raid was known of in advance from Ultra intelligence, and that these warnings were ignored in order not to jeopardize that source, have been scotched.) With radar not yet developed for night defence the Luftwaffe was able to cause serious damage at comparatively small cost to itself until the preparations for Barbarossa took the bulk of the bombers to the east, but once more Great Britain was able to fend off part of the attack by its technological skill. The German bombers were directed on to their targets by radio beams, flying along one beam until an intersecting beam told them that they were over the target, but British scientists quickly discovered how to jam the beacons transmitting the beams and so cause many German bombs to be dropped in the wrong place – preferably of course in open country but sometimes on an unintended target, as for instance when Dublin was bombed by a German force which had been making for Belfast.

Losses can be computed in different ways. No precise figure is unchallengeable. But, taking the Battle of Britain to have lasted from 12 August to the last day of September, the Luftwaffe may be said to have lost in operations over 1,100 aircraft of all types (not 2,698 as the British claimed at the time). The defence of Great Britain cost Fighter Command about 650 aircraft (not 3,058 as the Germans believed).

The reasons for the Luftwaffe's failure were various. Its previous triumphs were to some extent delusive. They had been won in the role of army support and not in combat with an enemy air force, and the handling of the Luftwaffe in this role had necessarily been governed in practice by the strategy of the army command. Having taken little or no part in the battles in France Goering took charge during the Battle of Britain with the enthusiasm of one who feels that his moment has come. It might have gone better for the Luftwaffe if he had not, for he must take the greater part of the blame for the Luftwaffe's ill-considered switching from one strategy and one set of targets to another. To some extent this mistake may be ascribed to bad intelligence. The gross overestimates of casualties made by both sides were more damaging to the attackers than the defenders. The German higher command, ignorant of the continuing powers of resistance of Fighter Command, made wrong decisions. Similar mistakes by the British were of less consequence, since the R A F's role was

to go on resisting in any case. But there were two other and more important reasons for the Luftwaffe's loss of the battle. The first was that it did
not have enough fighters. Of 1,050 fighters stationed in France and Belgium 800 were Me. 109s, excellent aircraft but not ideal for close escort
work and not numerous enough to provide adequate cover for bombers
on daylight missions which, ideally, required at least two fighters for every
bomber. The bomber squadrons in Norway and Denmark had no single-
engined fighter escort and only a small protecting force of twin-engined
Me. 110s. This secondary force in Scandinavia was intended by the
German Air Staff to split Fighter Command's effort by attacks on north-
eastern England, but only one such attack was made during the Battle of
Britain and the Me. 110s proved in general insufficiently manoeuvrable
for the role of bomber protection. Consequently the German commanders
found themselves in a constant dilemma, since every strengthening of the
fighter escort which they provided for their bombers reduced the number
of fighters available to engage the British fighters. In the event the bombers
failed to wreck Fighter Command on the ground and the fighters failed to
destroy it in the air.

The second principal reason for the defeat of the Luftwaffe was Fighter
Command itself – the spirit of its pilots and the quality of its machines, the
ceaseless toil in the factories where production kept ahead of losses, the
efficiency of the repair services which put damaged aircraft back into
service in the shortest possible time, and finally the higher strategy adopted
by Dowding and his principal lieutenant Air Marshal Park and persisted
in against mounting criticism which, after the battle, ensured the replacement and semi-disgrace of these two steadfast and wise commanders. The
greatest danger to Great Britain during these two months was the erosion
of its fighter force. The reserves were never exhausted but they were never
plentiful. Dowding and Park had therefore to minimize losses by cautious handling of their men and machines without thereby courting defeat
or lowering morale. They could not afford to indulge in unnecessarily
dashing tactics. They had to count the cost every day. In the end the sum
came out right.

The Battle of Britain was lost by Germany; the invasion of Great
Britain was never attempted; the blockade went on. But much was changed
that summer. Great Britain's prestige was raised high by the RAF and
Hitler was tempted into a blunder. Having failed to end the war with
Great Britain before attacking the USSR, he now proceeded to attack
the USSR none the less. He had always meant to attack the USSR at
some time in order to get *Lebensraum*. The fact that he now deluded
himself into attacking the USSR on the grounds that this was a way to

defeat Great Britain is an example of how disappointment can impair judgement. Moreover, the failure in the Battle of Britain prevented Hitler from concentrating all his strength against the USSR and eventually transformed a cloud in the west no bigger than a man's hand into the Anglo-American hurricane which, in concert with the blast from the east, was finally to devastate the Third Reich. The Battle of Britain was therefore one of the decisive events of the war.

Nevertheless Great Britain's position was still precarious and it is a measure of the continuing British crisis in this year that Churchill was prepared to contemplate two extremely un-British steps. The first, already mentioned, was the offer of a union with France – an offer so unreal that it faded almost immediately from the British consciousness. The second was even more startling and for that reason concealed. Although sceptical about the union with France, Churchill seems to have been in earnest when, in June, he offered to give Northern Ireland to the Irish Republic. The price was to be the use of Irish ports and the establishment of military and air bases in Ireland for the duration of the war, the cession of the northern counties to be effected when the war ended. De Valera countered with a proposal to permit the Americans to use Ireland in return for the immediate neutrality of a united Ireland. Churchill was ready to grant immediate unity but asked for Irish belligerence, not merely neutrality. De Valera doubted whether Churchill could deliver the unity of Ireland in the face of opposition from the Protestant rulers of the north (who got wind of the talks and were preparing to sabotage them) and of Churchill's own colleagues. So Britain forfeited a chance, albeit a slim one, to solve its Irish problem – just as, in 1915, it had proposed to trade Cyprus for Greek belligerence only to withdraw the offer within weeks and so saddle itself for half a century more with that intractable and unrewarding colony.

These two forays into the improbable did not obscure the crucial fact that from mid-1940 Great Britain was reduced to waiting for the Americans to come to Europe. Victory over Germany, as distinct from its harassment, could be achieved in no other way. Hitler's declaration of war against the United States at the end of 1941 ensured that the Americans would indeed come, but where many in Britain went wrong was in supposing that they would do so as reinforcement for Britain, ready and anxious to supplement British arms and execute British plans. This was perhaps the spirit in which Roosevelt, while his country was still at peace, proclaimed that one neighbour must lend his hosepipe to help put out another's fire, but it was not the spirit in which a great power sends millions of men and women to war. For this the Americans made their own plans. The British became the auxiliaries, occupying however an indispensable forward base.

To the Americans Germany was a great land power to be defeated by a greater land power. Stalin saw Germany the same way, but with the difference that Russians and Germans were at grips with one another from the first day of their hostilities, whereas the Americans had still to get to Europe. There must therefore be some delay during which two things must be accomplished: the Atlantic must be cleared of U-boats (Great Britain's last major contribution to victory) and a transport fleet must be built. Meanwhile American air forces would join the British and their continental and commonwealth allies in maiming German strong-points, German industry and the German people. From the American point of view the outstanding question was not what had to be done but how long the preliminaries would take before very large, mainly armoured, land forces could be brought face to face with the German armies – in northern France.

The British contribution to the ultimate victory included one further major and peculiar achievement in the breaking of many of the Germans' most secret ciphers, the theoretically unbreakable Enigma machine keys used by all branches of the German armed services including the Abwehr (military intelligence), by the SS and police, and by the railways and certain other specialist services.

To read enciphered wireless messages of any grade, high or low, it is necessary, first, to intercept them and take down the enciphered texts and, secondly, to render these back into plain language by deciphering them. The interceptors were men and women with earphones listening in relays round the clock at various points in the British Isles and elsewhere in the world to German (and other) traffic transmitted at strengths designed to carry to other Germans but not far beyond. This gruelling and tedious work was the essential precondition. It was capped by cryptographers who, concentrated at Bletchley Park in England, achieved the intellectually remarkable and operationally crucial feat of breaking Enigma keys, often promptly enough to make the contents of the resulting intelligence (called Ultra) operationally valuable to the waging of battles in progress. Bletchley Park began as a British venture but became in 1943 an Anglo-American one.

The Enigma machine was originally a commercial machine first put on the market in Holland in 1919. It was adapted by the German armed services (who gave it its name) in the twenties and progressively developed for their most secret communications. The first breaks were made by the

Polish secret service which reconstructed the machine's internal workings, solved the problem of setting it to read a particular key on a particular day, and read Enigma traffic between 1932 and 1938; but the Poles were then foiled by the complexities continuously added by the Germans, whereupon they disclosed to the French and British secret services all they knew about Enigma and what they themselves had achieved and handed over two Enigma machines reconstructed by them. The French disappeared from the picture with their defeat in 1940 but by then the British had overcome initial scepticism about breaking Enigma (they had assigned to it only one cryptographer in 1938 and two in 1939) and were making astonishing progress in penetrating Enigma keys.

At their wartime peak the Germans used about 200 different Enigma keys simultaneously among their various higher commands and special services. All these keys were changed every twenty-four hours and in minor respects every eight hours, and even in wartime the Germans continued to add complicating elements to the machine itself. The challenge to the British cryptographers, who possessed Enigma machines thanks to the Poles, was to set the many movable parts of these machines in exactly the same way as the German operators and receivers had set their machines at the given time and for the relevant key – a formidable task. A number of keys were never broken, chiefly owing to the paucity of the traffic which they carried; others were broken irregularly or tardily; but one in particular – the principal key used by all higher formations in the Luftwaffe – was broken every day from a date (still disputed) in April or May 1940 to the end of the war, frequently on the day for which it was valid.

This intelligence had two special features. It was authentic and uniquely credible since it consisted of what the Germans were saying to one another; and it could be operationally valuable since much of what they were saying was known to the allies almost as soon as they said it. But its beginnings were not dramatic. When war began it was by no means certain that Ultra would be of much use, even if it could be got. The first fruits were meagre, scattered and unexciting. They came from breaking the key used by the German *Wehrkreise*, the static administrative regions or home commands, each corresponding to an army corps, into which Germany itself was divided. These scraps of information dealt with recruiting, training, travel arrangements and so on. The first indications of Ultra's further potentialities came during the Norwegian campaign of April 1940. The key used by the inter-service command created for the occasion was read within a week of the beginning of the operation and yielded in all about one thousand decodes. Their operational value, however, was negligible because the breaks were usually tardy and the material in them was strange and largely unintelligible in the absence of experienced intelligence officers. It was a portent but not yet a weapon.

During the campaigns of May and June in the Low Countries and France, Ultra rendered some service although again its practical application was minimal. But in, or shortly before, this period Bletchley began its uninterrupted penetration of the principal Luftwaffe key. There had been sporadic breaks of this key since the very beginning of the year but on 1 May the Germans introduced changes into the Enigma machine which countered these successes. But the difficulties created by the new obstacles were rapidly surmounted and – a fact not realized at the time – this key would never again be lost.

Two developments converted these successes into a major weapon. The first was the establishment alongside the cryptographers of intelligence staffs whose business it was to collate and interpret the scraps of information contained in the decodes. In the vast majority of cases each decode was in itself trivial and uninformative; only in association with other snippets did it become illuminating. The value of Ultra derived from the volume of stored intelligence into which each day's new items – now running into hundreds per day – fitted and from the ability of experienced intelligence officers to appreciate these items in the light of broader knowledge. Secondly, a system was elaborated from 1941 for conveying selected and paraphrased items of operationally valuable Ultra to commanders-in-chief in the field and their special intelligence staffs.

Ultra's most characteristic service was its detailed disclosure of the German order of battle: locations of units, their strengths and shortages, day by day, in men, equipment and supplies. Such intelligence became for the first time significant in the Battle of Britain. Although it did not suffice to correct exaggerated estimates of the Luftwaffe's total strength and standards of serviceability or yet provide information on the output of German factories, it gave clues to the scale of impending attacks and also details of the units stationed in northern France, Belgium and Denmark and their precise locations. It also confirmed that Hitler had abandoned his plans to invade England, at any rate for that year. In the North African campaign intelligence of this kind was supplemented by regular information on the timing and routes of tankers and other supply vessels crossing the Mediterranean from Greece to the German and Italian forces. Even more decisive was Ultra's contribution to the Battle of the Atlantic where the breaking of the U-boat key at the end of 1942 was the crucial factor in giving the victory to Britain. Ultra continued to produce copious intelligence to the end of the war. Besides its specific uses, it transformed the conduct of war on the allied side by revealing the enemy as no enemy had ever before been revealed. It created in senior staffs and at the political summit a state of mind which transformed the taking of decisions. To feel that you know your enemy is vastly comforting. It grows imperceptibly over time with the regular and intimate observance of his habits and actions. Knowledge of this kind makes counter-planning less tentative and more assured, less harrowing and more buoyant. Directing a great war is immensely tiring and good intelligence reduces the strains wonderfully. When, for example, Churchill, Roosevelt and their Chiefs of Staff met at Casablanca in January 1943 to decide what they should do after clearing North Africa and recovering control of the Mediterranean, they had been receiving a steadily increasing stream of Ultra intelligence about their enemy for three years. Without it their view of the war would have been entirely different, very much less distinct. Their decisions were still difficult, but they did not have to feel that they were planning in the dark.

The British cryptographers at Bletchley Park might have read Enigma ciphers through their own efforts but the timing of their first successes – and timing can be crucial in war – owed much to the brilliance and ultimately the generosity of the Poles. The Poles owed much to the French in their dual task of reconstructing the internal processes of the German Enigma and in breaking particular keys on particular days. And the French got the information which they gave to the Poles from a German in the German cipher service who leaked precious documents to Paris from 1931 onwards. He was at all relevant dates a member of the Nazi party and he was called Hans-Thilo Schmidt. He was a traitor and a lecher, a man whom it is impossible to admire but to whom very great thanks are due.

CHAPTER 8

The Mediterranean, North Africa and the Middle East

FOR Hitler the failure to defeat Great Britain, following the fall of France and the entry of Italy into the war, created a new range of diplomatic and strategic problems. His hopes of peace in the west had been dashed first by Great Britain's determination to fight on and then by its success in doing so. He told those round him that Great Britain was sustained by the prospect of Germany being embroiled with the Soviet Union, and this misreading of the British mood gave him a new reason – besides the quest for *Lebensraum* – to deal with the USSR. He faced a complex situation in the Mediterranean which was a theatre of war so long as Great Britain refused to make peace and where the interests of Italy, France and Spain – an ally, a vassal and a coy courtesan – collided. And thirdly, the war at sea, which became once more the chief means of reducing Great Britain, involved some risk of war with the United States.

On 27 September 1940, before the invasion of Great Britain had been officially abandoned, Hitler revived a project for a Tripartite Pact between Germany, Italy and Japan. Each of the signatories undertook to come to the aid of another in the event of an attack by any state not yet at war. The Japanese Foreign Minister, Matsuoka Yosuke, was becoming alarmed about the possibility of Japan finding itself at war with the USSR, the United States and Great Britain all at once. He was therefore willing to fall in with Hitler's plans in order to deter Washington from joining Great Britain in a war against a two-continent coalition, and in order also to put pressure on Stalin to come to terms with Japan in Manchuria. (Matsuoka's manoeuvres were stultified when Hitler abandoned his pact with Stalin and invaded the USSR.) Hitler's aims were similar. He too needed to deter the United States and intimidate Stalin – although he professed to be anxious to improve relations with the USSR and even to get it to join the pact, which would then have become an anti-American four-power club whose members divided the world into spheres of influence among themselves and collectively dared the United States not to move out of its allotted sphere in the New World. But Molotov, who visited Berlin in November, asked awkward questions about the presence of German troops in Finland and the German guarantee of Rumania and

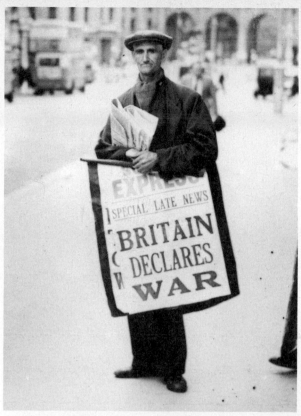

1   The first day

2   Munich: Chamberlain, Daladier, Hitler, Mussolini, Ciano

3 Czechoslovakia: the first
German invaders, October
1938

4 Poland: a village burns,
September 1939

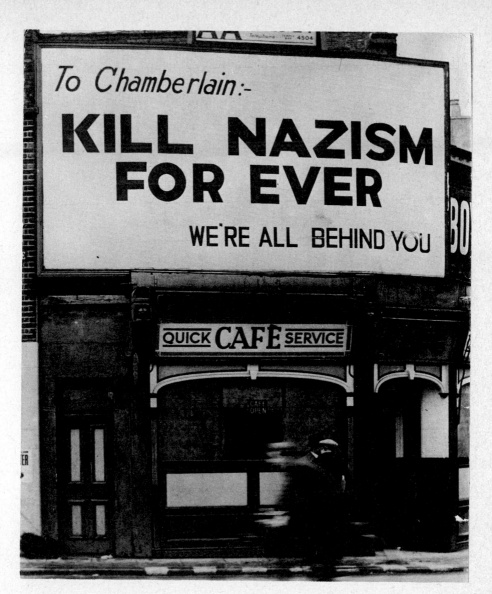

5 The voice of the people

6 *Top*: Ski troops in Finland,
1939

7 *Bottom*: German
loudspeakers patrol a Dutch
town, 1940

8   *Top*: The British
Expeditionary Force in
France, 1939

9   *Bottom*: The BEF in
retreat from France, 1940

10 *Top*: Dunkirk: makeshift
bridge

11 *Bottom*: Dunkirk: parting
shots

12 *Top*: France mobilizing

13 *Bottom*: Flight from Paris

14 *Top*: Goering and his staff
gaze across the English
Channel

15 *Bottom*: French warships
scuttled at Toulon, November
1940

observed that so long as discussion had to be conducted in an air raid shelter, there was something unrealistic about a plan for partitioning a world in which the British Empire was presumed to have ceased to exist.

Hitler's most immediate problem was the Mediterranean. This theatre was bisected by his ally Italy. At the western end were Vichy France and Spain, at the eastern end the Balkans. In France Hitler had established an occupational régime in the north and along the Atlantic coast and a satellite régime for the rest of the country. But this satellite was a satellite with a difference. Pétain had a certain number of cards in his hand – the not inconsiderable remnants of an important fleet, territories and strategic positions in North and West Africa and the Middle East, a degree of American benevolence, and a willingness to run France on lines broadly acceptable to Hitler and so relieve the Germans of administrative problems so long as they did not try to push Vichy too far. The Nazi leaders disliked the French but they could not treat France in the same way as Czechoslovakia or Poland. Therefore they could not give Italy the satisfaction, nor Spain the bribes, which these other Latin countries wanted at France's expense.

Hitler regarded Franco's Spain as a natural ally and as a debtor. A republican Spain he might have invaded without more ado but Franco's Spain he sought to bargain with. His aim was to lure Franco into active alliance in order to secure control of the western gateway into the Mediterranean and possession of one of the Canary islands as a base for the Battle of the Atlantic. The bait for Franco was Gibraltar. On his side Franco had allied Spain with the Axis by a Treaty of Friendship with Germany in March 1939 and by joining the Anti-Comintern Pact, and in June 1940 he had seemed on the verge of joining the war a few days after Mussolini did so. But there were arguments against as well as for. Hitler's attack on Roman Catholic Poland in partnership with Stalin had disconcerted the profoundly anti-communist Spanish dictator, and his innate wiliness and caution were accentuated by the need to keep Spain out of further trouble after the civil war and particularly by the need to import food. Franco, whose Ambassador in London was being cajoled by Churchill and was even given to understand that Spain might help itself to part of French North Africa, did not rise to the German bait of a joint German-Spanish attack on Gibraltar and at a long meeting with Hitler and Ribbentrop at Hendaye on 23 October he frustrated the German leaders in a bout of arguing in the course of which, besides pitching Spanish claims very high – Oran, the whole of French Morocco, large quantities of food, fuel and military equipment – he left Hitler in two minds about whether he intended to join in such an adventure at a date which he would not yet disclose or whether the securing of the western end of the Mediterranean would have to be undertaken not with him but against him. Further meetings at the end of the year between Hitler and Franco's Foreign Minister Ramón Serrano Suñer at Berchtesgaden and between Franco and Hitler's military intelligence chief Admiral Wilhelm Canaris in Madrid only increased the uncertainty. Mussolini was equally unsuccessful and Hitler toyed with the idea of a direct parachute attack on Gibraltar, which his advisers however had already considered and rejected. The German invasion of the USSR altered the atmosphere since this was something which Franco could wholeheartedly support and he sent 18,000 men to share in the anti-communist crusade of his fellow dictators. He was shocked by Churchill's prompt support for Stalin and even more by the Anglo-Russian alliance, which, Eden had assured his Ambassador in London, was unthinkable. But he continued to prevaricate over active operations in his own part of the world, so that Hitler was driven at one time to making inquiries about the chances of a coup to replace him by another general and considered as late as 1943 plans for an invasion of Spain.

If Hitler's dealings with Franco were a disappointment to the Führer, his relations with Mussolini went more seriously wrong. Mussolini's ideas were large, impracticable and not always consonant with German policy: if Hitler was to rule from the Atlantic to the Urals, Mussolini was going to rule the Mediterranean and all its circumambient lands (except presumably Spain). For Mussolini the rise of Hitler had offered a means not only of settling scores with Great Britain and France but also of winning an empire beyond Europe while Hitler kept him inviolable in Europe. The symbol of this vision was the Pact of Steel of May 1939. But at that date Mussolini was not ready for war. Like Hitler, but with more reason, he planned not to go to war until 1942 and the defeat of France in 1940 therefore upset his timetable. It did not, however, moderate his visions. At a meeting in October 1940 at the Brenner the Italian leaders made clear to their German partners that their first shopping list included not only a piece of southern France but also Corsica, Malta, Tunisia, part of Algeria, an Atlantic port in Morocco, French Somaliland and the British position in Egypt and the Sudan. Besides running counter to Hitler's plan to operate a limited accord with France, the creation of an Italian empire of this size, straddling the Mediterranean from the Atlantic to the Red Sea and marching with an equally vast German empire to the north of it, threatened to raise questions about the Middle East which Hitler was, vaguely, proposing to approach via the Caucasus and Mussolini, much more purposefully, via Suez.

Hitler had been generally content to leave Europe south of the Alps to

Mussolini. He had expected Mussolini to attack Malta in the summer of 1940 but Mussolini made no move; he was still intent on keeping out of serious wars. The Italian air force was obsolescent and the fleet, though large and in some respects first-class, was lightly armed by comparison with the British and French fleets and untrained in night operations. The army was gravely ill equipped and, although Mussolini did not know it at the time, its morale was poor: shouting fascist slogans proved a bad way of inspiring troops and the Italians were to fight badly until they were pressed back into Tunisia in 1943 and then changed sides later that year to fight the Germans on Italian soil. Mussolini's decision to go to war in 1940 was therefore the beginning of a series of disasters for Italy. Moreover, his opening of a campaign in Greece which he could not finish was seriously to distort Hitler's overall strategy.

Hitler had already in July decided to attack the USSR in the following spring and on 18 December he issued his first Barbarossa directive. In it he stated that the USSR might be invaded 'even before' the war with Great Britain was over. Since he assumed, correctly, that Great Britain could not help the USSR by opening a second front for at least eighteen months, he was not risking a war on two fronts unless the Russians held out that long. He expected to dispatch the Russians within six months and then revert to the problem of the British. But at the end of 1940 he was forced by the Italians, who attacked in Greece, and by the British, who counter-attacked the Italians in Africa, to undertake far more than he had intended in south-east Europe and eventually in Africa too. The Balkans, instead of being a flank to be secured before Barbarossa, became an independent theatre of war with extensions leading German troops and air squadrons away from the USSR into waters and sands beyond Europe's southern confines.

The Balkans and Hungary were already dominated by Germany before the war began. Annexed, by economic power, in the thirties they were to be lost in the military clash of the forties. These states had emerged as exemplars of the principle of national self-determination – which, however, they exemplified imperfectly since none of them was nationally homogeneous, although each was sufficiently a nation to have national quarrels with its neighbours. To other states they were chiefly of interest in the light of an older theory: the balance of power. Between the wars France made friends with Rumania and Yugoslavia because they stood for the maintenance of the Versailles settlement of 1919 and opposed any signs of a revival of German hegemony, but the waning of French influence in the thirties and its eclipse at Munich in 1938 forced France's friends to look elsewhere for salvation. Economically adrift and fearful of their Bulgarian and Hungarian neighbours (both of them hurt by the post-war settlement and waiting to alter the map once more), they were forced to turn to Germany. By 1939 all the states of the region, pro-Versailles or anti-Versailles, were wooing Germany with what they had – which was raw materials – in the hope either of protection or redress. To Germany they were important, as they had once been to France, not for any reasons connected with the politics of the area itself but for extrinsic reasons.

The Russo-German pact of 1939 recognized a Russian interest in the Balkans by assigning Bessarabia to the USSR. A year later Stalin, by annexing northern Bukovina as well, signalled that his interest was not limited to Bessarabia. Rumania thought of going to war but was restrained by Hitler who had other plans. Although in 1939 he had declared himself disinterested in this part of the world, he was not. Rumania's natural resources and its strategic position on the southern border of the USSR made it very important for him. In the autumn of 1940 he further partitioned Rumania by giving a piece to Hungary (the second Vienna Award, in August) and a piece to Bulgaria (the treaty of Craiova, in September). By this time King Carol was ready to throw in his hand. He had tried unsuccessfully to rule through a minor party and then through the Patriarch as Prime Minister, but after the humiliating territorial losses exacted by Hitler he abdicated and what remained of Rumania was controlled by Germany through Marshal Ion Antonescu with the title of Conducator. In November Rumania, Hungary and Slovakia – a Balkan northern tier along the Russian southern flank – all adhered to the Tripartite Pact. German troops appeared. Hitler was peacefully strengthening his control of the Balkans. He did not want it otherwise. He had no wish for a war in what was to him a storehouse and a waiting area. But on 28 October Mussolini had invaded Greece, and Hitler gradually found himself forced to make new plans and to interpose a military campaign in the Balkans before his invasion of the USSR.

Mussolini had given Hitler no proper notice of his attack on Greece. He sent a letter at the last moment and ante-dated it by five days. This was his way of retaliating against Hitler's habit of invading other countries without telling his ally in advance. In any case he knew that Hitler would object to his plans, because Hitler had been urging him to bide his time. This silly failure in cooperation was characteristic of the partnership between the Axis allies. Neither of the dictators was by nature a cooperator. They lacked – indeed despised – the habits of intercourse and interchange which are the everyday experience of democratic politicians. Moreover, by the time that their alliance had become formal on the eve of war, their relationship had begun to lose some of its strength. This was more Mussolini's fault than Hitler's, for while Hitler entertained a genuine admiration for Mussolini as his forerunner among men of iron will and retained a feeling of obligation to him, Mussolini had from the start been attracted to Hitler partly in spite of himself. He gravitated to the Axis more through repulsion from the western democracies than through any love of Hitler or of Germany, and he quickly allowed congenital jealousy to corrode an alliance which, although it had become essential for his policies, cast him as a manifestly junior, increasingly uncomfortable partner.

Jealousy and suspiciousness were strong features in Mussolini's character. He was a solitary. He had neither friends nor intimates. He had the singlemindedness and determination of the man who cares little for money or the other ordinary comforts of life (except sex), but he too often failed to relate his purposes to his resources. He was energetic without being industrious, so that his achievements were those of the gambler who leaves even the calculable to chance. His working-class origins, his poverty in early life and his consciousness of defective education and social poise made him aloof, secretive and assertive; he had neither the training nor the character to rectify his shortcomings by methodical hard work or by arguing (as Hitler sometimes did) with people who had ideas or knowledge to offer. He remained sketchily informed about public affairs and averse to listening to advisers who might be cleverer or better informed than he was; his energies, which were considerable until the last years of his life, went into posturing and rhetoric. He believed in the regenerative virtue of violence but much of the violence was, unlike Hitler's quests for *Lebensraum* and racial purity, pointless. There is something symbolic about the fact that the prelude to his rule was a spectacular event – the March on Rome – which never took place. Mussolini was appointed Prime Minister not because he advanced on the capital like a conqueror but because he outwitted rival politicians by devious scheming which he conducted at a distance in Milan and which made a grand coup unnecessary. He arrived in Rome by train.

Mussolini was a shrewd and stubborn politician who used the apparatus of tyranny because he was also a bully. Being ruthless and unprincipled he liked the short cuts which the strong arm of lawlessness provides, and very soon after becoming Prime Minister he discovered how well these methods can work in both international and domestic affairs. In 1923 General Enrico Tellini and other Italians who were members of a commission engaged in surveying the unsettled Greco-Albanian frontier were murdered on Greek soil. Mussolini bombarded and seized Corfu, berated the Greek government in extravagant style and had the satisfaction of seeing the British and French governments pressing Greece to accept Italy's humiliating and unjustifiable demands. In the following year Italy scored a substantial victory against Yugoslavia over Fiume because Yugoslavia could muster no outside support for its case. Foreign politicians were beginning to show respect for Mussolini as a statesman of consequence and were therefore contriving to turn a blind eye to such aspects of Fascism as the murder of the socialist leader Giacomo Matteotti (to which Mussolini's language certainly contributed, even though he may have given no precise order for the deed) and the suppression of personal and civil liberties in the name of efficiency and good order: they noted improvements in the public services but ignored the deterioration in manners and morals. By the time that Hitler came to power Mussolini had had a decade of experience in the techniques and fruits of brutality. He was secure at home and respected (by governments) abroad. He was ready to impress Hitler as he had impressed other leaders, but he had not bargained with the possibility that both he himself in relation to Hitler, and Italy in relation to Germany, might have to play a subordinate role in world politics. For the rest of his career he kicked ineffectually against these pricks. The invasion of Greece in the autumn of 1940 was the uncoordinated reflex of an ally who was not a good partner, of a secondary power seeking to establish parity with a first-class power by attacking a third-class one.

Mussolini wanted Italy to be a Balkan power as well as an African one. Greeks were well aware of this and Venizelos had begun in 1928 to mend Greece's relations with Yugoslavia and Turkey. He made a treaty with Italy in the same year but it became a dead letter. Venizelos wanted to end the old feud with Bulgaria too but in 1930 King Boris married an Italian princess. A Balkan pact concluded (without Bulgaria) in 1934 was mainly an anti-Italian mutual defence measure, but it lacked coherence and strength. By the summer of 1940, after Mussolini had won a little territory from France but not much glory, an Italian offensive in the Balkans seemed more than probable, the more so when the Greek cruiser *Helle* was torpedoed by an Italian submarine in the Aegean in August. The British guarantee could not be rated very high. The only hope was that Hitler would restrain his ally.

This hope was destroyed when Mussolini's Ambassador delivered an ultimatum in the middle of the night of 27–8 October. Italian troops had already crossed the Greek frontier with Albania. But the attack was a complete failure. It was undertaken against the advice of all three Italian Chiefs of Staff, who gave Mussolini accurate estimates of Greek resistance. The Duce preferred, however, to listen to his Commander-in-Chief in

Albania who promised to overrun the whole of Epirus in ten to fifteen days and secure the capitulation of the Greek army. He assured Mussolini that everything had been prepared down to the smallest detail which, since the attack had been envisaged nearly four months earlier, should have been the case. But there had in fact been little planning and the operation launched on 28 October was more like a whim than a campaign. The invading force of three divisions was totally inadequate and within a week the Greeks were counter-attacking and advancing into Albania. The Italians had attacked in three prongs. Their central prong was cut off, and the two prongs on either side had to be withdrawn. Italian casualties were heavy. Prisoners were taken by the thousand. By the third week in November there were no Italians left on Greek soil. In addition the British Fleet Air Arm damaged three Italian battleships in a night attack at Taranto on 11–12 November, as a result of which Taranto was abandoned and all Italian vessels of war were moved to harbours on the west coast. The British also moved forward into Crete and the Aegean – whence the R A F could threaten the Rumanian oilfields.

Things were also going badly for Italy on the other side of the Mediterranean. There Marshal Graziani had an army of 215,000 men in Libya. So long as France was in the war Graziani had a good case for lying low, since he was sandwiched between the French in Tunisia and Algeria and the British in Egypt, but as soon as France collapsed Mussolini began to urge him into action. Graziani was reluctant but in September, after having been ordered to fight, he began the first of the series of attacks and counterattacks which were to constitute the battle for North Africa which lasted until May 1943. In the first week of December, in a daring offensive of great political moment, the British retaliated. This move, by a force of little more than 30,000 men, was designed to show that Great Britain was still very much in the war. With remarkable daring, Churchill had sent reinforcements to the Middle East in the middle of the Battle of Britain. He hoped that a show of spirit far away from home might even get France back into the war, and although in this the desert campaign failed, it did make Hitler nervous about a rising in France and finally turned Franco against the Gibraltar plan and the entry of German troops into Spain.

Militarily the British offensive was an astonishing success. Throughout December and January the small British force under General Sir Archibald Wavell advanced from Sidi Barrani inside Egypt to Tobruk (which was captured in twenty-four hours) and then, both along the coast and across the desert, to Benghazi in the north-western corner of Cyrenaica. What had begun as a demonstration turned into a major victory. Wavell's mixed force of British, Indian, Australian, New Zealand, French and

Polish units covered 500 miles in two months and destroyed an Italian army six times its own size. This success also had wider repercussions. It forced Hitler to send help to the Italians, to revise and enlarge the scope of his contingency plans for a move into the Balkans on the basis that the British too might move into Greece in strength, and to make arrangements despite Russian objections for the entry of German troops into Bulgaria and that country's adherence to the Tripartite Pact.

But at Benghazi, which was captured on 7 February, the British advance stopped. The British cabinet had decided that it must be limited. Wavell had already been required to send four squadrons of aircraft (Blenheims and Gladiators) to help the Greeks on the Albanian front and anti-aircraft units to defend Athens; he had another war to fight in East Africa; he was responsible for the safety of Palestine and the Suez Canal, which could be threatened by an anti-British government in Iraq or by the Vichy French in Syria; and five days after the fall of Benghazi Rommel arrived in Tripoli, followed a couple of days later by the first of the German tanks which were destined to transform a desert war which now ceased to be an Anglo-Italian affair.

German intervention in North Africa had first been mooted and then dropped in October 1940. In November, during a not very amicable conference at Salzburg between Hitler and Ciano, Hitler began giving instructions and making promises. He urged the Italians to push on into Egypt and he promised air support. During that winter some 400 German aircraft operated in the Mediterranean protecting supply routes to Africa and attacking British shipping and air bases. Malta, which had been inadequately equipped to defend itself against air attack, was besieged by the German and Italian air forces which succeeded in interdicting it to the British navy and making the Mediterranean impassable by British convoys. The British continued their attacks on Italy, bombarding Genoa from the sea and bombing Spezia and Leghorn from the air in February. The Italians retaliated with hazardous but often successful attacks by small torpedo boats on British heavy units in harbour, but on 28 March British naval superiority was massively affirmed in a battle off Cape Matapan in which three Italian cruisers and two destroyers were sunk. Although the main target, the battleship *Vittorio Veneto*, got away, the Italian navy ceased to be a major factor in the war. (Italy also lost East Africa at this time. In August 1940 the Italians had forced Great Britain to leave British Somaliland and were threatening the Sudan and Kenya but the British returned in February 1941 and with the help of South African, Nigerian, Indian and French troops proceeded to invade Ethiopia and Eritrea. Addis Ababa was abandoned at the beginning of April.

Resistance continued in the north and the final, inevitable surrender did not come until November. The campaign was remarkable for the extraordinary exploits of Gideon Force which consisted of Ethiopian and Sudanese men under Lieutenant Colonel Orde Wingate and other British officers and took over 15,000 prisoners in three months.)

In the spring of 1941 the Germans attacked on the Balkan and North African fronts in campaigns which were subordinate to the attack on the USSR to come in June. Hitler had already left one front unsettled when he desisted from his attack on Great Britain in the autumn of 1940. Now, in the south, if he failed to conclude either his Balkan or his North African operations before beginning Barbarossa, he would again have multiplied his commitments. He concluded the one but not the other.

Forebodings of a German occupation of the Balkans raised forlorn hopes of a local alliance to deter it, with British support. After the Italian invasion of their country, Greeks hoped to induce the British to shift their weight in the eastern Mediterranean from Egypt to Greece, the better to attack the Italians, but the British lacked the resources for effective operations in the two theatres and were reluctant to risk what they held in the one for possible advantages in the other. The RAF gave modest aid against the Italians in Albania but although this help was increased from February 1941 it was not enough to eliminate the Italians before the advent of the Germans. There were, however, political considerations which weighed with Churchill – quite apart from the philhellene emotions roused in Great Britain by the unexpectedly successful Greek resistance. There was in the first place the British guarantee to Greece in 1939; it was time a British guarantee was honoured. Churchill hoped too that Turkey might be got into the war against the Germans; effective support for Greece would weigh with the rulers of Turkey. (Ineffectiveness did too. Turkey followed its instincts and stayed neutral.) Most importantly, Churchill had an eye on the Americans and the impact on them of the establishment of a Balkan front against the Axis. Great Britain had shown that it could win battles against Hitler but Churchill knew that Great Britain alone could never defeat Hitler on the continent. From the time he took office as Prime Minister Churchill kept his mind firmly on the big central issue of forming a coalition powerful enough to destroy Hitler's Germany, and the United States was the essential element in this design. A failure to help the Greeks, whose cause had been very popular in the United States ever since their brave riposte to the Italian invasion in the previous year, might discredit Great Britain; going to their help, even if unsuccessfully, would be accounted to Great Britain for virtue.

At the end of February 1941 Eden, now once more Foreign Secretary, went to Athens with the CIGS, Sir John Dill. By this date German intentions were apparent, Bulgarian adherence to the Tripartite Pact was clearly only a matter of time, and the chances of enlisting Yugoslavia or Turkey in joint operations with Greece and Great Britain were meagre. Bulgaria joined the Pact on 1 March and German troops began to move into that country. Yugoslavia was expected to follow suit sooner rather than later, while the Turks were refusing to join the war without assurances of British military supplies which Great Britain could not spare. Nevertheless from Athens Eden sent Churchill an optimistic assessment of the military possibilities and with this encouragement Churchill who, like Wavell, had been reluctant to prejudice the campaign in North Africa by deflecting ground and air forces to Greece, decided in favour of helping Greece and told Wavell that in the event of a German attack he would have to go to Greece's help. The Australian and New Zealand governments reluctantly agreed.

The Greek government was no less dubious. Help was welcome, but only if it were substantial. In the Greek view, token help would be worse than useless. Greek and British attitudes were now in some ways the reverse of what they had been two years earlier. Then Greece had wanted a firm British commitment in order to deter Italy while Great Britain had hesitated and recoiled for fear of provoking Italy. Now Greece was anxious not to invite a German onslaught so long as any hope of evading it remained and therefore opposed any British military involvement which would be large enough to provoke but not massive enough to deter or defeat the Germans. Greece had failed in 1940 to get enough British help against the Italians to turn their successes in the field into total victory, even though they had been willing at that stage to promise to enter Great Britain's war with Germany in return for substantial help against Italy. The Greek government feared, correctly as it turned out, that the only British help available would be inadequate to stop Hitler. Given the limits on Greek military power which remained almost entirely committed to holding the Italians in the north-west, the only possible anti-German strategy was a substantial British force in the north-east with merely token Greek support. But in spite of these doubts the Greek government agreed in principle in February 1941 to admit a British force into Greece and rejected a German offer of immunity from invasion in return for neutrality.

At this point there was a muddle. An attack through Bulgaria, Greece's traditional enemy, was taken for granted. But Yugoslavia's attitude was still uncertain. In the vortex of Balkan politics Yugoslavia and Greece had been over the years more friendly than unfriendly, and if this friendship

THE GERMAN INVASIONS OF YUGOSLAVIA AND GREECE APRIL 1941

Axis Powers and Allies.
Italian operations, October 1940.
Italian Albania, occupied by Greece.
German advances April 1941.
Italian advances April 1941.
Hungarian advances April 1941.
British, New Zealand and Australian troop positions.

Vienna

AUSTRIA

Budapest

HUNGARY

Ljubljana

Zagreb

Fiume

RUMANIA

Zara

Belgrade

Occupied 6 April.

Bucharest

Sarajevo

Y U G O S L A V I A

Split

Nish

BULGARIA

Adriatic

Dubrovnik

Sofia

Occupied 10 April.

Kotor

Occupied 7 April.

Sea

Skopje

ITALY

Durazzo

Tirana

Occupied 15 April.

Brindisi

Valona

Klisura

Salonika

Larissa

Occupied 9 April.

Yannina

G R E E C E

Thermopylea

Aegean

Corfu

Sea

Cephalonia

Athens

Piraeus

SICILY

Patras

Zante

Nauplia

Occupied 27 April.

Occupied by Italy.

Kalamata

Monemvasia

0   100

Miles

British evacuation 24-30 April.

CRETE

—ARTHUR BANKS—

held – indeed, until it was obvious that it would not hold – the Greeks wanted to keep their communications with Yugoslavia open. In order to do this, they must plan to meet the German-Bulgarian attack on a line north and east of Salonica, even though this line was unfavourable for natural reasons and harder for the British to reach. The British favoured the more southerly line along the river Aliakmon and even this position was likely to prove untenable if Yugoslavia allowed the Germans to invade through Yugoslavia as well as Bulgaria – or, as in fact happened, was unable to stop them. The situation was further complicated by the unfinished war with the Italians in the west, since a withdrawal south of the Aliakmon, without a matching retreat in the west, would expose the Greek forces facing the Italians to encirclement by the Germans – which is what happened. The Greek government hoped and expected Eden to clarify Yugoslavia's position and believed Eden to have agreed that there should be no Greek withdrawal to the Aliakmon line until this had been done. This was the first of a series of muddles for which the blame is still not clear. While the British imagined the Greeks to be regrouping on the Aliakmon line, they were in fact waiting in the north, where they were eventually caught.

In Yugoslavia the Regent Paul had hesitated about following the Rumanian and Bulgarian example and joining the Tripartite Pact. He was urged by Great Britain and the United States to resist German pressure and attack the Italians in Albania, but neither London nor Washington was able to offer any practical help, although Eden dangled territorial bribes before the Regent in return for Yugoslav belligerence against the Italians in Greece. The Regent equivocated. He was pro-British but no fool and he judged that the British wanted to pull him into the war for their own purposes and without any plan to save Yugoslavia from the Axis. In the end, impressed by the fall of France and hoping to get Salonica as his reward, he took the plunge and on 25 March joined the Pact. Two days later his government was overthrown by General Simovic, the leader of a group hostile to the Regent and supported principally by the Serb Orthodox Church. Simovic wanted to steer a neutral course by keeping clear of pacts and wars, and he continued to refuse to attack the Italians. But this was not good enough for Hitler, who was determined to scotch any possible British advance into the Aegean and Greece. He resolved to invade Yugoslavia and Greece and attacked both on 6 April, deploying against the former seven Panzer divisions and 1,000 aircraft. After heavy bombing and grievous casualties Belgrade fell on the 13th. The government capitulated four days later. Yugoslavia disintegrated. On the heels of the German conquerors Hungary, Bulgaria and Italy helped themselves to pieces of what they, wrongly, took to be a corpse; the Croat leader Anté Pavelic arrived from Rome to establish a separate Croat state; Serbia became a German puppet.

Greece was defeated only slightly less abruptly. The German attack had been preceded by a fresh Italian offensive in mid-March. Hopeful and ill-informed, Mussolini crossed to Albania, but had to go back again when his attack failed. The German attack followed. Fifty thousand British, Australian and New Zealand troops, supported by only one squadron of modern aircraft, could do little to succour the Greeks. Seven thousand Greeks were made prisoner and much valuable British material was captured. By the end of April resistance on the Greek mainland was over. Survivors from the Greek and Commonwealth forces were transported to Crete, which had been in British occupation for six months. Unfortunately for them little had been done to defend Crete in the mistaken belief that Great Britain's command of the sea made it impossible for an airborne invasion to be sustained. Churchill had urged that it be turned into a fortress bristling with everything from tanks to road blocks and defended by armed Cretans as well as British and other Commonwealth troops. He did not know that the requisite defences had not been constructed or that essential reconnaissance of the terrain had been neglected. The 3,500 Greek troops in the island had only one rifle per six men and three rounds of ammunition each; existing airstrips were not mined and proposals to build hidden airstrips in the hills not carried out; in spite of a plentiful supply of Italian prisoners of war landing stages were not constructed on the south shore nor roads to link north and south, with the result that supply ships from Egypt had to circle dangerously round the island and unload under intense enemy air attack; there were hardly any tanks and a fatal lack of radio and telegraph equipment.

The attack began on 20 May with glider and parachute landings from a fleet of 500 transport aircraft. These operations were very costly. Although air cover had been withdrawn from the defences before the invasion began, so that the approach of the air armada was unopposed, the reception was very hot and whole units were wiped out on landing or soon afterwards, many of them before they could reach the weapons which were dropped for them separately. Reinforcements were delayed because the airfields which the Germans were using in Greece were inadequately prepared dust bowls. But during the ensuing night Maleme airfield at the western end of the island was abandoned by the New Zealanders and the Germans started using it the next day. All efforts to dislodge them failed. This was a vital turn in events since, contrary to British belief, the German airborne forces were largely dependent on airfields and could not mount a concentrated attack with units dropped at random over the countryside.

A supplementary sea-borne invasion on the second night was baulked by the British navy, which suffered, however, seriously from air attacks. The defenders, believing that the main weight of the attack was bound to come from the sea, paid more attention to shore defence than to the recapture of Maleme, from which the Germans pressed eastward gradually and in increasing force. A week after the beginning of the attack it was clear that the main issues were the timing of the evacuation of the defenders and the number who would be saved. Withdrawal began on 1 June. Only half the defenders got away. The British Mediterranean fleet suffered seriously (three cruisers and six destroyers sunk, two battleships, three cruisers and an aircraft carrier damaged) in the attempt to thwart the invasion and the subsequent rescue operations and had to suspend the latter for fear of incurring further losses which would jeopardize its control of the eastern Mediterranean.

The capture from the air of an island defended by superior naval forces was a spectacular achievement but a freak. The defenders had failed to make good use of their six months' occupation of the island, denuded the island of its air fighter defences, failed with a force of 32,000 men to hold all of the three vital airfields and, having abandoned Maleme, failed to recapture it. These failures, leading to a further humiliating evacuation, blackened the reputation of the commander-in-chief, General Sir Bernard Freyberg, all the more so since he had received full and accurate intelligence from Ultra about German strengths and intentions. But the battle for Crete illustrated the limitations of Ultra as much as its value, for Freyberg had been verbally instructed by Wavell not to make tactical use of Ultra without corroborating intelligence from another source. This was standard practice and prevailed throughout the war. So important was Ultra that Churchill decreed that it was better to lose a battle than to lose this source. Consequently Freyberg was prevented from redisposing his forces on the basis of what he learned from Ultra and when he appealed to Wavell to be dispensed from the rule Wavell rejected his plea. Whether Crete would have been saved if the rules had been different it is impossible to say. But it is possible to assert that the rules were sound, since saving Crete at the cost of Ultra would probably have led in the next year to the loss of the far more crucial battle in the Atlantic.

The Germans considered themselves lucky to have won Crete so easily. They tacitly drew the conclusion that they should not have done so. Over a third of their airborne invaders were killed or wounded, the Luftwaffe lost 220 aircraft and no parachute operation of this kind was ever again attempted. Hitler, having won an extra base for helping Rommel and having driven the British beyond air range of Ploesti's oilfields, scrapped plans for a similar attack on Malta and turned his parachute units into infantry regiments.

It has been suggested that the Cretan operation delayed Barbarossa and so saved Moscow and even possibly the USSR itself in 1941. The Simovic coup in Belgrade occurred on the day, 27 March, for which Hitler had convoked a conference to discuss Barbarossa. The conference discussed Yugoslavia instead, Hitler decided to invade it as soon as possible and he postponed Barbarossa from mid-May to 22 June. Since the thaw came late that year there would have been some postponement anyway. The decision to interpose a Balkan war was chiefly important because the tanks used in it (800 of them) would need a breathing space for refitting between campaigns. This they were able to have. The further decision to take Crete caused some confusion (but nothing more serious) as the forces designated for Crete were moved south while the forces being shifted from Greece to the Russian fronts moved the other way, but the air squadrons left in Greece to cover the Cretan operation could move to their Barbarossa stations at shorter notice and the parachute troops were not intended for use in the USSR at all. Moscow was not saved by a mere alteration to the timetable of a week or two, and although the proposition cannot be incontestably proved or refuted it is very hard to see that the campaigns in Yugoslavia and Greece or the attack on Crete had any significant effect on Barbarossa. What might have helped the USSR would have been a successful defence of Crete and a prolongation of the battle there. At one time it looked to Halder as though Barbarossa would have to be further postponed but on 30 May Hitler confirmed the 22 June date.

The seizure of Crete was at the time more apparent than the cost and Cyprus seemed a possible next step. This was all the more alarming for Great Britain because the French in Syria and Lebanon recognized Vichy, in Iraq Great Britain's enemies had raised their heads and taken power, in Palestine the Mufti Haj Amin was strongly anti-British, and in Egypt King Faruq was not much less so. Consequently the whole British position in the Middle East was in jeopardy and might be scattered by a German attack.

The British position in the Middle East was anomalous. It rested on force, although with the lone exception of Aden no part of the area was constitutionally within the British Empire. During the nineteenth century the rivalries of the European powers had prevented any one of them from annexing portions of the Ottoman empire in Asia as they had annexed parts of Africa, but Great Britain had established *de facto* control over Egypt (and Cyprus). It also controlled the Persian Gulf and the lesser principalities along its western shores. The First World War produced the long-awaited withering away of the Ottoman empire and in anticipation the allied powers struck bargains for its partition in order to avoid fighting among themselves. The Russians, however, dropped out owing to the revolution of 1917 and the Italians withdrew when they scented the emergence of a Turkish national state out of the Ottoman imperial debris. Great Britain and France were left in control but the temper of the times required control to be veiled. France in Syria and Lebanon, and Great Britain in Palestine, Transjordan and Iraq established their rule under mandates. These mandates gave Great Britain a solid block of territory in the Middle East all the way from Egypt to the Persian Gulf. British forces dominated the area more effectively than Ottoman forces had ever done and this domination was practically unaffected by the grant of formal independence to Egypt in 1922 or the termination of the Iraqi mandate ten years later. Special treaties ensured the continued presence of British naval, military and air forces (although the treaty with Egypt took over ten years to negotiate) and the development of road, rail and air communications made assurance doubly sure. There was no Arab power to gainsay the British but there were Arab nationalists who, observing European politics in the thirties and remembering the interest of an earlier generation of Germans in the Middle East, hoped that Germany might come in useful to put an end to British rule over them. The German campaigns in the Balkans in the spring of 1941 stimulated these hopes, especially in Iraq.

The Arabs had also a second reason for being anti-British besides their nationalist resentment against the British imperialism which (with French imperialism) had frustrated their hopes of ruling themselves as soon as the Turks had been got rid of. In Palestine the British administration allowed a Jewish immigration which, given the background of the Zionist demand for a Jewish state, was a threat to Arab aspirations. During the First World War Great Britain endorsed the Zionist claim to a national home in Palestine (a camouflaged way of referring to the Jewish state which most Zionists wanted and which their founder, Theodore Herzl, had envisaged at the end of the previous century when he wrote his book *The Jewish State*). Under British rule the Jews in Palestine increased from less than 10 per cent of the population to nearly 30 per cent and the Arabs, who regarded the Jews as alien colonizers of Arab soil, began to look for foreign friends. The Nazis with their anti-Jewish tirades were an obvious choice for an anti-British flirtation. The Arabs were also impressed by the failure of Great Britain and France to check Mussolini in Ethiopia and encouraged by the extensive Arab revolt in Palestine in 1936. Upon the approach of war Great Britain tried to safeguard its position in the Middle East by dropping attempts, which were in any case futile, to find a way of pleasing both Arabs and Jews in Palestine and adopted instead a pro-Arab policy. In 1938 the BBC started broadcasting in Arabic, the first of its foreign language programmes. In May 1939 a British White Paper proposed severe limits on Jewish immigration (at the very moment when the case for it had been enormously enhanced by Hitler's concentration camps) and assured the Arabs that beyond these limits further immigration would be subject to Arab acquiescence. The White Paper saved Anglo-Arab relations and the British Empire in the Middle East for the war years – but not beyond.

One of the Arab politicians who wished to play the Germans off against the British and use the war to extract concessions from Great Britain about post-war Palestine was Rashid Ali el-Gailani, who became Prime Minister of Iraq in March 1940. A year later he was briefly ousted but returned with increased power. He was supported by four colonels picturesquely known as the Golden Square who were the principal spokesmen and pressure group for politically-minded army officers. The immediate question for Rashid Ali's government was whether to honour Iraq's treaty obligations to Great Britain and allow British troops to use the port of Basra at the head of the Persian Gulf on their way to reinforce the British position in Egypt. Rashid Ali and his friends, besides wanting to take a firm line with Great Britain, were afraid that the pro-British party led by Nuri es-Said would lead Iraq into the war in spite of the fact, as it seemed to them, that Great Britain was losing it. Rashid Ali therefore wanted to find out how much German help he would get if he resisted the British, but he found the Germans disappointingly vague. On the one hand Hitler was reluctant to give the Arabs what they wanted because Mussolini, who was still regarded as having at least an equal say in Middle Eastern affairs, had reservations. An Axis declaration endorsing Arab nationalistic aspirations did not square with Mussolini's intention to assume overlordship of Egypt and the Sudan in place of the British. Consequently Hitler hesitated over his Arab policy and eventually agreed to a declaration which fell short of Arab nationalist hopes. On the other hand Hitler did not want Great Britain to score a success in Iraq because such a success could swing Turkey (which had so far fallen down on obligations to Great Britain and France undertaken in a treaty of October 1939) into the British camp with embarrassing results for Germany's drive into the Caucasus and beyond. So in the end Hitler promised to give air support to Rashid Ali and to try to get Vichy to send him arms from French stores in Syria.

The British, fearful for their communications with India via Basra and their supplies of Iraqi oil, forced the pace by bringing what forces they wanted to Basra; they ignored Iraqi conditions limiting the numbers of British troops to be allowed on Iraqi soil at any one time and the length of stay of each unit in transit. On 2 May they attacked Iraq. A force from Palestine and another under Brigadier Glubb from the Arab Legion in Transjordan struck north towards Baghdad which surrendered on the last day of the month. Rashid Ali, having expected too much from the Germans, found himself a refugee in Teheran. The Germans, having expected too much from Rashid Ali and done too little for him, lost such chance as they had of taking the Middle East by frontal assault. Great Britain lost no time in making sure of Syria and Lebanon, and Iran too.

One consequence of the Rashid Ali episode had been a temporary intensification of German-French cooperation. The dominant figure at Vichy at this time was the acidly anti-British Admiral Darlan, with whom the Germans were engaged in negotiating the Paris Protocols which provided for extensive and active cooperation in the Middle East and Africa. In the Middle East Darlan agreed to give the Germans transit and landing rights for aircraft on their way to Iraq and to provide Rashid Ali with French arms, but this policy of resurrecting France through a working partnership with the Nazis was too much for Pétain who brought Weygand over from North Africa early in June in a manoeuvre to resist Darlan. The Paris Protocols thereupon lapsed but not before they had caused the British, with the Free French, to invade Syria and Lebanon.

The local French commander, General Dentz, proposed to resist with German help, but Vichy prevaricated partly through fear of British retaliation in Morocco and partly through fear of offending the Americans and so forfeiting the food and other materials which the Americans were sending to France. So Vichy attached conditions to the acceptance of German air support in Syria which caused the Germans to decline to give any help at all. They were in any case doubtful about the wisdom of helping a mandatory power which the Arabs, whom they were courting, wanted to see evicted. The British put pressure on Turkey to refuse facilities for French reinforcements and supplies (except oil which was covered by an existing agreement); Turkey refused, however, a British invitation to enter Syria from the north. General Dentz, strong in spirit and comparatively strong in numbers but weak in everything else, was forced to capitulate on 14 July after five weeks of fighting.

This British success not only extinguished Vichy's authority in Syria and Lebanon but also constrained de Gaulle to grant these two countries their independence – which was endorsed by Great Britain. But the Gaullists were not happy with the idea of recovering French territory from Vichy and then letting it go from the French empire at British behest, and no further steps were taken until 1943 when elections were held and governments installed with something less than sovereign status. In Lebanon a quarrel between the government and the French led to the arrest of the newly elected President and the dissolution of the newly elected parliament, but Anglo-American intervention forced the French to retreat and to concede real powers to the governments of both countries. Arab countries under British rule took note, waiting their turn. The United States and the USSR recognized independent Syria and Lebanon and although France tried at the end of the war to exact special privileges for itself like those enjoyed by Great Britain in Egypt, Iraq and Transjordan, and even bombed Damascus, it was frustrated by British action and forced to recognize that its defeat in 1940 had cost it its position in the Levant.

A few weeks after the capitulation of General Dentz in July 1941 Great Britain made doubly sure of its Middle Eastern position by occupying Iran in concert with the Russians. The Shah was bundled off to an island in the Indian Ocean and later to South Africa where he died.

Thus at mid-summer 1941 Germany had appropriated the Balkans and Great Britain had replied by dominating the whole of the Middle East. The first of these positions was not to be contested until the general German retreat at the end of the war, which liberated the Balkans. In the Mediterranean and North Africa the war went on. The battle for Cape Matapan in March and the withdrawal of the Luftwaffe for the Russian campaign in June eased the British position, and in July Malta welcomed the first convoy to reach port since January. Another followed in September and for a few weeks Malta became once more a naval base, but the loss of the aircraft carrier *Ark Royal* in the western Mediterranean and the battleship *Barham* in the east, and damage to Great Britain's two remaining battleships by Italian mines fixed to them in harbour at Alexandria, reasserted the challenge to British naval power.

On land Rommel advanced, retreated and survived. His first offensive, launched at the end of March 1941, carried him from Tripolitania through Cyrenaica and into Egypt. Benghazi fell but Tobruk was held by an Australian, New Zealand and Polish garrison. (The Australians were replaced by British troops during the siege. Their commander believed that their health had deteriorated so badly that they could not withstand a major attack. Also, the Australian government and commander-in-chief wanted to reassemble all Australian forces in theatre under a unified Australian command. The New Zealand troops remained. New Zealand was the only nation besides Great Britain to send fighting troops to every theatre of war.) Rommel's success offered tantalizing prospects of a German advance to Suez, Iraq and the Persian Gulf, but Hitler decided that all this must wait. The Balkans must come first because they were essential for the launching of Barbarossa before mid-summer. So Rommel had to pause. In May and June he and Wavell engaged in a series of dingdong battles for the Halfaya Pass on the borders of Egypt, and Wavell then made an attempt to relieve Tobruk which failed. In a trial of skill in armoured warfare Rommel came off best, the British suffered serious losses of newly arrived tanks, and Wavell was relieved of his command on the day of the German invasion of the USSR. He was replaced by General Auchinleck with General Cunningham in command on the desert front.

Until November Rommel remained on the Egyptian frontier, experiencing increasing difficulties with his supply lines across the Mediterranean. In that month Hitler sent Field Marshal Kesselring to Rome with the title of Supreme Commander South, reinforced the Luftwaffe's meagre strength in the Mediterranean and switched half his U-boats from the Atlantic to the Mediterranean. Generals Auchinleck and Cunningham attacked in mid-November. At the southern end of the front they defeated an Italian armoured division but in the north confused fighting, in which British and German tank formations often found themselves behind what would have been the enemy's lines if any lines had existed, produced no decisive result. At one moment the defenders of Tobruk attempted a break-out which failed. At another, Rommel, encouraged by British losses, made a dash for Egypt which also failed. Rommel's two armoured divisions were superior to the British in fire power but inferior in numbers, and in the first week of December he decided to retreat to avoid encirclement. Thus the siege of Tobruk was at last raised, but as Rommel withdrew once more into Tripolitania (his skill in withdrawal was as great as his dash in attack) leaving the British in control of Cyrenaica an acrimonious debate broke out on the British side. The main object of the campaign had not been achieved; the German Panzer army had not been destroyed. During the battle Auchinleck had dismissed Cunningham and summoned General Ritchie from Cairo to take his place. Since the battle and until the present day there has been controversy about the events of these weeks. It has been argued that if the British had waited for Rommel to attack they would have had a better chance of annihilating his forces, and it has also been argued that the retention of forces in the Middle East for this indecisive action contributed to the fall of Singapore in the following February. By this time Rommel had received new tanks via Tripoli and was planning a second eastward advance. The war in Africa was not concluded until eighteen months later and after the second front in North-west Africa, closed by the fall of France in 1940, had been reopened by the Anglo-American invasion of November 1942.

CHAPTER 9

Barbarossa

THE Russo-German treaty of August 1939 served its German purpose for almost two years. During that period Hitler made himself virtual master of the whole of continental Europe outside the borders of the USSR. A few neutrals existed on the fringes and one – Switzerland – in the middle, but nowhere was there opposition to Germany. These conquests had not been achieved without alarming Stalin. He had shared in the spoliation of Poland, annexed the three Baltic states after the fall of France and taken Bessarabia and Northern Bukovina from Rumania. Hitler then carved up Rumania and forced it, together with Hungary and Slovakia, to adhere to the Tripartite Pact. After Mussolini's unsuccessful invasion of Greece he added Bulgaria and Yugoslavia to the Tripartite Pact and moved into Bulgaria. Stalin protested – he had protested the previous year that the partition of Rumania was a breach of the Russo-German treaty of 1939 only to be met with the obvious retort that he himself had already broken it by helping himself to northern Bukovina. When the Simovic government in Belgrade repudiated the Tripartite Pact Stalin made a formal declaration of friendship with it but did not commit the USSR to go to its aid against a German attack. The two pseudo-allies were manoeuvring for positions in the one sizable undistributed area in Europe and the Germans were getting the better of the game because they did not mind provoking the Russians, whereas the Russians were still anxious not to provoke the Germans.

Stalin's agents abroad were reporting that Hitler was about to attack the USSR, the British and American governments were repeating the warnings, and German troop movements told the same tale. Most tellingly of all, German deserters were crossing what had become a Russo-German front line in Poland to give warning of the German attack. A week after the opening of the German campaign in the Balkans and on the day when Belgrade fell, Stalin concluded a neutrality pact with Japan. But he did not trust Japan to keep it and even after Hitler's attack he hesitated for some time before moving troops from his Asian to his European fronts. On 5 June he became President of the Council of Commissars or, as we would say, Prime Minister, in place of Molotov who became Deputy Prime Minister as well as Foreign Minister. (Stalin had hitherto held only

THE RUSSIAN BARRIER 1939 - 1940

The eastward advance of the German armies led the Soviet Union to establish a 'barrier' strip of territory between its western frontier and the potential aggressor. However, this proved of little advantage when the Germans launched their invasion in June 1941.

0   150
Miles

LATVIA
Russian before 1914
Independent 1920 - 1939

LITHUANIA
Russian before 1914
Independent 1919 - 1939

PART OF FINLAND
Russian before 1917
Finnish 1918 - 1939

ESTONIA
Russian before 1917
Independent 1918 - 1939

EASTERN POLAND
Russian before 1914
Polish 1919 - 1939

EASTERN GALICIA
Austrian before 1918
Polish 1918 - 1939

BESSARABIA
Russian before 1917
Rumanian 1918 - 1940

BUKOVINA
Austrian before 1918
Rumanian 1918 - 1940

FINLAND
Petrozavodsk
Helsinki
Viborg
Leningrad
Tallin (Reval)
Baltic Sea
Pskov
Riga
Memel
U S S R
Vilna
Königsberg
EAST PRUSSIA
Minsk
Grodno
Warsaw
P O L A N D
Pinsk
Lublin
Kiev
Tarnov
Przemysl
Lvov
SLOVAKIA
Uzhgorod
Kamanets Podolsk
Balta
HUNGARY
Iasi
Kishinev
Odessa
R U M A N I A
Black Sea

Occupied by USSR.
October 1939 to December 1940.

The German Reich by December 1939.

Under German control or influence
by December 1940.

-ARTHUR BANKS-the post of Secretary General of the Communist Party.) But during these last months Stalin continued to do everything he could to avoid or postpone the German attack. The ease of the German conquest of Yugoslavia and Greece showed him that the turn of events in south-eastern Europe would do little or nothing to interfere with Hitler's plans to attack the USSR. He increased Russian supplies to Germany, promising and punctually providing special facilities for the transit of rubber from the Far East and making other economic agreements favourable to Germany; he stopped arguing about the Russo-German frontier in the Baltic area; he expunged all criticism of Germany from the Russian press; he withdrew recognition of the Norwegian and Belgian governments in exile, expelled the Yugoslav Ambassador from Moscow, refused to recognize the Greek government in exile and recognized Rashid Ali's pro-German régime in Iraq. None of these things had been asked for by Hitler and the German press was told to make no mention of them.

At home Stalin had two paramount problems. The first was the state of the Soviet armed forces and the second was strategic. The USSR's western frontier was a long one. At no great distance behind it lay Leningrad in the north and the mineral and agricultural riches of the Ukraine in the south. In the centre Moscow, although more distant, was not beyond the reach of a powerful, mechanized enemy determined to seize it within six months. This central front was bisected by the Pripet marshes which impeded switches between one sector and another. In spite of the misgivings of his professional advisers Stalin had moved forces into newly occupied territories – Bessarabia, Poland, Finland, the Baltic states – and out of the so-called Stalin Line (whose powerful guns and tangles of barbed wire in difficult forest country later impressed the Germans who overran it), until by May 1941 170 Russian divisions were stationed outside the pre-1939 frontiers of the USSR. Stalin may have been hoping that Hitler's adventures in the west would give him a chance to attack again on the Finnish front (where he had twenty-seven divisions, including five armoured) or win further ground in the Balkans but this is surmise. The fact is that well over half the Russian army was occupying new positions whose fortifications and rearward communications were incomplete.

Furthermore, the forces which would be called upon to take the shock of the German attack were still recovering from the great purges. Where Hitler had tamed his officer caste, Stalin had killed his. The purges of the armed forces were a part of the Great Purge of the civilian and military establishments which Stalin began in 1936. An officer corps constitutes by its very nature a possible alternative to civilian government and Stalin was afraid of it. The Russian army had no tradition of revolution; its sole attempt to usurp the civil power – the Decembrist coup of 1825 – had collapsed after a day; but Stalin was obsessed with the example of Bonapartism and he proceeded in the thirties to emasculate the civil war generation whose leaders, military or civilian, might conspire against him. Because of his fears he was quick to lend an ear to accusations that his officers were plotting against him. One of his agents in Paris provided false evidence against Marshal Tukhachevski, the Chief of Staff of the Army, who was alleged to be in treasonable correspondence with German officers. This evidence was planted on Beneš who guilelessly passed it on to Moscow where it was used as reliable confirmation from an untainted source of prefabricated charges. In addition Russian agents persuaded German Intelligence to forge supporting documents which were likewise sent to Moscow to build up the case against Tukhachevski even further. Tukhachevski was arrested and executed after a trial lasting one day. Six of the eight officers who constituted the court martial were also executed. The further victims of the purge embraced three of the five Marshals of the Soviet Union, all eleven deputy Commissars for Defence (that is to say, deputy Ministers), seventy-five of the eighty members of the Military Soviet, all the commanders of the military districts into which the country was divided in peacetime, thirteen of fifteen army commanders, over half the corps commanders and 20–40 per cent of all officers below brigade. They were replaced by retired stalwarts or young party enthusiasts who were either too out of touch or too unprofessional to inspire confidence or to understand the new equipment which the army was beginning to receive.

This stupendous amputation of head and members, which affected the political as much as the military side of the Soviet army's dual control, disorganized and dispirited the services more than enough to prevent them from being a threat to the régime but also almost enough to prevent them from being a threat to an enemy. The invasion of Poland in September 1939 posed no fighting problem since the Poles had already been beaten by the Germans (it did, however, disclose organizational and logistic inefficiency), but the Finnish war was an inglorious shock, forcing the Russians to employ one and a half million men and to take three months over the sort of operation to which Hitler would have allotted a week or two. But this shock was also perhaps a boon. It forced Stalin to accelerate the reorganization of his defences. In May 1940 S. K. Timoshenko was made a Marshal and Defence Commissar at the age of forty-five, replacing the veteran Bolshevik K. E. Voroshilov. New training programmes were introduced. So were professional titles for ranks. Military commissars were abolished (they were reintroduced in 1941 and abolished again in 1942) and steps were taken to boost the prestige of the armed services. In February 1941 G. K. Zhukov, who had recently concluded a successful campaign against the Japanese in contrast to the deplorable performance of some of his colleagues on the Finnish front, was promoted full general and Chief of Staff of the Army; he became the pre-eminent figure among Stalin's Marshals but, like Marshal Soult whom he in some ways resembled (including the possession of a political temperament), was as heartily disliked by some of his fellows as he was lauded by others.

In the field, however, only a few of the army's new leaders had emerged, its divisions were below strength and its preparations – especially in frontier districts – had been impeded up to the last moment by Stalin's continuing obsession with avoiding provoking the Germans and so prolonging the respite. By ill chance the Russian forces were caught in the process of changing over to the T 34 tank which was only beginning to emerge from the factories. In addition they were, not for the first time, changing their tank tactics. In earlier years the Russians, like the Germans, had imbibed some of the new ideas about tank warfare propounded by Liddell Hart, Fuller and Martel, but in the thirties Stalin had changed his mind. The defeat of the Italians at the battle of Guadalajara in the Spanish civil war, perhaps also Marshal Tukhachevski's support for the new doctrine, and Russian experience in Mongolia and Finland, all undermined Stalin's faith in large tank formations and he decided that tanks should not be concentrated in tank corps and tank armies but should be spread through other formations in accordance with an older doctrine. Then the German successes in France made him change his mind again, although not in time to enable the Russian forces to be regrouped before suffering severe defeats.

Hitler's attack was launched on 22 June, two days earlier than the date on which Napoleon had led the Grand Army across the Niemen in 1812. It was the biggest military operation ever mounted. Although Hitler believed that the USSR would collapse, he was taking no chances and in any case he loved sheer size. His hosts, which included contingents of a dozen nationalities, attacked in three directions. Northern and Central Army Groups under Field Marshals von Leeb and von Bock headed towards the cities of Leningrad and Moscow, Southern Army Group under Field Marshal von Rundstedt for the Ukraine, the Don basin, the Crimea and the Caucasus with their wealth of grain, coal and oil. Their main objective was to surround and destroy the Russian forces in western Russia and prevent any 'battleworthy elements' from escaping into the interior: the capture of cities and provinces would then follow automatically. Surprise was complete: psychological surprise, because the Russian public had been allowed no hint of what was in store; tactical surprise, because the Russian forces in western areas were not forewarned. So began the most appalling, devastating and savage conflict in the history of warfare.

It was conducted on both sides by obsessively ruthless tyrants, battering one another like a pair of rabid rhinoceroses – with this difference that they used not their own bodies but those of millions of men whom, by the exercise of will, they committed to every kind of suffering, mutilation and death. Until nearly the end of its four years this fearful contest was remote from the other theatres of war, so that when it ended its impact on the rest of the world – on those who were neither Russian nor German – was incommensurate with its hideous actuality.

Stalin has been heavily blamed for his inept dispositions in the face of an invasion which was easily foreseeable. Apologists have suggested that he believed American and British warnings to be a ruse to induce him to mobilize and so provoke Hitler much as the Kaiser had been provoked to attack in 1914 by Russian mobilization. But this argument discounts the warnings received by Stalin from other quarters. While the timing of Hitler's invasion was a matter for conjecture until almost the last moment, it was virtually inevitable and, from several months earlier, imminent. Hitler had himself proclaimed his intention to annex parts of the Soviet Union as living space for the German race and he was deflected neither by his pact with Stalin in 1939 nor by his failure in the Battle of Britain to secure peace in the west before attacking in the east. For Stalin the pact of 1939 was never more than a means to a respite, a way to gain time not peace. The charge against him is that he made such poor use of the time he bought. He was already suffering from the two great diseases of the autocrat: vanity and isolation. His brutal domination over colleagues in the Communist party and the armed services deprived him of honest deliberation and advice; absurdly confident of his ability to fend off Hitler he was prone to play down warnings which clashed with his preconceptions, while some intelligence never reached him from subordinates who were too scared to tell him things likely to be unwelcome. From the winter of 1940–41 his own agents (notably Richard Sorge working in Japan for Red Army Intelligence) were reinforcing the warnings conveyed by the American and British governments but apart from his neutrality pact with Japan in April 1941 Stalin's attitude was almost entirely passive. Delay was his tactic and it was ineffectual.

Stalin's armed forces and his frontier defences, although in the process of reorganization and re-equipment, were hopelessly and chaotically inadequate when Hitler sent four fifths of his armies – three million men – across the dividing line in Poland, confident of making mincemeat of his enemy and of capturing Moscow, Leningrad and the Caucasus before the end of the year. Hitler was to be proved nearly right but yet disastrously wrong. The Russian fronts were broken in several places within hours of the opening attack. Whole armies and Fronts (the Russian equivalent of Army Groups) were annihilated in spite of desperate, if ill coordinated, resistance and suicidal counter-attacks. Stunned by the magnitude of disaster on every front, and perhaps fearful for his own life, Stalin stayed silent until 3 July but on that day he took control of the war. In a broadcast speech he appealed to Russian patriotism; in the field he dismissed generals and had them shot. From this point onward he functioned as supreme war lord. Although often suspicious of his generals he did not make Hitler's mistake of dismissing the best of them. At the end of July he removed Zhukov from the post of Chief of Staff and recalled the aged, infirm and only dubiously competent Marshal Shaposhnikov who might be expected, like Keitel on the German side, to do his master's bidding; but Zhukov, having been sent to take charge of the defence of Leningrad, was brought back in October to save Moscow and was thereafter uninterruptedly at the centre of war planning until the capture of Berlin.

The main weight of the German attack was in the centre. The striking power of each Army Group was concentrated in Panzer Groups. Army Group Centre had two of these; each of its neighbours one. The Panzer Groups struck swiftly and directly, disrupting the enemy front and outdistancing the rest of the German forces which advanced as a second wave in encircling movements to trap the Russian forces which had been severed from each other by the slicing Panzers. In this way the Russians were cut up into sections and surrounded in pockets, and the speed and success of the German Panzer Groups were so great that the pockets were very large. Some of them contained up to fifteen Russian divisions. Huge numbers of prisoners were taken. On the Russian side there was almost total disorganization. Roads and railways were made unusable by the Luftwaffe. Every kind of communication failed. Frantic reports from the front and appeals for instructions, sent *en clair* for want of time to encipher them, dismayed incredulous staffs at higher echelons which retorted that the reports must be wrong and reprimanded the senders for not using their codes. But amid this confusion the Russians faced forward and even counter-attacked, driving their tanks suicidally into German artillery fire and pouring uncoordinated masses of men into the path of the unstoppable Germans. Others retreated or fled, destroying such installations and livestock as they could, often themselves destroyed either by the Luftwaffe or by the machine guns of the N K V D. Their officers were summoned back to Moscow to be shot there. The Germans, advancing up to fifty miles a day, were equally amazed by their own success and by the violent, valiant and often ferocious resistance of men who should have been totally demoralized. They began from the start to perceive that the war in the east was going to be different from the other campaigns of the past two years.

In mere numbers the Russians could match the Germans at many points. They had more men and more tanks, field artillery and aircraft. They had about 20,000 tanks, of which some 7,000 were in forward areas, but most of them were obsolescent and according to Marshal Konev, writing after the war was over, losses were so heavy that by September there were only forty-five serviceable modern tanks between the Germans and Moscow. Konev, one of Stalin's outstanding tank commanders, regarded the Russian T 34 as the best tank in any army during the entire war, but it did not become the mainstay of the Russian forces until 1943. Russian manpower was immense but infantry divisions were still not motorized and shortages ranging from radio equipment to medical supplies were crippling. Large areas of the U S S R passed into German hands. Goebbels proclaimed on 10 July: 'The eastern continent lies like a limp virgin in the mighty arms of the German Mars.' As whole armies surrendered and cities fell (Minsk 28 June, Smolensk 16 July) the German victory in the field seemed complete. But the Russians were not quite overwhelmed. Their armies were not destroyed. Nor were their air forces.

The Russian air forces (the largest in the world) and Russian aircraft production were, like the Russian army, in a stage of re-equipment and expansion in the years immediately before war came. Although markedly inferior to the German and British air forces – in machines, output, design, technical equipment, training, maintenance, ground organization and airfield construction – the Russian air forces had reached a point where improvement in all these departments could be rapid. The most important feature of the air war in the east after 1941 was that this improvement was not only astonishingly rapid but far more so than the Germans or anybody else had believed possible. In the first half of the war the Russians were able to offset their all-round inferiority by superiority in one thing – numbers. In the second half of the war they had air forces which were not only bigger but better than the Luftwaffe.

Russian aircraft production passed German production about the end of 1937, that is to say, before Munich. It then rose steadily from around 800 a month to 900 in 1939 and 1,000 by the time of Barbarossa. The first deliveries from new factories built in the Urals in the early thirties began

OPERATION 'BARBAROSSA'
22 JUNE 1941

Under German rule or influence by June 1941.

General direction of the German advance.

Occupied by German forces between June and December 1941.

Cities besieged by Germans 1941.

NORWAY

SWEDEN

FINLAND

Murmansk

Kandalaksha

Archangel

Helsinki

BALTIC SEA

Leningrad

Tikhvin

Vologda

Novgorod

Riga

Pskov

Gorki

Danzig

Minsk

Smolensk

Moscow

Riazan

GREATER

Tula

Warsaw

Pripet Marshes

U

Orel

S

R

GERMANY

Kursk

Voronezh

HUNGARY

Kiev

Lvov

Kharkov

Stalingrad

Rostov

RUMANIA

Odessa

YUGOSLAVIA

Sevastopol

BULGARIA

BLACK SEA

GREECE

0   200
Miles

~ARTHUR BANKS~

to reach units in 1939, but when production and assembly plants in the west were overrun by the German armies total output was halved. It recovered by the middle of 1942 and then rose remorselessly to a peak of 3,000 a month. First line strength was 3,000–3,500 at the beginning of 1938, 4,000–5,000 a year later; after surmounting the crisis of 1941–2 it reached 10,000 by mid-1943, 15,000 by mid-1944 and over 20,000 before the war ended. But when war began reserves were poor. There was no pool of aircraft on which operational units could draw in order to replace their losses; new aircraft had to go straight from factory to units, so that the operational strength of units depended directly on the irregular factory flow and was sometimes down to half the prescribed establishment – with depressing effects on morale as well as on strengths. There were acute shortages of high-octane fuel at the front and essential raw materials for the factories. The Russian air forces had no radar, no ground control, not enough fighters and very few night fighters. Such fighters as could be spared from the fighting at the front were concentrated on airfields round Moscow for the defence of the capital. Strategic bombing of targets in the enemy's rear was impossible in 1941 and hardly developed at any time. Russian long-range bombers, unequipped with radar, engaged in danger-ous and largely ineffective missions in which a half to three quarters of modest forces of about one hundred aircraft failed to find their targets. Bomb loads never exceeded two tons, a light load compared with the ten tons carried by the British Lancaster. Finally, the Russian air forces were still divided in 1941 between a western front against the Germans and an eastern front against the Japanese, and in spite of Stalin's growing assur-ance that he had nothing to fear in the east he hesitated to denude his eastern front until the threat to Moscow forced him to transfer 1,000 fighters and fighter bombers westward in the autumn of 1941.

The first three months of the campaigns of 1941 were catastrophic but just not fatal. The Russian air forces, attacked by an enemy who was technically much superior, were caught by surprise, inadequately camou-flaged, undispersed, unsure of their supplies and communications: Russian fighters, 20–100 m.p.h. slower than the German Me. 109s, were outfought, frequently in the course of retreating from one airfield to another further back. Great numbers were destroyed on the ground, either by surprise attack or because they had to be left behind owing to shortages of fuel or spare parts. The Luftwaffe claimed to have destroyed 1,489 aircraft on the ground on the first day; a first attempt to retaliate by bombing German targets cost the Russians 500 aircraft. On the day after the battle opened one commander of a Russian bomber group committed suicide after losing 600 aircraft against only twelve German. Russian losses by the end of August probably amounted to more than 5,000 aircraft. A month later their front line strength in the west had been halved and the Germans believed that the Russian air force had ceased to exist. Significantly, they were puzzled by the continued arrival of reinforcements. They were handicapped by their inability to reach and bomb the factories in the east where many of these aircraft were being turned out. They continued to shoot down the new aircraft which were thrown by the Russians desperately into the battle as soon as they arrived, but the flow never ceased and the Luftwaffe itself began to feel the strain.

German front line strengths shrank too, sometimes to half establishment. Space and snow came to the help of the Russians. The Luftwaffe, however excellent, was too small for a 2,000-mile front. As units were switched from Leningrad in the far north to the Ukrainian or central front, operational efficiency declined. The Luftwaffe could not keep up its initial effort of 1,500–2,000 sorties a day. It was farther away from its bases at home than it had ever been, its communications longer and more precarious, its flying conditions more testing. Once again it was short of fighters, and although the Stukas made their final onslaught of the war they too were too few to deliver along this huge front the series of packed punches which had drilled holes in the armies on the western fronts. When the snow came and the airfields froze, the High Command of the Luftwaffe failed to provide its men with the right clothing or its machines with anti-freeze. Its difficulties were accentuated by the makeshift nature of some of the airstrips which it was obliged to use and which were inferior to the airfields round Moscow being used by the Russians. By the end of the year German operational strength along the whole front had fallen to 1,500 and in the Moscow sector the Russians had assembled twice as many aircraft as the Luftwaffe.

But this capacity of the Russian air forces to survive was secondary. The decisive fact was the survival of the Russian ground forces. At the end of the first four weeks of the campaign the Germans paused for breath – and for argument. The Panzer units were farther ahead of the infantry than had been expected and some of them were 200 miles from their depots in eastern Poland; spare parts had to be flown to them since many roads were only unsurfaced tracks and there were hundreds of thousands of armed Russians behind the German lines. How many it is impossible to say: certainly 250,000, perhaps twice that number, whole armies cut up and disoriented but not eliminated. Guderian and other tank commanders wanted to resume their advances as soon and as fast as possible in order to keep on hammering the Russians, prevent the consolidation of a new line of Russian defence, exterminate the enemy's fighting capacity and capture Moscow. Hitler on the other hand wanted to hold in the centre, strengthen his northern and southern Army Groups, bypass and isolate Leningrad with the one, and push south with the other until he was in a position to sweep round behind Moscow and the Russian armies to the west of it. Besides this strategic problem Hitler and his generals were worried by the gap which had already developed between the Panzers and the rest of the army and would be yet further increased if the Panzers were given their head, and they were worried because their advance not only extended their lines from west to east but also, fanwise, on a north-south axis – owing to the fact that the starting line of June had been considerably shorter than the line along which they were forced by geography to operate by the end of July.

The German forces were becoming stretched in all directions and it was not impossible to envisage the Russians inserting unused reinforcements between the Panzers and their supporting units, while at the same time breaking out of one or two pockets farther west and starting effective guerilla action against the German lines of communication. To give point to their fears several thousand Russian troops did break out of the Smo-lensk pocket. So from mid-July to mid-August the debate went on; the Germans failed to make the best of some of the most favourable weather of the summer or to exploit the chaos reigning in western Russia where local commanders and local party officials tussled with problems of dis-cipline and administration and no firm directives reached them from the top (except simply to attack Germans whenever they were seen); the battered Russians had time to breathe, to re-group and to rush reserve divisions into the gaps. These divisions were half-trained, poorly equipped, sometimes still in civilian clothes, but they arrived and played their part; the Germans had not thought that they could be brought into the line so quickly. So great was the urgency on the Russian side that when trains reached their destinations the locomotives were uncoupled and sent back post haste without waiting for the rolling stock.

During these weeks Stalin's authority became assured. It is not certain that it was so in the first disastrous weeks of war, or that he believed it to be so. A few days after the German invasion a defence committee to run the war was established under his chairmanship. The other members were Molotov, Voroshilov, Malenkov and Beria. Below this committee was the *Stavka*, a supreme planning staff which controlled the Fronts. The *Stavka* consisted originally of a dozen senior officers but Stalin, Molotov and Voroshilov were added to it soon after the outbreak of war. In July Stalin became, like Churchill, Defence Minister as well as Prime Minister; in August, like Hitler, Commander-in-Chief too. But titles do not make victories and his plight, as he himself saw it in this month, is revealed by his avowal to Harry Hopkins, Roosevelt's special emissary, that he would welcome American troops on any part of Russian soil under unrestricted American command. But by the autumn, he, like Russia, had weathered the first storm and was ready to face the next. He reorganized the higher commands and imposed his will on his commanders. The system of dual military and party control in the armed services, abolished shortly before the war began, had been reintroduced a few weeks after the German attack and command of three Fronts entrusted to Voroshilov and Zhdanov in the north, Timoshenko and Bulganin in the centre and Budyenny and Kruschchev in the south. Budyenny, a dashing hero with a big moustache but a little brain, was later relieved and succeeded by Timoshenko, who was replaced in the vital central sector first by Konev and then by Zhukov.

On 23 August the pause on the German side ended. The attack was resumed – in the south Guderian's armour was switched from Bock's Army Group Centre to Rundstedt's Army Group South. Two days later Dnepropetrovsk fell and the Russians blew up the great dam at Zaporozhe which supplied the power for the mass of industries in the Dnieper bend, a self-mutilation which proclaimed that they had little hope of recapturing lost territory in the near future. Kiev was now at the western tip of a Russian salient, half encircled and urgently threatened. To Budyenny and Kruschchev its loss seemed certain and its abandonment a strategic necessity, but Stalin insisted on a fight to the finish. This was not pure stubbornness. Stalin may have reasoned that Budyenny, whose forces were larger than those facing him, ought to be able to hold Kiev; that in any case any delay was worth while in order to check an advance which threatened to envelop Moscow; and that the retreat of so large a force at this juncture would be psychologically disastrous. Kiev had to pay the price, which turned out to be very high. Four Russian armies were surrounded and when they surrendered on 17 September the number of prisoners who fell into the German bag (even if they were fewer than the German claim of 665,000) was immense. Here, as elsewhere in this savage war, the prisoners were worse off than the dead, for the Germans frequently failed to give them medical assistance or to feed them properly. From Kiev the Germans swept on over the Ukraine; Odessa was abandoned, Kharkov taken; Rostov was lost but recovered.

In the centre Guderian's armour, switched back to this sector after a mere couple of weeks in the Ukraine, prepared for its last thrust of the year, the drive for Moscow. It was launched at the beginning of October. Again the Russians were taken by surprise – their air reconnaissance and their wireless intelligence were poor – and they suffered enormous losses. Something like panic developed in Moscow, accentuated by reports of how the Germans were treating prisoners and civilians and the NKVD shooting deserters. Some two million Muscovites were evacuated in due order and others simply fled. But Stalin and his principal military advisers and civilian subordinates remained. Reinforcements were rushed up from Mongolia – a switch which was less of a gamble than it appeared on the surface because Stalin had been told by the spy Richard Sorge in Tokyo that Japan had decided to attack in the Pacific and not in north Asia.

After the first week of the German October offensive the weather broke and converted the battlefields into mud swamps so thick that tanks and vehicles struggled in them in vain. The Germans slithered and stuck and prayed for frost to harden the going again. But they were unlucky once more. The mud was late in freezing over, and when it did in November the temperature fell not only late but sharply, causing them terrible suffering. In December came blizzards which reduced visibility to fifty yards. Clothing was inadequate. A request by Guderian for winter supplies had earned him a rebuke for implying that they might be needed. The men stuffed their clothes with paper to keep warm, often with leaflets sent to the front to be showered upon the enemy and tell him that surrender was his only sane course. By Christmas the Germans had 100,000 cases of frostbite. Dysentery was rife. Like their comrades in the Luftwaffe the army had no anti-freeze. Their guns would not fire. Yet they were constantly harassed, usually by small parties of Russians at night. The intense cold and snow also prevented supplies of food from reaching them. What food they had often had to be cut with axes or saws. Soup froze if a man paused for a minute in getting it into his mouth. The medal earned by these afflicted men was nicknamed the Order of Frozen Flesh. Some committed suicide. Looking back over the war when he came to write about this time Guderian recalled 'the endless expanse of Russian snow during this winter of our misery . . . the icy wind that blew across it . . . too thin shelter . . . insufficiently clothed, half-starved men'.

By the first week in November the Germans were within fifty miles of Moscow; by the end of the month twenty miles. The final German assault came on 1 December and failed. Stalin had already decided to counter-attack before the year ended. Local and limited counter-attacks during November had not been able to stem the German advance but a stronger and more coordinated attack launched on 5 December pushed the Germans back as Stalin harried his generals and these in turn drove their men forward. This was the first appreciable Russian victory and there were more crumbs of comfort in the south where the Kertch peninsula was

recaptured and Sebastopol held. Hitler failed to emulate Napoleon's feat
– in 1941 or ever. Perhaps if he had taken Guderian's advice to concentrate
on Moscow he might have succeeded; and perhaps he would then have
won his war in the east. But neither of these propositions is certain. What
is certain is that in the first week of December 1941 one of the most
precarious moments of the war was reached and passed.

Leningrad too survived, although threatened by famine as well as arms.
The siege of Leningrad became one of the epic events of the war. The
magnificent capital of Peter the Great, built on either side of the Neva
and on the islands in its estuary, contained three million inhabitants, of
whom close on one million died in the siege. When the German invasion
was launched desperate but belated preparations were made to withstand
an assault and the Russian forces renewed their attack on the Finns, who,
despite protestations of neutrality, were expected to make common cause
with the Germans. Finnish forces re-occupied territory lost in the war of
1939–40 but Field Marshal Mannerheim was unwilling to overstep the
1939 frontiers (which his troops reached in August) and, partly in response
to American pressure, refused persistent German requests for an alliance
and joint operations against Leningrad.

The northern group of German armies advanced rapidly. It reached the
river Drina in four days, pressed on to Pskov after a short pause and
might perhaps have captured Leningrad before the end of July. Its leading
units, which had covered 470 miles in three weeks, were only sixty miles
from the city but at this point they halted and did not resume the advance
until 8 August. Hitler – in a mood not unlike the one which had allowed
the British to escape from Dunkirk – wanted to nurse his armour and
reduce the city by siege and air attack, after which it was to be razed to
the ground as a symbolic extirpation of its eponymous guardian, the
founder of the bolshevist state. He seems always to have been in two minds
about Leningrad. On the one hand he willed its obliteration, but when he
was thinking in broad strategic terms he did not want to waste before it
large forces which should be advancing into the heart of Russia. The first
shells fell on it in the first days of September. Zhukov arrived to direct the
defences on the 11th. The city had been all but completely invested a few
days earlier.

Leningrad had been the scene of the most celebrated episodes in the
overthrow of the Tsars (whose capital it had been) and the jealous defender
ever since that date of all that was purest in communist tradition and
doctrine. Inside this city men, women and children now laboured ceaselessly on civil defence and emergency fortifications; to seaward the Russian
Baltic fleet, whether riding the waters or imprisoned in the ice, provided

an extra ring of guns; even the guns of the ancient cruiser *Aurora* which had been turned into a museum were removed and put into the first line; industries and population were evacuated to the east; patriotic enthusiasm was fanned by propaganda lectures. Leningrad was besieged from September 1941 to January 1944. It had at the outset only one to two months' supply of basic foods, much of which was then destroyed by air attack. Unlikely substitutes were turned into eatables. Uneatables were eaten. Equally catastrophic was the shortage of water for elementary cleansing and of medicines. Deaths from hunger began to occur before the end of 1941 and the monthly rate soon reached the annual average; deaths from privation ran at the rate of several thousands a day and created a serious threat to the morale as well as the health of the survivors, who were already exhausted by extreme cold, hard work, hunger, disease, and the collapse of public services. On Christmas Day 1941 about 4,000 died. The most serious threat came in November 1941 when Tikhvin was taken by the Germans. This town, due east of Leningrad, was on the railway by which the Russians hoped to keep the city supplied, and when it was lost the Russians were compelled to begin the construction of a road from a point safely east of Tikhvin to the eastern shore of Lake Ladoga, whence supplies would be taken across the water or the ice to the south-western corner of the lake thirty-five miles from the city. The first plan was to build a railway line across the ice but a large frozen lake is far from being a flat surface and the first train left its rails near the beginning of its journey. Next came a plan to tear up the city's tramlines and re-lay them on the lake but this scheme was abandoned almost as soon as it was thought of. Finally, the Russians began to build a road and collect lorries – from Moscow and from the American and British vehicles arriving in the far north – to make the passage by night, in the bitter cold of an exceptionally bitter winter (the temperature averaged twenty degrees below freezing over a whole month) and against the fierce north-east winds which constantly swept the surface of the lake. Some supplies got in this way but it was a desperate expedient which could hardly have saved the city. Fortunately the Russians recaptured Tikhvin in December. The encirclement of Leningrad was never complete because the Russians kept possession of the south-western corner of Lake Ladoga. Nevertheless starvation was sometimes only one or two days off during this first and most exacting winter of the war. In Berlin invitations to a reception in Leningrad to be attended by Hitler were printed but never sent out.

Leningrad won a further reprieve in 1942 owing to the resistance of Sebastopol where the German 11th Army, which was designated to switch to Leningrad after the fall of Sebastopol, was not freed from its southern

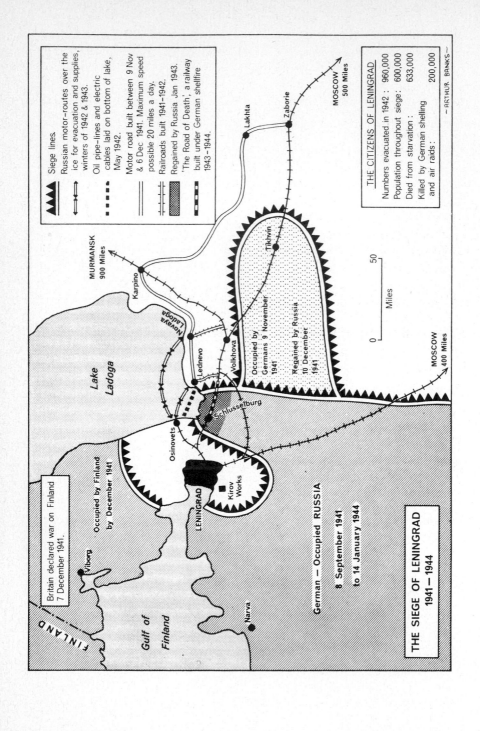

THE SIEGE OF LENINGRAD
1941-1944

German – Occupied RUSSIA

8 September 1941
to 14 January 1944

– ARTHUR BANKS –

THE CITIZENS OF LENINGRAD

Numbers evacuated in 1942 :   960,000
Population throughout siege: 600,000
Died from starvation :   633,000
Killed by German shelling
and air raids :   200,000

Britain declared war on Finland
7 December 1941.

Occupied by Finland
by December 1941

Occupied by
Germans 9 November
1941

Regained by Russia
10 December
1941

FINLAND

Gulf of
Finland

Lake
Ladoga

Viborg

Narva

LENINGRAD

Kirov
Works

Osinovets

Schlusselburg

Lednevo

Volkhova

Novaya Ladoga

Karpino

Lakhta

Zaborie

Tikhvin

MURMANSK
900 Miles

MOSCOW
500 Miles

MOSCOW
400 Miles

0   50
  Miles

Siege lines.

Russian motor-routes over the
ice for evacuation and supplies,
winters of 1942 & 1943.

Oil pipe-lines and electric
cables laid on bottom of lake,
May 1942.

Motor road built between 9 Nov
& 6 Dec 1941. Maximum speed
possible 20 miles a day.

Railroads built 1941–1942.

Regained by Russia Jan 1943.

'The Road of Death', a railway
built under German shellfire
1943–1944.

task until July and then only moved north partially. A German attack on Leningrad in the autumn of 1942 was forestalled and nipped in the bud by a Russian counter-offensive and shortly afterwards 11th Army was again concentrated in the south. A Russian operation at the beginning of 1943 eased, though it did not remove, the German blockade by opening a new corridor for supplies from across the lake but complete relief had to await the general collapse of the Germans. Leningrad was not freed from attack until January 1944. It received the Order of Lenin. Its endurance and its sufferings and triumph have been immortalized in Shostakovich's seventh symphony, not the greatest work of that great composer, but written and first performed in the most extraordinary circumstances – in the city during the siege. (The most poignant musical cries of the war are Richard Strauss's lament over the destruction of Munich, *Metamorphosen*, the thrilling pathos of the middle movement of Bela Bartók's Concerto for Orchestra, and Britten's setting of poems by Wilfred Owen in his *War Requiem*.)

At the end of 1941 the German conquests in the USSR were vast, but Hitler had not defeated the Russians. He had failed to take Moscow or Leningrad, had taken Rostov and lost it again, had overrun the Crimea but been baulked before Sebastopol, and had suffered in the USSR casualties of about three quarters of a million, of whom one in four were dead. The very arguments about priorities – Moscow or Leningrad, Leningrad or the Ukraine, Sebastopol or Leningrad – prove that from the very beginning the German forces were stretched. Once Russian resistance was not wholly broken within weeks, the German command faced choices because the tasks were too many. The same applied to the Luftwaffe. In the first four weeks of the campaign a force of 3,000 aircraft averaged 2,500 sorties a day and thereafter 1,500–2,000 a day for the rest of the year. Their performance was excellent (the Me. 109F, faster but less heavily armed than the Me. 109E, was making its first operational appearance) but in spite of this remarkable effort the force was too thinly spread for its commitments and again switches told the tale – to Leningrad at one moment and then back again to the central front for the main assault on Moscow. Air raids on Moscow were hardly more than token gestures. The city was attacked seventy-six times between the beginning of the campaign and the end of 1941 but the weight of the attack was often trivial. The largest force employed in a single night was 127 and in far more cases than not the bombers could be counted in single figures. The Luftwaffe's reserves were sometimes worryingly low and at the end of the year the mercurial Udet committed suicide. Thus the startling achievements of 1941 on the ground and in the air had by December essentially failed, and a fresh advance in 1942 was to culminate in the disaster of Stalingrad, whereafter the two great land powers of Europe were measured against one another until the Germans were utterly repulsed.

On the Russian side crippling casualties – at least three million men and probably 18,000 tanks in the first disastrous three months – were offset by patriotic determination and furious despair which mounted as the Germans resorted to monstrous cruelties. Sadistic and debauched proconsuls and their henchmen were invested with authority in the rear of the advancing armies (whose commanders preferred to turn a blind eye to proceedings which disgusted them – within limits). Mass executions and the deliberate burying alive of half killed victims united and fired all Russians who escaped this appalling demonstration of the dark side of human nature. At the top Stalin's nerve held, a new layer of brilliant field commanders was moving into the crucial positions and Soviet Intelligence from agents in Switzerland and Germany itself as well as Tokyo was providing a reliable basis for the conduct of the war. One of these agents was Richard Sorge in Tokyo, a handsome and talented German in Russian pay who had become a personal friend and confidant of the German Ambassador and had the almost incredible experience of discovering the answer to one of Stalin's most vital questions on the very eve of Barbarossa and on the day before the Japanese police arrested him as a spy. From his contacts with the Japanese cabinet Sorge was able to tell Stalin that the Japanese were not going to attack the Russians in Mongolia, but the Americans in the Pacific. When Sorge's information was confirmed by Japanese inactivity, Stalin began to nerve himself to denude his eastern frontiers. He did so just in time, although he still hesitated until he was within sight of the end of the short Siberian campaigning season. Reinforcements from the east, including 1,700 tanks and 1,500 aircraft, reached Zhukov on the Moscow front at the beginning of November at the point when the Russians had drained the last reserves from their training schools and the Germans thought that the Russians were finished.

The German failure to defeat the Russians in 1941 was the second and greatest turning point in the war in Europe. If Hitler could not beat the Russians in six months he could not beat them at all. He had prepared for a short war. He had not prepared for and he could not win a long one. Nor could his relations with his generals survive a long one. At the end of 1941 he took over command of the army himself from Brauchitsch and nine months later he would dismiss Halder, his Chief of Staff. More important perhaps, the handling of the 1941 campaign had produced quarrels with more highly respected field commanders and had deepened the mutual distrust between Hitler and the officer corps. By the end of the year Guderian, Rundstedt and Hoepner had all been dismissed. Others would follow later. In assuming personal command in the war in the east Hitler jettisoned his ablest generals.

It was at this point – the end of 1941 – that the European war begun in Poland in September 1939 was converted into a world war. On 7 December the Japanese attack on the American fleet at Pearl Harbor opened the war in the Pacific and made the United States a belligerent in that theatre. With one of the most startling gestures of the whole war Hitler immediately made the Americans belligerents in the Atlantic and Europe as well by a declaration of war. Germany was thenceforward engaged in a war that had spread right round the world.

CHAPTER 10
War with America

ON 11 December 1941 Hitler declared war on the United States of America. In retrospect the actual participation of the United States in the war in Europe and the hugeness of its contribution to victory obscure the fact that, all through 1941, the United States was still largely unwilling to become a belligerent. Many Americans felt that the war was not theirs, in the sense that it could affect no vital American interest; and those who nevertheless felt emotionally involved hoped that they could contribute to the defeat of the dictators without having to send their own sons to be killed.

Europeans have become used, during the twentieth century, to describing their wars as World wars, the implication being that everybody of any consequence automatically gets involved once Europeans start fighting. To many Europeans in both World wars American participation took the form of a belated recognition of the obvious. But it was not obvious that a European war must become a World war or that the United States must send fighting men to Europe. Even after the United States became a belligerent Americans regarded their country's intervention as assistance to friends in need rather than as the defence of essential American interests. There was a lot to be said for this view. The American continent was a long way from Europe. It could not be hit or invaded by German air or land forces and could only be marginally harassed by naval ones. Hitler showed in any case no desire to do any of these things. There was (save from Japan) no external threat to the United States, no enemy within sight. Moreover this commonsensical geographical view of the matter fitted comfortably into American history and mythology – the creation of the United States as a society detached from Europe and its ills, a community which had better things to do than get involved in the deceits and squabbles which constituted European politics.

Not that the United States had in fact been as isolationist as it believed itself, and was believed by others, to be. In the famous debates in the Senate after the end of the First World War about adopting the Treaty of Versailles and joining the League of Nations there had at no time been a majority against the new internationalism. Debate had been about the conditions to be attached to ratifying the treaty, and the combined forces of those who wanted unconditional acceptance and those who wanted conditional acceptance decisively outnumbered the isolationists who wanted no acceptance at all. The entry of the United States into the League was vetoed by the Senate only because the compact body of Wilsonian internationalist Senators joined forces with the small band of isolationists to defeat the amendments proposed by Republican internationalists. The event was decided by Wilson's determination to have all or nothing. The Senate's action was nevertheless interpreted as a signal of American withdrawal. Nor was this interpretation altogether wrong, for the League became the principal outward and visible sign and the principal organ of international involvement, and it never had the United States among its members. Yet the United States was willy-nilly enmeshed in European affairs because of the war debts owed to it by its recent allies, debts which these allies could not pay unless they in their turn were paid the war reparations owed to them by Germany. Consequently the United States took an active part in the attempts to sort out these problems, so much so that the two main plans for settling the German debt – the Dawes Plan and the Young Plan – were named after the American members of the teams which produced them. But this special kind of involvement, backward looking to the last war, was no pointer to a wider international involvement. On the contrary, it kept alive memories of the unpleasantness of war and added to them resentments about allies who, after the war, defaulted on their financial engagements.

Further than that, there grew up in the United States a suspicion that the American declaration of war in April 1917 had been engineered by chicanery. Catastrophic events tend to breed, a generation later, a critique which probes for hidden, and perhaps disreputable, motives. Americans were perturbed by the notion that the arms industry – the merchants of death as they were more picturesquely called before the invention of the sterner term military-industrial complex – had promoted belligerence for the profits to be made out of it, while yet other Americans blamed Wilson for feebly succumbing to cunning allied propaganda about the wickedness of U-boats. Criticisms of this nature became so strong that they were investigated, and given added circulation, by a committee of the Senate – the Nye Committee – between 1934 and 1936. This scrutiny contributed to the mood which induced Congress to pass the Neutrality Acts of 1935, 1936 and 1937. These Acts were intended to make clear the American resolve to keep out of another war and to prevent a President from leading the nation into one. Neutrality, a posture usually adopted by small states to avoid getting hurt in the quarrels of the great, became paradoxically the statutory refuge of the greatest power on earth. In order to give body to this general policy the Congress decreed that American arms were not to be delivered to belligerents or to be carried in American ships (but belligerents might buy non-military goods provided they paid cash for them and carried them away in non-American vessels); further, the President was empowered to take other precautionary measures by, for example, forbidding American citizens to travel in belligerent ships. It was in implementation of these Acts that Roosevelt issued in September 1939 a declaration of American neutrality.

There has been much debate over the attitudes of the American people towards external affairs, and even more about President Roosevelt's role in leading his country towards war. American isolationism was, as already noted, rooted in history and plausibility. The United States came into existence as a result of war against a European power and was peopled by migrants who left Europe out of distaste or discomfort. With an enormous and comparatively empty country to explore and exploit they concluded, as well they might, that other people's affairs were of no account and that they themselves had no vital interests beyond their own bounds (with the exception of the central American and Caribbean lands to the south which were not so distant as not to matter). The threat to the Union in the 1860s and the problems of reconstruction after the Civil War intensified the tendency to introspection, but two forces in particular were working against it. The first was the diversification of American economic interests and their consequent expansion overseas, coupled with a growth in American power which both tempted and enabled the United States to scan larger horizons. These material considerations were reinforced by the moralistic ingredient in American society, a factor in the American make-up which derived partly from the puritan origins of many of its communities and partly from that remoteness from events which allowed Americans to think of external politics in general terms of right and wrong instead of the more pragmatic categories of expediency and prudence to which Europeans, with their eyes on close neighbours and sensitive frontiers, were more prone.

This moralistic trend found expression, in political affairs, in a self-dedication to freedom and democracy, and this dedication made nonsense of isolationism. The isolationist attitude had found expression in neutrality, which is the formal expression of the emotion of isolationism. Covertly, however, neutrality negated isolationism, for whereas isolationism asserted that other people's conflicts could be overlooked, neutrality could mean that they were looked at and found to be equally lacking in merit on both sides. Thus neutrality was a Trojan horse in the isolationist camp, since Europe between the wars proved on inspection not to be an arena where unregenerate Europeans were simply tangling over issues of no significance. On the contrary, Fascism threatened democracy, Nazism threatened even more basic human norms; there were fights abroad in which all good men must join to put down brutality and faithlessness and uphold democracy and civilized manners. So a conflict developed within the United States. As the troubles of Europe and Asia became more troubled (by, for example, the Japanese attacks on Manchuria and China and the Spanish civil war), there was an atavistic and very powerful resolve to keep all the clearer of them, but at the same time a minority which concerned itself with foreign affairs developed a strong reprobation of the aggressive and fascist powers. Being neutral turned out to be more difficult than it used to be. To most Americans neutrality meant keeping out of wars, but to some Americans it began to appear that neutrality in Hitler's wars meant keeping out of a just war. Keeping out of wars was self-evidently sensible, but keeping out of a just war was not so clearly right.

The debate over Roosevelt's personal responsibility in bringing the United States into war has been not untinged by the emotions roused by Roosevelt in issues which have nothing to do with the war. Roosevelt was one of those men who can instil passionate enthusiasms and also intense hostility, even hatred. By his keenest admirers he has been credited with the foresight of genius; to his bitter enemies he was little better than a charlatan. The only common ground here is the acknowledgement that he had uncommon influence over the course of events. This is not the place for a complete assessment of Roosevelt as President, but we have to inquire into the nature of his influence, the use he made of it and the evolution of his policy in relation to international crises and to war.

Roosevelt was elected President in 1932 in the wake of exceptional turmoil in the United States. Although Americans had no external enemy to fear, they had experienced another kind of fear and disaster. The economic collapse which began so dramatically on Wall Street on 23 October 1929 took away from millions the basic material conditions of their lives and left them feeling helpless, bewildered and scared. The shock to morale was all the greater because, unlike the soldier who in some sense covenants with death, the brusquely impoverished father of a family had not contemplated this material bereavement, had done nothing to deserve it and scarcely understood it. There was more panic in the face of this economic blast than in the face of rifle fire or bombs. It was up to Roosevelt to do something about it and he did do, and was seen to do, lots of things. Not all these things were useful or even sensible but all of them, the failures as well as the successes, were activities and activity was a large part of what

was needed. One can argue about the value of planting thousands of trees
or of creating new government agencies, but it is impossible to doubt that
the sum total of sheer activity by government became transmuted into a
bank of popular confidence on which Roosevelt was ever afterwards able
to draw. He became at once a strong President, capable of weathering
storms and of giving a lead, the more so because the strength of his
political position was buttressed by exceptional (though not infallible)
political skill, superior intelligence and eloquence. But Roosevelt was no
revolutionary or visionary innovator, either domestically or in foreign
affairs. At home he was a compassionate, managerial conservative whose
New Deal meant some change in the distribution of power, little change
in the direction of policy. In external affairs his attitudes were at first no
different from those of millions of Americans. He was an isolationist in
the sense of wanting to keep out of foreign affairs on the assumption that
these spelt trouble, but he was not opposed to playing a part where no
trouble seemed to brew. Thus, he proposed in 1935 that the United States
join the Permanent Court of International Justice, but was defeated by
the Senate. He not only took an interest in disarmament but offered to
join a European collective security system if the Europeans would first
disarm. He was riled by the failure of the Disarmament Conference in
1933 and blamed Germany, which was seeking to increase its armament,
rather than France or Great Britain, which were simply declining to
reduce theirs. On the other hand he allowed Hitler's introduction of conscription in 1935 to pass without protest even though it was a breach of
the American-German peace treaty of 1921 (the treaty concluded by the
United States in place of the Treaty of Versailles). Again like millions of
Americans, Roosevelt, disposed though he was to criticize the fumbling
policies and imperial philosophies of France and Great Britain, was
coming to regard Nazi Germany as nastier and more dangerous – though
not in the same devilish category as the USSR. The remilitarization of
the Rhineland in 1936 added to the general uneasiness and to the share of
blame to be attributed to Germany. Nazi anti-semitism also began to
have its effect. It offended decent Gentiles as well as American Jewry
(which counted for more than something in Roosevelt's own state of New
York), but on the other hand there was good business to be done with
Germany and it entered nobody's head in Washington that government
could or should interfere with business. Roosevelt and the American
people, like European leaders and peoples, were divided and unclear about
trends in Europe during the thirties and about what initiatives, if any, to
take in respect of them. But they were becoming increasingly anti-Nazi

and so anti-German, and this trend was fed by the association of Japan with Germany. Both countries came to be seen as cruel and power-hungry, associated moreover not only by their domestic oppressiveness and external aggressiveness but also in their economic policies which were imposing a blatant economic hegemony in their respective spheres of influence in place of the American ethos of the Open Door which was not only more subtle and more amiable but also calculated to serve American commercial interests.

In November 1936 Roosevelt was re-elected President by a margin of 11 million votes (as against 7 million in 1932). Foreign affairs played little part in the electioneering and what Roosevelt had to say was along conventional keep-out-of-trouble lines. During his second term Roosevelt suffered a decline in popularity which was to be marked by the reduction of his majority to 5 million votes in 1940. The New Deal was not wholly successful and very far from being universally popular. The President's tussle with the Supreme Court and the manoeuvres by which he tried to pack it lost him the support and respect of many who had been among his warmest admirers. Moreover, if tradition was anything to go by, he would cease to be President in 1940 because no President had ever tried to serve more than two terms. He was still a strong President and an intelligent and eloquent one, but his strength was flecked by failures and by the running out of his time. He was not well placed to innovate in foreign affairs, especially if innovation meant running a risk of war. But foreign affairs imposed themselves on his attention. The Japanese attack on China in 1937 with its reminder of the growth of Japanese power and the consequent threat to American power in the Pacific posed for Americans a problem of a special kind. In Great Britain, where it was axiomatic that a war against Germany, Italy and Japan at once would be suicidal, the question debated was whom to conciliate: many people's first choice, notably in the Foreign Office, was Italy, but others, notably in the Treasury and in the services (the pledge that Australia and New Zealand would be protected from Japan by the Royal Navy was a constant consideration and was reaffirmed at the Imperial Conference of 1937) argued that the growth of Japanese power meant that Great Britain should revert to the alliance with Japan which had been abandoned after the First World War under American pressure. But Americans did not see Japan that way. An American-Japanese alliance was an impossibility and so American-Japanese rivalry created an external threat such as Hitler never posed. It was in the context of the Pacific and East Asia that the United States began to evolve a policy of meeting a threat by extending to an ally – in this case

China – all aid short of war and within the Neutrality Act. Moreover, Japanese aggression affected American public opinion owing to the extent of pro-Chinese feeling in the United States.

Partly in response to these worries on his eastern flank and partly because he wanted to be useful, Roosevelt tried in the last two years of peace to mediate in European affairs. He thought of meeting Hitler (as, later, he would hope to resolve other problems by personal contact with Stalin). He proposed a conference of neutrals to discuss modes of international behaviour, disarmament and access to raw materials. Although offended by the manners and behaviour of the dictators, he thought of himself at this time as one of the neutrals rather than as one of the democrats. Nor did the leading democrats do much to swing him to their side. Chamberlain, deep in his ineffective attempts to make friends with Italy and Germany, did his best to head off the American President. He wanted no joint Anglo-American initiative and preferably no American initiative at all – at this point; for it is only fair to add that, under some pressure from cabinet colleagues and the British Ambassador in Washington, he kept up his correspondence with Roosevelt and left a way open for an American initiative later on. Roosevelt might have overridden these obstacles if he had had any clear idea of what to do, but beyond offering his good offices in a vague and general way he was essentially without a European policy. It was hardly possible for him to have such a policy so long as the precondition of all American activity in Europe was to minimize involvement. He did not intend to fight the dictators and there was at this time no government in Europe which wanted him to. He was reduced to following events – in both senses of that phrase. He had little faith in Chamberlain's manoeuvring to avoid war over Czechoslovakia, but privately supported Chamberlain in the absence of anything else to do and publicly stated that the United States would not fight if France and Great Britain went to war for Czechoslovakia. Like most people he was relieved when war was avoided at Munich; like many people he was shocked by Hitler's breach of the Munich agreement and the annihilation of Czechoslovakia in March 1939. By this time his ineffectiveness in European affairs had strengthened Hitler's view that he did not have to worry about the United States, but round about this same time Roosevelt was becoming convinced that war was certain and American involvement at least a possibility. Within six months war had started.

Whereas Churchill was temperamentally a man of action upon whom full responsibility fell after war had begun, Roosevelt was an intellectual in a situation of half-peace half-war. His country was not equipped for war militarily or industrially and his fellow citizens were not ready for it psychologically. His nature and his circumstances alike made him gingerly in pace, and it was only as circumstances developed that he was able to resolve his hesitations about what American opinion would endorse and what he himself ought to do. To Americans the war in Europe presented itself as a contest between Germany on the one hand and Great Britain and France on the other. The question was who would win. A second question was whether it mattered to the United States who won. At the outset Roosevelt established a distinction: the United States was formally a neutral but it cared about the result of the war and, since it cared, it should use 'all methods short of war' to help Great Britain and France to defeat Hitler. This position did not go unchallenged. A not inconsiderable part of the American press and a number of influential public figures were either hostile to Great Britain or entranced with Nazi ideas or genuinely indifferent. Anti-British and anti-imperial groups were, if limited, vocal. There was no surge of pro-British feeling until the Battle of Britain (in which a number of American volunteers took part in defiance of the laws of their country), and even the Battle of Britain had only moderate effect in the western United States and less still in the psychologically more remote Middle West. On the other hand pro-German propaganda was an almost complete failure. The German-American Bund never had more than 6,000 members and could not efface the image of the Nazi as a bully.

But however partisan Americans might become it still did not follow that they could see the war as one which affected American national interests. It was difficult to believe that the United States, bounded by the Atlantic and Pacific Oceans, was not also protected by them. To the ordinary American it appeared that, although there might be a moral case for helping the democracies to defeat Nazism, there were no strategic issues of self-interest which required the United States to make war. The argument, a familiar commonplace in Great Britain, that no state must be allowed to become all-powerful in Europe did not make sense to a people separated from Europe by the Atlantic Ocean and not merely by the English Channel. In the thirties the speeds which were to be reached within a generation and the weapons which were to annihilate distances as well as cities were undreamt of by all save a few.

If there was a danger it seemed more likely to emerge from Latin America. Recollecting perhaps German attempts in the First World War to get Mexico, in alliance with Japan, to make war on the United States, and greatly exaggerating the potential threat from the Germans settled in the southern parts of the American continent, the United States turned immediately on the outbreak of war to the problem of immunizing the

New World from it. In October 1939 the American states met at Panama in an inter-American conference and agreed to quarantine the New World by proscribing transfers of territory within it from one European power to another and by designating a security zone extending 300–1,000 miles seaward from its eastern shores. Belligerents were required to abjure naval operations in this area. Great Britain, France and Germany contested the legality of this declaration but the British soon ceased to complain when they discovered that the United States was prepared to connive at infractions of the ban, even to the extent of helping to detect and locate German vessels.

Latin American attitudes to the war were compounded of three main strands. Through the historical Spanish connection and indigenous anti-communism there was sympathy for Franco and, by extension, for his fellow dictators in Europe. There was antipathy to the British blockade of European markets and, among the wealthier classes, grousing about the reduction in imported luxuries. Thirdly and perhaps most pertinently, all eyes were on Roosevelt and his manoeuvres between the traditional neutrality of the New World and his partiality for the democratic (if not the imperial) character of the anti-Axis allies. Pearl Harbor was therefore a climactic event since it precipitated the United States into open belligerence. Furthermore, many Latin Americans, while perceiving little real threat to their region from Germany, saw Japan as a more credible enemy. Within weeks of Pearl Harbor, all Latin America except Argentine and Chile broke off relations with Japan, Germany and Italy. Parts of Central America and the Caribbean were overrun by the United States in return for Lend-Lease and promises of financial and technical aid to sugar the pill of United States domination. Since Washington felt that this was no time for concern over the internal affairs of its neighbours, governments were strengthened by Washington's benevolence and liberal and revolutionary aspirations were stifled even more effectively than in German-occupied Europe.

In Mexico – the most delicate area because of its border with the United States, its nationalization of foreign oil companies in 1938 and memories of Japanese meddling in the First World War – ingrained antipathies were overridden by the exigencies and opportunities of war (some Mexicans did well out of exports of gold and other minerals to the United States) and Mexico took the extreme step of declaring war in May 1942 after U-boat attacks which sank Mexican vessels, drowned Mexican citizens and created popular outcry and a rare party political unity. A Mexican air unit was sent to the Pacific in the last year of the war – in order, like Cavour's dispatch of Sardinian troops to the Crimea, to raise Mexico's international standing. Only Brazil, which declared war on the Axis powers in August 1942 and on Japan in May 1945, sent a force to Europe (to Italy in 1944). It emerged from the war with the largest slice of Lend-Lease to Latin America and the strongest armed forces. The other major South American countries, Argentina and Chile, were the least keen to declare war, partly because of their mutual quarrel over the islands off the southern tip of the continent. They became nominal belligerents in 1945 under the threat of exclusion from the conference convened at San Francisco to create the United Nations. In Argentina a by-product of the war was the overthrow in 1943 of civilian rule, an event which led eventually to the elevation to the presidency in 1946 of Colonel Juan Domingo Perón. Washington regarded the post-1943 military régime as fascist and pro-German and attacked it with an outspoken vigour which was unusual among sovereign states and seriously alarmed the British who, besides stigmatizing Washington's handling of the situation as crude and crass, were nervous about the considerable British investments in Argentina and Great Britain's dependence on it for the meat ration.

The dangers from the German population of Latin America were largely a product of war nerves. There were 300,000 German nationals (*Reichsdeutsche*) and 1.75 million persons of German extraction (*Volksdeutsche*) in the sub-continent, and Nazi propaganda and German trade had both been intensified in the thirties, but the likelihood and consequences of pro-German coups were alike exaggerated. Here, as in other parts of the world, the *Reichsdeutsche* in particular were regarded as a disciplined fifth column which had been prepared by the External Affairs Department of the Nazi Party to play an active role in war. But out of about three million *Reichsdeutsche* living outside the Reich only 30,000 had been enrolled by the party by 1939, and the belief in the sinister efficiency of these people was a myth, a projection of the German reputation for thoroughness coupled with the glamorous novelty of the idea of the fifth column, a term coined during the Spanish civil war. (Absurd stories were spread with hysterical waywardness in many countries, particularly in Europe; these stories were reported by most of the world's leading newspapers and treated as undeniable by parliamentarians and others who raised a patriotic clamour for indiscriminate arrests; nobody was allowed to be what he seemed to be; thousands of innocent persons, including Jewish refugees from Germany, were seized and many of them were shot.)

In the two years and a bit which elapsed between Munich and the American elections of 1940 Roosevelt rearmed, tried to restore peace by diplomacy and gave what aid he could to the western allies. He had asked Congress in January 1938 for a 20 per cent increase in the navy allocations; his request had created an uproar but been granted. The same thing happened a year later when he asked for more money for the army and air forces. Early in 1940 he sent Under Secretary Sumner Welles on a tour of European capitals, sent a special emissary to the Vatican to initiate American-Papal mediation and tried to keep Italy out of the war. All these efforts were failures. The war went on and Ribbentrop, visiting Rome on the heels of Welles, extracted from Mussolini a promise to enter it at some unspecified date. The fall of France shifted American opinion, official and unofficial. After that catastrophe there was no significant opposition to huge and rapid rearmament, and a Selective Service Act was passed in September. The elimination of French power and the probable elimination (as it seemed) of British power too forced Americans to think about the consequences to themselves of the disappearance of two great friendly navies and the emergence of a new German-Italian naval power which had also annexed the French fleet. The United States made unconventionally strong representations to Pétain and his Navy Minister, Admiral Darlan, in order to prevent the French government from surrendering its fleet to Germany in the armistice negotiations. Here was a visible external threat similar to the growth of Japanese power in the Pacific. Roosevelt strengthened his cabinet by inviting two eminent Republicans, Henry L. Stimson (a former Secretary of State) and Frank Knox, to become his Secretaries of War and the Navy: unlike Churchill Roosevelt looked to the Right rather than the Left in constructing a war coalition.

When in 1940 it seemed that Hitler was winning the war rather easily Roosevelt still could do little to stop him. He had refused a request from the French government to send troops to Europe. But it was becoming plainer than ever that if Hitler was to be denied a complete victory more would be required of the United States than methods short of war. Helping the western allies meant ensuring the flow of traffic across the Atlantic against U-boats and German surface raiders. It meant supplies and protection; later it was to mean credit too. A first attempt to amend the Neutrality Act failed but Congress soon relented so far as to permit belligerents to buy military as well as non-military goods on a cash-and-carry basis. For the moment cash was not an immediate problem, but carrying was. Then, if the United States was to help protect the carriage, it would have to risk its own vessels and invite German retaliation, engaging in unneutral activities which might lead to war. Non-belligerence, which was essentially an attempt to get the best of two incompatible worlds – those of neutrality and partisanship – would be put at risk and would prove to be no more than the transitional stage from the one world to a full role in the other.

Roosevelt both saw and accepted the risks rather sooner than most people. Since the American people later proved by their actions that they accepted the consequences, Roosevelt might justly claim that his leadership had been endorsed and any deviousness which might have been involved condoned. But to some extent too his leadership determined the course. His simple presentation of the issues, his patience in unfolding his policies, his readiness to accept responsibility, and his calm handling of critical national decisions – for all the superficial detachment which he sometimes displayed as he turned from affairs of state to his stamp collection – these qualities inevitably led him to form and not merely observe the popular will. In which exercise of power he was giving an example of democratic leadership.

During 1940 Roosevelt resolved to seek a third term in the Presidency, an event not only unprecedented in American history but so obnoxious to American instincts that after the war it was prohibited by constitutional amendment. The war was not the only reason for this decision. He was deeply concerned to preserve the social innovations of the New Deal and he saw among leading figures in his own party no liberal Democrat upon whom he could rely to do this. But the conviction that the United States was going to become more deeply involved in war and that he should guide it also played a major part in his decision. At this stage Roosevelt developed the idea that the United States was in substance, if not formally, already under attack. He was a master of the art of democratic communication, and his regular fireside chats – one of the adroitest political uses of radio, which had at this period only been used effectively by politicians of a different stamp, Hitler and Mussolini – gave him the ear and the confidence of the people. They trusted him and when in 1940 they were asked to give him a third term 27 million of them decided to do so: his attractively unusual Republican opponent Wendell Wilkie (with whom in later years Roosevelt thought of making a progressive alliance and a new party) received 22 million votes, a big gap in a modern American presidential election. But it would be wrong to conclude that the 27 million who voted for Roosevelt did so because they were ready to fight against Hitler. They were with Roosevelt in wanting Hitler to be beaten – as were the great bulk of the 22 million who voted for Wilkie – but they wanted Hitler to be beaten by the British and were not yet convinced that the British could not do this without the United States as a fighting ally. Roosevelt himself still clung to the hope that the American role need not be a fighting one or that, if it came to fighting, the American share could be limited to sea and air and would not involve sending army conscripts overseas. During his campaign he promised again and again not to send Americans to fight in foreign lands 'except in case of attack' (on one occasion, subsequently much quoted against him, he left out the proviso) and there must have been many who voted for Roosevelt because he had kept the country out of war and who would have refused him a third term had they supposed that he would not continue to find ways of doing so. No opinion poll during the year before Pearl Harbor showed more than one in five Americans opting for war.

If in 1940 the defeat of France had been offset by the British success in the Battle of Britain, in 1941 the defeat of Great Britain became once more a possibility to be reckoned with. The threat to Great Britain at sea, which had come near to success in the First World War, was manifested on the first day of the Second when the German U-30 sank the British passenger ship *Athenia* (the victims included twenty-eight Americans). The threat at sea was posed by mines (laid by surface vessels, submarines or aircraft), surface raiders and U-boats. At the beginning of the war the magnetic mine did much damage to British shipping in coastal waters, but it was quickly mastered by technical counter-measures. Surface raiders, such as the pocket battleships *Graf Spee* and *Deutschland* whose exploits have already been narrated, caused much concern but comparatively little damage. The enduring enemy was the U-boat. Fortunately for the British, Doenitz's fleet was a small one. He divided his boats between Atlantic and North Sea raiding and mine-laying and in 1939 his operations were not too alarmingly successful: 114 merchantmen sunk, but at a cost of nine U-boats. (U-boats also sank the aircraft carrier *Courageous* in September and the battleship *Royal Oak* in Scapa Flow in October.) In 1940, however, the U-boat fleet, reinforced by a production drive, began to score abundantly. One convoy lost thirty-two ships in an attack which continued through four consecutive nights, and Hitler's new conquests gave him bases in Norway for U-boats and armed merchant raiders, bases for E-boats along the entire length of the English Channel, and bases for long-range aircraft – the F.W. 200 or Condor – which flew from Bordeaux over wide spaces of the western Atlantic and landed at Trondhjem in Norway, flying back the next day. Great Britain occupied the Faroes and Iceland when Denmark was overrun, but losses in this year mounted at an intolerable rate and Doenitz lost only twenty-two of his rapidly growing force.

Churchill turned to Roosevelt. A week after the British declaration of war in 1939 Churchill had begun, as First Lord of the Admiralty, an intimate correspondence with the President. He continued it when he became Prime Minister. The two men developed a very special relationship which was of incalculable benefit to Great Britain. This personal partnership, and its post-war institutionalization in the continuing Anglo-American alliance, appear so solid a part of the international scene that they have come to be regarded as a natural by-product of a common language and common traditions. In fact, however, Anglo-American relations were bad throughout the twenties and despite an improvement at the time of the London Conference in 1930 politicians on both sides continued to refer to each other privately in scathing, sometimes almost scurrilous, terms. There was neither trust nor liking between them. Their two countries were in the process of exchanging roles, particularly on the high seas where Great Britain's cherished naval supremacy was passing away, and against this background politicians sparred with conscious and unconscious jealousy. In constructing their alliance Churchill and Roosevelt had to work with a mixed legacy.

One of the first fruits of their special relationship was the destroyer-bases deal of September 1940 which placed in British hands fifty extra ships with which to prosecute the war against the U-boats. (A few weeks earlier Roosevelt, by the Ogdensburg agreement, had established a Joint Defence Board with belligerent Canada.) At this time Churchill was at least as worried about the war at sea as he was elated by victory in the Battle of Britain. Roosevelt, after lengthy study and intricate legal argument, agreed to transfer these fifty old but serviceable American destroyers to Great Britain in return for a promise never to surrender the British fleet and for the lease to the United States for ninety-nine years of six bases in the western Atlantic. (Two other bases were accepted as a gift. Churchill had wanted the two deals to be wholly distinct gifts but Roosevelt's advisers, already in difficulties about deciding whether the President could effect the exchange without recourse to Congress, insisted that there must be a substantial, related *quid pro quo*.) But by the end of 1940 British shipping losses were running at the rate of 300,000 tons a month and were destined to rise in February, March and April 1941 to 400,000, 500,000 and 600,000 tons. Great Britain was running out of cash too. The timing of American aid had become vital.

Roosevelt's policy was to aid Great Britain by all means short of war. So much was clear. What was unclear was how and how quickly aid could be made available and, more distantly, whether aid short of war was going to be enough. Soon after his re-election Roosevelt received an

urgent plea from Churchill. In reply he moved to depart from all sem-
blance of neutrality in order to ensure that Great Britain should receive
the tools it needed to survive. The device was Lend-Lease. He told the
American people that if a neighbour's house was on fire it was only
common sense and self-protection to lend him a hosepipe. The necessary
Bill, which the President always referred to as the Aid to Democracies
Bill, was introduced early in January 1941 and signed by the President on
11 March. Thereafter Great Britain placed orders for American materials
with the American government which purchased what was required from
American firms and paid them. The materials were then lent or leased to
the British in return for a promise of payment after the war: the United
States agreed to accept post-dated cheques in lieu of cash when there
was no cash left.

Lend-Lease was a gesture of very great moral significance. It buoyed
Great Britain up by promising to bring nearer the day when it would no
longer be fighting virtually alone. Churchill wanted American belligerence
even more than he wanted American aid, and to him, as to most people in
Great Britain, financial aid was the prelude to co-belligerence, not an
alternative. The material benefits of Lend-Lease were at first limited.
Until some months after Pearl Harbor and Hitler had forced the United
States into war on two fronts American industry was largely on a peacetime basis, the main exception being the Liberty ship programme which
launched its first ship in September 1941; Great Britain's own war production was greater than that of the United States. During 1941 Great Britain
got little more from the United States than it had imported in 1940 and
continued to pay cash for most of it. But what did come was important:
for example, in 1941 a million tons of food (a fifteenth of British imports
of food) and enough fuel oil to raise stocks from a danger point of 4.5
million tons to 7 million tons, which was maximum storage capacity.

The Lend-Lease Act was followed a few months later by an equally
significant act, drawing the United States closer to war. When Hitler
attacked the USSR, Roosevelt, following Churchill, promised aid to
Stalin. The attack was no surprise to Roosevelt and his advisers who had
known from secret sources from early in 1941 that Hitler had signed his
first directive for the campaign. Roosevelt and his Secretary of State,
Cordell Hull, had been doing their best to keep on reasonably good terms
with the USSR, but the anti-Soviet voices in the United States were
much more numerous than the anti-British ones had been. Anti-communism was a powerful emotion, especially among Roman Catholics.
Stalin's seizure of half Poland, his war on Finland and his annexation of

Estonia, Latvia and Lithuania caused bitter anger, which was not confined to the émigré communities from these countries. The time would come when admiration for Russian resistance to Hitler, especially during the battles for Stalingrad, would raise a tide of pro-Russian feeling, while at other levels and later in the war Churchill was to be criticized for being too anti-Russian, but American sympathy for the Russians never sufficed to efface underlying emotions of an opposite order and even at the fearful juncture of Stalingrad's agony – when Americans watched with genuinely bated breath and, perhaps, with less mixed emotions about the Russians than for many years before or after – there was (as too in the Battle of Britain) no plan to do anything to save the city if the last hour should strike. Roosevelt's promise of aid in 1941, therefore, was an act of leadership from which another President, heeding the cross-currents within his country, might have refrained.

Whatever the value of this act in time to come, when it was translated into $11.3 billions' worth of supplies, the immediate effect was slight and could not be otherwise. Even in relation to Great Britain Roosevelt was still treading warily. The Lend-Lease Act itself underlined the peculiar posture of the United States by once more expressly prohibiting the entry of American vessels into combat areas and the use of the US navy for convoy duties. But less than four weeks later the sinking in a single night of ten ships in a British convoy of twenty-one showed that further steps were necessary if the United States set more store by the defeat of Hitler than keeping out of a shooting war. Roosevelt ordered the occupation of Greenland and contemplated occupying the Azores. A force of three battleships with an aircraft carrier, cruisers and destroyers was transferred in May from the Pacific to the Atlantic. In the same month Roosevelt declared an unlimited national emergency. American shipyards were opened to British ships in need of repair. American ocean patrols were extended, shadowed Axis vessels and reported their positions to British units every few hours. A number of coastal cutters were transferred to the British flag. Roosevelt adopted and popularized a phrase of Jean Monnet dubbing the United States 'the arsenal of democracy'. But the United States remained officially non-belligerent and even the sinking of the *Robin Moor* by the Germans provoked no declaration of war.

In May the British scored a ringing success at sea. Raeder, who had more faith in capital ships than Doenitz and was continuously frustrated by Hitler's refusal to allow the indiscriminate use of submarines, renewed his surface challenge. Attempts to do this in 1940 had proved abortive, but in 1941 two new ships, the battleship *Bismarck* and the cruiser *Prinz*

Eugen, were ready. Raeder planned a great offensive with them in conjunction with *Scharnhorst* and *Gneisenau*, which had been at Brest since March. But these two battle cruisers had suffered damage and had not recovered by the time that *Bismarck* and *Prinz Eugen* were ready to sail from Gdynia on 18 May: they never sailed the high seas again.

Bismarck was sighted by a Swedish ship soon after she left her German berth, and London was quickly informed. From Bergen she proceeded with *Prinz Eugen* north-westward, passing north of Iceland and thence into the Denmark Strait between Iceland and Greenland. Emerging from the Strait into the Atlantic the two ships were spotted and shadowed. Battle was joined west of Iceland soon after dawn on 24 May by the battleship *Prince of Wales*, also newly commissioned, and the twenty-year-old battle-cruiser *Hood*. *Hood* was sunk within minutes by a shell which pierced her decks, and all but three of her complement of 1,419 died. Half an hour later *Prince of Wales*, also hit, was forced to break away, but the aircraft carrier *Victorious* came up and delivered a first attack before the end of the day. *Bismarck* managed to shake off her pursuers, turned for Brest, but then incomprehensibly gave away her position by breaking wireless silence with a long message to the German Admiralty. Even then she might have escaped – as her instructions required her to do – for the bearings obtained by shore stations from her intercepted wireless transmission were wrongly interpreted when relayed to Admiral Sir Francis Tovey's flagship *King George V* which led the chase in the wrong direction. The British Admiralty, however, correctly divined *Bismarck*'s intentions and early on the 26th an aircraft of RAF Coastal Command sighted her. A separate naval force which included the aircraft carrier *Ark Royal* intercepted her and *Ark Royal*'s aircraft, having first attacked but missed one of their own attendant cruisers, so wounded *Bismarck* that she became a sitting target for the British ships converging on her from all quarters. Encircled and doomed, she was sunk by torpedoes early in the morning of the 27th. One hundred and fifteen of her complement of about 2,400 were saved.

This German challenge on the surface was never to be renewed (although – with *Scharnhorst* and *Gneisenau* only damaged and *Tirpitz* about to come into service – the British Admiralty could not know this) and the Battle of the Atlantic was once more left to Doenitz, who built up his U-boat force to 120 during 1941 and was contriving to keep as many as half of them at sea at once. Although the pressure from the U-boats was relaxed when half of them were diverted to the Mediterranean at the end of the year, the newer boats were operating at longer ranges and the Atlantic crossing was as hazardous as ever. On the other side Roosevelt took yet further measures. The second half of 1941 was the period in which the Russians were now fighting but the Americans were not. In July Roosevelt nevertheless sent U S marines to Iceland to join the British troops who had been stationed there since May 1940. This extension of American arms entailed supply and escort duties by the U S navy in an operational zone. In August British and allied shipping was allowed to join American convoys and sail in them. American vessels of war were, without the knowledge of the public or the Congress, fighting an undeclared war farther and farther away from the shores of the American continent. Inevitably the German navy was in fact retaliating, although Hitler kept up the appearance and even the substance of restraint. He authorized in July attacks on American merchantmen but only in a restricted zone in the eastern Atlantic and not on the approach routes to Iceland.

In August, at Placentia Bay in Newfoundland, Roosevelt and Churchill held their first wartime meeting. It had been planned as early as January when Roosevelt's unconventional personal emissary, Harry Hopkins, paid his first wartime visit to London. Attended as it was by the Chiefs of Staff of both countries, the Placentia Bay conference looked like a joint council of war and many on the British side hoped that it was the curtain-raiser for an American declaration of war. Stalin too wanted such a declaration and had made his wishes and his plight clear to Hopkins in Moscow a week earlier. But Roosevelt was not yet ready to take that plunge, perhaps not convinced that he would have to, and the conference's main product was the Atlantic Charter, which many of the British participants regarded as a gust of high-sounding irrelevance. But the Atlantic Charter was more important than that. If the Americans were to go to war they must know why and wherefore, and the Charter set out war aims which would be worth fighting for. Merely contemplating war aims is a step towards war, while in the absence of war aims a democratic leader can hardly ask a people not under attack to start fighting. The Atlantic Charter was a part of the preparation of the American people for war, even though it turned out not to be strictly necessary since the issue of war or peace was decided by Hitler's act and not by the choice of Americans. The Placentia Bay conference was also a prelude to war in another sense, for after it the President ordered an inquiry into what the United States would require if war should come – a pre-war war plan. And thirdly, the conference inaugurated the personal acquaintance between service chiefs which was to grow much closer and be formalized by the creation of the Anglo-American Combined Chiefs of Staff Committee.

At sea the war continued to suck at the American resolve to avoid it. In

September, following an astutely publicized encounter between a U-boat and the USS *Greer* – an inconclusive engagement described by Roosevelt as an attack on an American vessel – the President announced that the United States would protect non-American as well as American shipping in the Atlantic security zone and would fire at sight on all German and Italian warships seen there. Incidents multiplied. American opinion was growing more anti-German than anti-war. In October and November 1941 the neutrality legislation was being progressively eroded by Congress. American merchantmen were armed and the President was empowered to send American ships into British ports. The United States was virtually making war in defiance of the rules. But it showed no sign of actually declaring war: undeclared war was serving the dual purpose of helping the democracies and keeping the bulk of Americans out of the firing line (those who wanted to go and fight were tacitly allowed to join the British or Canadian forces). When the United States was attacked at Pearl Harbor the President only asked Congress to declare war on Japan. Then, four days later, Germany declared war on the United States.

This act by Hitler has been described as one of gratuitous folly. It is certain that, by adding the United States to his overt enemies at a time when Germany was fighting both the British Empire and the USSR, Hitler sealed his doom. But the die was cast before December 1941. By the time Hitler declared war the United States was already an active ally of the British and the Russians. Up to the middle of 1941 Hitler had every reason to keep the United States out of the war at almost any cost and he did, as we shall see, set himself firmly not only to avoid provoking Roosevelt but also to ignore Roosevelt's provocations of him. After the turn of the year, however, the situation changed. With the launching of Barbarossa, Hitler was involved in the dreaded war on two fronts, while the United States was, though neutral in name, already decreasingly so in substance. Hitler therefore embarked on the policy of goading the Japanese into war partly in order to distract the Americans from Europe and the Atlantic and partly also because, obsessed with the British, whose survival forced him to fight the USSR with half a hand tied behind his back, he wanted Japan to deal Great Britain a knock-out blow in Singapore and India. In pursuance of this complicated aim he was forced, in November 1941, to promise Japan that Germany would declare war on the United States if Japan did. This policy failed because the Japanese blows at Pearl Harbor and Singapore were not knockouts and because of the unforeseen capacity of the Americans to fight, uniquely, a war in every quarter of the world.

Hitler badly misjudged the Americans, partly because of his preconceptions and partly because he was badly served. He entertained fantastically wrong notions of American society and politics. He believed that the masses of decent Americans (whose ancestors, he incorrectly recalled, had failed by only one congressional vote to adopt German as their national language) were on the verge of revolt against a dominant Jewish ruling class and that the United States, so far from being a bastion of democracy, was a corrupt and demoralized country fit and eager for the reception of Nazi ideas. To Hitler, Roosevelt, especially in his 1940 election campaign, was a desperate trickster clutching at any opportunity to win votes and retain power in defiance of a groundswell of popular enlightenment. On this view the United States was not nearly such a formidable enemy as its material power might make it appear. Besides being blinded by his prejudices Hitler was misled by exceptionally inept reporting by his emissaries in Washington, especially his service attachés who, pandering to these prejudices, devoted more ink to political nonsense than to technical reports. He overrated and misjudged the pro-Nazi German-American Bund; failed to appreciate the distaste of Americans for his racialism; overestimated the addiction of Americans to a comfortable neutrality; and mistook the prominence of men like Colonels Charles Lindbergh and Robert R. MacCormick, Senators Burton K. Wheeler and Gerald P. Nye and the 'radio priest' Father Charles E. Coughlin for real political influence.

He was also, and more pardonably, misled by the American record in the thirties. The economic crisis and isolationism prevented the United States from playing an effective role in world affairs in that decade. Hitler understood this, but he did not understand how far war would change American attitudes and policies. When Japan invaded Manchuria in 1931 (partly to forestall a possible Russian move which could precipitate a new Russo-Japanese war) the Secretary of State, Henry L. Stimson, had toyed with the idea of intervention. He was well aware of the force of isolationism in the United States but he hoped that by a show of determination he might influence the political balance in Tokyo where a civilian cabinet was at odds with the army factions which had provoked the fighting in Manchuria. This cabinet had no desire to begin a war with China in order to stave off a war with the USSR, but it fell. Stimson thereupon proposed economic sanctions against Japan but President Herbert Hoover did not like the idea (nor did the British government). Stimson pressed his interventionist policy again a few months later when Japanese troops were landed at Shanghai, but the President remained opposed to it and Stimson knew that American opinion would not tolerate it: he was using the prospect of sanctions as a counter, but in the knowledge that he could not play it. In the Ethiopian crisis Stimson's successor, Cordell Hull, instituted voluntary sanctions against Italy but there was little cooperation between the United States and the leading members of the League and Hull's initiative merely associated the United States with a failure. The remilitarization of the Rhineland, the Spanish civil war, the conclusion of the Axis and Anti-Comintern Pacts, the extension of the war in the east to China itself in the summer of 1937, the sinking of the American gunboat *Panay* and three tankers on the Yangtse in December all reinforced the American desire to keep clear of wars; and were seen to. Moreover, Roosevelt's unhappy attempts to intervene diplomatically in European politics in the late thirties, revealing his own hesitations and the hiatus between the American and British governments, roused only Hitler's scorn, and his attempts to avert war at the last moment were brushed off by Hitler. The war was going to be short. Either Great Britain and France would do nothing to help Poland or they would intervene and be quickly subdued. On this basis there was no American problem. But the basis was wrong. The war was not short and the Americans soon began to take a menacing hand in it.

The six months which embraced Hitler's invasion of the USSR and his declaration of war against the United States marked also the destruction, by his own acts, of his power of initiative in world affairs. The failure of Barbarossa was crucial, for had he defeated the USSR before the end of the year he would have been supreme in the European continent and either he would have issued no declaration of war against the United States or he could have done so without involving himself in the pincer movement which finally crushed him. It was the burden of Barbarossa which led him from a European to a world strategy, from a league in which he could certainly play and possibly win to a league in which he must lose.

But, secondly, the survival of Great Britain was also crucial because, without it, it is unlikely that the United States would have joined the war as an ally of the USSR against Germany.

Hitler's failures in Barbarossa and the Battle of Britain were both narrow ones. Something has already been said about both these engagements and more will be said later in this book about the sources of Russian endurance and victory. If Hitler had lived (as Napoleon did) to ponder his mistakes and failures in tranquillity, he would no doubt have fought the battles of the autumn of 1940 and the autumn of 1941 over and over again. He might also have puzzled no less over the incomprehensibility of the Americans and the British, who behaved in these critical years 1939–41 with what, to an outsider, could only seem perverse inconsequence. If Hitler made mistakes about the Anglo-Saxon peoples, whom in some moods he judged to be not much inferior to the German, he could claim that he was to some degree misled by their illogicality as well as by his own preconceptions and advisers.

He could hark back to the British declaration of war at the very beginning. This declaration, which was a formal consequence of the German attack on Poland two days earlier, had no discernible practical results at the time. If it was anything more than an empty formality it implied a determination to attack Germany. But neither Great Britain nor France had forces or plans for doing so, nor did they do so. (The only plans extant were for air operations in response to full-scale German action in the west.) In the event it was Hitler who attacked them and not the other way round. Seven months later he defeated France and prepared to defeat Great Britain. His plans posed a threat to American security which the Americans could, by the use of naval and air forces, have helped to defeat. Yet they too declined, as the British had declined in 1939, to take any direct action, and if they abstained at this critical point they might be counted most unlikely to intervene in a European war at any other. On this premise Hitler's own declaration of war at the end of 1941 was a formal act without practical consequences like the British declaration in 1939; the practical consequences, if any, would be in the Pacific where the Americans were already embroiled with the Japanese. But the Americans, who had abstained from direct action in the face of the threat in 1940, were ready by 1941 to throw themselves into the European war and even give it priority over a Pacific war. The intervention which had seemed politically impossible in 1940 became automatic in 1941. To Hitler it might have appeared that the British and Americans had leaders who did not understand power. The British had ostensibly engaged themselves in 1939 to do something which they had not the power to do; the Americans in 1940 had the power to intervene in a situation of critical importance to themselves but abstained from doing so. But in this assessment of the seeming political ineptitude of his adversaries Hitler failed to take account of Aristotle's diagnosis of the nature of the commercial state, slow to action but rich in the capacity to procrastinate and then triumph – not to mention Bernard Shaw's analysis of the Englishman's genius for triumphing through an insensitivity to the dangers of his own position amounting to a kind of sublime arrogance.

Hitler had for years intended to make war on the USSR but he never wanted a war against either Great Britain or the United States. These wars he merely accepted when they came. He tried to come to terms with Great Britain and then to defeat it, and when both these efforts failed he turned away. He tried for a time to avoid war with the United States. On the outbreak of war in 1939 he forbade attacks on passenger ships, and when the *Athenia* was sunk with its twenty-eight American passengers he had the crew of U-30 sworn to secrecy on their return to port and tried to persuade the world that the sinking was a British stunt to drag the United States into war. In October he permitted attacks on enemy merchant ships without warning and on enemy passenger ships after warning (the need for this warning was lifted at the beginning of November), but he still refused to sanction attacks on neutrals. He allowed the *City of Flint*, which had been captured, taken to Norway and there released by the Norwegians (who interned the German boarders), to proceed without further molestation and he kept to this reticent policy despite the insistent pleas of his naval advisers. If Roosevelt's only concern had been to avoid incidents in the Atlantic he would have had no great problem, for Hitler wanted to avoid such incidents too. As late as the summer of 1941 Hitler was still turning a deaf ear to Raeder's pleas to sanction indiscriminate retaliation in the undeclared war which the Americans were waging in the Atlantic.

Thus Hitler had pursued in the Atlantic a policy of avoiding conflict with the United States up to the last months before he declared war. But in the Pacific, where he operated at second remove through his Japanese allies, he had the choice between restraining Japan in order to prolong American non-belligerency and, alternatively, egging Japan on. He chose the latter course. Engaged in a war on two fronts in which the Americans were becoming unofficially or even formally involved, he wanted to create a second front for the Americans too. Japan could open this front and at the same time attack the British Empire which had so sadly failed to respond to Hitler's offer of an honourable place in a world partitioned on Hitlerian lines. Hitler knew from his agents that Japan had decided not to attack the USSR and, by relaying to Tokyo his own version of Great Britain's helpless plight and his contemptuous estimate of American valour, he encouraged the more bellicose members of the Japanese cabinet. Discussions in Washington between the Americans and the Japanese during the autumn puzzled and worried Ribbentrop and his Ambassador in Tokyo, who could not make out whether they represented a genuine attempt to avoid war. Even after the fall of the comparatively moderate Konoye cabinet and the appointment of General Tojo as Prime Minister on 18 October the Germans were afraid that the Japanese might fail them, and so in November Ribbentrop went so far as to promise to help Japan in a war against the United States and not to make a separate peace. On 11 December Hitler fulfilled this promise. Italy declared war too.

After 1941 Hitler started no more wars. He gradually lost those he had started.

Every war plan has two main elements: the instruments with which to wage it and the right time to begin it. On both counts Hitler's war on the USSR was not merely a conspicuous failure but also mismanaged and mistaken. Although his armies came within an ace of capturing Moscow and so perhaps of victory, they were inadequately equipped to pursue it after the first six months and 1941 was the wrong date, since Hitler, on his own statement of 1937 which there is no reason to disbelieve, intended to win *Lebensraum* in the east in 1943–5. It was furthermore no part of any plan of his to make war on the USSR when engaged in other wars elsewhere. In attacking Czechoslovakia and Poland, Hitler gambled on getting what he wanted without war. In the first case the gamble came off but in the second it failed and produced war not only with Poland but a war in the west which he could neither win nor conclude. By 1941, elated perhaps by his continental successes in the west, he gambled again by advancing the date for his war in the east and by discounting the significance of continuing British belligerence. By the end of that year his most serious purpose – the winning of *Lebensraum* – was in jeopardy; and his declaration of war on the United States further exposed his maladroitness, for it converted Great Britain from a relatively minor offshore enemy into an assembly area for the legions of a vastly more dangerous foe.

In retrospect it is clear that Hitler could no longer win the war after this date. But Germany was not yet doomed to the unconditional surrender which the allies were to exact, for the German U-boats might starve Great Britain of food and arms and prevent American armies from crossing the ocean, and German V weapons might force the western allies, if not to surrender, at least to negotiate a separate peace in the west.

Part III

EUROPE UNDER THE NAZIS

CHAPTER 11

The New Order

FOR four years Germany dominated the greater part of Europe more completely than it had ever been dominated before. How far was this domination also purposeful? Every conqueror sets out with a complex of aims. On the one hand he has ideas, more or less precise, about what he wants to do with the lands he intends to conquer. On the other hand his attitude will be to conquer first and leave the rest till afterwards. Among the Nazis there were some who regarded the conquests of 1939–41 as a prelude and an opportunity: they had a Grand Design, even though this design was more of a vision than a plan and even though they could not always agree among themselves about what they wanted or how to achieve it. There were also others, more pragmatic, who treated the gains of these years as assets to be exploited in the war that was still going on: in so far as they had a Grand Design, it was one with a low priority for the time being. Hitler himself belonged rather to the pragmatic school. He was concerned first and foremost with winning the war and one of his keenest interests – perhaps his main interest – was in military equipment and military tactics. But he was hardly less preoccupied with the two great questions of *Lebensraum* and race, and his ideas and writing were the stuff out of which men like Alfred Rosenberg and Heinrich Himmler, although often with different interpretations and opposing aims, began to create a New Order for Europe during the war years.

Politically the New Order was simple. German hegemony was to be extended by German arms and accepted by everybody else. Nazi values were to be exported from their German centre and the pattern of Nazi revolution and Nazi life repeated in other lands. The first pre-condition of the New Order was conquest: land had to be got. How much land was left vague. It adapted itself to circumstances. At the high tide of German successes the concept of the *Grossraum*, or Greater Germanic Estate, embraced Europe from the Atlantic to the Urals, although a little earlier it had seemed to make do with rather less of Russia. The determining features of the *Grossraum* were not its borders but its nature. Instead of finding where people lived and then drawing permanent or semi-permanent frontiers to fit the ethnic facts, the Nazis began by designating an area and then moved people around in order to make demography fit the facts of power. The *Grossraum* therefore might be any size and in 1942 one writer envisaged it as covering one sixth of the globe. It was not a fixed area but a biological habitat like a nature reserve. It was where the German family lived.

The Germans themselves were to be the proprietors and directors of the *Grossraum* but not its only inhabitants. It would also contain the other Nordic races, who were only a little inferior to the Germans but would have no effective political or economic power; and non-Nordic peoples who, suitably regrouped and assigned to their economic functions, would be the helots of the *Grossraum*. (Hitler liked reading history books and admired Sparta.) These sub-human varieties would be kept in subjection by, among other devices, depriving them of education. As Hitler himself put it, they were to 'know just enough to understand road signs, so as not to get themselves run over by our vehicles. For them the word "liberty" must mean the right to wash on holidays.' His aim in the USSR was to 'Germanize the country by the settlement of Germans and treat the natives as redskins'. An even more inferior variety of human being, too vicious to be allowed any place however menial, would be eliminated. Thus re-ordered, the *Grossraum* would be made economically self-sufficient, in-dependent of the other major areas in the world although specially linked, in some versions, with Africa in a Eurafrican super *Grossraum* which was partly just an even more grandiose vision, partly an extension designed to furnish Europe with the raw materials of which it had not got enough, and partly a way of finding an exciting but peripheral role for the Italians, whose position in a purely European *Grossraum* was, for obvious reasons, never spelled out.

Given these imaginings there were two main fields for action, the demographic and the economic. People had to be moved or removed; the work they did had to be reorganized to fit the plan for a Germano-centric autarkic Europe. During the war quite a lot was undertaken demographically, but the economic planning of the New Order was overshadowed by the exigencies of war economics.

The economic aspects of the New Order were never condensed into a single document or plan and it is to some extent misleading to propound any such plan by piecing together what was said about it by different people at different times. Nevertheless a general outline existed.

The Nazis were centralizers, but half-hearted ones. At one level they believed in the concentration of power. They converted federal Weimar Germany into a unitary state and they would have carried this centralizing process beyond Germany into Europe, making Berlin the political, econ-omic and cultural – in sum, the totalitarian – capital of a super-state.

But although they focused power on a single central capital, they also diffused it among the departments and agencies which were centred in the capital. This fragmentation was partly a reflection of Hitler's policy and his character: he was not an administrator and he ruled by dividing. It was also a consequence of lack of foresight. Especially during the war new problems thrust themselves upon Germany's rulers and the Nazi way of dealing with them was to create new agencies. In this respect they acted more like the Americans with their similar propensity for bureaucratic proliferation than like the British or French, who have characteristically preferred to accommodate new problems and new functions within the settled framework of the existing civil service and the existing machinery of government. The New Order, had it come into being, would have been controlled by a single but fissiparous and philoprogenitive machine.

This machine would have existed to serve Germany's interests but it would have claimed incidentally to serve other interests too. The core of the *Grossraum* – a Germany which had engulfed Alsace-Lorraine, Luxembourg, parts of Belgium and Silesia – would be to Europe what the Ruhr was to Germany. Here would be most of Europe's heavy industry and all its arms industries. Beyond it industries would exist on sufferance only and their primary purpose would be the production of consumer goods for Germans. Each conquered area would be a tributary, judged and regulated in terms of the needs of Germany. Besides consumer goods these areas would produce food, and their agriculture would be re-planned to suit Germany: more arable in Denmark, for example, and less dairy farming. In return Germany would provide a guaranteed market for all Europe's food production and abolish unemployment. The countries beyond the central core would, by virtue of centralized planning, become specialized producers knowing what they could export, how much credit they could have and how much labour they would need; an international labour pool would enable the planners to operate an effective international division of labour. This picture was neither entirely unfamiliar nor entirely unattractive to Europe. The notion of an economic entity larger than any existing political unity, and of the need for Europe to organize economically on a wider scale, had been propagated by various champions of European unity ranging from men in official positions like Aristide Briand in France and Paul van Zeeland in Belgium to the League of Nation's Inquiry for European Union and private enthusiasts like Count Richard Coudenhove-Kalergi. Europe moreover had had more than its fair share of economic instability between the wars and might therefore be persuaded that it was worth forgoing the freedom to choose for itself what it would make or grow if it could buy stability in exchange for economic sovereignty.

The German New Order was in this sense an attempt to construct an economy broader than a national economy and it suffered from the basic defect of most such schemes attempted in a nationalist world. Its scope was international but its purpose was national. Long-range planning, long-term agreements, guaranteed markets, fixed exchange rates, a European clearing system – plans to link the Baltic and the Black Seas by an Oder–Danube canal, the Rhine and the Po by another, plans to dam the Straits of Gibraltar in order to endow all Europe with cheap power – all these things could not conceal the fact that the basis of the New Order was German power and German requirements and not a European cooperative. The benefits to everybody else would be the crumbs from the rich man's table. It could hardly look otherwise during a war.

Ideas of this kind were peace aims rather than war aims and when the war turned into a long war and a losing war they were inevitably submerged. Up to 1942 the New Order was proffered with a kind of open-handed exultation and in the belief that it would strike some response, but from 1942 onwards the voice of Germany turned from allurements to warnings, prophesying communist horrors to come rather than a new Eden. At the same time the New Order, such as it was, had to be applied to keeping Germany going in a painfully immediate present. Instead of enlarging and fertilizing Europe's economy, it had to nourish Germany's war effort.

The lengthening war also held up the demographic planning of the New Order but it did not do so entirely. Some movements of population were undertaken and horribly much was achieved in the way of extermination. Both these aspects of the matter fell primarily, though not entirely, within the province of the SS and they acquired from the SS their overriding characteristic of ferocious brutality.

The SS grew out of a small blackshirted bodyguard originally called the *Stosstrupp Hitler* and renamed *Schutzstaffeln* (SS) in 1925. Even more than the Nazi Party itself they were the instrument of Hitler's personal will. They were drenched in Nazi ideology and they enjoyed a life of special licence which was nowhere better illustrated than on the very slopes of Hitler's own Bavarian eyrie where they could revel off-duty in an efficiently organized orgiastic hedonism calculatingly and cynically proffered to them by their non-alcoholic and near-chaste Führer. They were the principal beneficiaries of the destruction of the SA in 1934 and from that time their power expanded as they absorbed the police forces of Germany, built up a well-equipped private army of thirty divisions, became an economic force in control of a large part of the Reich's labour and of extensive factories, and duplicated their German functions and powers in occupied Europe. The SS became the rulers of Germany, the effective core within the amorphous mass of the Nazi Party. Their chief from 1929 (when their strength was under 300 men) was Heinrich Himmler, a man pre-eminent among the senior Nazi leaders for his mediocrity, a quality which ensured Hitler's confidence almost – but not quite – to the end. He was said to be so obsessed by blondness that he could not bear to have dark-haired people around. He had a little knowledge of Germanic origins and runic inscriptions which he pursued with the unintelligent concentration of a man whose hobby is his life, but paradoxically he was also a visionary with ambition who throve in the struggle for power because of his enthusiasm for a purer Germanic world on Nazi principles – which he accepted wholesale and uncritically without any of the cynical reservations of the sharper-minded Hitler or the softer-living Goering. Himmler was also acute enough and lucky enough to rise to the top in the Nazi jungle and stay there. Before the war ended he was not only *Reichsführer SS*, Chief of the German Police and Minister of the Interior but also Commander-in-Chief of the Home Army and he had twice – on each occasion briefly, ineptly and for the most part at a distance – held command of an Army Group in the field. He had become a contender for supreme power in succession to Hitler, although Hitler himself said in 1945 that Himmler would not do as his successor because he had no culture.

The annexation of the police by the SS was the vital step in the transformation of the SS from its modest beginnings within the Nazi machine into the power which ruled Germany and terrorized a continent. In Weimar Germany each province had its own government and its own police force. The most important of these forces was the Prussian police controlled by the Prussian Minister of the Interior, who was a more influential personage than the shadowy Reich Minister of the Interior. As Minister of the Interior and then Prime Minister in Prussia, Goering was, before he exchanged cruelty for easefulness, the most powerful policeman in Germany. Himmler was chief of the Bavarian police in Munich. But Himmler also got himself a subordinate post in the Prussian system.

The Prussian police was a rambling system whose branches included the Schupo (traffic police and men on the beat), the Orpo (*gendarmerie* living in barracks), the Kripo or criminal detectives, the Gestapo or secret state security service, and special services like the fire brigades and railway police. Himmler became deputy head of the Prussian Gestapo and he also became Chief of Police in various other provinces besides Bavaria. In

1936 a unified German police force was created with Himmler at its head, and in 1943 he became also Reich Minister of the Interior, an office which, with the centralizing tendencies of the Third Reich, had by then outstripped its Prussian counterpart in importance.

After 1936 the next step was to incorporate the detective and intelligence functions of the police into the SS. The new German police was divided into two main branches, the Orpo on the one hand and on the other the Sipo or Security Police embracing the Kripo and the Gestapo. As head of the Sipo Himmler appointed Reinhardt Heydrich who was already head of the *Sicherheitsdienst* (SD) or security services of the SS. For a short time the Sipo under Heydrich remained with the rest of the police within the Ministry of the Interior, but shortly before the outbreak of war it was transferred to one of the main branches of the SS, the newly created RSHA – *Reichssicherheitshauptamt* or Reich Security Division. Departments III and VI of the RSHA were the SD (Home) and SD (Foreign); Department IV was the Gestapo and its sub-department IV 4b meant Jews. In personal terms the RSHA was Heydrich until his assassination in Prague in May 1942, when he was succeeded by Ernst Kaltenbrunner; Department IV was Heinrich Müller; IV 4b was Karl Adolf Eichmann.

The chain of command Heydrich–Müller–Eichmann exhibits the variety of the SS. Müller, the head of the Gestapo, was the type of the faceless professional policeman who knew his job and did it; he was for a long time not a member of the Nazi Party; his origins were obscure and probably lowly and he had a chip on his shoulder. It was in a sense fitting that in April 1945 he simply vanished after walking out of Hitler's bunker to go back to his office and has never been heard of since. He has been suspected of being in Russian pay and of taking refuge in Moscow at the end of the war, where he is said to have died in 1948. Heydrich and Eichmann, his immediate superior and subordinate, were very different. Both had goals rather than jobs. Heydrich's driving force came from ambition, Eichmann's from obsession. Both were virulent anti-semites. Eichmann became in practice the principal agent in the destruction of the Jews, supervising and directing the application of Nazi racial policies first in Bohemia and Moravia and then in Poland and ultimately in Hungary. After the war he escaped to South America but in 1960 he was traced and kidnapped by a Jewish organization and delivered to Israel where he was tried, condemned and executed. Heydrich, a failed naval officer, was Hitler's right-hand man in the massacre of June 1934 and it was he rather than Himmler who ensured that the victors should be the SS and not the army. He pursued his course by vigour harnessed to ability and by intrigue served by his intimate knowledge of the personal weaknesses of the senior Nazi chiefs and the skeletons in their cupboards. As head of the R S H A he was one of the most powerful men in Germany, although not in the top rank, and it has been conjectured that when he took the office of Protector of Bohemia and Moravia in 1941 he did so with an eye to climbing higher by this circuitous route. He was as ruthless and violent as any of his colleagues and much more intelligent. (He also played the violin and at his funeral the cultivated, anti-Nazi Admiral Canaris wept.) His death removed Himmler's most formidable rival.

Heydrich was still a little-known figure in the thirties. Müller and Eichmann were even less well known, and comparatively few members of the general public would have recognized them. But the S S itself was not difficult to recognize. First in Germany and then throughout Europe its members strode along the streets or hurtled along the roads in cars in the special costumes designed to make them look as terrifying as possible – the sinister uniformity of the black shirt, no jacket to impede the swing of the arm, the expensive breeches and the hard shiny boots, and on every cap the head of death as a *memento mori* to every living citizen. The complexity of the German S S and police added to the terror. In occupied Europe the men of the Orpo were the visible intimation of police rule and police brutality. They were the men who could be seen rounding up one's neighbours and who might at any time of day or night come for oneself, while behind them in the recesses of buildings whose whispered addresses became household fears were the men of the Gestapo and the S D.

Himmler's long-term plans for the re-ordering of Europe were based on reducing the Slavs by 30 million and planting a German upper crust in selected parts of Poland, the Baltic states and the U S S R. In 1942 the S S produced a blueprint or Eastern Plan covering the next twenty-five years. It involved the establishment of temporary German strongpoints, partly garrisons and partly colonies, peopled by peasants under arms. These settlements would be at central points. At the same time permanent settlements were to be planted at the extreme edge of the *Grossraum*, where, at first under S S control, they would shield the *Grossraum* like the marcher principalities of feudal times. This Germanic population would reach 3.5 million at the end of twenty-five years. Among them would be a local population of landless poor. The plan was revised and re-issued but at the beginning of 1943 Hitler decreed that all these schemes must await the end of the war and so stopped Himmler from putting it into operation. At about the same time some Americans, including the Secretary of the Treasury Henry Morgenthau, were evolving a similar plan for turning Germany into an agricultural zone after the war.

Himmler was concerned not only to dispatch Reich Germans out into the *Grossraum* but also – and not without a degree of contradiction – to gather *Volksdeutsche* back into the Reich. (Hitler was more interested in the latter than the former programme.) As a first step *Volksdeutsche* in occupied territories were treated as a privileged class, given positions of minor authority where possible, allowed to use special shops and so on, but this policy, first adopted in Czechoslovakia and Poland, sharpened the Russians' natural distrust of *Volksdeutsche* and led to large numbers of them being deported to the east before the Germans could reach them. Himmler's plans were further confounded by disputes among the Germans themselves. While the S S started registering the *Volksdeutsche* whom they found round the Black Sea and elsewhere with a view to resettlement, for diverse reasons the army commanders, Rosenberg and Goering all wanted them left where they were. It also transpired that fewer of them still spoke German than had been expected. The only transfer of any consequence effected by the SS in the USSR was the eviction of a number of Ukrainians from the neighbourhood of Zhitomir and Kalinovka to make way for Volhynian Germans who did not want to go there. Significantly perhaps this single practical example had not been envisaged by the Eastern Plan. It created trouble in the German administration of the Ukraine and squabbling in Berlin and had no sensible purpose. Apart from this there was no considerable displacement of the *Volksdeutsche* of the USSR until the tide of war turned and about 300,000 of them were swept westward not as settlers but as refugees.

In other areas Himmler was less obstructed by rival authorities. One hundred and thirty-two thousand *Volksdeutsche* from Bessarabia and northern Bukovina and another 32,000 from southern Bukovina and the Dobrudja were earmarked for Germany and about 46,000 of them were settled in annexed territories; the rest probably spent the war in transit camps. Another 9,000 Germans from Warsaw and 14,000 from Slovenia had a similar fate. Poland was to be sorted out by moving 164,000 Germans westward from what had been the Russian zone in 1939 and an equivalent number of Ukrainians and White Russians from the original German zones eastwards. In addition 80,000 Baltic Germans were to find new homes in Poland. In the west Alsace-Lorraine and Luxembourg were prepared for Germanization by removing 105,000 inhabitants ('foreign elements') from the former and 7,000 from the latter. In practice these schemes produced chaos and a degree of incidental economic disruption which led to complaints about the damage done to the war effort by the S S. Some of the Baltic Germans found themselves moved back to where they had come from after only a few months, while the fate of the German-speaking Tyrolese was like a scene from Dante. In a plebiscite in

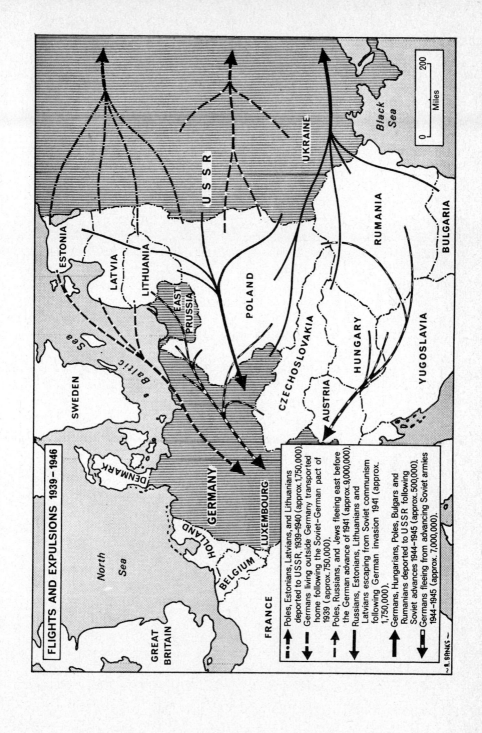

FLIGHTS AND EXPULSIONS 1939–1946

GREAT BRITAIN

North Sea

SWEDEN

DENMARK

Baltic Sea

ESTONIA

LATVIA

LITHUANIA

EAST PRUSSIA

U S S R

UKRAINE

Black Sea

POLAND

CZECHOSLOVAKIA

AUSTRIA

HUNGARY

RUMANIA

BULGARIA

YUGOSLAVIA

HOLLAND

BELGIUM

LUXEMBOURG

GERMANY

FRANCE

200

0   Miles

· ▬ · ▬ Poles, Estonians, Latvians, and Lithuanians
deported to USSR, 1939–1940 (approx.1,750,000).

▬▬▶ Germans living outside Germany transported
home following the Soviet–German pact of
1939 (approx.750,000).

─ ─▶ Poles, Russians, and Jews fleeing east before
the German advance of 1941 (approx.9,000,000).

▬▬▶ Russians, Estonians, Lithuanians and
Latvians escaping from Soviet communism
following German invasion 1941 (approx.
1,750,000).

▬▬▶ Germans, Hungarians, Poles, Bulgars and
Rumanians deported to USSR following
Soviet advances 1944–1945 (approx.500,000).

▭▬▶ Germans fleeing from advancing Soviet armies
1944–1945 (approx. 7,000,000).

~ R. BANKS ~

1939, 185,365 opted for the Reich; by 1941 this figure had somehow grown to 220,000 and the next year it was even bigger; but while somebody was apparently persuading more and more Tyrolese to ask to be moved to the Reich, nobody was making adequate arrangements for them to get there and it seems unlikely that more than 80,000 did so. At one time Himmler toyed with the idea of sending them all to the Crimea and many spent the war in camps waiting to be moved to nobody quite knew where. Few *Volksdeutsche* actually reached the Reich. A number were settled in the annexed territories and a greater number simply got lost.

These movements of population were only a part of the plan. There was also the elimination of undesirables, notably Jews and Slavs.

The attempt to exterminate whole peoples was a logical consequence of Nazi ideology, and the degree to which it succeeded was a result of the military conquests which placed millions of Jews within the Nazi grasp and of the reiterated propaganda which so transformed thousands of Germans that they were able to perform the cruellest obscenities. Many thousands more witnessed them or were otherwise aware of them.

The purity of the Aryan race did not require mass murder. It required the prevention of inter-breeding, but the prevention of inter-breeding required also the prevention of all human contact since even the strictest laws and the most intense propaganda cannot guarantee correct responses of the heart and the flesh. Moreover, in Nazi mythology the purity of the Aryan race was linked with the salvation of the human race, and since both doctrines posited a Jewish enemy, they together bred a hatred of Jewry and a determination to exterminate it. The discrimination against Jews, which was first prescribed by law immediately after the Nazis took power, led on to degradation, outlawry, pillage and murder; mass murder was methodically organized after the war began. By the laws of the first phase, culminating in the Nuremberg decrees of September 1935, not only were marriage and fornication between Jews and Gentiles condemned but also the slightest physical touch. Yet the accompanying pathological ravings of some Nazi zealots and a part of the press were not seen as a prelude to anything worse. There was some emigration and a few suicides, but even when a special Jewish Bureau was established without any concealment in 1936 (Eichmann was its chief) hope and incredulity were still allowed to prevail over desperation. Emigration moreover was baulked by prohibitions on the export of property and by the inaccessibility of the obvious haven, Palestine, where the British, caught between the irreconcilable promises given to Jews and Arabs in the First World War, refused to admit more than 1,500 Jews a month unless they brought £1,000 apiece with them.

But persecution was already grievous and in November 1938 a young seventeen-year-old Jew called Herschel Grynszpan decided to force it upon the attention of an unwilling world by a desperate deed. He murdered a German diplomat in the Paris embassy, Ernst vom Rath (whom he mistook for the Ambassador). Retaliation took the form of a pogrom which the Nazis were able to organize in advance because vom Rath lingered in hospital before dying. News of his death reached Hitler in Munich where he had gone to celebrate the fifteenth anniversary of his 1923 putsch. Local party and SS authorities had already been warned of what was coming and of the need to conceal the fact that it was pre-arranged. Traffic in selected areas was diverted, the telephone lines of Jewish subscribers were cut and at 2 a.m. organized squads wrecked 200 synagogues and other Jewish property (including a Jewish sanatorium), murdered seventy Jews in the Buchenwald concentration camp and arrested 20,000 Jews. So much plate glass was broken that the outburst of this one night was given the name of the *Kristallnacht*. In addition the Jewish community was collectively condemned to pay twenty-five million marks for the repair of damaged property and also a fine of one billion marks – which practically dispossessed it of the goods and enterprises which had not already been taken from it. Jews were expelled from hospitals, old folks' homes and schools, and public places were put out of bounds to them. A proposal to take away their driving licences was discussed but dropped. No foreign government protested. The British Foreign Secretary, Lord Halifax, ruled that a protest would constitute unjustifiable interference in the internal affairs of another state and warned his subordinates against giving unnecessary offence to Hitler. In this last year before the war the German Jews began to flee their fate, but the acquisition of Austria and Bohemia and Moravia added to the Reich as many Jews as left it. From the Nazi point of view the problem remained the same size – about 357,000. Then the conquest of Poland enormously increased that number, multiplying it by ten.

In 1938 Hitler discussed with Himmler the killing of whole sections of the population of Czechoslovakia and a year later similar discussions took place as a prelude to the Polish campaign. SS chiefs conferred with army chiefs about the modalities of this first instalment of the New Order. The ruling class, the intelligentsia, the Jews were to be collected and killed. The German Jews were not thrown into the programme at this stage partly because the Nazis had not finally made up their minds between deportation and extermination, and partly for logistical reasons: there was so much to be done first in Poland and later in the USSR that the mills of destruction could not grind fast enough.

The last serious attempt to purge Germany of Jews without killing them was the Madagascar plan. This plan had been adumbrated before the war and was revived after the fall of France, whose colony Madagascar was. The plan was to send all European Jews to this island in the Indian Ocean where they could be autonomous under German sovereignty and would, as Hitler put it, be hostages against the 'good behaviour of their co-racialists in America'. Problems of transport and the like were examined in some detail but the war did not end with the fall of France and so the Germans could not get hold of Madagascar or send Jews there. Instead they kept the German Jews in Germany until they could be sent to Poland to be killed along with Jews from other parts of Europe.

In the interval between the defeat of Poland and the attack on the USSR, Hitler set up a new agency, Operations Staff Rosenberg, which began as a research body for the collection of material about Jews, communists and Freemasons and the formulation of a policy for combating these pests. With a hideous simulation of scholarly application it assembled a huge library and, by combining pillage with study, amassed incidentally a fabulous art collection. It was expanded into a Ministry for the East, in which thousands of industrious, ingenious and even learned Germans worked away at schemes which had no relevance to the war going on around them; their activities were viewed with irritated scorn by the professional staff of the German Foreign Ministry and with even more irritated jealousy by Ribbentrop who considered that Rosenberg was being allowed to poach on his own preserves as Foreign Minister. Since the East meant the Baltic states and the USSR, Rosenberg became on paper the potential disposer of the Russian empire. His aim was to destroy the Russian state in perpetuity by fragmenting and pastoralizing it and by creating new separatist states out of the debris. Hitler had decided to give Leningrad to Finland and Bessarabia and Odessa to Rumania. From what remained Rosenberg intended to fashion at least four states: a Russian rump, renamed Muscovy, stretching from the Arctic to Turkestan and containing 60 million inhabitants; a Caucasian state; the Ukraine; and the *Ostland*, consisting of the three Baltic states and White Russia. All these states would be ruled by German Commissioners of proconsular dignity and two of them actually began to take shape in the *Ostland* and the Ukraine under Commissioners whose functions were similar *in partibus infidelium* to those of the Gauleiters of the Reich.

The *Ostland* was a hybrid. White Russia's function was to be a dump for undesirables who had not been murdered and could not yet be transported to Siberia. The fate of the three Baltic states was peculiarly poignant. These singularly well governed and civilized communities were first

THE ROSENBERG PLAN 1941

Germany before the invasion of the U S S R in 1941.

Territory to be annexed to Germany and controlled by Berlin.

Independent states to be under close German control.

Proposed Soviet national territory.

Proposed administrative centre for the entire eastern region.

500

Miles

0

—ARTHUR BANKS—

CHINA

AFGHANISTAN

PERSIA

TURKEY

SIBERIA

URAL

TURKESTAN

MUSCOVY

GREATER FINLAND

GREATER BELORUSSIA

POLAND

BESSARABIA

GREATER UKRAINE

CRIMEA

GREATER CAUCASIA

BALTIKUM

BALTIC SEA

BLACK SEA

CASPIAN SEA

Aral Sea

Lake Balkhash

Krasnoyarsk

Tomsk

Barnaul

Novosibirsk

Omsk

Alma Ata

Karaganda

Samarkand

Tashkent

Vorkuta

Svedlovsk

Keltas

Kazan

Ufa

Magnitogorsk

Krasnovodsk

Murmansk

Archangel

Vologda

Moscow

Ryazan

Stalingrad

Astrakhan

Leningrad

Helsinki

Riga

Minsk

Kiev

Kharkhov

Rostov

Novorossiisk

Tiflis

Batum

Odessa

Berlin

GERMANY

Warsaw

shackled by the USSR in 1939 and then absorbed in the next year. On the approach of war in 1941 the Russians started deporting and massacring the inhabitants, and they continued to do so as they slowly retreated before the Germans. The Germans began by treating the three states comparatively lightly and even accorded them a degree of administrative autonomy, but in 1942–3 they introduced their full programme of concentration camps, slave labour and the murder of Jews – to the accompaniment of public lectures on the superiority of German culture. (When the Germans were again evicted by the Russians, the killings went on none the less. A number of refugees, mainly Estonians, escaped to Sweden, though many died on the way. Depopulation was continued by deportations into the USSR after the war.)

In the Ukraine Rosenberg was encouraged by signs of welcome for the Germans (an autonomist, anti-Soviet movement raised false German hopes) and by the surrenders of Russian troops in the first weeks of the campaign (which he exaggeratedly ascribed solely to political rather than military causes). But his schemes never came to anything. Hitler was not interested in separatist vassal states. He told Rosenberg that the Baltic states, the Crimea, Baku and its neighbourhood, the Volga region and the Kola peninsula in the far north were to be entirely German. Erich Koch too, Rosenberg's Commissioner in the Ukraine, regarded his bailiwick simply as a source of food and labour for the Reich and derided his chief's political vision of a Ukrainian state as a stepping stone on the way to the Caucasus and a fender hung out to keep Russians and Poles at a safe remove. For Koch, as for Hitler, the Commissariat was a prelude to colonization. But Koch was a cleverer man than his chief Rosenberg. He soon sensed that this prelude had no sequel and he rarely visited the Ukraine. Rosenberg himself had to witness all his plans set on one side even before the turn of the military tide extinguished them. He experienced complete failure earlier than his equals in the Nazi hierarchy.

Rosenberg's activities provided a cloak for the operations of the SS. Although Rosenberg's Ministry, like the government of Hans Frank in Poland, was regarded by the SS as a nuisance and there was a good deal of friction between these different authorities, they became in effect collaborators in measures designed to kill even more people than the regular armed forces. They dealt death in the open and death in the camp.

Death on a grand scale by one or other of these methods was resolved upon in 1941 before the invasion of the USSR. A massacre programme was discussed between SS and army chiefs in May and four special squads or *Einsatzgruppen* were formed by the SS to round up and kill ideological opponents such as communist officials, political commissars

GERMAN RULE IN THE EAST 1941-1944

Six million Jews were murdered in the concentration camps and cities plus an equal number of non-Jewish Russians and Poles, two million of whom were children. Two million Soviet prisoners of war also were starved or beaten to death, and this policy of mass-murder led to partisan activity behind the German front line.

Baltic Sea

Reval
Novgorod

UNOCCUPIED
TERRITORY

Pskov

Riga
Dvinsk

Volokolamsk

OSTLAND
Kovno
Vilna
Vitebsk

Danzig ● ☐ *STUTTHOF*

TREBLINKA ☐
Bialystok

Minsk

GREATER
GERMANY

Orel

Kalisz ●
CHELMNO ☐

Warsaw
Lublin
MAJDANEK ☐ *BELZEC*
Cracow
AUSCHWITZ ☐
Lvov

☐ *SOBIBOR*

Rovno

Gomel

Kursk

Chernigov

Kiev

SLOVAKIA

Zhitomir

UKRAINE

HUNGARY

RUMANIAN MILITARY GOVERNMENT

Nikopol

Rostov

Melitopol

Stavropol

Odessa

RUMANIA

Krasnodar

Sevastopol
Yalta

Black Sea

Legend
- ⬛ Areas ruled by the German military.
- ⬛ Administered by the General-Government of Poland.
- ⬛ Administered by the Ostland and Ukraine Reichskommissariats.
- ⬛ Annexed by Germany.
- ☐ Main concentration camps.
- ★ Partisans active in these areas.

0 ——— 200
Miles

~ARTHUR BANKS~

and Jews. A special order for the murder of political commissars was issued by Hitler and transmitted through army channels at the beginning of June. A commissar was not defined, and, whether or not the vagueness was intentional, its effect was to license indiscriminate killing. Not only were suspected commissars shot out of hand or delivered by the army to the SD (which came to much the same thing): in addition recalcitrant or awkwardly sick prisoners could be dubbed commissars and summarily disposed of. The trigger-happiness of army officers and other ranks was encouraged by a further order, issued on the eve of the invasion, which did away with judicial proceedings in the military area and empowered battalion commanders and upwards to hear cases and impose penalties (including death) without the formality of assembling a court.

The four *Einsatzgruppen* were quite small – each was 500–800 strong – but their importance was shown by the choice of their commanders, who included the heads of Departments III, V and VIa of the RSHA. These men expected to end up in the four principal cities of the USSR where they would blossom into the local tsars of the New Order. Meanwhile their business was simply to kill. They began by inciting pogroms but were disappointed by the unenthusiastic response and were obliged to set to work more systematically. Leading Jews were required to assemble their fellows at given points, whereupon all were driven off to a nearby open space, stripped and shot. The dead and half dead were tumbled into trenches. Others were drowned or burned alive wholesale. No concealment was attempted or possible. The razzias were witnessed by thousands, talked about and even photographed. The executioners had to be kept up to their task by being made half drunk (which did not improve their aim), by treble pay and long holidays. A typical operation involved several hundred victims and took several hours. The largest single operation was the killing of over 33,000 Kievan Jews in two days in September 1941 as a reprisal for the blowing up of a hotel – the fearful inspiration of Yevtushenko's poem *Babi Yar* and the basis for Anatoly Kuznetsov's novel of the same name; the mass grave of these dead and dying Jews continued to be used as a dump for what the Nazis regarded as human refuse until it contained at least 100,000 corpses. A year later about 16,000 Jews were killed in a single day at Pinsk with the help of grenades, axes, dogs and SS cavalry. On the only occasion on which Himmler attended a massacre, it turned his stomach and made him order a change in technique: there was to be less shooting and more gassing.

Each of the *Einsatzgruppen* tended to magnify its achievements, so that it is impossible to take at its face value the boast by one commander, Erich Ohlendorf, that he had been personally responsible for the death of

90,000 people, most of them Jews, before he relinquished his command in June 1942, but it is probable that the number of Jews killed by Germans in the east was about two million. The disposal of the bodies was so rudimentary that the gases generated by decomposition betrayed the places of burial by a continuous barrage of small explosions, and a special squad had to be formed to open the graves and lay this ghastly evidence by chemical action, bonfires or mechanical pulverization.

The Jews of the rest of Europe were meanwhile being driven to their principal graveyard, the extermination camps of Poland. These camps were a specialized variety of the concentration camps which the Nazis had established in Germany immediately after coming to power.

A concentration camp is essentially a guarded area where people are sent and kept against their will, as though in prison. But a concentration camp is something different from a prison. A camp may be established because the prisons are full, but this is not why the Nazi camps were established. A man is sent to prison because he has been accused and convicted of a crime, and he is sent by a court. The men and women who were sent to the concentration camps were not accused or convicted of crimes; they were simply obnoxious to the régime, either because they were opposed to it or because they were – like the Jews – obnoxious by definition. And they were not committed to the camps by a court. They were sent there by party functionaries exercising a whim like an absolute monarch signing *lettres de cachet*. Further, the men and women in the camps were not meant to come out again. They were meant to rot and die there, and usually they did. Finally, the concentration camps were not created, like prisons, to hold men in durance and no more. They were also intended to intimidate those who remained outside them, and they did so by the cruelty of those who ran them and whose behaviour was no secret, and by the doubts which were allowed to circulate about citizens who abruptly disappeared from normal life.

The first concentration camp was established in March 1933, within a few weeks of the Nazis taking power. It was at Dachau, near Munich. Others were established in the years that followed, and the camp business received a boost when the *Anschluss* with Austria and the subjection of Bohemia-Moravia opened up new areas for the Nazi press gangs. With the beginning of the war the nature of the camps as well as their scale changed, for they became the scene of the Nazi policy of mass extermination. In the next few years millions were killed in them, perhaps seven millions – by hard labour, privation, epidemics, medical experiments on their bodies, fusillade, bastinado or asphyxiation.

During this period the camps were divided into two main categories.

Most of them were labour camps, in which people from all over Europe toiled for Germany for a certain number of months until they dropped dead or were killed off because they had become useless. Some of these camps were near important factories and were run by the captains of big industry. In a different category were the death camps, whose business was extermination. There were five of these, all of them in Poland. The first was established at Auschwitz (Oswiecim), near Katowice in Silesia, soon after the defeat of Poland in 1939. Auschwitz developed into a complex of camps, one of which was the showpiece of modern technical killing by means of the gas called Cyclon B (guaranteed to kill within ten minutes) and of modern technical disposal in the ovens of its crematorium. After the invasion of the USSR four more extermination camps were established in Poland at Chelmno, Treblinka, Sobibor and Belsec (not to be confused with Bergen-Belsen which was partly a Wehrmacht hospital camp and partly an SS internment camp near Hanover in Germany).

The Polish Jews had priority because they were on the spot. There were in Poland in 1939 over three million Jews. Their numbers made them a special case. Nowhere except in Palestine did Jews constitute so large a proportion of the population. Nowhere except in the United States were so many Jews to be found. Nowhere at all, probably, was anti-semitism so potent or the extermination of Jews so readily acceptable to Gentiles. The first German plan was to concentrate all Jews from the German zone of Poland in an area in the east of the zone, but the attempt to do this created such chaos on the railways that the plan had to be abandoned. Instead ghettos were established in the principal towns. A Jew found outside a ghetto could be executed. Those inside were starved and over-crowded. Epidemics developed fast. Jew-baiting was encouraged with the inevitable results of torture and private-enterprise murder. The Warsaw ghetto, whose sealing walls were completed in October 1940, contained about half a million Jews. The extermination camps began functioning at the end of 1941 with Chelmno destroying about a thousand human beings a day, and during 1942 the Polish ghettos were gradually emptied into them. At one time Treblinka alone was taking 6,000 a day, and Auschwitz, which killed well over one million people in less than three years, could take twice as many in its stride. The disposal of the Warsaw ghetto began in July 1942 when there were probably still about 380,000 Jews in it. By the beginning of October there remained only 50–60,000 hiding and starving in insanitary cellars and sewers (built to British design in the previous century). They were governed by a suborned Jewish police and a half honest *Judenrat* until, driven beyond the limits of endur-ance and faced with the extinction of all hope, an enfeebled residue staged in April 1943 a desperate and doomed rising. They fought alone: most Polish Gentiles were indifferent to their fate or worse. Yet their struggle lasted seven weeks before all were either killed or taken and shipped to the gas chambers. Their enduring memorial is Schoenberg's threnody for speaker, chorus and orchestra, *A Survivor from Warsaw*. A commemorative volume with some fifty illustrations was prepared by the SS and presented to Himmler.

By this time the stench of the camps had become so horrible and the danger of epidemics so great that mass burials and mass pyres had been largely superseded by cremation in specially designed ovens which would take half a dozen bodies at a time. The congestion in the extermination camps (sometimes aggravated by technical breakdowns which obliged trainloads of living victims to wait unloaded in sidings for several days) was caused by the international character of the Polish camps. Deportations from Germany itself and occupied countries swelled the traffic from the end of 1941.

In this year the Nazis finally decided to rid Germany of all its Jews. A plan to deposit them in the USSR having been frustrated by transport difficulties, they were routed instead to Auschwitz and eastern Poland for extermination. A conference on the Wannsee in January 1942 decided also to kill all Croat, Slovak and Rumanian Jews in occupied territory and to inform the governments of Croatia, Slovakia, Hungary and Bulgaria that the Germans were ready to deal with their Jews too. Jews from Austria and Bohemia-Moravia were treated as German Jews. Technically this extermination programme was based on an earlier programme for the 'euthanasia' of alleged incurables which accounted for some 90,000 victims of Nazi distemper before unwelcome disclosures in 1941 brought it to a halt and subsequently transferred its apparatus outside the Reich where its catchment was extended from 'incurables' to Jews, gipsies and Russian prisoners of war. (Of the many millions of Russian war victims two million were murdered prisoners of war.) The Wannsee conference made concrete Hitler's proclaimed aim to destroy the Jews, but action had already begun in the previous year when the *Einsatzkomandos* killed a million Jews.

The Wannsee conference came up against the problem which had been worrying Nazi racists for years: what to do about Germany's half-Jews and quarter-Jews. Heydrich proposed that the former should be sterilized instead of being deported, but Hitler objected, mainly because at bottom he opposed any solution except their removal from German soil. The problem of the half-Jew continued to be debated but was never settled one way or another. Quarter-Jews, who were exempt from the

Nuremberg laws, were to remain unmolested unless they were too obviously Jewish in appearance or – sinister opening for blackmail – there were special circumstances. There was a special category of privileged Jews. These included war veterans, Jews over sixty-five, holders of the Iron Cross First Class, senior civil servants, Jews with foreign connections or an international reputation, and others who still had the means to bribe the police. Their fate depended very much on the personal whim of the local Gauleiter and other officials. Privileged Jews remained subject to blackmail, often crudely expressed in such terms as 'going up the chimney' or 'making compost'. They had no legal status or redress and might suddenly find themselves dispatched to a concentration camp for talking in a tram or smoking in the street or receiving a food parcel. The camp at Theresienstadt (Terezin) in Czechoslovakia was reserved for them and was from time to time opened to representatives of the Red Cross. Privileged Jews died in Theresienstadt instead of in other camps, until the confusion of the last stages of the war caused them to be dispersed for extermination. When the war ended Theresienstadt had a residue of 20,000 inmates, one third of them not Jews.

The Greater German Reich was declared purged of Jews in November 1943. This was not strictly true. Many Jews who had married Gentiles, as well as half-Jews and quarter-Jews, survived. There were about 33,000 of them in Germany at the end of the war.

In western occupied countries Jews were removed immediately from public office and subjected to petty inhumanities such as being forbidden to eat in cafés or restaurants, use public transport or (in Holland) ride a bicycle. Next a census would be taken, property confiscated, segregation enforced. During 1942 many western Jews were driven into labour camps in their own countries and in the following year deportation began. It was substantially completed before the end of 1943. At first certain categories were exempted – for example, childless Jews married to Gentiles were given the alternative of sterilization – but these were administrative measures designed to ease the logistics of mass transport and mass murder and keep sections of Jewry quiet until their turn came. In 1943 Auschwitz was so busy that Jews from Holland and Luxembourg had to be sent all the way to Sobibor and Treblinka respectively. French Jews on the other hand went mainly to Auschwitz. Preparations for their deportation began in March 1942 and were extended in June to include the unoccupied zone: 100,000 Jews were to be collected and sent east. After the biggest single round-up – in July when 13,000 men, women and children were crammed into the concentration camp at Drancy and the Vélodrome d'Hiver in hideous conditions – French Jews were being transported to Poland at the rate of a thousand a day. The total was aggravated by Switzerland's refusal to admit or harbour Jewish fugitives. By a curious twist, however, a number of French Jews were saved by French anti-semitism. France had an anti-semitic strain of its own hardly less pronounced than Germany's. Even today, after the Nazi holocaust, no Jew has replaced the French Jew Alfred Dreyfus as the principal symbol of European anti-semitism. French anti-semites were given their heads by Vichy and at Laval's direction the French police helped the S D to round up the Jews in France, but Laval's perverted nationalism insisted that French Jews, as opposed to Jews of different nationality who had fled to France, should be dealt with by the French authorities instead of being sent to Germany or Poland. Some of them survived and after the extension of the German occupation to the whole country in November many escaped to the Italian zone and Monaco. Thus the Germans contrived to kill only about a quarter of French Jewry as compared with half the Belgian Jews and over three quarters of the Dutch. (The last were specially vulnerable in a small country in which it was difficult to hide. They had nowhere like the Ardennes, where many Belgian Jews and other refugees congregated, and as a community they had had little contact with the Gentiles who alone could have concealed large numbers of them.) In the west as a whole the 7,500 Danish Jews fared least badly. An attempt was made to round them up after the Germans took over in 1943, but all save a few hundred were saved. A German official leaked a warning of the plan and practically the entire Jewish community was first hidden and then transported in small vessels to Sweden, where they were looked after until the end of the war. When the Germans came to round up their victims, they found that the birds had flown. Of Norway's small Jewish community of about 2,000 some 750 were caught. Italian Jews were deported to Auschwitz and other camps by the Germans after the fall of Mussolini.

South-eastern Europe also provided its share of victims – about one million. In Rumania, with its large Jewish community of nearly three quarters of a million, pogroms were initiated without German encouragement and two thirds of Rumanian Jewry perished during the war in one way or another. In Bulgaria on the other hand the government's agreement to fall in with German plans by surrendering its Jews for deportation was thwarted by demonstrations of public disgust. In Serbia and Croatia most Jews were killed without being deported. A number of Croatian Jews escaped from the German to the Italian zone of occupation and thence later to the partisans. Of the 75,000 Greek Jews in Salonica at least two thirds were sent to Auschwitz in 1943.

In Slovakia the work of deportation and extermination was begun in

1942 with the cooperation of the puppet government but then suspended; it was resumed and completed after the Slovak rising of 1944. The Hungarian Jews were the last to go. Up to July 1944 they were persecuted but not exported for extinction. They numbered at this date about 440,000 of whom nearly half were in the Hungarian capital. The arrival of Eichmann heralded a grim turn but the Regent Hörthy (until the abolition of his régime by the Germans in October) was willing to offer an escape route and after some hesitations the American and British governments consented to discuss ways and means. A section at least of the S S seemed to be privy to these manoeuvres and two Hungarian Jews (Joel Brand and another) who arrived in Istanbul in July were thought to be instruments of an S S plan to secure from the allies food, soap and 10,000 lorries – the last for use on Russian fronts only – in return for allowing Hungarian Jews to escape their coming fate. Although Jewish leaders realized that western belligerents would not agree to help the German effort against the Russians, some of them hoped that the negotiations might be spun out in such a way as to stave off the killing of surviving Jews or to organize their ransom for money instead of lorries. But the offer was not taken seriously by the outside world and Brand was even put in prison by the British in the Middle East with whom he was supposed to negotiate. The Hungarian Jews were pawns whom the allies refused to buy on the terms proposed, while in Hungary Eichmann, more intent on the genocide of the Jews than on the provision of food and transport for the German armies, proceeded to round up and dispatch for extermination those Jews whom the fanatics of the post-Hörthy régime did not shoot, club or starve to death. Discussions with the Americans and British dragged on unrealistically until February 1945 when Hitler, perhaps previously unaware of them, put an end to them.

The separateness of the Jews militated against their survival. Cut off and marked out by their history and their circumstances, they were exposed to separate destruction in a way in which no other groups were exposed. Their alternatives were to resist in isolation or just wait. They did both: many waited but others, belying the passivity which had marked their people between their risings against the Romans and the outrages of the twentieth century, rebelled in arms as well as in spirit. Flight from the community was inhibited by family loyalties. It tended to be postponed from month to month in the desperate hope that, as in the past, the Jew would be saved because he was useful: in the *Ostland* a Jew's most precious document was his work certificate. In Germany a number of Jews passed themselves off as bombed-out refugees, resorting to every kind of disguise and desperate expedient to save themselves and their families; in

Vienna this was called 'doing a U-boat' – that is to say submerging. Gentiles were sometimes faced with the harrowing dilemma of taking them in or turning them away for fear that they might, by giving asylum to the outcasts, be consigning themselves and their own children to torture and death.

Many Jews resisted. In France Jews amounted to about a quarter of active resisters, many of them being Polish Jews who had left Poland during the pre-war period of anti-semitic, right-wing rule. In Poland several thousands of Jews took to the woods, formed bands of their own and fought, often in cooperation with escaped Russian prisoners. In Galicia they bought or took weapons from Italians who had been fighting on the Russian front but were on their way back to Italy. There were even risings inside the concentration camps, which were all the more remarkable in view of the utter exhaustion of most of the inmates. (Russian prisoners, for example, were driven on foot for hundreds of miles after the commissars among them had been shot and arrived in no condition to do anything except fall down.) The end of the extermination camp at Sobibor was highly dramatic. In September 1943 a first contingent of 1,750 Russian Jews arrived there, some of them former soldiers of the Russian army. All but eighty were immediately gassed but these eighty were kept alive to help build an extension of the camp and a few weeks after their arrival these and other Jews rose and attacked their guards with axes, knives and their bare hands. After ten S S guards had been killed about 400 prisoners escaped from the compound. Many of them ran into minefields and were killed. Others were rounded up again during the next few days in a hunt organized by the local S S command and yet others were killed by anti-semitic members of Polish right-wing bands. A few joined partisan groups and some eventually rejoined the Russian army. But Sobibor itself was destroyed by this act. Himmler ordered it to be abandoned and all traces of it to be expunged.

There were risings at Auschwitz too. The first, by a handful of surviving Russian prisoners of war in the summer of 1942, was largely a failure. Some were shot trying to escape, others were recaptured later; a few got away. Two years later a second attempt, organized by Jews in the Auschwitz extermination camp, was also unsuccessful. Four S S guards were killed but so were 455 prisoners.

As the war neared its end and the Russian armies approached Poland the surviving inmates of the extermination and labour camps were hurriedly destroyed by lethal injections or by being mowed down by gunfire. Some were removed to camps farther west, but although Himmler ordered the killing to stop in October 1944, a mere two or three per cent of all the

JEWISH EXTERMINATION 1941-1945

- ◉ German concentration camps and extermination camps.
- □ Approximate Jewish population 1941. (total: 8,500,000).
- ■ Number of Jews exterminated by 1945 (total: 5,400,000).

TURKEY

Black Sea

0   200
Miles

~ARTHUR BANKS~

RUSSIA (German occupied)
■ 2,500,000
■ 750,000

LITHUANIA
□ 140,000
■ 104,000

TREBLINKA
1942

POLAND
□ 3,000,000
■ 2,600,000

SOBIBOR
1942

MAJDENEK
1943

BELZEK
1942

RUMANIA
□ 750,000
■ 500,000

BULGARIA
□ 48,000
■ 40,000

Baltic Sea

STUTTHOF
1942

WARSAW
GHETTO

CHELMO
1941

AUSCHWITZ
1940

GREECE
□ 80,000
■ 60,000

LATVIA
□ 100,000
■ 70,000

RAVENSBRÜCK
1942

SACHSENHAUSEN
1936

GROSSROSEN

THERESIENSTADT

HUNGARY
□ 800,000
■ 700,000

ALBANIA

NEUENGAMME
1940

BELSEN
1943

GERMANY
□ 250,000
■ 180,000

CZECHOSLOVAKIA
□ 810,000
■ 60,000

MAUTHAUSEN
1938

YUGOSLAVIA
□ 70,000
■ 58,000

DENMARK
□ 6,000
■ 100

MITTLEBAU-DORA
1943

BUCHENWALD
1937

FLOSSENBERG

DACHAU
1933

AUSTRIA
□ 70,000
■ 60,000

Adriatic Sea

HOLLAND
□ 140,000
■ 104,000

VUGHT
1940

NATWEILER

SWITZ.

ITALY
□ 120,000
■ 9,000

BELGIUM
□ 85,000
■ 40,000

FRANCE
□ 300,000
■ 65,000

GREAT
BRITAIN

From Europe 280,000
Jewish refugees to U.S.A.,
South America, Great Britain,
and Japan 1933-1940.

Jews abducted during the war survived it. The number of deaths is incalculable. It lies somewhere between four and six million. The gipsies, who
were also marked down for total destruction, lost perhaps 200,000 lives;
the evidence about their sufferings is vague, but on one occasion at Auschwitz 4,000 of them seem to have been gassed in a single, if prolonged,
operation. Gentiles too were killed in droves, including Germans for
whom the first concentration camps were originally instituted: at least
half a million men and women died in the German concentration camps
during the war from illness and ill-treatment. Himmler's aim of reducing
the world's Slav population by 30 million was not attained, although the
losses suffered by the Russians in battle and at the hands of the SS went
some way towards realizing this abominable ambition. The apostles of
the New Order showed that, given time, their destructive plans were not
beyond the compass of human techniques and human will.

The massacre of millions of European Jews was a culminating act in the
history of the relations between Jew and Gentile. Hitler did not invent
anti-semitism. It was wrapped up in Europe's inheritance from Christendom. It lay ready to Hitler's hand and he used it with a pitiless thoroughness which made him a special kind of anti-semite. The myth of a
Jewish conspiracy to pervert the world is a Christian myth which has been
propagated by Christian writers of eminence and authority almost as far
back as the origins of their religion and right up to the present century,
and the same writers have also been responsible for the odious slanders
against the character and practices of the Jew which Hitler and other
modern anti-semites were able to cite and endorse. (One of the commonest of these myths is the charge that Jews murdered non-Jewish
children for ritual purposes. The first child alleged to have been killed in
this way, William of Norwich, who died in 1144, is still officially venerated
by Roman Catholics as a saint and martyr although there is no particle of
evidence about the manner of his death. Nor is there any better evidence
about any of the other cases of this kind.)

In the eighteenth century opponents of Christianity, such as the leaders
of the Enlightenment, who might have been expected to defend the Jews,
had their own kind of anti-semitism since they reprobated Jewry as the
forerunner of Christianity, while in the nineteenth century racist theories
sharpened the persecution of the Jews by making their offence inexpiable.
So long as the Jew was persecuted on account of his religion he might
escape its worst consequences by baptism, but when he was persecuted on
account of his race he had no way out except death. Whether Hitler, who
called himself a Roman Catholic, believed Christianity's anti-semitic
inventions or those of the racists is a question which he himself would

JEWISH RESISTANCE 1940–1944

Gulf
of
Riga

Baltic
Sea

LATVIA

Riga

LITHUANIA

Niemen

1942–1944 The 'Vilna Avengers.'

1943–1944 The 'Tobias Bielski' Division.

EAST
PRUSSIA

Vilna

Minsk

Lida

Mir

Jerusalem

WHITE

1943–1944 Jewish sanctuary in the woods.

Bialystok

P
O
L
A
N
D

Treblinka

Vistula

Bug

RUSSIA

WARSAW

Vistula

Sobibor

Lublin

Czestochowa

Koniecpol

Lutzk

UKRAINE

Sosnowica

Sielce

Zhitomir

Bendzin

Brody

Auschwitz

Cracow

Tarnow

Lvov

Stryzow

Tarnopol

■ Ghettoes in which the Jews organized risings against German rule.
▨ Areas of Jewish partisan group activity.
◉ Concentration camps in which Jewish risings occurred.

0   50
Miles

~ARTHUR BANKS~

have regarded as senseless. The point was not whether they were true but whether they were useful, and, as he once said to Rauschning, anti-semitism was an essential tool for spreading Nazism in Germany and beyond. On this issue his political cynicism fitted nicely with his deeper emotions, since besides using anti-semitism he hated Jews.

The enormity of what was done in the forties has led to a search for an explanation: what are the origins of this conflict and its Hitlerian solution? This is one of the most complex problems in the history of Europe, to which much learning and ingenuity have been devoted. Certain general factors appear at first sight: the religious differences, accentuated by Christendom's condemnation of the Jewish race for deicide; the recognizable physical features of many Jews; their own insistence on their religious and national identity, accentuated by their dispersal; the special functions which, historically, they filled in European societies, often unpopular ones such as money lending. At a deeper level theories about the vulnerability of the Jews have been advanced. One of the more interesting of these attaches importance to the fact that the special services which they once provided came to be no longer needed; for example, their function as the financiers of the state was essential so long as the state was financed through personal borrowing by monarchs but became otiose when this method was replaced by government taxation of the whole community. But the more that Jewish-Gentile relations are probed the more dangerous does it appear to generalize beyond a certain point, for it becomes clear that the position of the Jews in Christendom has varied greatly from time to time and from place to place, so that an explanation of the plight of the Jews in Poland in the twentieth century, for example, will not – except superficially – fit their circumstances in France at the same or any other date.

The premeditated execution of five to six million people by methods of singular barbarity should, one hopes, be difficult to explain. Part of the explanation is to be found in the fact that anti-semitism is ancient, widespread and irrational; yet this is no explanation, since it merely shifts the question back into the past and, by raising it again in a remoter historical context, makes it even more difficult to answer. The emotions which anti-semitism produces are fierce, and the ends which these emotions have compassed have been tacitly approved by thousands or millions of people who would themselves recoil from the methods used. Schemes for saving Jews from Nazi Germany were half-hearted at best. Before the war the Nazis would promise only a small annual exodus of workers without families or capital and tried to link this exodus with a boost to German exports by getting the receiving countries to undertake to increase their purchases of German goods. No country could be found willing to take substantial numbers of Jews; the British barred Palestine to them except in small numbers and on stringent terms; the Americans were so unimaginative as to require certificates of birth which few German Jews possessed and none could ask for from a German official (but a number of Christian priests forged baptismal certificates for them); a Bill to permit 20,000 Jewish children to enter the United States was killed by a 'patriotic' lobby in the Congress on the grounds that it offended against the sanctity of family ties and in spite of the fact that the immigration quotas from Germany were regularly underfilled. Hitler was able to exult that nobody wanted the Jews and so, since there was nowhere for them to go, he had no option but to destroy them.

Hitler's personal commitment to the wholesale murder of the Jews is incontrovertible. He himself proclaimed it more than once. He believed in it; he devoted considerable resources to its accomplishment in the middle of war; and Himmler, Canaris and others stated that it was ordered by Hitler and was therefore not to be questioned. The lack of any written order signed by Hitler is neither weighty nor surprising.

Allied leaders have not escaped some share of the responsibility for these terrible murders. Their culpability is at an altogether lower level but by the winter of 1942 – 3 at the latest the purpose of Auschwitz and its four companion outfits in Poland was known and published. The facts were so appalling and so unwelcome that most of those who became aware of them contrived to disbelieve or dismiss them. But in 1944 the truth became inescapable when two Jews who had escaped from Auschwitz arrived in the west to tell their tale. Jewish organizations pressed for action such as the bombing of access routes or the bombing of the gas chambers themselves. Allied governments tried to sidestep the issue, alleging that the camps were beyond acceptable bombing range. Yet Auschwitz was within range by August 1944 since a synthetic oil plant, adjacent to the camp and revealed by photographic reconnaissance in April, was bombed in that month and the camp itself was accidentally bombed in September in the course of an American raid on a target a few miles further east. One excuse for inaction against the camps – that the inmates might get killed or be put the more quickly into the gas chambers – seems peculiarly inappropriate in the light of the knowledge that 12,000 were being gassed daily at Auschwitz alone. While the greater number of the victims had been killed by this time, the minority who died later were nevertheless very many. The charge of moral myopia will not go away.

The Roman Catholic church had, it may be thought, a special obligation to do something for the Jews both because of its special contribution to

16 Women's work:
'somewhere in Wales'

17 *Top*: The latest in air raid
shelters: South Wales, 1938

18 *Bottom*: The London
blitz: nightly scene in Holborn
tube station

19 The London blitz:
Smithfield

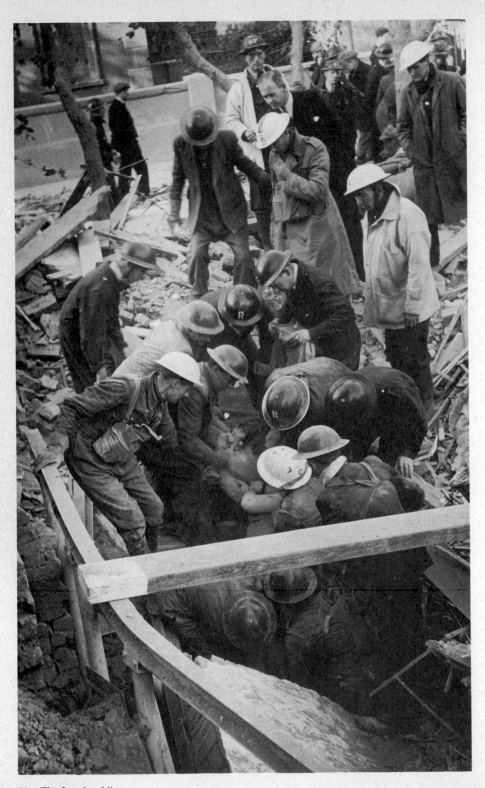

20 The London blitz:
retrieving the dead and dying

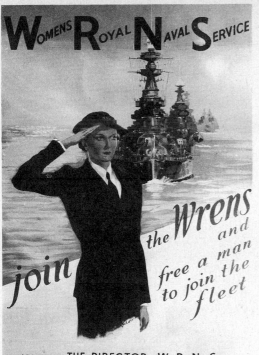

APPLY TO THE DIRECTOR W·R·N·S
50 CHARING CROSS. LONDON S.W.I

21 Join the Wrens

22 All for the front, all for victory!

23 *Top*: The Ukraine
welcomes Germans, summer
1941

24 *Bottom*: German defeat
before Moscow, winter 1941

25 Stalingrad: winter 1942–3

26 Stalingrad, 1943

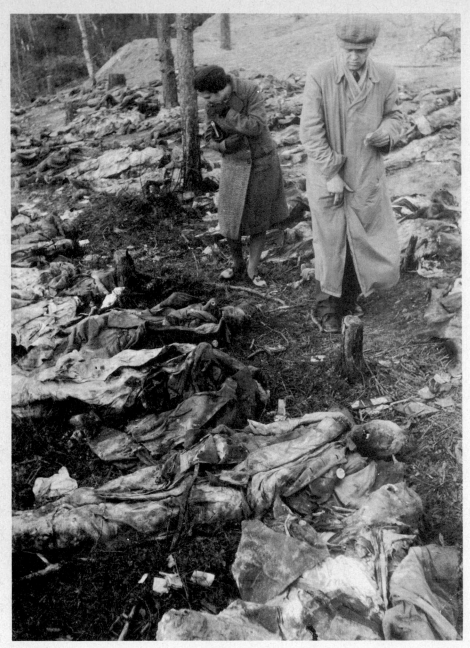

27 Discovery of the Katyn
massacre

anti-semitism over nearly 2,000 years and because of its own teaching on
brotherly love. Very many churchmen were compassionate men horrified
by Nazi crimes but the church as a body was caught in the toils of its own
propaganda, old and new. In modern times Jewry, besides being collectively charged with the judicial murder of Jesus, was associated with a
special kind of ungodliness. The French Revolution and the Bolshevik
Revolution were both blamed, again by professed Christian writers, on
the Jews, who were made the scapegoats for whatever was alarming to the
established order, and especially to the established ecclesiastical order, in
a world which had begun to change faster than seemed desirable to those
who were used to running it. Again, Hitler did not invent the equation of
communism with Jewry; but he was able to profit from it. The more
sophisticated and honest enemies of communism knew that the government of the USSR was very far from being run by Jews, but, because
they detested and feared communism, they hesitated to speak out against
Nazism for fear of undermining the German state and so helping Russian
communism to advance into the centre of Europe and join hands with
powerful communist parties in the west. The Jews – and the Christian
conscience – were sacrificed to this dilemma.

The Roman Catholic church in Germany was persecuted by Hitler. It
also came to terms with him and in 1933, on orders from the Vatican, the
Centre Party, which was the political face of the church, voted for the
Enabling Act which gave Hitler full authority to destroy the German
constitution and society. Most of the Roman Catholic bishops then made
haste to take back all that they had been saying about the beastliness of
the Nazis, Roman Catholic theologians set themselves the task of demonstrating the essential compatibility of Christian and Nazi doctrine,
and pulpits which had been used to denounce the latter emitted a new
view of the Führer as a man of God. The church so far attuned itself to
Nazism as to overlook the concentration camps and endorse Hitler's
foreign policy. When war came the German Roman Catholic clergy
broadly supported it and continued to do so in spite of the murder of
their Polish colleagues, officially reported, and in spite of Hitler's unwar-
ranted attacks on small, helpless neutrals; his attack on the USSR evoked
a crusading enthusiasm. But many Christians, priests and laymen, exerted
themselves and risked their lives to succour Jews. The Dominican and
Jesuit orders were specially mindful of their Christian duty.

In the Vatican two Popes, Pius XI and Pius XII, had to contend with
the spiritual and practical crises occasioned by the rise of Fascism and
Nazism. Pius XI, who became Pope in 1922, was faced with the problem
of the relations between the Vatican and first Italy and then Germany.

Pius VIII had faced a similar problem in his dealings with Napoleon. Mussolini and Hitler, like Napoleon, wished to establish treaty relations with the Vatican and both succeeded. In the case of Hitler, Pius XI and his nuncio in Berlin and eventual successor, Eugenio Pacelli, believed that a concordat with Hitler would do more good than harm because it would give the Vatican a stronger claim to interfere on behalf of persecuted priests. A concordat was concluded in July 1933. Its effects were disappointing since Hitler persecuted the German clergy more than ever once he had got it, but the motives of Pius and Pacelli were sincere and their reasoning could not be definitely condemned before the event. Both men were disgusted by the Nazis and by anti-semitism. In March 1937 Pius XI issued, in German, the encyclical *Mit brennender Sorge*, which was read from all Roman Catholic pulpits in Germany and, although it contained no explicit reference to anti-semitism, was understood as a clear and sharp, if belated, attack on Nazi policies; but again the effects were very limited. Pacelli, who was consulted by the Pope before the encyclical was issued, toned up its language. He himself more anti-Nazi than many western conservatives and diplomats, delivered in the same year an openly anti-Nazi speech at Lisieux and upon his accession to the Papacy was condemned by the Nazis as even worse than his predecessor.

Despite the ritual mystery surrounding the election of a Pope the elevation of Pacelli to the Papal see on the death of Pius XI in 1939 was a foregone conclusion. Pius XI, departing from all precedent, had practically designated Pacelli as his successor, and one of the shortest conclaves on record sufficed to fill the vacancy. Pius XII had served as nuncio in Munich and then in Berlin and had other special connections with Germany, but he was also at that date the most widely travelled Cardinal in Europe and beyond ever to become Pope. The breadth of his experience and of his intelligence were alike unusual. His opposition to inhumanity and aggression were beyond question. Yet he has been assailed for failing in his human and Christian duty. This supreme accusation against a supreme pontiff relates to his conduct in relation to both Christians and Jews. Directly and by his example he did much for thousands of Jews who were saved from death and given money, food, clothing and even employment in Roman Catholic institutions. But he made no public protest against the murders of Jews, did not use his awful weapon of excommunication against the murderers, refused to speak out against Vichy's anti-semitic laws (even when the French bishops did) and refused to intervene when, in October 1943, the Germans carried off over a thousand Jews from Rome itself to be gassed.

The Pope adopted one standard when he protested against the Russian invasion of Finland and another when he failed to protest against the German invasion of Poland. Although copiously informed about the Germans' treatment of the Poles he kept silent. He was chided by Cardinal Tisserant for even more unbecoming reticence over the misdeeds performed in his name by the *ustachi* in Croatia. This new state, which emerged from the dismemberment of Yugoslavia in 1941, was placed under the rule of Ante Pavelič, an Italian protégé since the twenties and a rabid Roman Catholic who was intent on destroying the two million Orthodox Christian Serbs in Croatia and on reviving the temporal sovereignty of the Papacy. Pavelič introduced a religious reign of terror, demanding wholesale conversions to Roman Catholicism, perpetrating atrocities which were ghastly even by the standards of these ghastly years, and encouraging his *ustachi* bands (often led by priests) to run amok. Roman Catholic bishops were appalled by his barbarity but judged it wiser to say little and accept compensation for their injured feelings in redeemed souls and enhanced church property. The Pope himself said nothing in public.

Pius XII could have argued, and perhaps did, that he must avoid the charge levelled against Benedict XV in the First World War of taking sides against Germany, that excommunication was no longer an incisive weapon (though he used it against communists after the war) and that public protest could do the victims more harm than good, but his posture in his dilemma was an unheroic one and contrasted unfavourably with that of some of his own nuncios and other Roman Catholic notabilities who were stirred to an open opposition which was often effective. He was in the uncomfortable dilemma of occupying an office whose pretensions were greater than its capacities and, in preferring the cautious to the outspoken course, he seemed to neglect his obligation to re-state the violated canons of human behaviour. Although he might not be able to save the victims, he could have pointed the finger of divine anger against the criminals. By keeping silent, he sanctioned the unheroic frailty of all those lesser men who prefer, unless exhorted and inspired, to pass by on the other side. He invited the charge of failing to keep the Christian conscience sharp and clean. That charge has since been laid. The record is mixed.

CHAPTER 12

Exploitation

THE pattern of German power in Europe was a patchwork. Very little territory was formally annexed to the Reich: Danzig, large slices of Poland and smaller ones of Belgium. Other areas were intended and prepared for annexation although not formally annexed and even formally assured of their continuing integrity and independence: Alsace and Lorraine, Luxembourg, parts of Slovenia. In these areas compulsory military service was introduced and the Reich Ministry of the Interior set about imposing German law and the German legal system, integrating postal, railway and customs services, changing place names and even personal names, adjusting citizenship rights and constraining the population to speak German. Formal annexation was only a matter of time. These were, from the practical point of view, districts which were contiguous with the Reich and had special strategic or economic value; from another point of view they were districts which had once been part of a medieval Germanic empire or were peopled by kinsmen of the German race.

Three other territories which were distinct from the Reich were nevertheless completely subordinated to it through a Governor General, a Protector and a Reich Minister. These territories, all of which lay to the east of Germany, were brought within the German customs area; their separate existence in international law was barely conceded; and various overlords within the Reich such as Goering as Commissioner for the Five Year Plan and Sauckel as Plenipotentiary for Labour were entitled to direct demands to their rulers. They were the Government General of Poland, ruled by Hans Frank with the status of a head of government but not a head of state; the Protectorate of Bohemia and Moravia, in which parts of the administration (justice, for example) were placed under Reich Ministries in Berlin but which had also a nominally autonomous administration in pseudo-diplomatic relations with Berlin and a Protector (first Neurath, then Heydrich and ultimately Frick) who advised this administration what to do and saw that it did it; and the Baltic and Russian territories which came under Rosenberg, who had theoretically the same executive and legislative powers as Hans Frank in Poland and exercised them through his Ministry for the East and its Reich Commissioners in Riga and Rovno for the *Ostland* and the Ukraine respectively.

~ARTHUR BANKS~

GERMAN CONTROL IN EUROPE 1942

Germany and her allies.

Annexed areas and areas scheduled for annexation.

Areas completely subordinated to Germany.

Areas under military government.

Areas under Reichkommissars.

Independent (in theory) until 1943.

Unoccupied France (until Nov 1942).

Neutrals.

The rest of occupied Europe was governed by military or civilian governors according to its continuing strategic importance. Greece, Yugoslavia, Belgium and occupied France were under military government. These areas were subject to decrees promulgated by the military authorities of the Reich and applied by the local military governor, who was in addition usually helped by civilian advisers posted to his staff to guide him in all but purely military affairs. The government of Belgium and north-eastern France, which formed a single administrative zone, was transferred to a civilian Reich Commissioner in July 1944 for the better supervision and regimentation of the local population. Greece and Yugoslavia both saw Italian and Bulgarian occupiers as well as German. The native government of Greece was put in the hands of a puppet government in Athens, that of Yugoslavia was divided between a puppet government in Belgrade and the separatist Croat state established under Ante Pavelič. This state comprised not only Croatia but also Bosnia and Herzegovina and part of the Dalmatian coast and was roughly co-terminous with the eleventh-century kingdom of the same name. Pavelič was a rabidly anti-Serb Croat who had curried favour with the Italians before the war as an enemy of the Yugoslav state and was then pressed on an unenthusiastic Hitler by Mussolini. After May 1941 Pavelič, who had had to cede most of the Adriatic islands and Dalmatian coast to Italy and accept a prince of the Italian royal house as king in Croatia, turned against the Italians. The king never visited his kingdom.

Norway and the Netherlands were placed under civilian Reich Commissioners – Josef Terboven and Artur Seyss-Inquart – who were directly responsible to Hitler and were empowered to legislate by decree and review all existing laws. The powers of crown and government were transferred to them, and each appointed deputies to overlord sections of the central administration and its regional offshoots. Obnoxious or potentially subversive elements in public life, such as parliaments and other elective bodies, the press and broadcasting, were abolished or brought under control, and the national police was subordinated to the German police and SS. Denmark was exceptional in that its head of state, the king, remained in the country throughout the war and in the exercise of his functions for most of it; the Danish cabinet continued to look to the sovereign and the Danish army remained in being in designated zones. There was no formal agreement but the military capitulation was made and accepted in return for recognition of Denmark's continuing independence and neutrality. Until 1943 relations between Germany and Denmark were conducted through diplomatic channels, although German officials had to be reminded from time to time that they must not treat Denmark as just another occupied country. In 1943 the Germans took over the country, the king was closely confined, the army was disbanded, the navy scuttled itself, and the government and parliament were dissolved. Thereafter Denmark was run by the SS.

If Germany had won the war Denmark and the Netherlands would probably have been annexed despite explicit assurances to the contrary. In both countries, although earlier in the Netherlands than in Denmark, political forms and economic activities were adjusted to German patterns and needs. Political parties – other than the local Nazi variant – were extinguished, Nazi laws introduced, production and labour treated as segments of the German economy. In the Netherlands trade-union leaders began by cooperating with the Germans in the hope of preserving their various auxiliary institutions and activities, but membership of unions dropped sharply and the creation of a labour front in 1942 caused union officials to resign too. Some unions were dissolved by decree when their officials resigned in protest against the appointment of pro-German overseers; one Roman Catholic union was dissolved when the Roman Catholic hierarchy ordered members to leave it on pain of being denied the sacraments. Dutch SS were formed as early as the autumn of 1940 (from candidates with untarnished ancestry back to 1800), took a personal oath to Hitler as the Greater German Führer and provided fighting units for the eastern front. Himmler planned to plant Nordic settlers from these countries in various parts of the USSR, whether they wanted to go there or not.

France, unlike every other defeated country, was run from two different capitals, Paris and Vichy. From Vichy Marshal Pétain's government exercised authority over the whole country except Alsace-Lorraine, virtually annexed to the Reich, and the zone in the south-east ceded to Italy by the armistice. From Paris Hitler's plenipotentiary, Otto Abetz, also exercised functions which covered occupied and unoccupied France: he was a career diplomat whose tasks were to advise the military commander in the occupied zone on political matters, to maintain permanent contact with the French government in Vichy and its representatives in the occupied zone, and generally to influence French politicians, the press and broadcasting. He straddled France, advising the German rulers in the north and bringing pressure to bear on Pétain and his ministers in the south. But in practice France was partitioned. As a defeated country waiting for a peace settlement it was subject to the interim arrangements accepted with the armistice. The Germans exacted the right to occupy the north with military and police forces, detached the north-east which, in terms of military government but not of civil administration, was controlled with Belgium from

Brussels, and created a prohibited zone running along the north and west coasts under strict military control. Abetz ruled indirectly in the unoccupied zone by addressing representations to Vichy, and Vichy's subservience to German power was never in doubt; although there was no outward German presence in the unoccupied zone until it too was occupied in November 1942, the SD operated there on a restricted scale from the beginning (for example, in tracking down wireless transmitters and operators).

In all these countries the pattern of German control at the top was invisible to most people who never had or were never given any clear picture of what role the Germans had assumed. What people saw was not a new pattern imposed by the conqueror but a series of random consequences of the impact of German rule on local administration. At the centre the Germans kept and even enlarged the powers of civil servants whom they converted from administrators into ministers-to-the-Germans with power to issue decrees, a form of indirect rule in which the Germans directed the civil service and the civil service directed everybody else. Local government bodies also remained in being, often with familiar faces in the same offices, but this reassuring continuity was contradicted by uncharacteristic behaviour on the part of mayors and other office-holders. Disturbingly these no longer did what they were expected to do. Nor did one mayor behave like the next one, for each reacted differently, the one more obediently, the other more defiantly or more slyly, to the directions of his superiors. Mayors whom the Germans regarded as satisfactory remained in office and were given enhanced authority, but since unsatisfactory mayors were replaced, those who survived became in effect appointees holding office during good behaviour. German observers were inserted into the machinery of government at the centre and also to some extent lower down – for example, on the governing boards of French *lycées*; Labour Offices were put under undisguised German control, so that an unemployed worker coming in to register even in a comparatively small town would find himself face to face with a German official who might direct him to work in Germany or in some occupied country other than his own. But for the most part the general public continued to deal with local authorities whom it knew, and was unaware of the extent to which or the methods by which they were subjected to German regulation. In fact German control, even where it was not obtrusive, was thorough and pervasive. Courts, like the administration, continued to function outwardly much as before, but the German police kept a watch on the sentences given in criminal courts and might override them, with the result that criminal justice became something of a lottery in which sentences differed widely from court to court and the accused did not know whether his sentence would stand. He even had reason to fear a light sentence since the Germans were more likely to step in and increase it.

In all occupied countries, whether under military or civilian rule, a great deal went on which did not meet the eye and was not meant to, and in particular Himmler's Higher SS and Police Führers were a law unto themselves. They normally held SS rank equivalent to that of the military governor or local troop commander and, *de jure* or *de facto*, circumvented the German military and civil power in implementing policies determined by Himmler. In the inevitable quarrels with local governors the SS had the advantage of knowing exactly where they stood, since the SS and police authorities in conquered areas were replicas by extension of the system familiar in the Reich. Most other offices were *ad hoc* creations in which a good deal of confusion prevailed.

The Germans turned out to be much less fond of local Nazis and pro-German parties than vice versa. They used such parties but felt no call to support them. In Belgium, for example, they made use of various collaborationist groups until these cancelled each other out by their competitive jealousies. In the Netherlands Seyss-Inquart paid very little attention to Adrian Mussert and the Dutch Nazis although some individuals were given minor administrative office. The Danish Nazi Party also proved valueless. In Norway a rather different situation arose because the German Commissioner Terboven was determined to retain power in his own hands, governing through a council in Oslo and regional deputies appointed by himself until ordered by Hitler to acknowledge Quisling and make him Prime Minister; Quisling's original role had been to subvert Norway in the German interest but this plan had been abandoned in favour of the military conquest of the country with the result that it was not clear to the new rulers sent by Hitler whether Quisling still counted or not. Only in France, under the aegis of Vichy, did native fascists flourish for a while. For day-to-day administration the Germans relied, where they could, on the existing machinery of government and its existing staff, supplemented by an injection of German officials at key points with the title but more than the status of observers. In the east, where the machinery was less good, the reliance impracticable and Slav sub-men by definition unemployable, they had to take over themselves except at levels or in matters which did not interest them.

One country escaped: Switzerland. In 1940 the general Swiss view was that Germany had won the war. The question was whether it would pay the Swiss better to be tough in this situation or pliant. They knew before the war that the Nazis treated Switzerland in their training manuals as

part of the Reich and showed it as such in official maps, and they also
knew that the German army had plans for an attack on Switzerland.
These plans were never put into operation but they nearly were on more
than one occasion.

Swiss planning for defence against Germany began in the mid-thirties,
ostensibly within the constraints of Swiss neutrality. In fact a very small
number of Swiss leaders deliberately transgressed this neutrality by entering into secret military discussions with France. They went so far as to
conclude, at the military but not the political level, plans for the entry of
French forces into Switzerland at the request of the Swiss government.
Documents captured by the Germans in France in 1940 gave Germany
grounds for invading Switzerland but they never did so.

Swiss airspace was infringed by both sides from 1940, for the most part
accidentally. The Swiss defences engaged aircraft, inflicting and suffering
casualties. A blackout was imposed in November 1940 in response to
German pressure when British bombers used Switzerland as a navigational
aid. As the air war grew fiercer but not much more accurate Switzerland
suffered increasing damage, for which it received reparation after the war
from the United States. It was blockaded by both sides and so forced to
introduce rationing of food and fuel. It was specially vulnerable on two
counts. Spies proliferated, and any undue toleration of their activities
could be dangerous: about 1,400 Swiss citizens and foreigners were arrested during the war years by a Swiss police determined to give the
belligerents no excuse to denounce Swiss neutrality. (But the famous Lucy
ring, frequently alleged to have been a British device for conveying Ultra
and other special intelligence to Moscow, was no such thing.) Secondly,
geography had set Switzerland in the eye of the hurricane – to quote the
phrase used by a post-war Swiss historian. Under a multilateral treaty of
1909 Switzerland was obliged to allow the passage in wartime of all non-
military material over its Alpine railways. This right was most valuable to
the Germans and Italians since the use of the Swiss route freed others for
military traffic, and there was therefore a corresponding fear that the
railways would either be seized by the Axis or sabotaged by their foes.

That Switzerland remained in spite of these hazards immune from
direct attack was primarily the reward of determination. The Swiss constitution provides for the appointment of a military, as opposed to a
civilian, commander-in-chief in times of emergency. On 30 August 1939
the Swiss parliament gave the cabinet emergency powers and on the same
day General Henri Guisan was named commander-in-chief. The appointment was controversial and contested and Guisan had to be on his guard
throughout the war against the intrigues of civilian and military per-

sonages who held that Switzerland's only chance of escaping a German invasion lay in a scrupulous emphasis on the Swiss tradition of neutrality: they believed that Switzerland must aim above all at avoiding any provocation of Hitler. General Guisan argued otherwise. He said that independence was even more important than neutrality, since without independence there would be no neutrality to protect; that the only threat to independence came from Germany; and that preparations must be made to meet this threat. On his orders a thousand factories, public works and public services, and Switzerland's numerous tunnels were prepared for demolition. In a dramatic, secret scene on the historic Rütli (where the Swiss confederation was inaugurated in 1291) 650 officers of the army took an oath to resist. A mountain redoubt was fortified where fighting would go on even if Switzerland's borders were forced and its frontier cities taken. Justified by results, Guisan lived to receive the acclaim of even the most timorous of his fellow citizens.

Germany's European allies complete the picture. They were Italy, Slovakia, Hungary, Rumania and Bulgaria. Slovakia was a puppet from the moment of its creation in 1939. In south-east Europe Hitler was prepared to let Rumania down as much and as often as it suited him, give Hungary most of what it wanted, enlarge Bulgaria to the dimensions tantalizingly glimpsed at San Stefano in 1877, and let Greece become an Italian province. If Hitler anticipated squabbles between Italians and Slavs he did so without distaste. Thus Bulgaria and Hungary were uneasy allies who made hay while the sun shone – Bulgaria at the expense of Rumania, Yugoslavia and Greece, and Hungary at the expense of the first two of these. When the sun stopped shining for the Germans in the middle of the war all these countries began to try to change sides. Rumania, which had tried to avoid taking sides between Germany and the western democracies, slid into alliance with Germany through fear of the Soviet Union but not without being forced by Hitler to yield territory to its neighbours and, indirectly, to evict its king. After being forced to cede Bessarabia and Northern Bukovina to the USSR King Carol sought territorial guarantees for the rest of his state from Hitler, but Hitler refused. The king, whose weak position was threatened not only by the loss of national territory but also by the hostility of the fascist Iron Guard (whose temper had not been improved by the murder in 1938 of its leader Corneliu Codreanu), tried to save himself by inviting the army leader Marshal Ion Antonescu and the Iron Guard to join his government, but they were advised by Germany not to. The loss of more territory by the second Vienna Award and the Treaty of Craiova (by which Hitler allotted parts of Rumania to Hungary and Bulgaria) made Carol's position impossible and he abdicated. Antonescu, a stupid rather than a sinister man, with a pushing wife, joined the government of the new King Michael and so too did the Iron Guard, but the mutual antipathy of the army and the Iron Guard produced a threat of civil war. The Iron Guard attempted a coup but Hitler, who wanted no trouble in Rumania and who had formed a favourable impression of Antonescu in the course of two visits by the Marshal to the Führer, decided to back the army which, with the help of German tanks, smashed the Iron Guard. Its leaders were lodged in internment camps until 1944 when, Antonescu having been overthrown by the tides of war, they were extracted to form a phantom Rumanian government in Vienna.

Italy was an ally of a different sort and its collapse in 1943 caused the biggest alteration to the pattern of German occupation before the retreat of the Germans themselves. The Germans were obliged to occupy those areas in south-eastern Europe which had been left to the Italians and to worry about the quantities of Italian arms which passed into the hands of Yugoslav and Greek partisans. Even more serious was the problem of Italy itself. Hitler was ill-informed about Italy. He had forbidden secret service activities there and the reporting of his civilian and service emissaries was deplorably poor. His belief in Mussolini made him reject warnings of the coming collapse. He helped Mussolini, rescued from captivity on the Gran Sasso by a spectacular piece of kidnapping in a small aircraft, to create a new Italian republic in the north, whose unreality and incapacity merely confused the picture but were not allowed by the German military and police commanders in the field to interfere with their respective businesses. Italy north of the allied line of advance became German occupied territory under military rule.

This patchwork of alliance and domination arose out of the needs and fortunes of war. It was not meant to endure. While it did, its function was to secure obedience to German wishes and, increasingly, to supply the German war machine with materials, goods, food and labour. As German needs became more urgent, German methods became harsher and resistance grew.

The German armies were accompanied in their invasions by special economic squads, whose first tasks were to seize what Germany wanted by way of pillage – raw materials and manufactured goods, gold and foreign currencies, machinery and rolling stock – and to protect valuable installations and essential factories, which were to be exploited as going concerns. Once these immediate aims had been achieved, the Germans began to look further ahead, but because they looked to an early peace and not to a long war they made mistakes. In either event the industries of non-German lands were to supplement the German economy, but expectations of an easy war led the economic planners to plan initially in terms of the New Order and, particularly in the east, to neglect or dismantle heavy industry: for over a year no attempt was made to repair factories and plants damaged by the retreating Russians, so that these were back in working order only shortly before the retreating Germans had to blow them up again.

The German economy had not been prepared for a long war. Hitler expected the war to be short and the German economy to take it in its stride. Production was adapted to the needs of the moment but not at first expanded. Thus in 1940 aircraft production was reduced (by 40 per cent) because the army needed more tanks and the navy more submarines, while in the next year factories which had made this switch were required to revert to aircraft because the Luftwaffe regained priority over the army and the navy in the light of its need to repair before Barbarossa the damage it had suffered in the Battle of Britain. But with the failure of Barbarossa to achieve its objectives by the end of the year it became inescapably clear that Germany needed a greatly expanded arms base and must also exploit the industrial potential of conquered countries both to contribute to Germany's arms production and to manufacture those other goods which Germany was ceasing to make for itself as its industry was converted to materials of war.

In areas formally or virtually annexed to the Reich, where there was no collision between short-term and long-term aims, industries were incorporated into German industry in order to enlarge its capacity. In Silesia, for example, coal production was very greatly expanded, synthetic oil refineries were built, and heavy engineering and arms production were developed. To the east of the areas which were treated as part of the Reich Goering ordered the transfer to Germany of all enterprises 'not absolutely essential for the maintenance of the bare existence of the inhabitants at a low level', unless transport difficulties made it more practicable to keep them at work on German orders where they were. In general, industry in the east was limited to producing goods and services required by Germany's armed forces and administrators, satisfying what Goering considered to be the bare needs of the local population and processing raw materials. In the west, after an initial few months of looting stocks and equipment, the policy was to exploit industrial capacity by nurturing and milking useful enterprises and to close down the rest by depriving them of raw materials. Factories which went on working had to deliver a high proportion of their output to the Germans; in some cases these levies reached 100 per cent (for example, of magnesium, heavy castings,

industrial precision parts). The equipment of factories which closed was
either taken to Germany or left to rot, while their labour was transferred
to war work in Germany or occupied countries or assigned to the Todt
Organization, which constructed the defences, installations and buildings
needed by the armed forces outside Germany. Production of non-military
goods was increased as German industry became more exclusively concentrated on war production, and towards the end of the war there was some
dispersal of war production from Germany as a result of bombing.

The German apparatus of control was very powerful. Allocations of
fuel and raw materials were regulated by licences issued by special agencies
which were either German or under close German supervision. German
specialists were often attached to industrial concerns. All contracts above
a certain value had to be reported to the authorities and any firm attempting to do business without such notification lost its allocations. This
relatively negative kind of control was supplemented by the active desire
of collaborationist governments to keep their industries going and to
maintain employment and the capital resources of the country. They
therefore welcomed German orders. In some cases the German authorities
placed orders with particular firms for goods which went straight to
Germany and were paid for either through a clearing system or by being
set against the occupation costs which the Germans charged for their
presence and sustenance in occupied countries. (These occupation costs
were far higher than the real costs of occupation. They were in fact huge,
continuing fines.) In other cases general agreements were made covering
whole industries, for example textiles, automobiles. In these cases the type
of the product was fixed to suit the Germans, who took what they needed
but set aside a proportion for the producing country: the Germans were
also able to fix prices since they were the principal purchasers. Thus
subordinate governments and foreign industrialists were largely in
German hands. Either they worked for the Germans or they were forced
to close, and if they were forced to close their employees would probably
be sent to do forced labour in Germany. By August 1942 it was estimated
that firms could only survive if at least three quarters of their output was
for the Germans. The firms which remained in operation lost their independence. If the directors collaborated they had to allow German observers into their plants; if they refused, they were evicted and replaced by
German managers and technicians.

Besides this subjection of industry by official processes, businesses in
occupied countries were taken over either by confiscation or by purchase.
Jewish property was confiscated without compensation. So, later, was the
property of enemies of the Reich, a category which was interpreted by

Seyss-Inquart to include those who had assisted, were assisting or might be expected to assist anti-German activities. In the USSR, where the German state was declared to be the successor in title of the Soviet state, property of the Communist Party or any political association was, together with state property strictly so called, transferred into German state ownership. The same rules were applied to the Baltic states even though property had only been transferred to state ownership in 1939 and the population was markedly pro-German. In Poland an organization was established to confiscate land without compensation and re-sell it to Germans at nominal rates. The German banks extended German control by buying shares in foreign enterprises or in foreign banks which themselves had substantial holdings in such enterprises. In these ways the commanding heights of the economies of conquered countries were captured at practically no cost either by the German state or by major German industrial and financial groups. If this dual approach to expropriation contained within it the seeds of a conflict in Germany between state control and private control, the conflict itself was averted, or postponed, by the loss of the war.

Control was likewise imposed on agriculture. Again, the annexed areas were integrated with the Reich. In western and south-eastern Europe the Germans preferred to exercise control indirectly by strengthening the powers of local Ministries of Agriculture and forcing them to use their powers to implement the requirements of the Reich's Food Office, which prescribed production and delivery quotas, prices, subsidies, and feeding and seeding rates. Germany looked to these territories for much of its food and so kept them at first well equipped with farm machinery and fertilizers – many eastern districts were better supplied than before the war – but from 1941–2 the exigencies of the Russian campaign disrupted this policy. Before the war ended food production in occupied Europe fell by about a quarter and much of it was requisitioned. The requisitions were generally addressed to the individual farmer, who was required to deliver up his produce in return for a claim slip with which he was left to get what compensation he could from his government. Other materials, such as coal, were requisitioned in the same way.

The food left over for civilian consumption became increasingly hard to move as the transport system failed. As a result of shortages of fuel, rubber and rolling stock, food was either not distributed at all or went bad during interminable waits at sidings. The use of canals and barges, where these existed, provided a partial alleviation, but shortages and distribution bottlenecks operating upon each other caused prices to rise steeply. Black markets flourished. Some governments tried to beat them by fixing prices and buying in essential products in order to regulate supply. They were unsuccessful: at one time it was estimated that nine out of every ten eggs marketed in the *département* of the Seine were being sold on the black market. Rations, which were introduced all over occupied Europe at a lower level (Denmark alone excepted) than in Germany, were frequently not honoured. Diets became increasingly vegetarian, and while country people often managed to live well enough half the population was required to exist on two thirds or a half of the pre-war normal.

Epidemics developed – tuberculosis, diphtheria, polio – and were made worse by a shortage of medicines. One of the by-products of undernourishment was an increase in industrial accidents which probably damaged production more than sabotage did. In particular areas at particular times the daily diet sank catastrophically. The worst examples were Athens and some of the Greek islands where it was 600–800 calories in the winter of 1941–2 and some Dutch cities where it fell to 500 calories in the winter of 1944–5. Hunger was made all the more insupportable by cold. Clothing and fuel both became desperately hard to get and – between the drop in real wages and the black market – impossibly expensive. Dutch city-dwellers were reduced to cutting down trees in parks and stealing any scrap which they could find to burn to keep their enfeebled bodies warm. In the east the situation became a tragic farce. The produce of the great granary of the Ukraine was garnered for the Reich but then left to rot because there were not enough trains to move it, until the Reich Commissar, Erich Koch, hit on the idea of doling out surplus stocks to service men going on leave in the form of 'Führer food parcels'. Germany got less out of the USSR after invading it than before. But occupied Europe was forced to yield 25 million tons of food to Germany, most of it requisitioned. During 1941 − 3 these supplies increased Germany's civilian ration by something between a fifth and a quarter.

It is difficult to give a picture of life in occupied Europe in terms of individuals as opposed to statistics because conditions varied enormously from place to place and from month to month. The constant factor was uncertainty – uncertainty about what could be got and, if it could, what it would cost. Necessities were frequently unobtainable and then suddenly on the market – the black market – at impossible prices. In France, for which reliable figures are easier to come by, the official cost of a kilo of butter rose from forty to sixty-one francs during 1941–3 but this price was entirely unreal, for when butter was available in, say, Paris it fetched by 1943 600– 800 francs. Tobacco and wine were rationed to a packet of the one and a litre of the other per adult per week but the rations were notional and black market prices were ten to twelve times the official price. Meat was frequently unobtainable for a month at a time. Meals could be got in subsidized works canteens or restaurants, but each lunch might cost a fifth of a weekly wage, so that a lunch a day more than consumed an entire pay packet. Shoes and clothes were already scarce and expensive by the winter of 1940 when a yard of woollen fabric or a pair of shoes cost the equivalent of half a weekly wage; by 1943 a pair of shoes absorbed six weeks' wages, a suit four to five months'. Coal and electricity were so rigorously restricted that the fuel ration was not enough to cook with, especially as the inferior food available could only be made edible by slow cooking. In Paris a ton of coal rose to the equivalent of two to four months' wages.

The most important of all the commodities which the Germans had to regulate was labour. Germany was short of labour before the war, while in a number of European countries there was appreciable unemployment. This imbalance was accentuated by the call-up of men for the German armed services and by the dislocations of war which put men and women out of work in conquered countries. The *Anschluss* with Austria and the annexation of the Sudetenland had automatically increased the Reich's labour force and there were in addition about 300,000 foreign workers in Germany in 1939 as a result of the operation of the law of supply and demand. During the war this force was enormously increased by three main methods: encouragement of more or less voluntary migration, the use of prisoners of war, and forcible recruitment.

In western and southern countries the Germans advertised the advantages of going to Germany for jobs: sure employment, good conditions, good pay, good holidays. Germany also made agreements with a number of satellite and allied governments, including Italy and Spain, for the supply of permanent and seasonal workers. The response was, however, inadequate, especially when reports of actual conditions in Germany filtered through and showed up the fraudulence of German enticements. Although a foreign worker from the west or south (as distinct from an eastern worker whose wage was derisory) was entitled to the same wage as a German worker, he was often put to less skilled work than he had been doing and so found himself earning less than he had expected. He had to pay German taxes and contribute to social insurance schemes from which he was not likely to benefit, since he did not expect to remain in Germany; and when inflation took hold of his home country without any corresponding increase in his German wage, he and his family found that the real return for his labours was drastically cut.

The Germans had therefore to stimulate volunteering by making work in occupied countries more difficult to come by and more unpleasant.

Men who were physically fit but who declined to volunteer to go to Germany lost unemployment pay; men in prison for civil offences were released if they promised to go; managements were forced to dismiss entire categories of workers needed in Germany; factories were closed; normal working hours were extended to a seventy-two-hour week or a thirteen-hour day; ration cards were withheld. These measures were the bridge between voluntary recruitment and the use of physical force. Between May 1940 and May 1941 the foreign labour force in the Reich rose by almost two million, the percentage of foreign labour from 3.2 to 8.4. By mid-1944 the percentage was 19.7. The voluntary element became very thin, the more so after allied bombing added to the discomforts of working in Germany. Sauckel estimated in 1944 that out of five million foreigners working in Germany fewer than 200,000 had come voluntarily.

The first prisoners put to work were some two to three hundred thousand Poles captured in the 1939 campaign and this number was greatly increased by the German victories in west and east in 1940 and 1941. Thereafter there were close on two million prisoners working for Germany until the war ended. The rules of war which Germany had accepted permitted the employment of prisoners other than officers, but the conditions which Germany's prisoners – most of them captured in the east – were forced to put up with during the Second World War contravened all the rules of war and of human decency. By 1944 about 40 per cent of them were, according to Albert Speer at Nuremberg, being used directly or indirectly in arms production. Non-commissioned officers were generally required to work and so too were Russian commissioned officers: the Nazis in effect did not recognize the validity of a Russian commission. Russian prisoners were paid half wages.

The German attitude to Russian combatants was one of calculated callousness. Since they regarded Slavs and communists as hardly better than Jews, the Germans killed them or allowed them to die with similar cruelty and, likewise, in millions. The total number of prisoners taken by the German armies in the USSR was in the region of 5.5 million. Of these the astounding number of 3.5 million or more had been lost by the middle of 1944 and the assumption must be that they were either deliberately killed or done to death by criminal negligence. Nearly two million of them died in camps and close on another million disappeared while in military custody either in the USSR or in rear areas; a further quarter of a million disappeared or died in transit between the front and destinations in the rear; another 473,000 died or were killed in military custody in Germany or Poland. (About 800,000 were released either on the grounds that they were not Russians or for volunteering to serve against the

Russians, leaving therefore about one million, of whom 875,000 were, by German standards, fit for work.) This slaughter of prisoners cannot be accounted for by the peculiar chaos of the war in the east. In such a war some prisoners will die through insufficient attention, but not millions of them. The true cause was the inhuman policy of the Nazis towards the Russians as a people and the acquiescence of army commanders in attitudes and conditions which amounted to a sentence of death on their prisoners. The Nazis encouraged barbarity against Russians by warning German troops to expect barbarity from them. The Russians were portrayed as uncivilized hordes. In addition the Germans made play with the fact that the USSR had not adhered to the Geneva Convention of 1929 on the treatment of prisoners of war, although it was known in Germany that the Russian armies had been ordered to observe the Geneva rules and the USSR had formally through Sweden requested reciprocal observance. In practice the Germans refused. Goering told Ciano that Russian prisoners of war, having eaten everything possible including the soles of their boots, had begun to eat each other and, 'which is more serious, had also eaten a German sentry . . . some nations must be decimated . . . there is nothing to be done about it'.

As the war went on forced labour became the only possible answer to Germany's problems. It was in addition sanctioned by ideology. On the day of the inauguration of Hans Frank's régime in Poland all Jews were formally condemned to forced labour and all other Poles were equally formally deprived of any right to leisure. The obligation to work included the liability to be sent to work in Germany. These regulations were copied by Rosenberg in 1941 for the Baltic states and the USSR. They were enforced by terror. Any person resisting recruitment was likely to see his house burned down and his family seized as hostages and sent to a labour camp. One of Rosenberg's principal officials compared the proceedings to the blackest days of the slave trade. He recorded that people were rounded up and shipped to Germany without any regard to health or age and that by 1942 over 100,000 had had to be sent back because they were utterly useless. Many of them died on the way and the next contingent of westbound workers would have to wait until the dead bodies of their rejected compatriots had been thrown out of the windows in order to make room for them in the disgusting trains (which incidentally were badly needed by the army). Women gave birth in the trains and the babies were thrown out onto the embankment. One German official charged with the provision of skilled Ukrainian labour for the Reich complained that his trains were held up by returning transports filled with discarded persons packed fifty or sixty to a truck and that eastward and westward bound trains stood motionless alongside each other for long periods; he added that his recruits often went hungry in these circumstances and that even the German Red Cross refused to feed them on the grounds that they were Russian swine. Another official complained of the propaganda effects when 400,000 Ukrainian domestic helps were being sent to Germany and before they arrived the German press announced that they would have no free time, would not be allowed to go to cinemas, theatres or restaurants, and might only be absent from the house where they worked for three hours a week at the most. His memorandum denounced the political ineptitude of treating eastern Europeans as second class whites in the sight of the whole coloured world and reminded his colleagues that the Russians were fighting 'with exceptional bravery and sacrifice for nothing more nor less than the recognition of their human dignity'. But the mixture of incompetence and callousness went on. By the end of the war the age limit for labour recruitment in the east had been lowered to ten.

The influx of foreign workers enabled Germany to shift labour from civilian to military employment – nearly six million by May 1941, nearly eight million a year later – without introducing compulsory service for women. In 1942 the number of women in civilian employment in Germany was lower by 189,000 than in 1939. But in 1942 the situation was radically altered by the failure to defeat the Russian armies in the field. In 1941 the German army had suffered heavy casualties for the first time and became a competitor with industry for men. In the autumn of 1942 Himmler concluded formal agreements with the Minister of Justice, Otto Thierack, and the Minister for Armaments, Albert Speer, by which the inmates of concentration camps and prisoners of war were released for work in factories in return for the allocation to the SS of a percentage of their output of weapons. The hours of work of the concentration camp victims were unlimited and the Himmler-Thierack agreement provided that 'antisocial' persons might be worked to death.

Forcible recruitment of labour was introduced in the west and southeast as well as in the east. Stricter controls were imposed in the Reich and in March 1942 Fritz Sauckel was appointed Plenipotentiary for the Deployment of Labour with extensive powers over the recruitment, use and distribution of German and foreign labour. Sauckel, whose appointment was part of no plan but a reaction to external events, collected over two million more foreign workers by May 1943 and increased the total labour force in Germany by just under two million in one year in spite of the drain caused by the demands of the fighting services. But his field for recruitment was narrowing. Poland had already been forced to contribute to the limit of its capacity. South-eastern Europe could not be denuded without imperilling the supplies of food which it provided for the Reich. In the USSR skilled labour had retreated eastward with the Russian armies and unskilled labour was largely required by the military and civilian authorities in the German occupied zones. In western Europe unemployment had been eliminated by earlier labour drives and by the demands of factories which were working for the Reich. From 1943 the difficulties became even acuter in both east and west – in the east because the advancing Russian armies reduced the area from which labour might be drawn, and in the west because labour was needed locally to make good the shortfall in German factories occasioned by bottlenecks and bombing. Moreover the machinery of German control was breaking down. Even in the west the Germans ceased to operate through local governments and began to round up labour in the streets of big cities – in one operation in Marseilles they kidnapped 1,000 French police by forcing them into lorries while they were on an exercise – and to seize the fathers of men who took to the woods and hills. Yet in Belgium 23,000 men evaded compulsory labour service by escaping to the Ardennes and in one area of France 95 per cent of those called for labour service during the winter of 1943–4 got away. Metaphorically Sauckel was being required to squeeze blood from a stone. In practice his minions squeezed it from human beings as they combed Europe for workers. Until the last year of the war Sauckel produced enough manpower to keep war production going and even to increase it, but after the middle of 1944 the economy began to crumble and not even the appointment of yet another plenipotentiary – this time Goebbels as Plenipotentiary for Total War – could keep the factories going.

The conditions of the millions of foreigners who worked for Nazi Germany varied according to their skills and racial ratings, but even the most favoured were shockingly treated. Jews as a rule were exterminated even if capable of working. Eastern workers fared worse than western or southern ones, Russians worse than Poles, Poles worse than the Baltic nations. The best treated were the skilled Danes, Flemings, Swiss and Hungarians, after them the French and Dutch, further down the scale the less skilled and racially inferior Balkan and Mediterranean peoples, including Italians and Spaniards, for whom the Germans had little respect even though they did not inspire the loathing directed against Slavs. For all of them Sauckel decreed that they should be fed, housed and treated in such a way as to ensure maximum production at minimum cost, and eastern workers in particular were kept in conditions which, besides being horridly inhumane, were also inefficient since they made them unfit for work and so reduced their output unnecessarily quickly. Agricultural workers were mostly housed and fed by their employers, but factory workers lived in barracks or in camps where they were segregated in huts by nationality. The camps, which were for western workers, were guarded by men and barbed wire; the inmates were not allowed out except to work. The huts were badly built, scantily furnished and scandalously lacking in sanitation. They were overcrowded, unheated and, as the war went on, unrepaired. Rations were in theory the same as those of German civilians, although in the case of eastern workers there was not even a pretence that they were: Goering ordered Russians to be fed lightly and without seriously interfering with German rations. In the camps ration cards were surrendered to the commandant who was free to provide what he thought fit in exchange. The diet of an eastern worker in a German labour camp was never within 1,000 calories of the lowest German ration, and the quality of the food was so poor that disease and mortality rates were preternaturally high. Concentration-camp workers received a diet roughly equivalent to the 1941–2 Athens famine rate.

But from the German point of view these miserable victims served their purpose. They constituted a fifth of Germany's wartime labour force; in 1944 there were seven million of them in the Reich. According to Albert Speer the western and Italian workers among them were at this date responsible for 25–30 per cent of the German effort. In addition Europe made, over the whole period of Germany's dominion from 1940 to 1944, contributions in kind equivalent to 14 per cent of Germany's own gross product and so increased by rather more than 50 per cent the resources available to Germany for the purchase of arms and equipment. No slave-driver could have hoped for more.

CHAPTER 13
Resistance

CONSCRIPTED labourers, prisoners of war, Jews, communists and gipsies were all minority groups. Even together they were still a minority of the peoples who came under German rule. The great majority stayed where they were or returned to their homes after having been temporarily scattered by the German advances. Some experienced life in a battle zone and in an army rear area; most of them a much longer spell under some form of occupational régime while the great bulk of Germany's front-line fighting forces was engaged on Russian soil. Only in the east, and to a lesser degree in Italy, did civilian populations live through protracted fighting.

The first shock left little room for anything except the sheer facts of defeat and abandonment. Those in the path of the *Blitzkrieg* were left dazed as the Germans swept away the familiar things of daily life from goods and houses to the governments and officials to whom a settled people is wont to turn for guidance or instruction in a crisis. Communities were atomized. The individual's first thought was to find his family, recover his belongings and get himself a job and a livelihood. The job became all important, first as a means for securing the necessities of life in a strange world and later in order to qualify for exemption from forced labour; a job meant also a renewal of contact with familiar routines, an assurance that some things remained the same. But jobs were scarce and in the immediate wake of defeat there was widespread unemployment. Many factories were reduced to a ten-hour week and earnings sagged until labour began to be required again for reconstruction and the occupiers' needs (building airfields, for example). Some employers paid reduced wages to help and keep their workers during temporary stoppages caused by lack of materials or power, but poverty spread alarmingly as the gap between earnings and prices widened at both ends and large quantities of food, clothing and other necessities disappeared into expensive black markets. Poverty caused neglect of children, social divisions and crime. The towns became resentful of the comparatively better-fed countryside; the law-abiding resented the profits made by black marketeers who, since they sold mostly to Germans, were beyond the reach of the law; the poor looked with rising anger at the advantages of the rich (in

Paris, to take an extreme case, the six most famous restaurants were exempt from all restrictions until 1943). Crimes such as theft, whether committed by adults or juveniles, multiplied and became respectable; in the Netherlands the crime rate almost trebled; stealing was both a symptom of poverty and a form of protest. Scruples of all kinds wilted in the face of need, and the hostility of the have-nots against the haves quickened. Prostitution increased by as much as tenfold as a result of financial hardship and the break-up of family life; women with no previous police records traded themselves to German soldiers in spite of the hostility which their conduct provoked among their more forbearing compatriots.

As a general rule everybody over fifteen had to have an identity card, observe a curfew and expect to have his movements restricted. The police state arrived on the heels of the German army. Jews had to produce baptismal certificates of grandparents or lose their citizenship. Few people possessed such documents but a number were forged by Christian clergymen. Freedom of movement was curtailed by the virtual elimination of private transport and severe limitations on public transport. Bicycle-taxis appeared in towns. Mail was censored and in some cases prohibited: between the zones of France the only kind of mail allowed was printed postcards with simple messages of the 'we are well/ill . . .' type, from which the sender could choose one by crossing out the rest. Newspapers either became pro-German and sparse of news or disappeared; about half of the national and local press ceased publication and the circulation of the survivors dropped sharply. Radio programmes continued under German control. The Germans offered good pay to well-known broadcasters, kept favourite programmes on the air and tried to use radio to propagate their views, but the nature of radio prevented them from securing a monopoly, and although they penalized listeners to enemy broadcasts they could not proscribe transmissions from neutral Switzerland, whose broadcasts became an important item in preserving for the conquered a window on the world. But life narrowed and this spiritual retrenchment was reflected in swelling attendances at cinemas and sporting events – even when, later, the Resistance admonished people to stay away. It also threw families together and sharpened the demand for books, including serious books about national history and culture.

Immediately after the end of the fighting there was a marked difference between those parts of a country which had seen the war at first hand in the form either of enemy armies or of refugees, and other parts which had learned of it by hearsay. Soon, however, all parts faced the same question: attitudes to the victors; to which was added the secondary question of attitudes to collaborators, which were often more bitterly intense. As people recovered they tended to divide into two groups, those who on the whole accepted the new world in which they had woken up again and those who felt too angry or too ashamed to do so. Although ultimately the Germans earned widespread hate, at first their coming raised more questioning than clear-cut emotions. The behaviour of the occupying forces in the west was for the most part correct and even affable and it was some time before their habit of strolling around singly in villages and towns was replaced by more circumspect promenading in pairs or groups and the abandonment of attempts at social intercourse with the natives; even where there was from the beginning a wall of silence, there was also that mutual respect which has been most tellingly portrayed in Vercors' *Le silence de la mer*. Some countries had an anti-German tradition but others – Greece, for example, which was anti-Italian but not initially anti-German – had not. The Germans were given the benefit of the doubt. Attitudes crystallized slowly in societies which had been atomized and people were thrown back on local or personal motives in deciding what to think and how to conduct themselves. There was something of a psychological vacuum in which the Germans had, and lost, their chances. There was no overall pattern. In a country like France, where the Third Republic had failed to command wide enough allegiance, the new order benefited at the start from adventitious aids such as the countervailing respect for Pétain (especially in the lower reaches of the social scale), an intensification of anti-British feelings among the bourgeoisie and a reinforcement of anti-radicalism. But these were not inherently pro-German feelings. They only gave a conditioned blessing to the German presence and perpetuated for a while after the armistice the confusion created by war. Only in the east did it swiftly become clear that the German occupation was a threat to the entire population and that the choice lay between resistance and extermination.

In most places there was a case for collaboration, for lying low for the time being. Moreover the disruptions of war and the contradictions of the occupation made it difficult for ordinary people to get a lead from their traditional mentors. In Belgium the king had declared himself a prisoner while his government had fled to London to continue the fight. In Denmark the king and government were undisguisedly anti-German. The king ignored German salutations on his daily rides through his capital, sent telegrams of sympathy to police wounded in a fight in which 300 Danish Nazis were arrested, gave an audience to a well-known historian just before he was arrested for spreading anti-German propaganda, and eventually threatened to abdicate if anti-semitic legislation were

introduced, but he and his government also officially discouraged anti-
German activities and recommended a policy of acquiescence for a considerable time.

Two things in particular resolved this ambivalence: the course of the
war and the behaviour of the Germans. A numb acceptance of Germany's
victories sprang not only from the shock of defeat but also from the
conviction that defeat was complete and final. Men like de Gaulle who
never accepted defeat at any moment were rare and had the logic of
events against them. But even before the end of 1940 doubt began to
spread. The failure of the Luftwaffe in the Battle of Britain and the
British initiative in Africa at the end of the year showed that the war was
not over. The entry of the Russians and then the Americans into the war
in 1941 showed that the Germans were going to lose it. These events
became well-known throughout occupied Europe through broadcasting
and a clandestine press which became amazingly extensive. One of the
most important facts about occupied Europe was that people in it knew
what was going on. This knowledge was due to radio which prevented
Europe from being totally cut off. The BBC's news services were widely
heard and believed; Swiss radio, with its built-in reputation for neutral
impartiality, played a similar role; communists, who took after June 1941
an exceptionally important part in Resistance, listened to broadcasts from
the USSR, which possessed the most powerful transmitter in the world
and the longest experience in broadcasting propaganda; governments-in-
exile in London reached their compatriots with news and exhortation and
gave them a factual and legal basis for opposing the Germans and their
satellite regimes.

Foreign broadcasts nourished indigenous clandestine newspapers. The
clandestine press became an industry of great potency in forming the will
to resist. In Belgium about 12,000 persons came to be engaged in it and
published 300 papers; in France underground presses produced books in
fine editions as well as over 1,000 papers and pamphlets (this figure
included regional editions of the same paper); in Denmark the number of
papers published rose from 222 in the whole of 1943 to 315 in the first
four months of 1945 and by the end of 1944 over 10 million copies of
these papers and pamphlets had been printed and distributed; in the
Netherlands some papers appeared three times a week after the confiscation of radio sets in 1943 and the five principal left-wing papers attained a
combined circulation of 450,000. The distribution of this quantity of
material was a well-organized and yet highly risky business, handled by
members of small local groups who took their lives in their hands with
every sheet which they delivered to a neighbour. These groups and their

newspapers recall the secret societies which carried on the revolution in France underground after the restoration of the *ancien régime* in 1814. Through their efforts the underground in Europe was in general better informed about the war than the regular combatants were about the underground. The flow of information was an essential factor in rebuilding the societies which had been smitten by the German victories and in stimulating opposition to a no longer invincible victor. It restored to the defeated a sense of coherence and a sense of purpose, and the clandestine press which raised the morale of Resisters likewise demoralized an enemy who, having thought that he had finished off the opposition, was presented with evidence of its persistence and even began to exaggerate it. The activities of the clandestine press led to other forms of resistance, as the confidence of these groups expanded and with their confidence their aims. Many active Resisters served an apprenticeship by helping to run a clandestine paper.

The German contribution to anti-Germanism was no less substantial. The natural nationalist opposition to the presence of Germans was swollen by opposition to their behaviour. Besides being aliens, they showed themselves inhumane: Jews were segregated, deported and killed – the round-up of Jews in the Vélodrome d'Hiver shocked Parisian opinion even more than the taking of hostages; human rights and freedoms were trampled on far beyond the necessities of war and occupation; the new rulers pillaged the material resources of the defeated, failed to provide them with enough food and conscripted them for labour in appalling conditions; prisoners of war did not come back; all in all the non-German individual was degraded body and soul. This inhumanity converted the resentment of the subject populations into hatred – which in Norway was given an edge of a very special kind, for in the First World War Norwegians had looked after German children, and they were filled with disgust at the thought that the invading armies of 1940 probably contained some of these very children grown to be violators of the charity shown to them twenty-five years earlier. Hatred of the Germans fostered various forms of opposition such as networks for helping fugitive allied servicemen who had been shot down or had escaped from prison camps; the collection and forwarding of military intelligence; the clandestine press; industrial sabotage, go-slows and strikes; and eventually the beginnings of organized and active armed resistance.

But the Germans went even further. Confronted with this opposition they took the iron fist right out of its velvet glove and began to use terror as a principal means of government. Hostages were taken and shot, concentration camps established, stunning reprisals exacted and picked areas devastated. Although the details varied in practice from country to country the overall pattern was uniform because it reflected not individual initiative or local eccentricity but a policy devised and commanded at the highest level in the German state, the Nazi Party and the armed services. Thus in December 1941 Keitel, as Chief of Staff of the Armed Forces, issued the *Nacht und Nebel* (Night and Fog) order which was designed to strike fear into whole populations. Hitler, he said, was interested in no penalty except death; no other deterrent seemed to him effective; even a sentence of hard labour for life struck him as a sign of weakness. Consequently the *Nacht und Nebel* order decreed that in cases where the death penalty was unlikely to be imposed by a court in an occupied country, offences against the Reich were to be visited with a substitute death. The offender was to be secretly spirited away to the Reich without trial, leaving friends and relations to tremble in suspense for his fate – and theirs.

The distinction between guilt and innocence had already been virtually abolished, for as early as September 1941 Keitel had instructed commanders on all fronts to ascribe all acts of resistance to communists and to execute batches of so-called communists for every German soldier killed: fifty to a hundred communists was the number recommended. A few weeks later fifty hostages were executed in France as a reprisal for the death of a German officer, and a further fifty a few days later when another officer was killed; the executions would have been twice as many but for strenuous intervention by Vichy. By the end of the war about 30,000 French hostages had been shot and the toll was comparable all over occupied Europe. In the Netherlands Seyss-Inquart revealed in May 1942 that 480 prominent Dutch personages were being held and that many had already been shot in retaliation for breaches of public order; on another occasion the village of Putten was burned down and all its males deported (very few ever returned) after a German motorcar had been attacked in the neighbourhood and one German wounded. In Poland a tally was established of one hundred Resisters to be killed for the death of every one German, and at Palmiry, a village near Warsaw, several thousand deaths were in fact exacted in revenge for a single attack. At Televaag in Norway 300 houses were burned down, 76 persons deported and a further 260 interned in April 1942 in an attempt to intimidate and quell Norwegian resistance. The first case of devastation and mass executions in Italy occurred at Boves in Piedmont in September 1943, while in Rome 330 people picked at random were executed in March 1944 after thirty-two German soldiers had been killed by a bomb. At Oradour-sur-Glane, selected by a mistake instead of a place of the same name a few kilometres

away, only ten persons out of a population of 652 survived the calculated
fury of the Germans, the men being shot and the women and children
being locked into the church and burned to death. This last enormity
occurred in July 1944.

The most famous of these razzias befell the village of Lidiče in Czechoslovakia where the entire population was killed or sent to concentration
camps with a horrifying sort of nonchalance in revenge for the assassination of Heydrich. At the end of 1941 two men from the Czechoslovak
army in England, one a Czech and the other a Slovak, had arrived by
parachute, with British assistance, in order to do this deed, which was
undertaken in the belief that Heydrich and his police chief, Karl Hans
Frank, were planning to destroy the entire Czech people. It was achieved
in the following May when the two executioners threw a bomb into
Heydrich's open car. He took a week to die. About 1,500 Czechs were
immediately killed, including the executioners and another 120 members
of the Resistance who had escaped into a church. In addition, 3,000 Jews
were removed from the concentration camp at Terezin (Theresienstadt)
and sent to Poland to be killed. But this was not the end. A few days after
Heydrich's death, Lidiče, apparently selected at random, was sealed off
by the SD. That day nothing much happened, although a woman and a
small boy were shot and killed for trying to escape. The next day the
entire male population over sixteen years of age was shot in batches – 172
of them in a leisurely massacre which took ten hours; the women were
sent to Ravensbrueck concentration camp and the children to a different
camp; pregnant women were first allowed to give birth to their children in
hospital and then joined their friends in Ravensbrueck, their babies having
been killed. Lidiče itself was razed to the ground. Lezaky, another small
village near Prague, was treated in the same way a few days later. These
savage reprisals were supplemented by some 10,000 arrests. The Czech
composer Martinů, who had fled from Paris to the United States in 1940,
composed an orchestral 'Memorial to Lidiče'.

As things got worse for the Germans, so did their behaviour. In July
1944 Hitler ordered all saboteurs to be executed on the spot and all
suspects to be handed over to the SD (which was worse). This decree,
called the *Kugelerlass* or Bullet Decree, was a form of words for transfer-
ring wide categories of prisoners to the SD for execution. It did not apply
to British or American combatants unless they were commandos (in which
case they were already covered by the Commando Order of 1942 requiring
them to be summarily slaughtered to the last man, even if they surrendered). The *Kugelerlass* was extended two months after its promulgation

to prisoners under sentence and to those whose cases were still pending. Keitel explained that there was to be no compunction about innocent persons who might accidentally get killed in the course of the measures needed to eliminate what he called dissidents. The response to these foul and frantic measures was active armed resistance on a militarily significant scale and, complementarily, a dwindling of the numbers of collaborators and *attentistes* as the complicity involved in siding with the Germans or even doing nothing amounted to condoning the unforgivable.

Such were the cumulative sources of Resistance. The word itself did not make its appearance at once. In France it does not seem to have been in general use before 1943, although Gaullism had by that time become a well-known term. The phenomenon of Resistance, however, appeared immediately after defeat, if only in modest, disconnected and often unsuccessful forms, spontaneous expressions of spirit by disbanded officers and men of the fighting forces which the Germans were usually able to master without much difficulty. Most people remained, then and for some time thereafter, very vague about their neighbours' activities and about Resistance movements, and also ignorant (as they were meant to be) about the separate intelligence and escapers' networks. People heard that something was going on without knowing what it was. The development of Resistance was to some extent dependent on growing awareness of its existence and endorsement of its aims and methods, and this interacting process took time. It was not until the butcher, the baker and the candlestick-maker felt moved to join active Resistance groups that there could be active Resistance groups for them to join. The process was one of awareness leading to complicity, and complicity leading to activity. Movements grew as householders sheltered Resisters, fed them, lent rooms for radio transmissions, failed to report raids on their farms by gangs who might be Resisters (though sometimes they were not), and so gradually became more deeply and sometimes more actively involved.

In point of time the earliest forms of opposition were intelligence networks which had in some cases been formed before the war began – in Czechoslovakia, for instance, in 1938. Some of these became so extensive that they were able to shadow and report on the entirety of the official administrative machine. Besides spying on German activities and installations they recruited their own agents and helped agents who arrived from outside (mostly by parachute). Belgium, partly because of its proximity to England, was specially active in this work, providing some 5,000 agents, supported by another 13,000 helpers. Czechoslovakia, to which aircraft from England could safely make the return flight only on moonless nights, was less closely linked but provided valuable information both to Great

Britain and, before Barbarossa, to the Russians, to whom it supplied detailed warnings of the impending German attack, including the names of the airfields which the Luftwaffe intended to attack; Czech Intelligence also unmasked a German sabotage group working beyond the Urals. In Poland an underground organization operated throughout the country, reporting on German troop movements, following the Germans as far as the Volga and the Caucasus and dispatching in 1942–4 some 300 reports to the west by radio or by courier via Hungary, Sweden and Switzerland. In Greece, to take a further example from another quarter, 1,072 agents – Greek, British, American and Polish – were dropped during 1941–4 and stayed in the country for varying lengths of time, usually a few months.

Similar to the intelligence networks were the escape routes along which escaped prisoners or airmen who had been shot down (and who, especially in England in 1940, were urgently needed back with their units) or Europeans seeking a way to re-enter the fight by getting to England were passed from hand to hand, sometimes by men and women who had performed the same service in the First World War or by their children. These routes were often long and intricate, running from Belgium or northern France or Germany itself through Switzerland and unoccupied France to Spain, Portugal or Africa; or from Poland through Czechoslovakia, Hungary, Yugoslavia and Italy; or northwards to Sweden. In Belgium alone some thirty-five groups were engaged in this work at one time or another, employing 10,000 persons and using their own teleprinter communications.

These were examples of the more obviously useful services which Resisters could render. They were of their nature clandestine. But Resistance was also effective in more open, if less concrete, ways. People came to realize that it was worth showing how they felt, and that strong feelings did not have to find vent in such dangerous activities as spying or such violent ones as guerrilla warfare. They used symbols and badges, like the red, white and blue knitted caps with which Danish students paraded their affinity with the RAF; or the Dutch habit of raising their hats when the traffic lights turned to the symbolic orange colour; or the Parisian students' mimicry of Germans, especially German airmen whose dress they copied by sporting their biros in the way that the Luftwaffe wore daggers. They even used silence, abruptly terminating all conversation if a German entered a shop or, again in Paris, rising and leaving university lectures if Germans came in to attend them. (The Germans closed the Sorbonne after a demonstration at the tomb of the unknown soldier at the Arc de Triomphe in November 1940.) Anti-German leaflets were slipped into licensed newspapers before distribution, a simple way of getting a large circulation. University laboratories were used to make bombs for the Resistance. Post-office workers intercepted denunciatory letters addressed to the SD by opening all SD mail and significantly impeded the activities of the SD which depended on a network of correspondents – amounting in Paris alone to eight to ten thousand persons. Police went into the business of forging false identity papers, a contribution which they were specially equipped to make owing to their familiarity with the genuine articles and their possession of genuine official stamps. Administrators turned their talents to losing dossiers and protracting discussions with the occupiers. A peculiar form of patriotic self-denial practised in France was hoarding instead of spending coins containing nickel and bronze in order to deny the metals to the Germans; this ingenious tactic not only created an embarrassing shortage of small change but also represented a considerable sacrifice by the poor, who had to go without the things which their coins could have bought.

From these non-violent declarations of hostility Resisters passed to equally non-violent but more positive protests, such as the resignation of the Norwegian bishops and nearly all the judges of the Norwegian High Court and the almost unanimous refusal of Norwegian teachers to sign an undertaking to teach in accordance with Quisling's party line, a protest which was backed up by hundreds of thousands of signed letters from parents. But moral resistance of this kind was possible only in countries where the Germans were, at least comparatively, lenient. In the east spiritual resistance could not be overt, but it occurred none the less, as witness the clandestine education of two to three thousand students in Poland and the continuance of scientific work and the secret publication of its results.

Economic resistance occurred everywhere. The methods were sometimes almost trivial but the results were considerable. Germany was denied the fruits of European labour and skill which, in an atmosphere less poisoned by hate, could have contributed extensively to Germany's war effort and home comforts. The means included going to work regularly a quarter of an hour late, mixing labels on packages so that they went to the wrong destination, more serious sabotage in factories and on railways, and strikes. Polish economic sabotage affected the delivery of Russian goods to Germany before Barbarossa and the supplying of the German armies on the eastern fronts after it, in both cases on a large scale. Sabotage in Czechoslovakia had become a serious worry to Heydrich before his assassination, and Czechs conscripted into the German army also engaged in sabotage. Strikes in Italy were the precursors of the fall of Mussolini and were repeated against the Germans when they occupied the northern half of the country. There were a number of extensive strikes in the Netherlands. But the strike was a dangerous weapon, which many workers were unwilling to use. It entailed not only loss of job and pay but, consequently, liability for deportation to compulsory labour service in Germany; and the leaders of the Dutch strikes were executed.

The more spectacular operations included two Anglo-Norwegian raids on the Lofoten Islands in 1941, when several thousand tons of shipping and eighteen cold-liver-oil factories were destroyed. These raids were a good example of the hazards of Resistance. Besides the material damage inflicted, they gave a boost to British and perhaps to Norwegian morale and kept Hitler guessing about his enemies' intentions, but they also provoked heavy reprisals and, when the British withdrew without warning on the second occasion after a week's stay which the local inhabitants had expected to be permanent, bitter resentment among the Norwegians left behind and an official protest from the Norwegian government in London. The reprisals severely damaged the Resistance movement in the same way, although not quite to the same extent, as the Czech Resistance movement which was virtually destroyed by the reprisals exacted after the death of Heydrich.

Limited operations could, however, be extremely valuable as well as less costly. The British were worried about German nuclear research. They wished to destroy the plant at Vemork in Ryukan in Norway where heavy water was being produced by electrolysis, and early in 1942 a first group of Norwegians from England was dropped in the region to spy out the land. In November a first attempt, by glider attack, to destroy the plant failed but in the following February a party of Norwegians succeeded in putting it out of action for five months. Later in 1943 it was bombed and partially destroyed by the Americans. The allies also wished to destroy the entire stock of heavy water. This involved the sinking of a ferry on which innocent Norwegians would be bound to be travelling. The Norwegian government in London was asked to decide whether this should be done. The government hardened its heart and gave the order to proceed. In similar limited operations valuable stocks of pyrites, iron ore and ball bearings were destroyed. Towards the end of the war sabotage groups were converted into anti-sabotage groups. One of their most notable achievements was the preservation by the Belgians of the port of Antwerp which was placed intact into the hands of the allies immediately they entered the city.

A large part of the Danish Resistance effort was directed to sabotaging Germany's exploitation of Denmark's food and strategic position. The Danish government refrained at first from encouraging sabotage for fear of reprisals, but the British pressed for more activity and got their way towards the end of 1942. The anomalies in the Danish situation were largely removed by the German take-over in 1943, when the official government ceased to function and a less inhibited, undercover government was formed under the name of the Freedom Council. From 1943 sabotage, and especially railway sabotage, increased: there were nearly 2,000 separate incidents in the first four months of 1945. At the other end of Europe the Greek Resistance, by blowing up the Gorgopotamos viaduct in November 1942, interrupted for six weeks the main route by which German supplies were going to Rommel in Africa and brought the port of Piraeus to a standstill. Subsequently Greek sabotage parties derailed 117 trains, destroyed 209 locomotives and 1,544 wagons, cut telephone wires and wrecked various tunnels, bridges and motor vehicles. Similar damage was inflicted on communications all over Europe. Much of it was quickly repaired by the Germans.

Economic sabotage merged into military action. The essential requirements were suitable terrain and climate and the support of the population. Without places to hide and people to help the dice were too heavily loaded in favour of the regular military and police forces of the occupiers. The Netherlands and Denmark, flat and bare, could not support a powerful militant movement, even with massive popular sympathy (in Denmark in elections in 1943 97 per cent of the votes cast were given to democratic parties and the Danish Nazis won only one seat out of 150); in the USSR partisan activity was impossible in the north and difficult in the Ukraine. Next, the Resistance forces needed training and organization which were to some extent of an orthodox military nature but also markedly unorthodox; and they needed arms. Secret armies had to operate on a cut-and-run basis until their German enemies were demoralized and themselves on the run. Attempts by partisans to fight pitched battles often led to disaster (as for example in the Vercors and at Montmouchet, as will be related in a later chapter). Active Resistance groups tended to form in the first place round regular officers adrift from defeated armies, but these first leaders were as a general rule superseded by new men who rose to command by proving their aptitude for the new kinds of warfare prescribed by circumstances. These leaders had to strike a balance between the need for caution in the face of a superior enemy – the need to score points but also to survive to carry on the fight – and on the other hand the need to engage the enemy frequently and effectively enough to satisfy their followers. Arms were not less important than tactics and there was a constant tug of war between the accumulation of arms (by raids or by parachute drops from outside) and the loss of arms through discovery of dumps by German Intelligence: this last danger put pressure on Resistance leaders to use arms when they had them instead of waiting for a more propitious moment.

Active Resistance contributed to the tribulations and ultimately to the defeat of the Germans by tying down units or preventing their orderly transfer from one front to another and by engaging them in battle. The threat of an armed rising in Norway by the Resistance movement called Milorg in cooperation with allied forces constrained Hitler to detail thirteen army divisions, 90,000 naval personnel, 6,000 SS men and 12,000 paramilitary troops to watch and control a country with a total population of only three million, and at the end of the war Milorg received the surrender of 400,000 Germans (ten times Milorg's own strength) and liberated over 90,000 prisoners of war, nearly all of them Russians. When the Anglo-American armies landed in Normandy in July 1944 French Resistance forces delayed the reinforcement of the crucial sector: the SS division *Das Reich* took nine days to get from south-western France to the battle area. In September the Dutch paralysed the railways at the time of the allied advance towards Nijmegen and Arnhem. The Danes harassed and impeded the withdrawal of German forces from Norway to the defence of Germany itself. National armies were reborn and rejoined the war: 120,000 Belgians were fighting as regular units by the end of the war, the Danish secret army was 45,000 strong, 60,000 Czechs fought with the Russian army in addition to the units which had been serving with British forces since the beginning. In France the Alpine departments and the Massif Central were liberated by the French Resistance, whose total contribution at the time of the re-invasion of Europe was put by Eisenhower – with perhaps a degree of pardonable exaggeration – at the equivalent of fifteen divisions.

This impressive resurgence of European nationalism in arms helped to salve the humiliation of the defeats in 1940–41 and by doing so contributed more to the spiritual rehabilitation of Europe, which was in the balance, than to the defeat of Germany, which was assured by other forces. It also emphasized the national character of European policies since the Resistance movements were nationalist not only in the sense of being anti-German but also in the almost complete absence of any contacts among themselves. At one point Resistance leaders met at a conference in Switzerland and discussed a new and less nationally divided Europe, harking back to Mazzinian ideas of a confraternity of nationalisms, looking forward to a *Europe des patries*, echoing ideas which were being discussed at the same time by anti-Nazi conspirators inside Germany; but so long as the war continued there was little opportunity for common action. Attempts to concert French and Belgian, Yugoslav and Italian Resistance came to little. A Resistance movement had to be ultra careful about its security and it was often suspicious of its neighbour's politics or ideology. So the international character of the external attack on Germany by the Anglo-American-Russian coalition could not be matched by any corresponding internationalism on the continent. Communism, which might have served as a link between Resistance movements, did not do so during the war because communist resisters were no more able than noncommunist resisters to make effective contacts beyond the bounds of their local field of operations. Thirdly, the patriotic aims of Resistance were yoked with objectives of national regeneration and revolution which will be more closely examined in the next chapters. Although Resistance movements began without any definite political purpose and were often antipolitical in the sense that they distrusted the political parties and institutions which had failed them before the war, yet at the same time these movements were obliged to be political in another sense. They responded to prevailing popular emotions and aspirations which were of a political nature and, because they were constructive and not merely hostile to occupiers or prewar régimes, imposed on the Resistance movements a distinctive blend of moral-political programme which was characteristically left-wing.

As Resistance developed it involved not only the Resistance movements themselves inside occupied countries but also governments in exile (all of them in London except the Greek government which was in Cairo) and the organizations established with similar aims by the British and American governments. The first of these in point of time, and for some time the most active, was the British Special Operations Executive (SOE) which was created in July 1940 as a department in the Ministry of Economic Warfare. The date indicated the need: to preserve or renew contacts with a continent from which Great Britain had been expelled and cut off. The Ministry indicated the prime aim: to injure Germany's war-making capacity by sabotage. The two together prescribed the method: to find, train and dispatch small groups of technically equipped demolitionists. At the beginning of the war the British government had made plans for interfering with Germany's supplies of iron ore from Sweden and oil from Rumania and although these had been attended by no success the notion of economic warfare had been embodied in a Department of State, and after Dunkirk Great Britain's inability to do much else in Europe, combined with the emergence of Resistance in the following year and Churchill's decision to foster it, focused attention on the possibilities of sabotage. SOE set to work to find saboteurs with the right aptitudes and languages (they were recruited in French-speaking Canada and polyglot

South America as well as among the refugees from Hitler's Europe) and it eventually established sixty training schools for operations in Europe besides others for Asia. These schools sent 7,500 agents, mostly nationals of the countries concerned, to western Europe and 4,000, mostly British agents and military liaison parties, to Italy and south-eastern Europe.

Almost at the outset these operations were extended from sabotage to intelligence. Many intelligence contacts had been broken by the retreat from the continent. In addition, military intelligence networks had been penetrated by the Germans before the war: in Holland, for example, the British headquarters, which was next door to the house made famous in the First World War by Mata Hari, had been under surveillance since 1935 and all visitors to it had been regularly photographed as they went in and out. There was therefore something of an intelligence vacuum and it seemed natural to ask SOE, which was organizing sabotage trips, to get its agents to do some intelligence work too. Unfortunately agents of the one kind are not necessarily the right people for work of the other kind, nor had they been trained for it, and the confusion of the two functions endangered SOE's work. It also endangered Resistance groups, since there were more agents around who had contacts with these groups and were at the same time liable to be picked up by German counter-intelligence or to become unsuspectingly involved with double agents.

A further extension of SOE's work occurred when subversion and insurrection were added to its brief. Churchill told Hugh Dalton, the Minister of Economic Warfare, that it was his business to 'set Europe ablaze'. Prizing variety and unconventionality for their own sake, and stirred perhaps by the historical recollections of chouans, carbonari and klephts, Churchill welcomed the chance to revive the fighting spirit and fighting forces of Europe's nations. He wanted to summon them to make life hell for the Germans and, ultimately, to cooperate with the allies' regular armies when the time should come to return to the continent. But this part of the programme raised unforeseen political complications. SOE's emissaries became charged with diplomatic tasks: persuading Resistance groups to adopt certain policies or tactics, reconciling them with one another for the good of the common cause, reporting on them and advising which were more worthy of support than others. Supplying one organization with arms in preference to another was a political act. The British tried to operate on the principle that the only thing that mattered was harassing the Germans and the only touchstone for deciding between competing groups was this anti-German fervour. But this simple rule of thumb ignored the facts. The Resistance movements were not simply, sometimes not primarily, anti-German. They represented for the time being

the domestic politics of their countries. Some of them were fighting against
the pre-war order and distrusted or opposed their governments in exile
with which the British government was in alliance; and they became more
definitely left-wing after Hitler's invasion of the USSR unshackled the
communists and set them free to join and try to dominate the Resistance.

To a man with Churchill's uncomplicated sense of purpose these were
secondary matters so long as the Germans had to be beaten. He knew
that war and politics could not be separated but he also knew which he
was going to subordinate to the other. The political issues would have to
be dealt with later, by which time they would doubtless present themselves
in a new context and a new light. Meanwhile he pledged Great Britain to
the restoration of the independence of Europe. He became a European
leader. The V sign for victory which he coined and its aural equivalent
· · · –, tapped out in Morse or played by the BBC to all Europe in the
familiar phrase from Beethoven's fifth symphony, were symbols of an
intimate link between Great Britain and the subject peoples of the continent without distinction between political creeds. Although a conservative
and a monarchist, Churchill discarded all tests except that of anti-
Germanism. Only when the war was manifestly won but not concluded
did he turn from battling to politics and set himself, unsuccessfully in
the one case, successfully in the other, to baulk the republicans in
Italy and Greece.

The Americans saw things otherwise. They were quicker to see the
communists than the klephts in the Resistance ranks. They were even
inclined to suspect all Resistance movements, including Gaullism, of being
either communist or stalking horses for communism. They appreciated
the political implications of helping the Resistance. They fell into a different kind of unreality from the British. Traditionally wary of European
politics and less well versed in them because of their distance from the
scene, they sought to separate strategic from political issues, to avoid
giving blank cheques to exiles and to get on with the war in the expectation
that victory would produce a return to stability in Europe, a withdrawal
of American intervention and a settlement of political problems by Europeans through the magic of free elections. But this expectation was
wishful thinking. It is almost true to say of Roosevelt that he substituted a
talisman for political analysis and had no political aim in Europe during
these years other than getting agreement, particularly from Stalin but also
from everybody else, on the holding of free elections all over Europe
(except in Germany) as quickly as possible after the end of the war. On
this basis it might be safe to help the Resistance. The Office of Strategic
Services (OSS) was created to emulate and in many instances surpass

SOE. American aid was lavish. It was given without acknowledging that this kind of intervention had political as well as military implications: whereas the British, in helping Tito for example, gave aid on the deliberate basis that military considerations overrode all others and that the obvious political implications must of necessity be subordinated, the Americans tended wishfully to believe that military and political considerations were so far distinct that military aid had insignificant political consequences.

Resistance created difficulties between the allied governments – in this case mainly the British – and governments-in-exile. Supporting governments-in-exile was not always compatible with the aid given by the British to armies-not-in-exile. The governments suspected the British of trying to dominate and direct a part of their national activity. They also protested on behalf of their nationals against what they regarded as foolish British tactics or serious British mistakes. There was an acrimonious feud between French and British authorities over which of them should employ French citizens as agents. The Norwegians and the British tussled ill-naturedly for control of Milorg and, as already mentioned, the Norwegian government protested sharply against experimental British coastal raids in 1940 which seemed to the unfortunate Norwegians in the places raided to achieve nothing beyond provoking frightful German reprisals. Relations with the Dutch were even worse and led to allegations that the British wanted to destroy the Resistance and that a senior SOE officer was a German agent. These accusations were the outcome of the so-called *Englandspiel*, the penetration by German Intelligence of SOE's networks in the Netherlands. An SOE agent was captured. He sent a pre-arranged coded signal to warn his headquarters in London of his capture and the vulnerability of his communications but London, in breach of its own rules, decided to ignore this warning and assume that the agent had made a mistake and could still be treated as secure. This basic error was repeated and was observed by the Germans who confirmed the illusion by staging bogus acts of sabotage to persuade SOE that its plans were working as intended. As a result all but two of sixty agents sent to the Netherlands were caught and sent to die in concentration camps, enough British equipment to train and arm 10,000 men was intercepted by the Germans, and many arms dumps and agents' networks were uncovered not only in the Netherlands but also in France where brave men and women fell into the hands of the SD.

Disgruntlement arose also from lack of communication and so lack of understanding on both sides. Resistance leaders did not realize that SOE and OSS were the poor relations of the traditional armed services, which tended to regard Resistance movements as amateur sideshows, a drain on their material and planning resources, an impediment to the more serious business of conventional campaigning and a distasteful adulteration of honest fighting with dubious politics. Resistance commanders complained of being undervalued and undersupplied. They asked in vain to be given the jobs which Bomber Command thought it could do better, felt bitter when innocent civilians were killed because a factory which could have been more easily and more cheaply disrupted by sabotage was attacked by hundreds of bombers, and blamed the allied organizations with which they were in touch. They did not know that SOE and OSS frequently shared their views, nor did they know how limited resources were (for a year SOE had only two aircraft) nor perhaps how difficult they themselves were to reach. To take an extreme case: at the beginning of the war Great Britain had no aircraft with the range necessary to fly to Poland and back without landing and but for the invention of wireless the Poles' feeling of abandonment would have been complete. The situation improved with the arrival in service of the Lancaster and Liberator and the conquest of air bases in Italy, but even then not many of the latest types of four-engined bomber could be spared for liaison with the Polish underground, eastern Poland remained out of reach of the western allies throughout the war, and Poles never felt satisfied that the British were doing enough to sustain what they regarded as a substantial arm of the general allied war effort. Of the operations attempted – 858 in all – only a little over half were successful. Polish complaints about the scale and purposefulness of British aid have to be judged against the Poles' own uniquely dangerous position. Caught in the German-Russian crossfire – and not for the first time in their history – they witnessed the fearful German onslaught on the Polish intelligentsia, were vaguely aware of a Nazi plan to deport 16–20 million Poles to Siberia after the war and judged from their experiences in 1939–41 that their treatment at Russian hands would be little less painful. Their appeals were attuned to their desperation.

Yet despite the mistakes and misunderstandings great and small, and despite the activities of double agents who were more numerous and more successful in their special brand of perfidy than the romantic would like to believe, the combination of Resistance and allied governments was an appreciable factor in winning the war and is not diminished by the fact that collaborators were more numerous than resisters. Men and women of many nations worked together with thrilling trust and courage even during the periods when the organizations to which they belonged happened to be quarrelling. SOE and OSS provided arms, wireless sets and a great range of ingenious equipment, invented new weapons and new gadgets, found, trained and dispatched thousands of remarkable men and women. The contribution to Europe's morale was also great. The BBC in particular not only linked the Resistance with Great Britain by providing news, encouragement and coded instructions but also created an *esprit de corps*. The Resistance could have become a separate war, but it did not. It has a special history and a special pride but they are part of the shared experience of the Second World War.

Sharing and cooperating imply communication. By the mid-twentieth century radio had put millions of people in direct touch with one another. In spite of prohibitions on listening, confiscations of radio receivers and jamming, a government could not prevent its people or its conquered subjects from hearing something of what other governments had to say. Radio propaganda became one of the most effective subsidiary weapons of the war. It was used for communicating with friends, keeping their spirits up and concerting active operations against the enemy. It created a sense of presence, or impending presence, which was invaluable between Great Britain and the continent after other normal links had been broken. It also enabled belligerent governments to address each other's peoples in attempts to shake their steadfastness, undermine their morale and generally sow doubt and unease. It was a difficult weapon to use because it was relatively untried and two-edged. On the one hand it provided, like the activities of SOE and OSS, an extra means to attack the enemy's military efficiency. From this point of view any statement which upset the combatants on the other side was useful and it did not essentially matter whether the statement was true or false. Lies, forgeries and rumours were all used in the course of what came to be called black propaganda. Radio programmes supposed to emanate from secret stations in enemy territory – the most famous was *Soldatensender Calais* – spread stories about, for example, how top Nazi bosses were enjoying themselves with blondes and plenty of food and spending more time in specially safe air raid shelters than in visits to the front. Leaflets and forged copies of well-known German newspapers were used in the same way. But the basis of black propaganda was nevertheless credibility, and credibility required a substantial degree of truth. Therefore black propaganda, however much it might embroider the facts, could not do without them. Its basic technique was to retail facts and insert among them one or two tendentious and alarming items. The tricks of the black propagandists (which make particularly entertaining reading in retrospect) were unfailingly ingenious but no more than marginally instrumental in directing the fortunes of war.

For white propaganda on the other hand truth was all important. White propaganda was directed against the enemy's civilian morale rather than his military efficacy. The distinction could on occasions be a fine one, but even in modern warfare there is a dividing line between the civilian and the military factors in the total war effort: white propaganda, like the mass bombing of civilian housing to which we shall come in a later chapter, was an attempt to destroy the enemy's will to fight as opposed to destroying his fighting forces. White propaganda also aimed to swing opinion in occupied Europe.

Neither side was very effective when it tried to subvert the other. German broadcasts to Great Britain were almost entirely ineffectual. British broadcasts to Germany, although much better informed and more imaginative, did not achieve their main object and Goebbels was able, as we shall see, to maintain German morale right to the end and against fearful odds. Suffice it to say here that the BBC's broadcasts to Germany, in which there was an almost dogmatic addiction to truth, were hampered because Goebbels could argue that they were not true. He repeated British bombing claims which the Germans themselves and neutrals could see to be greatly exaggerated and he was able for a time to decry BBC statements by recalling discredited accounts of German atrocities in the First World War and saying that the British were at it again. The BBC was also hampered by mass bombing which, although it had the same aim, proved to be counterproductive in the sphere of morale.

In their propaganda to occupied Europe the British and the Germans had opposite problems. The Germans, who were in occupation, cajoled, impressed and bullied. Their principal advantage was their monopoly of public entertainment and their principal instrument was the film. The British and the Americans, physically at a distance, exploited radio. Their principal advantage was that their audience wanted to believe what they were saying. Fostering and satisfying this desire required them to tell the truth and as the war progressed allied propagandists were in the happy position of having the truth working for them. It remains an open question, debated by psychologists, how far one man can make another act contrary to his basic wishes or instincts. Anti-German propaganda during the war had little effect on Germans for, although it may have penetrated their minds, it did not stir them to action against their leaders. But anti-German propaganda to non-Germans proved its worth.

CHAPTER 14

Revolution in the South-East

NONE of Hitler's European victims fought the war solely with the idea of defeating Germany and getting back to their pre-war circumstances. Even Great Britain, the most conservative of the countries involved, by turning massively to the Labour Party at the end of the war in spite of the risk of seeming ungrateful to an extremely popular national leader, recorded its dissatisfaction with the past. On the continent similar feelings were universal, but they differed greatly from place to place. Broadly speaking there were peoples who wanted to change the institutions under which they lived, if need be by force, and peoples who were content to retain their institutions but wanted to improve what went on within them. Again broadly speaking, it was in eastern Europe that the revolutionary current was strongest, while western Europeans aimed rather at reform – excepting perhaps the French (a case specially difficult to categorize and best considered separately). Thus the war against the Germans and Italians was crossed with civil wars, actual or incipient, whose roots lay in the pre-war past but which developed during the war because wars make men look more critically at their state and accustom them to action in pursuit of political goals.

Norway, Denmark and the Netherlands were relatively stable and united countries. They looked forward to the full restoration of their monarchies and parliamentary institutions. They participated in the war beyond their borders as well as by resistance at home. The Norwegian government had commandeered the Norwegian merchant fleet, 85 per cent of which was outside Norwegian waters at the time of the German invasion; it thus became the largest merchant shipping concern in the world. It was very much in the fight and also comfortably in funds. Contact with Norway was maintained by the so-called Shetland bus which conveyed persons to and from Norway and also several hundred tons of war supplies. Of the smaller but nevertheless appreciable Danish merchant navy over 60 per cent served with the allies. The Dutch also provided fighting men for the allied forces, and the Queen of the Netherlands, who escaped like the King of Norway to London, contributed to the unity and steadfastness of her occupied country by her broadcasts to them.

Belgium's case was superficially different because of its linguistic and

racial divisions and because the king became an object of controversy. He
was criticized for surrendering himself into captivity instead of accompanying his government to London, he was suspected (unfairly) of
undue partiality for the Germans, and his re-marriage during the war was
unpopular. The Germans exploited the differences between Flemings and
Walloons (as they had done in the First World War) and exacerbated the
social tensions in a country in which the monarchy had become a reflection
of division instead of a symbol of unity. After the war the king obtained a
popular vote of confidence but by so narrow a margin that he found
himself obliged to abdicate within a few days of the resumption of his full
functions. Yet here too there was no serious challenge to the country's
political institutions, other than the monarchy. There was, however, in all
four of these countries an intensified concern with social questions. The
discussion of such questions was a long-established feature of western
European political life, but during the war they became more real when
different sorts and conditions of men shared their experiences – in fighting
the enemy and helping one another, in receiving the same food rations
and facing the same firing squads. War made Europe more egalitarian
and more leftward inclined.

In eastern Europe this shift to the left occurred in situations in which
social reform was barely conceivable, or at any rate not at all likely,
without political revolution. Hence the special importance of the communists with their uninhibited attitude to violent revolution, an importance which is in the first instance distinct from the proximity of these
countries to the Soviet Union. In the countries which were allied with
Germany – the central strip comprising Hungary, Rumania and Bulgaria
– opportunity did not present itself until the Germans and the governments
under their protection began to fail, and when the opportunity came it
came not to reformist or revolutionary groups but to the Russian conquerors and the account of what happened belongs to the story of the
defeat of Germany and not of European Resistance. In Poland and Czechoslovakia too the decisive factor proved to be not an indigenous Resistance movement but Russian power. Czechoslovakia, less in need of reform
than Poland and the other countries of eastern Europe, had a moderate
government under Beneš which aimed to pursue a broadly based, middle-
of-the-road policy in post-war Czechoslovakia and to maintain friendly
relations with both Moscow and the western democracies; it succeeded
only up to 1948.

The Polish government, established in exile in London, was a right-
wing government which feared popular revolution and had every reason
to fear the Russians as much as it hated the Germans. Its policy was to

wait. It hoped, not unnaturally from its point of view, that the Russians and the Germans would exhaust and maim one another. It aimed therefore to build up a secret army in Poland but not to use it until German and Russian strength had been sapped and the pre-war régime could be restored with British and American help. Still less did it wish to provoke a national rising which would develop on similar lines to Tito's and leave the London government in exile for ever. Resistance to the Germans was therefore discouraged and until mid-point in the war was conducted almost entirely by Polish Jews and escaped Russian prisoners of war.

The secret army, or Home Army (A K), built up by the London government, was an amalgam of remnants of the old Polish army with bands which came into existence under German rule. Some of these bands were socialist, others consisted of right-wing Nationalists, yet others were affiliated to the Peasant Party. The socialists agreed in 1942 to become part of the A K, and the Peasant Party groups, although on the whole more hostile to the A K than friendly to it, accepted its authority the next year. Not all the Nationalist bands joined the A K. Some did so in 1944 after prolonged negotiation; others collaborated with the Germans. There were also left-wing groups which remained separate from the A K. Most of them were socialist and they created a small army of their own in 1944. The Communist Party, which had been harried by pre-war Polish governments and dissolved by Stalin before the war began, was being re-formed by Wladislaw Gomulka but it remained weak until the Russians began to send it arms at the end of 1943. In that year the London government's waiting policy was upset by the military successes of the Russian armies which destroyed the prospect of a long Russo-German bloodletting and also by a peasant rising in eastern Poland where Himmler, having discovered here the homeland of the ancient Burgundians, was creating a pure German colony – with *Volksdeutsche* from Rumania who had forgotten the German language. Owing to the A K's disinclination for risings the credit for supporting this rising against the S S went to the Peasant battalions and also to the communists who were able to score some anti-German successes in one or two areas including the country round Lublin. (Hitler's idea of reviving a Burgundian kingdom for Himmler was a typical piece of Nazi medievalism. Such schemes, although they may be dismissed as ridiculous extravaganzas, testify also to the hold of the romantic past on the German imagination. Historians – specially Treitschke who was as eloquent as he was eminent – had written excitingly about the way the Teutonic Knights had colonized and controlled eastern lands and had fired a new generation with the zeal to go out and do likewise. But Hitler was not unique in his historical romanticism. Roosevelt toyed with the idea of creating 'Wallonia' by putting together parts of Belgium and northern France, Luxembourg, Alsace and Lorraine.)

In south-eastern Europe revolution had freer play. In Greece and Yugoslavia civil war in fact occurred, in Greece hesitantly and ultimately unsuccessfully for the insurgents, in Yugoslavia on a full scale and successfully; in neither with Russian help. Albania, where various Resistance groups united against the Italians but then fell out and started a civil war from which the communists ultimately profited, was shifted from the Italian to the Yugoslav sphere of influence.

In Greece, General Ioannis Metaxas, who had been appointed Prime Minister by the king in 1936 and quickly converted his power into a dictatorship, had been placed in a dilemma by the unsolicited British guarantee of 1939. This guarantee, a promise of aid against Italo-German aggressiveness, ran counter to Metaxas' policy of relying on Hitler to keep Mussolini away. This policy failed when Mussolini attacked without telling Hitler and so forced Metaxas into a fight which he had neither wanted nor foreseen. By responding stoutly to Mussolini's ultimatum he made himself a national hero and temporarily united Greek monarchists and republicans, whose feud was the mainspring of Greek politics. But he was slow to accept British aid, which he did not relish, and his sudden death in January 1941 did not entirely remove the obstacles to British collaboration first against the Italians and subsequently against the Germans.

When the brief German campaigns against Greece and Crete ended, the king and his government had disappeared to Egypt leaving behind a political void which was filled by a pro-Axis puppet government, consisting mostly of generals who not implausibly believed that the war was over and won by the Germans. This government had little authority. The country was divided and roughly, sometimes very roughly, administered by German, Italian and Bulgarian occupiers. Away from the towns guerrilla bands began to form in the hills which constitute so much of Greece and make it unattractive to regular military formations. These bands were all predominantly left-wing and republican. Their members were largely uninterested in or contemptuous of the old struggle between royalists and Venizelist republicans and saw in the exile of its protagonists an opportunity to refashion Greek politics on less sterile lines. Few of them were communists, and at first they gave communism little thought, for it seemed hardly conceivable that the Greek Communist Party could play a leading part in Greek affairs.

Founded shortly after the First World War the Communist Party had

had a difficult row to hoe. It could make little appeal to the peasants, who formed the bulk of the population, because Venizelos had broken up big estates and given the peasants land of their own. Its anti-clericalism was equally lacking in appeal. Even more damning was its advocacy of separate Macedonian and Thracian states, which it had been forced to adopt by the international communist movement and which was regarded by practically all Greeks as the purest treason. After 1936 it was virtually destroyed by one of the few intelligent and sophisticated policemen to be produced by twentieth-century authoritarianism, Constantine Maniadakis, Minister of the Interior under Metaxas. Maniadakis' devices included the creation of a bogus Communist Party under his own wing and the publication of his own edition of the communist newspaper *Rizospastis* to the confusion of all concerned, especially communists. When the war came the party's principal leaders were either in prison or exile. But in the next three years they prepared to take over the country and came within measurable distance of success.

They did this in disguise. They created the National Liberation Front (EAM) which, with its armed bands (ELAS), became the principal symbol of Greek resistance to the occupiers and, carefully suppressing regular communist propaganda, provided the communist leaders with broad popular support on a basis of patriotic nationalism, calls for unity against the enemy and hopes of social reform after the war. Their aim was to establish their organization as the natural successor to the occupiers and the government of post-liberation Greece. There were three threats to this programme: the legitimate government which would try to return from exile; other patriotic Resistance movements which might thrive sufficiently to challenge EAM; and the British who appeared on the scene unexpectedly in order to organize sabotage of Axis lines of supply to North Africa.

The British military mission (it later became Anglo-American) was both an embarrassment and an opportunity. The leaders of EAM and other Resistance groups were ambivalent about waging war on the occupiers. Many of their followers were filled with a patriotic fury which they wanted to vent in action, but harrying the occupiers meant bringing down reprisals on the innocent country people upon whose goodwill the bands relied for sustenance and who were in any case their compatriots. Reprisals were exceedingly fierce. Hostages were taken and executed and whole villages were wiped out; 1,000 people were killed in a single incident at Kalavryta, 250 women and children were burned to death at Klisura. The total number of hostages executed in Greece has been put at 45,000.

In addition the Germans, Italians and Bulgarians executed another 68,000. (But the greatest killer in Greece was famine. Nearly half of the Greeks who died in the war starved.)

The bands had moreover a further reason for avoiding engagements with the occupiers. Each band was suspicious of its neighbours, usually rightly, and did not want to waste its energies and endanger its survival before the day of reckoning which would come when the occupiers withdrew. On the other hand the British mission had arms and golden sovereigns to give away and these precious supplies had to be earned. The price was cooperation with the British against the occupiers. The principal military result was the destruction of the Gorgopotamos railway viaduct, already mentioned – a feat of diplomacy as well as daring, since E L A S and its chief rival E D E S were persuaded to work together for the first, and last, time. A joint band of 150 Greeks engaged and destroyed an Italian force while British saboteurs blew up the bridge. Its destruction and the consequent interruption of the German supply line to Africa for a few weeks may have been militarily marginal. On the other hand an accumulation of marginals may be greater than the sum of the parts. Politically the operation had consequences that are easier to define, if contradictory. Its success heartened the Greek communists who began in the next year to construct a major movement of their own. Equally, however, their opponents derived from the same success an assurance of their continued separate existence, thus ensuring that the Greek resistance would not be unified under communist control.

The Anglo-American mission contrived to enlist the bands in further, if separate, activities in 1943 when an extensive railway sabotage plan was put into execution in order to deceive the Germans into expecting an allied landing in Greece rather than Sicily. This plan caused the diversion to Greece of a Panzer division and hampered its return. The Greek communists were also deceived. Thinking that the allies were about to arrive in Greece and that the war was ending, they attacked the anti-communist resistance and so started the first civil war which during the winter of 1943–4 they lost. But their miscalculation was not fatal to them owing to the fortuitous gains which they had already reaped from the Italian surrender to the allies in September 1943. This event gave E L A S all the arms it needed and so made it independent of the Anglo-American mission. It so happened that E L A S predominated in the areas of Italian occupation, and although captured Italian arms were meant to be allocated between all the bands, E L A S was able – as a result of this piece of luck and of some high-paced intrigue – to keep the lot. It became an armed force of about 19,000 effectives, ten times the size of E D E S. It had already attacked and destroyed some smaller bands and earlier in 1943 it had captured Colonel Stephanos Saraphis, one of the ablest non-communist leaders, and had persuaded him to become commander-in-chief of ELAS. Saraphis' ready acceptance, which surprised the communists, showed how far ELAS had established itself as the only band worth belonging to. Its most serious rival was EDES, a group formed by the republican Colonel Napoleon Zervas (its repute was later tarnished when it was joined by some shady right-wing characters seeking to escape the stigma of collaboration with the occupiers, and Zervas himself modified his republicanism partly to please Churchill); but EDES was confined to a small region in the west and as early as July 1943, when the allied mission persuaded the bands to sign an agreement establishing a joint headquarters, this was located at ELAS headquarters. From this year onwards the communists were less concerned with their rivals inside Greece than with the Greek government in exile and its army and navy.

The leaders of EAM aimed to sow division in the military and political ranks of the exiles and above all to delay the king's return until they could make it impossible. First mutinies in the Greek army occurred in February 1943. The king broadened his government (in Egypt) to the Left, whereupon a number of royalist officers resigned their commissions in protest. In order to assert its authority the Greek government asked the British to arrest these officers. The net result was a diminution of right-wing influence in the army. The king agreed in July to submit the issue of the monarchy to a referendum after the war but, when pressed also to undertake not to return to Greece before the question had been put to the vote, he refused. In this he was strongly supported by Churchill and Roosevelt. Churchill further advised him to refuse a request from EAM for seats in the government. EAM, influenced perhaps by the news that Great Britain had decided to back Tito and his communists in Yugoslavia and by the false hope that the Italian surrender heralded a general Axis collapse, made its first bid for power and opened operations against rival bands. But EDES survived, the war went on and this premature bid contributed to the ultimate defeat of ELAS by sowing dissension in its own ranks and stimulating the puppet government in Athens to recruit anti-communist security forces.

In March 1944 EAM established a provisional government inside Greece and so formally set up a challenge to the government in exile. In April more mutinies – this time in the navy as well as the army in Egypt – occurred and the conservative Prime Minister, Emmanuel Tsouderos, resigned under pressure from his left-wing colleagues. But his successors were no more able than he had been to control the situation and the

British had to intervene again. Thus the government in exile disintegrated at the same time as E A M had set up a rival to it. But E A M now changed its tactics and instead of insisting on its own creation as the only legitimate government it entered into negotiations for a share in the government in exile which had again been reconstituted under a new Prime Minister, George Papandreou, the political heir of Eleutherios Venizelos. After murdering Colonel Psaros, the leader of a smaller but not inconsiderable band, E A M sent representatives to a conference in Lebanon convoked by Papandreou in order to form a coalition between the exiles and the Resistance organizations. The upshot was a new government which included communists, but some of these feared that Papandreou had outsmarted them and reduced them to a subordinate role instead of the dominant one which they might attain by steering clear of all the politicians in exile. They were, however, under pressure from the Russians to put national and anti-fascist unity before communist power and they even agreed in September that all the bands should be subordinated to the new government and placed under the command of a British general. A few weeks later, in October, when Papandreou and his colleagues moved to Athens on the heels of the retreating Germans, it looked as though he and the British had pre-empted a communist take-over. A small British force followed in December.

But E A M controlled most of Greece outside the capital and in December, very probably on Tito's advice, it reversed its policy and made a second bid for power. (An alternative but less easily acceptable version is that E A M was provoked into hostilities by the British, so that it might be destroyed. There is evidence for the proposition that the shooting in the main square of Athens which opened the fighting was not begun by E A M.) E A M was without outside help. A Russian mission had gone to Greece in 1944 but reported that the Greek communists were not worth helping. In any case Stalin, as he told the Yugoslav communist Edvard Kardelj at the time, was convinced that the Americans would not allow Greece to be taken over by communists. Accordingly he had agreed to allot Greece to Churchill in return for a free hand in Rumania, a bargain which was sealed when the two of them drew up spheres of influence at Moscow in October 1944. E A M was therefore trying to emulate Tito's success in winning power for communists without external aid. It began by attacking E D E S, whose forces had to be evacuated by the British to Corfu, and openly assumed control of all Greece except a few islands and a small area in the centre of Athens from which the British could not be dislodged. The British, with tacit Russian support (evinced by the appointment of an Ambassador to the Papandreou government) and in spite of

fierce criticism in the United States and in Great Britain itself, sent reinforcements and defeated the insurrection after six weeks' fighting. E L A S
was not trained for regular as opposed to guerrilla fighting and its political
leaders were probably divided: in some parts of Greece E L A S did not go
over to the offensive and there were still those who preferred the tactics of
coalition to a coup. The failure of the insurrection was accompanied by
communist atrocities which left an indelible mark on a whole generation
of Greeks.

In the face of these events Churchill compelled the king to delay his
return until it could be legitimated *de novo* by a plebiscite. The archbishop
of Athens was appointed regent while the British defeated E A M and
negotiated a truce. A year later, in March 1946, the royalists scored
heavily in elections and six months afterwards King George II was summoned back by a popular vote of more than two to one in his favour. The
communists then renewed their insurrection with help from Yugoslavia,
Bulgaria and Albania. They were not defeated until 1949 when the re-
equipment and training of the Greek army by the Americans and the
defection of Yugoslavia from the communist block sealed their fate. The
communist domination of E A M and E L A S, the bitterness engendered
by the atrocities of 1944 and the subsequent onset of the Cold War altered
the nature of the political and social struggle which many Greeks had
taken to the hills to prosecute in the early days of the war. For Greece the
Second World War was an opportunity for change which came and went.
Greeks who wanted social change but not communism discovered that
they could have both or neither.

One of the many differences between the Greek and Yugoslav Resistance movements was the appearance in Yugoslavia of a commanding
figure, Josip Broz, later known to all the world as Tito. No national
Resistance fighter inside occupied Europe achieved anything approaching
his eminence; outside it only de Gaulle surpassed him. He possessed
courage, tenacity, intelligence, personal authority, and organizing experience gained in Moscow and the Spanish civil war (though he did not
actually go to Spain). He created the independent communist state of
Yugoslavia. He was helped by the divisions and weaknesses of his political
adversaries at home, by the disorders of the times, by the terrain of his
country and by outsiders – notably the British and Americans and to a
small extent the Russians – but of all the elements in his victory his own
personality was the outstanding one.

A second major difference between Yugoslavia and Greece was the fact
that Tito fought his enemies during the war instead of waiting. This policy
brought him into conflict with the other principal Resistance figure, Draza

Mihailovič, and eventually earned him the support of the western allies who had begun by backing Mihailovič.

Mihailovič was the accredited representative in Yugoslavia of the government in exile, which conferred on him the rank of general and the titles of Commander-in-Chief and Minister for War. He was also early in the field. But he failed to become a national leader for two main reasons: he was not truly national and he refused to lead. He was an impassioned Serb rather than a Yugoslav, as compared with Tito who, although half Croat and half Slovene, insisted on Serb-Croat cooperation and a federated Yugoslav state. Mihailovič too was reluctant to court disaster for his movement and reprisals for his compatriots by embarking on large-scale operations before the Germans were weakened by outside events. He and his followers, who were called *četniks* and were mainly former Serb army officers, were ready to undertake limited daring exploits but they had no thought of starting a national rising such as was in the minds and in the teaching of communist leaders. Mihailovič aimed to re-create a regular army against the day of German withdrawal and meanwhile, isolated exploits apart, to wait. In the course of waiting his hostility to Tito and to communism developed to the point where he opted for collaboration with Yugoslavia's national enemies in order to save it from communism. And in so adjusting his priorities, he destroyed himself.

The beginnings of the communist Resistance movement were small but professional and immediate. Tito began to organize resistance as soon as the Germans invaded Yugoslavia and in spite of the fact that Stalin was at that time still one of Hitler's allies. He himself moved from Zagreb to Belgrade in May 1941 and was ready with a call for action by the end of June when the German armies attacked the USSR. He had the beginnings of regional organizations, sabotage plans and groups of followers who, although critically short of arms, included some three hundred veterans of the war in Spain. They inherited the traditions of the *hajduks*, heroes like the pig-breeder Karadjordje who had become the leader of the Serb revolt of 1804 against the Turks and the founder of the modern Serbian state. Although the Communist Party was small (it had about 12,000 full members in 1941) it had non-communist contacts and sympathizers as a result of following the Popular Front policy adopted by the Comintern in 1935. By the autumn of 1941 these partisan groups had grown strong enough to undertake operations in Serbia and establish a headquarters at Užice where they ran an arms factory and a printing press. These successes led to discussions for joint operations with the *četniks* (some of whom were being attracted to the communist side), and until attacked by the *četniks* the partisans supplied the *četniks* with arms from their Užice factory. Mihailovič, however, had been directed by the government in exile, whose grasp of the situation was naturally imperfect, to assume command over the communist partisans. This Tito was neither prepared nor obliged to accept in spite of chidings from Moscow whence Stalin, anxious above all for allied cooperation, was urging him to forget about communist revolution for the time being and concentrate on a common anti-Axis front with all friends of the western allies. Fighting broke out between *četniks* and partisans. The *četniks* tried but failed to evict the partisans from Užice and suffered a series of defeats. These events eliminated all possibility of cooperation and induced Mihailovič to accept arms from the Italians to continue the struggle. The immediate gain went to the Germans who took the opportunity to clear Serbia of all Resistance groups.

In the following year the partisans were hard pressed by the Germans and Italians. Hitler had become aware of their potential danger, and they were forced to suspend operations and seek refuge in the mountains of Bosnia and Montenegro. A number defected. But thanks to Tito's leadership, reinforced by the professionalism of the Spanish war veterans and of former officers of the Yugoslav army who joined the partisans, the movement survived, recuperated and re-emerged as a well-ordered army of four brigades. It also began to assume the functions of a civil administration in the areas which it controlled, fixing prices and decreeing social changes as well as keeping order. In November 1942 an Assembly at Bihac foreshadowed the partisans' claim to become the government of Yugoslavia.

In 1943, when their strength had risen to about 20,000, they were attacked by forces about six times as large, lost half their equipment and a quarter of their men killed in battle or massacred afterwards, but they escaped once more from Bosnia to Montenegro in the spring and back from Montenegro to Bosnia in the summer. Their losses were all the more grievous because the wounded either died or had to be shot until this grim and tragic burden was relieved by British medical supplies and a medical airlift to British hospitals in Italy. Their enemies in these operations were a combination of Germans, Italians, Bulgarians, *četniks* and *ustachi*. (The last were organized brigades of toughs who clustered round Pavelič's court in Croatia in an atmosphere described by Ciano as 'cowboy'. They massacred Serbs and Jews on a scale which horrified most other Croats; hated the Orthodox church and the Cyrillic alphabet with pathological intensity; and became so corrupt that even Pavelič felt constrained to have two of their leaders shot.)

A few months after their defeat in Montenegro the fortunes of the partisans were transformed by the general Italian collapse. They gained control of most of Croatia including the Dalmatian coast and islands, seized large quantities of Italian arms and were able to recruit and equip an army of 250,000. They were now a formidable force, a nation in arms, and at the end of the year Tito was proclaimed Marshal of Yugoslavia and President of the Council for the Liberation, which was in effect an interim government. The king's return was to be conditional on a plebiscite in his favour.

For much of this time the outside world knew little about what was going on in Yugoslavia. A first British mission arrived in Montenegro in September 1941 with the dual purpose of getting information and giving such help as could be spared from the scant resources available in North Africa. It was assumed that help would go to Mihailovič, for although the British were already aware of the country's internal dissensions, they clung to the hope that Mihailovič could unite all opposition to Germans and Italians. Towards the end of the year a British officer who had visited the headquarters of both Mihailovič and Tito advised that no help should be delivered to the former pending the outcome of talks which were then going on between the two (Tito was receiving no aid at this date), but this advice was not followed and Great Britain, partly out of loyalty to the Yugoslav government in London which was an ally, decided to build up Mihailovič by broadcast propaganda and military aid. Then for a year all communication between the British authorities and their man in Yugoslavia was cut by Mihailovič. Among the British counsels were divided, as S O E in London continued to repose in Mihailovič a faith which S O E in Cairo no longer held, but by the end of 1942 Ultra revealed (to the select few entitled to see it) that the two leaders were fighting one another and, during 1943, that Mihailovič was collaborating with the Italians and then with the Germans also. Further emissaries sent to Yugoslavia, owing to the growing importance of the Balkans in overall strategy, told the same story and when the reconciliation which the British (and the Russians) desired was shown to be plainly impossible Great Britain decided to drop Mihailovič and his friends in London (who did not disown him until August 1944) and support Tito. This reversal of policy was influenced by the delayed discovery that Tito could be much more useful than Mihailovič (thus confirming simultaneous Russian arguments that Mihailovič had become no better than a collaborationist) and by the coincidence that a British mission to Tito in May 1943 arrived during a great battle in which 20,000 partisans, although defeated, proved that they were a disciplined army under skilled command and not a random collection of guerrilla bands. This engagement also provided first hand proof of the *četniks'* collaboration with the Germans as well as the Italians.

From this point aid to Tito became the largest item in the Anglo-American aid programme. A naval and air base was established on the island of Vis with a small naval detachment and a squadron of Hurricanes. Another air base was opened at Bari for operations in the Balkans. Yugoslav pilots and tank crews were trained in Egypt, and Yugoslav prisoners in Italy were collected and formed into a Yugoslav legion. Yugoslav wounded were flown to hospitals in Italy. Great quantities of equipment were sent to Tito, mainly by the Americans – 100,000 rifles, 50,000 machine and sub-machine guns, 1,380 mortars, 630,000 grenades, 700 wireless sets, 175,000 uniforms, 260,000 pairs of shoes. (The first Russian supplies did not arrive until April 1944.) When the Germans launched another major offensive against the partisans in May 1944, allied air forces came to their support, flying 1,000 sorties a day. Later in the year these air forces cooperated with the partisans in attacks on the Germans' lines of communication and harassed their retreat – in spite of Tito's suspicions that this cooperation was intended to pave the way for an allied occupation of the Balkans. In London King Peter dismissed Mihailovič and instructed the *četniks* to put themselves under Tito's command, but Tito made it clear to Churchill that the king could not return unless recalled by a plebiscite. Mihailovič made a final bid to retrieve his fortunes by an understanding with Pavelič, but the partisans engulfed all opposition and on 20 October 1944 they entered Belgrade. The Russians who had entered the country as allies from the north-east departed again (in accordance with a prior agreement between Stalin and Tito) and Tito ruled unchallenged. For nearly four years the Germans had been obliged to hold down Yugoslavia by force of arms instead of ruling it indirectly through complacent nominees. After the Italian collapse this necessity had cost them a standing force of fifteen divisions. Most of these were German, although they had some help from Bulgarians, *četniks* and the puppet régime in Belgrade. As the Russians advanced in central Europe the main concern of the Germans was the Russian front bearing down on Yugoslavia from the north-east but their troubles were increased and their forces distracted by the guerrilla fighters who had engineered a national uprising. The human cost to Yugoslavia was a population almost precisely decimated.

The final stage in the transfer of power to the communists was accompanied by some transient formalities. In an attempt to save the monarchy Great Britain forced King Peter to appoint a new Prime Minister, Dr Ivan Subasič, who went to Yugoslavia and concluded in December 1944 an agreement with Tito which provided for an interim regency and a parliament containing pre-1941 parliamentarians (provided they had not collaborated with the enemy) as well as members of the wartime communist assembly. A provisional government, formed in March with Tito at its head, included leaders of other parties, but they did not last long and before the end of the year the monarchy too was formally abolished after elections which the communists could hardly fail to win and did win. Yugoslavia had become a communist state and an independent one, the first since 1917. In this its war fortunes were unique, although the establishment of other communist states in eastern Europe at this time led many people to confound Yugoslavia with these under the generic name of satellites.

CHAPTER 15
France

FRANCE suffered during the decade which ended in 1940 two collapses which opened two debates. The spectacular collapse of France as a fighting force in 1940 was preceded by the collapse of the Republic itself, a collapse as complete as the collapse of the Weimar republic but unperceived; for although the symptoms of political and social disintegration were apparent and discussed, their full import did not become clear until the catastrophe of 1940 tore away the veil of illusion and showed that the Third Republic was no longer there. At this point Vichy took, temporarily, the place of the Republic. In the years before, France had become a vacuum governed by a *vis inertiae* deputizing for political institutions.

The failure of these institutions in the thirties was marked by parliamentary instability, by the growth of anti-parliamentary forces and by one significant but abortive attempt to arrest the drift of governmental incapacity. The political parties in the Third Republic were numerous, weak, young (none was as old as the republic itself or could even boast a foundation date earlier than the twentieth century) and usually unable to combine to produce positive programmes or policies. They combined in narcissistic and unproductive unions whose main effect was to keep Ministers in Ministries. This vacuity brought parliamentary democracy into contempt and encouraged the anti-parliamentarianism of those still unreconciled to the revolution of 1789 and of a more modern fascist brand, so that the republic was assailed from without at the same time as it was decomposing within. Both menaces were laid bare by a scandal which began, within a year of Hitler's seizure of power, with the suicide of a financial crook called Stavisky in January 1934. It continued with accusations against Ministers of complicity in Stavisky's swindles and against the police of hushing up the scandals and murdering witnesses, and it culminated in anti-government demonstrations which turned into drilled fascist riots. At this time various fascist and other right-wing leagues had a combined enrolled membership of about half a million and the sympathies of many times that number. At the centre of the storm was the Radical Socialist Party which was the pivot about which French politics turned.

The destruction of the Radicals would mean the destruction of the parliamentary system because the Radicals, as the centre party, were a *sine qua non* of any parliamentary coalition and because the party had personified the Third Republic almost from its inception. The Radicals were now, in the 1930s, the chief targets for charges of corruption and incompetence. Their lack of competence was partly a result of their position. They never won enough seats to form a stable one-party government and they found it difficult to make up their minds between alliance with socialists or conservatives. They had inherited a left-wing tradition of which they remained conscious and proud, but they had been moving steadily to the Right in their social outlook and their political programmes. Their inclination was to prefer the socialists, but the socialists were reluctant to join in government for fear of being outbid in the constituencies by the communists, from whom they had split off as a minority group in 1919. The socialists therefore resorted to the common but pernicious device of French parties of pledging support to another party but refusing to share office and responsibility – and then withdrawing their support, often sooner rather than later. These tactics, which the communists were to use against the socialists and Radicals in 1936, exposed all Left-inclined Radical governments to impermanence and eventually split the socialists themselves between those who wanted to give more support to the Radicals or less. The Radicals too were split between left- and right-wing groups, each hankering after a different kind of coalition. Further to the Right were a number of conservative parties, some more parliamentary and others more authoritarian.

The riots of 1934 had some cathartic effect and after an interlude of emergency 'national' government under Gaston Doumergue the socialist leader Léon Blum succeeded in creating a Popular Front stretching from communists to Radicals which, after an electoral victory in May 1935, took over the government with the hope of achieving parliamentary stability and social and economic reform. But the communists refused to join the government and displayed a chequered loyalty to it. A number of social reforms were introduced but Blum's administration was never able to concentrate attention, as its chief would have liked, on these overdue matters. The need to rearm absorbed funds required for social improvement and in 1936 the outbreak of civil war in Spain placed Blum in a dilemma from which he was unable to escape.

The Spanish government, also a Popular Front, appealed for help and Blum at first promised to give it, but his Radical colleagues represented middle-class Frenchmen who were afraid of the communist element on the government side in Spain and did not want to help it. Blum also feared that he could not count on the civil service or the armed forces and that, at the worst, he might even be risking civil war in France if he took sides actively in the civil war in Spain. Furthermore, the British government wanted to keep out and so Blum was forced by the balance of political power within France and by his principal ally to refuse help to the Spanish Popular Front. In June 1937, after little more than a year in office, his government was ousted by the Senate which had little liking for the Prime Minister's reforms and what they would cost the more prosperous sections of the bourgeoisie. A second Popular Front government was formed under a Radical Prime Minister with Blum as his deputy and the communists in undisguised opposition. This government was a Popular Front only in name. In substance it was a return to the old Radical-dominated merry-go-round and it was not long before the socialists quitted it. Blum did not so much fail to give France government and reform as demonstrate the impossibility of doing so. Long before 1936 the opposition to reform had become too strong to beat. His administration also gave a sharper edge to the danger of civil war in France as people gathered in the streets to shout: Better Hitler than Blum; and meant it. For Blum, personally an exceptionally generous as well as an exceptionally clear-minded man, was hated for what he stood for – social justice – and for what he was – a Jew.

The collapse of the political fabric of the Third Republic was not unwelcome to many Frenchmen but the collapse of its armies was a shock to all. There had been a feeling of weakness in France for a decade, but few had realized the closeness of the connection between social malaise and military impotence. The weakness of France was in any case puzzling. It was not the natural weakness of a small country like Denmark, but weakness embedded in strength. France continued to manifest, throughout the period between the wars, a vigorous artistic, scientific and cultural life, nationally and internationally renowned, and possessed not only one of the largest armies in the world but also one of the largest bank balances. Yet France was uneasy and pessimistic. The pessimism went deep. It came from the feeling that there were not enough Frenchmen. Between Waterloo (1815) and Sedan (1870) the population of France had risen from 30 to 36 million, while that of the hereditary enemy, Great Britain, had doubled from 13 to 26 million and the Prussia of 11 million had become the Germany of 41 million. During the 1930s the marriage rate in France was halved and the death rate overtook the birth rate. The annual call-up, which had produced 600,000 men in 1914, produced only 240,000 in 1936 and was then again halved in the next four years. The economic scene was as dismal as the demographic. The French theory of government required the National Assembly, as the embodiment of the sovereignty of the people, to be master of the executive, and the French political system contributed to the relative weakness of the executive power by proliferating numerous and undisciplined parties, none of which was capable of forming a government on its own. The resulting coalitions did not dare to affront the voters and since France was still a country of small farmers and small businessmen the voters to whom governments kowtowed were principally this section of the community. The kowtowing took the form of not imposing unpopular taxes and trying to find alternative sources of money for state expenditure. French insistence on war reparations from Germany was partly a consequence of this search, and when the reparations did not materialize governments resorted instead to unbalanced budgets and borrowing, devices which undermined confidence at home and abroad in the French economy and the capacity of the politicians to run it. In universities and schools the prevailing tone of the twenties and thirties was cynical – and the influence of intellectuals was in France pronounced. No less pervasive was the attitude of the lesser bourgeoisie, which noted with alarm the fact that production was static. In external affairs the bloodiest war ever fought on French soil had been followed by disenchantment and disillusion. The attitudes represented by the massive figure of Clemenceau and the forceful policy of the Ruhr occupation of 1923 passed away. They were succeeded by disinvolvement and pacifism, especially among ex-combatants and those who might be expected to continue the warrior caste, with the result that the Munich settlement of 1938 was greeted with relief and the mobilization of 1939 accepted with reluctance. But the ignominious collapse of 1940 was nevertheless an unforeseen humiliation.

Hence arose the two questions which occupied Frenchmen during the next few years. Who was to blame for these collapses, and what was to take the place of what had collapsed?

The first answers were provided by Vichy because Vichy was, at first, a fact in a country where most facts seemed to have vanished. Vichy answered that it was all the fault of the parliamentarians of the Third Republic, especially the left wing, and that their place was now filled by Vichy. The history of France in the next few years is the story of the rejection of these answers.

The Vichy régime was the parent and the child of the armistice. The armistice was demanded by the generals, Weygand and Pétain, who dominated the last days and the last cabinets of the Third Republic and who showed themselves less stout than some of their civilian colleagues. The last President of the Republic, Albert Lebrun, appointed Pétain Prime Minister on the advice of his predecessor Paul Reynaud, who resigned because there was nothing else he could do. Pétain and Weygand, who notoriously had never agreed about anything else in the course of their long lives, insisted on an armistice for political as well as military reasons, and Vichy was therefore from the start a politically defined and not a national régime. The military reasons were no doubt compelling, for the army had been defeated, but the defeat of the army was something more than a military event. It raised also the spectre of revolution, and the generals felt it their duty to preserve the army to prevent revolution. Nor were they eccentric in taking this view. Vichy may not have represented the broadest national consensus but its aims were widely sensed as sound preservative medicine: to retain the French empire by abandoning the fight, to gain for France an independent place in the German New Order, to mitigate and survive enemy occupation by judicious collaboration and to safeguard the traditions of France by firmly suppressing the degenerative forces of internal change. In order to achieve these aims the generals capitulated and agreed to set up a new government covering in effect only one third of France and to pay German occupation costs (which initially were nine times as much as the sums required of Germany under the Dawes Plan). Vichy left vague for the time being the extent of military, economic and political collaboration which would be needed in order to secure these aims. Like Hitler, Vichy did not foresee a long war or the demands that such a war would make.

The head of the new régime, and its symbol, was Pétain. Born during the Crimean War and taught his catechism by a veteran of Napoleon's *Grande Armée*, Pétain had been on the verge of retirement with the rank of colonel after a career that had been neither distinguished nor undistinguished, when the outbreak of the First World War opened the doors of immortality to him. At the end of that war he was one of half a dozen Marshals of France who were world famous – all of whom he then proceeded comfortably to outlive. His particular fame rested on two things: he had saved France at Verdun in 1916 and he had shown an unaccustomed humanity in the face of mutiny, preferring to decorate soldiers who had done well than shoot those who had failed. In person he was dignified, calm, unpretentious; in politics, so far as was known, he was detached, so much so that the Left trusted him as the sort of general who would not lend himself to coups; in religion he was a Roman Catholic but not a pronounced one like Weygand, a poor church-goer and married (at sixty-five) to a divorcée. He seemed the type of figure who could be relied on to do the right thing in a crisis.

From 1921 to 1931 he was vice-chairman of the Council of War and so Commander-in-Chief designate if war came, and he remained a member of the Council after 1931 because in France, as elsewhere, old Marshals never died professionally so long as there was breath in their bodies. Although succeeded in the vice-chairmanship by Weygand and, after 1935, by Gamelin he remained a potent figure and his continuing availability was emphasized when, after the fascist riots in Paris in 1934, he was made Minister of War in the Doumergue government at the age of seventy-eight – a military dugout called in to support a political back number. After a brief spell as Ambassador in Madrid, to which post he was appointed at the age of eighty-one, he returned to the centre of things in time to be present at the culminating crisis of 1940. In retrospect there is an element of slyness in the way he managed to be half a spectator and half a participant in the fall of France, observing in private conversation that Gamelin was incapable but refusing to give his opinion to the Prime Minister who, for all Pétain cared, might find out for himself. When the crash came he was stationed somewhere between the centre of the stage and the wings, so that only half a step was needed to carry him to the leadership of the nation.

At first the nation was on the whole relieved to have him. He was old but he had extraordinary physical fitness. He carried round with him a part of the glory of France at a time when this commodity was in short supply, especially in political circles. He was respected, if not vociferously popular; he was liked by the poorer people because he had been a soldiers' soldier as well as a Marshal of France. He had stood firm once before – *ils ne passeront pas* – and standing firm was again the vital need. He had never done anything blatantly wrong. What was wrong was concealed. He was vain as well as old and his physical fitness was beginning to be offset by declining mental powers. He was a narrow-minded, authoritarian reactionary and although his inertia created the impression that the sins of Vichy should be attributed to his entourage rather than to himself the pattern of Vichy was a reflection and emanation of his own ideas.

Vichy did not regard itself as a merely passive régime guarding France from its external enemies so long as the war lasted. No less than the Resistance movements, which opposed and eventually defeated it, Vichy had positive and revolutionary policies which were intended to transform France lastingly. The only thing that Vichy regarded as temporary about itself was its capital, which it had chosen in preference to Paris in order to keep a certain distance between itself and German headquarters (and possibly the Parisians too). This spa of 25,000 inhabitants in the Auvergne, famous for repairing the stomachs and livers of those who had lived too long or too hard in the colonies, could serve as a capital because the government would soon move back to Paris. But the government's work need not wait upon its move. Laws and decrees poured out. Besides

dealing with the immediate post-defeat problems of refugees, unemployment and rationing, Vichy charted what it called a National Revolution.
Full powers to govern by decree – powers more ample than those possessed
by Louis XIV but, in the eyes of reactionaries, none the worse for that –
were bestowed on Pétain as head of state, and the sufferings and humilia-
tions of France were declared to be the essential pre-condition for national
regeneration through the cultivation of the basic virtues and values of
labour, family life and patriotism. This, the conservative in contradistinc-
tion to the radical way to salvation, was the core of Vichy's ideology. (But
Vichy did not succeed in monopolizing it. Gaullism heeded it too: after
the liberation a film by Marcel Pagnol, *La Fille du Puisatier*, made to
extol Pétain and Vichy's cultural revolution, continued to be shown with
little alteration to extol the spirit of Gaullism.)

Vichy's constitutional revolution was the work chiefly of Pierre Laval
who was ultimately to be the principal scapegoat for the Vichy régime.
Laval was an ex-socialist, an ex-parliamentarian, many times a Minister
of the Third Republic, a man of humble origins and markedly un-
aristocratic appearance, a decidedly clever man but not a broadly intelligent one, a political manipulator of the first rank but one inclined to
mistake his own astuteness for achievement. When Pétain, Weygand and
their supporters in Reynaud's cabinet brought the war to a stop, Laval
appeared to talk deputies into giving the new government legitimacy and
plenary powers and so changed the nature of the state which Pétain was
to guide. By assiduous and insidious lobbying among the flotsam and
jetsam of the Third Republic which accumulated at Bordeaux and then at
Vichy, Laval got these representatives of legitimacy to turn Pétain, whom
he mistook for a mere figurehead, into an autocrat. The state still contained a Senate and a Chamber of Deputies but they could only meet
upon being summoned by Pétain and Pétain had no intention of convok-
ing them. The Vichy government operated through a series of committees
whose activities contrasted with the impassivity of the Marshal and so
gave the erroneous impression that Pétain reigned but did not rule and
ought therefore not to be blamed for all the enormities committed in his
name. Thus arose the Vichy myth of the martyr Pétain, beset by the
conquerors of France on the one side and its political riffraff on the other,
but preserving its dignity and its honour by his personal bearing.

Democracy and civil liberties were quickly abolished. Besides suppressing parliamentary rule at the centre Vichy decreed that local councils
should be appointed and not elected except in communes with fewer than
2,000 inhabitants. Trade unions were disbanded and political parties forbidden. The judiciary lost its independence. Public officials became liable

to arbitrary dismissal by the head of state and 2,000 were purged in Vichy's first six months. Those who remained in office had to take an oath of personal loyalty to Pétain. New laws were given retroactive effect so that people could be tried and condemned for doing things which had been lawful when done. They could also be tried and condemned for their opinions or for merely associating with persons who had fallen foul of the authorities. Prefects were empowered to arrest, without charge, anybody whom they judged to be imperilling the security of the state. By 1942 there were 80,000 in prisons or concentration camps. Their conditions were so appalling that some prisoners were reduced to eating the straw in their palliasses and in some prisons there were a hundred deaths for every one that had occurred before the war. Certain categories of person were deprived of the protection of the law. Vichy was profoundly anti-semitic and defined a Jew more strictly even than the Nuremberg decrees of the Third Reich: a woman with only two Jewish grandparents became a Jew if she married a Jew. Vichy's anti-semitism was more national and religious and less racial than Hitler's. It asserted the unassimilability of the Jew to French society and regarded him therefore as a threat to the coherence of that society, but it admitted that French-born Jews who had fought for France had become, by the baptism of blood, French rather than Jewish. The first anti-semitic laws were promulgated in October 1940. All Jews were excluded from the public service, from teaching and from positions of authority in industry and the press, radio and cinema. Foreign Jews – including Algerian Jews who were deprived of their French nationality – became liable to internment. Existing laws against libelling racial and religious minorities were repealed. A second batch of anti-semitic laws in June 1941 aryanized Jewish businesses. The owners, who had been promised in 1940 that they would not be deprived of their possessions, received inadequate compensation or none.

Vichy's national mystique did not stop at Jews. All foreigners and all persons with foreign fathers were made ineligible for the public service, and all naturalizations since 1927 became subject to review. This cleansing of the nation was reinforced by educational reform. Pétain was almost obsessively interested in education and had aspired at one time to become Minister of Education. He regarded education as a branch of morals rather than learning and he regarded physical exercises as the basis of sound morality. The body took precedence over the mind; sound thinking, as opposed to dangerous thinking, could be induced by setting all French children on the road to that physical fitness which characterized the Marshal himself; loose thinking meant morally faulty rather than intellectually untidy thinking. Therefore every child in a primary school had to do ten hours of physical training a week and this quota was reduced by only one hour in the secondary school. The rest of education consisted preponderantly of instruction about God and patriotic duties and Greek and Latin. In line with conventional Roman Catholic teaching Pétain, like Hitler, believed that woman's place was in the home and her purpose childbearing. Divorce was made more difficult, large families were encouraged, women could only get marriage grants upon undertaking not to go out to work, and abortion became not only a criminal but a capital offence. The family was the elemental institution in a collectivist scheme of things which denied the value of the individual. Pétain himself said that there was 'no creative virtue' in individualism and he regarded French society as a large family to be ruled firmly by himself and to some extent by God.

Pétain's Vichy was a reactionary, authoritarian, Roman Catholic, chauvinist, corporatist state, but it was other things as well. Pétain was both a comfort to conservatives of all kinds in need of a father figure and a gift to an assortment of extremists who were looking for a stalking horse. Consequently Vichy became an *omnium gatherum* of anti-republican and anti-progressive forces which attracted pro-German and pro-Nazi Frenchmen and uncommitted opportunists. It gave scope to the most diverse personages. There was Jacques Doriot, the ex-communist bully who had been in German pay for a number of years before the war; Joseph Darnand, whose followers were required to swear an oath to fight 'democracy, Gaullist dissidence and the leprosy of Jewry', whose *milice* was merged with the *Waffen SS*, who commanded a French SS expeditionary force on the Russian front in 1943 and who returned as Secretary-General for the Maintenance of Order, in which capacity he made the *milice* even more feared and hated than the SD; the anti-German, monarchist publicist Charles Maurras who set up as a sort of ideologist for Vichy; and, from 1943, the Bourbon claimant, the Comte de Paris, who went to Vichy with an eye perhaps to Pétain's job but was fobbed off by Laval with an offer of a minor post and later declared himself a Gaullist. The most pro-German of French right-wing leaders, Marcel Déat, preferred Paris to Vichy, against which he kept up a steady flow of criticism. Many French fascists disliked Pétain.

In external affairs Vichy had no choice. It was compelled to collaborate with Germany. Its options were limited to the degree and manner of collaboration, and within this narrow field the most important person was Laval. On 11 June 1940, Pétain issued the first of his Constitutional Acts which, with the disdain of grammar characteristic of monarchs, opened with the words '*Nous, Philippe Pétain . . .*' and appointed him

Chief of State. The office of President was by implication abolished. By
succeeding Constitutional Acts, issued on the same day, Pétain gave himself plenary powers in the appointment of Ministers and civil servants, in
legislation, budgeting and finance, in the control of the armed forces, and
in the making of treaties. He might also declare a state of emergency but
he might not declare war. The Senate and Chamber remained in being but
were prorogued and might be recalled only by Pétain. By a further Act on
the next day Pétain nominated Laval as his successor. Laval became
therefore the Caliph to Pétain's Mahomet, and since Pétain was much
older than Mahomet had ever been, Laval might regard himself as the
real manipulator of the totalitarian powers with which, largely by his own
efforts, Pétain was invested.

To Laval there was nothing shocking about the idea of collaborating
with Germany. He had long been a champion of a Franco-German entente. He had been in politics since before the First World War, had been
Prime Minister of France before Hitler came to power in Germany, and
like many Frenchmen of his generation he saw European politics in terms
of Franco-German conflict or agreement; and he preferred the latter. He
observed the American disengagement from Europe after 1919 and he
regarded the British with their extra-European empire as but dubious
partners in Europe. He was not pro-German in the enthusiastic way in
which some Frenchmen admired German achievements in the arts and
politics, but as a political realist he desired a Franco-German understanding and wished to promote it sooner rather than later because he accepted
the general view that, in relation to Germany, France would continue to
become demographically and industrially the weaker. Italy he regarded as
a natural and useful third member of the entente. As Prime Minister in
1931 he wished to settle the issues of reparations and disarmament in
order to clear the way for a triple entente which, had he achieved it, would
have anticipated the post-war cooperation of Robert Schuman, Konrad
Adenauer and Alcide de Gasperi.

He was out of office from the beginning of 1932 until October 1934
when he succeeded Barthou as Foreign Minister. During this interval
Hitler had become Chancellor in Germany. Laval had therefore a choice
between persevering with his German policy or dropping it and reverting
to the classical French policy of alliance with Russia against Germany
which Barthou had been pursuing. Laval chose to persevere because his
Franco-German vision of Europe still made sense to him – as it still did
after 1940. His anti-communism, which was pronounced, pointed in the
same direction and although he continued his predecessor's negotiations
with Moscow he did so only in order to have an alternative policy to fall

back on – and he even told the German Ambassador in Paris that this was his reason. The Ethiopian crisis wrecked his policy but did nothing to alter his belief in it.

In the summer of 1940 France, although decisively and humiliatingly defeated, still counted in the European balance, the more so because of its overseas colonies. Hitler had a vague plan for an anti-British, continental block which would include France as well as Italy and Spain; in such a block the French colonies could be strategically more useful to him than anything which Mussolini or Franco had to offer. German and French military chiefs seriously debated joint operations in Africa for the recovery of colonies which defected to de Gaulle and the transfer of British colonies to France. But Hitler was indecisive and half-hearted about cooperation with France. He himself and a number of his principal colleagues disliked the French and distrusted Laval personally. At Vichy the men round Pétain were also divided and uncertain; some agreed with Laval's policy of making the best obtainable bargain with a securely dominant Germany, while others cherished a lingering hope that Germany might fail to defeat Great Britain and believed that a British victory was not only possible but also better for France. Laval moreover discovered that Pétain was no mere puppet. This was not only a surprise and a disappointment but also a severe handicap since the two men had very little in common. There was life in the old Marshal yet and in December 1940 he showed it by dismissing Laval.

Laval's fall did not mean an end to the collaborationist policy. Pétain disliked Laval's pretensions rather than his policies. The Marshal's distrust of his deputy was also exploited by some of Laval's colleagues who were afraid that Laval might worm his way into the Marshal's confidence to their own discomfiture. For a couple of months it was not clear who was Laval's successor. It might be Pierre-Étienne Flandin, another leading politician of the Third Republic and a sincere admirer of much that Germany had produced through the ages, or it might be Jean Darlan, the anti-British admiral who was moved less by respect for Germany than by anger over the British attack on his ships at Mers-el-Kebir. In February Darlan was appointed Deputy Prime Minister and Foreign Minister and, the next day, Pétain's successor; a few days later he was Minister of the Interior too, and a week later still a cabinet reshuffle which excluded Flandin and other Vichy notables confirmed Darlan's pre-eminence. But Darlan's collaboration soon went too far for Pétain who, having got France out of the war on one side, was determined not to re-enter it on the other. In May 1941 Darlan negotiated with the Germans a series of protocols by which France would provide extensive facilities and war material in the Middle East in connection with the revolt of Rashid Ali in Iraq and would give the Germans free harbour and railway facilities in Tunisia and permit the harbour and airfield at Dakar to become German bases. Since the routes between Bizerta and Europe were to be protected by the French navy, Darlan was not only sanctioning active military cooperation in the Middle East but also upsetting the most delicate and contentious element in the French surrender: the undertaking to Great Britain not to allow the French fleet to join the Axis. Pétain refused to endorse Darlan's policy and demoted the admiral from his high position in the state.

Equally, however, Pétain refused to be lured back into the war on the allied side. From January 1941 Roosevelt had in Vichy as his Ambassador and personal representative Admiral William D. Leahy, whose task was at first to keep French aid to Germany down to a minimum by arguing that the war was far from over and that Hitler was going to lose it, and by supplying France with food and other necessaries. In 1942 Roosevelt went further and sent a secret emissary to entice Weygand into bringing the French in North Africa over to the allies in conjunction with the planned Anglo-American invasion. Weygand was not to be drawn and reported the conversations to Pétain whence they were conveyed to Berlin; and Pétain instructed Weygand to reply that an Anglo-American landing would be opposed by the (very numerous) French forces in Algeria and Morocco. In April Leahy's recall marked the end of this abortive American attempt to deal with Vichy.

A few weeks later Great Britain's seizure of the French colony of Madagascar to prevent it from falling into Japanese hands embittered Vichy and during the rest of the year the possibility of Vichy making common cause with the Germans was again mooted. When the Anglo-American invasion took place in November Hitler asked Vichy to declare war. Pétain refused but broke off diplomatic relations with the United States. The Germans occupied the whole of France and seized the use of French ports in eastern Algeria and Tunisia. At this point some Vichy leaders revolted: Darlan ordered French naval vessels in metropolitan France to sail for Africa and the French Commander-in-Chief in North Africa, General Alphonse Juin, ordered resistance to the Germans and Italians who were occupying Tunisia. Pétain himself, at the head of a government becoming increasingly irrelevant to the practical course of events, began to play a less effective part in it. He retained the allegiance of some of his compatriots and when dispatched to Paris by the Germans in April 1944 to attend a memorial service for victims of allied bombing he was so warmly received that the Germans themselves felt that their attempt to make use of the Marshal in this way had been a mistake. For the most part he lived secluded at Vichy or near Rambouillet. The composition of his cabinet was increasingly determined by the Germans and after he had been forced to accept Déat as a member in 1944 he ceased to attend its meetings. Four years earlier he had been the strong silent soldier who had sat in Reynaud's government until he undermined it. At the beginning of the occupation his *silences* were taken to be a guarantee of the honour of France. They were found to be a guarantee of nothing.

Laval had been restored to power in April 1942 with the title of Prime Minister which he kept until August 1944 along with the posts of Foreign Minister and Minister of the Interior. He still thought that France could bargain with Hitler and when the Germans sought French cooperation against the allies in North Africa he tried to get a German-Italian guarantee of the French empire. But Hitler, who had less than no use for Laval personally and was no longer as interested as he had been two years earlier in France's colonial assets, saw no reason to bargain with France. Germany was now more interested in French labour and Laval was caught up in the satisfaction of German economic demands. He became in the process so identified with the machinery of German exploitation that he was, by the end of the war, the principal scapegoat for all the crimes of Vichy and was subjected to a disgracefully unfair trial before a singularly ugly execution.

By the armistice agreement France was required to pay 300 million francs for every day that the occupation lasted. This sum was supposed to represent the cost to Germany of occupying the northern zone and when therefore the occupation was extended the daily price was raised to 500 million in token of Germany's new obligation to defend southern France and Tunisia. After the allied landings in Normandy in July 1944 the price went up to 700 million, the surcharge representing France's contribution to the general defence of Europe. All these sums greatly exceeded the cost of occupation and were used by Germany for general purposes, including the purchase of French natural resources and industrial enterprises. (The Germans kept the value of the franc high, since they were being paid in francs and were using them to buy up valuable properties.) Thus the armistice payments went much further than reparations, for which in any case the Germans, having suffered practically no damage, had no claim. The payments were a levy fixed by a victor who was using this method to appropriate the capital assets of the vanquished. In addition the Germans requisitioned, and Vichy ceded, supplies of food and other raw materials to which the former were not entitled under the armistice agreement, while even in the southern zone French factories worked for the German war effort, producing aircraft engines and other indubitably military equipment.

These exactions, which began immediately after the capitulation in 1940, were compounded and transformed in 1942 when the Germans began to press for labour. Laval hoped to satisfy the Germans and pacify his compatriots by a deal by which France would supply labour in exchange for the release of prisoners of war (the *relève*). At the same time, in June 1942, he revealed the depth of the anti-communism which was absorbing him more and more as the German campaigns in the east went wrong, by exclaiming that he desired a German victory since otherwise Bolshevism would triumph everywhere. Fulfilling Germany's need for labour became the measure of his commitment to Germany's victory, but at the time when he was coming to see the Germans exclusively as a defence against communism, his compatriots were increasingly concerned with their reprisals against the Resistance and their drive for forced labour. A first labour plan, negotiated between Laval and Sauckel and covering the second half of 1942, provided for the delivery of 250,000 men. It was almost precisely fulfilled. So was a second plan covering the first quarter of 1943. Thereafter Laval tried to apply a brake, offering to transfer French labour to German war work in France but objecting to sending Frenchmen to Germany. Frenchmen themselves took to the woods to avoid compulsory labour service, but a total of 641,000 workers was sent to Germany under the Sauckel programmes and in 1943 the French forced labourers in Germany outnumbered even the Russian conscripted and prisoner labour force – 1.7 million against 1.3 million. The French contingent included prisoners of war, workers enticed to Germany before the Sauckel programmes began and workers from Alsace-Lorraine and north-eastern France which were outside the Laval-Sauckel agreements. Vichy also shipped off to Germany thousands of Spanish refugees from the lost civil war. (Others, escaping Vichy's net and Hitler's camps, fought in various parts of Europe and some, flying their own flag, marched into Paris with Leclercq in August 1944.) France's sacrifice in labour lost to Germany during the war has been computed as the equivalent of the total output of the French labour force in a normal year. It was as if no work was done in France for a whole year. The value to Germany of the work done by French workers, including prisoners of war, has been estimated at 200 billion (1938) francs.

Laval's attempts to reconcile his countrymen to Sauckel's demands by securing the repatriation of prisoners of war failed. Between two and three million Frenchmen had been taken prisoner in 1940. Vichy's efforts to secure the return of these men were neither effective nor, in the eyes of many, wholehearted: returning prisoners might include obstreperous critics of pre-war and Vichyite policies and too high a percentage of communists. (To some extent the return of prisoners was feared by ordinary Frenchmen too because there were not enough jobs or food to go round.) During the Sauckel programmes prisoners were repatriated at the rate of about one prisoner for every six forced labourers. They returned to a country where production had been cut by a third since 1938, most foods had to be bought in a black market where they cost anything from twice to five times the official price, coal could only be had at ten to twenty or even thirty times the official price, rations were providing 1,200 calories a day or less than half the normal needs of an adult, and mortality was rising rapidly – especially among infants.

These conditions showed that at the most elementary level of material life Vichy had failed. It had also failed in three other respects. It had failed to lay the blame for the collapse of 1940 on its political enemies; it had failed to protect its own citizens; and it had failed to preserve the decencies of public behaviour upon which a conservative régime is wont to insist with special eloquence. Accordingly, even though no alternative French government was in the making, Vichy forfeited its own title to rule France.

The centrepiece of the attempt to lay the blame for France's disasters on the republican régime was the trial at Riom of Daladier, Blum and Gamelin. This trial, which opened on 19 February 1942, was meant to be a demonstration of treason in high places but became instead a counter-attack by the accused civilians on the criminal negligence of the French military establishment – which included Pétain himself, who had been Minister for War in the Doumergue government of 1934 and had stated, among other things, that it was impossible for an enemy to cross the Meuse at Sedan. (Because of Pétain's embarrassing involvement in the story of French inefficiency the scope of the trial was limited to the events of 1936 and later.) The principal issues were the extent of French unpreparedness for war, the failure of the army to use the credits allocated to it, and its inefficiency in the use of such weapons as it did have. In a welter of widely differing statistics the prosecution alleged material deficiencies of scandalous proportions while the accused (other than Gamelin who remained silent throughout) produced figures to show that the weapons had been made available in reasonable numbers but had then either been stored away by the military or so ineptly distributed that some formations had too much and others too little, while large stocks fell unused into German hands. The Riom trial was as unedifying a national *post mortem* as could be conceived and although the Vichy government was able to show that

France had been materially ill-prepared for a war against the modern German armies – a fact well known to everybody – it was unable to prevent the accused from retorting that the defeat must also be attributed to bad military planning and coordination before and after the outbreak of war. Since Vichy represented the military establishment which was the target of this counterattack, the trial was a failure – all the more important in that it left in possession of the field the rival view that Vichy, so far from being the high road to national salvation, was but the last refuge of those responsible for the republic's military ineptitude, political defeatism and moral unpreparedness, a cul-de-sac containing surviving specimens of the *deux cents familles* who were supposed, however exaggeratedly, to have dominated French industrial and social life for their own selfish ends. The trial was abruptly suspended after two months and was never resumed.

The authority of Vichy as a government was further eroded by the fact that on the one hand it lacked the power to protect French citizens against the Germans, while on the other it abetted German excesses. Some 30,000 French hostages were shot during the occupation, while countless other French men and women suffered transportation or mental anguish through the operation of *Nacht und Nebel*. France became a police state as well as an occupied country; Vichy's police assisted the German police and Vichy's administration and courts were progressively adapted to the requirements of the occupiers. Vichy's first anti-semitic law was passed in 1940, Darlan established a special Jewish office in 1941 and deportation of Jews began in 1942. With the increasing strength of Resistance movements all male relatives over eighteen of any Resister were made liable to the death penalty, his female relatives to forced labour and his younger relatives to detention in reformatories. Vichy fell back, in company with the Germans, on intimidation as a means of government, coupled with a proliferation of petty regulations enforceable by heavy fines (for example, the offence of carrying chickens to market with their legs tied together). But gradually, and without destroying the appearances of administrative propriety, local authorities, the police and the magistrature ceased to comply. Local officials either delayed or sabotaged instructions. The police, who frequently became covert allies of the Resistance, gave opportune warnings. Sentences passed by magistrates for breaches of occupation laws revealed so consistent a pattern of extreme lenience that the Germans protested to Vichy.

Public opinion began to manifest itself against Vichy at an early stage. Newspapers protested against increasing concessions to the Germans, applauded the Yugoslav revolution of 1941 and promoted a dialogue with their readers on such questions as censorship and the thinness of public information. Officials considered too zealous in their cooperation received miniature coffins as a warning. When Vichy broke off relations with the USSR in June 1941 popular reaction was so outspoken that Pétain felt obliged to broadcast – *c'est de vous-mêmes que je veux vous sauver* – and to double the police.

The ultimate condemnation of Vichy lies in the fact that for each French-man killed in the fighting in 1940 another died later as a civilian victim of the war. Vichy functioned as a satellite in Germany's New Order and was doomed to become nothing else, to sterility and transience. Neither its own roots in French society nor the shortcomings of previous governments were adequate to give it the credentials or the lifeblood of an independent French régime. Movements formed to sustain it showed by their wilting that it could not be sustained. *Les Amis du Maréchal* and, still more so, *Les Jeunes du Maréchal* were exposures of the barrenness of their own titles, while *Le Francisme* failed entirely in its functions as an anti-Resistance movement. Under Vichy the unity of France was a slogan which was belied not only by the physical disunity of the country but also by moral disunity. At the very best Vichy exercised a limited control over a minority; one third of the population lived in the non-occupied zone, while two thirds of France's home-grown food was produced in the north and so laid Vichy under the necessity to bargain with the Germans in order to secure fair shares for the south.

And Vichy was resisted from the start. Men demobilized from the defeated French forces did not cease to regard Germany as the enemy. Laying the blame for France's defeat on Great Britain – as Vichy tried to do but with only moderate effect – did not alter this fact, and Vichy was obviously Germany's creature: the hectic note of treason appeared from the first in the rejection of Vichy. Although there was at first little that they could do about the situation, the attitude of Resisters was clear to themselves and their friends and they took what opportunities they had of proclaiming and spreading it by such acts as scribbling slogans on walls or defacing propaganda posters. More purposeful sabotage was already in evidence by the autumn of that year. Personal and local protests of this kind provided the basis from which a mood might develop into a move-ment with nationwide organization and purpose. This development occur-red along two lines which had, at a point, to be merged. Within France local groups formed and came into touch with nearby local groups. Beyond France de Gaulle used the remnants of an army, the undecided loyalties of the French overseas empire and the force of his own personality and his own faith to create a new French régime whose authority would be accepted by all who were fighting against Germany – by French Resistance groups of all kinds and by the British, American and Russian governments.

When de Gaulle made his first broadcast to the French people from London on 18 June 1940 he was almost unknown. He was a general and he had been a junior Minister in Reynaud's last government owing to the accident of personal acquaintance with the Prime Minister. Within his profession he was noted for his intelligence and clarity of thought and for unorthodox ideas on tank warfare; he had also a reputation for incommunicativeness and intractability (he learned later how to communicate). Beyond the profession he was barely known, even by name. Among parliamentarians, for example, most of the members of the Committee on National Defence would have known something of him, but perhaps only a dozen other members of the Senate and the Chamber could have said who he was. When he began to be talked about, it was only with difficulty that a photograph could be found and for some months the face and figure which were to be so well known were only to be picked out in the back row of a formal photograph of Reynaud's last administration. There was no very strong reason why anybody listening to him on 18 June should imagine that this was a saviour and future President of France. He said that the war was not over and France not finished. Unlike many other Frenchmen at this time he did not argue about Great Britain's powers of resistance but about France itself: not about whether Great Britain could fight on but whether France could. And he did not so much argue as affirm. To argue about the fate of France at this point was almost certain to lead to a pessimistic conclusion. De Gaulle's resistance rested therefore on faith and action and he relied on these two forces to change the argument. He was able to do this because, besides being a patriot, he had in his bearing and his intelligence an authority which gave substance to his call for faith and action.

He was in this respect very like Churchill without Churchill's extraversion. Both men appealed dramatically to a people for sacrifices and in both cases the success of the appeal lay in the personality of the appealer, but whereas Churchill used words to make personal contact with his compatriots, de Gaulle used them in order to make himself not so much their leader as their symbol. To some extent the distinction was one of circumstances, for Churchill was among his people and was clothed with the legitimacy of office whereas de Gaulle was an exile without official standing of any kind (later in life he was to prove that he too knew how to move about among crowds); but the difference was even more a difference in character. De Gaulle's strength was that of the strong silent man of the English stereotype. His passions were under powerful control and during the early years of exile his natural reticence was reinforced by the fact that he was playing his hand from weakness. The poverty of his resources imposed on him the need to say as little as possible in order to reveal as little as possible. He was not interested in becoming a platoon commander in the Anglo-American host, for by doing so he might perhaps contribute to the defeat of Germany but without displacing Vichy and all it stood for. If as a Frenchman he was concerned to defeat the Germans, he was no less concerned, as a republican, to overthrow Vichy and restore and refine the post-revolutionary tradition of French republicanism. As a soldier from within this tradition he accepted the subordination of the military to the civil power but equally he wanted the wielders of civil power to behave better in future than they had behaved in the past. He was impatient of excessive parliamentary interference in the business of government and contemptuous of the past performance of political parties, but he wished to curb rather than abolish parliament and parties.

Consequently the simple solutions of the military dictator were not open to him. He wished neither to destroy the institutions of the republic nor to ignore the people, to whom on the contrary he appealed. But his respect for these institutions derived at least as much from his conservative temper as from any democratic conviction and his attachment to republic and people was long suspect in Resistance circles, especially on the Left where his sympathy and support for the Russians were as much a surprise as Churchill's. Like Churchill he envisaged a partnership between the populace and himself, but unlike Churchill he cultivated this union not only to win the war but also to restore and purge and to some extent refashion the republic. Unlike Churchill again, he was not a democrat in the Anglo-Saxon sense: he never used the word democracy and when he spoke of the republic he did so in the old Roman sense of the common weal. With regard to the war the movement which he set out to build was a military one, but with regard to *l'après-guerre* it was a civil movement which required the unification of all Resistance groups inside France with, and under, his own group in London and the empire. Gaullism was therefore *la France combattante* and also the next French republic. Since the Americans and, to a lesser extent, the British underrated the value of the first and refused for a long time to acknowledge the second, de Gaulle's role in exile became one of stubborn self-inflation.

De Gaulle's first task was to command the allegiance of as much as possible of the French empire, his second to command the attention of everybody else. Indo-China, the Middle East and North Africa had declared for Vichy, while in West Africa the attempt to acquire a foothold at

Dakar was a failure. In general too little was known about the Gaullist group in London and its prospects to tempt distant proconsuls into rejecting the armistice and Vichy's claim to legitimacy. De Gaulle had first to build up his own forces, create a following in France itself and show that Hitler's principal enemies accepted him as an ally. However, Félix Eboué, the governor of Chad in French Equatorial Africa, chose the Gaullist side and was followed by other African colonies, by Tahiti, the Marquesas Islands and New Caledonia, and by the French colonies in India. One other colony, the oldest, was seized by de Gaulle, who thereby earned lasting hostility in Washington.

St Pierre et Miquelon had been divided since the fall of France between a Vichyite minority which was in control and a Gaullist majority. The colony consisted of a group of islands a dozen miles off the south coast of Newfoundland. It had some strategic importance, for it lay off the mouth of the St Lawrence and could be used against convoys by harbouring U-boats and reporting the movements of shipping. Atlantic cables passed through its waters and after these had been cut the colony remained in close contact with Vichy by means of a radio station which, besides transmitting weather reports and Vichyite propaganda, reported on shipping and gave instructions to agents. Both Newfoundland (then a British Crown Colony) and Canada were suspected of designs against the islands, and the United States warmly advocated Canadian annexation. Great Britain, however, and also Canada after some wavering, preferred a Gaullist coup and were embarrassed by American schemes. The Canadian cabinet settled on a compromise whereby Canada would, by threats of economic sanctions and in the last resort by force, seize the radio station but not remove the Vichyite governor or overthrow his régime.

In October 1941 de Gaulle broached with Eden the question of a Gaullist coup. Eden, although sympathetic, felt obliged to refer to Ottawa and Washington. De Gaulle dispatched Admiral Émile Muselier to end the discussions by taking the islands; the coup was not difficult since the population was largely pro-Gaullist. But Muselier decided to go to Ottawa first. There he found the government undecided between its own plan to seize the radio station and the Gaullist plan to seize the colony. The Canadian government consulted Washington which objected strongly to a Gaullist coup, largely because it had just negotiated a general agreement about all the French possessions in the western hemisphere with Vichy's representative, Admiral Robert. Roosevelt was ill informed and badly advised on French affairs; he refused to regard Vichy as fascist or de Gaulle as a democrat, he was partly right in both cases, but he was wrong in imagining that this simple categorization was all that mattered; he exaggerated American influence at Vichy and tended to be combatively uneasy about his pro-Vichy policy which he knew to be regarded with scepticism by his British allies and with distaste by his own press and public. Roosevelt was therefore all the more hostile to de Gaulle who represented an additional challenge to his Vichy policy and whom he in return represented as no more than a fringe military figure. His objections to the St Pierre adventure prevailed. The British and Canadian governments gave way with reluctance and so did de Gaulle and Muselier. But in almost the same breath de Gaulle ordered Muselier to go ahead and take the islands.

This Muselier, with three corvettes, a submarine and grave misgivings about the probity of his undertaking, did. Great Britain and Canada were privately pleased but officially reticent; the American press and public were enthusiastically in favour of this first stroke against European dictatorship in the American continent; but in Washington Roosevelt and his Secretary of State Cordell Hull, who was more convinced than the President that Gaullism was insignificant, were so infuriated that they issued unnecessarily offensive statements about the Gaullists and tried to get the Canadians to mount an expedition to recapture the colony – a project which only incensed Ottawa against Washington. The rights and wrongs of this episode are still not entirely clear. The overthrow of Vichy's authority in the colony was in the allied interest. Roosevelt and Hull were wrong in their estimates of Vichy and de Gaulle and their reactions to the event were out of proportion to its significance. Roosevelt would probably have been glad to treat the affair as an irritating episode and forget it – he called it a 'teapot tempest', which is presumably something not much bigger than a storm in a tea-cup but Hull took it to heart to such a degree that he lost his judgement, nourished a personal animosity against de Gaulle and accused Great Britain of conspiring with de Gaulle against the United States. On the French side de Gaulle's action, of which Muselier disapproved, is less easy to assess. It is at least possible that, after accepting Washington's veto on his plan, he learned for the first time of the Canadian plan and thereupon, imagining himself deceived, reversed his decision. The most important consequence of the coup was to give de Gaulle and Gaullism great prestige throughout the French empire and in France.

For about a year the Gaullists were ill informed about happenings inside France itself. Resistance groups seemed to be small and uncoordinated. They might one day be useful adjuncts of a Gaullist army. For the time being their sabotage activities were good for French morale and good practice for the day when sabotage would help an invading force.

Activities on a larger scale raised problems. They were for the moment premature; they might do more harm than good; they might tend towards the emergence of a separate centre of authority in competition with the Gaullists and, after 1941, increasingly under communist control. Guerrilla operations did not seem to be a good idea. De Gaulle's headquarters, predominantly military and right wing, discounted the value of large-scale populist resistance and viewed it without enthusiasm. But this attitude changed during 1942, by which time Gaullism as a whole had edged leftward in reaction to Vichyite positions and in sympathy with the Russian stand against Germany, and had learned more about the Resistance movements inside France.

The main concern of the Resistance was the revival and consolidation of all that was best in the French spirit as a necessary precondition to action against the enemy. It was therefore at least as much concerned with Frenchmen as with Germans, for the defeat of the Germans was to be only an intermediate operation between a revolution in French public feeling and – the ultimate end – a revolution in the structure of French society and politics. When the Germans first entered Paris and other French cities their reception was far from universally hostile. Fraternization was common not only in shops and restaurants but in casual encounters on streets and squares where crowds gathered to listen to news broadcasts or concerts and rubbed shoulders with Germans, whom they were ready to treat as ordinary human beings. Resistance-minded Frenchmen regarded all this as a dangerous, even disgusting, self-deception. They were also concerned to combat Vichy's implicit claim to provide the right answers for France, and to demonstrate that Vichy, so far from serving France, was putting German interests before French ones. Vichy started with a major advantage since there was widespread acceptance of the view that France's disasters should all be blamed on the parliamentarians whom Vichy was attacking and displacing, so that the Resistance, which also accepted this view, was forced into the awkward position of damning political parties but at the same time advocating a restored, if regenerated, political system. Essentially, as postwar events proved, this was an illogical position, for the system demanded parties by whatever name they might be called (movements, rallies and so on became in fact parties as soon as they moved into action). But the Resistance contrived to evade the illogicality. It was joined by men of different parties and different social backgrounds. It did not at first look to de Gaulle nor know much about his movement except that it was a long way away in London and possibly under British control. In the south men of right-wing temperament often dropped out in the early days and accepted Vichy, so that southern Resistance movements had begun to wear a left-wing air even before they were joined by communists after the German invasion of the USSR. This ideological colouring of the Resistance was increased by the hostility or ambivalence of the ecclesiastical establishment: in general the Roman Catholic episcopacy had an outstandingly poor Resistance record, redeemed only partially by the heroism of a minority of the lesser clergy. Political parties continued throughout the war to be regarded in the Resistance with some distaste and there was a vague hope (except among the communists) that the unity forged during the Resistance would somehow dispense with the need to resuscitate the old parties after liberation. Postwar problems were, however, subordinated to the needs of the present, and old political leaders worked alongside new non-political chieftains to create forces which would cause real embarrassment and damage to the German occupiers.

Their efforts were aided by the revulsion against Vichy. This was at first gradual and patchy. Its principal sources were Vichy's own actions, the behaviour of the Germans coupled with Vichy's failure to take even a moral stand against it, and the recovery of courage effected by time, nationalism and the growth of the clandestine press from amateurish hand-outs to real newspapers. Particular events accelerated the general trend: the introduction of forced labour, which transformed the scale of the Resistance by hitting the middle classes as well as the working classes (comparatively well represented in the Resistance from the start); and the raids on the continent at St Nazaire and Dieppe which confirmed what people were hearing on the radio about the progress of the war (although the Germans decreed the confiscation of private radios, they were unable to confiscate enough of them to stop people knowing about the war).

The rejection of Vichy automatically turned attention to de Gaulle as an alternative government and by the beginning of 1942 a number of Resistance groups had decided to accept de Gaulle's leadership. In the south the principal Resistance movements were the *Francs-Tireurs et Partisans* (FTP), *Combat* and *Libération*, all of them active by the end of 1941 and all in contact with de Gaulle. In the occupied zone, where Resistance was in the nature of things more difficult and dangerous, *Libération-Nord* and *Organisation Civile et Militaire* (OCM) played the leading part, became effective in 1942 and also established contacts with the Gaullists in London. Although the Communist Party denounced the war until Hitler invaded the USSR, many individual communists joined Resistance movements before that date. After June 1941 the *Front National*, which covered the whole country and embraced diverse opinions under communist leadership, pursued a policy of cooperation between all Resistance movements and advocated extensive and immediate action, even courting reprisals in order to intensify anti-German feeling. Its object was to harass and kill the occupiers in order not only to end the occupation but also to transform French politics. To the rank and file of Resisters, and even to their regional leaders, the politics of the movement to which they belonged were very often unknown.

At the end of 1941 de Gaulle sent one of his principal lieutenants, Jean Moulin, to France. Moulin began by uniting the movements in the south, thus completing the elimination of Vichy as a force for the future. The further work of combining Resistance movements in northern and southern France, and uniting the Resistance with Gaullism, was facilitated by the German occupation of the whole country in November 1942 and by the consolidation of de Gaulle's position as the unrivalled chief of French forces overseas in spite of American attempts to prefer Giraud or Darlan. The communists accepted de Gaulle's leadership at the end of 1942. In March 1943 Resistance movements from all parts of the country combined in the _Mouvements Unis de la Résistance_, which gave birth to the _Comité National de la Résistance_ (CNR) which first met in Paris in May under Moulin's chairmanship and recognized de Gaulle as the national leader of France. A few weeks after this meeting Moulin and other French leaders were picked up by the Gestapo, tortured and killed, but during his last months in his native country Moulin had created the organs with which France would re-enter the war. (The CNR did not meet again until after the liberation. Owing to the activities of the German police it was forced to operate regionally.) The recognition extended to de Gaulle by the entire Resistance put him for the first time in command of considerable forces and greatly increased his political standing with his western and eastern allies.

Relations between the French Resistance and the western allies were uneven. Resistance leaders inside France (as elsewhere) suspected the British and American governments of not taking them seriously enough, of regarding them as a sideshow, and of sending fewer arms and other supplies than they could afford. They protested against the bombing of targets in France which they themselves could sabotage with much less loss of innocent civilian lives – although not, owing to the nature of sabotage, with lasting effect. Being in a position to observe the inaccuracy of strategic bombing they continually urged, without carrying conviction, that they had a better way of doing the job. Raids on Nantes from 16 to 23 September 1943 were a particularly grave example of the futility of the policy of total air warfare which the British and Americans had uncritically taken over from the Germans. Senseless destruction threatened to alienate the population not only from the perpetrators but also from the Resistance which was in a sense allied with them. On the other side the British and American governments, besides underestimating the effectiveness of the Resistance, exaggerated the tensions within it and, the Americans especially, were afraid that a civil war would break out in France before the Germans were defeated and that the communists would win it. With more justice they regarded the Resistance movements as insecure and not to be trusted with information of value. In fact Anglo-American assistance to France was very great but it was of a kind not always visible to Resistance leaders. While these anxiously awaited parachute drops which never came or seemed (until the eve of invasion) disappointingly meagre, Great Britain lent France £30 million and the United States gave de Gaulle all the facilities of Lend-Lease from November 1941 and helped to equip and maintain large French forces in Africa from the time of the Casablanca conference and in France itself in 1944, particularly after the Ardennes offensive at the end of that year when eight new divisions were formed out of Resistance units. But politically Roosevelt continued to drag his feet. In July 1944, when the CNR declared itself the provisional government of France, Washington recognized it as a *de facto* government, delaying until October the further step of recognizing it as the *de jure*, though provisional, government; and Roosevelt opposed de Gaulle's presence at Yalta.

Within France Resistance of a quasi-military kind was intensified from 1943 and organized in regions under the aegis of a three-man directorate which was established by the CNR and coordinated the efforts of the various military bodies in the field. Bands were mostly fifty to a hundred strong, although some were as large as 500–1,000. Nearly all their arms came from the Americans and British who supplied 1,000 tons of equipment by March 1944 (of which the Germans seized a third) and 8,000 tons in the next six months, the period spanning the invasion of France. Early in 1944 the movements joined forces as the *Forces Françaises de l'Intérieur* (FFI), by which time their combined field strength had reached about 30,000 and it was commonly assumed that an allied return to the continent was not far distant. Increasing strength meant increasing temptation to use it and sometimes action was premature and tragic.

At Glières for example, in Haute Savoie, a band of 500 men organized during 1943 by a former lieutenant in the *Chasseurs Alpins* attacked a considerable force of heavily armed Germans in February 1944 and lost half its men. Such incidents became more frequent as the great moment of liberation approached and misunderstandings over the role of the FFI and cooperation with the invading forces took their toll. Thus at

Montmouchet the Resistance, mistakenly believing that allied troops would arrive to join forces in an attack on the Germans simultaneously with the landings in the north, assembled a strength of 3,000–4,000 men and opened battle. Fighting went on for a week. The Germans suffered to begin with ten casualties for every one among their enemies but in the end they won a complete victory. A similar misunderstanding produced a similar tragedy in the Vercors. The Vercors, a natural fortress south-west of Grenoble, was occupied by Resistance units in the winter of 1942–3. From small beginnings – a group of local men in a small way of business, most of them socialists – the Vercors redoubt grew into an assembly centre and refuge of considerable importance, but it was not meant to be a stronghold to be defended in battle against regular German forces. Nevertheless such a battle took place. Again there were false expectations of outside help. Resistance leaders believed that plans for a joint operation had been endorsed by the French and allied authorities in London and Algiers when in fact these plans were, owing to administrative incompetence, not even known to many of the people who would have been involved. A few days before the landings in Normandy the Vercors Resistance mobilized and serious fighting began on 13 June. It continued for forty-one days, the Resistance force of 3,500 men holding an area where they expected allied reinforcements to land by air and so condemning themselves to static defence against two German divisions which eventually surrounded and liquidated most of them. This episode produced the sharpest disagreement between de Gaulle and his communist associates in the Provisional Government; the communists, who held among other posts the air portfolio, pressed for air support for the rising (which was rejected as impracticable) and accused de Gaulle of betraying the Resistance, in return for which de Gaulle dismissed the air member of his government.

But these episodes were not typical. Elsewhere the Resistance played a successful part in the defeat of the Germans. On a signal from the BBC the FFI mobilized 200,000 (lightly) armed troops and as many ancillaries in support. According to Eisenhower they were worth fifteen divisions and shortened the campaign by two months. They denied the French rail system to the Germans; disrupted road communications by felling trees and other devices; destroyed German minefields; cut down hedges in order to help the operations of allied tactical air squadrons; spread rumours of parachute landings which distracted the German command; obstructed the transfer of the German SS division *Das Reich* from the south-west so that it took nine days to reach the battle area in Normandy; forced 20,000 Germans to surrender to the Americans at Issoudun (and were very annoyed when the Americans gave their captives oranges, which no Frenchman had seen for years); successfully blocked off Brittany and then cleared it after the Americans had broken out of their Normandy beach-heads; took thousands of prisoners; protected works of art.

De Gaulle arrived in Paris on 25 August, the day after the surrender of the German military governor to General Jacques Leclercq of the revived French army and Colonel Rol-Tanguy of the Resistance as representatives of the French republic (the rising of the Parisians is narrated below in the context of the allied victories in France). He had already made careful preparations to assume the government of the country. The adherence of the Resistance to the Gaullist movement enabled him to do so by general consent. He was, however, apprehensive lest the communists might make a bid for power, using the local Liberation Committees which had been set up in each *département* and were mostly under communist control. Further, Roosevelt's hostility to him and the United States' continued refusal to recognize the CNR as a government or to come out against Vichy made him fear that the allies intended to impose a military government on France as they had on Sicily. He therefore chose and appointed *préfets* who were to be ready to assume authority as soon as invasion or Resistance had swept away Vichy's local government officials.

De Gaulle was also greatly concerned about the unity of the French people. He opposed the view, strongly held in the Resistance, that French society could be made healthy by a surgical purge of malign elements. The conflict between the Resistance and Vichy had generated much bitterness, which found vent during the occupation in the publication of lists of collaborators, the marking of their houses, summary executions (possibly 5,000 instances, plus another 5,000 in the throes and immediate aftermath of liberation) and an increasingly vocal determination to bring to trial and exact retribution from men and women of all ranks who had helped the enemy or served Vichy. In March 1944 a first Vichy Minister, Pierre Pucheu, was tried for treason and executed and a few months later another, Philippe Henriot, was assassinated in public and in daylight. Judicial and extra-judicial punishment of this kind was regarded by many in the Resistance and in de Gaulle's entourage as both inevitable and excusable, but de Gaulle himself deplored vengeance and regarded a purge, however conducted, as impracticable and likely to poison rather than heal French society. Some retribution was, however, inevitable and a special High Court was created to hear the principal cases. Fifty-eight cases were brought before this court, which passed eighteen death sentences (ten of them *in absentia*); three of the eighteen were executed. Altogether nearly 125,000 cases were heard by other courts and nearly 7,000 death sentences pronounced, of which 767 were carried out. Pétain was among those sentenced to death by the High Court. De Gaulle had hoped that Pétain would not be captured by French troops, nor return, and he was relieved when the death sentence on the Marshal was accompanied by a recommendation to mercy which he accepted. Pétain was consigned to a fortress on the Île d'Yeu off the west coast of France where he read de Gaulle's memoirs and remained until a few weeks before his death in 1951, when he was removed from the fortress but not from the island.

As Head of the Provisional Government of France de Gaulle saw his task in the same terms as he had seen it in 1940 as a junior minister and then as a refugee: to ensure and assert France's position as a major power. Although he might and did toy with the idea of presenting France as the champion of smaller powers or medium powers (the latter was a category which was recognized by the practice of the League of Nations and which France tried unsuccessfully to introduce into the structure of the United Nations), his basic aim was to range France unequivocally with the Big Three. He rejected the idea that France was a western equivalent of Poland or a power of the same consequence as Yugoslavia. This aim was formally achieved when France was accorded equal status with the Big Three in the administration of Germany and a permanent seat in the UN Security Council, but France still needed a special role to sustain this equal status. De Gaulle hoped that France might mediate between Anglo-Saxons and Russians and at the same time create and lead a western European group embracing the Low Countries, Spain, Italy and part of Germany as well as France itself – the countries touched by the Rhine, the Alps or the Pyrenees. In both these notions he was echoing Resistance aspirations for Great Power harmony and a European federation. But the harmony of the Resistance itself began to disintegrate under the pressures of peacetime politics and when the communists tried to refashion the post-war all-party government by forming an alliance and excluding the new Roman Catholic party, the MRP, de Gaulle decided to retire and leave the parties to conduct their despised manoeuvres without him. He announced his decision in January 1946. By the end of the next year the communists too were out of office. For a decade the government of France reverted to the political forces of the Third Republic until revolt in Algeria and a threat of a military coup in Paris itself drove them in 1958 to abdicate in favour of de Gaulle, who returned to save France once more and to pursue his interrupted task.

Part IV

THE MIDDLE GAME

CHAPTER 16

The Muster against the Axis

THE alliance which confronted Hitler in 1939 was a Franco-British one. When France fell Great Britain had to consider whether to carry on the fight. In retrospect it is easy to conclude that there was never any doubt about the answer to this question. It was never directly put, but there was a question all the same and there was a case for answering it in the negative. The defeat of France seemed to put Great Britain in a hopeless position, safe perhaps from military invasion but incapable of beating Germany and doubtfully capable of warding off intolerable air attacks. To the staid man of cool mind who was trained to assess a situation and then ask what was the most sensible thing to do about it – to the typical British statesman – the conclusion could well be that a government's job was to make the best of a bad business or, in other words, come to terms with fate in the person of Hitler. Some members of the British government reasoned this way. The historical importance of Churchill is that he did not. Having assessed the situation he refused to deduce his own course from it; he determined rather to alter it. He treated the concept of peace offers from Hitler as a contradiction in terms and ignored them. Moreover his famous speech on 4 June – 'we shall fight on the beaches, we shall fight on the landing-grounds, we shall fight in the fields and in the streets, we shall fight in the hills; we shall never surrender . . .' – gave the lead that the country wanted. Its reception showed how far the British mood had cleared since 1938. Then the question had been whether the British should fight, but now it was whether they should fight on.

But Churchill had been Prime Minister for only a few weeks. He was not the entire master of his cabinet, still less so of the Conservative Party, and both were substantially what they had been in the last years of appeasement. Official as well as popular feeling had changed since Munich, but it had not changed out of all recognition. Two weeks after Churchill's no-surrender speech his Under-Secretary of State at the Foreign Office, R. A. Butler, was telling the Swedish Minister that the Prime Minister's voice was not necessarily decisive, that the war might not have to be fought to a finish and that an opportunity to make a reasonable compromise peace would not be missed in spite of the 'diehards' in the cabinet. It is unlikely that Butler, a junior minister, was acting on his own. The Foreign

Secretary, Halifax, himself reinforced this appraisal by telling the same Minister that commonsense would prevail over bravado. (The Swedish government thereupon gave in to German pressure and allowed German soldiers going home on leave from Norway to travel through Sweden.) Another member of the old team, Hoare, who had wavered in the late thirties into toying with the idea of a Russian alliance and had then been relegated to the right wing as Ambassador in Madrid, was being similarly propitiatory. It was as a result of consorting too exclusively with people of this kind that the United States Ambassador in London, Joseph P. Kennedy, reported that Great Britain was finished – a judgement at variance not only with the facts but also with that of the Russian Ambassador, Ivan Maisky, who was assuring Stalin that the British would fight on despite the fall of France. (A year later Maisky found an ingenious solution to the reverse problem of persuading the British that the Russians would fight on and win in spite of Hitler's first victories in the USSR: he persuaded a British publishing firm to issue a cheap edition of Tolstoy's *War and Peace*.)

The question of a negotiated peace had been broached in the British Cabinet before the French capitulation, when some Ministers proposed invoking once more the good offices of Mussolini. Churchill was inflexibly hostile to any such move, even when faced with a threat of resignation by Halifax who argued that this was no time for obduracy. Yet Churchill's stance was not simply emotional bravado. Hitler was not likely to want to talk peace with the fall of France within his grasp, and Mussolini was even less likely to court a snub by making an inopportune and unwelcome approach to the lord of the continent.

Hints of peace in the summer of 1940 could have had two differing purposes. The more obvious purpose was to indicate that Great Britain was prepared to follow France in the acknowledgement of defeat: Lloyd George, who was known to be pessimistic about any other course, might play the role of Pétain and Churchill would leave the stage like Reynaud. Alternatively, defeatist talk might be a mere manoeuvre to gain time while British forces were evacuated from the continent. Although Churchill was anxious to get Lloyd George to join his government, there is no evidence that Churchill believed that the war should no longer be carried on, and his repeated overtures to Lloyd George are as consonant with a wish to muffle his old comrade-in-arms as to be supplanted by him. In the event there was no Pétainist peace. Butler and Halifax both left the Foreign Office before the end of the year and Churchill, more dogged and more passionate than the common run of politicians, became greatly more assured in his control of the government and his identification with the popular mood. But wars are not won by spirit alone. The British determination embodied in Churchill could hardly have prevailed against Hitler but for Great Britain's insular geography and its imperial past. As an island state Great Britain could parry and gain time. But this was only a negative advantage. It might enable Great Britain to get left out of Europe's catastrophic affairs but it could not directly affect them. As an island Great Britain was an anti-German perch, but there was in 1940 nobody to perch on it, for the Americans were unlikely to join a war which had dwindled to a formal state of belligerence and no more. But Great Britain was also an empire and it was the combination of British Empire and British Isles which kept the war alive: the American armies first joined this war not in Europe but in Africa.

Great Britain's imperial past had two major consequences. First, it provided a base in the Middle East to serve as an alternative point for accumulating forces and launching them against the European continent and, secondly, it provided the men and materials which India, the Dominions and the colonies contributed to the war. When Great Britain declared war in 1939 the Dominions did so too – in the case of South Africa by a vote of eighty to sixty-seven in Parliament, in the other cases wholeheartedly. This response was not the automatic reaction which it had been in 1914 but a freely formed resolve based on the close links of kinship and imperial solidarity and on revulsion against Nazi enormities. In India the Viceroy, acting with complete constitutional propriety but almost equally complete obtuseness, declared war without consulting any Indian leader. In spite of this tactless insensitivity Indians fought once more in Europe's wars at Great Britain's behest – to such good measure that Wavell felt bound to complain to Churchill in 1942 that the Indian army had the equivalent of seven divisions in the Middle East (more than it had in India) at a time when the country was dangerously threatened by the Japanese. Throughout the war there was never any shortage of volunteers for the Indian armed services. The Indian princes also pledged all their resources to the British cause and the independent kingdom of Nepal, the home of the Gurkhas, maintained its distinctive fighting reputation.

By mid-1941 the British Chiefs of Staff were making plans for the following year on the basis that they would be able to deploy about sixty divisions, of which slightly over one third would come from India and the Dominions (India eight, Australia five and a third, Canada four and a third, South Africa two, New Zealand one). The bulk of the armour, the equivalent of twelve divisions out of fifteen, would be British, but otherwise the imperial contribution was striking. Some Canadian units reached Great Britain as early as 1939 and took part in the battle for France next year; Australia and New Zealand agreed in January 1940 to the dispatch of a division each to the Middle East. Similar contributions were made to naval and air forces. The Commonwealth Air Training Scheme, established by the British, Canadian, Australian and New Zealand governments, trained tens of thousands of pilots, radio operators, gunners and observers annually at elementary and advanced schools in the various countries, and South Africa and Rhodesia set up schemes of their own, the latter with British instructors and aircraft. All this help was given with little restriction. South Africa did not allow service outside the African continent and restricted service outside the Union itself to volunteers: they served in North and East Africa. All the Dominion governments tried, as they were bound to do, to secure some say in broad strategic decisions and the right to be consulted on operational decisions of special moment to themselves. Australia and New Zealand complained about the dispatch of their units to Greece without adequate consultation, Canada showed concern about plans to commit Canadians to an assault on Trondhjem without express Canadian consent. But in general the Commonwealth commitment was unfettered as well as generous.

Thus, whether he fully realized it or not, Hitler was already in 1940 threatened from many quarters and by many peoples. The focus for this threat was the Middle East and it is conceivable that the threat to Hitler would not have materialized if Mussolini had not stirred it up by urging Graziani to attack in the desert and by invading Greece towards the end of 1940. By doing these things Mussolini opened a second front within range of British imperial power. He unshackled the British strategic initiative which had been neutralized when Great Britain lost in France its only fighting ally.

Churchill's problem after the defeat of France was how and with whom to get back to the continent. There were two possible ways of doing this. The one was to bring France back into the fight and the other was to make the journey back to within striking distance of Germany by way of the Balkans. A view of Europe from the south-east had been familiar to Englishmen since Egypt became to all intents and purposes a part of the British Empire and the Mediterranean, if not a British lake, at least a British highway signposted by Gibraltar, Malta, Alexandria and Suez.

Until the spring of 1941 the Balkans were debatable ground. Churchill built up British forces across the water in Egypt. But then Hitler conquered south-east Europe too, and the British in Egypt, their forces (mostly Australians and New Zealanders) thrown out of Greece and Crete, had to give up thinking of engaging the Germans anywhere on the continent; they were confined to the subsidiary problems of Libya and the Horn of

Africa. At this point Hitler himself again reopened the war in Europe and created for the German army an enemy who was to engage it until it was destroyed. His attack on the USSR in June 1941 transformed the war by carrying the bulk of Germany's ground forces to the east and out of occupied Europe, thereby making Resistance a serious practical possibility and opening for the British the prospect of returning to the continent either by assault on its weakened western defences or through ports captured by a French Resistance movement. Six months later Hitler's declaration of war against the United States ensured that this re-entry would be immensely massive. Hitler had dissolved the Anglo-French alliance only to create a convergence of British, Indian, Dominion, Russian and American forces against him. From 1942 onwards, the muster of these diverse enemies, joined by contingents from Hitler's victims, were on their several ways into Germany. But these had to be concerted.

The principal allies – the United States, the USSR and Great Britain – were united in their primary war aim but often divided about how to achieve it. Between the Americans and the British there was an accumulation of trust and fellowship which produced, for all its occasional rubs, an exceptionally efficient and harmonious alliance, but between them and the Russians there stood a generation of mistrust, thousands of miles and ineradicable divergences on post-war aims. There was also much mutual ignorance about attitudes and intentions, notably on post-war issues over which there was little meeting of minds, if only because – very often – minds were not yet made up.

The Grand Alliance which defeated Germany was fashioned by circumstances rather than by men. In the thirties the western European democracies had shunned the USSR because in a number of ways their rulers preferred Hitler to communism: either the USSR was weak, in which case it was no use as an ally, or it was strong, in which case it might dominate central Europe – an eventuality to be avoided at almost any cost. Stalin had no more liking for them than they for him and, concerned about how to keep out of trouble for as long as possible, he too had opted for Hitler in 1939: the victor in the ensuing war between Germany and the west would confront the USSR and probably be happy to attack it. But when in 1941, with that war still undecided, Germany invaded the USSR, an alliance between the west and the USSR became a natural sequel which imposed itself, or interposed itself, on the current of history. Although there was some surprise at the immediacy and wholeheartedness of Churchill's and Roosevelt's response, there was nothing surprising about the event itself. Hitler's decision to attack the USSR while he was still at war with Great Britain meant that an east–west alliance against him would precede the east–west conflict which he in effect postponed to 1945.

So long as the war lasted the maintenance of this anti-German alliance was a cardinal aim of the leaders on both sides of Germany. The war on two fronts was the war which Hitler could not win. A separate peace in west or east spelt danger for the other half of the alliance. For Great Britain the German attack on the USSR, because it came before Churchill had achieved his aim of seeing the Americans join the fighting, was an immense relief in a year of critical strain, and even after Hitler's declaration of war against the United States, six months after Barbarossa was launched, the maintenance of the Russian capacity and will to fight was essential to a western victory. Not until 1943 at the earliest were the German armies so mauled by the Russians that the western allies might hope to put their own great armies onto the continent without intolerable losses. Yet these forces must make their invasion not long after 1943 in order to be certain that new German weapons, such as chemical weapons, would not render it impossible. As late as the autumn of 1944 they were sharply reminded in the Ardennes that the Germans, even in a war on two fronts which they were clearly losing, remained dangerous foes.

On the Russian side Stalin, by his appeals for material aid and for the reopening of a front in France, proved his urgent fear of defeat in single combat with the Germans. He asked for British divisions to be sent to fight on Russian soil and for a no-separate-peace agreement, which was concluded between Molotov and the British Ambassador (Cripps) in October. His fears were allayed by the survival of Moscow at the end of 1941 and still more by the endurance of Stalingrad at the end of 1942 and were all but completely removed by the Russian victories in the summer of 1943. But the preservation of 'anti-fascist solidarity' remained a cardinal principle of Stalin's war policy, even to the extent of restraining communists like Tito and Togliatti, lecturing the one on the need to conciliate and collaborate with anti-fascists of all kinds and telling the other to mute anti-monarchism until the war was over. It is arguable that, if forced to a choice, Stalin might have put the control over eastern Europe above the preservation of the alliance once the USSR's moment of vital danger had passed, and that he never regarded eastern Europe as negotiable during the last two years of war; but he was never called upon to make that choice, an escape for which he could claim some personal credit since it was partly due to his refusal to confabulate with Roosevelt and Churchill until the end of 1943.

But although the overriding needs of the partners ensured its maintenance, the alliance was neither deep nor harmonious. Evidence to the contrary is to be found only in communiqués, notoriously misleading, and in descriptions of banquet scenes, traditionally unbuttoned. The persistent reality was a background of mistrustful manoeuvre and speculation. Although anti-Germanism was strong enough to hold the alliance together, it was – apart from a certain mutual martial admiration – just about the allies' only bond. Churchill and Stalin might admire as well as need one another but Stalin could remember the Churchill who had advocated the overthrow of the new Bolshevik régime not only by backing Russian Whites and enlisting British volunteers but also by using German troops, while Churchill could remember that one of the first acts of the Bolshevik government had been to desert the allied cause and make a separate peace with Germany. Difficulties appeared at once and were thereafter never absent. Churchill's declaration of sympathy and solidarity, made within hours of Hitler's attack, was followed by negotiations for an Anglo-Russian treaty which laid bare one of the problems which was never resolved until the Russians were strong enough completely to override their allies' views – the problem of the Soviet Union's European frontiers. What Stalin had got in his treaty with Hitler in 1939 he wanted his new allies to recognize and endorse – in the Baltic, Poland and the Balkans.

Churchill's general inclination was to mollify Stalin without entering into specific undertakings governing the shape of post-war Europe; in particular he could not concede Stalin's claims against Poland without flagrantly violating the Anglo-Polish treaty of 1939 and forgetting that Great Britain had gone to war in 1939 on behalf of Poland and was still host to a Polish government in exile. If Bessarabia presented no such problem (Rumania had joined in the attack on the USSR) the extinction of the three Baltic states raised political and moral principles which Great Britain did not care to flout in a formal diplomatic document.

In August 1941, on a battleship off the coast of Newfoundland, Roosevelt and Churchill had signed the document which became known as the Atlantic Charter and which was intended as a declaration of general war aims. For Roosevelt the Atlantic Charter was the equivalent of Wilson's Fourteen Points, a working paper setting out the basis on which a new and fairer world would be constructed. For Churchill it was less a document than a call or proclamation to stir the world. For Americans it was the equivalent of the Constitution, for the British of the Magna Carta – the one a document with continuing practical effects, the other a piece of secular religion. By the Atlantic Charter Roosevelt and Churchill renounced territorial aggrandizement, asserted the right of all peoples to choose how they should be governed, condemned territorial changes contrary to the wishes of the inhabitants of the territory and looked forward to an equitable distribution of raw materials, fair trading practices, freedom of the seas, disarmament and an international security system. They hoped to get Stalin to endorse this declaration but they got no further than a vague statement of approval from the Russian Ambassador in London, Ivan Maisky. At the end of 1941 Eden, on a mission to Moscow, discovered that Stalin's post-war aims included not only the recognition of the fruits of his pact with Hitler, but also fragments of Germany and the transfer to Turkey of the Dodecanese (which Great Britain's other ally, Greece, was expecting to be given as soon as Italy was defeated). But Stalin was not at this stage in a position to insist. Eden became privately convinced that it would be politic to concede Stalin's claims in the Baltic, but Churchill (and the Conservative Party) were not so minded, unmoved by Eden's arguments that when the war ended Stalin would take the republics anyway. The Anglo-Russian treaty, eventually concluded in May 1942, contained no undertakings about post-war frontiers and Stalin let the matter rest until the Teheran conference in November 1943, by which time his military position had greatly changed.

As important as Poland and more urgent was the question of a second front. Stalin pressed for one in July 1941 and again in September. Churchill's desire to help was genuine but he and many of his advisers were for a time sceptical about the value of the new ally which looked like being defeated and bundled out of the war almost as easily as France had been – in which event aid would have been wasted and Great Britain, once more alone, that much worse off. Churchill's spirit responded to the Russian needs but his strategic senses were more alert to the battles in the Middle East, the defence of the British Empire and the fear of a junction between the Germans and the Japanese. He had to count the cost of promises very carefully. Great Britain was a fighting ally of the USSR for six months before the United States too came into the war and the brunt of military aid to the USSR and the delivery of war material by the Arctic route must fall on Great Britain.

Roosevelt was less cautious. When, after the American entry into the war, Molotov visited London and Washington in the hope of getting more and quicker western aid, Roosevelt allowed himself to be less guarded than Churchill and half-promised a second front that year (1942). Churchill, who envisaged raids on the French coast in 1942 and a major invasion in 1943 at the earliest, felt obliged to record in writing his opposition to Roosevelt's imprudent engagement, and from this time the

Russians regarded Great Britain as a drag on more purposeful and generous American policies. In April 1942 the American planners produced, and the Chiefs of Staff adopted, proposals for an invasion of France by a million American troops in the spring of 1943 and for a smaller attack in the autumn of 1942 if either the Russians or the Germans showed signs of collapsing. The British did not object to this programme although they were convinced that any invasion in 1942 was out of the question. Churchill did not believe that so huge an American force could be assembled in England in time for a major invasion in 1943, especially if the war in the Atlantic had not first been won. Great Britain moreover was committed to the North African campaign, which could not on the most favourable estimates be completed in time to permit the opening of a new campaign thousands of miles away before the end of 1942; it was in fearful difficulties in the Far East, exemplified by the fall of Singapore and the Australian government's insistence on recalling troops from abroad for the defence of their homeland; and Churchill and his advisers were ceaselessly aware of their limited resources in men and materials.

In Great Britain Churchill's views prevailed, if not without question, yet without serious challenge. On the issue of the second front Lord Beaverbrook alone raised a voice of eminence and influence in favour of an immediate landing in France. Early in 1942 Beaverbrook had resigned from the government, which he believed to be crumbling, and had gone to the United States where he made a public appeal for the opening of a second front, recklessly if necessary. On his return to London he established an organization to campaign for a second front and lent himself for a while to anti-Churchill manoeuvres, but these came to nothing in spite of a certain amount of intrigue and gossip on the political fringes in which Beaverbrook's name was freely used. Beaverbrook then rallied to his old and loyal friend and found himself back in the government before the year was out.

Despite the loss of Singapore in February and Tobruk in June, Churchill's position was never threatened as Asquith had been threatened by the reverses of 1916. Public opinion saw no alternative to Churchill and wished for none. The Conservative Party, as a whole, having made Churchill its leader in 1940, knew that it could not prosper without him, while the Labour Party never aspired to the leading place. Churchill was master of his cabinet and of Parliament as neither Asquith nor Lloyd George (the latter dependent in 1917–18 on the votes of a party not his own) had ever been. He was also in undoubted control of his service chiefs whom he could dismiss if he chose – again unlike Lloyd George, who distrusted Haig but dared not dismiss him. As Minister of Defence and chairman of

the Chiefs of Staff Committee Churchill was a civilian warlord who had
no cause to fear military intrigues against him; no British general in the
Second World War complained to the king about civilian incompetence
and interference as Haig did in the first war; in his relations with the
military Churchill had an authority which no British Prime Minister – and,
in France, only Clemenceau – had ever had before. Churchill's conduct of
the war remained therefore remarkably uninhibited until it was curtailed
by Great Britain's declining share in the total allied war effort. But this
did not happen until there were more Americans than British under arms
in the European theatre and up to 1943 it was still difficult to ship American forces to Europe owing to U-boats, shortage of transports and the
competing claims of the war in the Pacific. At the end of 1942 there were
only 170,000 American troops in Europe (and 140,000 in North Africa)
out of 500,000 planned earlier in the year.

Roosevelt, as Commander-in-Chief as well as President, was confronted
throughout the war with two series of strategic problems: the claims of
the Pacific theatre against the European, and the alternative uses to which
American power could be put within a theatre. Until Munich the United
States had no plans for fighting Germany. It had plans of a vague and
general kind for a war against Japan. Munich stimulated thinking about
new problems and new theatres and in April 1939 the Chiefs of Staff,
faced with the possibility of a war on two fronts, provisionally recommended that Europe should come first. At the end of 1940, with war
palpably nearer, the Chief of Naval Operations, Admiral Harold R. Stark,
recommended a policy of attack in the Atlantic and defence in the Pacific,
which he was prepared to subordinate to the war against Germany and
the Anglo-American alliance. This policy had been affirmed at a joint
Anglo-American staff conference in March 1941 which hoped that war in
the Pacific might be avoided but recommended that, if it came, it be
subordinated to the war in Europe; but there were always dissentients on
the American side. In his State of the Union address to Congress at the
beginning of 1942 Roosevelt said that Hitler came first. By this time the
United States was actively involved in hostilities in the Atlantic, and
Hitler's declaration of war three days after Pearl Harbor had removed
any need to reconsider, in the light of Pearl Harbor, the priorities which
had governed American planning for the past few years: Hitler made the
Americans' war a war on two fronts from its first week.

But although American priorities were never reversed, they were inevitably questioned from time to time. At the beginning of 1942 American
strategy in the Pacific was largely dictated by the requirements of the
defensive, but the United States recovered from the blow at Pearl Harbor
with astonishing rapidity and was able after the naval victories of the

28 Sisters in a Polish field

29   *Top*: Rounding up
Warsaw Jews for the death
camp

30   *Bottom*: Polish hostages
hanging

31 A search in the Warsaw ghetto

32 Russian partisans near Minsk, 1941

33 Berlin: recovering in the
open after being bombed out

34 A Russian partisan about
to be executed, 1941

35 *Top*: Berlin: women and children take refuge in a hotel

36 *Bottom*: Berlin: the Tauentzienstrasse

37 *Top*: Stuttgart: the city
centre

38 *Bottom*: France, 1944: a
Frenchman kills a German
oppressor and welcomes
American liberators

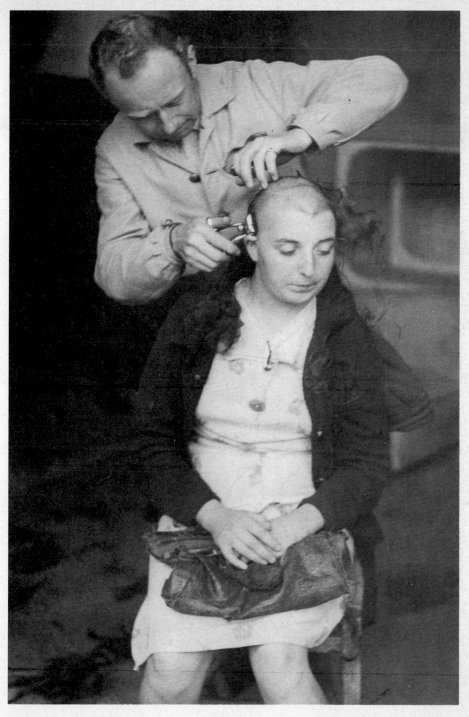

39 France, 1944: the
collaborator's fate

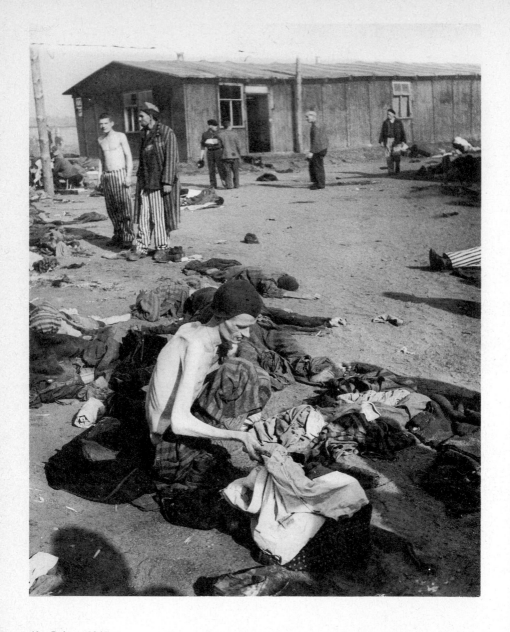

40   Belsen, 1945

Coral Sea and Midway in May and June to go over to the offensive sooner than had been expected. This turn of fortune lent strength to the pleas of the Pacific commanders, Admiral Chester W. Nimitz and General Douglas MacArthur, who were authorized to take the offensive and who therefore succeeded in altering to some extent the division of forces between the theatres. At the end of 1942 there were more Americans in the Pacific than in Europe.

In the European theatre Churchill dominated the strategic debate on the western side during 1942. Although he did not convince the American, or British, Chiefs of Staff he won a wavering Roosevelt over to his plan for a major Anglo-American landing in North-west Africa (Torch) which would join forces with the British army in the Western Desert, bring the North African campaign to a close and make the Mediterranean safe for the allies. Roosevelt was the more easily won over because he saw action in North Africa in 1942 as a partial redemption of the half-promise which he had given to Molotov of action in France in 1942, but to Stalin a second front in Africa was not the second front he wanted and in August Churchill set out for Moscow for his first meeting with Stalin in order to explain and justify this strategy. The meeting was boisterous but not disastrous and it formed Stalin's view of Churchill: he liked the man but not his plans. How far the two leaders ever understood one another is debatable, but so long as their common and overriding anti-German aim subsisted they preserved a mutual respect and did business with one another.

When the Grand Alliance came into being in 1941 the war in Africa was for the British, the senior combatants, nearly the whole of the war, but both the Americans and the Russians were dubious about it and regarded it as a sideshow. The Americans regarded battles in the eastern Mediterranean as battles to salvage the British Empire, battles in the western Mediterranean as battles to salvage the French Empire; and they had not entered the war to save or restore empires. The Americans, and the Russians too, thought of battles as much bigger affairs than anything that had occurred in Africa and could conceive of no vitally significant operation except the biggest possible battle in Europe at the earliest possible moment. Again, the Americans and Russians looked to a victory to be achieved preponderantly by ground forces, whereas Churchill clung to the belief in victory by air bombardments. (If he had been right, Great Britain would not have become so junior a partner in the Anglo-American effort.) In the final analysis Churchill and the British Chiefs of Staff did not question the paramount importance of an invasion of France and they agreed that other operations had to be justified by their contribution to the re-opening of a western front. Where they disagreed was in their assessment of the relevance of operations in the Mediterranean to this overriding aim. They were also more impressed than the Russians by the difficulties of landing in France (they seem to have given up the notion that the French Resistance would capture French harbours for them) and their hesitations on this score were increased in August 1942 by the costliness of the experimental raid on Dieppe.

In this atmosphere every British argument in favour of exploiting success in Africa by expanding the campaign in the Mediterranean was interpreted by the Americans as an attempt to turn this campaign into an alternative way of defeating the Germans without the necessity for a frontal assault in the west, and American suspiciousness was increased by the realization that Torch would rule out an invasion of France not only in 1942 but in 1943 too. On the American side there was a feeling of having been tricked by crafty British with ulterior motives. Churchill's strategic agility – his addiction to a strategy of ingenious pinpricks at spots as remote from a decisive theatre as northern Norway or Rhodes, which were the products of his lively sense of opportunity and often disconcerted his own advisers as much as his allies – was interpreted, wrongly, as unwillingness to face up to the serious business and daunting casualties of a landing in France.

Torch developed into an open-ended temptation. While the fighting in North-west Africa was still going on Roosevelt and Churchill met in January 1943 at Casablanca. They accepted the premise that for the time being their primary weapon against Germany was not direct invasion but air bombardment, and they sanctioned an invasion of Sicily as soon as possible after the defeat of the Germans and Italians in Africa, which was not completed until May. In that month they met again in Washington and decided to do something more in the western Mediterranean after taking Sicily, but what this was to be – an attack on Sardinia and Corsica or in Calabria or somewhere else – was left undecided and was still undecided when Sicily was invaded in July. This invasion, which caused the fall of Mussolini, led the allies on to an invasion of the Italian mainland but did not deliver Italy into their hands and effectively removed all prospect of a landing in France (Overlord) before 1944.

For twelve months therefore – from the end in Tunisia to Overlord – the three allies went their separate and barely coordinated ways towards Germany. The Russians won in July 1943 the battles in the Kursk salient which, even more than Stalingrad, spelt the end of Hitler's bid to subjugate the USSR. The western allies conquered Sicily in the same month, and then, landing at Salerno, set out in September for Rome, which, however, they did not reach for nine months because Hitler, after some hesitation, reinforced his armies in Italy and built them up by the end of the year to twenty-five divisions by withdrawals from both the Russian and western fronts. These latter operations involved the western allies in further disputes which were not without interest to Stalin both for their bearing on Overlord and their wider political import.

In the year before Overlord the western allies had in mind three principal operations. They could not, however, attempt all three because all of them required landing craft and there were not enough landing craft to go round. The first of the three possibilities was a second landing on the Italian coast to supplement the landing at Salerno and expedite the capture of Rome; this was effected in January 1944 at Anzio. The second was a landing in the Andaman Islands in the Bay of Bengal intended to lead to the recovery of Sumatra and Malaya; this was promised to Chiang Kai-shek by Roosevelt in Cairo in December 1943 but subsequently cancelled. The reason for the cancellation was the third operation – a landing in the Dodecanese. This was one of Churchill's pet plans and his strategic objective was the same as that of the Italian campaign: to win air bases (in the Aegean case, for attacks on the Rumanian oilfields) and to create a threat which would force Hitler either to evacuate the Balkans or reinforce them at the expense of more vital fronts (Hitler in fact built up his forces in south-eastern Europe to twenty divisions). Churchill was also keen to bring Turkey into the war. He argued that the Anzio and Dodecanese operations could be effected with the landing craft which were later to be used in support of Overlord by an invasion of southern France (Anvil), but that landing craft sent to the Indian Ocean could not be brought back to the Mediterranean in time. This argument won the day. (But the Dodecanese venture was a failure. Designed to coincide with the surrender of Italy, it was first postponed and then undertaken belatedly and with greatly reduced forces. An attempt to get the Italian garrison on Rhodes to change sides failed and the Germans put in troops of their own. The British nevertheless sent small detachments to take Kos, Leros, Samos and other nearby points. They were driven out of Kos after twenty days and out of Leros a month later and abandoned their remaining toeholds. The Germans made 900 allied and 3,000 Italian prisoners on Kos and shot Italian officers who had sided with the British. No attack was made on Rhodes. Turkey stayed neutral until the last week of February 1945.)

A successful British return to Greece, like the plan later proposed for an advance from Italy over the Brenner or through the Ljubljana Gap to Vienna, could have had political implications for the balance of power in central Europe after the war. But it does not follow that in 1943 Churchill sponsored his Dodecanese adventure for political reasons. It has been

ALLIED ADVANCES 1942 - 1945

November 1943   Russians
begin westward advance
reaching Berlin in May 1945

October 1942
British advance

German counter-
attack at the
Ardennes

'D' Day 6 June 1944

Allied advance held
up for a week by
Falaise pocket

8 November 1942, First U S
landings of the war

Stalingrad

Black Sea

Cyprus
(British)

El Alamein

Mediterranean Sea

Baltic Sea

Warsaw

Danube

Budapest

Vienna

Berlin

Leipzig

Dresden

Danube

Munich

Rhine

Milan

Rome

Malta
(British)

Paris

Rhône

Loire

Brest

Algiers

Oran

Gibraltar
(British)

Ft Lyautey

Casablanca

Safi

250

0   Miles

Advance of the Allies

~ARTHUR BANKS~

assumed on too little evidence that Churchill was attracted to the Dodecanese by his memories of the First World War when he was deeply enmeshed in the Gallipoli campaign and by a desire to establish a military
presence in eastern Europe which would limit Stalin's post-war hegemony,
but Churchill's concern about the position of the Russians in Europe does
not seem to have been aroused before 1944 – and then chiefly by events in
Poland – nor does he seem to have imagined that a minor British operation
in the Balkans was the right way to limit Russian power. His attempt to
regain a foothold in the Aegean was an aspect of exploiting the collapse
of Italian Fascism by reaching out a hand to the Greek and Yugoslav
partisans who had captured his imagination as doughty allies in the
common cause. It was opposed by the Americans and the Russians as an
unnecessary and perhaps harmful distraction from the engaging of the
German armies in the west.

   Nevertheless Churchill's strategies did acquire a political element which
became increasingly evident as the war went on. He was proud of British
achievements in Africa and the Mediterranean, aware that the victories to
come in western Europe would be more American than British, subconsciously anxious to make the most of what was, in Italy, still at least as much
a British as an American show. Like every great patriot he was a bit of a
chauvinist. He was also a European, whereas Roosevelt, like Woodrow
Wilson before him, was not a European and did not have the European's
sensitivity to the balance of power in Europe. Churchill, largely because
of his special interest in history, had this sensitivity to an unusual degree.
In the last year of the war the coming domination of Europe by the
Russians worried him quite apart from the fact that the government of the
USSR was a communist autocracy, and he was also worried by his inability
to get Roosevelt worried too. Roosevelt, again like Wilson, looked askance
at power political issues and attached more importance to the creation of
a new world organization which would impose universal harmony upon
particular disharmonies. For this purpose Russo-American cordiality was
all important and Roosevelt seized on the chance of wartime cooperation
as a means to establishing a more enduring entente. Everybody else's
salvation would flow from such an entente – a view of international order
which died with Roosevelt and the Cold War but revived with mutual
nuclear deterrence, the thaw of the 1960s and the fear of China to take the
place of fear of Germany. But Churchill, like Clemenceau *vis-à-vis* Wilson
in 1919, was more sceptical. In the heat of war Stalin might be pictured
as the benevolent Uncle Joe projected by wartime emotions; with the
approach of peace he could be looked at more coldly.

   The first meeting of the three leaders of the Grand Alliance did not take place until the Russian victory in the east had been assured and the preponderance of American over British might in the west had been made manifest. There were only two such meetings during the war in Europe: the first, which lasted four days, at Teheran in November 1943 and a second, which lasted eight days, at Yalta in February 1945.

Before Teheran Roosevelt and Churchill had had a series of meetings as well as a continuous and intimate correspondence. Churchill had met Stalin once, and Roosevelt and Stalin had met not at all. During 1943 distrust within the alliance had become serious. In the United States the view that Stalin was no better than Hitler was being freely expressed in the press and elsewhere; it was reinforced by the revelation in April 1943 of the Katyn massacre in Poland and by the constitution in Moscow in July of a Free German Committee which was taken as evidence of Russian flirting with Germany. From Stockholm came reports of Russian feelers, designed either to end the war in the east by a separate peace or to scare the western allies into thinking that Stalin was about to do so. The western allies feared that Stalin might be content to push the Germans back into Germany and then leave the Nazi régime intact. On his side Stalin, besides being embarrassed and angered by the publicity given to Katyn, feared that the Americans might divert most of their strength to the Pacific and resented, unreasonably, the suspension of the Arctic convoys for three months after disasters suffered in June 1942. Above all Stalin was trying to hold his allies to their promises to open a second front in 1943. By a second front he meant a landing in strength on the continent which would draw off great numbers of German divisions from the east. In the crisis of 1941 he had specified thirty to forty divisions. He accepted as adequate neither the western air offensive which engaged the best of the Luftwaffe's aircraft and aircrews (to the considerable advantage of the Russian armies) nor the operations in the Mediterranean which tied down a number of German divisions in the Balkans and diverted twenty-five to Italy. Although Churchill had given no promise of a cross-Channel invasion in 1943 he seems to have felt that, when in Moscow in August 1942, he had given Stalin grounds for expecting one; and Roosevelt had been much more explicit. Both western leaders had a feeling of unease about postponing the big assault to 1944.

Roosevelt and Churchill liked meeting for the sake of meeting. They believed in the value of man-to-man talks of a general nature, informal and on an assumption of shared aims and proved comradeship. Such meetings must, they felt, generate understanding and trust, eliminate the rubs in the alliance and so accelerate victory and lay a sure basis for post-war harmony. They envisaged not so much a diplomatic conference as a council of war. Stalin took a more professional view of summit meetings. He wanted a regular conference or nothing. He had exercised power and responsibility unremittingly for twenty years, during which he had got his way by always doing his homework more thoroughly than his adversaries, by never taking decisions in anybody's time but his own, by knowing how far to go at any given moment (unlike Hitler but not unlike Bismarck) – in short by arming an unusually clear mind and unusually ruthless character with the most rigorous professional techniques of the statesman and negotiator. Whereas Roosevelt and Churchill looked to their subordinates to supply these technical assets as required, Stalin embodied them in himself. He had neither the gifts nor the weaknesses of the amateur. He may have been a repulsive man but he was an exceptionally gifted and experienced master of his craft.

Roosevelt and Churchill, desiring a meeting on general grounds, thought that the sooner it took place the better. They pressed for it on and off throughout 1943. Stalin on the other hand had no use for a conference which was unlikely to further specific or particular objectives and he therefore blew hot and cold, favouring a conference when his fortunes and his bargaining power were in the ascendant, putting it off when they waned or when he was vexed. Early in 1943 he seemed willing to meet his associates. By this time the three great crises of the war, from the Russian point of view, were behind him: Moscow had been saved in 1941, Japan had not attacked when Germany did, Stalingrad had not fallen. Yet he still prevaricated, probably on account of the Anglo-American conference of May which resolved on further operations against Italy, and it was not until after the spectacular Russian victories on his central front in the summer which finally eliminated all prospect of a German victory over the USSR that he again reversed his position and agreed to a meeting in Teheran at the end of the year. The second front was no longer a condition of Russian survival. Rather the failure to open a second front could be used as a lever politically against the western allies. And the Polish problem had also been transformed by the certainty that Russian armies would soon be on Polish soil once more.

During 1943 Stalin broke with the provisional Polish government which had its headquarters in London. Relations with this government had been established after Hitler invaded the USSR by an agreement signed in London by General Wladislaw Sikorski, the head of the government, and Ivan Maisky; the agreement provided for an 'amnesty' for all Poles in the USSR and the raising of a Polish army on Russian soil. This was the season of Stalin's direst need. He was prepared not only to see American troops in the USSR but a Polish army too and General Anders, captured in the war of 1939, was disinterred from the Lubianka prison in Moscow to command it. The Poles in the USSR, however, were not enthusiastic about fighting alongside their hereditary and recent Russian enemies. Trouble soon came. The Russians accused the Poles of breaking the Sikorski-Maisky agreement by not committing their divisions to the front as quickly as they were formed. The Poles were probably reluctant to use up their fighting power in the defence of the USSR against the Germans, and as the pressure on the Russians eased, Stalin's priorities changed and he became more wary about a scheme which would take a Polish army, commanded by anti-Russian and anti-communist officers, into territories which he had recently seized from Poland and intended to keep.

Eventually, on Churchill's suggestion and with Stalin's consent, Anders's divisions left for Italy via Iran, thus incidentally ensuring that the liberation of Poland from the Germans would be accomplished by the Russians alone. Churchill, who established a personal friendship with Sikorski, hoped to be able to resolve the differences between his Polish and Russian allies by persuading Sikorski, who was in turn to persuade his compatriots, to cede territory in eastern Poland to the USSR in return for equivalent territory in the west to be taken from Germany: Poland was to be shifted westward. The Poles did not want to be shifted; they wanted the cancellation of the Russo-German deal of 1939 and the restoration of Poland's 1939 frontiers. But Stalin was determined not to give up what he had won before the German and Russian invasions of 1939, and talked of a new 'ethnic' Poland to the west of the Russo-German partition line. He was prepared to accept the somewhat less favourable 'Curzon Line' invented in 1920 by Lord Curzon and opportunely dug out by Eden, but he did not intend that the new Poland should have its old government, and in 1943 events enabled him to begin the process of displacing it.

During the short war of 1939 a great many Polish officers disappeared. They were believed to be in Russian captivity but they failed to reappear after the amnesty proclaimed in accordance with the Sikorski–Maisky agreement of 1941. They were in fact dead and in April 1943 thousands of bodies were found in pits in the forest of Katyn. They had been murdered. The temper of the times inclined western opinion to the belief that they had been murdered by the Germans and when Goebbels proclaimed that they had been murdered by the Russians few people in the west believed him. Yet it gradually became obvious that this was the case and that a massacre of some 10–14,000 prisoners had been perpetrated. The Polish government in London asked for an investigation by the Red Cross, whereupon Stalin seized the occasion to sever relations. A few months later, in September 1943, the death of Sikorski in an aircraft accident at Gibraltar removed from the scene the one Polish leader who, because he was a man of singular ability and vision, enjoyed the friendship of Churchill and had some personal credit with Stalin, might have been able to repair the breach between Moscow and the London Poles and implement Churchill's policy of making territorial but not political concessions to the USSR.

After Sikorski's death Churchill was virtually without any cards to play against Stalin on the Polish question. Sikorski's successor as head of the government in exile, Stanislaw Mikolajczyk, saw the need for an understanding with the Russians but he lacked Sikorski's authority and both his Minister of War, General Kasimierz Sosnkowski, and General Tadeusz Bor-Komarowski who succeeded to the command of the Polish Home Army (AK) when its first commander fell into German hands, were strongly anti-Russian. (They were also anti-semitic.) But Stalin, following his military successes of the summer, was about to take possession of the contested field, having turned Katyn to good account by divesting himself of the commitments in the Sikorski-Maisky agreement. At Teheran he was in a position to urge Churchill to acknowledge that Poland was his to dispose of, and Churchill, being already sufficiently in agreement with Stalin's case for securer frontiers in areas through which Hitler had attacked, went far towards doing so. He even took the lead in the discussions on Poland, leaving Stalin to concur. It was agreed that the Poles should be left out of the discussions until later. (About the three Baltic states nothing was said; the silence proclaimed their coming fate.)

Stalin had at Teheran other demands too: half East Prussia, a third of the Italian fleet (to be delivered in January 1944), the Kuriles, the southern half of Sakhalin and a free port at Dairen. In return he accepted an abortive plan propounded by Roosevelt for emasculating Germany by dividing it into five segments and putting the Ruhr, the Saar, Hamburg and the Kiel Canal under international control; agreed to join a world organization and to collaborate in a European Advisory Commission for the discussion of German problems; and repeated the promise already made by Molotov a few weeks earlier to join in the war against Japan as soon as Germany was defeated.

All these matters were dealt with in a single day. The other three days were devoted to military rather than political business. The principal outcome was a promise by the western allies to invade France in May 1944.

The comparatively long list of matters agreed at Teheran can be accounted for less by supposing a basic identity of views than by the fact

that both Roosevelt and Stalin attached comparatively little importance
to what the other most desired. Roosevelt was chiefly interested in establishing a personal relationship with Stalin, ensuring his entry into the
war against Japan and enlisting his participation in the new organization
which was to replace the League of Nations. Stalin had no objection to
any of these things. For him the real importance of the conference lay in
the territorial and political settlements which it might help to ensure in
eastern and central Europe and to a lesser extent in the Far East: he
intended to keep what he had won before Hitler's invasion from Finland,
the Baltic states, Poland and Rumania and to round off these acquisitions
by establishing a primary Russian influence in Bulgaria and the Straits.
These were matters to which Roosevelt was much less alert than Churchill.
How Roosevelt would have reacted to Russian meddling in western
Europe it is impossible to say because Stalin showed no interest in western
Europe. Beyond his immediate sphere of interest he postulated only the
restoration of an independent Czechoslovakia and Austria and he talked
vaguely about partitioning Italy. Churchill continued to have forebodings,
but his objections carried in 1943 less weight than they would have done if
the conference had been held at an earlier date, partly because of the turn
of the military tide in the USSR and partly because the preponderant
voice in the western alliance was no longer British but American. Stalin
even allowed himself to make during the conference half bantering, half
barbed attacks on Churchill which he would hardly have been likely to
make a year earlier; he treated Roosevelt with immaculate respect and
condescension. Roosevelt responded with what his detractors have called
naïvety.

The charge is in part valid not because Roosevelt was a foolishly vain
man, as lesser men have argued, but in the sense that Roosevelt seems to
have overestimated his superabundant political gifts. He had wanted to
meet Stalin without Churchill being present and had sent a personal
emissary, Joseph E. Davies, a former Ambassador in Moscow, to prepare
a *tête-à-tête*. He argued against the British that it was impolitic to engage
in a conference at which Stalin might feel himself outmatched by two to
one, but Roosevelt's deepest motive was his determination to talk Stalin
into a personal friendship which would be the counterpart of his special
relationship with Churchill. His own career had been based on his special
gifts as a manager of men, and he seems to have thought that he could
manage Stalin too in much the same way as he had managed American
politicians of varying degree and varying views. It is said that old and sick
men fall into the error of exaggerating their principal talents. Roosevelt,
long a cripple, had held one of the most arduous offices in the world for

an unprecedented number of years of unparalleled domestic complexity and external stress. Although at Teheran he seemed still to retain his extraordinary powers, at Yalta only fifteen months later he was dying. His mistake at the end of his life – if one can speak of a mistake in the case of a man whose faculties are deserting him – was to imagine that he could captivate a man like Stalin, a man of a kind uncommon even in American politics and placed in circumstances utterly remote from the imagination of any person raised in the American tradition. Roosevelt was the youngest of the three leaders – three years younger than Stalin, eight years younger than Churchill – but at Teheran and Yalta Stalin was the fittest of the three, not only fitter than Roosevelt but probably also fitter than Churchill, who succumbed to pneumonia after Teheran for the second time that year. It is not unnatural that Stalin had the best reason to be pleased with the way the conference went.

On the immediate strategic issue the Teheran conference agreed that the Anglo-American armies in Italy should advance to Hitler's Gothic Line (which ran from Pisa to Rimini). If necessary, Overlord might be postponed for a month, but once the Gothic Line was reached further operations in Italy would be entirely subordinated to the requirements of Overlord. This proviso meant in practice that the Supreme Commander in the Mediterranean, now Field Marshal Sir Harold Alexander, would have to relinquish a number of divisions for Anvil which was to take place simultaneously with Overlord. No thought was given to what would be done if the Gothic Line was not reached before the Anvil divisions had to leave the theatre to keep to the Overlord timetable. Yet this is what happened. The Anglo-American advance was so retarded by the Germans that Alexander had to request the cancellation of Anvil. The British Chiefs of Staff supported him; the American Chiefs were very angry but agreed to let him keep his divisions until after the capture of Rome. But Rome was not taken until two days before D-day for Overlord on 6 June with the result that Anvil, postponed until the middle of August, contributed nothing to Overlord and was proved by Overlord's success to be unnecessary before it took place. Alexander was denied the chance to press forward to the Danube, a plan of his which was warmly espoused by Churchill although regarded as over-optimistic by his military advisers, and the Mediterranean strategy petered out in the autumn rains of the Po valley.

On the eastern fronts the Russians gained in 1944 a series of military victories over the Germans and their allies which they were able to convert without impediment into political advantage. In the west the immense accumulation of American men and material for the invasion of France was accomplished without serious opposition from the German U-boats, and the invasion itself was successfully effected in June and equally successfully exploited until the German counter-attack in the Ardennes in November temporarily delayed the last stages of the overthrow of German power. These operations in east and west were affected by Germany's continuing need to defend itself on more than one front but otherwise the campaigns of the eastern and western allies owed little to one another. They were independent operations, usefully coincidental but only very loosely coordinated. In these circumstances allied cooperation became even more political and less military, more concerned with the post-war settlement and less with the conduct of the war.

In October 1944 Churchill went again to Moscow for his third meeting with Stalin (the second without Roosevelt who was campaigning for election for a fourth term as President). Churchill had now become much more worried about the fate of eastern and central Europe and the inability of the western allies to prevent the Russians from imposing communist rule in the countries which their armies were overrunning. He tried to strike a bargain with Stalin but since he was bargaining only about eastern territories, without being willing or indeed entitled to concede anything in the west in return, his position was not a strong one except in relation to Greece which, as a Mediterranean country, was more accessible to Anglo-American sea power than to Russian land power.

Stalin and Churchill agreed that all countries would be subject to the joint control of all three allies but that the degrees of interest of each of the three might be unequal and would vary from state to state. In a curiously offhand way in the course of one of their conversations they attempted to represent this idea arithmetically: the Russian interest in Rumania was put at ninety, the western at ten; the same interests in Hungary and Bulgaria were defined as eighty and twenty respectively, in Yugoslavia as fifty-fifty; Greece was rated 90 per cent a western sphere, 10 per cent Russian. This somewhat crude calculation gave offence to the Americans in particular who regarded it as a reversion to the worst practices of spheres of influence. It represented, however, certain realities, whether it was wise or not to put them down on paper. A mark of ninety or seventy-five to the one side acknowledged the impossibility of thwarting that side's wishes in that area; a fifty-fifty mark recorded uncertainty or a desire not to come to grips there for the time being. In central Europe it recognized what Stalin's armies had already ensured. In the Mediterranean it gave the British a free hand in Greece.

Poland was not in the list. Both leaders probably thought that, so far as frontiers were concerned, the Polish question had been settled at Teheran.

When Mikolajczyk, still apparently ignorant of what had passed at Teheran, flew to Moscow to try to get Stalin to accept Poland's pre-war frontiers, he failed and the Warsaw rising and its defeat by the Germans (described in a later chapter) eliminated the armed forces in Poland on which the London Poles were relying. Poland's fate had become settled, and both in Moscow and in London Mikolajczyk found himself treated as a wrecker whose inconvenient demands were imperilling the peace of Europe. He was even upbraided by Churchill in much the same terms as the Czechs had been chided by the appeasers of 1938.

The three leaders met again at Yalta on 4 February 1945. As at Teheran there was no formal agenda; each was free to raise or try to keep out whatever topic he wished to air or to pigeonhole. Since the Teheran conference Russian forces had entered Poland (and the Baltic States) and Stalin had allowed the Polish National Liberation Committee (communist and pro-communist Poles with headquarters in Lublin) to call itself a government. At Yalta Churchill tried to commit Stalin to early and free elections in Poland, but Stalin sidestepped these points by concentrating on frontiers. Poland was discussed briefly. Its frontier with the USSR was fixed and the city of Lvov was decreed to fall on the Russian side of it, but the western and northern frontiers were not agreed. Stalin, having discovered that there were two Neisses, tried to get his allies to agree to the western one but Churchill, arguing that the new Poland would have too many Germans in it, refused and Stalin had to wait for his armies to do the job. The government of Poland was to be reorganized under the direction of Molotov and the American and British Ambassadors in Moscow; it was to have an infusion of Poles from London to leaven the Lublin Committee and after the reorganization free elections were to be held with universal suffrage and a secret ballot. Thus what was left of the Polish issue was shifted out of the conference and onto a committee of three which was to meet later – in Moscow.

The conference was no more precise about the rest of liberated Europe. It adopted a general declaration promising free elections. Stalin agreed that France should have a zone of occupation in Germany and (after much argument) a place on the Allied Control Commission which was to administer Germany. He also conceded everything that Roosevelt wanted in relation to the United Nations: having asked for sixteen seats he accepted three without any fuss and even agreed to support an American demand for three seats if Roosevelt should consider that American public opinion demanded them. In separate Russo-American discussion on the Far East he sought and obtained reaffirmation of the promises already made to him together with an American undertaking to force Chiang

Kai-shek to accept them and a further American undertaking not to tell Chiang what was afoot until Stalin was ready for this disclosure. Stalin succeeded in other words in making Roosevelt his accomplice in imposing, at a moment of his own choosing, conditions on Chiang which included recognition of the independence of Outer Mongolia (and its virtual dependence on the USSR), a Russian share in the running of the Manchurian railways, and a Russian naval base in China. A vague notion of sweetening this large pill by getting Great Britain to transfer Hong Kong to China never came to anything. At first sight Stalin's gains over Roosevelt at Teheran and Yalta over the Far East are surprising, but they have to be seen against Roosevelt's growing awareness of the uselessness of Chiang as an ally against Japan and his need therefore for Russian help at a time when the coming nuclear weapon was still too mysterious to be relied upon.

With Poland on the way to the solution desired by Stalin and with these considerable Far Eastern advantages underwritten by the United States the only remaining item of real interest to Stalin was reparations. On this issue Stalin got much of what he wanted but not all. Roosevelt took comparatively little part in the reparations discussions. Although the American position was virtually the same as the British, the arguing was left to the latter. Whereas the Russians wished to impose reparations as a penalty, the Americans and British regarded them as restitution only for civilian damage. They considered that reparations should be paid only out of current German production and only after securing to the German people a minimum standard of living. They were opposed to the removal of capital assets and to the pauperization of Germany. Stalin on the other hand hoped to secure, besides regular reparations, payments spread over ten years, a German labour force to work in Russian devastated areas for ten years and something like 80 per cent of Germany's surviving heavy industrial plant. He proposed that the USSR's share of reparations payments in cash should be $10 billion and that the apportionment of the total sum should be made on the basis of the contribution which each of Germany's victims had made to the German defeat and not on the basis of its losses – a method which could have operated to give very little to countries which had been quickly defeated, however much they had suffered afterwards. Although the conference reached no final decisions on reparations Stalin succeeded in stamping the figure of $10 billion on future discussions. Most tellingly, Stalin abandoned at Yalta the policy of dismembering Germany. The simplest explanation of this change is that, confident of the departure of American troops from Europe, he thought he had a chance to dominate all Germany.

When the Yalta conference broke up, the Russian armies were on the Oder and the Danube and the western armies on the Rhine. The Grand Alliance had won the war in Europe. One of its leaders did not live to see the end: Roosevelt died on 12 April. His successor, Harry S. Truman, joined Churchill and Stalin at one more conference, at Potsdam in July. Its discussions were about war in Asia, but peace in Europe. But the shape of the new Europe was settled neither at Yalta nor at Potsdam, meetings which affected no more than the marginal details of the march of armed events. In earlier years Stalin had pleaded with Roosevelt and Churchill to open a second front in 1943, for want of which he feared defeat. Having survived and won, he benefited from the delay, for it gave him a mastery which he would not have enjoyed if the western armies had been able to begin their advances into central Europe a year earlier.

CHAPTER 17

The Clearing of North Africa

THERE is at first sight no obvious reason why a European war should be fought in Africa. The short reason why the Second World War spread from Europe to Africa was that the British and Italians were already there. The British had been the overlords of Egypt for sixty years and kept considerable military forces and military installations in Egypt. The Italians had begun to acquire an empire in East Africa at about the same time as the British occupation of Egypt in the 1880s and had extended it by taking Libya and Cyrenaica from the Turks on the eve of the First World War and by the conquest of Ethiopia in the 1930s. The campaigns of the Second World War in Africa were a consequence of these imperial positions, and the failures of the Italians in 1940–41 brought, as we have seen, the Germans into this field too. Nor was this all. France too had an empire in North Africa, exercising direct rule in Algeria which was juridically a part of France and indirect rule in the two flanking monarchies of Morocco and Tunisia which had been reduced to protectorates and where the French had steadily encroached on the authority of the native administration. This empire was preserved after the French collapse of 1940 so that the whole of North Africa from the Atlantic to the Red Sea was under European dominion throughout the Second World War. It was treated by Europeans as a campaign ground in their essentially European conflicts.

But these were not the only conflicts. North Africa was not a sand table. The military campaigns of 1940–43 were superimposed upon a further conflict between rulers and ruled, between imperial power and nationalist aspirations. The war provided nationalists with new opportunities in an old cause. The Americans, whom the war brought into the western end of this increasingly crowded scene in 1942, sympathized with the nationalists' hope of turning the evils of war to some good by accelerating the liberation of their homelands from foreign domination. To Europeans therefore Africa was one of the places where they vied among themselves, but to non-Europeans – whether African or American – one European was in this context much the same as another and none of them belonged there.

The system of government in Egypt was a three-cornered game between the British, the king and the Wafd. The British had been the real rulers of Egypt since 1882 and still had the ultimate power since, in spite of conceding formal independence after the First World War, they retained by treaty the right to station considerable forces in the country. King Faruq, the last descendant of the Albanian line of Mehemet Ali, wished to rule as well as reign but was hedged in by the British on one side and the Wafd on the other. The Wafd, founded by Zaghlul Pasha and led since 1927 by Nahas Pasha, was an upper-class nationalist movement which wanted to be rid of the British and the king. On coming of age Faruq had dismissed a Wafd government but kept the apparatus of parliament in spite of the fact that there was no political party of consequence except the Wafd; every other party was no more than the *clientela* of notabilities, incapable of giving the king enough backing against the Wafd or the British, let alone both. The Wafd, smarting under its treatment by the king, was inclined to ally itself with the British against the king and justify this policy *ex post facto* by getting true independence for Egypt by agreement with the British, but it was on delicate ground since too much friendliness between it and the British caused some nationalists to defect, Egyptians being divided among themselves about whether to get independence from the British by helping them to win the war in the expectation of later reward or by siding with their enemies.

When the war began, Egypt had at once broken off diplomatic relations with Germany and taken further pro-British steps such as handing over control of Egyptian ports and imposing a censorship, but the German victories in Europe in 1940 and the entry into the war of Italy, which had a much larger army in North Africa than the British, raised the question whether a more ambiguous policy would not be wiser. Egypt severed diplomatic relations with Italy but declared that it would not go to war unless the Italians invaded Egypt or bombed towns or military targets in it; Egyptian troops were withdrawn from the western frontiers to avoid incidents; and the Egyptian government refused to act as severely against the large Italian population (60,000) as the British authorities would have liked.

But the British were still powerful on the spot and were not willing to tolerate a government which hedged in this way. It was forced to resign and was replaced by a more pro-British one. The British also obtained other changes, including the retirement of the Chief of Staff of the Egyptian army, at the price of promising to buy considerable quantities of Egyptian cotton which they did not want. When the Italian advance into Egypt was repulsed by Wavell at the end of 1940 the pro-British policy was hailed as a success, but in April of the following year the Italians, now accompanied by the Germans, re-crossed the frontier and the champions of a stricter non-belligerence raised their voices once more. There were demands for the withdrawal of British troops and stores from Cairo and Alexandria. The Egyptian government was also beset by the economic problems created by its inability to buy and sell in foreign markets, by inflation and by the refusal of parties outside the government to join in forming a national coalition. In February 1942, following popular demonstrations in Cairo and a tiff with the king, it resigned.

The British Ambassador had already tried to persuade Faruq to retain his pro-British government. When it fell the Ambassador returned to the palace to demand the appointment of Nahas – by six o'clock that evening. The king refused. Three hours later British tanks and infantry entered the palace grounds. The king gave way. Afraid of retaining a mildly pro-British government when Rommel's star was in the ascendant, he was forced to accept Nahas, who was both more pro-British and a personal enemy, because that star was still at a distance. The drama at the palace when Faruq was forced to yield was a re-enactment of similar scenes in the past: not long after the British bombardment of Alexandria and the occupation of Egypt in 1882, Sir Evelyn Baring (later Lord Cromer) initiated the full British raj in Egypt by conveying to the Khedive Tawfiq (Faruq's uncle) the British cabinet's decision that the Khedive's government must either toe the British line or be evicted; and Tawfiq's son Abbas had been forced on his accession in 1892 to dismiss his chosen Prime Minister. Faruq in his turn was obliged to keep Nahas in office until nearly the end of the war, although Nahas was then dismissed as he was preparing to present to Great Britain his account for services rendered. After the war the Wafd blocked British attempts to re-negotiate the Anglo-Egyptian alliance with a non-Wafd government along lines which would have preserved some of Great Britain's favoured status, but its triumph was short-lived for after 1952 the more radical nationalist movement of Naguib and Nasser extinguished the Wafd as well as getting rid of both the king and the British.

By its show of power at the beginning of 1942 Great Britain had secured its base for the campaigns of the coming year. The first to move was Rommel. He entered Cyrenaica from Tripolitania in the first days of the year and so opened a series of campaigns in the North African deserts which took him almost to the Nile and the Suez Canal before the German and Italian forces were thrown back all the way to Tunisia and he himself, ill and defeated, laid down his command and returned to Germany to rest, to recover, to resume great responsibilities, to rebel against Hitler's judgement and ultimately to kill himself on Hitler's orders.

Rommel was the dominating figure in the desert war. There were exceptional commanders on the British side too – Wavell, Auchinleck, Alexander, Montgomery – but they were many and on the Axis side there was only one such figure of fame. Rommel, unlike most German officers, had been not merely an acquiescent Nazi but a keen one and his unconcealed enthusiasm for the new régime probably played some part in furthering his career in the years immediately before the war. But it was by his talents rather than his opportunities that he became famous. He was a first-class divisional commander and he proved his worth in the campaign in France in 1940 when he led an armoured division from the Meuse to the English Channel with all the personal dash and professional skill expected of the new wave of German tank commanders. When the time came for his promotion to a different type of command he was fortunate in finding, in North Africa, the one higher command of the whole war which required many of the aptitudes of the divisional commander. On the British side Wavell, Auchinleck and Alexander all at one time or another exercised tactical control of their forces to a degree unusual in a supreme commander. Rommel did so continuously and his fame as a desert general rests not so much on his exercise of his higher army command as on the flexibility, improvisation and quickness of judgement which he displayed in battle. Later in the war he was to command army groups, but never with that outstanding success which, as commander of the German Afrika Corps and the German-Italian Panzer Army, singled him out from his brother generals and field marshals.

The distinctive character of the desert war derived from the terrain as well as the personalities involved. The distances were great, the forces small. At Alamein the opposed armies deployed between them only 1,500 tanks and 1,500 aircraft, and in that battle the full tally of men on the Axis side was no more than a fifth of the German casualties in the battles in the Kursk salient the next year. The desert war was a war of movement and supply. The men on the ground were tormented by the heat and by the sandstorms which were the mechanics' worst enemies, while the men at sea, hazarding the passage in the Mediterranean, lived in constant expectation of a submarine or air torpedo. Each time the British advanced westward the Royal Navy was set a hard task in maintaining the supply route along the coast against Axis submarine and air attacks. The Axis armies were dependent on supplies from Europe which were intercepted in crippling quantities by British naval and air patrols acting on precise Ultra intelligence about the sailing of tankers and other vessels from Greek and Italian ports.

After Rommel re-entered the lists at the beginning of 1942 both sides

THE NORTH AFRICAN THEATRE

1 Mersa Breda
2 Agedabia
3 Beda Fomm
4 Msus
5 El Adem
6 Bir Hacheim
7 Fort Capuzzo
8 Halfaya Pass

~ARTHUR BANKS~

were preparing for a major effort. Churchill was urging Auchinleck to attack first. Great Britain needed a victory to offset disasters in the Far East. Singapore had fallen in February; the Japanese were occupying Burma; the War Cabinet ordered preparations for the destruction of the oil refinery at Abadan in western Iran and sent an expedition to take Madagascar before the Japanese did. The position of Great Britain again seemed critical. No American divisions could be expected to reach European or African theatres of war before the end of the year, while the Russians, although they had saved Moscow in 1941, could well lose the Caucasus in 1942. If they did, the British forces in the Middle East might have to face three ways: against Rommel advancing on Egypt, against new German armies descending from the north through Iran, and against the Japanese to the east. India too might be threatened from two sides – through Burma and through Afghanistan and Iran – in which event the Middle East command would lose its Indian divisions and all further hope of reinforcement from the Indian army. Hitler, who still regarded the Russians as mincemeat in the making, was not only dreaming of conquests of this kind but planning them. A special unit under General Helmuth Felmy (an exceptionally able army officer who had risen to the command of an Air Fleet but had been sacked after the episode of the crashed aircraft which gave away Hitler's plans for invading the Low Countries) had been formed with agreeable headquarters at Cape Sunion near Athens where it collected intelligence about the Middle East and trained Arabs for subversion. In 1942 it was moved to the Caucasus and began to take an interest in India too (although by the autumn it was back at Sunion with waning prospects).

Churchill's anxiety for an early victory in the desert was therefore not just a piece of impetuosity but a consequence of the disquieting view of the war seen as a whole from London. In the event Rommel attacked first and scored a great victory which carried him over the Egyptian border and produced the only occasion during the war on which Churchill is known to have allowed the strains to get the better of his emotions.

General Ritchie's Eighth Army was holding a series of positions stretching from Gazala, some thirty-five miles west of Tobruk, southward into the desert as far as Bir Hacheim which was garrisoned by a French force under General Pierre Koenig. These positions consisted of a number of strongpoints or boxes (not unlike the mile castles on a Roman wall) linked by minefields. They were meant to serve both as a shield for Tobruk and as a springboard for a British offensive. For this reason – and also because the longer the British line the farther would Rommel have to extend his supply lines if he planned to circumvent it – the British armour was dispersed, whereas Rommel's was concentrated for the attack which he launched on 26 May. Rommel moreover attacked in the south, whereas Ritchie had stationed the bulk of his forces at the northern or coastal end of the line. While the Eighth Army had the advantage in manpower and in tanks, the Luftwaffe was more than a match for the Desert Air Force.

Rommel's attack began with a feint in the north to distract attention from his main thrust which was made in the ensuing night by German and Italian armour in the south. Bir Hacheim held firm and Rommel fell into a dangerous trap which made his position desperate, exposed one Panzer division to air attack as it lay stranded for want of fuel, and brought a substantial part of his forces to within a few hours of surrender from thirst; but he was saved by his own resourcefulness and by the tentativeness of his opponent who failed to seize his opportunities. Bir Hacheim continued to hold out for two valuable weeks, at the end of which Koenig made good his escape with two thirds of his men. By this time the southern half of the Eighth Army's positions had been dissolved and Ritchie and Auchinleck were faced with the alternatives of a bold total withdrawal to the Egyptian frontier or a qualified withdrawal leaving a substantial force in Tobruk which, besides its considerable strategic importance, had acquired emotional and symbolic significance.

Neither British commander had intended Tobruk to stand a second siege and its defences were in no fit state to do so. There was a severe shortage of anti-tank weapons. Nevertheless Auchinleck decided to try to hold it and left a garrison of 35,000 which, misinterpreting or disregarding Ultra intelligence, he disposed ill-advisedly. Rommel attacked on 20 June. Tobruk fell to him in a day. Practically the entire garrison was taken prisoner, including one third of all South Africans on active fighting service. Rommel captured invaluable supplies, fuel, vehicles and other provisions without which he would not have been able to remain on the offensive. Churchill, who received the news at the White House in Washington, gave way under his emotions. He called the loss of Tobruk a disgrace second only to the loss of Singapore. Less than a month after launching his attack Rommel, promoted Field Marshal, entered Egypt on the heels of the Eighth Army. Cairo and Alexandria were seized with panic. Mussolini went to Africa where a white horse was waiting to carry him into the Egyptian capital.

Auchinleck took personal command of the Eighth Army in place of its defeated and dismissed commander and in a limited but nevertheless decisive duel in the first week of July, known as the First Battle of Alamein, he defeated the German and Italian forces opposing him so severely that the Axis command had to commit parachute troops (as ground troops) in order to save Rommel from having to retreat once more. Auchinleck's victory owed much to the picture of the enemy which he got from Y service intercepts and from Ultra.

The appearance on the borders of Egypt of these troops, which could more appropriately have been used in an attack on Malta, symbolized a strategic choice which the German and Italian staffs had to make in the first half of 1942. They lacked the resources to take Cairo and Malta at once. Voices were raised in favour of reducing Malta first in order to secure complete control of the supply routes through and across the Mediterranean. From the narrowness of their lucky victory in Crete the Germans had concluded that Malta could not be taken by airborne landing alone, but it might be battered and starved until ripe for capture by combined seaborne and airborne assaults: a force of 1,000 aircraft (mostly from the Russian front) was assembled at the beginning of the year under the supreme command of Field Marshal Albert Kesselring, who set up his headquarters in Rome.

Great Britain's position in the Mediterranean had been endangered by serious naval losses inflicted at the end of the previous year by U-boats in both the western and eastern basins, by minefields and by the 'human torpedoes' with which the Italians penetrated the defences of Alexandria in order to fix explosives to the hulls of warships. During the short period at the turn of the year when Rommel had been driven out of Cyrenaica five supply ships reached Malta, but with Rommel's first forward moves at the beginning of 1942 the Luftwaffe was able to reoccupy North African airfields which, together with its bases in Crete, were used to interdict the passage of east–west convoys. In February an entire convoy, attempting to make this passage, was destroyed; its last surviving ship was scuttled in desperation. In March a convoy of four vessels, attacked from the air and by the Italian surface fleet, managed to get two ships through, but in the ensuing months this attack on Malta's lifelines was redoubled by fierce air attacks on the island itself. These occurred several times every day. In the harbour repair soon ceased to keep pace with destruction. All ships which could be removed sailed away and the rest were scuttled. Without shipping and without labour – the population took to living underground during daylight – the docks became a silent testimony to the triumph of air power. The air defences were too feeble to interrupt the work of destruction. Reinforcements of Spitfires, flown in from an American aircraft carrier in April, were destroyed on their airfields before they had had time to engage the enemy. Further reinforcements in May fared better owing to the frantic efficiency of the ground crews which serviced them and got them into the air again within a few minutes of their arrival, but by the middle of May Malta was holding out with little hope of survival against the bombing and the blockade. At this point Hitler, hesitatingly, agreed to divert the Luftwaffe and give priority to the attack on Egypt which Rommel and Mussolini were urging upon him – Rommel because he wanted to attack Ritchie before Ritchie attacked him, Mussolini because he was enticed by the prospect of entering Cairo and adding Egypt to the Italian empire.

The blockade of Malta continued while Rommel fought his battles with Ritchie and Auchinleck. In June an attempt was made to run convoys simultaneously from east and west. Of the eastern convoy no ship reached the island but from the west two out of seventeen merchantmen made port. In August a further convoy of fourteen merchantmen sailed from the west. Five of its ships reached Malta; one of them, the American tanker *Ohio*, torpedoed on two successive days, arrived lashed between two destroyers. In both these operations the escort fleets suffered very heavily. The losses included the British aircraft carrier *Eagle* which went down with a squadron of Spitfires on board. Over Malta itself the air fighting became fiercer both in intensity and in temper. The chivalry of the desert war was notably absent. With the arrival of another convoy in November the situation of the defenders was eased. The siege was raised by events in Africa.

These events were the final defeat of the German-Italian Panzer Army, of which the battle of El Alamein was the centrepiece. Before that battle Churchill had drastically changed the structure of command in the Middle East.

After Auchinleck's victory in July Churchill urged a further attack to destroy the Axis forces in North Africa once and for all, thereby eliminating the possibility of a war in the Middle East on two or three fronts and setting the Eighth Army in motion to the west before the Anglo-American invasion of North-west Africa which was in preparation for the late autumn. From the purely local point of view the better strategy was to wait and then launch an attack with far better prospects of success – which was what Auchinleck preferred to do and his successors in fact did. But Auchinleck, yielding to superior orders and wider arguments, attacked again in the summer and failed. This failure confronted Churchill at a time of peculiar stress, for he was about to go to Moscow to tell Stalin that there would be no Anglo-American invasion of Europe in 1942 since the western allies had concluded that the African campaign must be finished off first. Churchill knew that an invasion of North-west Africa would be a poor substitute for an invasion of Europe in the eyes of the hard-pressed Russians, and he knew too that however sound his strategic reasoning his political good faith was bound to be distrusted by Stalin. But he had made up his mind, and had persuaded Roosevelt, that the sensible thing to do was to concentrate force in Africa before Europe and persuade Stalin that this strategic plan was conceived in the general allied interest and not in disregard of the Russian predicament. It would help him if he were able to show that success in North Africa was assured and likely to be prompt. He therefore decided to visit the African front on his way to his difficult assignment in Moscow and he arrived there in no halcyon mood.

It was clear that Auchinleck could not remain personally in command of the Eighth Army but Churchill was not satisfied that he should merely revert to his supreme command in Cairo. He had decided that Auchinleck's inability to pick the right commanders and the breakdown of morale in the Eighth Army after its defeats in the desert and the last failure in Egypt required dramatic changes, including the replacement of Auchinleck himself. He proposed to divide the cumbersome Middle East command, putting Auchinleck in charge of Iraq and Iran, and the Chief of the Imperial General Staff, General Sir Alan Brooke, in Cairo. For the Eighth Army Churchill wanted General Gott, one of its corps commanders, as opposed to General Montgomery, the choice of the CIGS. Auchinleck and Brooke both refused the proffered appointments. Churchill got his way over Gott but a few days later Gott was killed in an aircraft accident and the army command went to Montgomery after all. The higher appointments in Cairo and Baghdad went to Generals Harold Alexander and Henry Maitland Wilson. Auchinleck returned to India where he was re-appointed to his old post of Commander-in-Chief when Wavell became Viceroy in the following year. Both these men were great soldiers whose careers became tinged with sadness instead of the glory which their gifts might so easily have commanded. Many of their contemporaries felt that they were shabbily, perhaps even unjustly, treated.

At the end of August Rommel made a last and desperate bid to reach the Nile but was checked by Montgomery in two days of fighting in the battle of Alam Halfa. This was the first step in Montgomery's rise to a fame greater than that of any other British general in the Second World War. He had inherited from Auchinleck a battle plan but he introduced crucial changes into it: the victory was his.

Rommel's supplies were now down to 6,000 tons a month and only a quarter of the shipping attempting to reach him across the Mediterranean was getting through. In the air the Axis dominance had ended and the Luftwaffe and the Desert Air Force were now equals. On the ground the German and Italian tanks and motorized units were in constant danger of being halted by lack of fuel. After their failure at Alam Halfa the German-Italian armies had no choice but to await the attack of a stronger enemy who was able to pick his own time. Rommel himself was invalided home.

Montgomery had no intention of being hustled. When pressed to advance the date of his attack he threatened to resign. He was determined fully to repair the morale and the material of the Eighth Army before engaging the enemy and he had Alexander's full support. He won the confidence of his subordinates by the professional rigour of his training schemes and his (less professional) public relations encounters with all units under his command. He became personally known throughout his army and he was seen to be above all a commander who neglected no necessary detail in preparation and would know no hesitations in battle. His caution was not of the depressing kind: if he delayed giving battle, it was not because he was undecided but because he knew how he meant to win and was not to be deflected from his plan. In addition to his qualities as an excellent tactical commander and leader of men he had certain advantages denied to his predecessors. British industry was now in a state to meet the material needs of the fighting services. American Sherman tanks and Flying Fortresses added weight to the attack. Roosevelt had offered Shermans to Churchill as soon as the fall of Tobruk became known; 300 were dispatched at once; their engines, shipped separately, were lost at sea but promptly replaced. Roosevelt decided also to send complete formations of fighters and heavy and medium bombers to the Middle East and so made the coming battle the first Anglo-American engagement of the war (though not by any means the first in which American airmen had flown against the Luftwaffe). Last but not least, Ultra was giving British field commanders unparalleled assistance. Montgomery was a general who knew how to use it. The general who receives better intelligence than any of his predecessors has ever had does not cease to need generalship. He is not reduced to being an automaton. He is required to be tested in new circumstances, in which he may either fail or triumph. It is one of Montgomery's claims to fame that he was extraordinarily quick to weigh up, appreciate and act upon intelligence received, so that the campaigns which he fought provide an excellent illustration of generalship and intelligence in partnership in action.

When the (second) battle of El Alamein began on 24 October the German and Italian forces were outnumbered by about two to one in

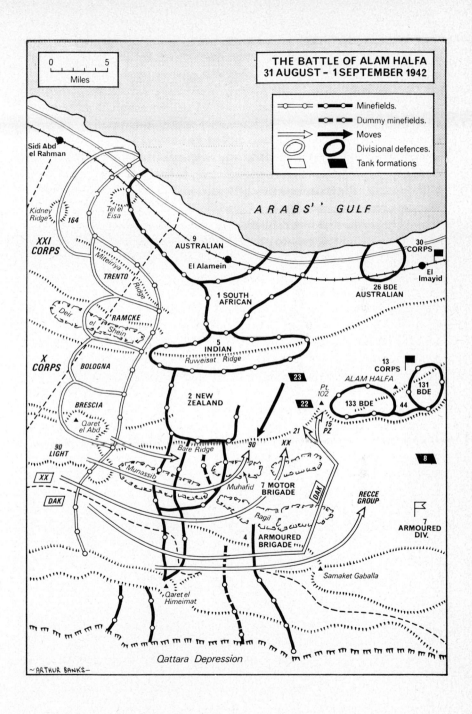

THE BATTLE OF ALAM HALFA
31 AUGUST – 1 SEPTEMBER 1942

Minefields.
Dummy minefields.
Moves
Divisional defences.
Tank formations

0   5
Miles

Sidi Abd
el Rahman

ARABS' GULF

Kidney
Ridge   164

Tel el
Eisa

XXI
CORPS

TRENTO

Miteiriya
Ridge

9
AUSTRALIAN

El Alamein

30
CORPS

El
Imayid

26 BDE
AUSTRALIAN

Deir
el
Shein

RAMCKE

1 SOUTH
AFRICAN

X
CORPS

BOLOGNA

5
INDIAN
Ruweisat Ridge

13
CORPS

ALAM HALFA

131
BDE

BRESCIA

Qaret
el Abd

2 NEW
ZEALAND

23

22

Pt.
102

133 BDE

44

90
LIGHT

Bare Ridge

Munassib

XX

90

21

15
PZ

XX

8

XX

DAK

Muhafid

7 MOTOR
BRIGADE

DAK

RECCE
GROUP

Ragil

4 ARMOURED
BRIGADE

7
ARMOURED
DIV.

Samaket Gaballa

Qaret el
Himeimat

Qattara Depression

~ARTHUR BANKS~

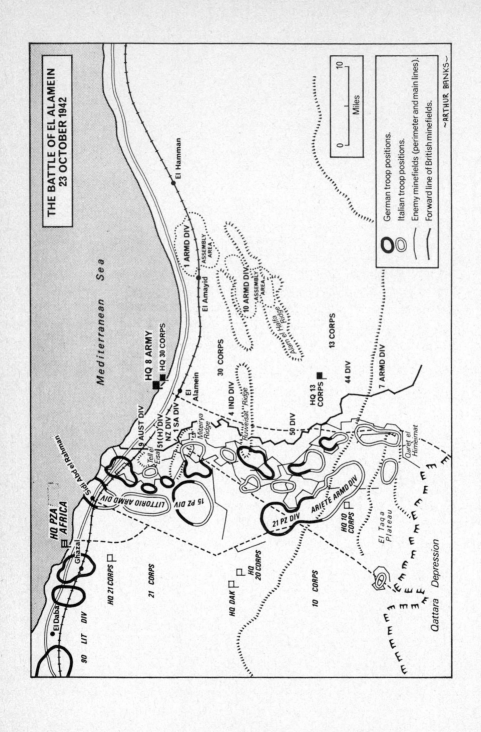

THE BATTLE OF EL ALAMEIN
23 OCTOBER 1942

Mediterranean Sea

El Hamman

1 ARMD DIV

ASSEMBLY AREA.

El Amayid

10 ARMD DIV

ASSEMBLY AREA.

Alam el Halfa Ridge

13 CORPS

HQ 8 ARMY

HQ 30 CORPS

30 CORPS

El Alamein

4 IND DIV

Ruweisat Ridge

HQ 13 CORPS

44 DIV

7 ARMD DIV

9 AUST DIV

51 (H) DIV

NZ DIV

1 SA DIV

Tell el Eisa

Miteirya Ridge

50 DIV

Qaret el Himeimat

Sidi Abd el Rahman

HQ PZA AFRICA

Ghazal

El Daba

90 LIT DIV

HQ 21 CORPS

21 CORPS

LITTORIO ARMD DIV

15 PZ DIV

21 PZ DIV

ARIETE ARMD DIV

HQ 10 CORPS

El Taqa Plateau

HQ DAK

HQ 20 CORPS

10 CORPS

Qattara Depression

Miles

10

0

German troop positions.

Italian troop positions.

Enemy minefields (perimeter and main lines).

Forward line of British minefields.

~ARTHUR BANKS~

men, guns and tanks. In the air the British advantage was narrower but the Axis unserviceability ratio was exceptionally high. Montgomery commanded an army of 195,000 men with over 1,000 tanks against a combined German-Italian army of 104,000 men with 500 tanks. The disposition of his enemies were known to Montgomery in great detail. So were their shortages of fuel and ammunition. Their supplies, particularly their supplies of petrol, were precarious and the intelligence available to Rommel (who was posted back to the front at once) about his enemy's strengths and intentions was of a completely different and inferior order to Montgomery's. The tide had turned against Rommel and the issue in the last week of October was not defeat or victory but the nature and extent of the defeat. Both issues were decided in little more than a week. Montgomery, using a brilliantly elaborate deception plan, took his enemy by surprise and scored a skilfully designed and executed victory. But in spite of fuel shortages and in spite of a final attempt to obey an order from Hitler to stand firm, Rommel got away with an army which remained a force in being for several months more. Montgomery has been criticized for not annihilating as well as defeating Rommel, but Montgomery's own resources were limited and he was determined to put an end once and for all to the see-saw character of the desert war. Fresh Anglo-American armies under Eisenhower had landed in North-west Africa three days after Rommel began his retreat and Montgomery followed Rommel westward through Cyrenaica and Tripolitania in order to join up with Eisenhower and finish off Rommel by trapping him in Tunisia between his Eighth Army and Eisenhower's First. But Hitler too put fresh forces into Africa and the first junction was not between Eighth and First Armies but between Rommel retreating from Egypt and a new German-Italian force put into Tunisia in order to hold at least a part of Africa and prevent the British and Americans from closing this theatre of war.

The Anglo-American invasion of North-west Africa (Torch) was originally proposed by Churchill to Roosevelt at their meeting in August 1941. Roosevelt at first fell in with the scheme, but he later inclined to prefer the unrealistic alternative of a landing in Europe in 1942, partly in order to succour the Russians and partly because the British retreats in the early part of 1942 had made an African venture less attractive. But Great Britain's further defeats in the summer of 1942 caused him to revert to Torch, largely in order to succour the British. On the military side, however, neither the American nor the British service chiefs (except the British Admiralty) were enthusiastic about a second front in Africa, and the American chiefs went so far as to try to force Roosevelt and Churchill into a European landing by proposing to give priority to the Pacific theatre if a European campaign were postponed.

The strategy of the invasion of North-west Africa, which was finally accepted by all concerned in July 1942, was British and naval. The idea was to clear the Mediterranean. To the British naval staff the need to do this was self-evident. The other services were slow to respond, especially the air staff which was concentrating on how to smash Germany on its own by air bombardment. The American staffs were largely unaware of what was going on until the early summer when they woke up to it and precipitately concluded that it was all a ruse to forestall an invasion of France in the near future. This was a misinterpretation, for the British regarded an early invasion of France as impossible anyway and never intended operations in northern Africa or southern Europe to supplant that ultimately essential operation. The naval strategy of clearing the Mediterranean did not necessarily imply a campaign in Italy or even Sicily, and the naval staff in fact preferred the occupation of Sardinia, Corsica and the Dodecanese as threats to the Germans in southern Europe, threats to be posed by occupying these islands without using them as springboards for more ambitious land operations. There were no long term plans or even blueprints, no conferences to take the big decisions about the future which, if books about strategy and policies are to be believed, have to be taken by identifiable groups of decision-makers. Subsequent events – the invasion of Sicily and then the landings on the Italian mainland – followed pragmatically, each born out of the success of its predecessor, links in a chain which grew but was never preconceived.

The invasion of North-west Africa was an essay in military cooperation with political complications. The political complications were provided by the existence of rival French authorities and American misreading of their comparative values. France's North African possessions had been made safe for Vichy by Weygand, the first High Commissioner appointed by Pétain, and by General Alphonse Juin who was made Commander-in-Chief in North Africa in 1941 after being released from German imprisonment. For both these generals and many of their colleagues the task of a patriotic Frenchman was to preserve French territory from Germany and also from any other aggressor – which, after the affairs at Mers-el-Kebir and Dakar in 1940, meant for the time being Great Britain. Gaullism, owing to de Gaulle's links with Great Britain, was therefore not much in evidence and was thought to be even weaker than it was, especially in the United States where Roosevelt's dislike of de Gaulle encouraged underestimates of both the man and his movement.

In April 1942 General Henri Giraud escaped from the prison in Germany where he had been kept for two years. He was sixty-three years old and his escape created a sensation which led the western allies to ascribe to him virtues which he never possessed. The Americans saw in Giraud an instrument for undoing de Gaulle. They smuggled him out of France to serve as an anti-Gaullist as much as an anti-Vichy rallying point but Giraud had neither the political sense, the intelligence nor the appeal of de Gaulle and he was a failure in the role for which the Americans cast him on the too slender grounds of being a senior general and a brave escaper. It was not long before the Americans wrote him off and reverted to their pro-Vichy stance. On the eve of the landings in Morocco and Algeria – whose precise date was not imparted to him – Giraud was taken by submarine and flying boat from France to Gibraltar and Roosevelt entered into an agreement with him placing all French forces in Morocco and Algeria under his command – apparently without properly informing Eisenhower, who believed that he had been given supreme authority over all forces, French as well as American and British. Meanwhile Eisenhower's deputy, General Mark Clark, had already been dispatched to Algeria by submarine to persuade the French political and military chiefs to collaborate with the coming invasion. Since the French forces in North-west Africa (about 120,000) outnumbered the Anglo-American assault forces, it was important to secure at least the neutrality of the French if the landings were to be successful and promptly followed by an eastward advance along the coast into Tunisia. Roosevelt was so apprehensive about the French reaction that he asked Churchill to keep the British fighting component out of action for at least a week. His policy was to win over Vichy's representatives in Algeria by keeping the British temporarily in the background and the Gaullists permanently out of the picture (a manoeuvre which de Gaulle never forgot).

Clark found that the senior French commanders, with the exception of Juin, were willing to accept Giraud as Commander-in-Chief but his limited time and limited instructions prevented him from probing the relative strengths of Vichyite and Gaullist sentiment. Had he done so, he would have found that the American partiality for Vichy did not correspond with the flow of French patriotism which Roosevelt and Churchill were seeking to re-engage in hostilities. Nor could he or anybody else on the allied side foresee that Darlan would be in Algiers on the day of the landings. This chance – Darlan had flown to Algiers to see his son, who was ill – capped all the existing confusions and misconceptions, since it gave the Americans the opportunity to do a deal with a senior representative of Vichy and so to outrage anti-Vichy feeling more completely.

The American and British armadas sailed from their home countries

ALLIED LANDINGS IN NORTH AFRICA
8 NOVEMBER 1942

100
0
Miles

Mediterranean Sea

Balearic Islands (Spain's)

Algiers

ALGERIA

Oran

SPAIN

PORTUGAL

Gibraltar

SPANISH MOROCCO

Tangier

FRENCH MOROCCO

Cape St Vincent

Mehdia
Rabat
Fedela
Casablanca

NORTHERN ATTACK

CENTRE ATTACK

Safi

Convoys pass Gibraltar from 5-7 November 1942.

Atlantic Ocean

NAVAL FORCES

from BRITAIN

ASSAULT CONVOYS

U-boat attacks 27-31 October 1942.

SOUTHERN ATTACK

ASSAULT CONVOYS from USA

CONVOY SL 125

1/11
3/10

30/10

~ARTHUR BANKS~

direct to their landing places on the Atlantic and Mediterranean coasts of Morocco and in Algeria. Their most easterly landing point was fifteen miles east of Algiers. The advantages and the hazards of landing farther east in order to make sure of Tunisia as well had been debated and the hazards were held to outweigh the advantages. Roosevelt's political representative, Robert Murphy, informed Juin of the landings on the evening before, but when they took place on 8 November the chosen date had been revealed to no other Frenchman. This precaution precluded assistance by well-disposed French commanders and occasioned some resistance, but surprise was justified in military terms and opposition was soon rendered manifestly pointless. On the 9th Darlan ordered a cease-fire. The political confusion was, however, ludicrously complete and in the course of the day almost every senior Frenchman was arrested by one or other of his compatriots. Darlan's readiness to change sides was at first suspect to the Americans and British, the more so since the depth of his anti-British feelings was well known, but he was a more useful counter than the disappointing Giraud since, unlike Giraud, he was in a position to give orders to Vichy's proconsuls – Juin, the Commander-in-Chief in North Africa, and Noguès and Estéva, the Residents-General in Morocco and Tunisia – who were showing regrettably little disposition to depart from their allegiance. The Americans – though not the British – had no basic objection to dealing with a Vichy Minister and were as willing to work with Darlan on this occasion as they – and the British – were willing to accept Badoglio as an ally against the Germans in the next year. Aware that they were giving serious offence to anti-Vichy feeling they tried to limit their commitment to Darlan but only succeeded in offending him as well. This tangle was only resolved on Christmas Eve when Darlan was assassinated by a fanatical Gaullist. The Americans fell back on Giraud who stepped temporarily into Darlan's shoes, which had already been adjudged too big for him, but Giraud had meanwhile displayed a considerable ineptitude for the role thrust upon him. At Casablanca in January de Gaulle and Giraud were persuaded to cooperate in the Committee of National Liberation established in Algiers, but Giraud gradually faded out of the picture. He later resigned from the Committee, leaving de Gaulle triumphant and resentful.

The invasion of North-west Africa introduced to the general public one of the major figures of the war, Dwight D. Eisenhower. General Eisenhower has too often been written down as a man who was lucky enough to rise to an eminence beyond his talents and there to contrive to make no disastrous mistakes. This judgement is wrong on both counts, for Eisenhower did make mistakes and yet he was bigger than this grudging estimate makes out. If he is not among the great captains, he was an exceptionally well-trained, methodical and unself-centred commander with in addition a humanity, perhaps unexciting but on occasions crucial, which enabled him to get on well with other people and also to help them get on well with each other. Few in 1943 expected him to go on from his North African command to even higher things, but his military and human competence so recommended him to his superiors that he was chosen to lead the allied invasion of France in the next year.

The German reaction to the invasion of North-west Africa was to occupy southern France and Tunisia and try to seize the French fleet at Toulon. This last endeavour failed. The fleet disregarded an order from Darlan to sail for Africa but it scuttled itself rather than fall into German hands. In Tunisia the Germans seized the opportunities presented to them by Anglo-American caution in making no landing east of Algiers. German and Italian troops occupied Tunisia and when the German commander, General Jürgen von Arnim, sent Kesselring pessimistic appreciations of the situation, Kesselring told him that he was not interested in appreciations and ordered him to hang on – an outstanding contravention of the Tolstoyan norm that supreme commanders are not the masters of events in battle. American and British forces occupied Bône in Algeria, near the Tunisian border, on 12 November and crossed the border four days later, but by the end of the year the Anglo-American attempt to secure Tunis had petered out and the Germans were pouring troops in by sea and air. In the east the Eighth Army had recovered Tobruk on 13 November and reached Benghazi on the 20th, while Rommel was retreating comparatively unmolested to join Arnim. Together their forces would outnumber their American, British and French adversaries and thwart them for six months.

Rommel had to strike before Eisenhower's and Montgomery's forces closed in on him. In mid-February he attacked the (mainly British) First Army under Eisenhower's command. Eisenhower was deceived by the excellence of his own intelligence. He knew from Ultra decodes that Kesselring in Rome had ordered Rommel to detach some of his units to Arnim for an attack in northern Tunisia. He did not know that Rommel preferred to attack further south and was prepared to disobey Kesselring rather than abandon his plans. So when Rommel attacked at the Kasserine Pass the allied command was divided, some (relying on Ultra) regarding this attack as no more than a feint in aid of Arnim; Rommel inflicted and even humiliated the American corps holding this sector. But First Army was not driven back and Rommel was obliged to disengage from his Tunisian front in order to counter the approach of Eighth Army from the east. On 6 March he attacked south-eastwards from the Mareth Line towards Medenine. Montgomery had only one corps approaching Tunisia, his second still east of Tripoli. Rommel's plan was to annihilate the forward corps and so send Montgomery's whole army reeling back once more into Cyrenaica or even Egypt and his reputation out of the history books. Rommel issued his orders but a few hours later, thanks to Ultra, they were in Montgomery's hands. Dropping all normal security precautions Montgomery drove his forces through the night with their lights full on. They arrived in time to thwart Rommel.

The battle of Medenine did not end the war in North Africa but it decided the issue. On 9 March Rommel left Africa never to return; at the end of the month Montgomery took the Mareth positions (which had been built in the thirties by the French to keep the Italians away from Tunisia); in the first days of April Eighth and First Armies joined hands; and on 12 May the Tunisian bridgehead, which the Germans and Italians had held for six months, was eliminated by a final capitulation. Almost three years after Mussolini had goaded the reluctant Graziani into action against a British Empire lying naked in the Middle East after the fall of France the last Italian and German combatants – 150,000 of them – were prisoners of war.

The end of the fighting left a more complex pattern in North-west Africa than in the territories farther east. The former Italian colonies were under British military occupation and Egypt was for the time being under British politico-military control, but in North-west Africa there were, first, French authority; secondly, the American and British military commands and their civilian representatives; and thirdly, the Sultan of Morocco and Bey of Tunis and the nationalist movements in their countries and in Algeria as well.

French authority had been unbroken, even by the collapse of 1940. Allowed by the armistice agreements with Germany and Italy to keep 120,000 troops in North Africa, the French had no difficulty in maintaining their control, particularly since nationalist leaders still at large had been picked up and put away just before the war began (the principal Moroccan leaders had been in prison since 1937). The humiliation of France was not unequivocally welcome to Arab opinion. The French empire had been a mixed experiment. On the one hand it represented the domination of one nation over another, a degradation and a denial of political rights and human values, but on the other hand it was a relationship between two cultures, a developing association which was prized so long as its fruits counterbalanced the thorns of unequal political dualism. Between the wars this balance had swung more and more the wrong way. The cultural association needed by its very nature to be an expanding one, but in France conservative views predominated, there was little awareness that the empire might be coming to a dead end and no willingness to grant more than minimal reforms. When the Popular Front produced a plan to extend the franchise and citizenship rights in Algeria – the *projet Violette*, so called after the Governor-General of Algeria – it was first blocked and then destroyed by the politically dominant and economically favoured white settlers or *colons* who threatened to disrupt the entire administration of Algeria if the plan were brought to the floor of the National Assembly. This rigidity sharpened nationalist animosities, and French governments were trapped between two increasingly hostile forces. But the nationalist movements were still weak. It took time for people at large to conclude that the nationalists might achieve more than abortive demonstrations and neither the bulk of the population nor, in Morocco and Tunisia, the sovereigns considered that conditions were ripe for a challenge to the power of France.

The defeat of France in 1940 changed this attitude only fractionally. That defeat was a shock which pained the Arab élite in spite of their quarrels with the French state. It also had unpleasant possibilities: Tunisia, for example, was immediately exposed to Italian covetousness and feared attack by land and sea. The Tunisian nationalist leader Habib Bourguiba, imprisoned at Marseilles, insisted that Tunisian nationalism must be anti-Axis. From the Vichy régime nationalists had nothing to hope for (Vichy's reaction was to apprehend any prominent nationalists still at large) and Bourguiba declared himself for de Gaulle and for the western allies. In Morocco, where General Noguès had established good relations with the Sultan after considerable disturbances in the early thirties, the Sultan had promised in 1939 to support the French war effort and the nationalists had promised not to impede it. The collapse of 1940 did not at first disturb these tolerances.

The year 1942 had profounder consequences, for in that year France suffered a second defeat when the Americans and the British landed in Morocco and Algeria without prior agreement with the French and opened fire on them. Moreover this second defeat was inflicted on France within the sight and hearing of the Arabs, it was followed by the quarrels between de Gaulle and Giraud which greatly harmed French prestige and it was accompanied by overt and covert American support for independence movements. In Tunisia, occupied by the Germans, there was the additional coincidence that a new Bey, more sympathetic to the nationalists than his predecessor, had just succeeded to the throne.

With the allied armies arrived thousands of copies of the Atlantic Charter which the Arabs had heard about and could now read for themselves. They concluded that the whole power of the invincible United States was now behind the independence movements. In Algeria Murphy, Roosevelt's political representative, encouraged nationalists to make claims designed to secure American and British pledges about the post-war government of Algeria. Algerian leaders offered their cooperation during the war in return for the immediate convening of a conference at which Algerians would draw up a new constitution for Algeria. The aims were unexceptionable but the tactics were dubious, since the French authorities were incensed by what they regarded as undercover blackmail and reacted indignantly not only against American interference but also against Algerian demands which otherwise they were not far from accepting – and went some way towards accepting once de Gaulle had established his authority over Vichy's minions and Washington's protégés.

In Morocco Roosevelt intervened personally. He had never made any secret of his detestation of imperialism in principle and his condemnation of the niggardliness of the French, British and other European empires in relation to their dependants, and during his stay at Casablanca in January 1943 he had a meeting with Sultan Mohammed V ben Yusuf, who came away from it with the belief that the United States would provide the political pressures and the economic aid needed to restore full Moroccan independence. The Sultan was already half-way inclined to make common cause with the Moroccan nationalists and his encounters with Americans encouraged him to lean still further that way. A year later the Istiqlal or Independence Party, formed by the merger in this climate of separate existing bodies, issued a declaration of independence which sought unilaterally to abrogate the treaty upon which Franco-Moroccan relations rested. It was followed by demonstrations which showed how the populace as well as the sovereign rated the French connection and France's ability to maintain it. Towards the end of the war the French arrested – but never charged or tried – nationalist leaders whom they accused of complicity in German plotting. There were more riots and Frenchmen were massacred. The French reacted with too much counter-violence and talk of too little reform. The war boosted nationalist hopes and activity and at the same time set an example of violence which was to be followed on both sides as the nationalists proceeded to their goals after the war was over.

In Tunisia the new ruler, Bey Moncef, was more than half a nationalist. He succeeded unexpectedly in 1942 and decided that his best policy was to take the leadership of the nationalist forces. Since the principal nationalist leaders were in French prisons this was not too difficult but it led to strained relations and ugly scenes with Vichy's Resident-General, Admiral Jean Pierre Estéva. Before the conflict could be resolved the Germans arrived in order to stop the Anglo-Americans from seizing Tunisia as well as Algeria and Morocco. For six uneasy months the German command and the French administration coexisted (Estéva was later condemned to life imprisonment for this collaboration), while Tunisian towns and villages were bombed in a war which Tunisians could not by any stretch of the imagination regard as their own. Some Tunisians collaborated with the Germans and some with the allies; most, including the Bey, waited as equivocally as possible.

A few weeks before the final defeat of the Germans, Bourguiba was released from prison, sent to Rome to be brainwashed with Axis seducements and then forwarded to Tunis. His policy was unchanged: independence and a treaty with France. But too many Frenchmen had come to regard him as an enemy of France and in addition Giraud, whom the allies had elevated to High Commissioner in North Africa, needlessly affronted Tunisians by deposing Moncef as soon as the Germans had been ousted. This tactless and illegal action – the Franco-Tunisian treaty gave the French government no power to appoint or depose a Bey – compromised the French at the moment when they were trying to re-establish their authority. Giraud shortly afterwards disappeared from the scene and the Gaullist régime in Algeria proposed some cautious reforms which, though they might have been acceptable before the war, no longer sufficed after the French setbacks of 1940–42. In March 1945 Bourguiba, concluding that discussions in Tunis would get nowhere, left secretly for Cairo where he established a Committee for the Liberation of the Maghrib with himself as secretary-general and the veteran Moroccan rebel Abd el-Krim as president. He did not return to Tunis for over four years.

In both Morocco and Tunisia the conflict was about the distribution of power between the French and native governments. Under the protectorate treaties the French had gradually assumed more power and more responsibilities and the nationalists were seeking to reverse the process by securing elected central and local councils with native majorities, freer access for Arabs to the upper reaches of the public services, equal pay for Arab and French employees and a strict application of the treaty provisions governing the role of French officials in the administration of the protectorates. These were questions of adjustment. What transpired during the war and immediately after it was that the adjustments would not be made. Each side calculated its position in such a way as to make it refuse to go near enough to the other side's position to effect agreement. The French calculation was a miscalculation, since in the end France had to concede complete independence and the ending of the protectorate status. The main source of this miscalculation was the blindness of pre-war and post-war French conservative governments which first failed to see the need for changes and then failed to see that changes which might have sufficed before the war did not meet the case after it. The brief Gaullist interlude of 1942–6 might have set a more generous course and so have reached the inevitable dénouement more quickly and less painfully, but it was constricted by American intervention and was impelled into an anti-Americanism which tainted its attitudes towards the nationalists, who were in turn tempted into believing that what they could not extract from France by themselves they could get by playing the American card. Gaullism, moreover, was a strange mixture of radicalism and conservatism. At Brazzaville in 1941 de Gaulle promised the Africans of France's sub-Saharan empire a bigger share in government, a wider franchise and more decentralization of public business, and in Algeria in 1943 de Gaulle and his chosen Governor, General Georges Catroux (who had been born in Algiers), showed that they appreciated the need for a new start. Yet the changes which were then proposed turned out to be disappointingly meagre and in Algeria, as in Tunis, the opportunity for an amicable and progressive re-ordering of relations passed sourly away.

On the last day of the war in Europe the inhabitants of the Algerian town of Sétif proposed to hold a procession distinct from the official one. They were given permission to do so provided no banners were displayed. The provision was ignored. Somebody started shooting. Twenty-one Frenchmen were killed. The affair developed into a revolt involving troops, air bombing and naval gunnery. Thousands more people were killed, mostly Algerians. Violence begot bestial ferocity on the one side which begot excessive reprisals and summary executions on the other. The established authorities prevailed but a number of the malcontents fled to the hills to carry on the fight. Although one war had ended in North Africa in 1943, two years later another and longer one had grown out of it, not to be ended until de Gaulle was brought back to power in 1958 to do so.

CHAPTER 18

The End of Fascism

THE allied victory in North Africa was only the half close of the Mediterranean campaign. Africa was not an end in itself but a part of a struggle for control of the Mediterranean and one way of getting back onto European soil. An invasion of Sicily was a logical sequel, for it could be argued that without Sicily and its airfields the free passage of the Mediterranean had not been unquestionably secured. At Casablanca in January 1943 Roosevelt and Churchill agreed that the forces which they had assembled in North Africa should be used to invade Sicily and so re-open the Mediterranean. They had not, however, taken any further decision. Whether Sicily, besides being a sequel to Africa, was also to be a prelude to mainland Italy was as yet unresolved, although studies were put in hand for crossing the Straits of Messina, landing in the heel of Italy as well as the toe, and taking Sardinia and Corsica. Nor was the purpose of a possible landing in Italy settled. If it led to the fall of Mussolini and the end of Italy's part in the war, the allied armies might either press northwards in a major attack into Austria or even Germany itself, or alternatively their task might be to draw German forces into Italy in order to weaken German resistance to an allied invasion of northern France. These two strategies were incompatible since the second would be best served if the allied armies made no rapid progress up the peninsula. On the whole the Americans (and Montgomery) saw Italy in this second light, whereas the British – or at least Churchill and Alexander – were intermittently seduced by the prospect of a major rather than an ancillary campaign in Italy.

The invasion of Sicily was launched on 10 July. The small island of Pantellaria had been easily captured a month earlier, but in spite of this pointer the Germans were preoccupied by a cover plan designed to make them fear a landing in Greece and wholly taken in by a piece of deception indicating an attack on Sardinia: a dead body with bogus plans was put in the sea in such a way that it would be washed up in Spain and in the justified belief that the Spanish authorities would hand the papers to the Germans. A genuine attack on Sardinia had been vetoed by Eisenhower.

Mussolini had no faith in the Sicilians. He did not dare to arm them and he had long since ordered all Sicilian-born officials to be transferred from the island to the mainland. The allies had command of the air. They landed at half a dozen points along the eastern half of the southern coast and along the east coast below Syracuse. An American plan for additional landings at Palermo and Catania was abandoned, largely at the instance of Montgomery, who had been impressed by the quality of German and Italian resistance in Tunisia and did not in any case want to see the allied forces spread too widely. The allied force, which sailed from American and British ports as well as North Africa and Egypt, consisted of a modest invasion force with very powerful naval and air cover. One hundred and sixty thousand men were put ashore in the first wave, with 600 tanks and 14,000 vehicles. They were supported by a fleet of 750 vessels and by over 4,000 aircraft. The British landings were completely unopposed and the Americans almost so, although there were 230,000 Italian and 40,000 German troops in the island. The first counter-attacks, which were directed against the Americans and almost dislodged them, were broken with the help of naval gunfire, and thereafter victory was swift. General George Patton's Third US Army, which had landed on the left flank of the combined force, reached Messina on 17 August by a round-about route which took his men swiftly across the centre of the island to the north coast and then eastward. They arrived just ahead of the British coming up by the shorter but more difficult east coast route. This was the end of an operation which, although successful, had again – as in Tunisia – been rendered costly and protracted by determined German intervention. It had also generated some blatant Anglo-American ill-will in the field. The Germans got away.

A military government was established in Sicily. In practice the island fell once more into the clutches of the Mafia. Mussolini, who understood gangsterism, had been the one ruler of Italy to get the better of the Mafia. His disappearance was the signal for its revival. *Mafiosi* from the United States, where they had been keeping their hands in, got themselves attached to the American forces because they could speak Italian and soon, partly by graft and partly from the need to fill local posts vacated by refugees, occupied most of the positions that mattered. Within a few months they were the government of Sicily. Later on, after toying briefly with Sicilian separatism, they entered into an alliance with right-wing politicians in Rome to defeat the Left and keep Sicily corrupt and miserable.

The conquest of Sicily spelt defeat for Italy but did not give the allies victory over the Germans in Italy. So far as it represented a way of defeating the Germans it left open the question whether a campaign in Italy was a worthwhile adjunct of the campaign in northern France which, everybody agreed, was to be the main blow. Italy itself, as a fighting force and as an independent sovereign state, was finished for the duration. It had undertaken a war for which it was neither equipped to fight nor willing to fight. Mussolini's Italy was hardly ready for any war in 1940, certainly not for a long one in two continents, but after attacking France and Greece it had become involved in wars in North Africa and East Africa and in the USSR. By the beginning of 1943 the Italians were not only dismayed and angered by the consequences of these gigantic miscalculations but were saying so. Strikes, beginning at the Fiat works in Turin, protested against rising prices and harsh working conditions and disclosed the workers' basic demand for peace. These strikes succeeded the defeats of the Italian armies on the Stalingrad front and were followed by the defeats in Sicily. Mussolini had already realized in 1942 that the war could only be won by negotiating a peace in the east but Hitler refused to consider such a thing. In February 1943 Mussolini in a general re-shuffle hedged his bets by demoting Ciano and Grandi, who were anti-German (and credibly rumoured to be plotting against him); he also appointed a new Army Chief of Staff who was suspected by Kesselring and Hitler of being ready to switch sides at the first opportunity. Ten days before the Sicilian landings Mussolini received Mihai Antonescu, who had come to suggest that Italy, Rumania and Hungary should all leave the war together and hoped that Mussolini would give the lead. After the Sicilian invasion he found himself compelled to fight on Italian soil with a million Italian servicemen engaged outside the country – 580,000 in the Balkans, 217,000 on the Russian front and 200,000 in France, not to mention those killed or taken prisoner in the Western Desert and Tunisia, who numbered at least 200,000 more. The defence of Italy required not only the recall of the Italian troops in the USSR (for which the landings in Sicily provided a welcome excuse) but also German reinforcements which would turn Italy into an occupied country.

Mussolini had no doubt what he ought to do but he did not dare to do it. In order to spur him on to ask for an armistice his advisers grossly exaggerated the size of the invading armies, which they represented as initially twenty-five divisions when they knew it to be eight. On 19 July Hitler and Mussolini met at Feltre, but Hitler did not allow Mussolini to get a word in and Mussolini's nerve, none too good by now even when Hitler was not around, failed him. After listening to one of Hitler's long disquisitions on the way the war was going, which included some very rude remarks about the Italians, he took refuge in silence. This failure sealed his fate.

The fascist chieftains or *gerarchi* feared for themselves and their régime. Mussolini's alliance with Hitler had proved a disaster. It had led to war, humiliation and defeat which, by 1942, were threatening the survival of Fascism. To save Fascism the alliance had to be broken. But Mussolini, who had made the alliance, was incapable of unmaking it. Moreover Italy was in no position simply to back out of the alliance unaided. It must change sides and make a new alliance in order to be rid of the old. There was no reason to think that this could not be done, although there was a question whether Mussolini himself might not have to be jettisoned in the process. The king might, if pressed by the anti-fascist members of the royal family, demand in a crisis the Duce's removal but he was very unlikely to insist on forming a government without any fascists at all. Similarly the allies would probably accept a partly fascist government. During the war they had made statements about the total overthrow of Fascism, but Churchill had also said that Mussolini was personally to blame for everything and until 1940 neither he nor Roosevelt had been notably anti-fascist. Both Great Britain and the United States had lived with Fascism for twenty years, for much of that time amicably enough.

The *gerarchi* therefore wanted a reversal of alliances, by and with Mussolini if possible, without and against him if necessary. After the Feltre meeting they knew that they must proceed the second way. On 24 July the Fascist Grand Council met for the first time since the outbreak of war. Twenty-eight men attended. Grandi proposed that the king should be restored to his post (taken from him in 1940) as Commander-in-Chief. He delivered a strong attack on Mussolini's conduct of the war. He spoke for over an hour and so impressed wavering members of the Council that when a pro-Mussolini resolution to adjourn was moved it was lost. There was a short pause during which Grandi and others moved around taking soundings. Mussolini himself seemed listless. Although only sixty, he was a sick man, his mind sluggish and his judgement gone. Upon the resumption Grandi's proposal was approved by nineteen votes to nine. It was a vote of no confidence in the Duce. It was now two o'clock in the morning. The members of the Council dispersed without any very clear notion of what their vote portended. During the morning of the 25th Mussolini worked as usual in his office. In the afternoon he went to the Villa Savoia for a private talk with the king whom he still regarded as an obedient puppet. But, if only out of self-interest, the king had become as dissatisfied with Mussolini as the fascist *gerarchi* and when Mussolini arrived the king dismissed him from the office to which he had appointed him over twenty years earlier. It is not known whether Mussolini argued in his own defence. The interview lasted only twenty minutes. As the ex-Prime Minister emerged he was politely arrested and driven away in an ambulance. He showed no fight and seemed to have no stomach for the stirring events which lay ahead.

Mussolini was succeeded as Prime Minister by Marshal Pietro Badoglio, a soldier who for twenty years had lent his prestige to the fascists in return for places and titles but had been dismissed in 1940 during the fiasco of the Italian attack on Greece. Upon succeeding Mussolini, Badoglio played an inglorious role, swearing loyalty to the Germans while negotiating with the allies. He and the king wanted to get out of the war but they did not see how to do it without turning Italy into one more German-occupied country, unless the allies could be persuaded to cut off and overwhelm the Germans. Badoglio was willing to capitulate to the allies but he wanted to make conditions: he would capitulate if the allies landed on the mainland, the farther north the better. He tried to persuade them to land at Genoa. If they would not venture so far he argued for a parachute operation to seize Rome; all the airfields round Rome were held by the one Italian division indubitably loyal to the House of Savoy, the Piedmontese Grenadiers. In addition Badoglio, while publicly professing loyalty to the German alliance, had circulated instructions for action against an assumed communist plot which he intended to put into operation by a pre-arranged code word, accompanied by the simple instruction to substitute 'Germans' where the original plan said 'communists'.

The discussions between Badoglio and the allies were protracted. They were conducted in secrecy in Lisbon and then Madrid and were complicated by the fact that the allies conceived themselves to be negotiating a surrender whereas the Italian emissaries considered that they were discussing joint action against the Germans in Italy. The Casablanca declaration had expressly committed the allies to demanding the unconditional surrender of Italy as well as Germany with the result that much time was spent in negotiating the conditions of a surrender which was none the less to be made to appear unconditional. Moreover the allies were divided about undertaking a major campaign on the mainland. They were tempted by the ease of their conquest of Sicily and by Mussolini's fall. An occupation of southern Italy would give them air bases for bombing Germany and would force Hitler to choose between abandoning Italy altogether or reinforcing it at the expense of the western front which the allies were about to attack. Naples, with its prestige and its capacious port, was a prize worth having and, unlike Rome or Genoa, was within the range of allied air cover. The Americans, in accordance with their broader strategy, had been reluctant to lodge large armies in a new Italian theatre but an attack towards Naples could be represented as no more than a variation on the operations which were in the planning stage and so half-way to being acceptable. They overcame their hesitations. The allies decided to cross from Sicily into Calabria, to land in the heel as well as the toe of

Italy and to mount a third operation to land at Salerno, thirty-five miles short of Naples. From there, in some as yet undefined way, a road to Rome would be opened.

As the first troops were crossing into Calabria the negotiations with Badoglio were finally concluded. An act of surrender was signed on 3 September. It was to be disclosed on the 8th, the day the allies landed at Salerno. Badoglio asked that publication should be delayed to enable him to redispose his forces. Eisenhower, who distrusted Badoglio, refused and had the news of the surrender broadcast on the appointed day. Badoglio was obliged to follow suit and later accused Eisenhower, incorrectly, of having promised not to invade before 19 September. The Italians were caught unprepared, the Germans immediately occupied Rome and its airfields, and a promised allied airborne coup against these airfields had to be cancelled. The king and his government fled to Brindisi. The Italian fleet, which put to sea and made for Malta, lost the battleship *Roma* – sunk by a new kind of bomb, controlled after release by radio by the pilot who dropped it. The formal Italian surrender was completed at Malta on 29 September and a month later, on 13 October, Italy declared war on Germany. Badoglio's flight from Rome to Brindisi committed Italy to civil war.

The Germans had expected an allied landing from the sea near Rome combined with a parachute operation and they proposed to withdraw all their forces south of Rome. This strategy was that of Rommel, who had been put in command in northern Italy. But Kesselring, who commanded in Rome and southwards, had other ideas. Decisive as ever, he believed that more of Italy could be held than the Lombard plain and circumstances helped him to wean Hitler away from Rommel's plan. For a time Rommel's plan prevailed and the Eighth Army was unopposed when it began to cross from Sicily into Calabria on 3 September. Montgomery proceeded sedately northward, the Germans withdrawing with equal circumspection. A separate landing at Taranto was similarly unopposed. In the early hours of 9 September the main assault on the Italian mainland was made at Salerno by an Anglo-American force of three divisions under the command of General Mark Clark which had sailed from ports in Algeria, Tunisia and Tripolitania. This landing was not unopposed. The defences, which had been manned by Italians, were in the process of being taken over by the Germans, who had just learnt of the Italian capitulation, and as they moved into their new positions they found themselves immediately in the path of the allied invasion. Their commander had no instructions covering this situation and he took it upon himself to resist. He was aware that the Eighth Army was advancing up the coast from

Messina and he planned to throw the main invading force back into the sea before the Eighth Army could arrive. He nearly succeeded. After initial successes in getting ashore the invading force was thrown onto the defensive and Clark took preliminary steps for an evacuation. But the allied units held their ground and by skilful use of parachute units Clark was able to check his antagonist, who broke off the engagement and withdrew northwards upon the approach of the Eighth Army.

While the invaders were struggling to keep their grip on the beaches at Salerno the people of Naples rose against the Germans and fought them savagely for three days, suffering terrible reprisals before the allies reached Naples on 1 October, their first staging point in a long slog to the north.

Hitler was now converted to the strategy of holding central Italy as well as the north. A new German line was formed along the Volturno thirty miles beyond Naples. The allies had added southern Italy, Sardinia and Corsica to their conquest of Sicily (but allowed the Germans to remove all their troops from Sardinia and Corsica); for anything more they would have to fight. Hopes of easy victories in Italy were becoming dampened. The allied armies moved from their landing places into the mountains and valleys where they were to spend long months toiling, fighting and sitting in the rain with the occasional respite provided by leave in towns where they could rest and revel and where – as Curzio Malaparte's *La Pelle* (*The Skin*) has most dramatically recorded – liberation became shoddily confused with corruption.

Hitler made political as well as strategic redispositions. Perhaps he had never intended to allow Mussolini to be kept in prison. He retained some respect for his fellow dictator and forerunner and he hoped that, with Mussolini as a mascot, he could re-establish a fascist régime, keep Italy true to the Axis and so protect his southern flank. After his arrest in July Mussolini had first been held for ten days on the island of Ponza in the Gulf of Gaeta and then for three weeks on the island of La Maddalena between Sardinia and Corsica where he passed the time translating Carducci into German; but in neither was he judged secure from a possible attempt at rescue. At the end of August he was moved to the Gran Sasso, where he was considered entirely safe. But two weeks later, on 12 September when the battle on the Salerno beaches was still undecided, he was kidnapped in an operation of uncommon skill and daring by the German SS officer Otto Skorzeny and flown in a small aircraft into which he barely fitted to Germany and thence to northern Italy where he was established as the head of a new government which never attained either power or dignity.

The restoration of Mussolini to the political stage and the flight of the

**THE INVASION OF ITALY
JULY 1943**

0 — 100
Miles

⟵ Allied advances.

Taken 26 April 1945

Entered May 1945

Milan

Turin

Verona

Venice

Trieste

Genoa

Bologna

Ravenna

Adriatic

Finally taken 18 May after five months.

Leghorn

GOTHIC LINE

Liberated by Free French Sept 1943.

CORSICA

ITALY

Sea

ROME

Monte Casino

GUSTAV LINE

Termoli

Sangro

Entered 4 June 1944

Anzio

Bari

SARDINIA

Beachhead 22 January– 22 May 1944

Naples

Salerno

Taranto

Mainland landings 9 September

BRITISH

Occupied by Anglo-American troops Autumn 1943.

Palermo

Messina

SICILY

Catania

Tunis

Licata

Syracuse

AMERICANS

BRITISH

Sousse

~ ARTHUR BANKS ~

king and Badoglio to Brindisi were minor episodes in the campaign joined in Italy between the western allies and Germany, but in the history of Italy they had greater significance for there were many Italians who wanted neither Mussolini nor the king and Badoglio. The appointment of Badoglio to succeed Mussolini sufficed the allies, who had no particular animus against the monarchy and were well enough suited by any government which was prepared to turn against the Germans. Churchill was by temperament a monarchist of a traditional and sentimental kind; like most conservatives he tended to think of society as a number of applecarts which must not be upset; he had not been among Mussolini's enemies until Mussolini attacked France and declared war on Great Britain, he was prepared to see some fascists in Badoglio's cabinet, he believed that Italy's choice lay between king and communism, and he feared a second E L A S in Italy if anti-fascist elements forced the pace of political and social change. But Italians wanted change, more change than was involved in a palace revolution effected by the Fascist Grand Council and the king and his entourage. If and so far as Italy in 1943 could be likened to an applecart, the apples in it were rotten. Italians were not concerned, as Churchill was, simply to undo what had happened since 1940 and chase the Germans out of Italy; they wanted to undo everything that had happened since 1922 and destroy Fascism. Anti-fascists had existed in Italy before Nazis had been heard of. To them Mussolini's dismissal was no more than a cabinet re-shuffle, an acknowledgement that his foreign policy had failed and been discarded. But they were more concerned with internal than external affairs.

The anti-fascists were the inheritors from the Risorgimento of a successful tradition of resistance and conspiracy within the country and by exiles. Both the exodus and internal resistance had begun immediately after the March on Rome, exiles and anti-fascists in Italy regarding themselves as true Italians whose mission it was to destroy Fascism in the same way as their grandfathers had been dedicated to the destruction of Austrian, Papal and Bourbon tyranny. Inside Italy anti-fascist groups formed, notably in universities. A clandestine press flourished as it had in the days of the *carbonari*. So did mural graffiti – slogans on walls played a prominent part in the struggle between fascists and anti-fascists. The Communist Party, well organized, covering the whole country and driven underground, managed to preserve some of the structure of the banned trade unions, organized strikes and other demonstrations (on May Day for example), displayed red flags and maintained active contacts with Italians and other sympathizers beyond the frontiers. Outside Italy the exiles spread over many countries from France, Switzerland and Belgium to Latin America and the United States. Many of them were comparatively humble people who were used to seeking seasonal work in other parts of Europe or who maybe had relatives more permanently settled in the New World, but they included also men who had made names for themselves in politics or the literary world. They too formed groups, issued newspapers and kept resistance alive.

In 1929 Carlo Rosselli made a dramatic escape from prison on the Lipari Islands and formed in Paris a movement called Justice and Liberty (with a paper of the same name) which brought anti-fascists of different political persuasions together and gave the anti-fascist crusade a distinctive flavour. For Rosselli and his friends it was not enough to be anti-fascist or to put the clock back to 1922. There must be a positive programme for putting the clock forward. These men not only hated Mussolini for his brutalities, especially after the murder of the socialist leader Giacomo Matteotti in 1924; they also regarded the Risorgimento as unfinished business and proclaimed once more the Mazzinian aims of democracy and a republic which had been submerged in Cavour's monarchist, bourgeois and capitalist Italy; and they added socialism to democracy and republicanism. They did not win the adherence of all anti-fascists. The more conservative of these formed a National Alliance which hoped to persuade the monarchy and the papacy to turn against Mussolini – but the Duce kept the king securely by his side and negotiated in 1929 a concordat with the Pope. The National Alliance issued pamphlets and disseminated them by getting each recipient to make six copies, of which at least two were to be sent to fascists. Its most famous exploit occurred in 1931 when the young poet Lauro De Bosis, taking off in an aircraft from the south of France, circled Rome for half an hour at dusk on an October evening and scattered 400,000 leaflets from 1,000 feet over the centre of the city before setting course for the sea, where, having run out of petrol or lost control of the aircraft which he had only just learnt to fly, he died.

Repression became severer as opposition persisted. Something like a small war developed between the fascist police and their enemies. Police agents followed the exiles abroad and this Italian civil war spilled over into foreign territory, particularly France and then Spain, where another civil war gave the anti-fascist exiles a chance to fight against Mussolini's fascist troops. In France consulates and other public buildings belonging to the Italian state were attacked. Men were killed on both sides. In 1937, on the thirteenth anniversary of Matteotti's murder, Carlo Rosselli and his brother Nello were murdered near Paris at Mussolini's bidding. When war came in 1940 the struggle, nearly twenty years old but still alive, was intensified. Mussolini now had fresh enemies and was beginning to lose some of his friends. The German alliance was unpopular; the Roman Catholic church was shifting away from Fascism. In August 1942 a conference of free Italians at Montevideo, presided over by the pre-fascist statesman Count Carlo Sforza, drew up a programme for a democratic and social republic of Italy. The next year the allied invasion of Sicily was regarded not as a conquest but as the beginning of liberation.

For thousands of Italians therefore, with all this behind them and within them, the Badoglio government was unacceptable. The government itself realized the precarious nature of its authority. It equivocated. It freed political prisoners and banned the Fascist Party, but it retained the censorship and the black-shirted fascist militia. Party politics were not resumed and all party politicians were kept out of the government. The war went on. Ordinary people were confused and then became angry. German troops began to pour in – and were resisted by Italians at three or four points along the frontier. Rome was hit by the allies from the air and suffered 1,000 casualties and the king's car was stoned when he visited the scene. Outside Italy local commanders and troops did not know whom to fight, if anybody; some of them turned against the Germans and on Cephallonia in the Ionian Islands 8,400 Italians were killed. By September when the king and Badoglio fled from the capital and Mussolini was carried off by the Germans to create a second fascist state in the north and two thirds of the country was under German occupation, the new government had disappointed the hopes and forfeited the respect of a great part of the population and was only sustained by the allies, particularly the British.

This period of uncertainty and disenchantment between July and September 1943 was followed by a second period, stretching from the events of the latter month to the German evacuation of Rome in June 1944. After its declaration of war against Germany in October 1943 the Badoglio government devoted much of its constricted energies to re-orienting the Italian army; by the end of the year regular Italian units were fighting in the Anglo-American forces, which also included French, Polish, Greek, Indian and New Zealand contingents and even Japanese from California. Allied generals were not enthusiastic about Italian help, but after Montgomery's departure the Eighth Army helped to train and equip a number of volunteer brigades which showed that Italians could fight as well as anybody when they wanted to. The Americans refused to copy the Eighth Army's example and the war ended before it got very far. Had the war gone on longer the Eighth Army would have fathered a first-class Italian army – composed chiefly of communists.

Owing to the slowness of the allied advance up Italy most Italians found themselves in German-occupied territory. They could not join Badoglio's forces even if they wanted to. The Disbanded soldiers and released prisoners-of-war – impelled by anti-German patriotism or fearful of being put to work or thrown into prison by the Germans or of being transported to forced labour in Germany – took to the hills. These men had not for the most part been anti-fascist but their defeats had caused a revulsion of feeling against Mussolini's senseless policies and a certain sympathy therefore for Mussolini's domestic enemies. These groups were at first small and basically anti-German; they were aware of the existence of other similar groups but not coordinated with them; they had no doctrine or political aims. But they grew. Where Germans were present in ordered strength and fixed positions they were obliged to coordinate their ventures in order to survive (many of them did not) and be effective. They needed the support and cooperation of the settled population and gradually became an adjunct of something quite different, the anti-fascist popular movement which had a political, as opposed to a merely anti-German, purpose and was planning a national uprising.

The term Resistance was not used in Italy during the war. (It was adopted after the war by extension from other parts of Europe.) This is indicative, because Resistance implied resistance to the occupier; the Italian movement which developed from 1943 was not primarily concerned with the occupation. It was an attempt, which ultimately failed, to make a revolution and take over the government of the country. It included republicans, socialists, communists, liberals and those left-wing Roman Catholics who looked backwards to pre-fascist Christian Populism and subsequently became a section of the Democratic Christian Party. Their common watchword was Renewal. They created a joint committee – the Committee of National Liberation (C L N) – which they regarded as the future government of Italy and, like Charles Albert of Savoy one hundred years earlier, they relied on themselves and not on foreigners: *l'Italia farà da se*. Two groups were particularly prominent: the communists with their Garibaldi brigades and the Action Party, the heir of Justice and Liberty, with similar brigades.

On the political front old parties reappeared and new ones were formed. Exiles returned. Barred from the government by the king and Churchill, they held a congress at Bari in January 1944 which demanded the immediate abdication of the king. Publicly and privately Churchill resisted them, speaking in the House of Commons against any change in the Italian government and instructing his representatives in Italy to support the king and Badoglio; but the British on the spot, more alive than Churchill to the trend of events, fostered the revival of democratic politics. Ironically the monarchy owed its reprieve not to the British but to the communists against whom Churchill was trying to protect it. The communist leader Palmiro Togliatti, returning from eighteen years in the USSR, joined in the demand for a new government but argued, on Stalin's instructions, that the fate of the monarchy should be deferred until the end of the war. The upshot was the withdrawal of the king from public life with a promise to instal his son Umberto as Lieutenant-Governor of the realm as soon as Rome was recovered. Badoglio remained Prime Minister but took representatives of six anti-fascist parties into his government. For the first time in history socialists and communists joined an Italian government.

When Rome fell the king transferred his powers to his son and Badoglio resigned. (The king still did not abdicate. He did so, belatedly, in 1946 when Umberto became king for a month. A plebiscite then abolished the monarchy by 12 million votes to 10 million.) The new Prime Minister was Ivanoe Bonomi, the penultimate pre-fascist Prime Minister and a respected figure acceptable to all anti-fascists in the short run. His government lasted until the end of the year when it was replaced by a narrower coalition, still under Bonomi. Another transient anti-fascist coalition was formed before the end of the war and lasted a few months after it. It was followed over the next twenty years by an unbroken series of Right-Centre governments. It is, however, tempting to see some consequences of the partisan movement in the post-war politics of north central Italy where much of the partisan activity took place. This part of the country has a tradition of opposition dating from at least the anti-Papalism of the Risorgimento; it has also a significant proportion of landless rural labourers. Since the war Emilia at its northern and Umbria at its southern end have given the communists their strongest base and their only popular majorities over the Christian Democrats, and between these two extremes the area, if less 'red', has still been consistently red with the exception only of a dent in Romagna where the radical but anti-communist Republican Party has been traditionally strong.

The attitude of the allies to the partisans was mixed. Churchill was in favour of guerrillas who harassed Germans. Most professional generals were hardly even that and all of them – generals, Churchill and other political leaders – were opposed to a national rising amounting to a civil war. Even in the midst of a Great War the idea of civil war was peculiarly repugnant with its moral implications of fratricidal strife and the special degree of unregulated cruelty which civil wars have evoked from early times down to the war in Spain still vivid in many minds. The allies looked with a favour which was exceptional on the national rising in Yugoslavia because it was successful and directed against their enemies and because they themselves were not there; but in Italy it was not so clear to the allies that the partisans were fighting against a common enemy and, besides, their activities might get in the way of allied military operations. The allies also, perhaps consequently, underrated the Italian effort. They were used to thinking of the Italian army as bad fighters and could hardly imagine that guerrilla forces might fight better than regular ones. Nevertheless allied aid, mainly British, was bountiful. It included 3,000 tons of supplies dropped by parachute – about half the partisans' total requirements.

After the fall of Rome partisan warfare in the countryside was intensified. So was sabotage by special action groups in towns. A series of strikes in northern cities in 1943 was capped in March 1944 by a general strike called by the C L N throughout the north. A million men and women responded and the strike lasted eight days. The Italian partisans became as numerous as any Resistance movement in Europe. By mid-1944 they numbered about 100,000 and were on their way to double or treble that strength before the war ended. Partisans killed, wounded or captured at least 50,000 Germans. Their own losses were heavy, particularly in areas where they assembled in large numbers and exposed themselves to organized German attack and also when the allied pressure was taken off the Germans and their northward advance blocked after the withdrawal of forces to France. Thirty-five thousand partisans lost their lives and another 20,000 were wounded. Another 10,000 civilians were killed in fights with the Germans or in reprisals. In addition 9,000 Italians were deported during the two years of direct German occupation, very few of whom were ever seen again.

As the winter of 1944 approached it became clear that the war would last into 1945. When General Alexander decided in November that he could undertake no further operations that year he advised the partisans too to suspend operations and go home. His message was broadcast *en clair,* so that it was received and read by German commanders who happened to be engaged at the time by substantial bodies of partisans. The partisans were infuriated by the message for many reasons. In the first place they could hardly go home without being arrested and shot. Further, they suspected that the allies wanted to deprive them of any share in the ultimate German collapse and make sure that the Germans should surrender to the Anglo-American command and not to any representatives of democratic Italy; they regarded the allied command as covert allies of the Right and knew that the popular rising with which they were preparing to end the war and inaugurate the new Italy was feared by the allies as a bloody communist revolution. They also resented the tone of the advice, which seemed to them too close to an order, and they had occasion to rue its consequences when the Germans, relieved of the necessity to bother about the allied armies, concentrated on the partisans and succeeded in killing thousands of them. Even Mussolini took heart and appeared in Milan and made a speech there.

The weather added to the stock of partisan troubles. The winter of 1944–5 was severe and the partisans suffered from it more than the German regular troops. But they were determined not to cease from their operations or to forgo their claim to be the liberators of Italy. They survived and, as the overall position of the Germans became more and more hopeless, they were able to renew the offensive in the spring. In April, when the Fifth and Eighth Armies launched their final attack, the northern cities rose; in Genoa 9,000 Germans surrendered to Italians and other great cities were captured by partisans. So was Mussolini who, politically, had survived the king after all and was trying in these last days to come to terms with the allies behind the backs of the Germans and through Cardinal Ildefonso Schuster, the Archbishop of Milan. At a meeting in the archiepiscopal palace of Milan on 25 April Mussolini learned that the Germans in Italy were negotiating with the allies behind his back and he thereupon dropped his own negotiations and set off for the Swiss border. He was captured and then recognized by partisans on 27 April and was shot the next day with his mistress Clara Petacci outside a small village. Their bodies with those of other fascists were displayed a day later upside down in front of a filling station in a square in Milan. They were suspended by meat hooks.

CHAPTER 19

Hitler's German Enemies

HITLER was hated by many Germans before the war began and, like Mussolini, he acquired fresh enemies when his wars turned to failures. There were plots against him before the war and more plots during the war. At first the conspirators aimed to displace him; later they came to believe that assassination was the only way to get rid of him. At first they were anti-Nazis of one kind or another; later they included Nazis who wanted to take his place or simply to save their own skins. The plots usually involved the army, since only the army had the organized power needed for a successful coup, but towards the end they involved also the SS which had grown into a separate and considerable armed force (the Waffen SS). Others, anti-Nazis or Nazis, might intrigue but only the leaders of the army or the SS had any hope of overthrowing Hitler's régime and taking control of the state.

Hitler's alliance with the army was crucial to his capture of power and to the prosecution of his external policies. He devoted a great deal of his political skill and his personal charm to this alliance. He was successful in the short run but even before war broke out he had become disappointed with the officer corps and distrustful of it; the build-up of the Waffen SS was a consequence of this disappointment and distrust. In its early days the Nazi Party had appealed to a number of German officers because they despised the civilian Weimar republic or were bored by it and were attracted by Hitler's promises of a better place for the army in a Nazi Germany and by Hitler's genuine personal interest in military matters. Hitler took care to moderate the radical strains in the Nazi Party which were likely to antagonize the preponderantly conservative officer corps and he traded on the political simplicity of a class which saw politics in black and white terms and was looking only for the most suitable partners with whom to fight socialism and communism. Field Marshal Werner von Blomberg, who became Minister for War when Hitler became Chancellor, had deluded himself into thinking that the Nazi Party was based on military virtues and military values and he saw no danger in letting Hitler gradually extend his influence by indoctrinating the services with Nazi propaganda. A handful of officers, notably General von Reichenau and Rommel, were openly enthusiastic about the party and its leader, although this enthusiasm began very soon to turn to disenchantment and then hostility. Others, like the Commander-in-Chief, Werner Freiherr von Fritsch, had reservations. Fritsch was appointed Commander-in-Chief by Hindenburg in 1934. He came from a civilian, not an army, background, but he had proved to be a brilliant officer. In character he was extremely reserved, inclined to self-doubt and – adopting the army tradition – non-political in the sense of not wanting to have anything to do with politics and not understanding much about it. He was not Hitler's choice for the post and he made Hitler uneasy.

Hitler's alliance with the army had been cemented in 1934 by the destruction of the SA and by the Soldiers' Oath but it was not followed by the wholehearted partnership which Hitler had hoped for. The army played along with Hitler without letting him feel that he was one of them. Hitler explained his aims and attitudes to selected groups of officers on more than one occasion and at great length, but their response was not enthusiastic. The more he made it clear to them that the army's role was to conquer *Lebensraum* in the east, the more sceptical and chilling did they become. Hitler did not understand that, like most professionals, the generals were conservative and cautious, nor did he appreciate the persistence of pro-Russian feeling inculcated by Seeckt's post-war policy of collaboration and by the respect learned on the eastern front in the First World War. By 1938, having sacrificed the SA to the army, he was finding the army an unsatisfactory tool. He decided to change its leadership and an outlook which seemed to him altogether too defensive and spiritless.

Two years earlier the SS had tried to tempt him into a plot against the army but he had refused to be drawn. Now, tempted a second time, he accepted the bait. Blomberg had just married a second wife. Hitler himself attended the wedding although the new Marschallin had been only a secretary. After the marriage the SS informed him that she had a police record as a prostitute. Hitler, who was easily shocked about some things as well as easily angered, agreed that Blomberg must go. He resigned, recommending Goering (as Commander-in-Chief of the Luftwaffe) as his successor, but Hitler dismissed the idea with the offhand remark that Goering was too lazy and abolished Blomberg's post. In its place he created a new Combined Services Staff (OKW) under General Keitel, weak in character and not particularly strong in intellect, through whom he proposed to exercise closer personal control over the services. This step was unpopular with the army.

Hitler also got rid of Fritsch. Fritsch was framed by the SS. He was accused of being a homosexual, which he was not. The SS dug out some police files concerning a certain Frisch who was. Fritsch resigned but his brother officers insisted that he should be given a trial. The case collapsed; the SS had to spirit away the now inconvenient Frisch who would have given the game away under cross-examination; and Fritsch was acquitted.

He was, however, only partially rehabilitated. In September 1939 he was wounded in the course of a patrol near Warsaw and died, apparently not unwillingly. The army was perturbed by the Blomberg episode and revolted by the Fritsch case but it did nothing beyond presenting a memorandum to Hitler against the creation of the O K W. Fritsch was succeeded by General Walther von Brauchitsch, an officer with a high professional reputation but only moderate strength of character: his wife, who nagged him, was a fervent Nazi.

By this time the officer corps as a whole had seen more of Hitler and the Nazis and come to like them much less. The army had acquiesced in and to some extent welcomed Hitler's rise to power because it was right-wing and anti-communist and looked forward to certain professional advantages from the new régime. It was also anti-semitic, though not so obscenely so as the Nazis; it wanted to be decently anti-semitic. But Nazi behaviour in power and the Nazi programme, especially Hitler's readiness to risk wars which the generals thought they could not win, disgusted and alarmed many officers who had not thought overmuch about the sort of people the Nazis were. By 1938 this was clear to all but the most determinedly blind. But it was not clear what should be done about it. The German army had no tradition of coups and did not know how to set about them. Its officers had exacting moral standards and a high sense of their duty to their country and they had come to believe that Hitler was a disaster. But they were by temperament neither political activists nor conspirators and they continued to serve Hitler while hating him. Hitler had every reason to distrust them but equally he had much reason not to fear them. They abhorred treason, particularly the graver form of treason which action against the head of state entailed. (Treason had two forms in Germany: the lesser *Landesverrat*, the betrayal of state secrets, and high treason or *Hochverrat*, involving action against an individual or a group.) Given their training and upper-class origins it is not surprising that few of them reached the conviction that treason was right; or that those who did so reached it only with extreme difficulty. They hated Hitler for being a murderer but did not want to be murderers themselves.

There were, however, exceptions and one of them was the Chief of Staff of the army, General Ludwig Beck. Beck was a quiet and industrious officer, a man with a wider culture than most of his fellows, much respected, perceptive and high-principled. He lacked, however, the talents of the successful man of action. In August 1938 he was retired by Hitler who may or may not have known that Beck was plotting against him. Beck had concluded that Hitler's foreign policies were insane and were leading to a war for which Germany was unprepared. Hitler must therefore be removed. As Chief of Staff Beck had ready access to all senior officers and he was also in touch with a number of civilians who thought like he did – including Ulrich von Hassell, an aristocrat and former Ambassador in Rome who was dismissed by Ribbentrop in 1937, and Carl Goerdeler, a former mayor of Leipzig. Admiral Wilhelm Canaris, the chief of the Armed Forces Intelligence Service (the Abwehr), Major-General Hans Oster, one of Canaris' principal subordinates, and other members of his department were also in the plot. This group tried in the summer of 1938 to get the British government to make an outspoken attack on Hitler whereupon army officers would arrest him on the grounds that he was leading his country into a suicidal war. But the British government did not speak out and Chamberlain's policies seemed to show that Hitler was running no risk of war and was far from insanely endangering Germany. Beck and his friends, appalled by Chamberlain's visit to the Führer at Berchtesgaden and conscious that German opinion after Munich was more likely to support Hitler than a group of conservative generals and diplomats, half of them retired, relapsed into impotence. This episode is characteristic. The British government believed that the foreign policies of the Beck group would not be very different from Hitler's (a judgement with some degree of truth in it) and concluded that there was therefore little to choose between it and Hitler (a wildly false conclusion). The conspirators' argument was that a British move would make all the difference, while the British response was to ask why the conspirators could not get on with the job without it. Even the more resolute army officers such as Beck looked for a first move by somebody else.

This military–civilian conservative opposition to Hitler was not the only one. There was intense and sometimes vocal opposition by students and among the clergy: many hundreds of priests, Roman Catholic and Protestant, were sent to concentration camps and killed. There was also opposition among former politicians from the middle-class world of the Weimar republic and among socialists from its dissolved trade-unions. Communist opposition was mostly of a different kind and consisted of spying for the USSR. The Rote Kapelle, a widespread, if overrated, communist network which penetrated even the Foreign Ministry in Berlin, succeeded in circulating an anti-Nazi periodical in six languages among foreign workers in Germany and later operated throughout much of occupied and neutral Europe. But the value of the information which it provided was not great, and it was destroyed in 1942 by the combined resources of the Abwehr, the SD, the Gestapo and the Chi-Stelle (the German code and cipher establishment at Potsdam).

Finally, there were groups of younger men, mostly belonging to the upper classes but radical or socialist rather than conservative and actively inspired by Christianity. They too objected to assassination on principle and toyed at first with schemes for arresting Hitler and putting him on trial. But they were more adept in conference than in conspiracy and their scruples complemented the efficiency of the secret police. Their interests were diffuse. They discussed plans for a post-war federation of European nations under an elective, revolving European presidency, as well as debating the removal or murder of Hitler. They took enormous personal risks which led many of them to the torture chamber and the scaffold. Although they shared the primary aim of the Beck group – getting rid of Hitler – they did not want the same kind of post-Nazi Germany. They distrusted Goerdeler, who was the conservatives' first choice for Chancellor but who appeared to them reactionary, incautious and over sanguine, and they proposed instead Martin Niemöller, an eminent Protestant divine and ex-naval officer who was in a concentration camp. Prominent in this set were Count Helmuth von Moltke, the pivot of the Kreisau circle, which was a small discussion and action group; Count Claus Schenk von Stauffenberg, an exuberant, widely travelled and widely read young Roman Catholic; Fabian von Schlabrendorff, a mildly conservative Prussian lawyer serving in a staff post in the army; and Adam von Trott zu Solz, a man of unusual physical and intellectual distinction, a socialist and a Christian with special links with Great Britain from his years at Oxford as a Rhodes Scholar. Trott's dilemma and fate were characteristic of his time. Deeply troubled about the right course for a patriotic and democratic Germany he decided, upon leaving Oxford, to temporize and postpone a decision between self-exile and returning to Germany to fight tyranny. After a spell as a lawyer in Germany he obtained, with the help of the chairman of the Rhodes Trustees, Lord Lothian, a semi-academic post in China. In order to secure the chance to return to Germany and enter the public service (which he ultimately did) he sent a number of reports containing anti-British judgements, but in the course of reinsuring his position on the German side he forfeited the trust of many of his British friends, who concluded that they had been duped. When therefore, after the outbreak of war, Trott tried to use his British and American connections in order to get allied support for anti-Nazi plots inside Germany he failed; so strong was the prejudice against him that even Sir Stafford Cripps, a friend who knew his true worth and had become a senior Minister in the British government, was forced by Eden (relying on reports in the Foreign Office about Trott's activities and on statements by some of his erstwhile friends) to desist from attempts to get his colleagues to take the German opposition groups seriously.

These groups were in truth relatively ineffective, although they were not, as many people in London believed, spurious, more German than anti-Nazi and so not to be trusted. Within Germany the Gestapo probably knew a great deal about their various activities but did not think it necessary to do much more than keep an eye on them, at any rate until after the attempted assassination of Hitler on 20 July 1944. In 1941 General von Witzleben, one of the more determined anti-Nazis, was dismissed from his post as Commander-in-Chief in the west on the eve of Barbarossa – possibly a precautionary move. In November 1939 two British Intelligence officers in Holland who believed that they were in touch with plotters in the German army were lured across the German border and seized. These officers, Captain S. Payne Best and Major R. H. Stevens, had been outwitted by the S D and had been having interviews with an S D officer, Walter Schellenberg, who was posing as an emissary of a group of disgruntled German officers. Schellenberg had had four meetings with Best and Stevens in Holland and had established a regular radio link with them and he was preparing to go to London to pursue his game there when he was ordered, much to his annoyance, to go instead back to Holland and kidnap Best and Stevens. On 8 November, the anniversary of the 1923 putsch, there had been a bomb incident in Munich and Hitler may have believed that this incident, although probably arranged by the Gestapo in order to enable it to spring a few traps, was a genuine attempt on his life in which British Intelligence was involved.

With the outbreak of hostilities plotting within the army became more difficult. The army officer's congenital reluctance to plot was greatly strengthened by war, which made treason peculiarly heinous, and the worse the war went – the nearer the dreaded Russians came – the more untimely did revolt seem. In addition war scattered the officers who might have concerted effective action. Brauchitsch and Beck's successor as Chief of Staff, Franz Halder, a capable but stolid Bavarian, listened to plotters, swayed this way and that, but could not bring themselves to do more than not give them away. The plotters hoped for a military reverse which would serve as a prelude to overthrowing Hitler. The Abwehr tipped off the Danes and the Dutch about the impending invasions of their countries, and others hoped that something would go wrong with the campaign in France. There were attempts to suborn senior commanders – Bock, Rundstedt, Kluge, Manstein, Guderian – who showed where their sympathies lay by not reporting these moves and showed also their own temper and perplexities by doing nothing else. Goerdeler displayed his lack of judgement by persisting in his belief that the generals could be made to act, and the Beck group discussed whether to try to rope some senior Nazis into an anti-Hitler conspiracy. Goerdeler was prepared to accept Goering as an interim Chancellor but Beck did not like the idea. At this time the group's aim was to get rid of Hitler, open negotiations with Great Britain and France and end the war. The emphasis was on the restoration of peace and Christian morality – but without the restoration of Czechoslovakia; parts of Hitler's conquests in Czechoslovakia and Poland were to be retained and the *Anschluss* was to be undisturbed.

The war made cracks in the Nazi Party. The first to show were in the troubled mind of Rudolf Hess who, on 10 May 1941, arrived in Scotland out of the blue. He had flown from Munich in a Me. 110 fitted with extra tanks and after failing to find the landing ground he was looking for had parachuted to earth and twisted his ankle. He was rescued by a farmer to whom he gave a false name and he asked to be taken to the Duke of Hamilton, whom he had met when the Olympic Games were held in Germany in 1936 and whom he knew to be commanding a Fighter Command sector in southern Scotland. Hess was, like a number of Nazi leaders from Hitler downwards, an *Auslandsdeutscher* or expatriate German. He had been born in Alexandria, where he lived until he was fourteen. As a young man of twenty he had served in the First World War and at the end of it, unemployed and somewhat feckless although anything but destitute, he ran into Hitler and was immediately enthralled. He took part in Hitler's Munich putsch and shared Hitler's cell after the fiasco, thus earning a minor part in the composition of the most celebrated prison book since Boethius and Bunyan – Hitler's *Mein Kampf*. Shortly after becoming Chancellor, Hitler nominated Hess as his deputy in the Nazi Party and in March 1939 he was declared second in line of succession to the chancellorship (Goering came first). He was therefore a very elevated Nazi, close to Hitler and intimately involved over many years in the enormities of the Nazis within Germany. He was also a hypochondriac and a devotee of astrology and his wife was a member of the miscalled Oxford Group – later renamed Moral Rearmament – founded and led by Dr Frank Buchman, who had on one occasion thanked God for Adolf Hitler.

Hess was not clever like Goebbels or devious like his party successor Martin Bormann, no heavyweight but entirely loyal to Hitler. Like too many of the senior Nazis Hess liked to try his hand at foreign policy, a pastime which provoked angry scenes with Ribbentrop (whom later he had to sit next to in the dock at Nuremberg), and in 1941 he evolved a plan for getting Great Britain to make common cause with Germany against the USSR. He tried to get in touch with Hoare in Madrid and with the Governor of Gibraltar, and after failing in these endeavours he decided to go himself to Great Britain, where he imagined there to be an alternative anti-communist and anti-Churchill government waiting to come into existence. Since he left a letter explaining his motives to Hitler it is reasonable to assume that Hitler, who flew into a rage on learning of his flight, had no foreknowledge of it, but it is not possible entirely to discount the view that Hess was the bearer of an official peace proposal. In Great Britain Hess's arrival was treated as a bizarre phenomenon and a propagandist opportunity (reduced, however, by Goebbels' promptness in giving the news of the flight before the British did) but not as a serious political event; the Russians on the other hand may have taken Hess's escapade more seriously, given their abiding fears of a western alliance (including Germany) against the USSR. Hess's position as deputy to the Führer was filled by Bormann, a protégé of Hitler who made himself indispensable by being always around, a mean-spirited man who came to be specially feared and disliked by the other party chiefs. Hess remained in detention in Great Britain until he was taken to Nuremberg at the end of the war to stand his trial on charges of complicity in murder and other crimes. There was some doubt about his sanity, but doctors in Great Britain and at Nuremberg declared him to be sane enough to stand trial (although an amnesiac) and he was sentenced to life imprisonment. The doubts about his mental state saved him from being hanged and his lingering longevity – he lived until 1987 as the sole prisoner of Spandau gaol in Berlin – gave him fame of a different sort.

More significant was the discontent of Himmler, who began to see the writing on the wall after the failure of the Russian campaigns of 1941. Goering's star had fallen with the defeat of the Luftwaffe in the Battle of Britain and the bombing of German cities, but Himmler's was rising with the wartime expansion of the Waffen SS into a considerable pretorian army. This expansion got under way in 1942 as Hitler's distrust of the regular army grew. The Waffen SS, so named in 1940, had grown out of the small but independent SS *Verfügungstruppe* which Hitler had created as a military (not a police) force as early as 1935. He had shown his affection for it by donning its uniform when he appeared before the Reichstag in 1939 to tell Germany and the world that Germany and Poland were at war and he had given it special tasks and opportunities in one campaign after another. He also gave it the best equipment, but its expansion from 1942 onwards perforce diluted its ethnic and ideological purity and even its prized standards of physical aptness and it became a mixed force which included even Slavs and Indians. Himmler, who thus found himself at the head of a personal army of eventually thirty divisions and so a power in his own right, began about 1942 to weigh the advantages of negotiating with the western powers instead of pursuing a war on two fronts which was coming to look more and more like defeat on two fronts. (Later on Himmler's doubts were greatly stiffened by the disclosures of Cicero, a German spy who, for £20,000, stole secret documents from a safe in the bedroom of the British Ambassador in Ankara. At the time of the Teheran conference these documents showed, among many other things, that Hitler's and Ribbentrop's reliance on the collapse of the East–West alliance was unfounded.)

In May 1942 the Bishop of Chichester, Dr George Bell, who happened to be in Stockholm on ecumenical business, was approached by German Christians who asked him to impress on the British government the reality of German resistance to Hitler. Their plans envisaged the overthrow of Hitler by the SS, followed by the overthrow of the SS by the army. The Bishop reported these matters to Eden at the Foreign Office but without effect. The approaches in Stockholm coincided with other feelers put out in Spain and Turkey and the British government suspected that, wittingly or unwittingly, the Bishop's Christian friends were being used by the Nazis to initiate discussions designed to lead to a compromise peace which would leave the Nazis in power in Germany and in possession of much of their ill-gotten gains – or at least designed to sow discord between the western allies and the USSR.

In January 1943 at Casablanca Roosevelt suggested and Churchill hesitantly agreed that they should declare that the only acceptable conclusion of the war was the unconditional surrender of Germany, Italy and Japan. Roosevelt got this idea from the State Department (which later became lukewarm or cooler towards it). He wanted at first to leave out Italy but it seemed simpler to include it. The phrase 'unconditional surrender', with its echoes of General Grant's ultimatum to General Buckner in Fort Donelson in 1862, sprang readily to the mind of every American but there were also more immediate reasons for adopting it: memories of the end of the First World War and of Germany's later claim that it had never really been defeated; the need of the two western leaders to find something ringing to proclaim at a moment when they could not foresee any very powerful military action against Germany for the immediate future; and their need to assure Stalin that they would negotiate no separate peace with Germany and to prevent him from doing so.

The most pressing aim of the declaration was to hold the Grand Alliance together at a time when Stalin was disappointed and angry and when both Japan and Italy were working for a separate peace between Germany and the U S S R — a policy which Ribbentrop was known to favour. In retrospect the overriding importance of this aim still cannot be gainsaid. To risk letting the alliance fall apart implied either that the western allies could win on their own or that they could find another ally. Neither during the war nor since has it been seriously argued that the western allies could defeat Germany if the German armies were released from their commitments in the east. The only alternative ally that has been suggested is the anti-Nazi Germans. But there was too little reason to suppose that Hitler was going to be overthrown by an internal revolt or that Nazism would be eliminated if Hitler were murdered. The anti-Nazi Germans were no substitute for the U S S R. Nor would a victory over the Nazis with the help of the German army cut down the disturbing power of the German state and the German threat to European stability and freedom which had been among the causes of the war.

The declaration on unconditional surrender, whatever its strategic necessities, may nonetheless have done something to consolidate German opinion and discourage Hitler's enemies at home. Although it was intended to proclaim an uncompromising opposition to Nazism, Fascism and Japanese militarism and not any intention to eliminate the German, Italian or Japanese states, still less their peoples, it inevitably acquired wider and fiercer connotation. Yet in fact the declaration did not quench German opposition to Hitler. The army plotters were becoming convinced of the necessity for Hitler's assassination rather than a coup aimed at no more than his removal from office. First in a senior staff post at army headquarters and then as Chief of Staff at Army Group Centre on the Russian front General Henning von Tresckow was working to put conspirators in key positions. He also tried to win the active support of the Commander-in Chief of the Army Group, Field Marshal von Kluge, but Kluge could not make up his mind and consequently a plan to shoot Hitler when he visited the headquarters in March 1943 had to be abandoned. Instead a bomb, secreted in a bottle of Cointreau, was put on board the aircraft carrying Hitler back from Smolensk to Germany. But the bomb failed to go off. At least five more attempts on Hitler's life were made in the latter months of 1943, all of them equally unsuccessful because the determination and daring of the conspirators were not matched by technical efficiency.

There was then a pause before the famous and nearly successful attempt on 20 July 1944, when Colonel Count Claus von Stauffenberg carried a bomb in a briefcase into the Führer's conference room in his headquarters in East Prussia, placed it beneath the table and left to fly to Berlin where

Beck, Witzleben and other officers were waiting to take over the capital and the government. But Hitler had not been killed – he was only slightly hurt and was able to show Mussolini the workings of Providence a few hours later – and the group in Berlin, who might have achieved something all the same, did nothing for the two hours during which Stauffenberg's aircraft was in the air and out of contact. On landing, Stauffenberg announced that Hitler was dead but a few telephone calls proved that he was not. The telephone lines between Berlin and East Prussia had not been cut – a vital slip on the part of the conspirators. There was confusion in Berlin, arrests and counter-arrests, with the established order quickly coming out on top. Beck shot himself. Stauffenberg and three others were executed at once. Then the shootings stopped and a longer and more comprehensive hunt began. In the east Tresckow committed suicide by walking east into no man's land. In Germany the principal result of this ill-fated scheme was the slaughter by the S D over the next six months of many fine men whom post-war Germany could ill afford to lose.

From 1938 to 1944 the conspirators against Hitler had sought outside help, especially from Great Britain, because they believed that without it they must fail. Denied it in 1938 they desisted for a while. Later, driven by a desperate patriotism, they acted without it and failed. By 1944 the worst horrors of the war had been perpetrated and, had they succeeded then, they would have done no more to it than shorten its final phase. Some uneasy questions remain. Were they right in their belief that outside help was essential? Probably they were, for they were never more than a small band attacking the centres of power of an exceptionally well-armed, well-disciplined and well-informed organization – the Nazi Party and police at the controls of the German state. Potentially the conspirators represented a powerful counterforce, for they had brains and devotion and the concurrence of some men in positions of power. But they failed to make the all-important step from conspiracy to success in action and there is something to be said for the argument that the missing additive could have been supplied by the British. This is a very serious argument, for it amounts to saying that the British missed a chance, first, of averting war and then of shortening it. To this argument there is no certain conclusion. What is certain is that the conspirators failed to impress the outside allies whom they needed. For this they were, partly and negatively, themselves to blame. They were a diverse group, at times a number of groups, and their schemes seemed imprecise and variable, their effectiveness doubtful. It was not always clear what sort of help they wanted. But there was failure on the other side too. Plotters start at a disadvantage because most governments, even governments which share their aims, are congenitally opposed to plotting. The characteristic members of a British or American government have some difficulty in making mentally common cause with conspirators of any kind and are inclined to underrate them. There was a lack of imagination, a failure to understand the drive which animated the conspirators, the counterpart of the failure of conservative ruling classes to understand Fascism.

And finally there was an aversion not only to plotters but also to Germans. Many of those caught up in the war fought it with good spirit and a clear conscience because they hated Nazism and wanted to destroy it, but anti-Nazism would never have started the war. In order for there to be a war for the destruction of Nazism there had to be a war about something else. The signal to start a war, or to accept a war challenge by an enemy, is given by governments and no government in the thirties asked itself whether it should go to war to destroy Nazism. What governments did ask themselves was whether they would have to go to war to stop Hitler – by which they meant stopping the territorial expansion of the German state. So the war, when it came, was a war against Germany. The part of Hitler's programme which provoked it was not the beliefs and practices of Nazism but the infringement of frontiers by Germany. The German conspirators against Hitler were the natural allies of anybody fighting Nazism but they were not the natural allies of a state at war with – or contemplating having to fight – Germany. The common ground between the German anti-Nazis and the enemies of the German state was not as large or as open as it seemed to those for whom the struggle was about righteousness rather than territory. In the last analysis the conspirators failed to find outside allies because, besides being anti-Nazi, they were also German. They were therefore doomed to be the bravest but the least effective of Hitler's serious enemies.

Hitler died in the end by nobody's hand but his own. From 1943 all his principal subordinates were thinking of how to end a war which could not be won. He himself was not. Once he had lost all chance of ending it on his own terms he gave little thought to ending it at all. He became obsessed with continuing it and, regardless of the true state of affairs, conducted increasingly hopeless operations by issuing nonsensical orders to armies which were shrinking to the size of divisions. His principal associates did not share his monomaniacal delusions. They tried, first by persuasion and then by conspiracy, to make peace with one part of the Grand Alliance or another. To a man like Ribbentrop who had signed the Russo-German treaty of 1939 a second essay in *Realpolitik* on these lines was tempting; he was supported by professional diplomats who had favoured such an alignment since the early 1920s and by the Japanese who tried in September 1943 (on the eve of the fall of Mussolini) and again in the spring and autumn of 1944 to end the Russo-German conflict. (But Ribbentrop later became disenchanted with the Russians and offered to arrange a conference with Stalin at which he would shoot Stalin with a specially designed fountain pen.) From the German point of view a peace or truce on the eastern front would release all Germany's forces for new victories in the west and re-open the flow of food and other materials with which the (then unravaged) USSR had supplied Germany before Barbarossa. During the winter of 1943–4 German emissaries were taking soundings in Stockholm, probably with the knowledge but not necessarily with the endorsement of Himmler, but such prospects as they might have had were eliminated by the German belief that Germany was still successful enough to lay down conditions, such as the establishment of an independent Ukraine.

But if Ribbentrop wanted to make peace with the USSR Goebbels, who neglected no opportunity to denigrate Ribbentrop, took the opposite view and developed a lively concern for the preservation of western civilization against the barbarous east – at the same time equating the Nazi with the Anglo-American view of what that civilization stood for. The invasion of Normandy strengthened the ranks of those who wanted a separate peace in the west, since they saw the impossibility of fighting on two fronts and the certainty of defeat in the east unless they surrendered in the west. The success of Overlord meant that Germany no longer had the slightest hope, without western help, of preventing the Russians from doing to Germany what the Germans had done to them. To prevent this retribution even Hitler should be discarded. Himmler, who had been fully informed about anti-Nazi plotting from 1943 at the latest but preferred not to take action, was toying with the idea of an alliance between the army and the SS for the removal of Hitler and the installation of himself as Chancellor in a new government consisting of a few Nazis and representatives of the military and the civilian oppositions to Hitler. His Waffen SS had grown to a force of a million men with the best equipment. (The other irregular army, Goering's twenty-two Luftwaffe Field Divisions, was of poor quality; its failures hastened Goering's decline.) Himmler wrongly supposed that the western allies would accept the substitution of himself for Hitler as an adequate consummation of the war in the face of the Russian menace and he entered into clandestine correspondence with the western allies through intermediaries in Sweden, Switzerland and Italy. These schemings played a minor part in the surrender of the German forces in Italy and in Hitler's barren last-minute switches of posts in the Third Reich.

Judgement on the German opposition to Hitler is not easy. Before the war, and during it, this opposition was ineffectual but it has been argued that the allies, Great Britain in particular, were partly to blame. Anti-Nazi conspirators existed in influential positions in the armed forces and the secret services and by September 1938 they had brought themselves to accept that Hitler's intention to conquer the whole of Czechoslovakia constituted a sufficient threat to German interests to warrant a coup against him and the dishonouring of their oaths of loyalty to him. A day for a putsch was fixed but one condition remained to be fulfilled. The conspirators wanted some assurance that the western powers would applaud and, if necessary, intervene. But the signal that they got was the wrong one: at Munich, Great Britain and France proclaimed in effect that they preferred to deal with Hitler and try to restrain him. This is not surprising, since governments are conditioned to deal with other governments, not with private plotters. Their appraisal of the effectiveness of the anti-Nazi activists was low, even scornful, and in looking for ways to avert war they put no faith in the hazards of a domestic German coup. What is surprising is that they found, and apparently sought, no way of encouraging the putsch without aborting the meeting at Munich in which their hopes for preserving peace principally reposed. Doing one thing with the right hand and another with the left is a common diplomatic technique. In this instance the western allies did not think it worthwhile.

After war had broken out only mutiny at high levels in the armed forces or the assassination of the Führer could have altered the course of events but the psychological and practical obstacles to either coup were formidable. There was plotting by some generals but it amounted to little more than risky talk. There were a number of assassination plans but not even Count Claus von Stauffenberg's attempt on 20 July 1944 came to anything. Again it has been argued that, particularly after the German disaster at Stalingrad, leading figures in the Abwehr made potentially fruitful overtures to the western allies who refused to take them seriously. These overtures were intended to elicit western support for a military coup against Hitler and his régime, leading to a separate peace with the west which would scupper both Nazism and a Russian victory over Germany. Alternatively it has been alleged that these approaches were not so much ignored as sabotaged within the British secret services, so that they never reached the right ears. That Admiral Canaris, General Oster and others in the Abwehr and elsewhere hated Hitler and desired a separate peace is evident enough. How far they disclosed their hopes to western contacts is less clear and what is not clear at all is how the British and American governments would have reacted if they had formally debated the conspirators' intentions. There is no evidence that they ever did so. The prevailing mood was deeply sceptical about all anti-Nazi Germans, and even had they felt it expedient – and found a way – to support such plots they were, to say the least, ambivalent about a separate peace involving the betrayal of their eastern ally. The anti-Nazi Germans wanted to save Germany, the allies to vanquish it.

CHAPTER 20

Great Britain at War

THE British experience of war between 1939 and 1945 was unique in that Great Britain was assailed and blockaded without having any of its home territory overrun and that its war effort was accompanied by changes in society and in the scope and structure of government which were presided over and directed by an established and virtually unchallenged government. In meeting their emergency the British were not able to superimpose a war economy on their existing peacetime economy, as the Americans did in the comparatively unruffled circumstances vouchsafed to them by physical inviolability and economic elbow room; nor could they, as the Russians did, fall back on the vastness of space and the rigours of autocratic rule to get the most in human labour and human endurance out of a patriotic people fighting against an enemy within the gates; nor, finally, were they left, as many continental Europeans were left, to face the present and shape a post-war future in the absence of a native government or in defiance of it.

To the question why Great Britain fought on in 1940 only an impressionistic answer can be given. It would take in an accumulation of factors, of which the most important are these. The Munich agreement of 1938 was a relief to a great many people who sensed the onset of a war which was never represented to them as a national or patriotic necessity. But Munich was also felt as a disgrace, and the sense of shame was compounded six months later when Hitler tore up the Munich agreement and completed his annexation of Czechoslovakia. That action finally revealed to the British that they had had enough of Hitler. The full story of the concentration camps was still to come but revulsion was now pressing hard against the dam of incomprehension. Moreover when war came, it came with a weird slowness, so that for nearly a year the British watched the approach of the storm; and all they saw nerved them for a fight where others had been unnerved. When prognostications of an unimaginable rain of death proved ill founded, the British found themselves spectators in a phoney, unnatural and yet humiliating war: no help was given to the Poles; no help reached the Finns, whose gallantry was at least equal to that of the Poles and more effective; Norway, a much respected country, was occupied by the Germans under the British nose. When the campaign in the west opened, the bombing of Rotterdam revived the German reputation for Hunnish atrocities in the First World War. France collapsed – a shock but in a sense also a release, since the British as a nation had no great opinion of the French and were as happy to fight, if need be, without a French ally as with one. Whereas Munich and the occupation of Prague and the growing evidence of Nazi barbarity had braced the younger generation for a fight, the bombing of Rotterdam stirred an older stratum of anti-German patriotism which, inclined also to be contemptuous of France, was undismayed by the prospect of single combat. And old and young were equally fortified by the retreat from Dunkirk which with a glorious perversity they regarded as a victory.

Something must be said too about British society. Although socially stratified to an extraordinary degree, this society was ideologically more coherent than most in Europe, less distraught by fascist or communist fissures, readier to respond unitedly to the generous humanity, the aristocratic chauvinism and the courage of a Winston Churchill. Furthermore, Great Britain was a singularly law-abiding, government-conscious and well-governed country. It was well governed not in the sense that the government was good for the people as a whole, but in the sense that government worked well within the limits set for it by the people who did the governing. Great Britain between the wars was not an agreeable place to live in. It was crowded with misery and injustice: estimates of the underfed in the worst years in the thirties go as high as twenty million. Little was done by government to help this large section of the nation and much of what was done was silly, for the governors were for the most part men of limited awareness and only moderate intelligence. Yet the temper of Great Britain did not become revolutionary. Rather did it become resigned in the face of chronic unemployment, killing poverty and the obscene slums which were among the most frightful places in which Europeans had ever been expected to live; and one of the main reasons for this resignation may be found in the fact that Great Britain had strong government. Strong government does not in this case mean repressive government but a government which never looked like breaking down or running down and which remained fully competent to perform its allotted tasks and preserve the formal framework of the nation's life. Although government was bad in the sense that it was inadequate in conception and in performance, it worked. It accepted a deplorably narrow view of its functions, but this view was traditional and excited little rebellion (except of the intellectual kind) with the result that the machinery of government did not become discredited. There was in 1940 in Great Britain neither a feeling of disintegration nor a movement to take the opportunity to alter the system of government. The British did not rebel against inequality and injustice because on the whole they did not believe in equality or expect justice. These things were too abstract or remote to be pursued or regarded as ingredients in real life: real life in Great Britain was steeply graded, material goods and opportunities were seen to be unfairly distributed, and even the law was accepted as one thing for the rich and another for the poor. But this did not mean that the British were supine. It meant that their demands were peculiar. What they did require of their rulers was freedom for themselves – the note which was struck in the seventeenth century and has dominated all others ever since in English history – and financial honesty at the top, and because they got these things in large measure Great Britain was, despite blatant social inadequacies, law-abiding. Freedom and incorruption were the secular religion of Great Britain (religion in its essential Latin sense of something that binds to-gether), and *in hoc signo* the British engaged the enemy as a united people. At Mons in 1914 desperate men had seen angels in the sky; at Dunkirk in 1940 they saw German aircraft; but what mattered on both occasions was not in the sky but in tradition.

For the British the crisis of the war came with the fall of France. This event left Great Britain alone, exposed to direct attack, committed to a vast industrial effort to re-equip its armed forces, and uncertain about its food supplies. Alongside the military problems of survival and riposte was a twofold problem of government. First, the direction of the war consisted in a series of choices. Great Britain could not simply do what it had not done earlier. Doing some things meant not doing others. Men, women and materials were needed in more places and for more purposes than they could fill and somebody had to decide which came first. Only the government could take such decisions and so the government found itself involved in a range of activities which it had not undertaken in peacetime. Secondly, the direction of the war had to command popular approval. This was to some extent assured by the very nature of the emergency and by the confidence inspired by Churchill personally, but British society was sufficiently sophisticated and emancipated to require to feel in broad terms that the conduct of the war was efficient and to see that it was fair. The military front was left by the public and also by Ministers themselves very much to Churchill and his professional advisers, but on the home front the government acknowledged the need to assume new responsibilities for an equitable distribution of the burdens of war and for post-war reforms. Churchill promised blood, toil, tears and sweat. But his government had to do more than promise what Clemenceau had called the grandeurs and miseries of war.

Social awareness and a social conscience were not a product of the Second World War. They can be glimpsed in British history in the earlier part of the century and indeed much earlier than that. In the thirties unemployment had thrust itself, with the help of the press, on public attention. Most people knew that slums existed, even if they had no idea what they were like. But the depression between the wars frightened members of the ruling class even more than it touched their consciences. They feared for their own standard of living (which they were apt to confuse with the wealth of the nation) and they were as much afraid of the poor as sorry for them. So they nailed their slogans to the mast of orthodox economics, demanded reduced expenditure even if it meant wage cuts, imposed heavy import duties to keep prices up and opposed schemes for the relief of poverty as utopian and a threat to the value of sterling which, by inverting their priorities, they regarded as more vital than finding work for the unemployed. The war, like previous wars, affected this emotional muddle in two ways. By throwing people together, whether in the armed forces or in fire-watching posts or in civilian billets or in the reception areas where urban evacuees migrated, it forced people to become rather less ignorant of each other's circumstances than they had been, or had preferred to be, before. Shock, shame and comradeship created a positive desire for reform for idealistic reasons. Secondly, by creating an emergency which required the mobilization of the whole nation, war forced government to take note of the whole nation, to make it fit for the fight in body and spirit and to cater for its basic needs. The health and morale of the entire population became, in the Second World War, a matter of the first concern in the same way as the stamina of professional armies and their loyalty to their princes had been the essence of warmaking in earlier times. Looking after the whole population, in and out of uniform, became a function of government for practical reasons. On the material side it included the provision of food, accommodation, medical services, adequate working conditions, fair wages; on the spiritual side it involved justifying the war morally (not difficult with the Nazis as enemies), making people feel that their hardships were being equitably shared and assuring them a better society when the war was over and not merely a return to things as they had been.

The relief of poverty, however poverty may be defined, had long been regarded as a proper function of government, as witness a series of acts from the Elizabethan poor law to industrial insurance. During the war government came to provide for people for other reasons too: because they were pregnant or because they were old (even if they were not necessitous) or because they were very young. Therefore the war became a stepping stone in the slow and piecemeal progress from the concept of relief to the concept of welfare. Further, attitudes to poverty itself changed too. The old poor law had been administered locally; the right to relief existed only within the parish. But many people no longer lived all their lives in the places where they were born, and the increased mobility of the population in wartime finally destroyed a basis for poor relief which had long been out of date as well as inhuman. The poor became a charge on the nation instead of a charge on the parish, and local authorities ceased to have an interest in chasing away poor people who might by tarrying acquire claims on the local budget.

The immediate need in the early summer of 1940 was to re-equip the armed forces and survive the air bombardment which was bound to come. This meant specially hard work in specially difficult conditions. Many basic pre-requisites were missing. British industry was short of equipment, notably machine tools, and of certain raw materials, notably steel, rubber and aluminium. It was also short of factory space and of statistics about factory space: neither industry itself nor government knew how much space there was or how it was being used or how it might be adapted for war. Much effort was put into new building when it could more economically have been employed in conversion. There was not a serious overall shortage of manpower but there was a shortage of some special skills. There was also a ludicrous and throttling lack of statistical information about manpower – information about how many people were doing what where, for example, how many people were employed in the building industry. The first wartime government had done little to remedy these deficiencies and the second, taking office on the day when Hitler attacked in the west, still did not know what was scarce and what was not: it assumed, for example, that there could be no shortage of coal or shipping. Its difficulties were compounded by the losses of men and material in France, by the primitive inefficiency of much of British industrial management, and by unforeseen shortages of foreign currency. Required to build and equip new factories, to replace lost weapons and design and produce new ones, to feed the population, ensure a bearable standard of living and bearable working conditions, and to import essential minima of overseas raw materials, it was forced to plan in a time of unprecedented stringencies and turmoil.

There were three principal domestic upheavals during the war. They were caused by evacuations, the blitz and the break-up of families through the direction of men into the armed forces or to industrial work away from home and the flow of women into factories, agriculture and the services. The government assumed the task of regulating these changes and mitigating their unwelcome consequences. The complex series of measures introduced for these purposes covered the provision and rationing of food and other goods, the control of manpower and the regulation of working conditions, the control of prices, the provision of new social services for all classes of the population and the preparation of social reforms for post-war Great Britain.

Because the damage which the Luftwaffe would do to London and other big cities had been greatly exaggerated, the government had prepared, among other things, a plan for moving several million people out of the main target areas. The general principles, adopted in 1938, were: the designation of evacuation, reception and neutral areas; no compulsory removal, except from special areas where national security rather than personal security so required; schoolchildren to be moved *en masse* with their teachers; and the government to take compulsory billeting powers. When war came, close on 1.75 million people were moved by train and boat under the government's scheme. They included very young children with their mothers, pregnant women, the blind and crippled, inmates of hospitals and prisons, and government departments. In addition two million people moved themselves (and over 8,000 went to the United States and Canada, one quarter of them with government aid). This migration of close on four million persons was smaller than had been expected, but the private enterprise element was larger: in some specially attractive areas official immigrants were outnumbered by eight to one. In general the arrangements at the points of departure were fair to good, the arrangements in the reception areas fair to bad. Owing partly to official parsimony and partly to the filling of prospective billets by unofficial, and usually more welcome, refugees the accommodation of the government's charges sometimes verged on the chaotic, and the refugees were made to perceive the distaste of country people for what were called, and sometimes were, urban dregs. Elsewhere their reception was all that generosity could desire. But everywhere there was a bit of a shock. Town children were not only put out by the change of scene, they were also disturbed by being separated from their families and became the more prone to obstreperousness by day and bedwetting at night. The hosts looked with horror and for the first time at children whose clothes were thin and dirty and torn and whose hair had lice in it; some of them began to feel that much was being asked of them, even if there was a war on, others that not enough had been asked of them in peacetime to remedy the social ills of slum life which had never before been brought home to them. Such encounters may be salutary but they are hardly ever easy for either side. By the end of the year a million of the evacuees had decided that they would rather go back to the cities again. The discomforts of social adjustment, and the false sense of security engendered by the phoney war, repopulated the target areas. In 1940 a second evacuation took place when, after the fall of France, 200,000 schoolchildren were moved from London and other cities and some of the more exposed coastal zones were redesignated evacuation areas, but the partial failure of the first wave of evacuation caused a number of people to opt for bombing and death.

A secondary consequence of evacuation was an enormous increase in the mobility of the population. Military service and compulsory direction of labour had the same effect, and over the whole period of the war the number of moves made from one home to another inside Great Britain exceeded the total number of the population.

The London blitz, which began on 7 September 1940 and continued for seventy-six consecutive nights with only one intermission, caused great dislocation and some discontent, which were countered by solidarity and comradeship in adversity, by the efficiency of voluntary bodies and by the active sympathy and interest of superior beings like Churchill and the king and queen. Although the weight of the attack had been so far over-estimated that the tonnage of bombs dropped on London in the whole war was less than what had been expected in the first two weeks, the damage per ton was higher and the trouble and danger caused by un-exploded bombs (5–10 per cent of the total) unforeseen. Casualties per ton on the other hand were lighter – fifteen to twenty per ton in place of the estimated fifty to seventy, a reflection not only of happily inaccurate forecasting but also of the effectiveness of precautions ranging from shel-ters in basements, gardens and subways to rescue, ambulance and hospital services. On the other hand victims often did not know what relief services existed or where they were to be found. There was much improvisation, for the homeless turned out to be a bigger problem than the dead, and the raids came by night instead of by day. Sleeping facilities had to be provided in underground railways and other public places, and rest centres – mostly provided at this stage by private effort – were initially too few, under-equipped and overcrowded. At one point in 1940 there were about 25,000 homeless people in London and, in addition to death and destruction, human beings had to contend with lack of sleep, more dirt and more broken glass than most people had thought about, the blackout, sirens (reduced on Churchill's command from a two-minute to a one-minute wail), an increase in the accident rate especially among children, queues, and a continuous strain which was not totally lifted until the war ended. Outside London air raids were less concentrated. In the attacks on cities and ports which began at Coventry on 14 November 1940, when 554 people were killed and much of the city including its cathedral destroyed, the dispersion of the effort over two dozen major targets lessened the impact on each. The renewed attack in 1942 – the so-called Baedeker raids – was a tip-and-run operation which did comparatively little damage, and the V weapons, arriving only in the summer of 1944, were too late to be a prolonged menace. Air raids killed 60,000 people, seriously injured 86,000 and slightly injured 149,000. Half these casualties occurred in London and two thirds of them while Great Britain was fighting alone.

The evacuation and the blitz were the two sides of a single coin depicting the parrying and withstanding of the enemy's attack. In this attack the family, the basic unit in British society, was buffeted in its two vital parts: the link between the spouses and the care of the children within the family group. The British family had become smaller since the First World War, more compact perhaps but also more vulnerable. It no longer had so many older children to look after the babies; the older children were fewer and not enough older. With the father away and the mother perhaps doing part-time work there was no reserve for emergencies. Older relatives and friends, who might have been expected to lend a hand, were also more likely to be out at work and when the bombing began there were soon many houses with a room or two damaged and so without the extra space for taking somebody in for a night or a week. People who had moved might not have got to know their neighbours well enough to ask for the little services of neighbourliness. Looking after a family with these traditional longstops gone became a constant worry.

The separation of the spouses was another worry. Husbands and wives do not normally want to live apart. During the war one or both of the separated spouses was often in danger. Sometimes neither knew for certain where the other was. Letters took a long time and in any case not every-body was used to conveying feelings by letter; many letters were awkward, stilted compositions which said nothing of consequence except that the writer was alive and well, or alive and recovering from something or other; they were, as Wilfred Owen wrote in the earlier war,

> . . . the sighs of men, that have no skill
> To speak of their distress . . .

Many separations began on the morrow of marriage, and many of the married were unusually young. Although the marriage rate fell during 1942–4 (it had been abnormally high in 1939–40), there was an increase in the proportion of marriages contracted by persons between twenty and twenty-four and a very notable increase in the number of persons marrying under twenty-one – nearly one third of the women who married for the first time during the war were under twenty-one. The birth rate, which fell in 1941 to its lowest recorded level, rose sharply from 1942 onward.

The number of illegitimate births rose dramatically – from 26,574 in 1940 to 64,743 in 1945; the percentage of single and widowed women bearing children rose from a pre-war average of 0.55 per cent to 1.04 per cent. Separation was one cause: the number of husbands separated from their wives by military service may have reached 2.5 million at its peak, about a quarter of a million men served overseas continuously for the full five years of war, and very many more were absent long enough to promote the conception of bastards on one side of the family or the other. Civilian husbands too were separated from their families when they were sent to work in distant factories or their offices were moved wholesale from one place to another. Although attempts were made to keep families together, it was impossible in wartime to provide the necessary accommodation. The number of foreign servicemen in Great Britain varied between a quarter and half a million and rose to 1.5 million before the invasion of Normandy. Many of them contributed to the illegitimate birth rate along with the relaxation of moral conventions occasioned by war, separation and the shortened expectation of life.

But although the number of illegitimate births rose so that something like 100,000 children were born illegitimate during the war who would otherwise have been born in wedlock, there is no evidence of an increase in extra-marital sexual intercourse and the proportion of extra-marital conceptions in fact fell. One seventh of all children born in the last year before the war had been conceived extra-maritally, and nearly 30 per cent of mothers had conceived their first child out of wedlock. During the years 1940–47 one eighth of children were so conceived. The war affected what happened after conception. Whereas before the war 70 per cent of the parents who procreated before marriage got married before the child was born, during the war they did so less and less until in 1945 only 37 per cent married in these circumstances. In sum, the rise in the number of illegitimate births in wartime betokens no change in sexual behaviour but a decline in the opportunities available to couples to regularize the status of their misconceived offspring. The result was a magnified social problem, often misinterpreted as a moral one. The percentage of unmarried mothers under twenty-five dropped during the war, although in the higher age groups it increased. The biggest increase (41 per cent) occurred among the thirty to thirty-fives.

There were more divorces. The grounds for divorce had been extended by statute in 1937 and a number of men and women found in the services advice about divorce and a cheaper way of getting one, but the increase from 10,000 petitions a year just before the war to nearly 25,000 in 1945 reflected also a general loosening of family ties. Juvenile delinquency also increased, although it still concerned only a small proportion (between 1 and 2 per cent) of the young. Cruelty to children and neglect increased. So did truancy from school. But drunkenness was halved.

The government had to take cognizance of these social trends. The armed services adopted a liberal attitude towards applications for compassionate leave or compassionate postings by anxious husbands or fathers. By the end of the war requests in these categories were being made at the rate of 200–300 a day and about half of them were being granted. At home the government established and paid for services for pregnant women, young children, old people and even, with some reluctance and a good deal of secrecy, unmarried mothers. State care for pregnant women was a new idea. Before the war local authorities had been empowered – but not, except in the case of midwives, obliged – to provide services, but where they did so the quality varied extensively, some were very bad and the death rate was shockingly high. There was little comprehensive care embracing pre-natal, midwifery and hospital services because these services often came under different authorities. The war exacerbated the problem since displaced mothers were seldom able to have their babies in billets and there was an acute shortage of maternity beds in hospitals. The government therefore established emergency maternity homes, which had high standards and a low death rate and which proved to be one of the most successful of the government's wartime incursions into the field of social welfare.

The unmarried mother remained a being apart. Practically her only recourse was to the old poor law and the workhouse; when she left the workhouse, even to go to work, she had to carry her baby with her in order to satisfy the authorities that she was not running away and abandoning it. She could get no public assistance outside the area to which she belonged owing to the rigid administration of the poor law by districts and the determination of each district to guard its territory against trouble and expense from beyond its borders; she was, for these as well as other reasons, unwelcome as an evacuee in a reception area. Apart from the workhouses there were in 1939 only four publicly assisted homes for unmarried mothers in the whole of England and Wales and further accommodation provided by voluntary organizations for 3,000–4,000 mothers per year – against a total of illegitimate births which, as already mentioned, passed 25,000 before the war began and then rose steeply. The death rate for illegitimate babies was twice the normal. The armed services assumed during the war some responsibility for the illegitimate children and so--called unmarried wives of servicemen, and the government, with a similar eye on morale, gave some niggardly assistance to those similarly situated in war industries, but for moral and financial reasons the government's scheme was run in such a hole-and-corner way that many possible beneficiaries never got to hear about it. The war dented attitudes to the livelier consequences of adultery and fornication, but not much.

The government was bolder in grasping the nettle of venereal diseases, whose incidence roughly doubled during the war. New centres for treatment were established (some existed before the war) and considerable publicity was given to the dangers, causes and cures. Some newspapers, putting prudery before health, refused to accept the government's advertisements. Doctors were given power to order patients to submit to treatment for venereal disease, as also for scabies, which, according to the Ministry of Health, was developing into a threat to the war effort. At one point the Rubber Control stopped the manufacture of contraceptives but this particular exercise of administrative discrimination in relation to a scarce commodity had to be reversed as a result of representations by interested parties – an example of the power of the consumer.

The care of children under five presented special problems since they were not evacuated with their schools like their older brothers and sisters and many of the mothers who had been expected to stay at home and mind them went out to work. The call-up of women was one of the more contested and controversial decisions of the war on the home front. It was foreshadowed early in 1941 when women were required to register on a limited scale. This step was partly a precaution and partly an appeal. It was hoped that women who had neither jobs nor household duties would go to work, but the number of such women turned out to be small and when industry, notably the aircraft industry, began to run into serious labour shortages the net was extended and the power to direct women to work was used. The lower age limit was eighteen and a half and the upper, fixed in October 1942 at forty-five and a half, was raised by steps to fifty. Women with husbands at home or children under fourteen were exempt, but they were nevertheless asked to work and 13 per cent of those with young children did so. Older women also volunteered for work. By the end of 1943 the female labour force had increased by over two million, half of whom were working voluntarily and for no pay. The consequences, during the war and afterwards, were considerable. Women undertook work which they had not done before and persisted in it after the war: the diversity of female labour was greatly increased (the main cause, together with higher taxation, of the decline in domestic service – from 5 per cent of households to 1 per cent). Women also became more accustomed to working after marriage, another change which stuck. It was discovered, to the surprise of some men, that in most jobs undertaken by women a woman was the equal of a man except when she came to be paid.

Day nurseries for very young children had first been established in 1880. They were expanded during the First World War but allowed to dwindle and in 1938 there were only 104 in existence. In addition there were nursery schools and classes, mostly in very poor districts, taking about 185,000 children, that is to say, one in ten of all children under five. There were also a number of children in workhouses. Voluntary and official bodies supported welfare centres, health visitors, medical attention and free meals. These services were cut when war began owing to a complete failure to foresee the problems which would arise when labour became scarce and even women with young children would be exhorted to go to work. Despite anxious prodding by the Ministry of Labour little was done for two years but thereafter the exigencies of the situation – and demonstrations in London and elsewhere – caused the government to pay more attention to this section of the population and before the war ended there were over 200,000 children in day nurseries or nursery schools. They were mostly run by voluntary organizations and paid for by the state. A small number of residential nurseries was also established, largely through American and Canadian generosity although the government ultimately agreed to foot the bill; they accommodated about 20,000 children. Finding premises, equipment and toys for all these establishments proved difficult; it so happened that the makers of cots had been specially unlucky in the blitz and at one point there was a shortage of rubber teats which had to be imported from the United States owing to a shortsighted prohibition on their manufacture in Great Britain; toys were made by air raid wardens waiting for raids and by prisoners, as well as being sent by sympathetic foreigners. Finding staff was also difficult and the number of mothers released for industry was not very much greater than the number of women employed to mind their babies, although it does not follow that the scheme was of minimal value since many of the child-minders could not have been usefully employed in anything except child-minding. The standards prevailing in the nurseries were high, epidemics very few and the idea of nursery schools caught on and survived the war.

In making provision for young children and pregnant mothers the government was extending to whole categories services which it had previously supplied only to the indigent, thus removing the stigma of poverty which had inhibited people from asking for what they needed. It had also to provide certain necessities for the whole population without distinction of class or category. The most important of these necessities was food.

Much of Great Britain's food came from overseas. Enemy action and shortage of shipping endangered the nation's food supply and created a corresponding need to produce more food at home. But Great Britain had very little surplus land to bring into cultivation. Therefore more food involved changes in uses of existing agricultural land and greater productivity per acre. This in turn meant more machinery, especially more tractors, and the modernization of agriculture which had been neglected during the pre-war years. Imports could be cut by increasing arable farming at the expense of livestock since feeding stuffs were largely imported. At the beginning of the Second World War Great Britain's arable acreage was smaller than it had been in 1914 by 2.75 million acres. The government therefore gave generous grants for ploughing up unploughed land and for improvements such as drainage. It also helped marginal farmers – a policy which was continued after the war. In the course of the war ploughland expanded from under 13 million acres to over 19 million and tillage from nearly 9 million to 14.5 million. The number of tractors rose from 52,000 just before the war to around 200,000 at the end. Cereal crops increased by 50 per cent and so did potatoes. Milk production was maintained but the country's population of pigs, poultry and sheep contracted sharply as imports of feeding stuffs fell from 8.75 million tons to 1.25 million. Yet the food value of this diminished animal population was considerably increased by more intelligent farming and its money value rose by 30 per cent at constant prices.

The needs of war changed both the structure of farming and even the landscape itself. In some areas small farmers retreated before the economics of a machine age until the average size of a farm was ten times what it had been. Much ploughed land did not return to pasture after the war. The Wiltshire downs, for example, which had been pasture land since neolithic times, were ploughed and have continued to be ploughed.

Local War Agricultural Committees were established to give advice (which was not always well received) on such comparatively new subjects as chemical weed control and soil analysis, to chide and if necessary evict bad farmers and to reclaim and work any derelict land that could be found. They had considerable powers and they used them. They also owned and hired out machinery. These committees consisted of unpaid local people assisted by paid officials, one of many examples of the blending of the voluntary system with the new expertise and the new concept of central direction. Although they were regarded by a conservative countryside as a regrettable and temporary necessity, their effects were salutary: output per acre was increased by 10–15 per cent, total production rose by 35 per cent with only a comparatively small increase in the labour force, neglected land was restored, finance became available and profits were made. The farmers with the most and best land did best, but all did better than before. After the war the powers of the wartime committees were perpetuated by statute (in more circumspect language) but the new committees used their powers much less.

Hardly less important than the production of food was its equitable distribution. Great Britain's wartime rationing system was almost a work of art. The simplest form of rationing is to assign to every individual a given quantity of a limited number of specified substances. This system becomes somewhat less simple when the quantities assigned vary according to categories of consumers – infants, pensioners, heavy industrial workers, diabetics, etc. Furthermore even a comparatively simple system of this kind will not work unless the authorities can ensure the continuous provision of adequate stocks of the rationed goods at all places and times, a task which was particularly difficult in Great Britain's case owing to the uncertainties of imports. But the British system was far more extensive and flexible than specific rationing of this kind. It embraced foods beyond the basic necessities and gave the consumer a certain range of choice. The system was tripartite: first, it specified precise rations of some foods, for example, butter. Secondly, it rationed meat by price instead of by quantity, so that a family might either pool its rations to buy a good joint once in a way or choose to have less good stewing meat more often. (Offal, rabbit and chickens were off ration.) Thirdly, the system imposed a general limit on purchases in a wider area – biscuits, jam, oranges, sweets were examples – within which, however, the purchaser was free to choose. This was achieved by a brilliant, if simple, device called the points system. Every individual was allotted a certain number of points, represented in his ration book by tokens of varying point-value which he could exchange for rationed foods at any time in a prescribed period. The goods which fell within this scheme were graded so that, for example, a packet of biscuits or a tin of sardines cost so many points. The gradings were altered from time to time, upwards or downwards, in accordance with the availability of stocks, and the individual's aggregate number of points in a quarter was also varied in order to increase or restrain his overall demand on rationed goods (other than specifically rationed ones). The points system introduced administrative difficulties since the consumer's freedom of choice made it impossible precisely to predict the demands which were likely to be made in a given period in different parts of the country – people in the south-west might develop a marked taste for biscuits while people in the north-east were making a run on sardines – but the flexibility in demand and consequent alleviation of the monotony of wartime diet were worth the extra effort, and the scheme as a whole was a major success for government planning as well as a triumph for fairness. The opulent could not (in theory – though appearances sometimes seemed otherwise) get unfair advantages by eating large meals in restaurants because for any meal costing more than 5s. (25p) coupons had to be surrendered. No coupons were required in works canteens but these meals were limited to a value of 5s. – and usually to baked beans and a mass-produced wartime invention called, after the Minister of Food, a Woolton pie. There was little cheating or black marketeering. Besides food, clothes and household goods were similarly rationed. Each individual had a separate book of coupons for these goods. Overall purchasing power was restricted but within this general limitation the purchaser could choose whether to buy half a dozen yards of cloth or a pair of sheets or a new dress.

Food and household goods were also cheap. The government's policy was to keep people healthy and vigorous by keeping the price of food down. Price controls were introduced in stages until by the end of 1942 they covered all goods in general demand. Special attention was paid to children, who, in this and other respects, were exceptionally well looked after during the war. They had different ration books and were provided gratis with milk, orange juice and cod liver oil (for vitamins) and meals in school. Standard – 'utility' – clothing and furniture were introduced, and utility clothing was exempted from purchase tax. These controls brought the cost of living down and, since wages were not brought down too, many people were financially better off during the war than they had been before it – a particularly grim commentary on the social outlook of pre-war governments. Average personal expenditure on food rose from 10s. 8d. (53p) to 14s. 6d. (72½p): that is to say, people continued to spend roughly between a quarter and a third of their net income on food, although by the end of the war they were buying at 14s. 6d. slightly less than they could have got for their 10s. 8d. at the beginning of the war. This stability was remarkable in view of the great increase in the cost of food. Home-produced food doubled in cost; imports, although reduced in volume (by 25 per cent), also doubled their cost. All in all the annual cost of food rose by £726 million, of which £472 million was paid directly by the consumer and £254 million was met by government subsidies. The extent of government intervention is shown by comparing this last figure with the pre-war cost of food subsidies – £72 million.

By this combination of measures – food production, rationing and price control – the government succeeded in ensuring an adequate, if monotonous, diet and an adequate, if uninspiring, supply of other basic goods. The first two years of war, with meat severely rationed and all imports of fruit discontinued, were a period of shortage but no danger to health. Civilian consumption was rather restricted by the shortage of steel, timber and aluminium, of which there was little left over for such things as kitchen utensils, furniture or sports goods. Textiles were also reduced by the transfer of labour from the textile industry to more urgent war production; part of the textile industry never recovered the labour and the markets which they lost. These were the years of the biggest cuts in civilian standards, personal expenditure on food dropping by 20 per cent during 1941, on other household goods by more than 40 per cent and on clothes by 38 per cent. There was, however, a compensating gain. The quality of what was available improved. The government imposed minimum standards on such goods as 'utility' furniture and fabrics, so that although richer people had to make do with goods inferior to what they had been used to, most people were getting a better buy than before the war. Design too, as well as the material itself and the workmanship, improved over a whole range of goods which had previously been turned out tastelessly for a public which was supposed not to care. Cheapness was no longer synonymous with shoddiness.

From 1942 life continued on a reduced plateau, which people at large accepted and the government maintained with such variations as it might introduce when supplies could be improved and the balance between military requirements and the demands of civilian morale could be adjusted. Housing began to present a bigger problem than food or goods. By the end of 1941 300,000 families were living in sub-standard houses and no fewer than 2.5 million persons in houses which had suffered bomb damage of varying degree. There was overcrowding and discontent, but the building industry was using the bulk of its depleted labour force (reduced by two thirds by July 1944) to build airfields and camps and to repair factories, railways and docks. From 1943, however, some of this labour had to be diverted to repairing domestic housing and converting large houses to accommodate more families. This work was given a high priority and in 1944 nearly 3.5 million men were engaged in repairing houses and maintaining and renewing industrial plant. They themselves created a lodging problem when they were drafted into cities in large numbers and their work was offset by the arrival of the V weapons but by the end of the war 40,000 houses were being repaired per week. Nevertheless the war left a massive housing problem which was only partially and temporarily eased by spending £150 million on 'pre-fabs'.

Although enough food of the right sort is the basis of fitness, diet is not the answer to everything. People still get sick or tired or bored. The government was therefore obliged to assume responsibility for hospital services, to intervene in the regulation of working conditions and even to provide entertainment and other resources for filling in time.

Great Britain's pre-war hospital services were an uncoordinated muddle, partially masked by the excellent and devoted work which went on in some sections of what could hardly be called a system. Hospitals included over a thousand voluntary hospitals which were unrelated to each other, many of them in shocking condition, short of equipment, antiquated and bankrupt

The War Office had its own hospitals; local authorities, of whom the independent voluntary hospitals were inherently suspicious, ran others. Apart from London and a few other rich areas there was a serious shortage of doctors and nurses. Plans had been discussed before the war for a comprehensive state hospital service but they made little headway against the rivalries of the different hospital bodies. Estimates of likely civilian casualties produced an irremediable problem: about 250,000 beds could be made available by cramping patients and staff and lowering standards of care and hygiene as against an anticipated need for 1 million to 2.8 million beds. Fortunately the problem never materialized and the government was granted the right combination of breathing space and exigency to impose (against the protests of the War Office and by overriding the independence of local authorities) a regional system in which new hospital boards, covering wide areas, allotted varying functions to hospitals of all kinds in their areas. The coming of war was an accelerator which forced a highly unsatisfactory state of affairs on the attention of government, provided an excuse for the beginnings of action and laid the basis for a new system in which the distinctions between the different kinds of hospital would be eliminated by overall state control, and a more sensible area of management – the region – would replace both the single voluntary hospital and the variety of local authorities which were often too small or too poor to do the job properly.

Hospitals clearly existed to perform a public service. In 1939 this was not true of the railways, which were generally considered to exist to make a profit. They were also unprepared for war and barely fulfilled their function in it. Before the war it was assumed that there would be no lack of carrying capacity on the railways and that they could cope with twice the amount of normal goods traffic provided the turn-around of wagons was accelerated and passenger travel drastically curtailed. But curtailing passenger facilities has psychological, not merely statistical, consequences and there were in any case no solid statistical grounds for this optimism, the main effect of which was to absolve the government from making any overall plans for war transport. The first winter of war exposed the fallacy.

The distribution of coal was held up to such an extent that a quantity had to be diverted to coastal shipping and for several weeks coal was given absolute priority on the railways in order to prevent a national outcry. This was only the foretaste of a crisis which was compounded by the strains of a population on the move, by bombing and by the closure of ports, which forced traffic away from the coastal and into the inland system. During 1940 deliveries of coal to London, to take a single example, were all but halved and the points of intersection of the main railway lines nearly quivered to a standstill; cooperation between the different railway companies was far from good. In the next two years, with less bombing and more planning, more coordination between the Ministries of Transport, Supply, Food and Mines, the institution of central control over rolling stock and road transport, and the loan of 400 locomotives from the United States and the War Department, things improved. By 1943 the government had established effective control over inland transport but it could not in wartime remedy the capital depreciation and mismanagement of the pre-war years and even as late as the penultimate winter of war about a hundred factories stopped work because they were short of coal. At this time the railways had increased by 50 per cent their capacity in terms of tons of goods carried per mile but they were also on the verge of collapse: government intervention and regulation were a salvage operation which averted disaster but could do no more.

Few things so frustrate industrial effort and fray tempers as traffic failures, and the railway failure during the war not only hampered production but also exasperated individuals who were kept waiting for trains (and buses) after long stints of overtime. Workers who had been moved some distance from their homes became specially disgruntled. Train fares were higher than corresponding bus fares with the result that trains were not used to full effect until fares were reduced and travel allowances given to the less well-paid workers. Transport was beginning to be regarded, at least in wartime, as a public service run for people and not as a commercial enterprise run for profit.

The government greatly extended its supervision of industrial life. Ernest Bevin secured the transfer of the Factory Inspectorate and the administration of the Factory Acts from the Home Office to the Ministry of Labour and expanded the whole concept of government intervention from safety in factories to welfare in industry. One of his first steps as Minister of Labour was the creation of a Factory and Welfare Division in his Department. All factories employing 250 people or more could be directed to install amenities such as canteens and to appoint welfare officers. Bevin considered that adequate transport for workers, day nurseries for their infants and the rehabilitation of the disabled all fell within the scope of government responsibility. The numbers of factory doctors and industrial nurses were increased; when the war began there were only thirty-five full-time and seventy part-time factory doctors in the whole country but by the time it ended there were 181 and 890. On the lighter side the BBC introduced 'music while you work' and outside working hours the government encouraged entertainers to make life as normal as possible. On the outbreak of war places of entertainment had been closed, but it was soon perceived that this mood was unhelpful and dance halls, cinemas, theatres and dog tracks were quickly re-opened and football matches resumed. Museums too re-opened, although their most precious possessions were removed from danger and stored in caves, country houses and other refuges.

The main tool for the regulation of the pre-war economy, in so far as it had been regulated and not left to sort itself out, was monetary – the budget. The main tool in wartime was, however, not monetary but human – the allocation of manpower. The armed services, which employed fewer than 500,000 men and women before the war, topped 5 million before it ended. If civil defence and munitions workers are added to the armed services the total number required in these occupations of first importance was 8 million in 1941 and 10 million by the middle of 1942. The civilian labour force remained roughly static but had to be considerably re-deployed. On the one hand a manpower budget was introduced. All users of manpower, military and civilian, were required to assess their future needs. These assessments were always excessive, sometimes falsified, and they always added up to a total that was not available. The reconciling of these competing claims was a cabinet matter. Secondly, in the civilian sector sweeping powers were given to the Minister of Labour and National Service (Ernest Bevin from May 1940 to July 1945) to direct labour from one occupation and one place to another and to forbid workers to leave specified kinds of employment. Bevin was at first slow to use the powers given to him because he was so short of accurate statistics that he did not know what directions he ought to give. He was also careful not to introduce compulsion until the need for it had become evident to those who were to be compelled. He himself gave much thought and personal energy to explaining the needs, thereby creating a sense of participation and comprehension without which direction of labour would have been exceedingly unpalatable. There was virtually no hostility to the idea that certain categories of persons having special manual or intellectual skills should be exempted from military service if they could make a better contribution to the war effort in some other way. The basic criterion was no longer the equal exposure of all to the dangers of the enemy's bullets but the graded contribution of each to a complicated mesh of national services. In one much debated instance Bevin directed young men away from military service not because they were specially skilful or specially clever but because a civilian service, coal getting, was desperately short of labour. At the beginning of the war, when there was unemployment in the coalfields, miners had been allowed to join the forces and the labour force had declined by 10 per cent before the government began to suspect that it might face a shortage of miners. Shortages of coal in the winter of 1940–41 were due to transport difficulties and not to supply. Coal was not rationed, but consumption was kept down by restricting the supplies allocated to coal merchants, and steps were taken to ensure that householders with storage space might not build up stocks in cellars at the expense of their less favoured neighbours. By 1942 it was clear that a serious crisis was at hand. With an ageing labour force, ailing machinery, incompetent planning or none, and a heritage of exceptionally bad labour relations the industry was unable to deliver the coal and the government created a new Ministry as a way of asserting central control. It also expedited and paid for the installation of modern machinery and decreed a national minimum wage – an important step in view of the low scale of pre-war wages in an industry noted for its insecurity and risks to health and life. In October 1943 Bevin directed that a proportion of the young men being called up for national service should be selected by lot for work in the mines instead of joining the armed forces – a direction which was popular neither with the recruits nor with the miners but which was necessitated by the decline of the industry and worked well enough to stem a further drop in the labour force and production in the mines. In the last eighteen months of war 21,800 'Bevin Boys' were directed into the mines. In 1945 175 million tons of coal were mined, 56 million less than in 1939.

Control over labour was matched by control of industrial materials (through a Production Executive established in 1942 and later expanded into a Department of State) for the purpose of keeping a just balance between production for the armed forces and production for civilian consumption and morale. By these two main instruments the government indirectly controlled British industry and sought to make the wisest allocation of the nation's resources in men and materials. Until the last year of war British industry produced 60 per cent of the munitions and weapons of war needed by British and Commonwealth forces, the United States contributing 25 per cent and the Commonwealth the remaining 15 per cent.

The manufacture and purchase of all these war materials and of essential civilian requirements had to be paid for. In financing a war a government has few options in the area of military supplies. It must buy or make all it can and pay for them by taxation and borrowing. Its choice is restricted to adjusting the balance between taxation and borrowing (when it does not have to do both to the hilt) and to spreading the burden of taxation in one way rather than another. In the area of civilian supplies, however, a government may feel less constrained. Subject to the obvious limitation of not calamitously underfeeding or overstraining its own people it may control the volume of goods supplied and their price with some regard to the financial implications. In other words it may screw down the level of privation more or less, and the less it does so – the more, that is, it eases the living and working conditions of the population – the more financial problems it creates for itself. In particular, a policy of cheap food and cheap household goods unaccompanied by wage control produces infla-tion. Great Britain did not abandon during the war the principle that wage rates ought to be fixed by bargaining and not by edict, the govern-ment accepted the principle that wages ought to be increased where they were particularly low or where productivity was boosted, and a steep rise in the cost of living early in the war produced inevitable wage claims. When these claims were met the working population had more money with which to buy cheapened goods. Wage rates were kept in check by voluntary restraint and a readiness to accept sacrifices, but nevertheless they rose substantially: between 1939 and 1945 money earnings increased overall by 81 per cent from a variety of causes, including wage increases (32 per cent) and overtime (20 per cent). Earnings rose faster than the cost of living index. (The figures were as follows. The rise in the cost of living index in 1939–41 was 26 per cent. Thereafter it rose only 3 per cent more. Since the index was an antiquated one it did not accurately reflect the real rise, which was somewhat greater. Given a pre-war base of 100, wage rates rose by the end of the war to 150, earnings to 180. The size of the civilian working population remained static.) But the gains of the working classes did not greatly disturb the economic gradation of British society. The rich and the very rich, although hard hit by direct taxation, found their com-pensations – the rich recovering after the war their ease and affluence through expense accounts and capital gains, and the middling and profes-sional classes finding, somewhat to their surprise, that they were the principal beneficiaries of new social services such as subsidized further education of which the poor were often still too poor to avail themselves. Within the working classes the average wage of the unskilled worker rose from 70 per cent to 80 per cent of the basic wage of the skilled worker.

To contain inflation and keep borrowing within manageable proportions the government relied primarily on big increases in direct taxation: income tax, which stood at 7s. 6d. (37½p) when war began, was up to 10s. (50p) less than two years later. Purchase tax was introduced in 1940 – in two grades, 16.6 per cent and 33.3 per cent. An excess profits tax, designed to forestall complaints of war profiteering, was introduced at 60 per cent in 1939 and raised in 1940 to 100 per cent. The government laid down how much profit was too much – excess meant any increase over a specified pre-war standard and this incursion into the operation of a market economy was accepted as not only inevitable but, in the circumstances, proper. But purchase tax was to a large extent a concession to popular feelings against war profiteering and economically a disincentive to production, and in 1941 the government tried to resolve this dilemma between social and fiscal policy by promising to repay 20 per cent of the tax after the war. Revenue from direct taxation was trebled. Indirect taxation rose by 160 per cent. But the government still had to borrow. Half of all national expenditure during the war (other than purchases covered by Lend-Lease and similar credits) was met by borrowing, at home or abroad. The government introduced a variety of savings certificates and defence bonds to attract the pennies and the pounds of different classes of person. The bulk of the national deficit was met by home borrowing.

The country's external debt rose by £3,500 million and a quarter of its overseas assets were sold. The United States government supplied Great Britain with materials to the value of $27,025 million under the terms of Lend-Lease (the pound sterling being at that time worth $5.00); taking into account goods and services rendered to the United States to the value of $5,667 million (in, for example, building camps and airfields for American forces in Great Britain) the net British debt to the United States was $21,358 million. Canada made a loan of $700 million free of interest in 1942 when Great Britain's liquid resources in Canada ran out. This loan was followed by a gift of $1,000 million and by further loans totalling $1,800 million. Great Britain's total bill for Canadian goods and services was $7,441 million, of which rather more than half was paid in cash. The United States and Canada were much the most important of Great Britain's suppliers and creditors, but non-dollar aid from various other sources amounted to £4,000 million, that is to say an addition of nearly half the total of North American aid.

American Lend-Lease was a blessing but a mixed one. It became available when Great Britain was left with no other way to pay for American goods, and all British dollar holdings and other assets in the United States had first to be sold, sometimes at considerable loss. For more than two years after the passing of the Lend-Lease Act the value of the goods paid for in the United States in cash exceeded the value of the goods acquired on deferred credit under Lend-Lease. The conditions attached to the loans were stringent. No British goods manufactured even in part with raw materials supplied under Lend-Lease might be exported; goods for civilian consumption were excluded, so that Great Britain had to use gold or hard currencies to buy such things as tobacco, thus depleting its dollar reserves, which the United States had (privately) resolved ought to be allowed to stand no higher than $1,000 million; and Great Britain had to undertake to eliminate discrimination from its post-war trading system and therefore to abolish imperial preferences. Reverse Lend-Lease was given to the United States without any strings. In 1944 Lord Keynes led a mission to Washington to salvage Great Britain's export business by persuading the American administration that exports were so vital to Great Britain that some conversion of industry to exports must be permitted during the war. Predicting a complete British collapse after the war, he was largely successful in his mission but in August 1945 Lend-Lease stopped in peculiarly damaging circumstances: goods to the value of $650 million which had either arrived in Great Britain or were on their way had to be paid for in cash. Great Britain, being completely incapable of earning dollars in this quantity immediately after the end of the war, had to borrow $3,750 million from the United States and accept burdensome conditions including a promise to make the pound convertible within a year of the ratification of the agreement by Congress. Until the end of the war Great Britain, like the United States, was in favour of free trade as the basis of the international post-war economy and had expressed this view in the Atlantic Charter (which declared that all states should have access on equal terms to the world's trade and raw materials) and at the Bretton Woods conference which evolved the International Monetary Fund. The convertibility of currencies was an important element in this scheme of things and the British government was sufficiently optimistic to imagine that the pound could be made convertible within five years of the end of the war. It was shocked by the American demand for convertibility within one year and unable to persuade the United States that this was impossible – as it proved to be when the free convertibility of sterling in July 1947 caused such a rush for Great Britain's reserves that it had to be discontinued after five weeks.

The purchase of war equipment in the United States was forced on the British government by the inadequacy of its own resources. American industry was not only bigger than British industry and immune from war damage but also more efficient technically and managerially and so quicker. By buying in the United States instead of at home the British government forfeited a measure of control over the nature of the product. It had, especially after Pearl Harbor, to persuade the Americans to part with materials and weapons which they needed for themselves and it had also to argue for designs which, although they were to be produced in the United States, were to be used by British troops and had to be as nearly as possible what British commanders wanted. These matters were handled through joint boards in Washington and by constant coming and going between the two capitals. Inevitably there were disagreements about weapon design and for the most part American rather than British designs were put into production. When placing orders with industry the American administration would order more than it needed for itself in order to cover possible, but not yet precisely ascertained, British requirements. What the British did not eventually want was sold on Lend-Lease terms to the Free French.

It remains to consider the post-war measures adopted in Great Britain while the war was still being fought, and here a *caveat* is needed. It is temptingly easy to see in the conduct of the war on the home front a compact in which people agreed to work and endure, to postpone attempts to better themselves and even forego some hard-won gains in return for promises of post-war reform. This is, however, a misleading analysis if it implies that the work and endurance were conditional on the promises. Post-war reforms were not needed as a bait nor were they offered as a reward. They were worked out – in the exceptionally difficult circumstances of war – as an instalment of something due, to which the accident of war and the ferment created by it in Great Britain contributed.

The impulse came from the Labour Party, which was the more insistent on wartime action because it did not expect to win the first post-war election. It was supported by Liberals and Tory reformers with similar aims and ideals, but opposed by the larger part of the Conservative Party and press which denounced social inquiry as a diversion from the war effort and, in extreme cases, as opening the door to communism. Churchill himself was hostile but consented under pressure to the setting-up of an interdepartmental committee of civil servants with Sir William Beveridge as chairman to consider Social Insurance and Allied Services. The first initiative had come from the TUC, and the appointment of the Beveridge committee was partly a way of fending it off. But the committee came to life in an unusual way. Beveridge was not only an exceptionally well-equipped civil servant but a much less retiring one than most with a keen desire for radical reform and a no less keen political sense. He perceived that a report of the usual kind signed by the whole committee would be too tame and he got everybody concerned to agree that it should carry his own signature alone. The report, published in November 1942, was a closely reasoned and numerate technical document but its main lines were clear enough and radical enough to evoke great enthusiasm and great hostility. Beveridge proposed the extension of social insurance to the entire population on a compulsory contributory basis by which the cost would be shared between employers, employed and the Exchequer. He also declared that social insurance required new policies in relation to health, education, housing and unemployment. The opponents of welfare on this scale, reading the signs rightly, had begun attacking the report even before it was published. Alarmed by the spectre of continuing high taxation, which they regarded as a temporary war phenomenon not to be sanctioned for fighting any evils save those of Nazism, they denounced Beveridge's proposals as sapping the spirit and health of the nation. They were at the same time heatedly opposing Bevin's Catering Wages Bill which was designed to prevent employers from taking advantage of employees in a notably disorganized and therefore ill-paid industry. This opposition ultimately failed but Conservative hostility to Beveridge succeeded in preventing him from being invited to pursue his work. He thereupon produced on his own a second report on Full Employment in a Free Society which placed the prevention of mass unemployment at the centre of politics, argued that a return to mass unemployment after the war was immoral, uneconomic and avoidable, and attacked the view that government intervention in social policy must lead to an unacceptable destruction of freedom. The government so far accepted the paramount duty of maintaining employment as to issue its own White Paper on Employment Policy. These documents ensured that post-war governments for at least a generation would at the very least pay lip service to the doctrine that a government should plan to prevent unemployment instead of hoping not to be plagued by it; they asserted, even though without gaining universal assent for it, the proposition that a high level of employment (rather misleadingly called full employment) might be a prior aim to the maintenance of a particular ruling exchange value for the pound.

In 1943 a Ministry of Reconstruction was set up to think about post-war problems. These included the control of the environment and land use, about which three reports were issued during the war; a Town and Country Planning Act was passed in 1944. New Education Acts were also passed for England and Wales (1944) and Scotland (1945). They extended free education to children beyond the elementary stage. They also introduced a test to be taken at the age of '11 plus' in order, by dividing children into a clever minority and an ordinary majority, to enable the grammar schools to survive as separate and superior establishments. In terms of Great Britain's past achievements in providing education for all these Acts were a definite step forward. They were comparatively un-controversial since the need for better education was evident on material as well as social grounds; the country needed more and better education in order to prosper and it had been shocked by the degree of ignorance and illiteracy revealed by the call-up of the nation to the armed forces. More controversial was the question of health and who should pay for it. A White Paper in 1944 on a National Health Service, raising the issue of a free and full medical (not merely hospital) service, was vague. It was welcomed by doctors as well as the general public but there was significant opposition to the idea of a salaried service and to the extinction of a private medical sector. It was, however, the precursor of the National Health Act which was introduced after the war by the Labour government along with a Family Allowance Act, a New Towns Act and a National Insurance Act.

The extension of the scope of government, whether to fight a war or to undertake a social transformation, affected the structure of government. Early in the war the Chamberlain government took sweeping powers by a series of legislative enactments, but it made sparing use of these powers and remained fundamentally a peacetime administration grappling with war problems rather than a war directorate prepared to accept and use the huge concentration of power foisted upon it by the nature of its re-sponsibilities. The British system was government by the executive tem-pered by the executive's own distrust of power; the executive could do pretty much what it wanted but was traditionally shy of straying far outside the tracks delineated by *laissez-faire* dogma. This reluctance to take and use power was fortified by British belief in the value of voluntary effort, a belief grounded in experience and justified in war when voluntary organizations old and new played a highly important role in conjunction with officialdom. Nevertheless the business of war required the creation of nearly a dozen new Ministries, an expansion of the central government and a complication of the machinery of coordination in Whitehall which accustomed Ministers, civil servants and the public to think of government in widening terms. War also raised questions about government away from the centre. During 1937–9 the country was divided into a number of regions under Regional Commissioners, appointed, not elected – prefects, in the continental vocabulary – whose functions extended beyond the strict problems of civil defence. The Regional Commissioners were general factotums of the central government. As such they could be expected to be suspect, but they became in fact popular owing to the manifest inadequacy of the existing patchwork of elected local governments, which were very uneven in size, financially weak and endowed with only partial authority in a number of fields. There developed a popular demand for increasing the powers of the Regional Commissioners and so an opportunity to reform the geography and structure of local government by combining the old elective principle with the new pattern, but this opportunity was missed and the regions were allowed to expire. A unified fire service and regional hospital boards were the principal survivors of a reorganization which was otherwise expunged because, war being regarded as an ephemeral and malevolent phenomenon, most of its products were so regarded too.

More specialized but more enduring was the acclimatization of science and scientists in the machinery of government and the processes of decision-making. This was another pre-war trend accelerated by war. It belied the view often expressed that modern science had become a world unto itself, inaccessible to non-scientists, however clever they might be. The Second World War saw – not of course in Great Britain alone – a revival of the term military science in the broad sense in which it had once been used to designate a partnership between the field commander-staff officer and the inventor-designer, of whom Archimedes and Leonardo da Vinci were the archetypes. This partnership had been broken in the post-Clausewitz age when war became a profession for professional soldiers (notwithstanding that many nineteenth-century commanders were very amateurish indeed), but it was reconstituted in the twentieth century for two main reasons. First, new weapons became increasingly complicated. The tank, the aircraft and the submarine were already very different from the rifle even before radio and radar made them more different still. Designing them, and thinking of defences against them, were highly technical matters. The purely professional soldier could no longer tell the expert what he wanted because he did not know. He had to rely on the expert to diagnose his problem and find an answer to it. This was how the scientists came to present the air force with radar as the answer to the problem of how to stop the bomber. The scientist, tackling problems instead of waiting to be given specifications, acquired an initiative in war, which however he could only exercise in close consultation with the non-scientist. Secondly, scientists developed a new role called operational research. In cooperation with the fighting services they watched the battle and evaluated results with their analytical tools. Having invented new weapons they did not merely hand them over but took part in a continuing debate about the most effective way to use them. Thus hard tests of the effects of

41   The Arab Legion

42   *Top*: Kismayu, Ethiopia:
the British evict the Italians,
February 1941

43   *Bottom*: Malta: a crippled
tanker in harbour

44 *Top*: Tobruk: January 1941

45 *Bottom*: Libya: the British advance, November 1941

46 *Top*: Briefing Mustang
aircrews, 1943

47 *Bottom*: Sicily, July 1943:
invasion

48 *Top*: Sicily, July 1943:
Militello turns out for the
British

49 *Bottom*: Italy: Americans
land at Salerno, September
1943

50   *Top*: Italy: Anzio,
February 1944

51   *Bottom*: Monte Cassino:
May 1944

52 *Top*: General Mark Clark
ascends the Capitol, Rome,
June 1944

53 *Bottom*: Americans on
their way to France through
an English village, 1944

54 *Top*: D-day in Normandy,
6 June 1944

55 *Bottom*: The Battle of the
Bulge: identifying civilian
victims at Malmédy, Belgium,
December 1944

bombing during the German-Italian retreat in North Africa and in the capture of the island of Pantellaria before the invasion of Sicily served to build up the case for using bombs in tactical attacks on rail and road communications rather than in the mass bombing of civilians, housing and factories. The debate on this particular issue was protracted and bitter, but the significant thing is not that this was so but that scientists took part in it at the highest and most intimate levels.

These activities – together with the less ferocious aspects of science such as the uses of penicillin, the development of sulphonamides, skin-graft surgery and shock therapy – altered the popular conception of the scientist as a special kind of being who resided somewhere in the wings. Science acquired a place at the heart of the machinery of government, in the practical business of the conduct of war and, by analogy and under the name of technology, in the development of industry. In addition people began to recall that science simply meant knowledge. They felt that they ought to have more of it, even if its arcaner specialities were beyond them. Hence the debate on Two Cultures in which educated people lamented their inability to understand what other educated people were talking about and deplored the division of their culture into parts. They raised their voices against this estrangement partly because it was intellectually unhealthy and partly, whether they perceived it or not, because the war had shown that the gap was not unbridgeable. Hence too the growing suspicion that a system of government by men and women versed in only half a culture might not suffice to keep the country abreast of the times.

When the war ended the cost had to be counted. There had been much death and destruction. Damage to life and property had been less than anticipated and less than in the First World War; deaths in action, including the merchant navy, were 380,000, half the total for the earlier war, to which had to be added another 60,000 who lost their lives as civilians. But the blitz had been short as well as sharp, the V weapons had arrived mercifully late and the battles which were specially British – the Battle of Britain, the Battle of the Atlantic and the North African campaigns were all fought by quite small bodies of men. Industrially there had been overstrain in some places. Inferior labour and materials had had to be used. The retail and distributive trades, the textile and clothing industries, building and pottery had all lost 50 per cent or more of their labour. Timber had been over-felled. There was a permanent loss of some craft skills. Some overseas investments had been sold and the reserves had been depleted; Great Britain parted with a third in value of its foreign investments and a third of its gold reserve. But the investments were recovered or replaced within a few years of the end of the war, and exports, cut by more than 60 per cent during the war, were restored to their pre-war level by the end of 1946. Here was vigour. The government was itself spending three quarters of the country's gross national product in place of one quarter before the war. It was doing so because its military expenditure had been doubled and it had undertaken expensive social obligations. The latter held promise for the future. It had constructed buildings and plant, much of it transferred to private industry when the war ended. It had trained more skilled workers than the country had ever had before and spent more in scientific research and development. All major industries except the clothing industry were producing more than before the war despite bombing and other tribulations, and Great Britain emerged from the war as a pioneer in nuclear technology and with an electronics industry stimulated by wartime investment. It had the makings of a more sensible control of economic policy in the practice, initiated during the war, of making estimates of the national income and expenditure – a practice which was unheard of in pre-war Great Britain and which amounted to a revolution in budgeting. The foundations had been laid for radical reform after a generation and more of economic and social failures. Even the arts were recognized as something more than a peripheral eccentricity; a Council for the Encouragement of Music and the Arts, created in 1939 with the help of the Pilgrim Trust, was later given a government subsidy and was preserved after the war under the name of the Arts Council. The strain and the achievement had been tremendous; there had been irreparable pain; the prospect was inspiriting.

War intensifies and simplifies emotions. Because of the pressures of an enemy at the gates the British people experienced a sense of community which loosened its class structure. Before the war the rulers saw their main enemy in Bolshevism, which was a threat to their class rather than to the state. During the war the threat was Nazism, which was hateful to all, and Germany, which was challenging the existence of the European nation state. Nazism enslaved human beings, Germany enslaved states, and both reminded the British of all classes that they were determined never to be slaves. The enemy therefore stimulated national unity – as Napoleon and other conquerors had done. In Great Britain this national unity was further fed by a new richness of communication between governors and governed. On the military side Churchill's personality and talents not only inspired confidence but gave people the feeling that they were all in it together. On the social side – and it became more accurate to refer to non-military affairs as social rather than civilian – wartime planning and post-war planning added to the sense that the nation was one and that post-war Great Britain would be a better place than pre-war Great Britain had been. In terms of institutions war menaces democracy by requiring the suspension of democratic safeguards and processes, but in terms of popular participation and involvement in affairs war may – and in Great Britain did – nourish the substance of democracy even when it was temporarily dismantling some of its trappings. It gave more of the people more concern for and knowledge of affairs of state. They became, if not insiders, at any rate less outside than they had been. There was an enlargement of the body politic to something nearer the bounds of British society as a whole. The governors who had to look to the safety of the state and to the welfare of society were to that extent distracted from their pre-war pre-occupations with the class interests and the imperial interests which had seemed to be their natural and proper business but which had either alienated or failed to stir the mass of their fellow citizens. The war made the British state more national and less imperial, more democratic and less oligarchic. It produced more social change than had ever been compassed anywhere in so few years, save only by revolution – and not often then. The ruling class abandoned the resistance of a generation to reform and therewith its own integrity. Society was no longer the same and the ruling class was no longer the same. The question for the future was whether, how far and for how long this impetus would be maintained; or how soon an enlarged ruling class would revert to the traditional role of ruling classes to keep things pretty much as they are, to institutionalize, to put a brake on change for fear of putting the skids under themselves. In July 1945 the British people manifested in a general election an uncommon seriousness and optimism about their common future. The main source of these feelings, and the main condition of their survival, was not simply the baneful fact of war but the clearing by war of the channels of com- munication within the nation. Soon after the end of the war these channels began to silt up again.

Part V

THE DEFEAT OF GERMANY: 1942–5

CHAPTER 21
The Battle of the Seas

GREAT BRITAIN's survival in 1940 did not remove the danger of defeat. The U-boat might still succeed where the Luftwaffe had failed. The crisis of 1940 was followed by the crises of 1941 and 1942, when Great Britain's imports of food, weapons and materials for industry dropped to within sight of a war-losing level.

The essence of the crisis was shortage of shipping. Ships were needed for many purposes and all over the world. Supplies had to be brought to Great Britain across the Atlantic and from many distant sources of vital raw materials; troops and their equipment had to be moved to different battle-fronts, including the Middle East, East Africa and the Far East; the blockade of Germany had to be maintained around the coasts of Europe, a task which was magnified every time the Germans won control of a fresh country; and there were special obligations like the dispatch of aid to the Russians by convoys which gathered in Scotland and Iceland to make the passage to Murmansk or Archangel. The fulfilling of these tasks against the U-boats, the German high seas fleet and the Luftwaffe entailed a battle which lasted several years and cost many lives.

The idea of a shipping shortage did not come naturally to the British. It seemed almost as absurd to suppose that Great Britain would lack ships as to suppose that it might run short of coal. In fact it did both and the reasons were similar. The neglect and mismanagement of the coalfields by their owners had become proverbial and had created so much ill will that it smouldered on and produced strikes even in the all-forgiving and all-compelling atmosphere of war. The shipyards were in not much better case. They were antiquated and inefficient, but such is the force of habit that the government did not wake up to the consequent dangers until some time after the war began. The provision of ships seemed to be one thing that Great Britain did not need to worry about. This complacency was fostered by the months of phoney war which were nowhere more deceptive than at sea. Great Britain lost 150 dry cargo ships in the first nine months of war and made good the loss by new building or capture. But this simple sum told only part of the story. Imports were affected by many factors: few foreign ships ventured to British ports; British ships had to take roundabout routes which delayed them (carrying capacity cannot be measured simply in numbers of vessels); at home, when the east coast ports had to be closed, unloading facilities elsewhere became over-burdened; there was a shortage of hard currency to buy goods with; the fall of France increased voyage times by 30–40 per cent; the convoy system reduced the speed of all but the slower ships.

Imports began to sink rapidly. In 1941 they were 30.5 million tons of dry cargo against a peacetime norm of about 50 million. This was only very slightly more than in 1917 when population and industry were ap-preciably smaller, and yet the ports which were still working had difficulty in handling even this limited volume. 1942 was worse again – 22.9 million tons. Throughout this period cargo space declined. But in 1942 consump-tion at home was exceeding imports by the alarming amount of 2.45 million tons and half the imported raw materials consumed by industry had had to be drawn from stocks. Running down stocks at this rate was potentially catastrophic because stocks had not been built up before the war (wheat stocks at the beginning of the war were for three weeks, for example) owing to a facile and false view in the Admiralty that the inven-tion of radar had put paid to the U-boat. The exploding of this view turned complacency into something like panic, aggravated by gross exag-gerations of needs by the Ministries of Supply and Food and by the absence of any reliable statistics. Consumption was screwed down so that, until 1942, it was even lower than imports, but the corollary of this rigour was that rations could hardly be further reduced, or imported raw mater-ials economized, without direct danger to the war effort, the creation of unemployment and a possibly lethal blow to morale.

In 1943 the decline was checked and stocks were replenished as imports topped consumption by 2.8 million tons. The balance swung into deficit once more in 1944 when imports fell by 1.3 million tons and consumption rose by 3.4 million, but by this date the U-boat had been beaten, the pattern of imports had been altered by Lend-Lease which enabled goods to be imported manufactured or semi-manufactured instead of in bulkier raw forms, and the government had learned by experience at what point it need get alarmed. But these figures tell the gravity of a situation which gave Germany its one chance of a substantial victory after the failure of its air forces over Great Britain and its armies before Moscow. For three years Great Britain was closely beleaguered and Hitler could entertain some hope of reconverting the war to a war on one front. Great Britain's survival at sea, which could never be confidently predicted in these years, saved the United States from the predicament posed for Great Britain by the collapse of France in 1940: whether to carry on or call it defeat.

There were two critical phases in this battle. The first followed the conquest of western Europe by Hitler and the second followed Pearl Harbor. Both events made Great Britain's position worse. The first cut Great Britain off from sources of supply, especially food. It put the Germans in possession of bases for submarines and long-range reconnaissance aircraft on the Atlantic coasts of Norway and France; U-boats took up new stations in concrete pens in Atlantic harbours and the long-range F.W. 200s began making wide sweeps over the ocean, flying from Bordeaux to Trondhjem one day and back another. From this time all traffic to London had to go north of Scotland (the trip round Scotland to London and back took more than half the time required to cross the Atlantic) and many ships were routed into ports unaccustomed to handling the cargoes they were carrying; there was much confusion in these ports. Finally, by closing the Mediterranean, Hitler's continental victories doubled the distance between Great Britain and Bombay and more than quadrupled the distance to Suez. Great Britain obtained some compensation in the muster of European shipping which took refuge in British ports and took service alongside the British merchant navy as one European country after another was overrun. Largely as a result of appeals and veiled threats put out by the BBC no ship at sea at the time of the conquest of its home port returned there, although not all of them went to British ports. Neutral shipping too carried goods for Great Britain. More than four fifths of Sweden's dry cargo shipping outside the Baltic did so. Not all of this can be ascribed to sentiment. Great Britain invented a warrant scheme and refused to issue warrants to ships sailing in conditions or under contracts which were damaging to the allies. Ships sailing without such warrants were denied facilities in ports under British control and in American and some other neutral ports, and found it almost impossible to get insurance.

Pearl Harbor inaugurated a second crisis by multiplying the calls on American shipping and unleashing a successful U-boat campaign against it. South African ports became so crowded with ships in search of asylum or in need of repair or on their way to the Middle East that by mid-1942 nearly eighty vessels at a time could be found waiting to berth or go into dry dock. The advance of the Japanese overland and at sea disrupted the economies of southern Asia by stopping the export of Burma's rice, oil and rubber and Bengal's coal: India's east coast ports were closed, the feeding of India, Ceylon and parts of east Africa became an allied responsibility, and countries round the Indian Ocean faced starvation and a general breakdown of public services. In Bengal in the summer of 1943 1.5 million people died of hunger. Thus commitments increased as carrying capacity was once more drastically reduced. It was at sea, much more than on land, that the several wars which together made a world war interacted.

The British government, besides welcoming the merchant fleets of its continental friends, bought second-hand vessels in any part of the world where they could be found, but this source was exhausted by the end of 1940. There remained the United States. But the American shipbuilding industry was in no better shape than the British. It had been allowed to atrophy after the First World War and in the years 1921–36 it constructed, tankers apart, only two ocean-going freighters. In 1941 total construction was under 1 million tons (lower than Great Britain's) as against an assessed need of 8 million tons for the war in Europe, excluding tankers and troopships and quite apart from whatever the United States might want for itself elsewhere. In May Roosevelt ordered 2 million dry weight tons, including tankers, to be found for Great Britain and other democracies at war. The British had hoped that it would be 2 million gross tons, excluding tankers, and all of it for Great Britain alone. (Two million d.w. tons equal 1.3 million gross tons.) So there was some disappointment as well as relief. Later in the year Roosevelt gave more help by sanctioning American escorts for allied vessels, by opening American ports to allied ships in need of repair and by Lend-Lease; but substantially Great Britain had to get through 1941 on its own. Rations were severely cut and some foods, including fresh vegetables and fruit, were deleted from overseas cargoes. The government budgeted on imports of 30 million tons, half in food and half in arms and industrial raw materials, and Churchill ruled that any reduction below 30 million tons must be borne by the Ministries of Supply and Food in the proportion of two to one. In the same year shipping was also needed to move an average of 29,000 men by sea per month, and it was estimated that the figure would rise to 70,000 a month in 1942. (The latter figure was almost reached. It included the transport of 16,500 men a month to the Far East in January–March 1942. The situation was eased by commandeering six large passenger liners which sailed fast enough to dispense with escorts and were refashioned to carry up to 15,000 men at a time.)

At the end of 1941 Pearl Harbor dashed hopes of increased American assistance. American construction was immensely increased in 1942 – to the 8 million tons prescribed a year earlier and then to 13.5 million in the following years, tankers and naval construction excluded – but these astonishing achievements hardly sufficed to keep pace with the American need. The ships sunk by the Japanese at Pearl Harbor had to be replaced, while on the east coast the German U-boats, whose successes against British shipping were doubled in the first months of the new year, sailed zestfully into American territorial waters where the Americans, disdaining Great Britain's experiences in two wars, refused for several months to introduce a convoy system and lost in consequence a disabling number of vessels. In response to the crisis in the Pacific the great bulk of civil shipping requisitioned by the Administration after Pearl Harbor was committed to the Pacific theatre, and when the Anglo-American invasion of North Africa took place at the end of the year, Great Britain had to lend the United States troopships, dry cargo ships and practically all the tankers used in that operation.

Moreover, the estimates of the number of ships needed, and the time for which they would be needed, were both misjudged. For four months North Africa absorbed 106 ships a month in place of an anticipated sixty-six, and instead of going over to a maintenance basis in February 1943 the armies had to be kept supplied on a fully operational basis until May – the most serious consequence of the decision not to attempt any landing east of Algiers. These operations coincided with the U-boats' record month – 729,160 tons sunk in November 1942. In the second half of 1942 the United States was lending shipping to Great Britain but only on a modest scale, on a short-term basis and in smaller quantity than reverse British lendings to the United States: each American vessel was made available for a single voyage at a time. American aid increased Great Britain's carrying capacity by 7.5 per cent to 10 per cent in the second half of 1942, but British loans to the United States over the period of the North African campaign ran at the rate of 17 per cent of all the dry cargo tonnage sailing on British account (net of American loaned shipping) during the seven months October 1942 to April 1943. Great Britain's total dry tonnage cargo committed wholly or primarily to the needs of the armed services was greater than the total of American shipping committed in the same way – 8.5 million tons against 6 million. British requirements were at this time also greater since British troops overseas were more than twice as many as American troops overseas, British theatres of war were about twice as distant from their principal bases as American theatres, and the concurrent British civilian needs had no American counterpart since the United States did not have to import food or, to the same extent, raw materials. During 1942 Great Britain lost on balance 1.4 million gross tons while the United States merchant fleet rose by 2.7 million gross tons. By and large Great Britain's basic problem was its inability to match sinkings with new building. The United States built in most periods more than it lost, but the net increase in its fleet did not keep pace with the increase in its needs, so that there was a continuing conflict between satisfying the expanding needs of the US armed services and helping Great Britain and other allies.

The turning point in the Battle of the Seas came in the winter of 1942–3. In that period the U-boat was defeated. The Luftwaffe had been eliminated from this battle in 1942. Its anti-shipping force, though skilled, was always small. Its torpedo-carriers were a neglected and minor branch of the service; its long-range F.W. 200s were reduced by bombing of the Bremen factory where they were made; it was too deeply absorbed by prior commitments on the eastern front and in the Mediterranean. The U-boat was the weapon which threatened to turn the allied shipping shortage into an allied defeat, for the U-boat accounted for two thirds of all British, allied and neutral shipping losses during the war – 14.7 million gross tons out of a total of 21.6 million. Aircraft accounted for 13.4 per cent. Surface raiders came third. Of the tonnage sunk by U-boats nearly half – 6.3 million tons – went to the bottom in the year 1942. Over half of all these sinkings were in the North Atlantic.

The U-boats of the First World War had come so close to victory that Great Britain tried after the war to get submarines abolished by international agreement. Yet Germany began the second war with very few. Admiral Karl Doenitz, the commander of the U-boats, had argued in the thirties against the building of capital ships on the grounds that they would not be ready in time and that the space and effort could more profitably be used to build the fleet of 300 submarines with which he reckoned that he could starve Great Britain into surrender. Essentially Doenitz's argument was the same as that used by the champions of strategic bombing (whom we shall come to in a later chapter): he said that his weapon was a war-winning one on its own. It is not clear whether the verdict of history is that no single weapon can ever do the trick or that no government can ever be persuaded that it will. In any case Doenitz failed to convince Hitler and Germany began the war with fifty-seven submarines, of which thirty-nine were operational when war broke out but only twenty-three were capable of ocean-going operations. With such small numbers Doenitz could not essay the pack tactics which he had been elaborating and the first months of the war produced, as we saw in Part II of this book, no sensational results at sea. Then for eighteen months Germany's operational submarine force declined and it was not until the summer of 1941 that new construction so far outpaced losses as to give the force a real boost.

The task of defeating Doenitz and assuring Great Britain's sea-borne supplies fell first and foremost on the Royal Navy. But this was not its only task. It had also to secure its own bases, not one of which at home or overseas – even Scapa Flow – was adequately defended against air and submarine attack at the outbreak of war. It had, until 1940, to be ready to foil an invasion of the British Isles and it had to maintain – and, when lost, re-establish – important strategic routes in the Mediterranean. It had to nullify the German surface fleet. It possessed an impressive number of battleships: *Iron Duke*, a solitary survivor of the days before the First World War which spent the second war at anchor; ten survivors of the First World War of the *Queen Elizabeth* and *Royal Sovereign* classes; and *Nelson* and *Rodney*, both launched in 1925. The tally of capital ships was raised to sixteen by three battle cruisers, also survivors of the First World War. In addition a new class of battleships – *King George V* and her four sister-ships – had been laid down and the first of these were about to be commissioned. The decision to build these ships has been criticized as an obtuse failure to see that the battleship had had its day and that the money could more profitably have been spent on aircraft carriers, but it has also been pertinently argued that it was impossible in the radarless mid-thirties to foresee that an aircraft carrier and its aircraft could be any use except by day and when there was no fog.

From cruisers downwards the Royal Navy was uncomfortably short of modern vessels. It had sixty-one cruisers, but a third of them had been launched in 1919 or earlier. It had to obtain fifty old destroyers from the United States. Six of its ten aircraft carriers were old or converted, and it lost three soon after the war began. It was primarily designed to fight big fleet actions in which heavy capital ships would be ranged against each other and would prevail through the weight and accuracy of their gunnery; but so far as fleet actions were fought at all in the Second World War they were won by aircraft. It had paid too little attention to the design of aircraft suited for operations at sea – partly because it did not secure full control of its own air arm until 1937 – and it could call on very few long-range reconnaissance aircraft. The weakness in both these categories was not cured until the Americans remedied it. Between the wars it had, unlike the German navy, neglected the magnetic mine which both sides had used successfully in the First World War. It found that the Germans could lay mines faster than it could sweep them. During the crucial years to 1943 it was short of torpedoes, although the torpedo was the most destructive of all the weapons used at sea in the second war. But in spite of this backlog of deficiencies it prevailed because it was a highly professional and valiant force, because its adversaries had even more serious deficiencies and because it was seconded in its tasks by the R A F.

The lesson of the First World War on the protection of merchant shipping was clear: convoys and close escorts. This lesson had, however, been learned late in the war and after Churchill had left the cabinet. The problem was debated again intermittently during the thirties and the convoy system was adopted, hesitantly and conditionally, shortly before the second war broke out. But Churchill did not like close escort work. His conception of the war at sea was a series of sweeps, which he likened to cavalry sweeps. He believed that the emphasis should be at least as much on seeking out and destroying the enemy as on guarding the merchant ships. So the escort vessels available were split between close escort and wide forays. These tactics consumed fuel and wasted bombs and depth charges for comparatively little return, while the merchantmen plied their course at unnecessary risk. They were based on two false assumptions: first, that a convoy was more easily spotted by enemy forces and so more vulnerable than single ships and, secondly, that single ships could fight back successfully if attacked. Not until 1942 did the figures and arguments of operational research convince Churchill that he was wrong, as the British cabinet had been wrong at the beginning of the first war and the Americans continued to be wrong in the second even later than the British.

The risks run by the merchant ships were accentuated by two other factors. Up to mid-1943 the Germans were able to read British naval ciphers which gave them the positions of British surface and submarine vessels and convoys. Secondly, the Royal Navy had been unable before the war to come to any arrangement with the RAF for operational control over the squadrons of Coastal Command, and even when it did so in 1941 that Command was still kept short of modern long-range aircraft which were allotted in priority to Bomber Command. Bomber Command undertook (among its many missions) bombing raids on U-boat bases and building-yards but the effects of these raids were disappointment and some of the aircraft employed in them could have been used to better purpose on Atlantic patrol.

The Battle of the Seas began in earnest after the fall of France. To defend their precious merchantmen the allies had insufficient escort vessels, insufficient reconnaissance aircraft, inadequate intelligence and inadequate gear for detecting submarines and destroying them. The German occupation of French and Norwegian Atlantic ports laid shipping under an aerial surveillance which forced it to take long and devious routes: an average crossing of the north Atlantic took fifteen days, a southerly crossing by way of Freetown in Sierra Leone twenty-one days. Great Britain lacked not only enough escorts to cover the convoys constantly at sea for this length of time but also escorts with enough range to accompany the merchantmen the whole way. At first close escorts accompanied convoys only as far as 15° west longitude – about 200 miles beyond the west coast of Ireland. This limit was gradually extended during 1940 to 19° west. At this point the escorts halted and made rendezvous with an eastbound convoy, which had been escorted by Canadian destroyers for the first 300–400 miles of its journey. But there was a gap in the middle and after the fall of France even short-range German surface forces could operate as far as 25° west. This gap could only be closed by providing escort vessels with a wider radius of action and by routing convoys farther north and giving air cover from Iceland and refuelling facilities there. The sloop, the only escort vessel which could go all the way across the Atlantic, eventually provided continuous protection but sloops were few when war began. Iceland, although occupied in 1940 when Hitler invaded Denmark, was not brought into the Battle of the Atlantic until 1941. Coastal Command was kept busy looking for invasion barges in the North Sea throughout most of 1940, and a request by the Admiralty for a reconnaissance squadron to be stationed in Iceland was not granted until early the next year.

From this date, however, things began to improve. Close escorts were provided up to 35° west, more than halfway from east to west, and from July 1941 convoys were given continuous protection in three stages, covered by groups based in the Western Approaches, Iceland and Newfoundland. But the cover, though continuous, was still thin. Up to the end of 1941 the average number of escorts per convoy was only two. At the same time the continuing lack of long-range reconnaissance aircraft enabled U-boats to patrol on the surface with fair immunity. The older boats took the risk of being spotted, and the newer ones which came into service in 1941 were able to operate beyond the range of British aircraft.

Losses at sea in 1941 of ships sailing on British account totalled 4.3 million gross tons (1,299 vessels). Losses of this order were not replaceable. In 1942 they were much worse: 7.8 million tons (1,664 vessels). The share of the U-boats in the latter year rose to four fifths and the U-boat fleet was growing. A force of ninety-one boats at the beginning of 1942 had grown to 212 by the end of the year despite the loss of eighty-seven boats during the year. In one battle in March 1942 U-boats caught two convoys at once and sank twenty-one out of ninety-eight vessels with the loss of only one U-boat. An action of this kind, which sent over 140,000 tons of shipping to the bottom, went a long way towards giving Doenitz the 800,000 tons a month which he was aiming at. A few months later, when American escort vessels were almost completely withdrawn from the regular Atlantic convoy service for tasks in the Pacific or to support the coming landings in North Africa, the U-boats scored heavily and consistently. They developed new tactics whereby one boat acted as a tracker which signalled the position of a convoy to other boats which then assembled for a surface attack by night. The weakness of these tactics was the need to break wireless silence and so reveal the position of the tracker to the allied listening services, but the risks proved worthwhile and Doenitz was not far wrong when he concluded that he was achieving his monthly target and his Führer's aim. But the sinkings of March 1942 – 273 ships totalling 834,164 tons – were only once exceeded – in June when 173 ships totalling 834,196 tons were lost. These were sinkings from all causes. In November exceptional successes by U-boats pushed the total above 800,000 once more and for the last time.

The Atlantic was the one place where Great Britain could still lose the war. The U-boats might starve Britain of food and weapons of war and prevent the Americans from assembling in Great Britain the vast strengths needed to force a re-entry into France and so beat Hitler. In London an anti-U-boat committee was formed, consisting of British and American brass and boffins under the chairmanship of Churchill himself. During 1942 new radar detectors and new offensive weapons, such as new kinds of depth charge, were introduced; at the end of the year the strategic bombers of both nations were directed to attack, as first priority, U-boat construction yards in Germany and U-boat bases in France; and in December the Ultra cryptographers delivered a critical blow by breaking the new U-boat Enigma key.

Bletchley had been reading the German navy's principal cipher from March 1941. This cipher was used by the Atlantic U-boats until early in 1942, when these boats were given a new cipher of their own, thus blotting out for an unforeseeable period the British Admiralty's chief source of information about the movements and intentions of the U-boats. Naval Enigma was always more difficult to break than other keys because the machines used by the German navy were the most complex. Nevertheless the new key was broken in December and the U-boat threat began immediately to fade. In March 1943 the boats scored their last major victory when they sank thirty-two vessels for the loss of only one boat (they had at this time over one hundred boats at sea at a time) but a few weeks later they broke off an engagement in which they had lost six boats, and after further defeats of this kind they completely withdrew for a time from the Atlantic. New boats continued to be commissioned, but the rate of sinkings began to catch up with the rate of production and by 1944, when the Atlantic became a highway crowded with men and munitions making for France and Germany itself, U-boat sinkings exceeded in tonnage the allies,

BATTLE OF THE ATLANTIC 1939-1942

GREENLAND

ICELAND

Murmansk

Reykjavik

Julianehaab

CANADA

Belfast

GERMAN OCCUPIED OR CONTROLLED

New York

North

St Johns

CONVOY ROUTE FROM MAY 1941

UNITED STATES

Atlantic

Bermuda (GB)

Azores (Portuguese)

Gibraltar

Casablanca

WEST INDIES

Ocean

Puerto Rico (USA)
Virgin Is (USA)
Antigua (GB)
St Lucia (GB)
Trinidad (GB)

Dakar (French)

AFRICA

Georgetown (GB)
Paramaribo (Dutch)

Freetown (GB)

GUIANA

CONVOY ROUTE FROM JULY 1942

CONVOY ROUTE

Recife (Pernambuco)

SOUTH AMERICA

South

Rio de Janiero

Atlantic

Cape Town

Ocean

Montevideo (Uruguay)

Battle of the River Plate 14 December 1939.

to EGYPT, MIDDLE EAST & RUSSIA

Symbol	Description
⊙	US & British bases.
▨	Occupied by Britain 1940.
▥	US Protectorate 1941-1945.
●—	Limit of Allied air patrols.
Ⓡ	Allied coastal convoy system established July 1942.
■	Main U-boat bases.
▦	U-boat activities Sept 1939 - March 1941.
▤	U-boat activities April 1941 - July 1942.
☐	Areas not possible to patrol by Allied land based bombers.

0   1000
Miles

~ARTHUR BANKS~

losses in merchant shipping. Altogether 1,162 U-boats were built and commissioned during the war and 941 of them were sunk or surrendered in the course of it. One of these was captured by an aircraft.

The latter phase of the war against the U-boats was waged simultaneously with the battle in Arctic waters in which the German surface fleet and the Luftwaffe joined to prevent the dispatch of allied aid to the Russians and to sink the allied vessels carrying it. After the loss of *Bismarck* in 1941 Hitler had little use for his capital ships but during 1942 he concentrated them in Norway, chiefly because he was afraid that the allies intended to invade that country. *Bismarck*'s sister-ship *Tirpitz* was moved to Trondhjem in January. The battle cruisers *Scharnhorst* and *Gneisenau* and the cruiser *Prinz Eugen* were recalled in February from Brest on Hitler's direct order (once again he had to override his professional advisers, Raeder considering the order so crazy that he refused to take responsibility for it). They succeeded in running the gauntlet of the English Channel by day to reach home ports, whence *Prinz Eugen* was directed to Norway. She was damaged by a torpedo on her way and had to turn back but Germany's strength in northern waters was further increased by the dispatch of the cruiser *Admiral Hipper* and the two battleships *Scheer* and *Lützow* and, in the following winter, two more cruisers and *Scharnhorst* and – once again – *Prinz Eugen*. Although *Lützow* ran aground and was out of action for several months, this build-up was alarming for the British Admiralty, the more so since attempts to cripple ships by air attack in harbour had proved disappointing. *Scharnhorst*, *Gneisenau* and *Prinz Eugen* had survived a winter's battering in Brest before making their successful dash up the Channel and it was proving impossible to do any real damage to *Tirpitz* in her narrow anchorage up the Trondhjem fjord.

Tirpitz, like *Bismarck* before her, was the most powerful vessel on either side in the Atlantic war. Yet she took part in no battle. Launched in April 1939, she did her trials in the Baltic during 1941 and was dispatched to Norwegian waters at the beginning of 1942. The British Admiralty feared another sortie into the Atlantic, like *Bismarck*'s the year before, and these fears gave rise to one of the most brilliantly daring ventures of the war. If *Tirpitz* made for the Atlantic, she would probably sooner or later need to put in at St Nazaire. An old American destroyer, *Campbeltown*, disguised as a German ship and filled with explosives, was sailed up the Loire estuary to St Nazaire, deceiving the German gunners defending the harbour until the last few minutes. Her captain and crew sailed her straight at the dock gates and rammed them, while commandos landed to destroy other selected installations. The next day *Campbeltown* blew up. The dock at St Nazaire was never repaired by the Germans.

BATTLE OF THE ATLANTIC 1942 – 1945

0   1000
Miles

SUBMARINE WAR 1939-1945
1,200 U-boats involved
700 U-boats sunk
32,000 German sailors drowned
2,700 Allied ships sunk.
30,000 British merchant seamen
       drowned.
36% of the total British merchant
Fleet was sunk between June 1940-
December 1945.

GREENLAND

Reykjavik
ICELAND
Julianehaab

CANADA

St Johns
Halifax

UNITED STATES

New York

Belfast

GERMAN OCCUPIED OR CONTROLLED

Azores from Oct 1943

Gibraltar
Casablanca

North Atlantic Ocean

Bermuda (GB)

Key West USA
Exuma (GB)
Guatanamo
Jamaica
Puerto Rico (USA)
Virgin Is (USA)
Antigua
St Lucia (GB)
Trinidad

Dakar from Nov 1942

AFRICA

Freetown (GB)
Monrovia (Liberia)
Takoradi (GB)

Panama Canal
Georgetown (GB)
Paramaribo (Dutch)
Cayenne (French)
Belem

EXTRA CONVOY ROUTE

SOUTH AMERICA

Recife (Pernambuco)
Salvador (Bahia)

Ascension Is (GB)

FROM

Rio de Janeiro

South Atlantic Ocean

Cape Town

1943

Montevideo (Uruguay)

⊙	US & British bases.	▦	U-boat activities August 1942 - May 1943
●	Limit of Allied air patrols.	▨	U-boat activities June 1943 - April 1945
▣	Main U-boat bases.	☐	Areas not possible to patrol by Allied land-based bombers.

~ARTHUR BANKS~

But although *Tirpitz* never attempted a foray like *Bismarck*'s she indirectly inflicted grievous losses on allied shipping in Arctic waters. Churchill's response to Stalin's request for help in 1941 had been not merely generous in spirit but incautious in degree. He promised a convoy every ten days, to the dismay of the Admiralty which was thinking in terms of one every forty days – if it had to run any at all against such suicidal odds. The run of 1,500–2,000 miles lay through seas made dangerous by icebergs, tempests, fogs and interference to radar by natural causes. It was almost entirely within the range of the Luftwaffe, to which the interminable daylight of the summer months was an extra boon. The convoys could not sail eastward beyond a certain point without courting the risks of attack by shore-based German bombers and of a major fleet action should German capital ships put to sea. It was therefore necessary to consider in advance which mattered more, the merchantmen or the escorts. If the merchantmen, then the escorts must be committed to the risk of heavy losses. If the escorts, then the merchantmen must in a crisis be abandoned. The Admiralty, faced with this predicament by Churchill's insistence on the overriding need to get supplies to the USSR by this route, decided that if and when a choice had to be made the merchantmen would be abandoned.

The first convoy sailed from Iceland in September 1941 and was followed by others at the rate of one about every two weeks. Their destination was Archangel or Murmansk, the former being seasonally, and the latter permanently, ice free. Murmansk's more temperate clime was offset by the fact that in 1941 it was only thirty miles from the front, and the Russians therefore preferred Archangel and undertook to keep it open with eight to ten icebreakers. But only two of these materialized and after one had been hit by a bomb in January 1942 five British ships were frozen into the ice for the rest of the winter. The principal problems of these early convoys were the shortage of escort vessels, the natural hazards of the journey, the inadequacy of ice-breaking and unloading facilities at the Russian end and the failure of the Russians to provide coal, ballast, stores or fresh water for the return journeys. The ships employed on this task, which were among Great Britain's newest and best, had to be specially fitted to withstand the climate. Once so equipped they were virtually restricted to the Arctic run, and the tying up of six or seven merchant ships a month was an appreciable drain on Great Britain's hard-pressed merchant fleet.

German opposition did not at first make itself felt. Twelve convoys reached their destinations intact. But PQ 12 was the last to do so. Goods were piling up in Iceland and with the knowledge of this situation Stalin

ARCTIC CONVOYS
TO RUSSIA

ARTHUR BANKS

Arctic convoys (winter route).
Arctic convoys (summer route).
Limit of Allied shore-based air cover.
Limit of German air strikes.
British air bases. Ⓑ
German air bases. Ⓖ
Naval anchorages. ⚓

GREENLAND

DENMARK STRAIT

ICELAND
Akureyri
Seydisfjord
BREYKJAVIK
Hvalfiord

Approximate ice edge: August—September.
Approximate ice edge: April.
Jan Mayen Island

Faroe Islands

SCOTLAND
Loch Ewe
Scapa Flow
ORKNEY ISLANDS
SHETLAND ISLANDS
Sulkom Voe

SPITZBERGEN
South Cape
Hope Island
Bear Island

North Cape
Altenfiord
Banak
Tromso
Bardufoss
Lofoten Is
Narvik
Vest Fiord
Bodö
Namsos
TRONDHEIM
Aandalsnes
OSLO

NORWAY

SWEDEN

FINLAND
Gulf of Bothnia
Gulf of Finland
LENINGRAD

Kirkenes
Petsamo
Kola Inlet
MURMANSK
Kola Peninsula
Vaenga
White Sea
Molotovsk
Ekonomiya
ARCHANGEL
Bakaritsa

U S S R

NOVAYA ZEMLYA
Moller Bay
Gusini Nos
Kolguev Island
Kanin

BALTIC SEA

75° N
70° N
65° N
60° N
75° N
70° N
65° N

50°E
40°E
30°E
20°E
10°E
0°
10°W
20°W
40°E
30°E
20°E
10°E
0°
20°W

was pressing for the fulfilment of the ten-day pledge. Early in 1942 Churchill, against the advice of the Admiralty, promised three convoys of twenty-five to thirty-five ships every two months. In June P Q 17, consisting of thirty-five merchantmen and one tanker, set sail for Archangel.

The British Admiralty was not only a Department of State and a General Staff but also an operational headquarters. It conducted battles. There was therefore a division of authority between the Admiralty and – in this case – the Commander-in-Chief of the Anglo-American covering force, Admiral Sir John Tovey, who was flying his flag in the newly commissioned battleship *Duke of York*. The Admiralty, fearful of the powers of *Tirpitz* and mindful of the dilemma posed by each P Q convoy in turn, had decided that if a German surface force appeared the cruiser and destroyer escort force was to be ordered to withdraw and the convoy to scatter, each merchant vessel being left to make its way to its destination as best it could on its own; the convoy was to be dissolved upon any threat of hostile surface action; an attack by *Tirpitz* on the allied navies was not to be faced.

The convoy was spotted by the Germans on 1 July and air attacks began on the 4th, when four ships were sunk. Before this attack Admiralty intelligence gave strong indications that *Tirpitz* had put to sea. The order to scatter was given and the naval escort was withdrawn westward. *Tirpitz* had not in fact left Trondhjem (although she did so later). Thus the convoy was left exposed to air and U-boat attack. The result was a massacre. Twenty-four of the thirty-five ships went to the bottom. The German surface forces did not need to join in the action. They had achieved their object without doing so.

This catastrophe dictated a pause. P Q 18, sailing in September, was escorted by an aircraft carrier and lost no more than thirteen of its forty ships, and P Q 19 was not dispatched until December. Between-whiles thirteen ships attempted the passage singly. Only five of them made it. During 1943 no convoys sailed in the light months. But the pressures on the Russians had been eased by the victories of their own arms. The northern convoys caused hard feelings and produced bitter words between the allies so long as allied aid seemed a matter of life and death to the Russians, while the carrying of it was not only a severe strain on specially strained shipping resources but also peculiarly dangerous to the men engaged in it. These convoys lost 7.5 per cent of their cargoes, as compared with losses of 0.7 per cent in the Atlantic. Forty convoys in all sailed east, thirty-seven back; 811 merchantmen set out on the passage east, 715 back; 100 ships were sunk, 2,800 men died.

Not all aid to the U S S R went this way. In fact rather less than a

ALLIED CONVOY PQ17 JULY 1942

Miles
0   200

~ARTHUR BANKS~

Spitzbergen

Bear I.

Hope I.

ICE

WASHINGTON
BOLTON CASTLE
PAULUS POTTER

EMPIRE BYRON

EARLSTON

PANKRAFT

RIVER AFTON

ALDERSDALE

HONOMU

ZAAFRAN

DANIEL MORGAN

Trawler AYRSHIRE with SILVER SWORD
                              TROUBADOUR
                              IRONCLAD

Track of PALOMARES

FAIRFIELD CITY

PETER KERR

PAN
ATLANTIC

Position of PQ17
on scattering
4 July 1942.

ZEMLYA

NOVAYA

Matochkin
Str.

Kara Str.

Sukhoi
Nos

HARTLEBURY

EMPIRE TIDE
WINSTON SALEM (ashore)

OLOPANA

ALCOA
RANGER

JOHN WITHERSPOON

ICE

HOOSIER

EL CAPITAN

Kolguev I.

C. Kanin

Goulo

Iokanka

Vaenga

Kola Inlet

Murmansk

Petsamo

Kirkenes

Banak

North Cape

2130
5 July

TIRPITZ, SCHEER,
HIPPER, 8 destroyers,
sailed 1145, 5 July.

Altenfjord

75°N

70°N

20°E   30°E   40°E   50°E   60°E

quarter of it did, the principal route being through Iran. After the war the Russian economist N. A. Voznesenski estimated allied aid at 4 per cent of the USSR's own production; western estimates range a little higher. In figures the United States delivered supplies to the value of $11.3 billion, Great Britain £428 millions' worth. In retrospect the lists are long, dry sets of figures which are difficult to take in: 22,000 aircraft, 13,000 tanks, 2.7 million tons of petrol, 15 million pairs of boots, 2,000 telephones and a million miles of field telephone cable; but while the war was being fought these shipments were very much more than sets of figures, especially in 1941–2 when the Russians were recovering from the first shocks and, as we shall see in the next chapter, struggling to salvage and move factories and get industrial production going again. One tenth (in value) of American supplies consisted of food and this, together with the miscellaneous deliveries of vehicles, chemicals, clothing, tents, blankets, leather goods, radio equipment and medicine were probably even more welcome than the tanks and aircraft which the Russians soon began to turn out for themselves, of excellent quality and in huge numbers.

The harassing of the northern convoys was the last exploit of the German high seas fleet. In September 1943 British midget submarines – craft of fifty feet manned by specially intrepid crews of four – attacked *Tirpitz* at her anchorage up Trondhjem fjord and put her out of action for six months. But the British Admiralty dared not let this powerful vessel remain in being. Her very existence was a threat, even though she remained inactive. Aircraft of the Fleet Air Arm, flying off aircraft carriers, inflicted further blows on her in April 1944 but the damage was comparatively light and further attacks failed. Then Bomber Command was called upon. A first attack by Lancasters operating with 12,000 lb. bombs from Russian airfields crippled her in September but left her afloat. A second attack by Lancasters in November sank her. *Scharnhorst* had been sunk a year earlier and the German surface fleet had long since ceased to play the role which Grand Admiral Raeder had looked forward to. He had resigned his command at the beginning of 1943 when his fleet was already crippled by fuel shortages and the loss of the Führer's confidence. Hitler felt that the men could be better used in other ways and talked of de-commissioning all capital ships. Above and below the waters the command of the seas was no longer disputed anywhere except between the Americans and the Japanese in the Pacific.

The high seas and the ships sailing upon them had been used to ensure or interdict supplies, not to stage major naval battles. There was nothing like the Battle of Jutland, let alone Trafalgar. The vital issues in the Battle of the Seas were, first, whether the British people should get enough to eat, British factories get enough to keep going and the British armed services get enough to fight on; and secondly, the movement of troops across the seas. The worst months of the blockade were also the months in which command of the seas was an issue all over the world – in the Pacific and Indian Oceans as well as the Atlantic – and all the active theatres of war depended on the movement of tens of thousands of men and their equipment every month. The Americans, unaided, were fully committed in the Pacific, so that the armies which they had promised to send eastward in fulfilment of their pledge to put Europe first had to be transported largely in non-American vessels. The major role in keeping the routes open was played by the British with material help from some of their European allies. The British merchant service was maintained throughout the war at a strength of about 145,000 men. Volunteers could and did enter it at the age of sixteen. Employment was traditionally by the voyage, that is to say, any seaman could leave his ship upon his return from any voyage; but none did so. After March 1941 the government had the power to prevent seamen from leaving the service and to direct former seamen back to it, but the flow of volunteers was such that it never had to worry about the manning of the ships. Thirty-two thousand died directly or indirectly through enemy action and many more were disabled.

The defeat of the U-boat was, like the Battle of Waterloo, a 'damned nice thing – the nearest run thing'. The Germans came closer to victory at sea than anywhere else after 1941, and at the time of their defeat in 1943 they had not exhausted their capabilities. They lost, not because they had no more cards to play, but because they played them just too late. They had a new long-range torpedo which could be fired from ranges outside the scanning range of the victim's detecting apparatus; with this torpedo they could strike before being seen. They also had a faster U-boat equipped with the new device called Schnorkel. Thanks to its speed this boat could overtake and then outdistance vessels previously immune and thanks to its Schnorkel, a tube which just broke surface and enabled it to breathe without surfacing, it could remain virtually concealed from sight and from radar. These innovations did not have the chance to take effect in the battle because allied skills had beaten the U-boat back to a position of no recovery.

The U-boat had started the war in a theoretically winning position because it was too difficult to detect and destroy. Sailing faster and deeper than the submarines of the First World War and more strongly built it was almost out of sight and, except when directly hit, it was impervious to depth charges which had improved little over twenty years. Yet, fortunately for Great Britain, it was still essentially what it had been in the First World War – a submersible surface craft and not one which could live permanently beneath the waters. It had to surface to live and it was therefore still vulnerable to detection and destruction by an enemy who knew where it was and had good enough weapons. Its main weaknesses were its inescapable need to surface to recharge its batteries and the practice, enforced by the German High Command, of maintaining contact with home and so betraying its position from time to time by breaking wireless silence. These weaknesses, coupled with the small number of available U-boats in the first two years of war, enabled the allies to turn the tables. As in the air, Great Britain's lead in radar was crucial. Radar was used to find the U-boats when they were forced to surface and a variant of radar – asdic or sonar, developed in both Great Britain and the United States – probed beneath the seas to find submerged boats. The Ultra breakthrough robbed the unwitting U-boat of its invisibility, and as Coastal Command acquired aircraft which could fly farther, detect at great ranges and with greater accuracy and carry more lethal weapons than the pre-war depth charges, so the U-boat was forced from the offensive to the defensive. It did not recover in time to stage another round. Its reverses in 1943 added up to final defeat.

CHAPTER 22

The Victory of the USSR

THE USSR presented Hitler with a problem which was not only different in scale from his British problem but, militarily, diametrically opposite to it. Stalin had resources – of manpower, raw materials and space – which were greatly superior to Germany's. Against them Hitler had to pit superior skill and superior organization in a bid to win a quick victory. He had to break the USSR, not wear it down. In the west he could lose the Battle of Britain but still hope to win the long-drawn-out Battle of the Seas. In the east time was not on his side. He not only hoped to win in six months but needed to win in not much more. He threw the immensely efficient armed forces of a thoroughly modern industrial power against a colossus which had not reached the same stage of industrial sophistication and was, in addition, weakened both materially and psychologically by a generation of turmoil: revolution and civil war, followed by ostracism, the destruction of the peasantry, political and military purges, and a police tyranny and an inquisitorial system of government extremely ill calculated to elicit loyalty. Hitler relied on his military engine to destroy the enemy's power to resist and, at second remove, to encourage the peoples of the USSR to turn against their own government. Although at the end of 1941 he had failed to achieve the decisive victory which he had hoped for, the successes of German arms had been so great that the USSR was like a man who has had his weapon dashed from his hand and does not know where to turn to get himself another. A third of the USSR's industrial capacity had been overrun and another third was under fire from the German armies and air forces, its output gravely cut. The next three years produced fighting more ferocious and devastating than any experienced by man. Both in scale and temper and therefore in its consequences the war in the USSR was altogether different from any of the other campaigns embraced by the Second World War.

Although Stalin had played every available political card in order to fend off a war with Germany and although his military dispositions could be criticized for unpreparedness, he had taken a number of steps to prepare the USSR for war on the industrial front. He introduced measures at the end of 1938 to curb absenteeism in factories and restrict the excessive movement of labour which were a debilitating feature of the Soviet economy: absenteeism became grounds for dismissal and eleven months' employment in one job a prerequisite for two weeks' holiday. In 1940 new measures punished slacking and forbade certain changes of job without permission. In the same year the government took power to direct workers from one place to another. The costs of transporting and re-housing the worker and his family were to be paid by the state; he was to receive six days' pay on arrival at his destination; and he was promised that his wages would not fall. The government also tackled the problem of training. It had an alarming shortage of technicians, especially below the top ranges. It established vocational schools to take nearly a million trainees a year who were then assigned to jobs and were required, military service apart, to stay in them for four years. Young people who were not exceptionally clever or exceptionally privileged were diverted into these schools and away from high schools and universities, where fees were introduced for all but the favoured few; in the face of the emergency created by the threat of war higher education was denied to all but a small élite.

With the advent of war the armed services made big demands on manpower and their losses were so heavy that they continued to do so to the end. The population of the USSR in 1941 was about 200 million but at least one in ten of these died, in uniform or out of it, before the war was over. The territories annexed by the USSR in 1939–40 – an area larger than the United Kingdom – added to its population a million Poles and perhaps half a million Balts, but the total labour force fell from a pre-war total of 28 million to below 20 million by 1943. Half the workers in war industry were women and the proportion of women in agriculture was much higher. Something like half the male peasantry was conscripted into the army, leaving the fields to be worked by women, children and old men, or not worked at all. Millions of these peasants never returned to the countryside, for when the war ended the survivors among them were needed in the towns and factories and for many years after 1945 women continued to provide two thirds of agricultural labour.

The labour available for war industries was not only reduced by the needs of the fighting services and, by western standards, inadequately trained; it was also in the wrong places because industry itself was to a very large extent in the wrong places for a war which began with a German invasion. The removal of industry from threatened areas under the stress of war and the expansion of production in eastern regions of the USSR became a crucial factor in the USSR's victory – the most crucial factor after the Soviet armies had survived the first six months of war. This effect has been presented as nearly a miracle. Like all miracles it had a basis in hard fact.

The USSR was not in 1941 an industrial power like Germany or Great Britain or, least of all, the United States, but it was in process of becoming one. The industrialization of Russia had begun in the nineteenth century, albeit patchily, later than in western Europe and under the heavy disabilities of an ailing political and social system. The revolutionary régime which came to power in 1917 had ambitious ideas about modernizing and urbanizing the USSR and making it self-sufficient but the government's plans were severely hampered by the destruction caused by the First World War and the ensuing civil war and by its own political and economic isolation. The conditions were harsh and the base low. Capital was scarce; communications were poor; technical skills, even secondary education, were thinly spread; the USSR was rich in natural resources but they had never been properly surveyed. But a poor beginning makes for (statistically) impressive achievements, and during the first Five Year Plan (1928–32) and again during the second Plan capital investment, industrial output and gross national product were all doubled and transport facilities increased in even greater proportion. Education was extended and the shift of the population as a whole rose by a third between 1914 and 1940, the urban population from the country to the towns was accelerated while the population was multiplied by 2.4. There was therefore a considerable alteration not only in the number of people at work but even more so in what they were doing.

The main industrial effort remained where it had been – in the areas round Moscow and Leningrad, in the Ukraine and the Don basin. The development of existing facilities had first priority. Nowhere else was there an adequate supply of skilled labour. But the development of other areas – the Urals, western Siberia and Kazakhstan – was a theme which appealed to communist propagandists as well as to the romantic imagination. These areas were known to be rich in minerals. The pre-revolutionary regime could be blamed for doing too little about them. Lenin had said that the right thing to do was to create industries where raw materials were to be got. Consequently the repair and extension of industry in the traditional centres in European Russia was to be matched by exciting new schemes farther east. This eastward trend was gradually intensified. Up to 1930 the traditional centres absorbed the bulk of the effort. During the thirties they still retained their primacy but at the same time vast sums began to be lavished on other areas, particularly the Urals and the Siberian district round Kuznetsk (the Kuzbas), and under the third Five Year Plan, which began in 1939, other areas in western Siberia and central Asia were promised increased attention of the same kind. Railways were built, electric power provided, resources surveyed and populations moved to where labour was required. In the new development areas there was not only a total lack of skilled labour but a considerable shortage of any labour at all, to remedy which the government compelled migrations and used convicts and political prisoners ruthlessly. (In 1941 the NKVD was responsible for a sixth of all new construction in the USSR.)

This relocation of industry, which was to prove strategically vital, was at first economically irrational. Thus coal was mined in the Kuzbas in Siberia and iron ore round Magnitogorsk in the Urals, but there was no iron ore near Kuznetsk or coal near Magnitogorsk and the two centres were well over a thousand miles apart. This situation was, however, later redeemed by supplying Magnitogorsk with coal by rail from Karaganda in Kazakhstan (half the distance away) and by opening up the new iron-fields of Gornaya Shoriya in Siberia to be fed with Kuzbas coal. Thus nature justified the huge expenditure of capital and labour and the USSR found itself endowed with two new industrial complexes in place of one barely cohesive one. (The development of the Kuzbas illustrates the pace of expansion. In the decade 1928–38 its production of coal rose from 2 million to 16 million tons a year.) As the production of iron and coal rose upon the basis of improved communications and technology, more power and more labour, so the USSR began to be supplied with the quantities and the varieties of steel to sustain its expanding industries and, an increasingly more urgent preoccupation, its armament as well.

This wider distribution of the steel industry was the most important single element in the development of the eastern regions, but not the only one. Western Russia is poor in non-ferrous metals, which Tsarist Russia had imported on a significant scale. But copper had been mined in the Urals and the Caucasus since the seventeenth century, and the USSR planned to exploit the copper, lead and zinc of Kazakhstan. This work was put in hand before the war and greatly developed during it, so that Kazakhstan became second only to the Urals in sustaining the Russian war effort. The chemical industry was also diffused, although it remained preponderantly European, and was so severely damaged that American, British and Canadian imports were required to make good the losses. The radio industry was also expanded. Besides 120 large broadcasting stations the USSR was operating 2,000 local stations before the war and had begun a public television service in 1938 (discontinued during the war).

In sum, the Ural, Siberian and central Asian areas, which had been opened up as ancillary industrial enterprises primarily in order to modernize the USSR and make it economically independent of capitalist countries, had become in addition an alternative arms base. Without this

SOVIET INDUSTRIAL RESOURCES
1941 — 1945

German-occupied territory
by December 1943.

Soviet-occupied centres
throughout the war.

OIL Soviet-controlled materials
1941–1945.

Soviet-controlled railways
1941–1945.

Routes of Allied aid
1941–1945.

Scapa Flow
GREAT BRITAIN
North Cape
Berlin
Murmansk
Kandalaksha
COPPER
IRON
Warsaw
Leningrad
IRON
Archangel
Vologda
Kotlas
Moscow
COPPER
Kirov
PLATINUM
Odessa
COPPER
OIL
Kuibyshev
Sverdlov
Saratov
COAL
Tobolsk
MANGANESE
IRON
COPPER
BAUXITE
From the Pacific Coast of
the USA via Vladivostok
Black Sea
Astrakhan
Orsk
Omsk
OIL
OIL
Novosibirsk
IRON
TURKEY
Neutral
OIL
Caspian Sea
Aral Sea
Barnaul
TIN
COPPER
ZINC
LEAD
COPPER
COPPER
MERCURY
OIL
Krasnovodsk
OIL
Lake Balkhash
COPPER
ZINC
COPPER
Ashkhabad
Bukhara
Begovat
Alma Ata
CHINA
IRAN
LEAD
Tashkent
MERCURY
Joint Anglo-Soviet
Occupation
Persian Gulf
AFGHANISTAN
Neutral

0   300
Miles

~ARTHUR BANKS~

alternative the USSR might well have collapsed at the beginning of 1942. The German victories of the previous year had eliminated much of the fruits of the Russian industrial effort of the thirties: between a half and two thirds of its productive capacity in coal, pig iron, steel and aluminium, a quarter of its engineering output. Over 300 ammunition factories had been put out of action. By November 1941 the USSR's overall industrial output had been halved, and during November and December no coal whatever was delivered from the Moscow or the Donets minefields. Industry in the Urals and eastward could not immediately fill the gap but it supplied a base.

A gigantic movement of people and plants took place. The number of people involved may have been as high as 12 million. From Leningrad more than two thirds of the city's capital equipment, building excepted, were conveyed away. According to N. A. Voznesenski, the head of Gosplan (the State Planning Commission), these movements involved 'millions of people . . . hundreds of enterprises, tens of thousands of machine tools, rolling mills, presses, hammers, turbines and motors . . . 1,360 large enterprises – mostly war enterprises – were evacuated to the eastern regions of the USSR.' The impressive aspect of this undertaking was its hugeness, not its organization. The railways, although they had been singled out for improvement under the third Five Year Plan, were reduced to chaos as west-bound trains carried men to the armies at the front while east-bound trains, loaded with machinery, workers and deported Volga Germans and Polish prisoners of war, were pushed into sidings where some of the equipment stayed to rot and men and women to die. At the new sites wooden structures were thrown up to house machinery, but there was often neither time nor materials to build houses for the workers. They sometimes set to work, in temperatures below zero, before the roof was on their makeshift factory and they slept on the floor among the machines. Their privations were terrible. Food was scarce, hospitals (and schools) non-existent. They just worked as long as they could. Mortality was high, output per head poor. The wonder was that they were not worse. By their efforts war industry kept going. But the early months of 1942 were critical. Thereafter production in these regions expanded dramatically until their aggregate war production reached 2.5 times the total pre-war production of the entire USSR. Labour, while it declined overall, rose in 1940–43 from 1 million to 1.5 million in the Urals and by similar degrees in western Siberia and Kazakhstan, each of which had employed nearly half a million in industry on the eve of war.

The principal features of this victory on the home front were two: the rigours which an authoritarian government (aided by the appeal to patriotism) could impose on the people, and the adaptability of the Soviet economy, which partly made up for its technical weaknesses by its ready response to central planning and direction. Once the corner was turned and production resumed, expansion was astonishingly rapid. By the middle of 1942 arms production exceeded its pre-war level. In the next years output in the east continued to rise, while industry in the occupied western areas was rehabilitated with amazing vigour as fast as they were liberated. The Moscow coalfields, for example, whose pre-war production was 35,000 tons a day, resumed output in January 1942 at the rate of 590 tons a day, increased it to 22,000 tons by May and were back to normal by October 1942. Electrical generating capacity, nearly half of which was physically destroyed by the Germans, was also back to its pre-war volume before the war ended. Russian production of tanks and aircraft surpassed German production in 1943. At their peak they reached 40,000 aircraft and 30,000 tanks and other armoured fighting vehicles a year – alongside an output of 150,000 pieces of artillery, 500,000 machine guns and at least 2 million sub-machine guns and 3 million rifles. Stalin had won, by however narrow a margin, the fight for the material resources of war; but there was also the question of human responses.

The response of the people of the USSR depended not only on how they were treated during the war but also on how they had been treated before it. Wartime privations, however severe, were expected and attributable to the enemy, but the history of pre-war relations between government and governed gave rise on the German side to hopes of rebellion and, one may suppose, to equivalent fears on the Russian side.

The intensive industrialization of the thirties was Stalin's special contribution to the evolution of Soviet society. Through it he established his totalitarian authority and because of it he waged a savage fight against the peasantry which had been one of the protagonists in the revolution of 1917. The question of the peasants is the question of food. The food which peasants produce can either be bought or seized. During the confused years of revolution and civil war after 1917 it was most frequently seized but seized with some justification and consent, since the struggling revolution – to which the peasants adhered – had no money to pay for it and no means to produce the goods which the peasants might have taken in exchange for their produce. The peasants understood this, but they also learned the strength of their position and when the civil war ended they in effect bargained with the central government and forced it to reward them for their labours instead of merely appropriating its fruits.

For the next six years (1921–7) the New Economic Policy sought to provide goods to satisfy and stimulate the peasants, but some of the richer peasants continued to demonstrate their power by keeping food off the market when they were dissatisfied with the returns offered to them. A series of good harvests increased their power and the temptation to hold back supplies for the towns and play the markets, so much so that the government had to import grain to save the towns from starvation. The New Economic Policy not only derogated from the basic principles of the Bolshevik Party by making concessions to private operators and to the profit motive, so that bolsheviks like Stalin came increasingly to resent the power of the peasants and to determine to destroy it, even at the cost of another revolution; it also made the peasantry a rising power opposed to the party and opposed to the towns. So instead of running consumer industries to pay for peasant produce the government would force the peasants to pay for heavy industry by reverting once more to the civil war practices of exploiting their labour and taking their produce on the state's own terms. There was in fact no other way of paying for industrialization, since the USSR was neither forming the needful capital within its borders nor able to borrow it abroad. Peasants had paid for industrialization before – for example, in the Industrial Revolution in western Europe – but not nearly so harshly or so fast as Stalin made the Russian peasants pay.

They paid for internal reasons, but the way they were forced to pay was largely dictated by failures in foreign policy, in particular the rupture with Great Britain and the collapse of the attempt to foster communism in China. These failures were all the more dangerous, given the failure to promote communism in Europe a decade earlier. Industrialization could no longer wait and so with the first Five Year Plan the peasants were brigaded into collectives in order the better to be coerced. In the course of his war on the peasantry Stalin sharpened the totalitarian machinery and police terror of the state and converted the Bolshevik Party from a policy-making organization, which to some extent it still was in the twenties, into an apparatus of arbitrary power to be used not only against the peasants but also against townspeople and enemies or imagined enemies of all kinds. The more prosperous peasants were ruined, great numbers of peasants were killed and agricultural production was disastrously reduced. The horrors of these years made their contribution to the industrialization which Stalin had resolved to effect, but at a price which raised the question of how far the peoples of the USSR could be counted loyal to it in war. Unable to pay the Russians to work harder or inspire them to do so as perhaps Lenin or Trotsky might have done, Stalin had been left with only the modern equivalent of flogging them – a police régime in which the workers, trapped by informers and false accusations, were consigned wholesale to hard labour camps. Stalin was not blind to the risks inherent in this ferocity. His first wartime speech on 3 July 1941 appealed, in terms unwontedly similar to the appeals to patriotism made by democratic leaders, for sacrifices, ruthlessness and unity, for a scorched earth policy and guerrilla warfare to help the desperately struggling armed forces.

The sacrifices which the peoples of the USSR may have braced themselves to make in 1941 can hardly have been as gruelling as they turned out to be in fact. Life in the USSR during the war became not only grim but so difficult to sustain that about a million people died of starvation. The armed services and workers in war industry got enough to eat. By and large other people did not. The total amount of food provided and purchased was almost halved. Personal consumption fell below that of the frightful famine year in 1932. The sugar ration, to take an extreme example, was reduced to half a pound a year. The supply of vegetables was cut by nearly two thirds, of meat by more than half, of flour by nearly half. There was no attempt to keep up tobacco stocks, which fell by three quarters, nor the flow of vodka, which was halved. Production of consumer goods was not much more than adequate for the needs of the armed services. Real earnings were cut by a half or more. Compulsory saving was increased by contributions to war bonds which were to be redeemed after the war – but lost nine tenths of their value when the currency was reformed in 1947. Prices had begun to rise with fear of war in 1939 and rose sharply during 1940. After the outbreak of war in 1941 prices of rationed foods and goods were pegged at their, already enhanced, pre-war levels, but they were scarce in the state shops which sold rationed and price-controlled commodities, while in other shops prices rocketed upwards and reached by 1943 about fourteen times their 1940 levels. (After the war the prices of price-controlled commodities were re-adjusted, in a number of cases by trebling them. When rationing ended in 1947 basic prices were about three times what they had been in 1940. But vodka had gone up ten times.)

Hours of work were lengthened. Holidays, other than the weekly day of rest, were cancelled. The seven day week was reintroduced in 1940 – that is to say, one rest day in seven instead of one in six or (before 1929) one in five. The normal working day was extended from seven hours to eight, but plant managers could extend it up to eleven hours, for extra pay at higher rates. The state offered some palliatives. The USSR had a well-established, comprehensive social insurance scheme which worked on a non-contributory basis, was financed by central and local government authorities and the state's business enterprises, provided sickness and other benefits graded according to wages and length of service, and gave pensions to men at sixty and women at fifty-five: pensions ranged from 50 per cent to 100 per cent of the basic wage (the latter for the lower paid), but there was a ceiling which, although not ungenerous in the thirties, became niggardly with wartime inflation. The state also recognized the need for solace of a different kind. From the outbreak of war, churches became packed with people praying that their country would be saved from its enemies and that they themselves would have the fortitude to bear their increasingly intolerable burdens of mental anguish and physical pain. In 1943 Stalin re-established the Holy Synod of the Russian Orthodox church and allowed it to elect a patriarch and re-open seminaries.

A large proportion of the population of the USSR lived outside big towns and their attitudes were specially difficult to control or predict. While Stalin appealed to them from the one side, the Germans were hoping to find among them a substantial number of disaffected who would take the first opportunity to turn against their government. Both sides wanted them to take an active part in the war, the one as guerrilla partisans against the invaders, the other as auxiliaries on the German side.

Stalin seems to have envisaged guerrilla resistance before the German invasion took place, for instructions for it were issued within a few days. The civil wars after 1917, still a living memory in the USSR, had made partisan warfare less esoteric than it was in the west, and communist doctrine tended to blur the sharper distinction made in more traditionalist societies between professional and popular campaigning. The rapid advances made by the Germans in 1941 placed them in control of large areas from which the inhabitants had not had time to flee. German control was unevenly spread and Stalin could have ordered the civilian population to escape eastward; broad corridors, more or less unpoliced by the Germans, could be traversed without much danger. But no such withdrawals were made. Many of the inhabitants may have been unwilling to leave their homes, even though they were in enemy occupied territory, in order to be drafted into Stalin's armies, but it seems that Stalin did not in any case want to use them that way. They could be more useful as guerrilla fighters within the enemy's lines.

Bands were quickly formed to harass German units and communications, to collect intelligence and to exact vengeance upon anybody who collaborated with the enemy. From these beginnings a considerable force grew, although not without some initial setbacks. Moscow's first plan was to provide a core of organizers, with some elementary training in partisan warfare and of indubitable party loyalty, who would be reinforced by local anti-German patriotism and enthusiasm. This plan was not at first very successful. Local enthusiasm was not as marked as had been hoped and the first groups had to contend with some pro-German attitudes as well as the attentions of the SD. Problems of supply and communication were extremely severe during 1941 and these first groups achieved little beyond a few hit-and-run raids and enough reprisals against collaborationists to make people think twice before helping the Germans. A number of these bands were completely eliminated. In the same period other bands came spontaneously and haphazardly into existence. Out of the flotsam and jetsam of the defeated Russian armies, groups 300–1,000 strong formed, but their first aim was survival rather than further action against the Germans who, until the end of 1942, still looked like the winning side. During 1942, however, the government was able to impose a degree of organization and direction on the bands and began to draft the local peasantry into an effective, if subordinate and ancillary, fighting force.

The Germans employed around 250,000 security troops (usually substandard or foreign conscripts) in the USSR, partly in response to this activity, but shortages of men and materials limited their anti-partisan operations. The partisans harassed German communications and retarded reinforcements, notably in conjunction with the Kursk offensive in 1943 and before the Russian attacks in White Russia in the summer of 1944; they also inflicted about 35,000 casualties. They were helped from the start by the Germans themselves. The horrors, already related, perpetrated by the SD and the *Einsatzkommandos*, the destruction of over three million prisoners of war, the deportations to extermination camps and forced labour, the killing of a further million partisans and civilians in the USSR, the burning of villages and shooting of villagers by way of reprisal – on one occasion 158 villages were burned down as a single act of reprisal – all these things inflamed anti-German hatred and made villagers think that they might as well join the partisans instead of waiting to be killed or enslaved by the Germans. Thus, although the Germans sent agents (operation Zeppelin) to infiltrate the bands and the *Volksdeutsche*; although the Ukraine contained the seeds of a separatist and anti-Soviet movement; although the Germans appointed a Russian civilian governor of Bryansk as an experiment; and although they captured a potential anti-Soviet leader in General A. A. Vlasov, their excesses (like those of the Poles in the same parts in 1920) ruined whatever chances they may have had of subverting any appreciable number of Soviet citizens and swelled the active ranks of their adversaries.

By mid-1942 the partisans probably numbered about 150,000. Their strongest ground was White Russia, where wooded country provided the best terrain; Bryansk became a principal base and from it they extended their operations into the Ukraine. But the government still could not spare them much in the way of up-to-date equipment. A year later the Germans put their strength at 200,000 and eventually they may have reached half a million. From 1943 they received new equipment from the USSR's reorganized factories, including mortars and artillery, special anti-tank guns for attacking locomotives, radios which kept them in touch with one another and with the Russian High Command, and medical supplies which had been almost totally lacking. They were supplied by air and constructed and maintained airfields for this purpose. Most of them were between seventeen and thirty-five years old, conscripted peasants with a sprinkling of army officers and other ranks and party officials. Whereas in the early days the emphasis was on reliable party members, the proportion of these inevitably fell as the movement became bigger; the consciously and actively political element may have been around one tenth in the later years. Towards the end of the war partisan brigades moved into other countries as an advance guard of Russian retribution and in order to help form local committees of reliable residents. In Poland they fought some minor engagements against the Polish Home Army and in Slovakia some 3,000 of them joined with Slovaks parachuted from the USSR in the Slovak rising against the Germans at the end of 1944, but in Rumania and Hungary their activities were insignificant and in Latvia they were driven out again.

The partisan movement had also a political purpose. The Germans occupied areas of the USSR containing a population of 70 million. These areas included large tracts, with a population of 20 million, which had only very recently come under Russian rule, and where anti-Russian feeling was intense. In all these areas, temporarily lost, Stalin was concerned to preserve some vestiges of the presence of the Soviet state. He had no reason to assume that the peasantry of the USSR would remain loyal to his régime and even less reason to suppose that the population of the Baltic states and eastern Poland would not jump at any chance, even a chance presented to them by the Germans, to repudiate it. The destruction by the Germans of the apparatus of government was a threat to the communist system, especially in areas where local separatism – political as in the Ukraine or religious as among the USSR's Muslim peoples – reinforced dislike of Stalin's communist autocracy and police rule, dislike of forced collectivization and dislike of war. The partisan movement was a reminder, if necessary a forcible one, that the government of the USSR was still in being and still in the fight. The partisans actively combated German attempts to subvert local leaders. Village elders appointed by the Germans were killed, so that fear of the German conqueror was more than offset by fear of the continuing capacity and omniscience of the central government of the USSR and its servants.

Yet a number of Soviet citizens did collaborate with the Germans or take service with them. There is more than a suggestion of severe disaffection in the fate of the Tartars, Kalmucks, Chechens and other minorities, about a million of whom were deported from the Caucasus in the winter of 1943–4, charged with collaborating with the Germans. The brutality with which they were treated (later acknowledged by Khrushchev), the thoroughness with which all traces of their homes and even their cemeteries were obliterated, and above all the date, betray a grim punitive intent persisting after all need for precautions had disappeared. In more lastingly occupied territories perhaps half a million or a million Russians, the so-called *Osttruppen*, took German pay. Their main reason was not a desire to serve against their own country but the appalling way in which the Germans behaved in the areas which they occupied. Joining the *Osttruppen* was a way out. Most of the *Osttruppen* were used as rear units in various parts of Europe but the Germans also made some attempts to form more active Russian fighting forces. In 1941 they established a Russian National Liberation Army (RONA) for anti-partisan warfare. It was later converted into the SS Division Kaminsky. In 1944 it participated in the suppression of the Warsaw rising where, even by current SS standards, its barbarous behaviour was outstanding and caused Guderian to protest to Hitler himself; its commander, Kaminsky, was killed by the SS themselves. There were one or two other formations of this nature, such as the XXSS Cossack Cavalry Corps. The SS overcame their prejudices against Slav sub-men by dubbing any Slavs who came over to their side Cossacks and pretending that Cossacks were not Slavs.

Another Russian formation on the German side was the Russian Liberation Army (ROA), which is connected with the name of General Vlasov. Vlasov began the war by deserving well of his country. Like Zhukov he had seen service in the Far East. After commanding a corps on the southern front in 1941 he was posted to the Moscow front as commander of the Twentieth Army at the age of forty-one and had a share with Zhukov in saving the capital. He became appalled by Stalin's ruthlessness in the sacrifice of lives and when, in the following summer, he was captured by the Germans on the Leningrad front he was ready to be transformed into an anti-communist leader.

The ROA was more of a scheme than an army. Hitler was afraid of creating a substantial all-Russian force and he refused to incorporate the *Osttruppen* in the ROA. He preferred to use it in non-combatant, paramilitary roles; it was a piece of window-dressing which was meant to imply massive Russian disaffection within the USSR, serving Goebbels's anti-Russian propaganda and helping to keep up the morale of the *Osttruppen* who might begin to wonder how prudent it was to go on working for the Germans. Late in 1944, however, Hitler toyed with the idea of assembling all his Russian bits and pieces into an army under Vlasov and recognizing Vlasov as the head of a Russian government in exile. As a result Vlasov found himself in 1945 in command of two divisions totalling about 50,000 men. A part of this force was sent into action on the eastern front in March. Whether designedly or not, it suffered very heavy casualties. In May further units under Vlasov himself went to the Prague front where they joined the Czechs and turned against the Germans. The commander of a Russian force moving south from Berlin towards Prague proposed joint action with a neighbouring American force, but the American commander refused, and when it became clear that Prague was about to fall to the Russians alone, Vlasov tried to escape to the west. He was caught and hanged by the Russians with nine of his associates. Several thousand of his army were turned over to the Russians by the Americans.

Vlasov was one of those Russians who had imagined that nothing could be worse than Stalin's rule. Before the Germans undeceived him on this point by their own bestialities he and others who thought like him had welcomed and incited desertions from the Russian forces to the German side. His supreme aim was another Russian revolution, to be achieved if necessary with the help of the Germans (he was never interested in cooperation with the Americans or British who were Stalin's allies). His crime and ultimately his fate lay in continuing to hold to this course after the Germans had displayed their own beastliness and had moreover become the losing side. He regarded Stalingrad as a defeat. He was therefore a traitor in the strict sense of the word. He was moreover a traitor who found in the end that he had misplaced his trust, so that he had doomed himself to a death without compensations. Like a number of traitors with a cause he is entitled to be remembered as a tragic figure. He was a premature anti-Stalinist whose anti-Stalinism involved aiding the invaders of his country.

In the field the decisive events, after Hitler's failure to score a knockout victory in 1941, were the bitter, yard by yard struggle for Stalingrad in the following winter and then the huge tank battles of the Kursk salient in July 1943.

Stalin's aims for 1942 were to repel Hitler's central Army Group, relieve Leningrad and recover the Ukraine. These plans, which probably assumed a second front to be opened by his allies in the west that year, were not fulfilled. In January the Russians attacked with determination on all fronts against an enemy who was pitifully ill-equipped for the Russian winter, but Stalin was so over-ambitious that these attacks were damaging without being decisive, and so ruthless that they inflicted on his own armies losses as heavy as those suffered by the Germans. As in the previous year large Russian formations were often surrounded and had to be rescued (or not) by further attacks which detracted from Stalin's main aim of inflicting a major defeat on the Germans in the central sector. The German armies, although badly battered, remained in being and in March Stalin was compelled to desist. The rest of the year was coloured by the ill-directed exertions of the first quarter which left Stalin without the men or munitions needed for anything but defensive operations. In addition Stalin made a series of serious mistakes. He refused to allow Timoshenko to break off his offensive towards Kharkov in May although it was evident that the Russian attack had been forestalled. Large Russian losses included the capture of 200,000 men. Furthermore, and in spite of convincing evidence to the contrary, Stalin insisted on believing that major German preparations in the southern sector were merely a feint to cover a second attack on Moscow.

This was a complete misreading of Hitler's intentions, all the more fateful since Hitler, in spite of his disappointments the year before, still held the initiative. His plan was to clean up the Crimea, capture Stalingrad and occupy the Caucasus up to the Turkish border. Thus the main weight of the renewed German attack was to be in the north and south, with the centre remaining relatively static. In the south the programme – the Crimea, Stalingrad, the Caucasus – entailed a number of differing and ultimately diverging operations. The whole of the Crimea was overrun by May except Sebastopol which, having heroically sustained a siege of 250 days, did not fall until July. Manstein's Eleventh Army, which had won these victories, was then switched to the Leningrad front although Manstein himself would have preferred to cross the straits of Kerch (which run along the eastern shore of the Crimea), strike northward with the sea of Azov on his left, make contact with the forces designated for the capture of Stalingrad and preserve the contacts between these forces (Army Group B) and others (Army Group A) which were heading south-eastward into the Caucasus.

In July 1942 Hitler moved his headquarters to Vinnitsa in the Ukraine, whence he had the satisfaction of seeing his armies advance without serious check across the Don to the Volga and to the Caucasus mountains. But these favourable beginnings were the end of Hitler's joy. Very unwisely Hitler had succumbed to the temptation to attempt simultaneously two operations which he had originally planned to put in motion one after the other and which, the more either of them succeeded, were bound to open a gap between Army Groups B and A, the one making for Stalingrad and the other disappearing right-handed into the Caucasus.

In the air the Luftwaffe was still supreme. Although the Russians had two or three times as many aircraft as the Germans (and four or five times as many fighters), and although they were also receiving American Tomahawks and British Hurricanes, and although the Germans had relinquished some squadrons for the Mediterranean, the Luftwaffe was able, when called on to make a maximum effort, to fly as many as 3,000 sorties a day – ten times as many as the larger Russian forces. But on the ground the Russian armies, reorganized, backed by reorganized industries and enjoined by Stalin in an order of the day of 1 July to yield no more ground, met their enemies with a new effectiveness and a new confidence. The German advances slowed down. Army Group A failed to reach the Caucasian oilfields before it had to turn round and fight its way back again. Army Group B crossed the Don, won a series of engagements in the narrow zone between the easternmost sweep of the Don and the Volga, and reached the Volga in the last days of August. But the capture of Stalingrad, which would put Hitler in command of one of the most important points in the rail and waterways system of the USSR, proved just too much for it.

The battle for Stalingrad has become one of the most celebrated episodes of the war. Its importance was realized at the time. In the summer, as the Germans approached, Stalin relieved Timoshenko who commanded what had become the South-west Front and appointed General V. N. Gordov in his place. In August Zhukov was dispatched to the Front with special powers – which caused, among other things, jealousies and disputes which had to be referred to Stalin. Stalin may have recalled how he had himself been a commissar on this front in 1919 and had attached to himself a group of officers and commissars antagonistic to the supreme warlord, Trotsky: Khruschchev was now unwittingly building a similar group of loyal friends who would stand by him in the decade after Stalin's death. As German pressure increased the South-west Front was divided into two, confusingly named, new Fronts: the Stalingrad Front, subsequently renamed the Don Front, and the South-east Front, subsequently Stalingrad Front, the latter commanded in turn by Generals A. I. Eremenko and K. K. Rokossovski. But the most famous name on the Russian side was to be that of General V. I. Chuikov, second in command of the Sixty-fourth Army and then picked by Khrushchev on 12 September to command the Sixty-second Army. Chuikov had been an army commander before the war began. He was relegated early in the war but was soon reinstated. He was still an army commander when the war ended. He was ready in criticism of his superiors and sometimes unfair, and like a number of Stalingrad heroes he fancied that too much of the credit for that famous victory was taken after the event by Stalin, Zhukov and to a lesser extent Rokossovski.

Chuikov and the Sixty-second Army were penned into a city which was in the grip of the Germans; all industry within it and all traffic along the Volga were stopped. From the middle of September the city itself was the battleground and its principal buildings, which sometimes changed hands as many as five times in a day, the tactical objectives. The German Sixth Army under General Friedrich Paulus occupied seven eighths of it and twice – in the third week of October and again on 11 November – almost succeeded in overrunning the defenders. The Germans still had a definite superiority in the air. Although their sorties dropped from about 2,000 a day during the autumn to half that figure during the height of the siege, and although the Russian effort was growing, the Luftwaffe was flying about twice as many sorties as the Russians. The Sixty-second Army, inspired by its commander who was always in the thick of the battle, maintained itself by winning back by night ground lost during the day. It was never completely cut off, for it had its back to the river which the Germans failed to control at every point and beyond which was sited all the Russian artillery.

In November the Sixth Army was itself surrounded, when the Russians attacked and defeated the armies on its left and right. This stroke had been planned by the Russian command in September and nervously anticipated by the German generals, but they had been unable to get Hitler to guard against it and when it happened they were taken by surprise. Hitler had dismissed the Chief of Staff of the Army, General Franz Halder (he also took over personal command of Army Group A in the Caucasus from Field Marshal List, who was also dismissed), and replaced him by General Kurt Zeitzler who – although not noted for disagreeing with Hitler – warned him that his forces were dangerously strung out, especially in the Stalingrad sector where the Sixth Army, the spearhead of Army Group B, was worried about its flanks. Hitler refused to withdraw the Sixth Army and abandon the attack in Stalingrad. Instead he tried to buttress it by sending the Rumanian Third and Fourth Armies into positions to the left and right of the Sixth Army and by putting in some Luftwaffe Field Divisions, of whose value the army generals were rightly dubious. Army Group B consisted therefore of the Sixth Army with a Panzer army (Fourth Panzer) on its right, this German core being flanked on either side by the two Rumanian armies and, on the left, by Italian and Hungarian forces. The Army Group's contacts with Army Group A to

THE BATTLE FOR STALINGRAD SEPTEMBER 1942 - FEBRUARY 1943

Built-up areas of Stalingrad and its suburbs.

German forces, 13 September 1942.

Lines of German advance, involving street fighting and hand to hand fights.

Sole part of the city in Soviet hands on 12 November.

ORLOVKA

Orlovka

GORODISCHE

RYNOK

Volga

Mokraya Mechetka

MATVEEV KURGAN

'Important factories'

Tsaritsa

Sta.

STALINGRAD

Sta.

MININA SUBURB

Volga

0	1	2	3	4

Miles

The Germans planned to capture Stalingrad followed by a northward advance along the Volga. This operation was frustrated by the Soviet defence which endured for five months.

~ARTHUR BANKS~

the south were very tenuous. This was the position when the Russians attacked on 19 November (twelve days after the Anglo-American landings in Morocco and Algeria). The Rumanian Third Army was routed at once. So was the Rumanian Fourth Army the next day. There was now a gap between the Sixth Army and the Italians and Hungarians further to the left and a wider gap than ever between Army Groups B and A. And the Sixth Army, which consisted of twenty-two divisions and 220,000 men, had to be supplied by air or extricated.

The strains of the autumn months of 1942 made Hitler singularly moody and intractable. He stayed at his headquarters conducting the war on paper, refusing to allow his plans and his hopes to be upset by reports of what was actually happening in the field. The German staffs had good intelligence about the Russian forces and their dispositions; their intentions were not difficult to guess. But Hitler, pitting his will against the Russians' resources, continued to believe that he could prevail by insisting that that was how it was to be. The arguments of his generals failed to persuade him that he must give up the idea of taking Stalingrad and concentrate on saving the Sixth Army. By November the generals, now deeply pessimistic, were reduced to hoping that something would happen to change Hitler's mind before it was too late, but even after Paulus had been surrounded Hitler found arguments for sticking to his guns: the new Tiger tank would do the trick and meanwhile the Luftwaffe would keep the Sixth Army supplied.

But the Tiger was not yet in service and the Luftwaffe could do nothing of the sort. Goering, confronted with the question whether he could deliver 700 tons a day to the Sixth Army, declared that he could. This irresponsible pledge was partly the result of a successful supply operation earlier in the year to other forces surrounded on the Russian front. This operation, however, had been conducted in much better weather and before the Luftwaffe had had to send squadrons (including Ju. 52 squadrons) from Russia to Africa; and it had cost crippling losses. But Goering preferred to undertake, however vainly, to save the Sixth Army than to incur reproaches for not stepping forward to say he could. The generals at Hitler's headquarters knew that Goering's promise was absurd but their protests, muted by fear of the Führer, were passed over. The daily target of 700 tons was reduced to 300, but the Luftwaffe never came anywhere near it. It had no adequate landing grounds near the Sixth Army or within its shrinking perimeter, and the cold, which set in early in November and was accompanied by thick fogs from the middle of the month, made flying extremely hazardous when at all possible and the servicing of aircraft on the ground a torture for frozen mechanics. The lift began on 25 November. On that day and the next sixty-five tons were delivered, on the third nothing. A big effort was made in mid-December but the fog came down again and although a few F.W. 200s continued to drop a few tons on most days until the end, the Luftwaffe's contribution was wholly ineffectual. The total supplied by drops and landings was 3,295 tons. The Luftwaffe lost 488 machines and 1,000 men.

At the end of November Manstein was given command of Army Group B (renamed Army Group Don) but it was still not clear whether he was to save the Sixth Army by opening an escape route for it to the west or by breaking the Russian ring round it and so enabling it to remain on the Volga. Hitler equivocated. Manstein's own plan was twofold: an eastward offensive by the Fourth Panzer Army and a simultaneous westward attack by a part of the Sixth Army, leaving however the rest of the Sixth Army still on the Volga; and, at a later stage, a breakout by the whole of the Sixth Army to the west. The operation began on 12 December and the German armour advancing from the west got to within forty miles of the Sixth Army's position, but nine days later it was halted. Neither Manstein nor – still less, since he was Manstein's subordinate – Paulus was willing to give the order to the Sixth Army to break out without Hitler's approval, which they could not get. Without it the first part of Manstein's plan was pointless and, as the events showed, also impracticable. By mid-December therefore the fate of the Sixth Army was sealed. The Russians, after inflicting further defeats on Italian, Hungarian and German armies north-west of Stalingrad, offered Paulus on 8 January honourable terms of surrender. Hitler made Paulus a Field Marshall and told him to stand his ground.

By this time the city had been turned into something which none of those who fought there had ever imagined and none who survived could ever forget. The closest and bloodiest battle of the war was fought among the stumps of buildings burnt or burning. From afar Stalingrad looked like a furnace and yet inside it men froze. Dogs rushed into the Volga, to drown, rather than endure any longer the perils of the shore. The no less desperate men were reduced to automatons, obeying orders until it came to their turn to die, human only in their suffering. The Germans were on half rations from the end of November. By the middle of January the German zone, which had measured twenty-five miles by twelve when Paulus was first surrounded in November, had been halved. A little later it was cut in two. Again the Russians called for surrender and again Hitler refused to permit it. The final capitulation came on 2 February. Ninety-one thousand survivors, including a Field Marshal and twenty-four generals, were taken captive. The Russians had already taken 16,700 prisoners during the last weeks of the fighting. Some 70,000 Germans died during the siege, many of them from exposure or starvation, some by suicide.

At Stalingrad the Russians first demonstrated the material strength which was to overwhelm the German armies in 1943 and 1944. They concentrated over a million men against German armies which were numerically slightly stronger and, although still inferior in aircraft, they had the measure of the Germans in tanks and guns. Even in aircraft the balance was shifting. A new Russian fighter, the La. 5, made (like the British Mosquito) of wood, came into service and helped the Russians to achieve local air superiority. Although at Stalingrad the Luftwaffe committed 1,000 aircraft – about half its strength in the Russian theatre but diminished in October when Hitler ordered some squadrons to Leningrad – its numerical superiority was beginning to be offset by growing experience, skill and morale on the Russian side and by anxieties about repairs, reserves and replacements on its own. From 1943 onwards the Germans continued to keep between a half and two thirds of the Luftwaffe in the east, but some of its best pilots, newest aircraft and latest equipment were reserved for the defence of the Reich and for other theatres, and the shortage of pilots and aircraft gradually increased to the point where at times new aircraft, even new types, were given to the Rumanian and Hungarian air forces, which had pilots to fly them, while at other times German squadrons were obliged to make do with obsolescent machines. The Russian air force on the other hand was not only growing in quantity and quality but, since it undertook very little strategic long range bombing, was able to devote almost its entire strength to attacking the German armies and their installations and communications.

There was after Stalingrad also a qualitative change in the war in the USSR. The importance of Stalingrad was much more than statistical. This battle destroyed the idea that the German army could not be beaten: here, on the contrary, was defeat unmistakable. The surrender of the Sixth Army was a tremendous psychological as well as military blow to the Germans and an equally powerful boost to Russian morale and to Stalin's campaign to show that Russia's great patriotic war could be won. The effect on Hitler was to accelerate his physical and mental decline. In 1942 his speech and handwriting began to show the effects of Parkinson's disease, a general decay of the nervous system which destroys a man's coordination and eventually his understanding. A year later he had become a shambling, shaking wreck, pathologically suspicious of his generals, contemptuous of the qualities of his fighting men, driven increasingly to substitute his personal stubbornness for the divisions which he pretended to direct but which were often not really there. He showed at

Stalingrad, in catastrophic degree, his inability to accept even the concept of defeat. His astonishing memory and grasp of detail, his energy and quickness, his serious application to the art of war and the way with men which he sometimes displayed – all these things were destroyed, first, by the distortions induced by failure in a mind of terrifying rigidity and irrationality, and then by disease. The nemesis of will was upon him and his people.

The defeats of Army Group B in the winter of 1942–3 exposed Army Group A to the risk of being bottled up entire in the Caucasus. The Russians planned to advance from the Don to the Donets and then turn about and capture Rostov at the mouth of the Don from the west. This manoeuvre would have established a Russian line from Stalingrad to Rostov, cutting off Army Group A's line of retreat. The Russian plan was, however, frustrated and the Fourth Panzer Army succeeded in making contact with Army Group A and opened an escape for it, thereby enabling its forces to survive and fight another day. The thaw in March eased the pressure on the Germans who recaptured Kharkov which they had lost a few weeks earlier. Thus the Russian victories, although massive, were not decisive and the Germans were able to regain the initiative and hold much of the Donets basin. This, if anything, was the Sixth Army's posthumous reward. But the losses of the German armies could not be replaced; after the middle of 1943 the eastern fronts had even to surrender units for Italy, the Balkans and the west, and by the end of that year thirty divisions – 15 per cent of those on the Russian fronts – had been disbanded for want of replacements to fill the gaps in their ranks.

As a result of the fighting in February and March 1943 the Russians held Kursk, a hundred miles south of Orel and a hundred miles north of Kharkov, both of which cities remained in German hands. The Russian position was therefore a huge bulge extending westward from Kursk for seventy miles and measuring some hundred miles from north to south at its eastern end. After some hesitation Stalin decided to wait for Hitler to attack first. By this time his air reconnaissance had greatly improved his intelligence about German dispositions and he was also receiving valuable information from an infiltrator in German headquarters and from the spy ring in Switzerland called Lucy which had excellent contacts in Berlin and elsewhere and provided him with the date chosen by Hitler for his attack.

Hitler's aim was to re-establish German mastery and morale by eliminating the Kursk salient. The German attack was launched on 5 July by Kluge in the north and Manstein in the south with a combined force of a million men and 2,700 tanks. The Luftwaffe, despite its commitments in other theatres, was able to fly 3,000 sorties a day and Hitler hoped that after cutting off the Russian armies in the bulge he would be able to turn about and dash for Moscow, 200 miles north-east of Orel. On the Russian side two Fronts, commanded by Rokossovski and Vatutin, were backed by a reserve Front under Konev which had been constituted in their rear. The Russian armies were plentifully supplied by Russian industry, and although the Russian Marshals had somewhat fewer tanks than their opponents, the Russian air forces were for the first time able to put many more aircraft into the air than the Luftwaffe. Russian field intelligence was detailed and accurate.

The ensuing battles in the Kursk salient were the main encounter of the war between the Russian and German armies and they were astonishingly short. The German attack in the north was held from the beginning and by 10 July Kluge was forced onto the defensive, partly by the weight of Rokossovski's artillery and the effectiveness of his anti-tank weapons, and partly in anticipation of a Russian counter-attack on his left flank. The Russians also used air to ground rockets which, although not much more destructive than other weapons, were more demoralizing. In the south Manstein was initially more successful and Konev's reserves had to be called upon to help Vatutin. The result was the biggest tank battle of the war. By 12 July it was a clear Russian victory. The German offensive had failed. The Russians counter-attacked, took Orel and Kharkov and extended the fighting along the whole front from the Baltic to the Black Sea. Their gains included Kiev which fell to them in November.

The battles for the Kursk salient cost Hitler half a million men and when they failed, all possibility of avoiding total defeat had gone. The rest was retreat. The Russian armies, under the meticulously competent overall direction of Stalin (who achieved a more effective relationship with his generals than Hitler did) now outnumbered the Germans. The German Tiger tank, which had appeared in the previous autumn, and the Panther, which made its first appearance in these battles, failed to give Hitler the decisive superiority in the tank war which he had hoped for and which had been eluding him ever since 1941. His Tiger II, first used in 1944, was too late to affect the issue. The Russians, with the heavy Joseph Stalin tank, the medium T 34 (which had reached units just in time in 1941) and the light T 70, proved themselves at least the equals of the Germans in quality, and in 1942 Russian production outstripped German. The Russians were great war builders, the peers – given the circumstances – of the Americans. From 1943 their annual production of armoured fighting vehicles (that is to say, tanks, armoured vehicles and assault guns) was around 30,000. In Germany, where after Stalingrad Hitler had charged

SOVIET ADVANCES 1942–1944

Soviet–German Frontier October 1939.
Front line November 1942.
Soviet gains to April 1943.
Retaken by Germans June–July 1943.
Soviet gains July 1943–April 1944.
German-controlled territory April 1944.

—ARTHUR BANKS—

Caspian Sea

Kazan
Gorki
Volga
Volga
Stalingrad
Astrakhan
Grozny

MOSCOW

Don
Rostov
Kharkov
Orel
Dnieper
Kalinin
Kiev
Odessa
Sebastopol

Black Sea

Lake Ladoga
Leningrad
Helsinki
Gulf of Finland
FINLAND
ESTONIA
Riga
LATVIA
Minsk
LITHUANIA
Vilna
Memel
Pinsk
Brest-Litovsk
Lvov
Cernaut

Baltic Sea

SWEDEN
Neutral

DENMARK

EAST PRUSSIA
Berlin
Warsaw
P O L A N D
GERMANY
Prague
Vienna
Budapest
HUNGARY
RUMANIA
Bucharest
BULGARIA
YUGOSLAVIA
Belgrade

0   300
Miles

Guderian and Speer jointly to overhaul and increase the output of armoured fighting vehicles, production reached a peak of 19,000 in 1944.

Despite defeat Hitler maintained his refusal to sanction any withdrawal, rationalizing his stubborn strategy by his need to keep Rumania, Bulgaria and Hungary in the war and Turkey from joining his enemies – none of which he succeeded in doing as he was pushed back from the Dnieper to the Bug to the Dniester. A fresh Russian winter offensive, beginning in December, relieved Leningrad early in 1944, cut off a German army in the Crimea and brought the Russians to the Carpathians and into Rumania. As his entire southern front collapsed Hitler dismissed Manstein and other senior commanders.

The Russians paused before beginning a new series of attacks in the summer. These began on 22 June – the third anniversary of the launching of Barbarossa – in White Russia where the German Army Group Centre had been instructed to hold and protect Lithuania, East Prussia and northern Poland. Hitler was deceived into expecting that the main Russian attacks would be in the north and south rather than the centre. Army Group Centre was first split into two and then destroyed in a couple of weeks. The German losses were around 400,000 and this huge defeat left Poland and eventually Germany itself defenceless. In the north Army Group North, defending Latvia and Estonia, was cut off as the Russians advanced to the sea west of Riga. In the autumn it was pressed back into the Courland peninsula where it survived until the general capitulation. In Finland a Russian attack in June led to an attempt by the Finns to negotiate peace and a visit by Ribbentrop to Helsinki to stop them. President Ryti gave Ribbentrop his personal promise not to make peace but this was a trick to enable Finland to get German aid for a few more weeks and then come to terms with the Russians, as occasion served, by changing president. In August President Ryti was replaced by Field Marshal Mannerheim and an armistice was signed in September. Finland had to pay an indemnity, lease the naval base of Porkkala, ten miles from Helsinki, to the USSR for fifty years, and provide the Russians with other military facilities so long as the war against Germany lasted. In the farthest north the Russians forced back German troops until they crossed into Norway and operations were suspended by the weather.

The Russian victories in the summer of 1944 posed a grim problem for the Polish government in exile in London and its forces in Poland, the Home Army (AK). They regarded the advancing Russians with at least as much dread and hatred as the defeated Germans. The Russians' winter offensive of 1943–4 had carried them across Poland's pre-war frontier and the ensuing summer offensive across the dividing line fixed by the

Ribbentrop-Molotov pact. The commander of the A K, General Tadeusz Bor-Komorowski, first instructed his men to harass the Germans and neither attack the Russians nor be drawn into the Russian army. He later ordered them to occupy towns abandoned by the Germans and, if absolutely necessary, to defend themselves against the Russians rather than allow themselves to be evicted from their positions. These later instructions amounted to a recognition of the fact that the Polish army might be required to fight the Russian army in order to assert the Polishness of Poland's eastern territories. The Russians for their part declared these territories to be Russian, refused to recognize the A K as a regular combatant force (as the United States and Great Britain did), arrested A K commanders in their westward progress and sponsored in July the Polish Committee of National Liberation (the Lublin Committee) which at the end of the year they recognized as the provisional government of Poland. In this situation the London government decided to play a major card. In order to gain control of the Polish capital before the Russians, and to prevent its rivals within Poland from taking the lead in opposing the enemy, it ordered Warsaw to rise. In doing so it gravely underestimated the German opposition. It also failed to notify either its western allies or the Russians, from all of whom it would quickly be obliged to beg desperately for help. Its 20,000 armed insurgents had ammunition for only seven days. When the battle ended half of them had been killed as well as some 200,000 of Warsaw's population of one million. The survivors were transported to the extermination camps. Nine tenths of the city itself was destroyed.

Preliminary signals for the rising were sent out by radio in the last week of July and the rising began on 1 August. It lasted two months. It was met and defeated by the Germans with an appalling barbarity, particularly on the part of the S S which used half-crazed gangs of criminals and prisoners of war (notably the S S Kaminski brigade) to gas whole clutches of people trapped in the city's underground workings and to burn others alive after sousing them with petrol.

At Teheran in the previous November Roosevelt and Churchill had tacitly accepted that the imminent invasion of Poland by the Red Army left them with few weapons to gainsay Stalin's plans for post-war Poland. The Poles' hope that Churchill would send a British army to Poland was no more than a measure of their political incomprehension and Churchill, with mounting irritation, failed repeatedly both before and after the rising to get the London Poles to see that they must take the Russian victories into account. At Teheran the three leaders agreed in imprecise terms that Poland should be shifted westward to an area between the Curzon line in the east and the river Oder in the west (but with the city of Lvov switched to the Russian side of the Curzon line). At this time Stalin was, if only for tactical reasons, willing to arrange some cooperation within Poland with the AK and to allow the London Poles a minor position in the new embryonic Polish government; but he was plainly determined not to allow the London Poles, whom he rootedly distrusted, to restore pre-war Poland and become its government, nor could he be forced to do so except possibly by an extreme Anglo-American threat tantamount to the determination of the anti-German alliance.

The stronger Stalin's military position became, the weaker was his need to cooperate with the AK or accommodate the London Poles, while his distrust was accentuated by Polish attempts to get arms by air from the west – arms which, in Stalin's view, were designed for use against his forces rather than Hitler's. On 21 July he unveiled the Polish National Committee (the Lublin Committee) which was to be as subservient to him as the London Poles were hostile. At Churchill's prompting Mikolajczyk flew to Moscow where he found Stalin obdurate and engaged in fruitless wrangles with the Lublin Poles as Warsaw's sacrifice began.

That the London Poles should have failed to take Moscow into their confidence about the rising is hardly surprising since it was in large part an anti-Russian venture. That Stalin should prove unhelpful is no more surprising. He disliked most Poles and most distrusted the London Poles and the AK. He was certainly irritated and possibly embarrassed by their sudden and unheralded initiative which happened to come at a moment of strategic debate about the next phase of his general offensive. He had some justification for his repeated accusation that the rising was reckless. He may have been expecting to take Warsaw himself by the end of the first week in August but he was disconcerted by local German successes which dislocated his planning. General V. I. Chuikov, the hero of Stalingrad and now serving on the central front under Marshal Rokossovski, later testified that German air attacks were intense in the Warsaw area, that the Russians lacked bridging equipment vital for forcing the passage of the Vistula and that Rokossovski believed (erroneously, as it turned out) that the Germans had an armoured force east of the Vistula which might attack southward and endanger any Russian positions established across the river. Finally, Stalin may be credited with some ignorance of the barbarous nature of the German suppression of the rising. Nevertheless his refusal to help or to facilitate Anglo-American aid is one of the grisliest examples of the triumph of calculation over humanity in the history of *Realpolitik*. Stalin had some excuse for some inactivity at the beginning of the rising, but thereafter it is impossible to avoid the judgement that

Stalin saw the rising as an opportunity and took it. The rising played into his hands. The responsibility of the London Poles for what happened to Warsaw is great. So is Stalin's.

The London Poles had asked for and been refused Anglo-American air and parachutist support before the rising began. Such aid, they were told, would be too costly without Russian cooperation. This judgement was proved correct. From Italy Air Marshal Sir John Slessor reported that, in the absence of permission to land in Russian-held territory and refuel (which was not granted), operations to Poland were so impossibly dangerous and comparatively useless that he would not undertake them unless ordered to. He made, however, an exception in favour of a Polish squadron under his command. It suffered very heavy losses. The RAF and South African Air Force later joined in a desperate attempt to supply the insurgents and, with the Poles, dropped 233 tons. When the Poles pleaded for direct and massive American air drops to supplement this inevitably meagre effort, the Russians refused (15 August) to allow the aircraft to land at Russian airfields before returning to base. At one point Churchill suggested to Roosevelt that aircraft should land on Russian airfields without Russian permission and see what happened, but Roosevelt was not willing to go as far as that. On 10 September Russian ground forces made a successful attack on the suburb of Praga. They then began an attempt to cross the Vistula, established a number of bridgeheads but were forced by the Germans to retreat. On 13 September Russian aircraft began dropping food and ammunition to the Poles in Warsaw. At least fifty tons – perhaps considerably more – were dropped, most of it accurately but in damaged condition because parachutes were not used. At the same time Stalin lifted his veto on the use of Russian airfields by the Americans and on 18 September the US Air Force undertook a single daylight operation with 110 Flying Fortresses, most of whose drops fell wide of the mark. By 2 October there was nobody left in the city to save or help.

Later that month, in Moscow, Churchill tried to persuade Stalin to accept the revised Curzon line as a *de facto* arrangement to be reviewed at a peace conference but Stalin would have none of it. His armies were now not merely in Poland but, since mid-August, on German soil too, and Finland and Rumania were suing for armistices. Churchill's efforts to persuade Mikolajczyk that all these things were part and parcel of Poland's future fate led to angry scenes between the two men, as the one berated the other for betraying the undertakings given by Great Britain to Poland in 1939. By the time the three leaders met for the second and last time at Yalta in February 1945 Poland was completely occupied by Stalin's forces. Warsaw, held by the Germans for three months after the defeat of the rising, had just been entered by the Russians, Polish contingents under their command leading the way. At Yalta Churchill and Roosevelt continued their expostulations about the composition of the new Polish government but they held even fewer cards than they had held at Teheran: Stalin was in Poland and they were not. The A K had been dissolved by the Russian winter offensive and in March seventeen non-communist Polish leaders, proceeding under safe conduct and at Russian invitation to meet a Russian general, were dispatched to Moscow where all were imprisoned and some died.

Upon recovering the Ukraine the Russians entered Rumania as well as Poland and posed an increasingly awkward problem for Germany's other allies: Bulgaria, Slovakia and Hungary. These allies had already seen the writing on the wall. The German defeats in 1943 and the capitulation of Italy in the same year had set them thinking about how to secure their future in a Europe which was going to be dominated by the USSR in place of Germany.

In Rumania Ion Antonescu's attempt to concert action with Mussolini in 1943 was fruitless. He was then recaptivated by Hitler and his talk of secret weapons but in August 1944 he was dismissed by King Michael after a stormy interview. Attempts to secure western help against the Russian wrath to come were fruitless, for there was nothing the western allies could do for the Rumanians and they were left to make the best terms they could. The king broke off relations with Germany and made contact with the Communist Party (which had been outlawed before the war). After a short period of confusion, during which Bucharest was bombed by the Germans and the German Ambassador committed suicide and his colleagues disappeared for good into the Soviet Union, a new and essentially communist government was installed under Petru Groza. Rumania was required to ratify its territorial losses to the USSR in 1940 but was promised the return of what it had lost to Hungary (but not what it had lost to Bulgaria); it was also required to pay an indemnity to the USSR and fight against Germany.

In Bulgaria, which was at war with Great Britain and the United States but not with the Soviet Union, the government declared itself neutral but failed none the less to stave off a Russian invasion and declaration of war. Bulgaria, under a new government, was compelled in September to declare war on Germany. In the same month Russian troops entered Yugoslavia. They shared with Tito's partisans in the capture of Belgrade in October and then retired a few days later.

The Slovaks, like the Poles, rose against the Germans as the Russian armies approached. Slovakia was an ally of Germany and a co-belligerent but in October 1943 an entire Slovak division had come over to the Russians and in the same period partisan warfare flared up inside eastern Slovakia. In 1944 the country was in a state of general revolt. National committees emerged and commandeered factories and the property of collaborators. An army 65,000 strong engaged the Germans. It hoped to be joined by the Russian army and there is still controversy about why it was not. Marshal Konev seems to have been approached by Slovak officers with a plan for a rising in conjunction with a Russian attack, and to have recommended Stalin to adopt this plan. A Russian advance began early in September. But the Russians had to cross the formidable Carpathians against stiff German opposition and it was the middle of October before they set foot on Slovak soil. By this time the Germans, who had been forewarned of the rising, had defeated it and burned sixty villages and filled at least 200 mass graves with slaughtered Slovaks. The Russians later complained that they had been given too little advance notice of the actual date fixed for the rising. They may also have been sceptical about Slovak estimates of the importance of the operation.

In Hungary the Regent, Admiral Horthy, Europe's senior head of state (he had been one of the leaders of the movement which overthrew Bela Kun's communist regime in 1919), was forced by events to try to abandon the German alliance which had served him well for a number of years. He had joined it because he belonged to a small, nostalgic and illiberal ruling caste for whom anti-Bolshevism was an overriding issue. He had benefited from the two awards of 1939 and 1940 which had given him chunks of his neighbours' territories, he had been happy to help Hitler invade Yugoslavia and the Soviet Union in 1941 and he had been gratified to find that Hitler did not want to oust him in favour of the leader of the local equivalent of the Nazi Party – Ferenc Szalasi of the Arrow Cross (who wanted even more of his neighbours' territories than Hitler was prepared to concede). Up to 1944 Horthy tried to persuade himself that Hitler, after abandoning the Balkans, might succeed in holding the Carpathians and Transylvania and so keep the Russians away from central Europe, but the impending collapse of Rumania showed him that he had no choice and he prepared – too late – to make his escape from the war, even at the price of turning to the communist USSR.

For Hitler, however, Hungary had exceptional strategic significance. He had to hold it so long as he had troops in south-eastern Europe and even if these were safely withdrawn the loss of Hungary would set the Russians well on the way into Vienna. He therefore took over Hungary (thereby initiating anti-Jewish razzias) and sent Otto Skorzeny, the saviour

SOVIET ADVANCES
IN SOUTH-EAST
EUROPE 1944

Front line 20 August 1944.
Soviet advances 20 August – 20 October 1944.
German withdrawals.
British attacks October 1944.
British paratroops land 13 October 1944.
Tito's partisans.
Albanian partisans.

—ARTHUR BANKS—

BULGARIA
GREECE
Athens
Piraeus
YUGO.
ALBANIA
Patrai
Corinth

Black Sea

Odessa
Jassy
U S S R
Bucharest
Danube
R U M A N I A
B U L G A R I A
Sofia
Istanbul
TURKEY
GREECE
CZECHOSLOVAKIA
Vienna
Danube
H U N G A R Y
Budapest
AUSTRIA
Drava
Sava
Belgrade
Y U G O S L A V I A
Tirana
A L B A N I A
Adriatic
Sea

of Mussolini, to kidnap Horthy. Skorzeny first kidnapped the Regent's son and then, in a singularly bold escapade, seized the citadel of Budapest with one car and four tanks. The Regent escaped but immediately afterwards resigned and was taken to Germany under guard. The Germans installed an Arrow Cross government under Szalasi, who was however an incompetent visionary and was hated by the Hungarian army. At the end of 1944 Budapest was beleaguered by Marshal Malinovski. The Germans tried to relieve it but failed, and the city surrendered on 12 February 1945. In this case the Russians made no effort to restrain their troops, who proceeded to eliminate the *ancien régime* in the most direct and gruesome manner. Horthy's long reign ended, as it had begun, with terror and bloodshed, and Hungary virtually lost its independence too.

The Russo-German campaigns were the most terrible war that has ever been waged. The numbers of the dead were huge. The great sieges of Leningrad, Stalingrad and Sebastopol recalled the war-making of other times but the field campaigns were something new. They were the acme of (pre-nuclear) industrial warfare. The mechanized armies of tanks and workshops were industrial plants in motion attended by hundreds of thousands of technicians. These ponderous devastators, made of steel and moved by oil, churned up the countryside and at intervals blazed away at each other, leaving the land covered with warped steel, stinking oil and corpses. In between these armadas men in various kinds of armoured or unarmoured transport, and sometimes still on foot, covered great distances because they were winning or losing or simply because they were required to shift themselves laterally from one part of the front to another. Sometimes there were long lulls, passages of normalcy embedded in senselessness and horror, and if the weather was fine, men might go through the motions of ordinary life and, with their singing and their horseplay, behave as though they were on an excursion rather than a highly organized killing. But then for many months there would be slush and mud and clothes never really dry, or the intense cold which made it dangerous to take off a glove. The most remarkable thing about this war was that, on both sides, men went on fighting it for nearly four years.

Part of the price demanded by Stalin was the repatriation to the USSR, after the war, of all those who had given aid to the Germans and were captured, or could be tracked down and apprehended, in the allied sphere of operations. That deserters and persons who had served the enemy should be tried and sentenced by the state which they had betrayed was nothing new. What was new was a situation in which such traitors should be apprehended not by their own state but by an allied state. This situation raised questions, juridical and political, which gave rise to embarrassment and heartsearching when the war ended and, a generation later, to bitter controversy. The surrender to the Russians of Soviet citizens who had put on German uniforms did not, during the war, seem outrageous or even unusual, and the case for doing so was fortified by two things: many of the persons concerned were known to have behaved with a brutality exceptional even in so awful a war, and there was on the British side an awareness that the advancing Russian armies would soon have in their power British citizens liberated from German prisoner-of-war camps. All these circumstances contributed to the agreement, finally concluded in 1944 and affirmed at Yalta, to exchange all nationals accused of desertion or treason. It was obvious that the Soviet victims of this agreement would receive harsher treatment than their western counterparts and might well be shot without trial, but these surmises were deemed to be irrelevant (as pertaining to the internal jurisdiction of another state) or, if not irrelevant because outrageous, then so impossible to reconcile with the political imperatives of the alliance as to be best forgotten. What was overlooked at the time was that the captured Soviet citizens were in law the nationals of a state with which neither Great Britain nor the United States had an extradition treaty, so that there was no sound juridical basis for their repatriation, however justified the USSR might be in treating them as criminals once they were within its jurisdiction. (Persons who had not become legally Soviet citizens after 1917 were not covered by the agreement.)

Decades later attempts were made to stigmatize this agreement as a piece of political cynicism or disgraceful kowtowing to Stalin. When the war ended British and American tribunals lent over backwards to rule that individuals sought by the Soviet authorities were not liable to repatriation because they were not Soviet citizens as defined by the agreement, while in the field many fingered for repatriation to the USSR were encouraged to jump off the backs of lorries or trains and take to the woods. Nevertheless appalling scenes took place as those destined for repatriation, aware of what was in store for them, committed or tried to commit suicide; and in the general post-war chaos some persons not covered by the agreement (mostly Ukrainians) were wrongly included among the repatriated and so presumably consigned to penal settlements or death.

CHAPTER 23

Mass Bombing

FRIGHTENING your enemy is the fundamental and presumably the oldest weapon of war. Starving him – hitting him where it hurts most – cannot be much less old. Mass bombing is the most modern way of trying to destroy both his morale and his economy at one and the same time. Where earlier warriors rushed upon their foes with painted bodies and hideous screams, or poisoned wells and beleaguered towns, their more sophisticated though hardly more civilized successors rain high explosives on factories and homes and set fire to whole cities. Only the techniques and the scale are new.

Perhaps the hallowed antiquity of the aim explains the fact that these new and fearful means were generally accepted in the Second World War. Air raids involving the indiscriminate killing of enormous numbers of civilians were the current step in the natural evolution of the art of war. The very concept of the civilian hardly remained valid. The traditional distinction between men setting forth to risk their lives and those who stayed behind out of range of death disappeared in the first half of the twentieth century. All were now combatants in their several ways. A civilian was a combatant who did not happen to be enrolled in the traditionally recognized fighting services; he was constantly proclaimed to be in the front line, a description implying that he was risking his life as much as anybody and would not think to complain about staking it. Even the deaths of children were accepted as, if not legitimate, yet logical consequences of war, occasioning special grief no doubt but relatively little indignation: that was the way things were.

At the beginning of the war Great Britain and France had promised, in response to a plea by Roosevelt, to confine bombing to strictly military targets provided the Germans did so too, but what was a military target was unclear and changeable. Yet there seemed to be one rule which still survived. There was still a sense of proportion and a feeling of uneasiness if it were disregarded, an acceptance of the ancient Greek tag that means must bear some relation to ends. To destroy factories or the people who worked in them, or the homes of people who worked in them, was perhaps legitimate; but to do these things – as for instance in the bombing of Dresden – without being able to point to a commensurate strategic advantage was not just a sad necessity but also uncomfortably hard to justify – either in general moral terms or in the strict application of the medieval doctrine of Just War.

But if a majority acquiesced in what seemed to be the inevitability of the deplorable, a minority clung to an older teaching. This minority, trying to bend modern capabilities to the Christian faith instead of adapting the latter to the former, said that since all killing was wrong in the absence of special justifying circumstances, indiscriminate mass killing needed to be very meticulously justified indeed – and was not. Champions of this tradition such as Dr George Bell, Bishop of Chichester, accepted that the nature and context of war had so changed that many deaths, hitherto regarded as unjustifiable, must be accepted, but they alleged that there was still a line to be drawn somewhere and that the destruction of closely packed residential areas, because they were closely packed residential areas, was a sin and – even in the absence of any international convention on air warfare – a crime. Even if it was permissible to kill men and women at work in factories, it was not permissible to kill men, women and children in their homes. For keeping these Christian ideas before men's minds in spite of the clatter of arms the Bishop of Chichester was not elevated to the highest Christian office in England when the see of Canterbury, for which many inside the church and out considered him pre-eminently qualified, fell vacant at the end of 1944. He was even denied the lesser see of York many years after the war was over and after it had virtually been promised to him.

The advent of air power had brought with it a school of theorists who alleged that this new weapon could contribute to war-making by doing something that had never been done before, and could do this independently and without the help of the older sea and land forces. The Second World War put this theory to the test and (with air power as it was before the introduction of nuclear weapons) found it wanting. The prime aim of assailing industry, communications and morale was to compel the surrender of the enemy even though his armed forces had suffered no irreversible defeat in the field. Defeat in workshop and homestead was to take the place of defeat in the field as the first aim of strategy. This had been the aim of naval blockade, but no navy had ever succeeded in making a blockade more than an ancillary element in war-making. It had neither broken morale nor brought the machinery of war to a halt. If air power could succeed in these tasks, then the bomber aircraft would prove a truly revolutionary weapon, more revolutionary than either the submarine which upset a number of military concepts in the First World War or the tank which did the same in the Second.

Although aircraft had appeared in time to take part in the First World War, their role had been too limited and tentative for any settled conclusions to be drawn about the nature of air power. Consequently the question was much debated, *a priori* and often acrimoniously, between the wars. The importance of air power was conceded, but the best way to use an air force was hotly contested between those who thought of aircraft as a sort of extended artillery operating in conjunction with and under the control of army commanders and, on the other hand, those who held that air power had superseded land power. There were no even approximately accepted estimates of the amount of damage which a bomber force could inflict and most estimates were wildly excessive, largely owing to the unjustified assumption that if a bomber could reach its target, it would have relatively little difficulty in hitting it.

In 1917 Churchill, then Minister of Munitions, said:

It is improbable that any terrorization of the civil population which could be achieved by air attack would compel . . . surrender . . . we have seen the combative spirit of the people roused, and not quelled, by the German air raids. Nothing that we have learned of the capacity of the German population to endure suffering justifies us in assuming that they could be cowed into submission by such methods, or . . . not be rendered more desperately resolved by them.

But in 1940 he thought that 'only the Air Force' could win the war. It is not clear what changed his mind, but it is probable that the champions of bombing had succeeded between the wars in implanting in many minds the belief that precision bombing could win a war. This involved considerable loss of life in the factories hit, but it did not envisage the mass bombing of civilians in their homes as well as their factories. But when it came to the test, precision bombing failed to be precise and area bombing was substituted for it as a means whereby an air force could live up to its claim to win a war.

The weightiest of the early champions of the independent role of the bomber were to be found in Italy and the United States – in particular General Giulio Douhet and General William Mitchell – but its most effective protagonist between the wars was the Royal Air Force under Air Marshal Sir Hugh Trenchard. The US Air Force was the most powerful of all bomber forces before the war ended, but the RAF was the first to acquire and operate a heavily armoured four-engined bomber; the Luftwaffe never had one in any number which counted. In spite of the urgent need to equip Fighter Command with modern fighters, the Air Council decided simultaneously to provide Bomber Command with four-engined bombers, ordered prototypes of the Stirling, Halifax and Manchester (later redesigned as the Lancaster) in 1937 and placed an order for 3,500 heavy bombers in October 1938 for delivery in the spring of 1942. Although these aircraft were not available as early as the Hurricane and Spitfire (with the result that Bomber Command's best crews had to fly antiquated Blenheims and die in them) they were brought into service in 1940–41. This decision by the Air Council, like the decision to build the eight-gun fighter, was undoubtedly justified, although it was partly the outcome of a conflict of views which was resolved by adopting both – by allowing Dowding to have his eight-gun fighter while at the same time going part of the way with the opposition to Dowding which decried the fighter arm and wanted to concentrate on a smashing bomber force, the symbol and justification of an independent air force.

In Germany a similar conflict was resolved in a different way. The accidental death of the protagonist of the heavy bomber, General Walther Wever, led to the cancellation of plans for such an aircraft, to a decision to rely on speed rather than armour, and to a disproportionate concentration on fighters, dive bombers and the role of army cooperation. The bomber became the Cinderella of the Luftwaffe. The Battle of Britain showed how ill judged this policy was. The Luftwaffe's relatively fast but lightly armed and lightly armoured medium bombers were defeated – as the RAF's obsolescent Blenheims had been over France a year earlier. For a time both sides were restricted to operations under the cover of darkness which were clearly not a war-winning effort. But although both sides were thus reduced to similar tactics, their circumstances were very different. The RAF's Bomber Command was conserving its strength, making few sorties in mass, keeping its losses down to about 3 per cent and awaiting the early delivery of the four-engined aircraft which were to take over from the two-engined Wellington, Whitley and Hampden; between the outbreak of war and the end of 1941 it increased its strength from 200 to 500 and the latter figure included the first few dozen Stirlings and Halifaxes. The Luftwaffe had nothing of the kind in view.

On the British side a further consequence was the evolution of a singularly independent Bomber Command under a Commander-in-Chief less amenable than his fellows to the overall strategic control of the Chief of the Air Staff and dedicated to proving the proposition that his force could win the war independently and was doing so and ought not to be impeded by diverting new bombers to Coastal Command's war against the U-boats. This position was further enhanced when the heavy bombers reached the Command in strength in 1943, their radar aids became increasingly precise and the invasion of France was postponed to 1944. Moreover by this time Bomber Command's pertinacious activity had won for it a position of independence from the Americans which the British army, preparing for the role of minor partner in Overlord, could never claim. British independence, which had been saved by Fighter Command in 1940, was symbolized thereafter by Bomber Command.

The first test of air power as an independent war winner as distinct from the army support provided by the Luftwaffe in Hitler's land campaigns in the west in 1940 came with the Battle of Britain. From the Luftwaffe's point of view this battle had two entirely different phases. The aim of the first was to destroy the Royal Air Force as a prelude to invasion. This attempt failed. It was succeeded by the attempt to destroy from the air British installations, homes and people, and in this phase the Luftwaffe operated wholly independently of the other two services and its bomber arm came into its own.

London and the industrial midlands were the principal targets in night-time attacks of which the most celebrated was the raid on Coventry on 14 November. Decades later a sinister myth about this raid arose, when it was put about that Churchill and others were forewarned about it by Ultra but failed to take steps to prevent or mitigate the deaths and destruction on the grounds that the safeguarding of the Ultra source was paramount. None of this is true. Ultra did not mention Coventry and the question of securing the Ultra secret did not arise.

Three days before the raid a decoded procedural Enigma message gave a list of frequencies and other directions for a German operation called Moonlight Sonata. It was evident from the message that the operation involved an exceptional effort. No date was given. No target was specified but broad target areas were referred to by code names. From other available evidence these were believed to be areas in and near London. In a separate part of the message appeared the word Korn. In retrospect it has been suggested that Korn stood for Coventry – on the grounds that the initial letters were the same, a common German practice with cover names. A day or two later another routine message set out bearings from a series of beam emplacements in northern France used by the Luftwaffe to direct its bomber raids. The bearings intersected at Birmingham, Coventry and Wolverhampton. These targetings indicated that, at some unspecified future date, these cities were likely to be bombed (which was probable in any case). At almost the same time a prisoner stated that Birmingham and Coventry were shortly to be bombed. His was the only specific reference to Coventry by name. These pieces of information were taken to portend a major raid at the full moon (15 November) with London as the main target and the west midlands the most likely alternative. Certainty would have to await the activation of the beams which could be relied upon to point to the night's target a few hours before sunset. Between 3 and 4 p.m. on 14 November monitoring of the beams' frequencies showed that Coventry would be the main target that night. The usual counter-measures were put in hand, including special precautions prescribed some weeks earlier, although one of these – the jamming of the beams – was rendered largely ineffective by a mathematical error. In addition 'intruder' operations were flown that night against German targets all the way from Berlin to the west coast of Brittany. Churchill, so far from pondering whether to save Coventry or safeguard Ultra, was under the impression that the raid was going to be on London and ordered the car that was taking him to the country to turn back to the capital.

Throughout the winter the Luftwaffe's bombers wrought a vast amount of destruction but with no strategic gains. If day bombing was too costly, night bombing was too inaccurate. In the first year of the war the British discovered that even fair-sized towns were missed by two thirds of the then inexperienced crews; during the winter of 1940–41 photographic reconnaissance and other intelligence revealed that results were not much better at night even though the enemy's night fighters (not yet equipped for night fighting) were virtually impotent. Bomber Command's claims, advanced with partisan fervour and, some thought, with a degree of partisan recklessness, were shown to be very wide of the mark. One solution was to choose larger targets. Attacks on oil refineries were abandoned but attacks on rail centres continued, because these could be significantly damaged even if the bombs fell as much as 1,000 yards wide of the aiming point. But even rail targets could not be usefully attacked without the help of the moon and rather than do nothing on moonless nights Bomber Command began raiding areas of population and hoping for the best. Intelligence continued to report a significant number of misses by miles. This combination of operational imprecision and reliable intelligence drove the Command, under the forceful leadership of Air Marshal Sir Arthur Harris, increasingly to area bombing. It was powerfully supported by Churchill's fiercely singleminded Principal Scientific Adviser, Professor Frederick Lindemann (Lord Cherwell), who believed that it was both possible and legitimate to destroy half the working-class houses in all the larger German cities, but was strongly contested by other eminent scientists, notably Professors Henry Tizard and P. M. S. Blackett, who alleged (correctly, as it turned out) that expectations were greatly exaggerated and argued for more selective operations such as the war against the U-boats. The policy in action cost the lives of over 55,000 aircrew in Bomber Command – and twice as many in the American air forces in Europe.

When Harris assumed command in February 1942 his force was ready to make massive attacks within a restricted radius and in March Bomber Command's main campaign of the war opened with a raid on the ancient and inflammable city of Lübeck which was chosen because it was lightly defended and easily accessible from the sea. This was the first operational appearance of the Lancaster. Four raids on Rostock, east of Lübeck and also on the Baltic, followed in April. These raids were experiments and demonstrations. They provoked a German counter-attack on cities in England which were also lightly defended and historically and artistically noteworthy – the so-called Baedeker raids on places like Bristol and Exeter. In May Bomber Command hit back with the 1,000-bomber raid on Cologne, for which training machines and crews were pressed into temporary service. The material damage was not great, but the boost to morale in the force and among civilians, the shock to the Germans and the impression made on allies, Resistance movements and neutrals may be thought to have justified the effort and the cost. German retaliation was ineffective.

In the latter part of this same year Bomber Command's effectiveness was increased by the formation of a corps of specially equipped and trained Pathfinders, which preceded the main body of aircraft to locate and mark their targets. Other technical aids to navigation and aiming followed. The ground operated Gee was supplemented by Oboe, which helped pilots to keep to the right course but had limited range and was subject to jamming, and from 1943 by the airborne radar H 2 S which enabled the bomb aimer to 'see' his target in spite of poor weather and the heights to which he might be forced by anti-aircraft guns and searchlights. Nevertheless precision bombing remained impossible except at ruinous cost. When in May 1943 the Möhne, Eder and Sorpe Dams were breached in an attempt to immobilize industry in the Ruhr (by dispersing the waters stored to provide energy for industries), the attack was made from the perilous height of sixty feet by a select band of nineteen Lancasters carrying a specially designed mine and crews who had been trained for months over replicas of the target area. On the night of the raid bad weather added to the perils: one aircraft and its crew made ten runs over the target before releasing its mine. Eight of the nineteen aircraft were lost, fifty-four of 133 men killed. This extremely heroic operation had been conceived before the war but rejected, and its outcome justified that rejection inasmuch as it proved to be horribly costly and only moderately successful. Six dams were attacked, two were breached; a number of German workers were drowned but the German grid was able to prevent serious industrial disruption. The air weapon was still at the stage of the bludgeon; precision bombing was suicidal. No comparable raid was ever carried out. The bombing of cities remained Bomber Command's main way of proving the claim of air power to be a war-winner, the civilian population being the principal target with factories as, in the words of a Bomber Command directive, a bonus.

In this context the Ruhr was marked out as the Command's main target. But it was very heavily defended. Essen and Düsseldorf were both attacked in the summer of 1942. In retrospect these raids underline how far Bomber Command was and remained an élite force. Essen was attacked by 1,000 aircraft but this was the last time that Bomber Command put 1,000 aircraft into the air for a single raid before 1944. During 1943 it gradually intensified its campaign against the Ruhr and extended it to more distant targets such as Hamburg and Berlin. Its strength in aircraft was not much greater at the beginning of 1943 than it had been a year earlier, but half of these were four-engined aircraft. In addition the Mosquito, one of the outstanding aircraft of the war, designed in the mid-thirties but comparatively unnoticed until now, had the range and speed to enable it to brave the German defences all the way to Berlin with a 4,000 lb. bomb. On the other hand the Luftwaffe's early warning system, ground controls and night fighter tactics were being greatly improved. When the war began Germany had radar which was more accurate than British radar but of shorter range and not linked with a ground control system of the same complexity and sophistication. As a result the bombing operations of 1942 defeated the German night defences, but in 1943 the tables were turned and the German night fighters began to strike almost as freely as though they were operating by day. Bomber losses rose to over 5 per cent of the attacking force. For several months it was not clear who was winning. Nerves were taut on both sides and in August 1943 the Chief of Staff of the Luftwaffe, General Hans Jeschonnek, committed suicide.

In Berlin, which suffered sixteen major night raids spread over four months in the winter of 1942–3 as well as additional American daylight raids in the latter part of this period, the damage was severe enough to cause a considerable exodus and close all schools, but even in the immediate aftermath of the raids less than half of the city's industries stopped work and many of the stoppages were brief. Hamburg on the other hand, which was attacked by night and day seven times in nine days in July and August 1942, was savagely and to some degree permanently wrecked with the assistance of two new techniques: the dropping of strips of tinfoil called Window which so confused the defence's radar scanners that bomber losses on the first night were only twelve out of 800; and the raising of fire storms by incendiary bombs which created fierce currents of flame rushing at temperatures of 1,000° centigrade to the centre of the storm at speeds of 100–150 m.p.h. and incinerating people above and below ground. At least 50,000 were killed in this way and a million more fled from the city: half the houses were destroyed and more than half the remainder damaged.

Yet morale broke in neither city. Bomber Command failed to bring German industry to a halt and the German defences pushed bomber losses up beyond 5 per cent and, early in 1944, even to 10 per cent. A new German airborne radar called Lichtenstein gave the night fighters longer range and a wider angle of vision and also enabled them to overcome Window. In an attack on Nuremberg in March the Command lost ninety-four aircraft out of 791 (12.5 per cent). In four and a half months 1,000 aircraft were totally lost and 1,682 more seriously damaged. Such losses were not tolerable. The Command's onslaught had been parried. No other arm suffered such casualties during the Second World War. The cost and the results were horribly reminiscent of Passchendaele. The only consolation was that German counter-attacks on London and elsewhere in the early months of 1944 had been thwarted by the defences, and the Luftwaffe could no longer even carry out reconnaissance flights over Great Britain.

The American strategic bombing offensive was showing the same pattern of destruction at great cost and without commensurate results. At the Casablanca conference of January 1943 Roosevelt and Churchill had agreed that strategic bombing was for the time being their principal weapon against Hitler and their principal way of helping Stalin. At that time, however, the U S air forces were comparatively small and stretched over many theatres (the Pacific and Atlantic, North Africa and the Middle East), and it was not until the second half of that year that the U S Eighth and Fifteenth Air Forces were able to add significantly to the British effort: the first American raid on Germany was made on 17 August 1942 by eighteen aircraft of which twelve found their target.

The Americans entered the battle with the conviction that area bombing was useless and precision bombing possible. The main instrument of American bombing was the four-engined B17 or Flying Fortress, an aircraft bristling with guns and designed to fight off any enemy's daylight fighter attacks. But the B17s were badly mauled by the German fighters and the American commanders drew the conclusion that effective precision bombing of the German economy as a whole must be preceded by the destruction of German fighter production – by precision bombing. The duel which followed was weighted against the Americans because the

ALLIED BOMBING OF GERMANY

Legend:
- Main centres of civilian casualties
- Main areas of bombing
- Industrial areas
- Aircraft industry factories
- Main railways
- Canals
- International boundaries

~ARTHUR BANKS~

May 1942
First 1,000 bomber raid

0 — 100
Miles

North Sea
Baltic Sea

EAST PRUSSIA
POLAND
CZECHOSLOVAKIA
AUSTRIA
HOLLAND
BELGIUM
LUX.
FRANCE

Breslau
Dresden
Berlin
Rostock
Tutow
Magdeburg
Bernberg
Leipzig
Halle
Chemnitz
Regensburg
Munich
Hamburg
Kiel
Lübeck
Hannover
Brunswick
Halberstadt
Aschersleben
Gotha
Schweinfurt
Nürnberg
Fürth
Augsburg
Stuttgart
Bremen
Bremerhaven
Dortmund
Wuppertal
Cologne
Kassel
Frankfurt
Darmstadt
Coblenz
Wiesbaden
Duisburg
Düsseldorf
Essen

Elbe
Weser
Ems
Oder
Rhine
Danube

fighter factories were not only specially well defended but numerous, dispersed and far away. An attack in August 1943 on the Messerschmitt factory at Regensburg coupled with an attack on ball-bearing factories in Schweinfurt came to grief with excessive losses. A further attack on Schweinfurt two months later caused the loss of more than a quarter of the attacking force. The conclusion drawn this time was that successful precision bombing at tolerable cost was impossible without a fighter escort capable of going all the way with the bombers. The right aircraft happened to be at hand. The American P51 (Mustang), already in service with the RAF in a modest way, was chosen for the job and equipped with long-range tanks which enabled it to cover the required distances without losing too much speed or its capacity to outmanoeuvre the German fighters. This aircraft played a role as remarkable in its way as the Spitfire or the Mosquito, for after it had been put into production with the intensity for which American manufacturers were famous, it enabled the B17s, withdrawn from the battle in the autumn of 1943, to resume their offensive, and this combination overcame the German defences. The German fighters were eliminated from the battle by their fighter foes and the American and British bombers were together able to undertake round-the-clock bombing of Germany and, from the summer of 1944, to pound an economy which had abruptly begun to disintegrate irretrievably fast.

Hitler had not prepared his economy for a long war and Germany was not ready for one when it came. In 1939–41 Germany was able to fight and win a series of campaigns on a half-stretched economy, but it could not overrun the whole continent on this basis, and after 1941 it had to convert to a war economy in the face of the crippling campaigns in the east and the increasingly severe bombardment from the west. Germany was not short of equipment or factory space; it started the war with twice as many machine tools, and multipurpose ones, than Great Britain and probably still had more than the United States half-way through the war. Its vital industries were as efficient as any in Great Britain or France and its output of coal and steel was greater than the combined British and French output; but it was economically inferior to the United States and the USSR, it was short of practically all minerals, and its steel and aluminium industries were dependent on imported iron ore and bauxite until sources had been overrun by the German armies. Stocks of some raw materials were low when the war began but they were replenished for a time by the bonuses of conquest. Germany's greatest economic weakness was the inefficiency of its administrative machine. Hitler's government was ill adapted to make the huge adjustments required in order to fight and beat the Russians and the Americans at one and the same time. Nazi Germany had no single central administrative authority; it was run by discordant authorities dominated by potentates more attuned to mutual in-fighting than to working together against outside enemies; its industries as well as its administration were a tangle. Hitler himself was in no sense a planner or an organizer. He seems to have regarded talk as a substitute for planning and, from the records that have been left behind of his sessions with his favourite associates, it would appear that the talk, which was of a miserably low intellectual order, was intended less for use than for ostentation. Nevertheless Germany was astonishingly successful for two years in sustaining an enormous war effort and expanding its war production.

The conquests of 1939–41 were regarded, from the economic point of view, as bonuses which enabled the government to fight wars and increase the German standard of living at the same time. Domestic consumption in Germany rose to the end of 1941. More significant, however, in the longer run were the failures of 1939–41; the failure to finish off Great Britain and, more serious still, the failure to defeat the Russians before the first winter of the war in the east. These failures forced Hitler to expand his arms base, his labour force and also his armed forces. The latter, which stood at 5.6 million in May 1940, expanded voraciously and, at the same date in the next three years, reached 7.2, 8.6 and 9.5 million; the rise of nearly a million in 1942–3 was achieved despite losses of the same extent in the same period, and with further losses of 1.6 million in 1943–4 the total armed manpower began to fall. In October 1944 all available males between sixteen and sixty were mobilized in the *Volkssturm*, to fight and not to labour.

During these same years the German labour force had dwindled steadily, until by the end of the war it had been reduced by a quarter. This decline was not made good by the conscription of women (as was done in the much more tightly regimented British war economy), and although the proportion of German women at work in wartime Germany rose, their numbers did not, partly because of the Nazi doctrine that woman's place was in the home and partly owing to the afflux of foreign labour which obscured the need for a more extensive conscription of German labour. During the war the numbers of Germans at work increased by no more than the natural increase of the population, whereas in Great Britain and the United States the number of workers rose by 15 per cent over and above natural increase. (If, on the other hand, the significant manpower figures should embrace the armed services as well as industry, then Germany was using in these joint occupations a smaller proportion of its population than Great Britain.) As we have seen in an earlier part of this book, the German labour shortage was met by putting prisoners of war onto war production and raiding conquered countries for slavelike labour, but although the labour so acquired ran into millions of men (three million by May 1941, over four million a year later and over six million from May 1943), foreign labour was no substitute for German labour, especially in skilled jobs.

The re-orientation of German industry was begun by Fritz Todt, a brilliant technician who created at short notice an organization which stood up to unparalleled enemy bombardment for nearly three years after his death in an aircraft accident in February 1942. He was succeeded by Albert Speer, an indifferent architect with an aesthetic taste akin to Hitler's but also a gifted and versatile amateur with a flair for organization and an excellent sense for capturing and retaining Hitler's trust and friendship. Like Schacht, Speer has been judged, not without equivocation, to have been a non-Nazi technocrat who served the Nazi government in spite of his better nature and his better intelligence. Again like Schacht, he escaped the death penalty at the Nuremberg trial, where he was sentenced to twenty years' imprisonment for crimes against humanity (Schacht was acquitted on all counts), and he has since been treated by historians with some leniency, partly owing to his courage in refusing at the end to obey the (now decrepit) Führer's orders to lay Germany waste and partly because he survived the Nazi era to talk and write about it with some intelligence and show himself decent after the event. Speer's wartime achievement was considerable but not perhaps as remarkable as has been made out. He kept the German aircraft industry going in spite of crippling shortages and furious bombing, but what he and it produced was quantity rather than quality and the last aircraft of the Third Reich were inferior replicas of finer models. He believed in centralized capitalist control with the emphasis on the large leading industrial concerns as opposed to the Nazi partiality for the little man and the regionalism embodied in the local boss-rule of the Gauleiters. He kept the conveyor belts moving. Hitler backed him for three years, made him Minister for Armaments and Munitions (later Minister for Armaments and War Production) and defended him against satraps like Goering (as head of the Four Year Plan) and Funk (at the Ministry of Economics) and also against the army's own Office of War Production in his efforts to rationalize the German economy in terms of the overriding need for weapons. But Speer never won a completely dominant position. Goering and Milch managed to exclude aircraft production from his empire (except partially in 1944–5), and the odious and jealous Sauckel retained the control and procurement of labour to the end. Nevertheless Speer succeeded in more than doubling Germany's war production by the middle of 1943 and more than trebling it by the middle of 1944. Under his direction Germany produced arms in great quantities; in the latter part of the period it produced more weapons than the available divisions could use.

The areas of principal concern in the defence of Germany's war machine against air attack were the aircraft industry, the synthetic fuel plants, the Ruhr's coal and steel production and the rail, road and water services which linked these activities and distributed their output. In the end the interdependence of the different parts of the German economy proved to be its Achilles' heel. This was shown most clearly by the experiences of the aircraft and fuel industries.

Aircraft production, which reached a first wartime peak in the middle of 1943 and then fell back, rose again in 1944 and surpassed all previous records in the autumn of that year. But the squadrons had by then no fuel for their aircraft, because for a time there had been too few aircraft to defend the fuel plants. The pre-war target for the German aircraft industry was 2,000 a month, increased to 2,300 shortly after the war began. Actual production was 700–800 a month from 1935 to 1940. During the first part of this period the types which played the biggest part in the war were being evolved. During the first two years of war Hitler, still planning on a short war, was not worried about production or interested in the development of further new types since he believed that the war would be over before they could be brought into service. In 1941 there was a modest increase in production and in 1942 a well-organized expansion in Germany and occupied Europe which raised production from 1,000 to 1,600 a month. In the summer of 1943 the damage inflicted by allied bombing – although it was repaired before the end of the year – forced the German Air Ministry, which still had more than thirty different types in production, to streamline the industry. Production, which had risen by June 1943 to 2,316 and had been set a new target of 3,000, was cut back by the raids to below 1,900.

In 1944 the industry was put under new management. Speer and Milch severely cut back the production of bombers, introduced a seventy-two hour week with high wages and improved working conditions, created new factories underground and provided the older ones with better defences, improved the repair services and raised the target first to 6,400 a month and then to 7,400. As a result production, which had again fallen at the beginning of the year to 1,369, rose in September to 3,538 new aircraft, while damaged aircraft returning to squadrons provided another 776, almost twice as many as in January; the production of single-engined fighters was more than doubled between February and June. Of a total of 113,514 aircraft produced during the war 40,593 were produced in 1944. The annual production of fighter aircraft in 1939–44 inclusive was 605: 2,746: 3,744: 5,515: 10,898: 25,285. Even in 1945 production of fighters almost reached a total of 5,000 for the four months before the war stopped. But this astonishing riposte to the bombing of the aircraft industry was in vain.

Until the end of 1943 Speer had been able to answer the allied bombing offensive. Reconstruction kept pace with destruction, stocks of vital materials (mostly large at the beginning of the war) were not dangerously run down and essential imports were maintained in spite of damage to railways and rolling stock. In 1944 the allied air forces were required to combine their attack on Germany with preliminary operations in aid of Overlord, but their own resources in the production of aircraft and the training of pilots enabled them, ominously for Germany, to fulfil both roles; the weight of the American attack was enormously increased, so much so that in one month in 1944 more American bombs were dropped than during the whole of 1942. Bomber Command similarly dropped in the last quarter of 1944 a bomb load four times as heavy as in the same part of 1943 and twenty times as heavy as in the same part of 1942. The synthetic oil industry, which was singled out for special attention in 1943–4, began to falter. Although the damage inflicted by a first series of raids was repaired, Speer's miraculous reconstruction services did not manage to cope so fully with a second series, stocks began to be drawn down alarmingly and production fell below demand. During nine consecutive days in September 1944 no aviation fuel whatever was produced except on one day, and production for the month was the hopelessly inadequate total of 9,400 tons. A pause in the bombing owing to bad weather gave some respite, but Germany's air defences were, if not totally eliminated, at least rendered negligible for the last six months of the war. When Dresden was bombed in February 1945, there was no defence of the city. Yet the aircraft industry was still producing 1,000–2,000 aircraft a month when the war ended.

This critical interdependence of aircraft and fuel production was made the more acute by the concentration of German heavy industry in the Ruhr and the dependence of industry outside the Ruhr on coal from the Ruhr. Germany was never short of coal but the damage done to communications in and around the Ruhr prevented Ruhr coal (80 per cent of Germany's output) from being moved to where it was needed. At the end of 1944 coal was being transported out of the Ruhr at one quarter of the normal rate and a few months later, after the winter's respite, this traffic was again halved. This dislocation of the Ruhr, combined with the conquest of Silesia and Lorraine by the Russians and Americans, strangled the steel industry which produced in the last quarter of 1944 less than 4 million tons in place of a projected 37.2 million. Other sectors of the economy collapsed with equal or greater suddenness in a chain reaction. At the end all fronts, except one, collapsed together – the fronts where the armies were still fighting and the economic front which finally succumbed under air attack.

The one front which held out with incredible tenacity was morale at home. This was the achievement of Joseph Goebbels, Minister of Propaganda and one of the few masters of his craft among the Nazi chieftains. What Speer did for Germany's war industry Goebbels did for its morale. Ultimately Hitler's greatest debt was to Goebbels whom he had once described – in an interview with a right-wing editor as early as 1931 – as his Field Marshal on the spiritual front, the man whom he would make Minister of Propaganda when he came to power and who would occupy a post as important as that of Foreign Minister or Chief of the General Staff.

Propaganda – the attempt to make an impact on large numbers of people in order to affect their mood and their actions, to get them to change their minds or not to change their minds, to get them to act in a certain way or not to – is an ancient instrument. It was modernized and immensely extended in the twentieth century by the invention of radio, and Goebbels was one of its master practitioners. He was not universally successful. In addressing himself to foreigners he was less adept than some British propagandists who had a better understanding of the society – and the language – of their enemy than Goebbels ever had. Also, like all propagandists, he found there was a limit to the extent to which he could affect people who basically did not want to believe what he had to say. But with German audiences he was very successful not only before the war but even in the face of the horrors of the Russian campaigns and mass bombing. He was appointed to his post a few weeks after Hitler became Chancellor and he held it until he and his entire family died with Hitler in Berlin.

He staffed the executive side of his Ministry with bright young men, half of them with a university education, and he taught them how to appeal to the emotions and the reason of the masses at one and the same time, so that an audience which had had its feelings roused would be captured not merely for the moment but also enduringly because a message had lodged in their minds. There were no limits to Goebbels's emotive appeals. He set out to intoxicate audiences and throw them into hysteria. The most rabble-rousing speeches of western politicians were by his standards sedate. In the years before and after the Nazi capture of power in 1933 Germany was in a state of crisis and Goebbels's techniques were designed to benefit from this feeling of crisis and to perpetuate it. People were screwed up, perils and evils were emphasized, the situation was presented as one which called above all for action – and for a man who could lead into action and must therefore be followed. From 1933 to 1939 German opinion was never allowed to let up, still less when war came. Goebbels could not make the Germans want war – there was a wild outburst of joyful relief in Berlin in October 1939 upon a false report that the British government had fallen and the war was over – but he created a mentality of endeavour and was able during the war to foster, against the odds, a solid mood of endurance. A crucial element in his technique was simplicity. Even in the most febrile and far-ranging tirades Nazi orators pinpointed and repeated one or two essential facts or arguments, eschewing generalization, representing issues as conflicts between good and evil, making them concrete and personal. While hammering away at favourite themes like the wickedness of Jews, the ill treatment of the Sudeten Germans, the need for *Lebensraum*, the western democracies' sinister but feeble attempts to encircle Germany, atrocity stories from the republican side in the civil war in Spain or, after the war began, successes in the field, Goebbels and his disciples held their audiences by the actuality of specific illustrations, true or false, which went home.

Goebbels made great use of shows: sporting events, funerals, festivals of every kind. Using entertainment to capture the public was not new – Thomas Cromwell had subsidized plays which were performed in town squares and on village greens throughout England in order to rub in Henry VIII's case against the papacy – but Goebbels made the most of its vastly increased scope. The Olympic Games of 1936 were turned into a propaganda event of the first magnitude. Goebbels also realized the importance of films, commissioning documentaries and newsreels and bringing pressure to bear on the film industry (which was not brought wholly under government control until it was nationalized in 1943) to make the sort of films he wanted. War films were used to impress neutrals as well as to fortify morale at home, where newsreels were compulsorily shown in all cinemas. These films, like Nazi oratory, were simple and repetitive. The press was not only regimented and bullied, but overwhelmed by official hand-outs, press conferences and special briefings. The number of newspapers in Germany sank during the Nazi period from 4,700 to fewer than 1,000. Uniformity, imposed by decree and by fear, produced dullness but once again it simplified the issues. The reader did not get the impression that one paper was saying one thing and another another, so that it was impossible to know what to think.

In the first years of war Goebbels's task was made comparatively easy by the turn of events. He extolled Hitler as the infallible leader who told his people what he was going to do and did it. A cheap radio set (with a limited range) had been marketed just before the war and about 70 per cent of German households had a radio. Goebbels made play with the taunt that the British were fighting to the last Frenchman and ascribed the collapse of France to racial miscegenation, but by July he was restraining overconfidence about the collapse of Great Britain and was soon advising editors not to tell their readers that London was a heap of ruins: British resistance was futile but it might go on for a time.

The invasion of the USSR gave him a new line. He represented the German attack as pre-emptive, alleging that Hitler had certain intelligence of a Russian attack, and he plugged the theme of the brutal and subhuman Slav. He did not minimize the rigours of the new war. After a calculated pause of a week came twelve special announcements (*Sondermeldungen*), all issued on the same day – a Sunday – and taking up practically the whole of the day. This battery of victory communiqués created an overwhelming effect commensurate with the scale of operations in the east and gave anxious Germans, who had been struggling to make sense of unfamiliar names scattered about their maps, the assurance that details did not matter. But Goebbels was careful not to commit himself to the statement that the war was won and he was therefore all the more horrified when Hitler and his press chief, Otto Dietrich, declared in October with premature exuberance that it was. Goebbels had already foreseen that his theme was as likely to be the preaching of total war as the proclaiming of total victory, and as winter came on he reverted to his sober warnings, started a campaign to collect clothes for the men freezing at the front and made regular reports on the response to this appeal. On the more optimistic side he could at least claim that Hitler had done better than Napoleon in spite of General Winter and the brutish tenacity of the Russian soldier, and that the gains in oil, grain, iron ore and other materials were considerable. Rommel's victories also provided good cheer.

From 1942 Goebbels, as the chief upholder of the home front, had to counter the general decline in Germany's fortunes and two major catastrophes in the defeats of the German armies in Russia and the heavy bombing of German cities. At first the army's communiqués about Stalingrad had been optimistic, the strategic importance of the city was underlined and its capture was to be the climax of the war in the east. The capitulation of the Sixth Army was a tremendous blow and Goebbels, not without courage, took the unique step of issuing a *Sondermeldung* about a defeat instead of a victory. It was accompanied by muffled drums, the national anthem and a three-minute silence, and all places of entertainment were closed for three days. Two weeks later a vast – and picked – audience was assembled in the *Sportpalast* in Berlin. Ten questions were put and answered to counter enemy propaganda that Germany had had enough and to pledge total war. In the shadow of Stalingrad this demonstration probably stiffened morale but it also made people think that total catastrophe might be on the way.

The tenth anniversary of Hitler's coming to power was marked by the first assertion that capitulation was out of the question: it was also the first mention of capitulation. The eastern battles in 1943 and 1944 increased the foreboding. There were only three *Sondermeldungen* in 1943; there had been sixty-five in 1941. The fall of Mussolini did not help. Hitler himself became remote, seldom appearing or speaking. Allied propaganda suggested that he had been driven to silence by his own mistakes; he had no words to explain what had gone wrong. Goebbels countered with a new image of Hitler as the supreme sufferer, stoically enduring like Frederick the Great in adversity, shunning the limelight unlike his flashy and temporarily successful opponents. At the same time, as disaster threatened, Goebbels worked to inculcate the feeling that the only way to avert it was to stick by Hitler.

Mass bombing was Goebbels's biggest problem. When bombing first began, Goebbels had repeated with sarcastic comment the exaggerated claims made by the British Air Ministry on the basis of aircrews' instant reports, but these tactics no longer sufficed when the destruction became heavy. Goebbels did not seek to deny it. He used it to stir up hatred against the enemy. He also showed himself all over Berlin, inspecting raid damage, showing that a Minister cared and was in control, and so forestalling panic and a break in morale. He initiated an anti-defeatist campaign (strengthened by a few death sentences) and although he could not prevent the German mood from drooping he succeeded in preventing it from turning into action against the government. His plea that this was the time for government and people to hang together was sufficiently widely accepted. Appointed Plenipotentiary for Total War in 1944 he extended normal working hours, conscripted women up to the age of fifty, cut entertainment, schooling and university courses and by these and other means ensured that Germans should go on fighting not just because they were afraid of the Gestapo but also because they were persuaded that this was the right thing to do. With a part of their minds they knew that they were defeated and that fighting on meant postponing the end without altering the outcome. But because Goebbels spoke to them straight, they took what he said as straight. By telling them, as one adult to another, that things were bad, he dissuaded them from facing the fact that they were hopeless. They behaved like a man who knows that he is condemned to death with cancer but prefers to believe the doctor who tells him that he has appendicitis. At the same time Goebbels piled on the horror of Slavic hordes about to sweep over Germany devastating the land and debauching its maidens. The nearer it came, the worse did Goebbels make fate sound, so that there seemed to be no purpose in doing anything except go through the motions of warding off the inescapable.

In the final assessment the bombers' contribution to the defeat of Germany must be judged a weighty one in the final stages of the war. In the light of the pretensions of the Douhet-Mitchell school of air strategists two questions arise: Did the bombers win the war? If they did not, could they have done? The answer to the first question is no. The German armies were fatally defeated by the Russians in July 1943 and at that point the bomber onslaught had barely begun and had caused no decisive damage; it did not do so for another year. The second question is hypothetical. Air power equipped with nuclear weapons may be a war-winning weapon in the sense that it can compel the surrender of an enemy whose armed forces in the field are undefeated. There was, however, no such air power in the European theatre in the Second World War. On the other hand it can be plausibly argued that the surrender of Japan after two nuclear bombs was a consequence of the overwhelming superiority of American air power over Japan's total defences. It is all a question of degree and there is nothing to prove that the fatal imbalance between attack and defence could be achieved by nuclear weapons alone. If the allied air forces had been even stronger than they were, and if allied air policy had not wavered between general attacks on population and morale and selective attacks on economic nerve centres and bottlenecks, then Germany might have been brought to surrender without the necessity for a major invasion and the hard-fought campaigns from Normandy to the heart of Europe. Such a possibility cannot be disproved, but the experiences of the American and British air commands show that this strategy would have been exceptionally costly in lives. It is moreover all but certain that, in a war in which Germany was being attacked by the USSR as well as by themselves, the western allies would never willingly have confined themselves to strategic bombing or have delayed their invasion in such a way as to allow the Russians to occupy the whole of Germany.

Leaving aside the inadmissible claim that bombing did win, or could have won, the war on its own, there emerges a different question: how far bombing, judged as a contributory instead of an independent factor, shortened the war. No precise answer to such a question is possible, but in general it is pertinent to recall that allied bombing diverted German air power from the offensive fronts to the defence of the Reich and diverted German labour – 1–1.5 million men, many of them skilled – to repair and reconstruction works. Perhaps these contributions should be adjudged significant subsidiary sources of Germany's defeat. They cannot be held to be decisive but they must have made the allied victory somewhat easier and somewhat quicker. Both area bombing and precision bombing made this kind of contribution, for even if a government at war is more intent on protecting its factories than its industrial proletariat, there is nevertheless a point beyond which it cannot leave its people undefended and unhoused. Speer's evidence after the war was that precision bombing could do crucial damage; but until the last phase the allies were not able to carry out effective precision bombing operations. Area bombing, to which they resorted instead, paid only a small dividend and one which those who bring ethics into the equation may well regard as too small.

CHAPTER 24

The Western Fronts

AMERICAN and British armies set foot on the mainland of Europe in Italy in September 1943 and in France in the following June. The armies in Italy reached Rome two days before the invasion of France. They had spent over eight months fighting their way up the peninsula against tough German opposition in harsh mountain country and horrible weather.

When they landed in Italy the allies hoped to be in Rome before the end of that year. Hopes in the Italian theatre were apt to be exaggerated. Churchill in particular had got into the habit of regarding anything to do with Italy as soft. The Americans were more sceptical. The opposition was German, not Italian, and it was commanded by Kesselring, who had prepared three defensive positions south of Rome. The allies' best hope was to strike rapidly northward with Clark's US Fifth Army, while Montgomery supported his advance on the eastern side of the peninsula. But both Clark and Montgomery made slow progress. Heavy rains helped the defenders. Both armies gained ground but no road to Rome was opened. For the Germans the worst consequence of the landings in Italy was the establishment of the US Fifteenth Air Force on Italian airfields whence it could attack targets in Germany, northern Italy, Austria and Rumania.

At the beginning of 1944 the attack towards Rome was renewed with a frontal attack in the centre and a simultaneous landing at Anzio forty miles south of Rome on the west coast – the place where Nero was born and the Apollo Belvedere found. The Germans, crediting the allies with an adventurousness which they did not display, believed that they would land north of Rome at some place like Leghorn. The Anzio landing was hurriedly planned and timidly directed. The initial landings on 22 January were practically unopposed and a daring commander might have made a dash for Rome and got there, but General Lucas, the commander of the expedition and a man of basically pessimistic temperament, on discovering that there were no Germans in his path behaved as though there were. Kesselring was given time to organize a defence and seized it. He disposed of reserves which his opponents, ignoring intelligence assessments, had underrated. By the end of a week the expedition was in trouble and when the Anglo-American force made a bid to advance from its carefully consolidated beachhead on 30 January, it incurred savage losses (one unit lost 761 men out of 767). The Germans counter-attacked in the first week in February; allied losses mounted, morale and confidence sank; the allies were all but evicted; the German attack was renewed in mid-February and after four days of heavy fighting the allies were again on the brink of total defeat when they saw to their surprise that the Germans, unaware how close they were to victory, were drawing off. The Anzio venture had failed to achieve its purpose but the Germans had failed to eliminate the beachhead.

In the centre of the peninsula the allies were equally frustrated. The two sides were roughly equal in numbers on the ground but the Germans were more easily reinforced, as well as exceptionally well equipped; the allies offsetting these German advantages by superiority in the air, in intelligence and in deception. The main allied thrust was not successful until the middle of May and then only after one of the more questionable actions of the war – the destruction from the air of the abbey of Monte Cassino.

Of Kesselring's three defensive positions the strongest – the Gustav line – contained the famous Benedictine abbey, founded in 524 by the creator of western monasticism and the repository of one of Europe's most prized libraries. Although it no longer held the bones of the saint, which had been removed to the banks of the Loire thirteen centuries earlier in order to save them from the Lombards, the abbey had been temporarily enriched with pictures and other works of art removed from Naples to escape the war. The Germans supervised the removal to Rome of the abbey's treasures and most of its monks in October 1943 when the U S Fifth Army, by crossing the Volturno and then the Sangro rivers, threatened the Gustav line. Monte Cassino, although an obstacle to allied progress, was not of prime military importance since it was surrounded by higher peaks and the combatants were understood to have assured the Pope that the abbey would be neither fortified by the one side nor attacked from the air by the other.

At the outset of 1944 the allies were moving arduously towards the town and abbey. A British corps under Clark's command crossed the Garigliano and French troops under Juin (campaigning with Chateaubriand in his pocket) crossed the Rapido north of Monte Cassino. The abbey, in which the abbot and five monks still remained, was hit for the first time in January but a first allied attack on the town failed after three weeks of heavy losses in foul weather. Although American and French forces got to within striking distance of both town and abbey they could not cover the last thousand yards and a final assault by New Zealand and Indian units was thrown back by superior German numbers and artillery fire.

On the allied side opinions differed about whether this artillery fire came from the abbey. The Germans denied that the abbey was being used for military purposes but their enemies were not prepared to believe anything they said and General Ira C. Eaker, who was one of a number of senior commanders to make a personal air reconnaissance, reported that he had seen German troops in the abbey. The allied command declared that the abbey would no longer be spared and although American, British and French generals opposed its bombardment it was attacked on 15 February by 142 Flying Fortresses and destroyed.

This operation was, however, fruitless. The town and hill were not taken and the battle was resumed a month later with a heavy air and artillery bombardment which reduced the town of Monte Cassino to a shambles. The New Zealanders went in again, only to be checked by German resistance and uncleared rubble. They failed to reach the heart of the town. A complementary attack by the Indians on the monastery likewise failed after getting within 400 yards. A week later both town and monastery were still in German hands and the attack was called off after a final New Zealand attempt to dislodge the defenders. The road to Rome remained blocked. The best that the allies could claim was that they were holding twenty-two German divisions out of some other battle. The strategy of the Italian campaign had postulated the surrender of Italy and the creation of fresh options leading the allies to the Balkans or the Danube or into Germany itself. The collapse of Italian resistance had, however, produced a German resistance stout enough to bar all these routes, and the longer the campaign lasted the more pointless it became. Its object had been to give the allies useful victories in the interval between the re-conquest of the Mediterranean and the re-conquest of France, but the nearer the French invasion approached the more the Italian campaign became a sideshow producing nothing important which could not be obtained by invasion in the west.

But Kesselring's position was never more than a defensive one in a theatre of secondary importance. He could expect little in the way of reinforcements and in May he was finally forced to abandon all his positions south of Rome. British and Polish units of the Eighth Army opened a new attack which was at first held but French forces then executed a spectacular turning movement in almost impossibly difficult mountain country and forced the Germans to evacuate Monte Cassino at last on 17 May. On the next day the Poles entered the ruined abbey and the British the town, and the Germans began to retreat all along the line. The forces in the Anzio bridgehead broke out but were too slow to cut off the Germans who retired north of Rome in good order. Kesselring abandoned the Italian capital after declaring it an open city and established a fresh holding line through Lake Trasimene and a stronger one, the Gothic line, in Tuscany.

Clark entered Rome two days before Overlord, not six months as Churchill had hoped. General Sir Harold Alexander, the overall commander of the Fifth and Eighth Armies, was now in a position to exploit their successes, but the timing was wrong. Alexander's dual purpose was to entice German divisions into the Italian theatre and then keep them there or cut them off. He wanted to maintain both his armies at full strength, force the Gothic line and then move either left into France or right into Austria, sucking more German troops into the theatre as he intensified the threat to Germany itself. Although the soft underbelly of the Axis had proved less soft than Churchill had imagined, it was now pierced and the Italian campaign was on the verge of justification. On the last day of May Churchill promised Alexander his full support for keeping his armies up to strength, but Churchill's was no longer the deciding voice and Alexander was obliged to relinquish part of his forces for an invasion of southern France (operation Anvil or Dragoon) complementary to Overlord. The Americans, supported at first by Maitland Wilson and believing that Kesselring was more likely to be milked than reinforced, wanted to make a bigger thrust up the Rhône valley than up Italy, and after bitter argument they prevailed. Anvil turned out to be an unnecessary reinforcement of Overlord but Alexander lost seven divisions and part of his air strength and was told to go ahead with this reduced force; Kesselring on the other hand got four extra divisions.

Retreating in his own time, Kesselring reached the Gothic line in August and then held up the allies long enough for the autumn rains and mud to come to his assistance. Churchill and Alexander were still hoping to make for Vienna, but the Americans refused to reinforce a theatre which had become decidedly secondary, and after a limited German counter-attack in the last week of the year operations were suspended and more allied troops were withdrawn from Italy. The last hope of staking a claim to be heard in the post-war settlement of central Europe by effecting a junction with the Russians in Vienna had gone.

It had never been a realistic one. Victory in Italy in 1943 was beyond the allies' grasp and victory in 1944 was pointless because there was never any thought of making the winning thrust anywhere but in France. By 1944 no other front could hope for the men and material needed for so decisive a role.

In November 1943 Rommel was sent from a semi-active command in northern Italy to inspect the coastal defences of the western front from Dunkirk to Brittany. He found them rusty, uncoordinated and manned by second- or third-rate divisions which were well below strength. By this date the allies had already chosen the general area in which they would land but their decision was not known to the Germans. The alternatives were obvious. Either they might cross the Channel at its narrowest point and make their landings east of the Somme, or they might land in Normandy west of the Somme. The principal argument in favour of this latter plan was the unsuitability of south-east England for the accumulation of the vast quantities of men and stores which were to be put into the invasion and above all the meagre capacity of the Kentish ports compared with the Portsmouth-Southampton area. In addition the latter was less vulnerable to attack and less open to reconnaissance; and on the other side the strongest German defences were in the Pas de Calais. These considerations outweighed the disadvantages of the longer sea passage and the opening of the new front further away from the frontiers of Germany, and the allies settled without much debate on the bay of the Seine.

When Rommel arrived in France he found that the Commander-in-Chief West, Field Marshal von Rundstedt, inclined to the view that the invasion would come in the Pas de Calais. OKW took the same view. Rommel, however, queried it and as the months went by the pattern of allied air activities and the absence of mining in the bay of the Seine strongly supported him. By the spring the Germans were nine tenths convinced that the main attack would be delivered in Normandy but some of them, Hitler in particular, expected either diversionary or follow-up operations in the Pas de Calais: they were deceived by spoof radio activity simulating the presence of large forces in south-east England and their inferiority in the air was by now so marked that they could not survey even Kent accurately enough to establish that there were no armies there.

More important than this initial divergence about where the invasion was to be expected was the dispute about how to meet it. Rundstedt saw no hope of preventing a landing. His strategy was to accept it and then throw the enemy back into the sea by a counter-attack. Rommel on the other hand believed that, in France as in North Africa, Sicily and Italy, once the allies had gained a foothold they could not be forced off it again. He proposed therefore to deny rather than repel the invasion, by mining the shore and the beaches and by engaging the enemy before he could cross the vital hundreds of yards between the water's edge and the first natural cover beyond the open sands and rocks. Hitler decided in favour of Rommel and appointed him to command, under Rundstedt, the group of armies deployed from Holland to Brittany, but insisted with characteristic caution on retaining large forces east of the Somme after as well as before the invasion and with characteristic indecision on holding much of the armour in reserve outside Rommel's immediate command and immediate operational area. These prevarications proved specially perilous because allied air supremacy, and the extensive destruction of communications in the weeks before the battle began, immobilized German forces caught in the wrong place. On the eve of the invasion Rundstedt had sixty divisions, of which forty-three were available to Rommel (the remaining seventeen were south of the Loire), but of these forty-three only eighteen were in Normandy; five were in Holland, one in the Channel Islands and no fewer than nineteen in Belgium and France east of the Somme.

The preparations on the allied side were of the utmost thoroughness and ingenuity. There had been disputes about the timing of this operation but none about whether or not to launch it. Preliminary planning had been put formally in hand after the Casablanca conference of January 1943 and before that raids on the continent – at St Nazaire, for example, in March 1942 and at Dieppe in August – had been undertaken with an eye to gaining information and experience which would be valuable for a full scale invasion. Detailed and daring reconnaissances of the landing beaches were carried out in order to establish the lie of the land, the obstacles below and above the water line, the state of the going for tracked and other vehicles and a thousand and one other pieces of information. Elaborate feints were devised to keep the defenders guessing and dispersed. Entirely new accessories of war were designed and constructed, from the two artificial harbours (Mulberries) as large as medium-sized ports which were towed across the Channel in sections (beginning on D-day) and the oil pipelines (Pluto – eventually twenty came into use) which were laid under it, to a variety of strange adaptations of tracked vehicles for carrying prefabricated bridges, laying carpets on the sand and destroying land mines.

The principal commanders had been designated in 1943 and had been working together and training their subordinates for much longer than is usually possible in war: General Dwight D. Eisenhower in supreme command with Air Marshal Sir Arthur Tedder as his deputy and General Walter Bedell Smith as Chief of Staff; Vice-Admiral Bertram Ramsay, General Bernard Montgomery and Air Vice-Marshal Trafford Leigh-Mallory in command of the three services in the assault phase; Generals Omar N. Bradley and Miles Dempsey commanding the two invading armies, the former destined to command an Army Group after the build-up. One and a half million Americans were transported across the Atlantic with all their own equipment and food and crammed into southern England. Unprecedented and often very irritating new security measures were introduced, affecting even the embassies of neutrals and allies. A fleet of over 5,000 vessels was assembled for the initial phase: 1,200 naval vessels, including seven battleships, to bombard the coastal defences, sweep mines, escort the invaders and tackle enemy sea- and air-craft; and 4,000 transports, barges, tugs and other sea-going and amphibious craft for the conveyance of the armies with their tanks, armoured cars, guns, vehicles, ammunition and the lavish variety of modern fighting gear. In the air the allies mustered 7,500 aircraft in direct support of the invasion and 3,500 bombers which could be and were used in this battle as well as for the continued strategic bombing of Germany. Eisenhower failed to get the heavy bombers included in his command but succeeded in getting them used for the destruction of German communications to the battle area (in accordance with a plan worked out in great detail by a civilian professor of anatomy). Naval and air supremacy ensured the passage of the thirty-seven divisions assembled to strike the decisive blow in the west.

Two hazards remained: the weather and the issue of the first engagements. The invasion was once postponed by twenty-four hours and Eisenhower seriously pondered a second postponement which would not only have been a much longer one but by ill chance would have re-timed the operation to coincide with a serious and unseasonable storm which blew up on 19 June. In the event the first invaders crossed the Channel by air at two o'clock in the morning of 6 June to be dropped some miles behind the five landing beaches, and at dawn five separate groups approached these beaches from the sea. These men – 20,000 airborne and 70,000 seaborne – were the advance guard of a force of two million drawn from a dozen nations which was to be set ashore in France within the next two months. Their first objectives lay along a line which stretched for forty miles from the eastern base of the Cotentin peninsula eastward to the mouth of the river Orne which flows into the sea eight miles northeast of the town of Caen. The task of the first invaders was to get onto the beaches and then get off them again as quickly as possible.

The first day's objectives included Caen. Fortunes were mixed. At the westernmost beach the Americans secured their first objectives with the loss of only twelve men before the end of the day. At the next beach, however, the second American landing was an almost complete disaster and, after suffering 3,000 casualties, was saved only by the successes in neighbouring sectors. At the remaining three beaches British and

THE PRE-INVASION SCENE MAY - JUNE 1944

ALLIED PRE-INVASION CONSIDERATIONS

0   50
Miles

The longer route across Channel, but further from German aircraft. Also, German defences weaker in Normandy than in the Pas de Calais.

The shorter route across Channel, but German forces heaviest in Pas de Calais. Also Kentish ports unsuitable for large ship and troop concentrations.

ENGLAND

Weymouth
Southampton
Portsmouth
Dover
Strait of Dover
Calais
PAS DE CALAIS
Boulogne

ENGLISH CHANNEL
Dieppe
Cherbourg
Rouen
Caen
St.Malo
NORMANDY
Seine
Paris

GERMAN PRE-INVASION CONSIDERATIONS

0   50
Miles

ENGLAND   Allied bogus radio activity

KENT
Dover
Southampton
Weymouth
Portsmouth
Strait of Dover
Dover Calais
PAS DE CALAIS
Boulogne

ENGLISH CHANNEL
Cherbourg
Dieppe
Rouen
Caen
NORMANDY
Seine
Paris

Rommel (and later, Hitler) believes the invasion will occur here and, thus he strengthens beach defences. He is anxious that the Allies do not achieve a foothold.

Von Runstedt and OKW expect invasion to occur here. German strategy accepts the initial landings but envisages a counter-attack will dislodge the invaders.

ALLIED PRE-INVASION BOMBING

+++++ Railways.
★ Targets destroyed.
☆ Targets heavily damaged.

ENGLAND
Southampton
Weymouth
Portsmouth
Dover
Ostend
Dunkirk
Ghent
Cologne
Calais
Lille
Brussels
BELGIUM
GERMANY
Rhine
Moselle
LUX.
Trèves
Abbeville
ENGLISH CHANNEL
Dieppe
Cherbourg
Amiens
Le Havre
Rouen
Laon
Soissons
Reims
Metz
Caen
Seine
St Lô
Nancy
St Malo
Falaise
Meuse
Strasbourg
Chartres
Paris
F   R   A   N   C   E
Rennes
Troyes
Rhine
Le Mans
Orleans
Chaumont
Belfort
Nantes
Loire
Tours
Dijon

0   50
Miles

~ARTHUR BANKS~

THE ALLIED INVASION OF EUROPE 6 JUNE 1944

THE ALLIED ATTACK

3 US ARMY

CHANNEL

ENGLISH

CONCENTRATION AREA

Guernsey

Jersey

A B C D E

NORMANDY

Paris

0   50
Miles

ALLIED DISPOSITIONS AND MOVEMENTS

BRITISH SECOND ARMY

British and Canadian assault formations.

'Follow-up' units.

FIRST US ARMY

United States assault formations.

'Follow-up' units.

THE NORMANDY BEACHES

A   Utah
B   Omaha
C   Gold
D   Juno
E   Sword

● Allied airborne dropping zones.

GERMAN DISPOSITIONS

- - - Army boundary

⊞ GHQ   ▣ Army Group

⊟ Army   ⊏ Corps

⊠ Division   ···· Reserve

⊠ Forming

THE ALLIED LANDINGS

Roads.
Railways.
Flooded areas.

Areas held by Allies at 2400 hrs on D-Day.

Areas held by Germans at 2400 hrs on D-Day.

First Allied assault waves.

- - - Line of planned Allied beach-head at 2400 hrs on D-Day.

⇐ XXI Panzer Division counterattacks.

↑↑ Assault areas.

| US 1 ARMY | 21 ARMY GROUP | BRITISH 2 ARMY |
| Bradley | Montgomery | Dempsey |

| US 7 CORPS | US 5 CORPS | BRITISH 30 CORPS | BRITISH 1 CORPS |
| Collins | Gerow | Bucknall | Crocker |

Montebourg

St. Mere Eglise

UTAH

BAY   OF   SEINE

OMAHA

Vierville

Port-en-Bessin

GOLD

Arromanches

JUNO

SWORD

Douvres

Cabourg

Colleville

Carentan

Isigny

Bayeux

Creully

CAEN

XV ARMY (Salmuth)

VII ARMY (Dollman)

Vire

Balleroy

Aure

Tilly-sur-Seulles

Bures

0   5
Miles

~ARTHUR BANKS~

Canadian troops fought their way onto and beyond the shore against German opposition which stiffened uncomfortably after noon. At the end of the day the fate of the paratroopers was still uncertain and some of the Americans were in serious trouble, but the seaborne invaders had made their lodgements.

Montgomery, who was in overall command of all land operations, aimed to take Caen with his British-Canadian left, but although his forces came within four miles of it they did not enter it until 10 July or gain complete possession of it for another week. This was a serious setback since Montgomery's first plan was to drive through Caen to Paris. It was compounded by bad luck. By 18 June 629,000 men had been put ashore and the Mulberries, although not yet completed, were handling 6,000 tons a day. But on the next day a strong and unseasonable gale blew up and lasted for five days. It wrecked one Mulberry, damaged the other and blew about 800 craft onto the shore. Supplies directed onto the beaches and through the Mulberries, which had reached an average of 22,570 tons a day, were drastically cut and when the gale abated the armies had 20,000 vehicles and over 100,000 tons of stores less than they had been counting on. This shortfall was not made good for a month. Moreover Cherbourg, at the tip of the Cotentin, was only belatedly captured on 26 June with its port facilities wrecked and the harbour blocked; it could not be used at all for weeks, not fully for months. Nevertheless a million men were in France at the end of the first week in July and over a million and a half before the end of the month.

Once they had got ashore the allies' principal fears were stalemate in Normandy and the imminent threat of Hitler's V weapons. Their principal uncovenanted advantage was the persistent success of their deception plan which kept Hitler from reinforcing his armies in Normandy from his substantial forces east of the Seine. Combined, a stalemate and the arrival of the V weapons might give Hitler, not victory, but a negotiated peace; but stalemate became impossible as the German armies in Normandy remained unsupported from outside. Nevertheless the failure to take Caen and so open the short and direct route to the Seine and Paris kept the issue in doubt from mid-June to mid-August. A series of costly attacks on Caen failed. In mid-June a British corps suffered defeat at Villers-Bocage, a battle which coincided with the release of the first V 1s. An attempt at the end of the month to outflank Caen to the west also failed. A direct attack, preceded by heavy air bombardment, in the second week of July caused terrible casualties on both sides but gave the allies only half the city. A renewal of these tactics a few days later had to be called off on the third day but forced the Germans out of the city. Meanwhile Montgomery and Bradley (who was still subordinated to Montgomery and not directly to Eisenhower) planned to end the battle for Normandy by breaking westward into Brittany and then encircling the Germans to the south. Although still plagued by the tardy capture of Cherbourg and by continuing bad weather, Bradley launched his forces out of the Cotentin peninsula on 25 July and, having defeated a German spoiling attack across the base of the peninsula, sent Patton's US Third Army into Brittany and so round to Argentan, which it reached the day after the Canadians, coming south from Caen, reached Falaise (16 August), thus trapping the Germans in a bag with an escape route only fifteen miles wide. This gap was closed on the 19th when American and Polish units joined hands. About 60,000 Germans were killed or captured and huge quantities of arms and vehicles lost in the Normandy pocket.

On the German side these battles were fought by Field Marshal von Kluge who succeeded both Rundstedt, dismissed by Hitler on 1 July, and Rommel, accidentally put out of action when his car was hit by an aircraft on 17 July. Kluge was in turn dismissed on 17 August. He committed suicide, probably because he knew that Hitler knew that he had been cognizant of the plot to kill Hitler on 20 July. For the same reason the convalescent Rommel was forced by the SD, acting on Hitler's orders, to kill himself.

The new Commander-in-Chief, Field Marshal Model, managed to extract a not negligible number of the encircled troops in Normandy, but two days before his appointment fresh American and French armies under General Devers landed in the south of France (15 August) and two days after it Patton reached the Seine north-west and south-east of Paris. On the 19th Paris rose. Within the Paris Liberation Committee there were differences about whether to wait for the nearer approach of the regular armies or not, the communists being for action now, the non-communists for delay. The pressures for action became irresistible and the order was given for the liberation of the capital by its own people. There was fighting in the streets between the Germans and the Resistance. A truce was arranged but Hitler would have none of it and ordered the destruction of the city, if necessary by bombing. The truce degenerated into confusion and fighting started again. At one time the bells were ringing for victory while the guns were still firing as the last of the SS and their French accomplices defended all that remained to them: their lives. De Gaulle urged that General Jacques Leclercq's Second French Division be sent forward since, left to themselves, the Parisians could be overwhelmed by the Germans and their city destroyed: 1,500 of them were killed in the rising and twice as many were wounded. After some hesitation de Gaulle's

THE FALAISE POCKET
AUGUST 1944

Approx. German front, evening 16 August.
Approx. German front, evening 19 August.
German forces.
Allied thrusts.

GERMAN COUNTER
ATTACKS

Touques
Livarot
Vimoutiers
Gacé
Vie
Les Champeaux
Coudehard
Chambois
Orne
Hordouseaux
Trun
St Lambert
Jort
Dives
Argentan
Ecouche
Pierrefitte
Putanges
Falaise
Orne
Rouvre
Briouze
Condé
Flers
Tinchebray

CANADIAN
ARMY

AMERICAN
ARMY

BRITISH
ARMY

Miles
~ARTHUR BANKS~

request was granted and Leclercq entered Paris on 25 August (the British tactfully declining an American suggestion that a token British contingent with a Union Jack should accompany Leclercq). The German military governor, General Dietrich von Choltitz, who had disregarded and defeated Hitler's orders, surrendered to Leclercq and to Colonel Rol, alias Tanguy, one of the military leaders of the Resistance and a communist veteran of the Spanish civil war. Choltitz surrendered to the French Republic and not to the allied command, an action which the Americans, though riled, took in good part. The allies had already discovered that they could not get away with their facile assumption that upon the defeat of the Germans France would be provisionally administered by them. (They had prepared an occupation currency but de Gaulle's indignation on learning of its existence had blown it away.) De Gaulle arrived in Paris and proclaimed a provisional government of France at the Hôtel de Ville on 30 August.

After the end of August the allied advance slowed down. Hitler had ordered the German garrisons, which still held a string of ports, to resist to the last man in the hope that the allies would divert forces to invest these places and so be delayed. For the most part the allies ignored the garrisons which were therefore simply isolated and kept out of battles farther east until they were obliged by events to surrender, but in one or two cases German stubbornness paid off, notably at Brest which did not surrender until 18 September and so could not be used to supply the increasingly large and increasingly distant allied armies. On 1 September, the initial phase being completed, Eisenhower assumed command in the field in northern France and thenceforward exercised it to the end through his two Army Group Commanders, Bradley and Montgomery. Eisenhower's principal concern was the supply of his large and rapidly moving armies. He himself, underrating the Germans' capacity to pull themselves together for a last round, seems to have thought that he could keep up the pace along his whole front with the resources available to him. Montgomery was the most eloquent of those who said that this was impossible. He argued that the logistical problems produced by the unexpectedly swift advances after the break-out at Caen had made it essential to concentrate a punch either on the left or the right, and he naturally made the most of the case in favour of the left. He wanted all the support that the Supreme Commander could give him for a drive across the Somme, through Belgium, into the Ruhr and on to Berlin. This way, he believed, he could finish the war before the end of the year.

Montgomery may have been right but neither then nor in retrospect was he obviously so and he pressed his point of view regardless of the

THE ALLIED ADVANCE FROM NORMANDY TO
THE RHINE 6 JUNE 1944 – 7 MARCH 1945

D-DAY
6 JUNE 1944

D-day + 49 (13 July).
D-day + 68 (24 August).
D-day + 81 (26 August).
Falaise pocket.

——— Allied line December 1944.
⇑ Last German counter attack.
= German border and
Siegfried Line.

German held until
8 May 1945

American armies from
Southern France.

SWITZERLAND

Miles
0   50

~R. BANKS~

Cologne 6 Mar
Remagen 7 Mar 1945
Aachen 21 Oct
Rhine
16 Dec
ARDENNES
Brussels 3 Sept
Antwerp 4 Sept
BRITISH & CANADIANS
Calais 30 Sept
Amiens 31 Aug
Rouen 30 Aug
Le Havre
Falaise 23 Aug
Seine
Paris 25 Aug
Orleans 17 Aug
Yonne
Metz 18 Nov
Nancy 16 Sept
Epinal 15 Sept
FRENCH
Dijon 11 Sept
AMERICANS
Tours 26 Aug
Loire
Nantes 6 Aug
Rennes
St Malo
Cherbourg 22 June
Channel Islands
Lorient
St Nazaire
Brest 19 Sept

political pressures on Eisenhower and even beyond the limits prescribed to a loyal or considerate subordinate. Eisenhower was sceptical of Montgomery's strategy and, although an exceptionally honest and fair man, he could not avoid giving weight to a political problem. He was an American general in command of a preponderantly American force, and giving preference to Montgomery meant favouring a British general whom the American public and many American senior officers disliked. Not only Eisenhower himself but also Marshall felt that the voice of Congress and the voice of the American press had to have some weight in these strategic decisions. Their sensitivity on this score was the more acute because the commanders on the American side included in Patton a soldier who was no less colourful than Montgomery and readier to resort to insubordination if he did not get the orders he wanted. Holding back Patton's drive from the Seine to the Saar in order to enable Montgomery to knock out the German army somewhere else was something that Eisenhower was not prepared to attempt.

On the last day of August Montgomery took Amiens, due north of Paris, and crossed the Somme and less than a week later he had taken Brussels and Antwerp and developed a bold plan for a further advance. The obstacles to continuing eastward into the Ruhr, apart from his difficulty in getting the undivided support of the Supreme Commander, were stiffening German resistance and the prepared defences of the Siegfried line (the West Wall) which guarded the German frontier from Switzerland up to and including Belgium – but excluding Holland. Montgomery proposed to strike north instead of east, advancing from Belgium into Holland instead of the Ruhr. By doing this he would cut across the German supply lines in Holland, isolate and surround the remaining German forces in Belgium and western Holland by extending his own lines to the coast at the Zuider Zee, get beyond the northern end of the Siegfried line and then turn east into the north German plain. He might also catch the Germans where they would least expect a major blow.

The operation was to be a dual one. Airborne troops would seize a series of bridges over the principal waterways in Holland and so gain control of key points along the north–south line Arnhem–Nijmegen–Eindhoven. At the same time ground troops would advance from the south to Eindhoven, thence to Nijmegen and finally – the crucial link – to Arnhem. Eisenhower approved the plan and gave Montgomery the Hundred-and-first and the Eighty-second US Airborne Divisions for the Eindhoven and Nijmegen drops. The bridge over the Lower Rhine at Arnhem was to be captured by the British Airborne Division. But there remained some misunderstanding about how far Eisenhower had decided to give Montgomery all the material support he needed, even at the cost of staying Patton's advance.

This operation, which was launched on 17 September, was intended to revitalize the allied advance which had been petering out since the beginning of the month. It came to grief after a week's bitter fighting, one of those failures which nearly succeed but are turned into disaster by the chances of war and by muddle – but not, as has sometimes been supposed, by betrayal. The two American divisions accomplished their tasks, the Hundred-and-first Division comparatively smoothly and the Eighty-second Division on the fourth day after one of the most dashing exploits of the war in the west. The British ground forces (XXX Corps under General Horrocks) made punctual contact with the Hundred-and-first Division and then sent forward armoured units in time to follow up and consolidate the Eighty-second Division's successful capture of the bridge over the Waal at Nijmegen. But XXX Corps' further advance towards Arnhem was impeded by mines and the skilful and vigorous recovery of the Germans, and meanwhile the British Airborne Division had got into trouble.

The airborne drops were spread over three days and the defences of the bridge at Arnhem were reputedly so fierce that it had been decided to drop the British division about eight miles from the bridge. In this way the division could expect to find itself on Dutch soil more or less intact and would then proceed to attack the bridge like an ordinary ground formation. In other words the defences at the bridge had persuaded the British, before a shot was fired, not to attempt a direct airborne *coup de main* but to mount a hybrid attack which was part airborne and, in the second and decisive part, a straight fight through fields and villages. Given these tactics it was peculiarly unfortunate that German strength in the area had been seriously underestimated. Ultra intelligence pointed with some but not complete certainty to the presence within striking distance of the German II SS Panzer Corps comprising the Ninth and Tenth Panzer Divisions, but this intelligence was poorly evaluated. These divisions were in the area for refitting, had been excellently equipped and were ably commanded. Moreover, by a piece of grave misfortune, the British orders for the entire operation were captured on the first day off an American soldier whose glider crashed.

Nevertheless the first day's operations were everywhere successful and on the Arnhem sector the British units began their advance towards the town through a friendly population anxious to show their delight by hospitality of every kind. On the second day, however, German opposition surprised the British and the situation began to get confused. Poor weather intervened and airborne supplies to the units which had already been dropped miscarried to such an extent that most of them were collected by the Germans. Aircraft losses were heavy. From the third day the British were being forced to make local withdrawals and it soon became clear that the fate of the Airborne Division depended on what speed XXX Corps could make to its relief. As hope faded, the story became one of endurance, heroism and the gradual strangulation of the perimeter, while the prematurely exuberant Dutch awaited the return of the Germans in the cellars of houses where they had been dispensing good cheer to the British but which were now being wrecked above their heads. The attackers' losses were 1,200 dead and over 3,000 taken prisoner. The Arnhem bridge remained in German hands until the middle of April 1945. The Arnhem operation, the last major parachute operation of the war, summed up the experiences of four years which had begun with the successful German operation which opened the campaign in the Low Countries in May 1940. These experiences showed that parachutists could play an important role as the advance guard of a main force which was not too far away and was advancing rapidly, but that they could not yet take an independent giant stride ahead on their own.

The failure at Arnhem gave the Germans a last chance to consolidate a line beyond Germany's own borders. On 5 September – the day after Antwerp had fallen in the north and Lyons to the Americans advancing from Toulon in the south, and two weeks before the Arnhem operation – Hitler had recalled Rundstedt once more and had given him the task of holding what was left of Belgium, Holland and the Siegfried line. But Hitler also intended Rundstedt to do more than that. He would take advantage of a lull on the eastern front to switch troops to the west for an offensive in the Ardennes at the end of November from the Meuse to the sea. His main target was Antwerp, captured by the allies on 4 September. For it he assembled twenty-five divisions grouped in three Armies, including the newly created Sixth SS Panzer Army commanded by General Sepp Dietrich. Hitler did not, however, tell his principal commanders in the west of the plans which they were to execute and it was not until the end of October that they were informed. Rundstedt, Model and their senior commanders and staff officers immediately objected that the plans were too ambitious. They proposed a watered-down version designed to encircle a part of the American forces west of Aachen with the option, in the event of speedy success, of going on to Antwerp at a second stage, but Hitler refused to consider any alterations to the plans which his own staff had already worked out in detail. All he would grant, under pressure of circumstances, was the postponement of D-day to 16 December.

The last German offensive of the war of any note was accordingly launched on that day. It caused immense perturbation because it came as a complete surprise to allied commanders. This should not have been so. Ultra intelligence, which was copious from start to finish of the campaigns of 1944–5, gave numerous indications of a substantial offensive in the offing and in the general area of the Ardennes (but, as usual, no date). It had reported in September the creation of Sixth SS Panzer Army and, early in November, the reinforcement of the Luftwaffe in the relevant sector by units switched from further north and from the Russian fronts. German railway ciphers, which were being read at Bletchley Park, gave detailed information of movements of men and material, and orders to Luftwaffe reconnaissance units showed that the Germans were specially anxious to conceal something that was going on to the east of the Ardennes. In addition signals intelligence, monitoring German army traffic, noted the appearance of new formations which had been ordered to keep radio silence – itself a significant order but one that could not be completely obeyed since the units had to break it once or twice a day in order to make sure that they were still in proper touch with one another. Why these pointers were missed is still unclear but it has been surmised that allied staffs were so convinced (and in fact correctly) that Hitler could no longer launch such a venture successfully that they overlooked the fact that he might nevertheless try. With their minds concentrated on how best to cross the Rhine they had become immune to the notion that the Germans might re-cross the Meuse.

But not even the element of surprise could give Hitler's gamble any chance of success. After four days it had failed. Eisenhower placed all troops north of the German thrust – including two American armies – under Montgomery's command, a redisposition of some courage in view of the prevalent American animus against Montgomery and the contrary advice of Bradley who underrated the gravity of the situation. The Germans were lucky with the weather at the outset, for fog in England for the first three days, followed by fog on the continent, prevented the allied air force from taking part in the battle. Yet the German advances were not as great as had been planned and an order by Patton (who feared that the Germans might break left rather than right and so cut across his rear) to withdraw was not executed, so that the town of Bastogne was held and became an American strongpoint, brilliantly defended by the US Tenth Armoured and the Hundred-and-first Airborne Divisions and supplied by air. By the 22nd Rundstedt, under pressure on both flanks, was counselling the abandonment of the attack. The Fifth Panzer Division under General Hasso von Manteuffel continued to advance until Christmas Eve but was then diverted to Bastogne. From this point the Germans were forced onto the defensive and began to suffer increasing casualties. The battle of the Ardennes was substantially an American victory under a British commander. The German thrust failed, but it was a nasty shock to the allied commanders and publics because of the surprise which cast doubt on allied intelligence, its initial successes, and Eisenhower's alteration in the command which stirred up national animosities.

In January Hitler abandoned his offensive in the west. He had hoped for a quick victory, to be followed by a massive counter-attack on the Russians in the east. He had been defeated by allied air superiority, by the defenders of Bastogne, by poor cooperation among his own forces (especially between the Fifth and Sixth Panzer Divisions) and by a new weapon, the proximity fuse. This fuse contained a tiny radar which, in conjunction with radio waves and their echoes, made a shell go off at a distance from its target. It was estimated to increase the effectiveness of artillery tenfold. Although used against Japanese aircraft in 1943 it was not used in the European theatre before the emergencies of the V1 and Ardennes offensives.

The end of the attack on the Ardennes coincided with a lesser attack in Alsace begun on the last day of the year, although originally conceived as a move to cover the left flank of the Ardennes offensive. This operation gave rise to a major row between Eisenhower and de Gaulle, about which there are many accounts, including accounts by Eisenhower, de Gaulle and Churchill. These accounts cannot be reconciled and so it is still impossible to produce an unassailable version. By the time the attack in Alsace came it was – whatever the original German plan – distinct from the flagging Ardennes offensive and a comparatively minor affair. But Eisenhower may not have seen it that way. Rundstedt's attack had forced him to contemplate a major switch of Patton's forces northward and a consequent re-deployment of his southern Army Group which, under Devers, had come up into the line from the south of France: Devers's forces might have to take over part of Patton's front and perhaps even withdraw from the Rhine to the Vosges. Such a withdrawal meant abandoning Strasbourg.

Devers's Army Group included a French army under General de Lattre de Tassigny, but Devers did not tell de Lattre, and Eisenhower did not tell de Gaulle, that a withdrawal was anything but a hypothetical contingency. Their reticence was no doubt due to their knowledge that a withdrawal, exposing Strasbourg to recapture and reprisals by the Germans, would be strenuously resisted by the French. De Gaulle meanwhile had instructed de Lattre to defend Strasbourg, the arch-symbol of Franco-German rivalry ever since 1870. In doing so he was ignorant of Eisenhower's instructions to Devers and convinced, correctly as it happened, that a withdrawal was unnecessary. The upshot was that Eisenhower and Devers got themselves into a position where they were trying to outwit de Gaulle and de Lattre by putting into execution a plan which had been represented as something less than a plan, while the French commanders were taking decisions into their own hands to the extent of denying the superior command powers of the American commanders. Upon discovering what was afoot de Gaulle sent Juin to Eisenhower's headquarters where a battle of threats developed between him and Bedell Smith, and sent a signal to Churchill who flew at once to France to smooth over the controversy. Strasbourg was not evacuated.

On 12 January a new Russian offensive opened. Hitler had already begun to switch part of his armour in the west back to the east in order to meet it. Since 6 June the Germans had lost three quarters of a million men in France. They were now defending the Rhine.

The imminence of victory cast a number of shadows before. The anti-German alliance was a military combination created by, and unlikely to survive without, German aggressiveness. So long as the war lasted the allies' reciprocal needs overbore their mutual distrust but the evaporation of the German threat twitched aside this cloak of common concern. Months before the end of the war both the Anglo-Americans and the Russians were preparing to forestall one another in a dash to seize secret German installations and valuable German scientists. Both sides had been manoeuvring to set battle lines, which might later become political lines, separating their respective zones of operations and occupation in Germany. And both were uneasy about the fate of their citizens in German captivity or German employ who would be found in areas which they did not control.

Some of these persons were prisoners of war taken by the Germans on their western or eastern fronts. But prisoners of war were a relatively small category; prisoners from the west were not very numerous, while prisoners from the east had been comprehensively murdered. Much the largest number of non-Germans in Germany were Russian and other citizens of the USSR who had been overrun by the German victories of 1941–2 or had defected to the German side. When the war ended over two and a half million of them were sent back to the USSR from the American, British and French zones of occupation in Germany and Italy and years later it was alleged that they had been forcibly returned in defiance of the most basic rules of humanity. The great majority – about nine out of ten – were Displaced Persons who returned voluntarily; probably it never occurred to them to do otherwise. The bulk of them were back in the USSR within three months of the end of the war. They may have been hideously disillusioned when they got there but nobody forced them to return.

Of the remaining quarter million about 200,000 were Soviet citizens who had been captured in German uniforms which they had donned for a variety of reasons. Some did so in order to survive, others because they hated the USSR. They had given aid to the enemy, although mostly in humble capacities and simply to save their skins. They too expected to be able to return to their homes unnoticed and unpunished, even if technically they were deserters or traitors. They went back of their own accord. But a residue of about 50,000 did not. They were forcibly repatriated and paid, presumably atrociously, for what they had done. They comprised three main groups: some 10,000 survivors of the Ukrainian SS Division; some 5,000 survivors of the two Vlasov divisions; and about 25,000 Cossacks, including 5,000 women and children. There were also, in Italy, remnants of the Turkestan Division, central Asian and Azerbaijani Muslims who had served in the Wehrmacht and had exhibited appalling ferocity to men, women and children. All these groups consisted of Soviet citizens who had fought for the Germans against the USSR and had committed dreadful atrocities which made them war criminals as well as deserters and traitors. They were liable to forcible repatriation under agreements made in 1944 (and confirmed at Yalta) – agreements which applied to citizens of all the anti-German allies and were in line with commonly accepted rules of international law. Given the large numbers involved, and given post-war chaos, it is impossible to show or even to suppose that no mistakes were made. In particular a number of Ukrainians not covered by the agreements because they were not Soviet citizens at the prescribed date were nevertheless delivered to the Russian authorities and barbarously treated. Chaos also worked the other way. Guards of camps and convoys allowed or encouraged their charges to disappear into the woods to escape a fate which they expected to be worse than death, and the most culpable groups evaded retribution in substantial numbers: many members of the Ukrainian SS Division claimed, successfully if falsely, that they were not Soviet but Polish citizens, and more than half the Vlasov survivors did the same, thus escaping not only the net prepared for deserters and traitors but also arraignment for war crimes. In Italy, where a first trawl through the Displaced Persons camps had yielded 2,000 Soviet citizens taken in German uniforms, further investigations carried out by special tribunals with painstaking thoroughness condemned to forcible repatriation only 264 men out of a much larger number of grave suspects whom the tribunals exonerated, since by this time (1947) they were looking for any excuse to save the accused from Russian vengeance. The tragedy of the 264 was not that they were innocent victims but that they encountered a fate out of proportion to their offences.

CHAPTER 25

Disintegration

By the beginning of 1945 the accumulation of Germany's reverses had produced disintegration. It is surprising that the war lasted into May. Even in the previous summer Montgomery had believed that Berlin could be reached before the end of 1944, and on the other front Chuikov, the defender of Stalingrad and ultimately the conqueror of Berlin, chafed at his superiors for not allowing him to make straight for the city at the beginning of the new year. Hitler no longer had an army capable of sustaining the fight, he had so little fuel that his soldiers had standing orders to siphon off the fuel in a disabled tank before abandoning it, he scarcely had an air force at all, his anti-aircraft units were manned by a mixture of regulars, prisoners of war and teenagers down to sixteen, and his secret weapons had not worked the miracles that were expected of them.

After 1942 the Luftwaffe had performed one function brilliantly at the cost of relinquishing all others. It had created a fighter defence of Germany which defeated American and British strategic bombing until the final phase of cumulative disintegration was reached. But otherwise – apart from limited local successes, as when it drove the British out of the Dodecanese in 1943 – it ceased to count in one theatre after another. Its formations were outnumbered, its airfields bombed and its new types and new weapons failed it. In 1943 the Do. 217 was equipped with a 1,000 lb. radio-controlled glider bomb (Hs. 293 – first used against the Italian fleet as it escaped from Italy to Malta upon the Italian surrender) and also with a 3,000 lb. radio-controlled anti-personnel bomb (FX), but these were primitive prototypes of things to come and neither was successful. The He. 177 four-engined bomber appeared in 1943, but in small numbers only and after Germany's chance to affect the issue by heavy bombing had passed; the Luftwaffe was never able to drop the super-bombs which were dropped by its enemies on German cities (the heaviest bomb used against Germany was 22,000 lbs.).

The Me. 262 jet fighter and the Me. 163 rocket-propelled fighter appeared towards the end of 1944, but by then it was too late. Both these aircraft were the successors of earlier models which had flown before the war began and in both Germany was the pioneer, but their champions had been unable to persuade Hitler or Goering to adopt them because it was assumed that the war would be finished and won without them. The Me. 262 was, however, put into series production half way through the war (1,294 were made) because Hitler mistakenly supposed that this 500 m.p.h. fighter could be usefully converted into a bomber.

During 1942–3 the Luftwaffe had been called upon to fight on four fronts. It was not strong enough to do so. Its own bomber offensive was defeated, it failed to succour the German armies in the east or in the Mediterranean, and it was squeezed out of the Battle of the High Seas. The Russian campaigns acted like a magnet and a churn. Great numbers of aircraft were drawn into battles in which the Luftwaffe was gradually ground out of existence. In 1944 a new front was added in the west. This was the last straw. The destruction of the Luftwaffe was accelerated by a training crisis, a fuel crisis and a breakdown in its intelligence. By 1945 it was out of the fight.

Germany did not manage to produce the Second World War's most startling new weapon – the nuclear bomb. In the aftermath of defeat some German writers and scientists sought to ascribe this failure to the reluctance of German science to place so terrifying a weapon in the hands of so terrifying a man as Hitler, but the truth seems to be that the Germans failed to produce nuclear weapons because they took a wrong turning. They did, however, produce at the end of the war special weapons which, had they been brought into service earlier, might have had a considerable effect. These were the V weapons, V standing for *Vergeltung* or retribution. With them Hitler hoped to flatten London and force Britain to capitulate by the end of 1943, while Churchill was so alarmed that he considered using gas in retaliation.

There were three V weapons. The V 1 was a jet-propelled pilotless aircraft twenty-five feet long with a ceiling of 2,000– 3,000 feet, a range of 200–250 miles, a speed of 470 m.p.h. and a one-ton warhead. It cost only £125 and consumed in flight only 150 gallons of low-grade fuel. Beginning in June 1944 2,448 of these weapons hit Antwerp, 2,419 London (out of 10,492 aimed at it) and 3,132 hit other parts of England. The V 2 was a rocket. It was fifty feet long and six feet in circumference and carried a one-ton warhead. It rose into the air for fifty to seventy-five miles and could reach a speed of 3,600 m.p.h. Its range was 220 miles. Its motor, controlled from the ground, was cut at the crucial moment, thus setting it on course. It was impossible to intercept and arrived without warning since it travelled faster than sound. The V 2 was therefore a more terrifying weapon than the V 1, but each V 2 cost about £6,000, exclusive of research and development costs. Again Antwerp was the chief sufferer, receiving 1,265 hits. London received 517 and other parts of England 537.

The V 3 was a long-range gun. One weapon of this kind – originally there were to be two – was installed at Mimoyecques, near Calais. It had twenty-five barrels, each of them 416 feet long, entirely embedded in limestone and concrete, and the whole weapon was serviced and controlled by an extremely elaborate underground network. Its construction absorbed 1,000 tons of steel. It was to fire one shell on London every twelve seconds, but although the site was well prepared the components did not start arriving until early in June 1944. Allied bombing first severed its electricity supply and then scored a direct hit with a heavy bomb. In any case trials in the Baltic had not been completed when the site at Mimoyecques was overrun by the allied armies.

Development and production of the V 1 and V 2 were held up by rivalries between the army, which was in charge of the V 2, and the Luftwaffe, which was responsible for the V 1. These jealousies were accentuated when the SS tried to get control of the whole programme and at one point in March 1944 arrested the brilliant young researcher Werner von Braun and other key scientists. Allied Intelligence had wind of these inventions from November 1939 when the 'Oslo Report', a comprehensive report on German war science, was received in London from an agent or well-wisher (who is still anonymous). A year later Peenemünde was identified as the experimental area for these weapons by an agent who appears to have been in or near German military intelligence under Admiral Canaris. No further clues became available for over two years but early in 1943 prisoners of war (including two generals) were overheard talking about Peenemünde and photographic reconnaissance began to disclose some of the test station's activities. In August of the same year Peenemünde was bombed for the first time and Ultra began to provide information about the nature and capabilities of the V 1 and V 2. Ultra put an end to a debate about whether Hitler was counting on a pilotless aircraft or a rocket by showing that he meant to have both but conflict and confusion persisted on the allied side, particularly over the size of the warheads which the new weapons might carry. These doubts arose chiefly from ignorance about the fuel used, there being a correlation between bulk of fuel, range and size of warhead. In London these differences caused some of the bitterest quarrelling of the war because Lord Cherwell – who was not only an exceptionally stubborn and often ill-mannered man who allowed scientific disagreement to invade personal relations, but who also resented the fact that the coordination of intelligence about Hitler's secret weapons had been assigned to a committee under Duncan Sandys, Churchill's son-in-law, whom he did not like – pooh-poohed the existence of any threat from rockets or pilotless aircraft.

The first V 2 was launched at the experimental station on Peenemünde in the Baltic in October 1942 after three earlier failures, and a first V 1 a few weeks later. Attempts were made to cripple the programme by bombing Peenemünde and other places where parts of the apparatus were being manufactured but most of these targets were at long range. On the night of 17–18 August 1943 600 bombers of Bomber Command attacked Peenemünde in three waves in the hope of interrupting research and killing key scientists. As a result of a successful feint towards Berlin the first and second waves suffered only slight losses in spite of a full moon, but fighter attacks on the third wave brought the total loss to forty-one aircraft. At Peenemünde 732 people, mostly non-Germans, were killed, some projects were abandoned or moved elsewhere, but work on the V 1 and V 2 was only interrupted for a short time. The attack on Peenemünde itself and related industrial targets was supplemented from December 1943 by attacks on sites along the north coast of France which had been identified by photographic and other intelligence as launching sites for the V 1. There were about a hundred of these sites known, from their appearance, as ski sites. These attacks were moderately successful but they were countered by swift repair and then by a German ruse. The Germans pretended to be repairing the sites when they were in fact abandoning them, using them as dummies and constructing new sites by a new method which enabled them to build a site in a matter of days. This deception was not discovered until May 1944 and during the first half of the year the allies wasted more bombs on these abandoned sites than the Germans had aimed at London during the eight months of the 1940–41 blitz.

The German failure to bring the V 1 and V 2 into operation before the summer and autumn of 1944 respectively, by which time allied armies were approaching, was largely due to teething troubles. British estimates of the production and effects of these new weapons were unduly pessimistic. Plans were made to evacuate the population and the government from London on the assumption that V 1s would arrive at the rate of 45,000 a month, and that the V 2s, arriving at the rate of one an hour and carrying a ten-ton warhead, would cause 108,000 casualties a month. At the beginning of the war the German production targets for the V 1 and the V 2 were 3,000 and 900 a month. In 1944 the former target was raised to 8,000. This figure was never reached but the earlier one was passed in 1945. Altogether 32,000 V 1s were produced. Production of the V 2 rose from fifty in January 1944 to 253 in April when it fell back because priority was given to the V 1. It picked up again later in the year, was steady at around 630–60 in the last four months and reached 690 in

January 1945. Nearly 6,000 were produced in all. These figures were creditable to the Germans and would, timing apart, have been alarming for the British.

Hitler's plan of attack on England was to fire a salvo of V 1s at dawn and dusk every day with intermediate single launchings every twenty to thirty minutes, but when the attack began on 12 June from fifty-five sites it was a rushed fiasco. On the first day ten V 1s were launched, of which four arrived. Appreciable damage was caused to rail traffic, factories, hospitals and housing, mostly south of the Thames. There was then a pause of three days but in the ensuing two weeks 2,000 were launched. At first spotter aircraft gave warnings but the number of V 1s destroyed was small. Anti-aircraft guns in the London area had to cease firing after the first two days because they were bringing the V 1s down in the city. Batteries were re-deployed along the south coast and, with the help of radar and proximity fuses, gradually succeeded in hitting half and then three quarters of their incoming targets. Some V 1s were destroyed by aircraft. The attack on London was suspended in September (Antwerp and Brussels came under fire a few weeks later) but it was followed by the V 2 attack.

There was still much doubt about the potency of this weapon. In June parts of a V 2 fired from Peenemünde had come down in Sweden and valuable information about it had come into allied possession. Another came down in Poland without exploding; it was hidden, dismantled and secretly conveyed to England. But there were still controversies about the size of the warhead; estimates varied between ten tons and one ton (the latter being correct). On 6 September two V 2s were aimed at Paris but the firings were a failure. On that day Duncan Sandys announced in London that 'except possibly for a few last shots, the Battle of London is over'. Two days later the first V 2s struck London. They were fired from Holland. The worst aspect of the attack was the number of men, women and children who were blinded by flying glass before they knew that anything had struck. In spite of doctors working round the clock on delicate eye operations many lost their sight for life. There was also severe material damage, but the firing sites were already threatened and had to be removed as the British armies approached them. The weight of the attack was diverted to Antwerp which was more seriously damaged than London and did not get relief until March 1945.

There has been a tendency to laugh at Hitler's V weapons. This is partly because it seemed in 1944 the best thing to do. But the weapons were not negligible and would have been extremely dangerous if they had been available earlier. In the first two weeks the V 1s killed 1,600 people, seriously injured another 4,500 and damaged 200,000 houses; the casualty rate in England in June 1944 was as heavy as it had been in September 1940, although the weight of attack measured in tons of explosives was much lighter. Over the whole period of the V 1 and V 2 attacks 29,400 houses were completely destroyed in London and over a quarter of a million damaged. It may be argued that Hitler could have used to better purpose the 200,000 persons engaged in the development and production of the V 2 – he might, for example, have got more from their brains and their labour if they had worked on defensive projects – but against this must be set not only the chance that the V weapons might have been ready sooner, but also the hard facts that the British had to increase their fighter, anti-aircraft and balloon defences, suffer appreciable material damage and divert a significant air effort to Peenemünde and the launching sites. The V weapons failed but their failure does not prove that they were ridiculous. They were the forerunners of much that has been developed since the war. They may not have been the weapons that Hitler hoped for to settle the result of the war, but if their appearance had not been delayed by allied bombing by a few months, they could hardly have failed to affect its course.

The V weapons were Hitler's last offensive expedients. After their failure he continued to produce expedients but they were defensive. In October 1944 he called into existence a new force, the *Volkssturm*, a Home Guard of last resort under Himmler's command and consisting of all available men between the ages of sixteen and sixty. The Werewolves, another desperate expedient, were to constitute armed bands operating like marauding partisans after the defeat of Germany. The Alpine redoubt, where Hitler said he would make his last stand, was even more phantasmal. It never existed, it had no men in it or prepared defences, and the Führer himself did not go there.

The first front to go was the Italian. Early in 1945 senior S S figures in Italy made approaches to Swiss contacts and indirectly to the head of the American intelligence services in Switzerland, Allen W. Dulles. These S S officers wanted to negotiate a separate surrender to the western allies of the entire Italian front. Dulles was not interested in a partial surrender, but he was concerned to keep the discussions alive in the hope that they would contribute to a total and unconditional surrender on all fronts. In March the German Supreme Commander in Italy, Kesselring, the Luftwaffe commander, Pohl, and Hitler's Ambassador in Italy, Rudolf Rahn who was in command of Mussolini and his government, were all brought into the discussions. Although they thought at first that they were discussing a negotiated and partial surrender, they quickly came to realize that what was in train was capitulation on all fronts and that the western allies would neither accept any vestige of Nazism in a new German government nor envisage any split between themselves and the Russians. The Russians, however, who knew that Himmler was trying to do a deal with the west via Stockholm, not unnaturally assumed (as for a while did some in the west) that the talks initiated by the SS in Switzerland were part of an anti-Russian venture. After a delay caused by the transfer of Kesselring to the western front and the need to initiate his successor, Vietinghoff, a surrender of all the German forces in Italy was made on 1 May by the army and air commanders acting on their own authority. It was botched by a farcical succession of arrests and counter-arrests among the Germans themselves but clinched when the news of Hitler's suicide reached Italy on the next day.

On the main fronts the German armies were overwhelmed by superior numbers and material. After the retreats of 1944 Hitler hoped to hold the line of the Vistula in the east (where Himmler was appointed to command an Army Group) and the Rhine in the west. The Russians, opening a new campaign in mid-January, crossed the Vistula, turned northwards to the sea to envelop the German forces in East Prussia and overran Pomerania and Silesia up to the Oder and Neisse rivers which they reached at the beginning of February. In the south they captured Budapest on the 12th. In the west German commanders tried vainly to obey Hitler's orders to give no ground and transport neither men nor material eastward across the Rhine. They were weakened by the transfer of a Panzer division to the east after the failure of the Ardennes offensive. This German armour, which was to defend the Hungarian oilfields, was believed to be routed through Dresden but when Ultra revealed the division's orders this belief was found to be wrong. The mistake was pointed out to the British and American bomber headquarters concerned; the latter expressed willingness to cancel the raid if the other would do so too but the former saw no reason to alter its plans. The presumed passage of the German armour through Dresden was only an ostensible reason for the operation. Equally dubious is the plea that the raid was executed in aid of the advancing Russians. There was no Russian request for a raid on Dresden although the western allies had been asked to attack Leipzig (a request which was taken to be a pointer to Stalin's plans for his line of advance on Berlin, about which he gave his allies no direct information). Dresden, so far barely damaged, was chosen because it was big, famous and crowded, so that its destruction might stampede the enemy towards surrender. So on 13 and 14 February one of Europe's most splendid cities was recklessly destroyed. Industrial targets were barely hit and the rail services were put out of action for only three days. The number of people killed has been estimated at 135,000, although the true figure may be half or even less than that huge total. The slaughter was in any case immense, most of it by burning people to death in buildings or in the streets. All this destruction was done in two night raids lasting an hour each, and a third raid of ten minutes at midday on the next day. One thousand two hundred and twenty-three aircraft dropped bombs. They faced no opposition.

On 7 March an American unit, seeing to its surprise that a bridge at Remagen, south of Bonn, had not been destroyed, crossed the Rhine and in the next weeks large forces followed at several points. Three of the western armies hoped and believed that they were on their way to Berlin. In addition there existed a plan for airborne attacks on key points in Berlin by a force of 20,000 paratroopers. But in the event the western allies made no attempt to reach the German capital. The reasons for this abnegation were two: Eisenhower's strategic decisions and the existence of an agreed division of Germany into separate administrative zones, with Berlin inside the Russian zone.

The zonal agreement grew out of administrative planning which had not been intended to have – but did have – political consequences. At their conference in Teheran in November 1943 Roosevelt, Churchill and Stalin agreed to create a European Advisory Commission which, sitting in London, would produce preliminary plans for the occupation of Germany. This Commission inherited a plan prepared in London by the Anglo-American planning staff which subsequently became part of Eisenhower's headquarters. This plan divided Germany into three zones – a British one in the north-west, an American in the south-west and a Russian in the east: Berlin was inside the Russian zone. Roosevelt had indicated to his own officials before Teheran that he did not like the arrangements proposed for the American and British zones and wanted them the other way round. But the dispositions had evolved logically from the planning for Overlord which always put the American armies on the right of the allied forces and the British (and Canadian) armies on the left, and in addition Roosevelt's reservations and objections got lost in Washington and were not conveyed to the American member of the European Advisory Commission until too late. A separate American proposal for a corridor linking Berlin with the north-western zone also got overlooked. The Russians were well satisfied with an arrangement which gave them 40 per cent of Germany and its capital (subject though the capital would itself be to tripartite division and control), while the western allies, who continued to be afraid that Stalin might run out of the European war or refuse to join the war against Japan, were loath to suggest amendments of any kind. The plan was therefore adopted by the Commission in March 1944 and confirmed at Yalta in February 1945.

It was not meant to settle anything more than immediate military and administrative matters. The future of Germany in a larger sense was left vague. Germany was *tabula rasa* with no agreement about what to inscribe there. At Casablanca Roosevelt had enunciated his demand for unconditional surrender and Churchill had fallen in with a design which was at once bold in outline and entirely imprecise in everything else. Stalin too endorsed unconditional surrender later in the war. Churchill was disposed to curb and isolate Prussia, thus implying decentralization or perhaps partition, but he gave relatively little attention during the war to post-war problems. At Quebec Roosevelt and Churchill, to the horror of their principal political advisers, Hull and Eden, endorsed the Morgenthau plan for constraining Germany by converting it from an industrial to an agricultural economy, but this vision quickly evaporated. At Teheran the three leaders were in favour of some kind of partition, which Churchill opposed at Yalta and the new trio all rejected at Potsdam. Events, not plans, eventually reshaped Germany.

It did not, however, follow that western forces were not to advance to Berlin or anywhere else so long as the war lasted. The plan only bound them to observe fixed lines of demarcation when the war was over and the occupation had begun. Stalin expected the Americans and British to race him for Berlin and the western allies had strong motives for doing so as they speculated about the future of an alliance which was about to pass from military cooperation to political manoeuvre.

Montgomery's and Bradley's Army Groups both crossed the Rhine in the third week of March. Montgomery, commanding Canadian, British and American armies – the last was the Ninth US Army under General William H. Simpson which had been subordinated to him during the Ardennes offensive – was heading across northern Germany for Berlin; Bradley with three US armies under command was heading across central Germany. Further south the American-French Army Group under Devers was making equally rapid progress. A few days earlier Hitler had signed the first of a number of orders for the total destruction of everything. On the 28th the Russians made their first air attacks on Berlin. At this time Eisenhower, to the dismay of his subordinates and still more of Churchill, took his eyes off Berlin. Although there were no longer any meaningful German armies in the field Eisenhower clung to the view that his task was to seek out and destroy the enemy's forces rather than seize his capital and he held to this resolve even after the US Ninth Army crossed the Elbe on 12 April. He instructed Bradley, reinforced by the re-allocation to him of Ninth Army at Montgomery's expense, to push eastward towards Erfurt, Leipzig and Dresden – on a line, that is, running well south of Berlin, which he declared to be irrelevant, and through Saxony, which was. He now adopted the policy of the concentrated thrust which Montgomery had urged upon him in the previous summer but he had chosen the wrong thrust. Further, in an unprecedented message to Stalin – which was probably dictated by anxiety to avoid an unpleasant clash between American and Russian forces and partly also by a genuine belief in the importance and practicability of post-war Russo-American cooperation – he disclosed his intention not to go for Berlin and gave Stalin a detailed account of the allied order of battle. Stalin was so surprised that he thought the message was a trick, did not send the equivalent information on Russian plans and dispositions which Eisenhower had asked for, and immediately accelerated his own measures to take Berlin. Churchill was not only surprised but appalled at this assumption of politico-strategic authority and by the revelation that the Supreme Commander had so little notion of the political importance of Berlin. To his own Army Group commanders Eisenhower remained for a time vague, so that when the first Anglo-American crossings of the Elbe were made the troops were still under the impression that they were on the last lap to Berlin. On 15 April, however, Simpson received a precise order to go no further. He was expecting to be in Berlin two days later. Thus it was at Torgau on the Elbe, on 25 April, that Americans and Russians first exchanged salutations.

Farther south too the Americans, spurting across Germany to Czechoslovakia, were reined back by punctilio. A line of demarcation had been agreed on 30 April. On 4 May, with German resistance vanishing, Eisenhower asked Moscow to let him keep up his momentum. He was only fifty miles from Prague and in a position to reach it before the Russians. Stalin, who had conceded to Eisenhower the right to advance as far as Pilsen, was not prepared to see him advance farther, and when Bradley offered at a meeting with Konev on the 5th to cooperate in the taking of Prague Konev declined. On that day Prague rose against the Germans. But the Americans neither advanced to their assistance nor felt able to send supplies by air. Eisenhower and Truman felt that they had done their best; Truman had already told Eisenhower at the end of April that he was 'loath to hazard American lives' for what he described as 'political purposes', and neither leader saw much point in taking a city which would then be immediately turned over to the Russians. Konev began to move towards Prague from Saxony to the north-west on the 6th and Malinovski and Eremenko from the south-east and east respectively a day later. The first Russians entered Prague on the 9th. But by then the 30,000 insurgents had been overpowered by the Germans and 8,000 of them killed.

For his main central thrust in 1945 Stalin had grouped his armies in three fronts under the overall direction of his Supreme Headquarters in Moscow. These fronts were commanded, from north to south, by Rokossovski, Zhukov and Konev. D-day, originally fixed at 20 January, was advanced to the 12th at the request of the western leaders when hard pressed in the Ardennes. Rokossovski was directed north of Warsaw to Danzig and then westward. Zhukov, who relinquished his senior staff appointment in Moscow in order to become the captor of Berlin, struck straight towards the German capital from south of Warsaw. Konev, moving further south through Silesia, also had Berlin in his sights. The last barrier of any consequence was the river Oder, especially the fortress of Küstrin (which, bypassed, did not surrender until the end of March) at the junction of the Oder with the Warthe due east of Berlin. Chuikov's Eighth Guards Army reached the Oder on 1 February and began to cross the next day. Chuikov wanted to press on despite logistic difficulties and the risks, which he rightly discounted, of a last German stand. But Stalin, like Eisenhower, was wary. He ordered Zhukov to consolidate on the Oder and turn northwards into Pomerania and clean it up. Stalin overestimated German strength in Pomerania as well as the opposition lying between Zhukov and Konev and Berlin. Chuikov fumed against the restraints imposed on him and after the war he complained that Zhukov had failed in his duty by not urging a more adventurous strategy on the overcautious Stalin. He was probably right since Guderian had already expressed the opinion at the end of January that Berlin would fall in a few days and Hitler was sending such reinforcements as he could muster not to eastern Germany but to Hungary. But Stalin may have had a political motive when he reined Zhukov in. By doing so he enabled Konev to draw up. The two Marshals were rivals and it suited Stalin to promote compeition between them and let them both share the glory of taking Berlin rather than let one of them garner too many laurels singlehanded.

Stalin's delaying has also been explained in other terms. It can be argued that in the opening weeks of 1945 he was anxious not to take Berlin too soon. Chuikov crossed the Oder on the eve of the Yalta conference and Stalin had no wish to disrupt the conference or the Grand Alliance. Berlin was doomed, its fate only a matter of time, and it was more important for him to safeguard the ravaged USSR against western hostility than to deliver the *coup de grâce* to Germany in one week rather than another. So long as Roosevelt lived Stalin probably felt that the American President's determination to remain on good terms with the USSR was a cardinal factor in his own foreign policies, but Stalin knew enough about western democracy to understand that Roosevelt was not the sole maker of policy and that there were significant anti-communist and anti-Russian forces in the United States and Great Britain. To take Berlin, assuming that he could have done so, while his western allies were still on the wrong side of the Rhine involved ending the war in a way which would have given him so dominant a position in Germany as to alarm the western powers and even revive visions of an anti-Russian alliance between them and the still not totally inconsiderable remnants of German military power. A dominant position in Germany could be more of a hazard than an asset so long as the war-weary USSR had not the strength to sustain it against a western coalition, and although Stalin banked on Roosevelt's determination to withdraw from Europe, he must also have recalled that Churchill had in 1919 not only supported western intervention in the USSR but had advocated the use of the German army to effect it. Whether such fanciful calculations did or did not pass through Stalin's mind remains unknown. The final onslaught was in fact delayed until April.

It was then mounted at short notice and, in the belief of Stalin's Marshals, under the impression that Montgomery had been ordered to get to Berlin before them. At a conference on 3 April Zhukov and Konev told Stalin that they could beat Montgomery and were told to produce their plans in forty-eight hours. Stalin drew a line on a map from east to west, dividing their zones of operations but stopping fifty miles east of Berlin with the implication that beyond that point the leading Marshal might be free to move on the German capital by any route he chose. The attack was launched on 16 April with 2.5 million men, 6,250 tanks and 7,500 aircraft against one million men, 1,500 tanks and 3,300 aircraft. Prolonged resistance by the Germans was impossible and by the 22nd the Russians were fighting in the streets of the capital. Konev's men had a slight lead over Zhukov's and there was some confusion as the two Fronts converged, but the suburbs were gradually reduced and in the early hours of 1 May General Krebs, Hitler's last Army Chief of Staff, acting under instructions from Goebbels and Bormann, sought out Chuikov to ask for an armistice. He told Chuikov that Hitler was dead and that he had come to negotiate with the Russians on behalf of a new German government which had been formed in compliance with Hitler's will and in which neither Goering, Ribbentrop nor Himmler had any part. Chuikov telephoned Zhukov. He was told that Stalin refused to negotiate. The Germans must surrender unconditionally on all fronts. Shortly after midday Krebs went back to the centre of Berlin where he shot himself. The next day, 2 May, the commander of the garrison capitulated.

Hitler had been dead two days. He spent the last weeks of his life underground in Berlin. By the Chancellery in the middle of the city was a complex of heavily protected underground shelters arranged in two floors. Hitler and his mistress Eva Braun had a set of rooms in what was called the Führer's Bunker at the deeper level. With them were Goebbels, his wife and five children, a doctor, a cook, a valet, a couple of secretaries and an Alsatian bitch which had just pupped. Nearby, in similar shelters, were Bormann, Artur Axmann, the Hitler Youth leader, and an assortment of adjutants, guards and so on. Other people came and went. Ten days before his end Hitler emerged from his delusion that the war could still be won and told Keitel that he accepted the fact of defeat and would shoot himself. He told Speer the same thing the next day. But from time to time hope still flickered and every day the increasingly senseless conferences took place in the war room. Goering had gone south but he quickly learned of Hitler's decision and sent him a signal proposing that he should immediately take over as though Hitler was dead. Since Goering was officially Hitler's successor there was nothing very odd about this proposal but it infuriated Hitler who ordered Goering's arrest and dismissed him from his command of the Luftwaffe.

A few days later Hitler was still further incensed on learning that Himmler, at a personal meeting with the Swedish Count Folke Bernadotte, had taken it upon himself to propose capitulation. (Since he proposed to capitulate in the west but not in the east the western allies rejected his advances.) Hitler ordered Himmler's arrest and had his SS adjutant, Hermann Fegelein, who was in the Bunker, shot there and then. That same night, 28–9 April, he married Eva Braun. After the ceremony and a wedding meal Hitler retired to write his two last documents. His will dealt with personal matters. It contained nothing particularly unusual except the gift of his pictures to found a picture gallery in Linz. His political testament, a much longer document, rehearsed all his old attacks on the Jewish race and reaffirmed his belief in the German need for *Lebensraum* in the east. Next to the Jews he blamed the German officer corps for all that had gone wrong. Having dismissed Goering and Himmler, he appointed Doenitz President and Commander-in-Chief of the Armed Forces and Goebbels Chancellor. He also appointed a number of other Ministers and a new Commander-in-Chief of the Army to succeed himself. On the afternoon of the 30th Hitler said his good-byes. He then poisoned the dog and Eva and shot (or possibly poisoned) himself. Their bodies were burned

THE SOVIET DRIVE TO BERLIN 1945

GERMAN UNITS

(PZA) Panzer Armies.
(A) Armies.
(PZD) Panzer Divisions.
(ID) Infantry Divisions.

0 ____ 20
Miles

To Rostock
To Stralsund
Karow
To Hamburg
Starsow
STETTIN
2nd White Russian Front
3 PZA
Wittenberge
Gransee
Army Group Vistula
Hohenzollern Canal
3 PZA
9A
US UNITS
Fehrbellin
Havel
Lanke
Bernau
1st White Russian Front
Stendal
Elbe
Nauen
9A
Küstrin
Warte
BERLIN
Buckow
Spree
Frankfurt
Fürstenwalde
remnants
Möckern
12 A
9A
4 PZA
Oder
Treuenbrietzen
(13 Divisions in all)
Wittenberg
To Leipzig
Dessau
Army Group Centre
4 PZA
17A
Cottbus
1st Ukrainian Front
Schlieben
US UNITS
Torgau
4 PZA
Neisse
Ruhland
Diesa
Elbe
2 PZD
17A
DRESDEN
2 ID
To Prague

OPERATIONS APRIL–MAY, 1945

Front line 16 April.
Soviet thrusts 16–20 April.
Front line 19 April.
Soviet thrusts 20–26 April.
Front line 25 April.
Soviet thrusts 26 April–9 May.
Front line 8 May.
German counter-attacks.

~ ARTHUR BANKS ~

outside in accordance with instructions which had already been given. That night the surviving inhabitants of the Bunker made their escapes, but not the Goebbels family. After the failure of the Krebs mission to Chuikov Goebbels gave poison to his children and either shot or poisoned his wife and himself – the second Chancellor of the Third Reich.

Doenitz, its President for a week, was also its undertaker. On 2 May he sent Admiral Wilhelm Friedeburg to Montgomery to negotiate a surrender in the west. Montgomery refused to negotiate. On 7 May representatives of all three of the Reich's fighting services arrived at Eisenhower's headquarters at Reims and there, in the presence of senior American, Russian, British and French officers (but not of Eisenhower himself) surrendered unconditionally to the western and Russian commands. After the formal act there was a brief encounter between Jodl and Eisenhower at which Eisenhower asked Jodl whether he fully comprehended what had been done and Jodl said he had. On the next day, towards midnight, and again in the presence of senior officers of the four principal victors, the act of surrender was ratified at Russian headquarters in the German capital, Berlin.

Epilogue

THE Second World War was fought to a finish in Europe and had to be. Hitler could have ended it by negotiation because he was fighting for material things and might have decided at some moment or other that he had won enough of them. He wished to do so after the defeat of Poland and again after the defeat of France, although with the reservation that making peace on either occasion was only a prelude to a fresh bid for *Lebensraum* in the east. There was no lack of peace-makers: the Pope, Mussolini, the massed sovereigns of the Low Countries and Scandinavia, the King of Rumania, all tried to mediate in various ways and at various dates in the closing months of 1939. The inactivity of France and Great Britain during the obliteration of Poland gave Hitler and others grounds for believing that their declarations of war had been retractable formalities. Hitler could hardly conceive how, although they had been silly enough to go to war on behalf of Poland, they would continue at war on behalf of what had become non-Poland. With the Right preponderantly and the communists wholly for peace and with the knowledge, leaked by German counter-intelligence, that Hitler had given orders for an attack in the west in November, France and Great Britain could logically be expected to give up. But 1939 brought neither peace nor war. Hitler had to postpone his attack in the west and the peace offensive continued in 1940 up to and again after the German campaigns in Scandinavia and the west. Roosevelt sent his Under-Secretary of State, Sumner Welles, on a long exploration in European capitals in February and March, and the Pope and Mussolini kept up their feelers. After the fall of France Hitler tried again to secure his gains and close the account but Churchill refused.

The hesitations in London about whether to seek terms or not in 1940 reveal the differences between Hitler's war aims and those of his enemies. Great Britain, the sole effective combatant at this point, was fighting for no specific or material gain. It was fighting against Hitler and Nazi Germany. On the British side therefore negotiation meant not compromise but the abandonment of British war aims, which, in so far as they could be rationalized at all, were the surrender of Germany and the collapse of Nazism. Unconditional surrender was implicit in the nature of the war long before it was proclaimed at Casablanca. The alternative, for Great

Britain, was to acknowledge that it had no war aims and had got into war by a mistake; but, once in, it could get out in this way only with the utmost difficulty, for a declaration of war is so weighty a pronouncement that it is intolerable to regard it as meaningless. To retire from a war with nothing accomplished and without being beaten requires a very unusual psychological effort. In this particular case it entailed also a sense of shame, for the evils of Nazi Germany had sunk in and making peace with Hitler seemed iniquitous. Although fearful of war in 1938 and glad to be spared it, the British were by 1940 determined to see it through.

So the war went on and the aim of surrender was achieved, although at great cost. Fighting on had not only a certain inevitability nor was it only the fulfilment of a praiseworthy obligation. It involved the deaths of millions of people, including victims of Nazism – like the Jews – who might have been killed anyway but might not, and countless other civilians who certainly would not have died the premature and often horrible deaths which came to them. To ask whether the frightful cost was worth it is to ask an exceptionally painful question, but Hitler's régime was as horrible as any that Europe had ever seen and more horribly well equipped to pursue its fearful ends, and it may be thought that hardly any price could have been too high to pay for the elimination of the German Nazis. The tragedy was that the price had to be paid by so many people and so innocent.

As the Nazis recede into history they become objects of interest to historians, sociologists and psychologists, but they were in their own generation objects of pure horror. This horror can be expressed by saying that they represented a threat to civilized values and standards of behaviour; it can only be conveyed by recalling, with increasing effort over receding time, the things which they did to individual human beings. The battered but living skeletons found in the stinking degradation of the torture camps in 1945 are Hitler's truest memorial.

Hitler was many things, including an archcriminal, a criminal over and above criminals. His principal surviving accomplices were arraigned and tried in a series of trials in which they were charged with violations of the laws or customs of war, with 'crimes against humanity' and with 'crimes against peace'. The first of these categories includes offences such as the refusal to give quarter, the use of certain proscribed weapons (for example gas, expanding bullets) and the execution of prisoners of war, that is to say, acts which have become illegal by custom or have been declared illegal by international conventions. The most flagrant violations of these agreements during the Second World War were the execution of commandos after they had surrendered and the execution of commissars, or anybody said to be a commissar, among captured Russian soldiers. The expression 'crimes against humanity' was coined to designate acts which, although not explicitly proscribed by international pronouncement, are clearly contrary to law in civilized states independently of the existence of a state of war, such as the killing of men and women simply because they belong in certain categories and without any allegation of criminal acts committed by them; or forced labour. 'Crimes against peace' denoted the preparation and waging of aggressive war in contravention of international law.

War crimes trials are not new. The notion that wars have rules which must be observed is at least as old as classical antiquity. It was reasserted by such eminent Renaissance jurists as Vitoria, Suarez and Grotius, and the first adequately recorded war crimes trial in Europe took place nearly 500 years ago. During the Second World War Germany's enemies and victims gave early warning of their intention to bring war criminals to justice. At the beginning of 1942 nine countries jointly declared that the punishment of war criminals by judicial process was one of their war aims, and shortly afterwards a War Crimes Commission was established to collect and sift evidence and consider what should be done about it. In November 1943 Germany's three principal enemies declared that when the war was over criminals would be handed over to the governments of the countries where their crimes had been committed and that major criminals, whose crimes could not be attached to specific areas, would be tried by an international tribunal.

This tribunal, the International Military Tribunal, was formally constituted by an agreement signed in London in August 1945 on behalf of the American, British, Russian and (provisional) French governments and it subsequently conducted the most famous of all war crimes trials at Nuremberg in 1946. In addition the American authorities conducted twelve trials in their zone of Germany during 1946–9 under the provisions of a four-power ordinance (Control Council Law No. Ten) and the French held a smaller number of similar trials. The British, more tardily, put Manstein on trial on seventeen charges on nine of which he was found guilty, but dropped a plan to try Rundstedt, who had issued the commando order, on the grounds that he had become too old and feeble. The Russians held no trial under Control Council Law No. Ten. In Italy Kesselring was among the accused in trials held by the British. He was sentenced to death but this sentence was commuted to imprisonment, first for life and then for twenty-one years; and he was released on medical grounds in 1952. All over the rest of what had been occupied Europe, Germans from the SS, the armed services and the civilian administration had to face charges of murder, plunder and offences against the person of varying magnitude. Finally, the Germans themselves instituted similar proceedings when they recovered their juridical independence. Such trials were still occurring over twenty-five years after the end of the war as fresh facts came to light and criminals who had successfully lain low for years were discovered.

The first protests against war crimes in the Second World War and the first enunciation of a determination to prosecute the criminals were attempts to put a curb on the atrocities which were being perpetrated in Europe, by reminding people at all levels that even in war certain things were not permitted and that those who ignored the law might be brought to account. Further, there developed during the war a desire to assert both the existence of international penal law and the practicability of enforcing it by judicial process. And if the perpetrators of local crimes were to be indicted and perhaps executed, it seemed right and necessary to indict also those at the top who had either inspired or commanded these crimes. Hence the trial at Nuremberg in which twenty-two men who had wielded exceptional power and authority were put in the dock. (The indictment named twenty-four but one, Robert Ley, committed suicide in prison and a second, the industrialist Gustav Krupp von Bohlen, was found unfit to plead because of age and infirmity.) The Nuremberg defendants included the principal surviving political figures of the Third Reich but this and later trials were not confined to Nazi Party leaders since the prosecutors wanted to establish also the accountability of all, irrespective of party affiliation, who had wielded and abused power: service chiefs, police chiefs, industrial chiefs, holders of high judicial office, scientists and doctors who had used human bodies for inhumane experiments, etc. Twelve of the twenty-two accused were sentenced to death, three to life imprisonment, four to terms of ten to twenty years and three were acquitted. All the death sentences were carried out except that on Goering, who committed suicide after he had been sentenced, and Bormann who was either dead or in hiding and was convicted and sentenced *in absentia*. In the next most important trials – the twelve American trials under Control Council Law No. Ten – 185 defendants were indicted. Of these 177 stood trial, twenty-six were sentenced to death (but two of these sentences were remitted), thirty-five were acquitted and the remainder received sentences ranging from life to small terms which in fact resulted in their immediate release.

These proceedings commanded something less than universal approval among the general public and in the legal profession. The general public was worried by the appearance of unfairness resulting from the fact that the defeated were tried by their conquerors. Even though the trials were not unfairly conducted they were, from this point of view, not unassailable. Alternatives had been considered but rejected as impracticable. A trial by Germans was ruled out by the farcical outcome of the attempt to get the Germans to do the same job after the First World War, and a trial or trials by selected neutrals offered complications of procedure and language even more daunting than those involved in the solution adopted – quite apart from the fact that there were few neutrals and they did not want to assume the required role. (There was at least one trial in the French zone of Germany at which French judges were joined by one Belgian and one Dutch judge.)

From the legal point of view the principal objection to the trials was the argument that, since there existed no international legislature to make international law, there was no offence of which the accused could be guilty or with which they could be charged. This argument raises a fundamental question about the nature of law: is it made by enactment, so that without enactment it does not exist; or can it evolve from some other source, so that it may be valid without enactment, in which case the enactment is not creative but declaratory? Murder, to take a simple example, has been regarded as a crime and punished in certain states before any legislative act declaring it to be a crime and saying how it would be punished. War crimes, properly so called, have existed independently of the Hague and Geneva conventions which regulate conduct in war. Neither in the case of crimes against humanity nor in the case of war crimes could the criminals of the Third Reich claim that they did not know that the actions which were subsequently held against them were criminal. Nor, given the warnings issued by their adversaries from 1940 onwards, could they claim that they had not been warned that they would be tried. Many of the offences laid to their charge were committed after this date.

The category of crimes against peace is not so clear cut, but the International Military Tribunal, presided over by a Lord Justice of Appeal from Great Britain sitting with eminent judges and jurists from other countries, held that preparing and waging aggressive war had been a crime at least since the conclusion of the Kellogg-Briand Pact of 1928; that it was a crime which could be committed by an individual; that although it might be difficult to define aggression in general it was possible to recognize it in particular cases; and that eight of the accused had committed this crime.

Some of the Tribunal's negative decisions were as striking as its positive conclusions. It refused to make any pronouncement on genocide in peacetime within a state's legitimate boundaries. After the war a convention banning genocide was adopted by the United Nations and ratified by a number of states but this convention contains no adequate provisions for enforcement. The Tribunal also refused belligerent rights to non-uniformed partisans and held that there is nothing in international law to prohibit in all circumstances the execution of hostages. Finally, the Tribunal did nothing – because it was not asked to – to adapt the laws of war to the age of mass bombing. Since the international code of war had not been revised since the Hague Convention of 1907, throwing a bomb from a balloon was expressly prohibited but dropping one from an aircraft was not (unless the target were totally undefended) and it appeared that, although gassing people was clearly unlawful in the same way as poisoning wells was clearly unlawful, the unlawfulness of indiscriminate bombing remained open to debate.

As a normative body the International Military Tribunal had serious limitations. It was an international body created by agreement among only a few nations. Even though the laws which it applied were not new, their codification was *ad hoc* and *post hoc*; its Charter was devised for the specific purpose of trying individuals who, however much they deserved to be tried and condemned, were in everybody's mind before the Charter or the indictment was drawn up. None but losers were tried. The judges, however fairly they discharged their judicial office, were provided by the victorious prosecutors from among their own nationals. There was therefore a risk that the principles enunciated at Nuremberg would lack moral backing and legal endorsement and that the trial itself would become a piece of history without contributing to international law.

In order to give them a wider sanction the General Assembly of the United Nations in 1946 unanimously affirmed the principles recognized by the Charter and by the Tribunal's judgement and asked the International Law Commission to re-formulate them. The Commission formulated in 1950 seven principles which have therefore, as a result of the war, become part of the corpus of international law. They proclaim: that a person who commits an act which is a crime under international law may be punished for it; that this liability is not avoided merely because the internal law of the accused's country provides no penalty for the criminal act, or because the accused was acting as a head of state or government official, or because he was following an order from his government or a superior (provided, in this last case, that he had a moral choice); that any person charged with a crime under international law has the right to a fair trial on the facts and the law. The principles also defined three kinds of crime: crimes against peace, war crimes and crimes against humanity; and stated that complicity in any such crime was itself a crime under international law.

Crimes against peace are defined as planning, preparing, initiating or waging a war of aggression or a war in violation of international compacts, or participating in a conspiracy to do any of these things. War crimes consist (as they have done since ancient times) of violations of the laws or customs of war: examples given include the murder, ill-treatment or deportation – for slave labour or any other purpose – of civilians, the murder or ill-treatment of prisoners of war or persons on the seas, the killing of hostages, plunder of public or private property, wanton destruction of cities, towns or villages, or devastation not justified by military necessity. These definitions leave a lot of things open to argument, but they assert that it is proper to open the argument, to bring it before a judicial tribunal and to demand punishment. Finally, crimes against humanity are defined as certain acts against the civilian population when these acts are done in connection with any crime against peace or war crime. The acts are: murder, extermination, enslavement, deportation and other inhuman acts, and persecution on political, racial or religious grounds.

The Nuremberg trial and its aftermath were an attempt to establish that war is not so much a visitation like a plague or an act of state like a treaty of alliance, nor even a duty like a just war, but pre-eminently a crime and a punishable one.

The prime cost of war is measured in death and destruction. By this reckoning the cost fell most heavily on the USSR. Perhaps 20 million died – more than all the dead of all nations in the First World War and a staggering death roll for the short period of four years. Another twenty-eight million were made homeless. In the territories which they had occupied the Germans (whose scorched earth policy in retreat was much more efficient than the Russians' own destructiveness in 1941) destroyed half the living quarters in the towns and three quarters of it in the countryside. Two thirds of the wealth of these areas was extinguished. Over thousands of square miles the land was bared, neglected and almost uninhabited: no towns, no villages, no buildings to shelter man or even beast, hardly any beasts, hardly any people. There was one cow where there had been ten, one sheep or one goat where there had been four, one pig in place of two. Crops had to be sown by hand. Such machinery as could be seen was unusable rusting monuments to war but no longer aids to livelihood. The unoccupied areas had suffered too from neglect: in the oil industry, for example, technicians had had to go away and fight, leaving their machinery and installations to fall into shocking condition.

Recovery was at first slow. Communications had been wrecked or worn out – 40,000 miles of rail track and a vast quantity of rolling stock destroyed. Production of many peacetime necessities had been all but abandoned – the output of tractors reduced from 116,000 a year to 8,000. Political conditions prohibited a quick reconversion of the economy – the American nuclear bomb had to be countered by a Russian one. So when in 1946 two thirds of the inhabitants of Stalingrad had returned to the city, only one sixth of its buildings had been patched up. Many of the rigours of war continued. There was little real improvement in living conditions for a decade. The memories of war were ineradicable and its consequences were prolonged with deep, if incalculable, effects on post-war domestic and international politics.

The next heaviest burden fell on the Germans. At least four and a half million of them died, including about a million civilians; their military dead were twice as numerous as in the first war. In Germany as well as the USSR material damage was very heavy. These two peoples – the Russian and the German – were the chief victims not only in the European war but also in the World War, since Japanese casualties were around two million. The one possible exception is the Chinese whose death roll, peculiarly difficult to assess, has been put as low as 2.5 million and as high as 13.5 million. Great Britain, France and Italy all suffered fewer deaths than in the first war. British fatal casualties, including civilians, were 450,000 with another 120,000 from the British Empire; in the first war the imperial total was nearly a million. France lost 200,000–250,000 in action and about as many civilians, as against nearly a million and a half in 1914–18. Italy, whose loss of life was greater than the French and not far short of the British, sacrificed 410,000 (one in every five a civilian) as against its earlier total of 615,000. Belgium's military casualties were approximately the same in both wars but in the second it lost more civilians than servicemen. Norway, Denmark and Holland had been spared the first war. Their losses in the second were small by comparison with the figures already quoted but sizable in relation to their own populations and Holland had the highest number of civilian deaths (200,000 or more) of any country in western Europe other than Germany itself. In central and eastern Europe the civilian deaths were very heavy indeed, since they included 5 million Jews, another 4 million non-Jewish civilians and a further million Yugoslav Resisters. In their regular armies the chief sufferers were Yugoslavia and Hungary, which lost some 400,000 each, and Poland and Rumania, which lost 300,000 each. The price paid by Austria was also around 300,000. Bulgaria escaped comparatively lightly with 20,000 deaths, half of them civilians, but in Greece the dead exceeded

250,000, two thirds of them civilians. American casualties on all fronts, Pacific as well as European, were 290,000, nearly six times as many as in the First World War. These casualties would have been higher if the Americans had not had the best medical services among the combatants. All these figures are, in the nature of the case, not only approximate but disputable. They add up to something like 50 million.

No great European war since the Seven Years War has so little changed the map of Europe or so much changed the map of the rest of the world. If Hitler had won, his New Order would have transformed Europe, but since he did not win states and frontiers were more restored than altered. Estonia, Latvia and Lithuania were the principal victims, engulfed in the USSR, their populations removed wholesale. Parts of Finland, Czechoslovakia and Rumania (and Afghanistan) were also annexed to the USSR. Poland had to submit to being shifted, partly because the boundaries which it had won after the First World War were not ethnically easy to justify. In eastern Europe a few provinces changed hands. But there was no post-war conference to allocate real estate, as after the defeat of Napoleon. The reason was not merely the fact that territorial annexation was out of favour (although this was so) but also the fact that real estate was ceasing to be an index of power. Stalin, who was an expansionist and was in a position to incorporate large areas in the USSR, did not do so because he did not need to. Communists believed that new Soviet Republics would be created; that Yugoslavia, for example, would become one of the Republics of the USSR. But Stalin decreed otherwise. He told Tito that Yugoslavia and other nearby countries were to become People's Democracies, juridically outside the USSR. He may have been deterred by the fear that the Americans would not tolerate the territorial expansion of the USSR but he did not need to put the issue to the test because Russian power sufficed to establish a new kind of Russian empire in central and eastern Europe – extending over much of the old Habsburg and Ottoman lands in Europe as well as those of the Tsars. Its authority could be assured by indirect rule through obedient communist cliques. It did not work in Yugoslavia but it worked everywhere else for the rest of Stalin's life and many years beyond. Where the First World War had dissolved Europe's empires, the Second resuscitated one of them and vastly enlarged it – in modern dress. The main thing for Stalin was to implant a particular social system where he could: annexation was not necessary for this purpose, occupation sufficed and occupation could be vicarious. He said to Djilas in 1944: 'This war is not as in the past: whoever occupies a territory also imposes on it his own social system.

Everyone imposes his own system as far as his armies can reach. It cannot be otherwise . . .' But the determining factor was the radius of power of the army and not the legally established frontiers of states.

This new Russian empire was the product of circumstances and not of compact. The western leaders have been accused of handing over half Europe at Yalta to Stalin – as they have likewise been accused of cheating China at Teheran of its rightful claims in Asia. But Stalin would have established his empire even if there had been no Yalta conference. In the war on Hitler's eastern front, which was largely independent of the land, sea and air campaigns in the west, the Russian armies beat the German armies. Power in central Europe passed therefore by conquest from Germany to the USSR. What Roosevelt and Churchill tried to do at Yalta was to prescribe limits within which Russian power would be exercised. They have been criticized for not doing more to shackle that power. It is conceivable that, at Teheran fourteen months earlier, they could have driven a different bargain but it is unrealistic to forget that the circumstances of 1943 were inappropriate for driving post-war bargains at all. The Teheran conference was a war conference between partners intent on keeping each other in the war. Post-war problems – which is a euphemism for foreseeable and foreseen post-war disagreements – could only be raised at Teheran at some risk to the common war effort. Yalta was a different kind of conference, but by February 1945 Stalin's local power in eastern Europe could not be gainsaid. Roosevelt and Churchill extracted from him the declaration on liberated territories which was intended to assure basic democratic rights and procedures, but when Stalin disregarded this declaration there was nothing that any western power could do in the Russian sphere of influence created by Russian arms. All they could do was retaliate elsewhere. The creation in 1949 of the German Federal Republic and of Nato was a kind of retaliation against Stalin's exclusive and authoritarian hold over eastern Europe.

The biggest changes occurred in Germany. Since Hitler was not displaced by his army or his people, the surrender of Germany and the collapse of Nazism occurred simultaneously. They were a single event. Germany therefore was laid completely low. This had been envisaged: German power would disappear at the end of the war, in some versions for ever. There would of course be Germans and they would inhabit a place called Germany but this Germany would not exist as an independent unit in the power political structure. It was easy to see that this would be a fact immediately after the war. Less thought was given to how it would be perpetuated. Germany might be deprived of its industry, pastoralized, occupied, but the essential requirement for its indefinite subordination was the maintenance of an invincible alliance against its resurrection. This was assumed, if only superficially, and did not turn out to be so.

One of the main reasons why it did not turn out to be so was that Germany ceased to exist as such. Instead of persisting as a unit reduced to insignificance, it became divided into two units which rapidly became politically and militarily significant. This consequence of the war was entirely unforeseen and by removing Germany as a unit from the political scene it removed also the allies' main incentive to maintain their alliance. There was no Germany for them to keep down: the alliance brought about in 1941 for a limited purpose had achieved that purpose with the surrender of Germany and its subsequent partition. There were instead two Germanies to be kept up, each appropriated by the one side or the other. The Cold War might have developed in any case. Probably it would, but the division of Germany fundamentally impelled and shaped it. To some extent a consequence of the Cold War, this division was also – more perhaps than has been appreciated – a major formative factor. Moreover the division of Germany, besides dividing the allies, did more than anything else to keep the Americans in Europe. They stayed, first, to administer Germany and argue about its future; later to defend Western Germany and their own positions in it. When the anti-Nazi alliance was converted into a duel between the victors, the Americans were still in Europe and acquired new reasons for staying there.

The Nazis and their fascist like had been defeated by the combined forces of liberal democracy and totalitarian democracy. In the exuberance of victory there were those who hoped that the alliance of the anti-fascists would endure, but soon these two traditional streams – the sources, as noted earlier in this book, of the collapse of Europe's *anciens régimes* – found themselves no longer side by side but face to face. Europe's triangle of forces resolved itself into the duel called the Cold War.

In terms of Europe the Cold War was an ideological contest between liberal democracy and totalitarian democracy; the simpler description of it as a contest between communists and anti-communists is misleading since not all anti-communists are liberal democrats. The Cold War was at the same time a power struggle between the United States and the USSR. Had this contest remained European the principal issue would have been the possible revival of Fascism, the reconstitution of the triangle of forces, and the manoeuvres of its three elements to make a pattern of two against one either in the same way as during the war or in some other way. War, being by its nature dual, had forced the triangle to conform for a few years (1941–5) to its law which says that there can be only two sides.

56 *Top*: Paratroopers landing
in southern France, 1944

57 *Bottom*: British units
arrive in Bayeux, June 1944

58   *Top*: De Gaulle at the Arc
de Triomphe, 24 August 1944

59   *Bottom*: Paris 1944: a last
sniper causes an alarm

60   Churchill and de Gaulle
in Paris, 11 November 1944

61   *Top*: Americans in what is
left of Saarbrücken, March
1945

62   *Bottom*: Americans cross
the Rhine, 26 March 1945

63   *Top*: Field Marshals
Montgomery and Rokossovski
take a salute from Cossacks
on the Elbe

64   *Bottom*: Eisenhower and
Montgomery

65 Franz von Papen, captive,
April 1945

66 Pierre Laval, captive in
Lins, Austria

67 Berlin, the Reich
Chancellery: Hitler's office

68 Berlin, the Reich
Chancellery: the reception hall

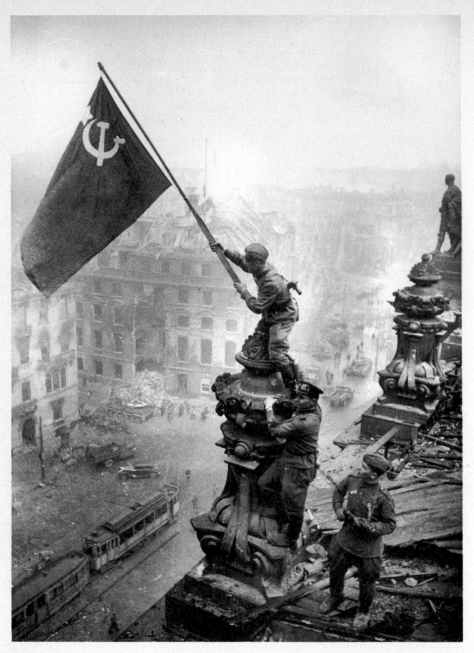

69   Red Flag over the
Reichstag, Berlin: May 1945

After the war and the elimination of the one side the surviving forces moved from identity to opposition and so formed a new pattern, rigid until the appearance of some third element to give it mobility.

In the late forties and fifties this third element was neither European nor fascist. The Second World War, as has already been said, changed the map of the rest of the world as markedly as it left the outlines of the map of Europe recognizably familiar. The Seven Years War had decided that Great Britain and not France should have the lion's share of the dark continents in which Europeans had been seeking profit and adventure. North America and much of southern Asia were secured for Great Britain. France, the Netherlands and Portugal retained positions in Asia and, with Belgium, Germany and Italy, also shared in the later partition of Africa. The nineteenth and early twentieth centuries were the heyday of these European empires. The Second World War was the centrepiece of the last act of the story; the generation after the war was kept busy with the epilogue. As a result the nature of world conflict changed. This conflict had been a dispute centred in Europe, a dispute over political forms coupled with a struggle for power. It became a worldwide contest, still ideological and strategic, but one in which the third element was the significantly dubbed Third World which ceased on decolonization to be part of the Western World.

The new states which emerged from the dissolution of Europe's overseas empires, in far greater number than those which had emerged from the dissolution of its continental empires after the First World War, decided for the most part not to attach themselves to either side in the Cold War but to take up a distinct, non-aligned position. So far as the Cold War was ideological they sensed, correctly, that the ideological issue was a European one and had little to do with their immediate needs. Further, they diagnosed the Cold War as essentially a struggle for power which was bound to hurt them and which they must therefore try to stop. They rejected neutrality – opting out – as neither possible nor desirable. The Second World War had shown how little a neutral could rely on having his neutrality respected; the changes in the nature of war suggested that neutrality was a thing of the past. The neutral's claim to stay out of a war required certain conditions which were disappearing. It rested upon the assumptions that a state of war was clearly distinguishable from peace and that a given war could be restricted to certain areas and prevented from leaking through the frontiers of the neutral state. But the very expression Cold War showed that the concept of war as something overtly declared and conducted with lethal weapons against proclaimed opponents no longer sufficed; guerrilla and subversive wars, whose techniques had been expanded in many parts of the world during the Second World War, also increased the uncertainty about what was a war and who was a belligerent. Air warfare eroded the significance of frontiers; nuclear fall-out abolished it.

For all these reasons attempts to keep out of war by choosing the classic posture of neutrality seemed to make little sense. Keeping out was no longer a guarantee of safety. Those who wanted to fend off war could no longer seek to barricade themselves against it; they must actively try to prevent or extinguish it. Thus third parties came to believe that they must in their own interests – to which it was easy to add the moral imperatives of the peacekeeper – play a part in international affairs rather than abstract themselves from the scene. Leaders of new states were in any case inclined towards a negative non-alignment: their consuming preoccupation with independence made them eschew alliance with a dominant power, their pressing economic needs made them seek trade and aid in all quarters, their concern for the cohesion of their new and often divided societies counselled them against a foreign alliance which would offend a particular domestic faction of the Left or the Right. But their non-alignment was not merely negative. Despite their weaknesses, of which they were only too well aware, they adopted a policy of positive non-alignment, that is to say intervention, in order to ensure the survival and independence which other states had tried in the past to safeguard by going into political purdah. And because they mattered to the protagonists in the Cold War, at least to the extent that each of these wanted to stand no less well than the other with the non-aligned, their emergence from European dominion into statehood after the war altered the terms and area of international politics.

Yet important though they were this widening of the scene and multiplication of the cast were almost trivial beside the irrefragable involvement of the United States in the world's proceedings. This involvement after the Second World War has become as much a commonplace as American isolationism after the First, and at times pushed to equally questionable limits. It was the war which marked the change.

The American experience of war was different from all others. First, the United States had war aims, in the sense of purposes to be accomplished by going to war as opposed to the bare winning of a war that had happened. Taking part in a European war which they did not feel obliged to fight in response to an external threat, the Americans needed war aims. A people which is not forced to fight must have a reason for doing so. A people which has no choice needs no aims, but a people which has a choice must have aims. To Europeans the American preoccupation with war aims seemed either unreal or hypocritical. Europeans had no war aims except the aim first to survive and then to win, and these were not aims freely considered and adopted but simply a formulation of the force of circumstances. (The Resistance did develop war aims, but these were adopted in the course of the war and not as a reason for going to war; and they touched only a proportion of Resisters and a very small proportion of the whole people, which is one reason why they were so thinly attained.) But Americans, who had not been attacked and were not fighting for survival, could not be led into war without some explanation of why they should do any such thing, and the simplest way of satisfying this natural requirement was to present a statement of what the war was about and how the world could be made better by helping the right side to win it. Such statements are necessarily vague and often grandiose. Therefore they are easy to contemn. But for a people not under compulsion they are a necessity.

They also colour that people's outlook after the war is over. If a war is fought and suffered for certain purposes, there is a duty – not least to the dead – to see that the purposes are achieved. Where victory is the end of war, the war ends with the victory. But Americans believed that there were other ends and that the war had been fought to rescue and restore values such as freedom and justice, which Nazis and fascists had scorned and destroyed (and imperialists, in their less brutal ways, were also ignoring). Americans were not more devoted to these values than good men elsewhere but they were more committed to doing something to secure them. The sins of communist governments could not be overlooked. Therefore the war spirit which had animated the United States in the war was not assuaged when the fighting – against the dictators – ceased but oppression and injustice did not; and Americans carried into the more complicated world of peace politics the guiding principles which had sufficed in the simpler world of war. They remained campaign-minded.

Secondly, the American homeland remained inviolate. Although the American contribution in manpower and materials was enormous, the men and women with their equipment went out of the United States to battle and never imagined doing battle in it. Nor did those left behind know, at first hand, anything of bombardment or the fear of bombs, resistance, evacuation or privation. At second hand, through press and radio, they knew more about distant events than a people at war had ever known before, but the events themselves remained distant. It was the kind of war which had once been familiar to Europeans but had ceased to be so. Although in material terms the American war effort was the most up-to-date imaginable, in social terms it belonged still to an era in which combatants set sail while non-combatants stayed safely behind. War fosters and sanctifies material effort: in the United States the materialism promoted by military exigencies was not countered, as in Europe, by the social emollients produced by shared dangers. In this respect the American experience of war brought changes which were comparatively less abrupt during the war but, as with the effects of war aims, comparatively more potent after it. The United States took the war in its giant stride but did not afterwards look nearly as much the same as Europe did ten to twenty years after the war ended.

Thirdly, there was the sheer size of the achievement. Over 15 million men and women were summoned to do services of one kind or another – as compared with 22 million mobilized by the USSR, 17 million by Germany and 12 million by Great Britain, the Dominions and colonies. Gross national product was nearly doubled, rising from $91 billion to $166 billion. Overall industrial output was doubled, while at the same time agricultural output also increased by more than a fifth. New industries were created (synthetic rubber) or given an enormous boost (electronics). The expansion of American shipbuilding from one to 19 million tons a year has already been mentioned. Such efforts were common. Aircraft production rose from below 6,000 a year on the eve of war to more than 96,000, the numbers employed in the aircraft industry from 46,000 to more than 2 million. Altogether the Americans made 275,000 aircraft, of which 40,000 went to their allies. American aircraft provided the RAF with an increment of 20–25 per cent over and above what it obtained from the British aircraft industry.

So too with tanks. American tank production, negligible in 1941, rose to 14,000 and 21,000 in the next two years. The American Sherman became the mainstay of the western allies. The British army possessed 3,300 Shermans on the day when it returned to France in 1944. The Sherman did not give the western allies the superiority over German models which they were looking for, but the Pershing, which came into service in 1944, proved a match for the last German tanks, the Tiger and Panther. British industry, obliged after Dunkirk to replace losses as quickly as possible, began by supplying current obsolescent models and the newer Churchill and then developed the Cromwell and the Comet which reached fighting units towards the end of 1942 and 1944 respectively, but tank design and production were, by agreement, primarily an American commitment and the resulting models were American designs with the incorporation of as many British ideas as fitted them. In addition to the first essentials of aircraft, tanks and shipping the United States produced a total of 64,000 landing craft (to Great Britain's 4,300) and equipped its allies as well as itself with practically all the transport aircraft, self-propelled artillery, amphibian vehicles and heavy trucks which they required. That remarkable vehicle the jeep was produced in such quantities that the Americans were able to spare 86,000 for the British. (The Germans had a jeep too, which was water and sand proof.) As a result of this war effort the United States, uniquely among the combatants, began the next phase of its history materially better equipped than before.

Fourthly, the war altered the distribution of power in the United States geographically and politically. It accelerated the shift of money and people from the east to the west coast and gave the south the boost which it had never had since the Civil War. Industry invaded the west where it had been relatively inconspicuous and the south where – outside Texas, already well supplied with capital from oil – it had hardly been at home at all. As the aircraft and telecommunications industries expanded into the south, employment and communications boomed. Atlanta, for example – designed by geography to be as much a natural centre in the age of aircraft as in the age of rail – a city where the complete devastation of the Civil War had opened the way for a *post bellum* entrepreneurial class to supplant the old upper class which had remained sufficiently dominant elsewhere (in Mississippi for example) to impede rejuvenation – had at last the opportunity to join the mainstream of American modernization and prosperity. The demands of war gave a new mobility both to southern whites who moved to the nearest city and to negroes who, whether through the calls of economic expansion or through conscription, moved to all parts of the country, including parts where they had been little seen before. These shifts and needs helped the anti-discrimination cause. Roosevelt gave a pledge of no discrimination in industry, wrote non-discrimination clauses into the government contracts upon which industry increasingly lived during the war and created a Fair Employment Practices Commission. (But the pledge was widely evaded and the Commission harassed. In the armed services negroes continued to be relegated to subordinate positions. Secretary Stimson debarred them from equal opportunities on the grounds that they were incapable of learning the necessary skills. Secretary Knox was even firmer. The negro was not integrated in the armed services until the Korean War.) Thus the primacy of the old centres of wealth (and liberalism) in the north-east was eroded and movements of population, begun in the First World War but arrested by the great depression, were resumed. The consequences of these economic and social movements began to become apparent only in the generation which followed the war years.

The balance of political power was affected by more than geographical shifts. As the British and the Germans both discovered, war is a mighty centralizer. For the United States too the same proposition held good. War necessitated an immense increase in federal budgets and federal spending. The proportion of federal to other taxes grew. This centralization of authority accelerated a constitutional trend, as between the federal government and the states, but did not inaugurate any economic or social revolution, as between government and private interests. Roosevelt had to combat the marked reluctance of American society to entrust the government with regulating powers. His administration had at first no adequate control either over the estimates made by the armed services of their requirements and so of their demands on industry, or of industry itself, and it was not until 1943 that Roosevelt succeeded in imposing centralized government control over activities traditionally jealous of government interference. American capitalism produced the goods but it wanted also to remain sovereign in its own house, and resisted government direction until complaints of the monopolization of government contracts by the bigger corporations and rumours of scandals gave Roosevelt the opportunity and the necessary backing to create new government agencies to fix priorities, allocate orders and at the same time check inflation by price, wage and rent control. The Congress mistrusted the vast increase in the government's powers which accompanied the vast increase in the nation's efforts. It was only with difficulty persuaded that the one required the other. The unions too bridled against the shift which the war imposed on the balance of power between government and unions, and at one point Roosevelt was forced to nationalize the coal mines in the face of strike threats from John L. Lewis, the leader of the mineworkers. Roosevelt eventually secured control over the economy through the Office of Economic Stabilization, the Office of Price Control and his annual Finance Acts. The latter raised the income tax and extended it to whole classes which had never had to pay it before; federal income tax rose, at the top level, to 94 per cent. A corporation tax rising to 50 per cent was imposed and an excess profits tax was introduced which rose by stages to 95 per cent of the excess. Yet government expenditure on the war grew so fast that during the four war years only 41 per cent of it was covered by taxation. For the rest the government had to borrow and to control the consequent inflation by the statutory regulation of wages and prices.

The war finally brought the great depression to an end, but at the same time the semi-socialist New Deal gave way to a fully capitalist war economy. This war economy performed prodigies of productive valour in the service of the military. The achievements of the partnership were miraculous, so much so that they stamped a pattern on the further development of the American economy and American society in the nuclear age.

Fifthly and finally, the United States was not only transformed domestically but also was seen to have become to an unprecedented degree the world's most mighty power. This power, however reluctantly acknowledged, had played some part in propelling the United States into war. Even before the mobilization of its resources in manpower and production the United States possessed enormous industrial and military might. Its low posture in the twenties and thirties was out of line with its capacities and Americans were perhaps readier than appeared at first sight to be up and doing – preferably with a good cause – because the sense of power possessed is itself an incentive to the use of power. The war destroyed reticence. Victory destroyed bashfulness, since victory was seen as a triumphant use of power for good ends. Then the power itself was vastly accentuated by the American monopoly of the nuclear bomb, but neither victory nor the bomb was the source of American power. They were on the contrary among its consequences. Yet the bomb created a new situation since it made the United States more powerful than all other states put together, not merely more powerful than any other state or any conceivable coalition of states. It could impose its will universally, should it be prepared to threaten and resort to nuclear war. And, so it seemed in 1945, it might maintain this position indefinitely since it was widely, if wrongly, assumed that no other state would be able to make nuclear weapons for a long time to come.

The appearance of nuclear power as a military factor coincided with the disappearance of a system of international politics in which several states of roughly equal strength predominated. Although this system left its mark on the nascent United Nations, where five states were held to be superior and were given a permanent place and a veto in the Security Council, the new reality was a bipolar system in which predominant power belonged to the United States and the USSR, each of whom was accepted as markedly superior to everybody else. Since these two powers were presented and accepted as the protagonists of two opposed ways of life, the bipolarity was also inherently an actively hostile confrontation. Europe was the chief object of this ideological and power conflict.

Yet the universality of American power was, despite first appearances, limited. The Americans recoiled from the use of nuclear weapons. The novelty of these weapons made them more awful than anything that had gone before, even though the two occasions on which they had been used (described in the ensuing part of this book) had not caused as many deaths as some more conventional instances of slaughter. Their continuing toxic effect, vaguely apprehended, added to the revulsion. There was widespread feeling in the United States that nuclear weapons should not be used again. But if this were so, the threat to use them was not a threat but a bluff. Thus, even before the USSR itself constructed a nuclear bomb, the American monopoly had been negated and the American omnipotence converted into a predominance paralleled by Russian power. The American monopoly was both a fact and a myth.

In Europe in particular, American power was countered by Russian power. The Russians occupied half Europe and maintained very large armed forces within and beyond their borders after the war ended; Stalin, with a ruthlessness reminiscent of his war on the peasants in the thirties, gave an absolute priority to war industries and war research, in particular to discovering the scientific and technological secrets of nuclear power which Russian experts were already close to mastering. By postponing for a generation the amelioration of the quality of life in the USSR Stalin ensured that power in Europe should be shared.

The Cold War, which is the name for the rather novel way by which this contest for power was initiated and then conducted, was something that Roosevelt certainly, and Stalin probably, would have wished to avoid. It represented Europe's continuing claim on the attentions of the world's two super-powers and it was the principal outward and visible sign of the post-war involvement of the United States in international affairs. This involvement would probably have come about in any case, but historically it followed from the recognition of the facts of power and geopolitics, brought about by war and Roosevelt. The direction of the involvement, on the other hand, was determined by pre-war concepts and Truman. Shortly after Hitler's invasion of the USSR Truman, then a Senator, said that the United States ought to help the Russians so long as they were being beaten by the Germans but that, if the Russians began to win, then the United States should help the Germans, so that as many as possible of both might be killed. This was a denial of the thesis that the war was a war against Fascism and a reassertion of the thesis that liberal democrats and communists could not live together amicably. Truman, like Stalin, belonged emphatically to the pre-war generation. He was also, unlike Roosevelt, relatively inexperienced in international affairs and so more dependent on the State Department and more receptive to an official line on the USSR which was harder than Roosevelt's had been. Those who believe that men make history will say that two men in particular, Truman and Stalin, made the Cold War. Those who believe that men operate only on the surface of deeper currents will point to Truman and Stalin as examples of the strength and direction of those forces which, having been driven underground for a space like the fountain of Arethusa, re-emerged after the defeat of Fascism to take control once more of men's conflicting destinies and destinations.

How events were shaped is a matter for debate. The events themselves are clearer. In June 1948 the United States formally abjured isolationism by the Vandenberg resolution adopted by the Senate, and ten months later it signed the North Atlantic Treaty in company with Canada and ten European states. These two events marked the end of isolationism – with a particular intent.

The cost of a war in men and materials, and the redistribution of territory and power which it brings about, are only two parts of the consequences of war. There is a third, less tangible but at least as important.

Wars intensify simple emotions and they also create opportunities and heighten expectations. Wars are horrible and bearing them is only made possible by hating one's enemy and by believing in a better future for one's self.

The hatred cannot be switched off. It may abate, though slowly, but since the Second World War the hatred felt for Germans in those years among Russians, Jews and others who suffered terribly has remained a factor in European affairs. It may be exaggerated for purposes of propaganda but it exists to be exaggerated and is easily rekindled. One of the war's many causes was the madness which took hold of Germany and one of the war's effects was to spread this madness and fill all Europe with violence and with the toleration, even the applause, of violence. There was in this respect a difference between the war in eastern Europe and the war in the west, and this difference has affected post-war emotions and therefore post-war political attitudes. The German onslaught in the west was less savage than in the east and German barbarity in western occupied territories was episodic whereas in the east it was planned and persistent. Consequently the western response was less vicious too. It is difficult to gauge the feelings of those who rejoiced, in Great Britain for example, at the news of the destruction of German cities. There was a certain grim Old Testament satisfaction, but there was little exultation and the dominant feeling was probably the thought that such blows must hasten the end of the war. There was much bitterness but little of the sheer hatred which disfigured the First World War, and although the two catastrophes were only a quarter of a century apart the generation of the second war would have considered it absurd to boo dachshunds in the London streets as their fathers had done. There was a certain sobriety.

There were also expectations and, after the war ended, a balance to be struck between satisfied and unsatisfied expectations. Making the world a better place to live in meant, in Europe, political, economic and social changes, a further instalment of the long-drawn-out revolution promising freedom, equality and brotherhood; outside Europe it meant, in the first place, the end of foreign and colonial rule. Of these twin aspirations the second was substantially satisfied in less than a generation after the end of the war and in some places within a few years. The British, French, Dutch and Belgian empires in Africa and Asia (but not yet the Portuguese) dissolved. They were doubtless already dissolving but the war accelerated the process by weakening the resources and the nerve of the metropolitan powers and by a revolution in thought which made empire seem in 1945 much more old-fashioned and dubious, as well as impermanent, than it had seemed six years earlier. By 1960 these empires were extinct or vestigial. Their demise constituted the greatest change ever made in a short space to the map of the world and to the mechanisms of international relations.

Within Europe the revolutionary current stimulated by the war was less successful. The old order proved remarkably tenacious, perhaps because the economic stringencies of the aftermath of war, on top of the strains of the war itself, drained the life out of reform movements. There were gains. In Great Britain, for example, the creation of a free public health service transformed the lives of millions of people not only by relieving or preventing sickness but also by removing the hideous worries of those who had had to endure illness or watch it in their children without being able to pay to do anything about it. In other countries too social services and social experiment received a fillip and even right-wing parties and governments took to thinking and acting in terms which they would have abhorred before the war. In eastern Europe civil liberties were obliterated by the political repression and economic obscurantism, worthy of Tsar Nicholas I, which Stalin and his successors in Moscow felt impelled to adopt, but in the USSR itself the government was the legatee of its own wartime promises of a better life and of wartime measures of toleration – such as the toleration of religion, the reappearance of priests, more freedom for writers, the appeal to popular sentiments in place of the use of disciplinary threats. Post-war stringencies produced a retreat from this tentative liberalization but did not altogether kill its seeds. War, it has been said, is the midwife of revolution. But nobody has said what is the period of gestation. The revolutions of 1848 occurred thirty-three years after the end of Napoleon's wars.

Finally there is the Middle East. Hitler's climax to Gentile persecution of the Jews – a drama unequalled for shame in the history of European civilization except by the slave trade – was effected with horrors even more appalling than the pogroms in Russia and Roumania in 1881 and 1905. It piercingly and urgently sharpened the desire of the survivors to depart to Zion. It probably also sharpened the desire of guilt-laden Europeans to see them go and it certainly accentuated the sympathies of some Gentiles for a people whom they had too often and now too fatally reviled. But Zion was no empty haven waiting to receive them. For half a century Zionists had been resolved to find a home in Palestine for the Jews and to create a Jewish state there. Some of them had imagined a state under Ottoman suzerainty and later some of their successors thought of an autonomous dominion within the British Empire, but most Zionist leaders realized from the first that what they sought must be an independent sovereign state. They also realized that it would be impolitic to say so, since the creation of this new state would entail the dispossession, or at least the subjection, of the existing Arab inhabitants of the lands for which Zionists yearned as a refuge and a religious fulfilment.

When the war ended, the Zionists, who had refrained from harassing the British in Palestine so long as the war lasted, resorted to violence in their turn. They took up arms and drove the British out. They then defeated the Arabs who came against them, jointly but hardly unitedly, and so won their state and enlarged it by provoking the Palestinians by terror into flight. Zionism was not only rendered more urgent by Nazi brutality; it was also itself brutalized. Israel's doors were, as a matter of principle, open to all Jews whencesoever, and the Jews of Europe hurried to it – except those in the west who were too comfortable to move and some in the east who were not allowed to. This migration, which was supplemented by similar migrations of non-European Jews, opened a new chapter in the history of the Middle East by implanting the state of Israel in a part of the world which Arabs regarded as theirs, which they had hoped to inherit from the Turks with British help in 1919, which they had seen the British take for themselves, and from which they were now not only debarred but actually – by arms or by fear – evicted. The Jewish problem had been off-loaded by Christendom onto Islam. But it did not cease to concern Europe: for the Middle East remained what it had been for centuries – one of the world's most convenient highways – and what it had become in the twentieth century – one of the world's primary sources of mineral wealth – so that the world's Great Powers could not ignore it.

But their continued intervention took new shapes. The Second World War destroyed the pattern imposed after the First. Then the British and French had established a post-Ottoman condominium, in despite of the

Arabs and to the exclusion of the Russians. But the Second World War eliminated first the French and then, more gradually, the British and so created new opportunities for Arabs – and Russians. These new opportunities coincided with swelling revolutionary and nationalist currents in the Arab world which offered Arabs a new Arab-Russian alliance in place of the Arab-British association which had governed Middle Eastern politics during the First World War and after it. Against this potential Arab-Russian entente Israel and the United States constituted, however loosely, a counter-system. Thus the Superpowers who, in Europe, were the protagonists in the Cold War were, in the Middle East, antagonists in an area where keeping the peace would require them to restrain not themselves but others.

It has been said that wars settle nothing. This is too caustic a dismissal of human endurance and human striving. At the end of this great war in Europe the Nazis and their fascist allies were beaten. Things would have been very different had they not been. Fascism, perhaps not irretrievably but yet at this point decisively, was defeated.

A famous Russian historian of classical antiquity has judged that Greece declined because men came to distrust reason and Rome fell because it tried to maintain an exclusively privileged society wherein the rich were enervated and the poor alienated. If these judgements on the ancestors of Europe's civilization have any bearing on its own fate, then the Fascism of the twentieth century begotten of anti-rational and anti-democratic authoritarianism was a malign cancer and its defeat in 1945 at least a reprieve.

Chronological Skeleton

WESTERN FRONT	THE MEDITERRANEAN, AFRICA AND THE MIDDLE EAST	EASTERN FRONT	ASIA AND THE PACIFIC THEATRE
1937			
			July 7 Japanese attack Chinese at Marco Polo Bridge
			Dec. 14 Fall of Nanking to the Japanese
1938			
			July 11 Japanese-Soviet battle of Chang-kufeng
			Oct. Chiang Kai-shek's Government withdraws to Chungking
			Oct. 21 Fall of Canton to the Japanese
			Oct. 25 Fall of Hankow to the Japanese
			Nov. 5 Prince Konoye declares 'New Order' in Asia
1939			
Sept. 3 Great Britain and France declare war		Sept. 1 Germans invade Poland	May–Sept Battle of Nomonhan between Japan and USSR
		Sept. 17 USSR invades Poland	

1939		Oct.	USSR exacts mutual assistance treaties from Estonia, Latvia and Lithuania
		Nov. 30	USSR invades Finland
Dec. 17	Graf Spee scuttled		
1940		Mar. 12	Finland capitulates
		Mar. 30	Setting up of Wang Ching-wei's puppet Government at Nanking
Apr. 9	Germans invade Denmark and Norway		
May	British occupy Iceland		
May 10	Germans invade Low Countries and France. Churchill Prime Minister		
May 15	Dutch lay down arms		
May 20	Germans reach English Channel		

May 28 Belgium capitulates

May 27–
June 4 Dunkirk

June 10 Italy declares war

June 14 Germans enter Paris

June 22 France signs armistice

July 3 British action against French fleet at Mers-el-Kebir

July 10–
Sept. 15 Battle of Britain

Aug. 4 Italians invade British and French Somaliland

Sept. 3 Anglo-US bases destroyers deal

Sept. 14 Italians invade Egypt

Sept. 27 Tripartite Pact between Japan, Germany and Italy

July–
Oct. Closing of the Burma Road

Oct. Hitler confers with Mussolini (4), Franco (23), Pétain (24)

Oct. 28 Italians invade Greece

Nov. 5 Roosevelt re-elected President

Nov. 11 British attack Italian fleet at Taranto

Nov. Hungary, Rumania and Slovakia brought into Tripartite Pact

1940	Dec. British offensive in North Africa captures Tobruk (Jan. 22) and Benghazi (Feb. 7) 1941	Dec. American embargo on sales of scrap iron and war material to Japan
	1941	
Mar. 11 Lend-Lease Act signed	Mar. 1 Bulgaria joins Tripartite Pact	
	Mar. 27 Simovic coup: Yugoslavia refuses to join Tripartite Pact	
	Mar. 28 Battle of Cape Matapan	
	Mar. 31 First German offensive in North Africa: takes Benghazi and invests Tobruk	
Apr. US occupies Greenland	Apr. 6 Germans invade Yugoslavia and Greece	Apr. 13 Non-Aggression Pact signed between Japan and Russia
	May 2 British invade Iraq	
	May 20– June 2 Germans take Crete	
May 27 *Bismarck* sunk		

June 8   British defeat Vichy French in Syria and Lebanon

June 22   Germans invade USSR

July   US joins occupation of Iceland

July 2   Japan decides on extensive moves into Indo-China

July 12   Anglo-Soviet Treaty of Mutual Assistance

July 28 and 29   US, British and Dutch East Indies impose embargoes on the sale of oil and steel to Japan

Aug. 14   Roosevelt–Churchill conference, Placentia Bay: Atlantic Charter

Aug. 17   Fall of Kiev

Aug. 25   Anglo-Russian occupation of Iran

Sept.   US 'shoot at sight' order

Sept. 8   Leningrad invested

1941

Oct. 17 General Tōjō replaces Konoye as Prime Minister of Japan

Oct. 30 Sebastopol invested. German thrust for Moscow

Dec. 1 Russian counter-attack

Dec. 7 Japan sends a declaration of war to the US

Dec. 7 Japan attacks Pearl Harbor, the Philippines, Hong Kong and Malaya

Dec. 8 US and Great Britain declare war on Japan

Dec. 9 China officially declares war on Japan and Germany

Dec. 10 Japanese sink the *Prince of Wales* and the *Repulse*

Dec. 10 Japan captures Guam

Dec. 11 Japan attacks Burma

Dec. 11 Germany and Italy declare war on US

Dec. 23 Fall of Wake Island

Dec. 24 British re-capture Benghazi

1942

Jan. 28 Germans re-capture Benghazi

Jan. 11 Japan attacks the Dutch East Indies

Feb. 8 Fall of Rangoon
Feb. 15 Fall of Singapore
Feb. 19 Japanese bomb Port Darwin in Australia
Feb. 27–29 Battle of the Java Sea

Mar. 2 Fall of Batavia
Mar. 11 Cripps mission to India

Mar. Bomber Command raids Baltic towns

Apr. German 'Baedeker' raids

Apr. 4 Japanese raid into the
Apr. 9 Indian Ocean, bombing Ceylon
Apr. 9 US surrender of Bataan
Apr. 18 US air raid on Tokyo
May 1 Surrender of Mandalay
May 6 Surrender of Corregidor
May 6–8 Battle of the Coral Sea

May 30 '1,000-bomber' raid on Cologne

1942			
June — Destruction of PQ 17			June 4 — Battle of Midway Island
			June 4 — Japanese attack on the Aleutian Islands
July — Regular raids on Ruhr and Hamburg begin		July 3 — Fall of Sebastopol	
			Aug. 7 — US landings on the Solomon Islands
			Aug. 9 — Civil disobedience campaign announced in India
Aug. 12–15 — Stalin–Churchill meeting in Moscow		Aug. 12–15 — Stalin–Churchill meeting in Moscow	
Aug. 17 — First US raid on Germany			
Aug. 19 — Dieppe raid			
	Aug. 31 — Battle of Alam el Halfa: German–Italian advance stayed		
		Sept. 13 — Battles for Stalingrad begin	
			Sept. 21 — Opening of the Arakan offensive under Wavell
			Sept. 21 — Opening of US offensive in New Guinea

Nov.   Record months for sinking by U-boats

Nov.   Regular raids on Berlin begin

Oct. 23   Battle of Alamein

Nov. 8   Allied landings in Morocco and Algeria

Nov. 11   Germans occupy southern France and Tunisia

1943

Jan. 14–24   Casablanca Conference

Jan.   German retreat from Caucasus

Jan. 11   Treaty relinquishing extra-territorial rights between the US, Britain and China

Feb. 2   German surrender at Stalingrad. Russians recover Kursk (8) and Rostov (14)

Feb. 8   Wingate's expedition into Burma

Mar. 2   Battle of the Bismarck Sea

Mar. 29   Battle of the Mareth

Apr. 18   Death of Admiral Yamamoto, at Bougainville

Apr. 19–May 16   Rising and extinction of Warsaw Ghetto

1943

May 11 US begin to liberate Aleutian Islands

May 12 German-Italian surrender in Tunisia

May 17 Attack on Ruhr dams

May 26 Discovery of Katyn massacre and severance of Russo-Polish relations

June 29 US landings in New Guinea

July 5– Battles in the Kursk
Aug. 6 salient and Russian recovery of Orel and Belgorod

July 10 Invasion of Sicily
July 25 Dismissal of Mussolini

Aug. 17 US daylight raids on Regensburg and Schweinfurt

Aug. 17 Quebec Conference: setting up of South-East Asia Command, under Mountbatten

Aug. 23 Russians recover Kharkov

Sept. Russians recover Novorossisk and Smolensk (25)

Sept. 3 Invasion of Calabria and signing of Italian surrender

Sept. 9 Landings at Salerno
Sept. 12 Rescue of Mussolini

1943

Oct. 13   Italy declares war on Germany

Oct.   Russians recover Zaporozhe (14) and Dnepropetrovsk (25)

Nov. 5–6   Greater East Asia Conference held in Tokyo

Nov. 6   Russians recover Kiev

Nov.   US landings in the Gilbert Islands

Nov. 22–26   Cairo Conference: unconditional surrender demanded of Japan

Nov. 28–Dec. 1   Teheran Conference

Dec.   Opening of the assault on the Marshall Islands

1944

Jan. 12   Landings at Anzio

Jan. 27   Leningrad relieved

Feb. 15   Bombing of Monte Cassino

Feb.–Mar.   Beginning of Japanese offensive on borders of India, siege of Imphal and Kohima

Apr. 2   Russians enter Rumania

Apr. 17   Renewed Japanese offensive in China

Apr.–July   US advances through Dutch New Guinea

1944

June 6 Invasion of Normandy
June 12 First V1s hit London

July 20 Attempt on Hitler's life

May 17 Germans evacuate Monte Cassino
June 4 Americans enter Rome

May Russians recover Sebastopol and Crimea

June 23–
July 3 Russians recover Byelorussia

July 23 Russians take Lublin and establish Polish Committee of National Liberation

June 15 Americans invade Saipan
June 15 First B29 raid on Japan

July 4 Japanese defeated at Imphal
July 9 Fall of Saipan
July 18 Resignation of General Tōjō

Aug. 15 Allied landings in southern France	Aug. Kesselring mans the Gothic Line	Aug. 1–Oct. 2 Warsaw rising against the Germans	Aug. US recovery of Tinian and Guam
Aug. 17 Final victories in Normandy. Paris rises			
Aug. 24 Leclercq enters Paris			Sept. Allied counter-offensive in Burma, under Mountbatten
Sept. 3 Brussels liberated		Sept. 5 USSR declares war on Bulgaria	
Sept. 8 First V2s hit London		Sept. 12 Rumania signs armistice	
Sept. 17–30 Arnhem operations fail		Sept. 19 Finland signs armistice	
		Oct. 20 Partisans and Russians enter Belgrade	Oct. 20 US landings in the Philippines
			Oct. 25 Battle of Leyte Gulf
			Nov. Beginning of systematic US bombing of Japan
Dec. 16 German offensive in the Ardennes			

1945

Date	Event
Jan. 9	US landings on Luzon
Jan. 12	General Russian offensive begins
Jan. 17	Russians enter Warsaw
Feb. 4–12	Yalta Conference
Feb. 13	Surrender of Budapest
Feb. 13–14	Dresden raids
Mar. 7	Americans cross the Rhine at Remagen
Apr. 1	US landings on Okinawa
Apr. 4	Japanese Prime Minister Koiso resigns and is replaced by Suzuki
Apr. 12	Death of Roosevelt
Apr. 13	Russians enter Vienna
Apr. 16	Last Russian offensive begins
Apr.	Russia refuses to renew her non-aggression pact with Japan
Apr. 28	Death of Mussolini
Apr. 30	Death of Hitler
May 2	Berlin in Russian hands. Germans in Italy capitulate
May 3	Japanese surrender Rangoon

May 7 Germans surrender at Rheims

July 17 Potsdam Conference

May 5 Prague rises

May 9 Russians enter Prague

July 26 Allies at Potsdam call on Japan to surrender

Aug. 6 Hiroshima

Aug. 8 Russia declares war on Japan

Aug. 9 Nagasaki

Aug. 14 Japan capitulates

Sept. 2 Japanese surrender signed

Books: The Western Hemisphere

Books on the Second World War are legion. The lists which follow embrace only a small proportion. By and large they contain books written in or translated into English but this is not a rigid rule.

The contribution of official historiography is itself substantial both in the number of books published, and their bulk and importance. The forbidding nature of official histories should not be allowed to obscure the fact that they contain numerous volumes that are uncommonly good and as readable as they are scholarly. The British official History of the Second World War runs to more than eighty volumes divided between Military, Civil and Medical series. The US collection is longer still; its volumes on the US Army alone almost equal the entire British *oeuvre*. Other English-language collections – Canadian, Australian, New Zealand, Indian, South African – are commensurately weighty. Their subject matter ranges from Grand Strategy and Foreign Policy to particular topics and services such as Merchant Shipping, Manpower, Civil Defence. The lists below do not include these official publications.

ORIGINS

(i) *General Surveys*

Christopher Thorne, *The Approach of War 1938–39* (1967); A. J. P. Taylor, *The Origins of the Second World War* (1961, reprinted with new introduction 1963); Elizabeth Wiskemann, *Europe of the Dictators* (1966), *Czechs and Germans* (1967); D. C. Watt, *Too Serious a Business: European Armed Forces and the Approach to the Second World War* (1967); A. Adamthwaite, *The Making of the Second World War* (1977).

(ii) *British Policies*

Michael Howard, *The Continental Commitment: The Dilemma of British Defence Policy in the Era of Two World Wars* (1972); C. G. Peden, *British Rearmament and the Treasury 1932–39* (1979); L. R. Pratt, *East of Malta, West of Suez: Britain's Mediterranean Crisis 1936–39* (1975); R. P. Shay, *British Rearmament in the Thirties: Politics and Profits* (1977); S. W. Roskill, *Naval Policy between the Wars*, vol. 2: *The period of Reluctant Rearmament 1930–39* (1936), *Hankey,*

Man of Secrets, vol. 2: *1919–31* (1972), vol. 3: *1931–63* (1974); Lt-Gen. Sir
H. R. Pownall, *Chief of Staff: The Diaries of Lt-Gen. Sir Henry R. Pownall*
(ed. B. Bond, vol. 1: *1933–40*, 1972, and vol. 2: *1940–44*, 1974); T. Jones, *A Diary with Letters 1931–50* (1954).

(iii) *Appeasement and Munich*

M. Gilbert, *The Roots of Appeasement* (1966); C. A. Macdonald, *The United States, Britain and Appeasement* (1981); A. A. Offner, *American Appeasement: U.S. Foreign Policy and Germany 1933–38* (1969); R. Ovendale, *Appeasement and the English-speaking World: Britain, the United States, the Dominions and the Policy of Appeasement* (1975); R. Parkinson, *Peace for Our Time: Munich to Dunkirk, the Inside Story* (1971); Telford Taylor, *Munich: The Price of Peace* (1967); K. Middlemas, *Diplomacy of Illusion: The British Government and Germany 1937–39* (1972); I. Colvin, *The Chamberlain Cabinet* (1971); J. A. Cross, *Sir Samuel Hoare: A Political Biography* (1977); S. K. Newman, *March 1939: The British Guarantee to Poland, a Study in the Continuity of British Foreign Policy* (1976); Sir A. M. Cadogan, *Diaries 1938–45* (ed. D. Dilks, 1971); R. G. Vansittart, *The Mist Procession* (1958); D. E. Kaiser, *Economic Diplomacy and the Origins of the Second World War* (1980); D. Calleo, *The German Problem Reconsidered: Germany and the World Order 1870 to the Present* (1978); G. Niedhart (ed.), *Kriegsbeginn 1939* (1976); M. Baumont, *Les Origines de la Seconde Guerre Mondiale* (1969; English trans. 1976); R. Douglas, *The Advent of War 1939–40* (1978); W. J. Mommsen and L. Kettenbacker (eds.), *The Fascist Challenge and the Policy of Appeasement* (1983).

HITLER, NAZISM, FASCISM, THE AXIS

(i) *Hitler and the Third Reich*

Adolf Hitler, *Mein Kampf* (17th edn 1939), first, abbreviated, English translation: *Mein Kampf* (1933); A. Bullock, *Hitler: A Study in Tyranny* (2nd edn 1965); J. P. Stern, *Hitler: The Führer and the People* (1975); J. F. C. Fest, *Hitler: Eine Biographie* (*1973*), English translation: *Hitler* (1974); N. Stone, *Hitler* (1980); W. Maser, *Adolf Hitler: Legende, Mythos, Wirklichkeit* (1972), English translation: *Hitler* (1973); F. Jetzinger, *Hitlers Jugend* (1956), English translation: *Hitler's Youth* (1958); A. Kubizek, *Adolf Hitler: Mein Jugendfreund* (1953), English translation: *Young Hitler* (1954); K. Heiden, *Hitler: A Biography* (1936); W. A. Jenks, *Vienna and the Young Hitler* (1960); E. Calic, *Ohne Maske* (1968), English translation: *Unmasked* (1971); H. Picker (ed.), *Hitlers Tischgespräche im Führerhauptquartier* (1951); H. Rauschning, *Conversations with Hitler* (1939); M. Domarus, *Hitler: Reden und Proklamationen 1932–45* (1953); H. R. Trevor-Roper, *The Last Days of Hitler* (4th edn 1971), *Hitler's War Directives 1939–45* (ed., 1964), *Hitler's Table Talk 1941–44* (ed., 1953); Maj.-Gen. J. M. Strawson, *Hitler as Military Commander* (1971); P. E. Schramm, *Hitler als militärische Führer* (1965); K. D. Bracher, *Die deutsche Diktatur* (1969), English translation: *The German Dictatorship* (1971); J. F. C. Fest, *Das Gesicht des Dritten Reiches* (1963), English translation: *The Face of the Third Reich* (1970); M. Broszat, *Der Nationalsozialismus* (1960), English translation: *German National Socialism* (1966); W. Shirer, *The Rise and Fall of the Third Reich* (1960); P. Ayçoberry, *La question nazi* (1979), English translation: *The Nazi Question: An Essay on the Interpretation of National Socialism 1922–1975* (1981); W. S. Allen, *The Nazi Seizure of Power: The Experience of a Single German Town 1930–35* (1966); J. Nyomarkay, *Charisma and Functionalism in the Nazi Party* (1967); H. Krausnick (ed.), *Anatomy of the SS State* (1968); G. H. Stein, *The Waffen SS* (1966); A. Speer, *Erinnerungen* (1969), English translation: *Inside the Third Reich* (1970); P. Schmidt, *Statist auf der diplomatischen Bühne* (1951), abbreviated English translation: *Hitler's Interpreter* (1951); H. B. Gisevius, *Bis zum bitteren Ende* (1946), English translation: *To the Bitter End* (1948); N. Rich, *Hitler's War Aims: Ideology, the Nazi State and the Course of Expansion* (1973); R. J. O'Neill, *The German Army and the Nazi Party 1923–39* (1966); Telford Taylor, *The Sword and the Swastika* (1952); F. L. Carsten, *Reichswehr and Politics 1918–1933* (1956); J. S. Conway, *The Nazi Persecution of the Churches 1939–45* (1958).

(ii) *Nazism and Fascism*

B. Moore, *The Social Origins of Dictatorship and Democracy* (1967); J. L. Talmon, *The Origins of Totalitarian Democracy* (1952); H. Arendt, *The Origins of Totalitarianism* (1958); F. Meinecke, *The German Catastrophe* (1950); E. Nolte, *Der Faschismus in seiner Epoche* (1963), English translation: *Three Faces of Fascism* (1965); H. Kohn, *The Mind of Germany* (1961); G. L. Mosse, *The Crisis of German Ideology* (1966), *Nazi Culture* (1966); D. Gasman, *The Scientific Origins of National Socialism* (1971); R. Butler, *The Roots of National Socialism* (1941); P. Gay, *Weimar Culture* (1969); A. J. Nichols, *Weimar and the Rise of Hitler* (1968); F. Neumann, *Behemoth: The Structure and Practice of National Socialism* (1942); B. Granzow, *A Mirror of Nazism* (1964); F. Chabod, *Storia del fascismo italiano* (1960), English translation: *A History of Italian Fascism* (1963); G. Carocci, *Storia del fascismo* (1972), English translation: *Italian Fascism* (1974); C. Seton-Watson, *Italy from Liberalism to Fascism* (1967); D. Mack Smith, *Mussolini* (1981); R. De Felice, *Mussolini il duce: gli anni del consenso* (1974); I. Kirkpatrick, *Mussolini: A Study of a Demagogue* (1964); C. Hibbert, *Benito Mussolini: The Rise and Fall of Il Duce* (1962); G. Ciano, *Diario 1937–43* (ed. R. De Felice, 1980), partial English translations: *Ciano's Diary 1937–38* (1952) and *Ciano's Diary 1939–43* (1947); E. Wiskemann, *Fascism in Italy: Its Development and Influence* (1969), *The Rome–Berlin Axis* (1949); M. Toscano, *Le origini diplomatiche del patto d'acciaio* (2nd edn 1956), English translation: *The Origins of the Pact of Steel* (1967); F. W. Deakin, *The Brutal Friendship: Mussolini, Hitler and the Fall of Italian Fascism* (1962); M. Knox, *Mussolini Unleashed 1939–41* (1982).

THE FRENCH COLLAPSE

M. Bloch, *L'étrange défaite* (1946); A. Beaufre, *Le drame de 1940* (1965), English translation: *1940: The Fall of France* (1967); A. Adamthwaite, *France and the Coming of the Second World War* (1977); G. Chapman, *Why France Fell* (1968); P. Stehlin, *Témoignage pour l'histoire* (1964); G. Warner, *Pierre Laval and the Eclipse of France* (1968); H. Cole, *Laval: A Biography* (1963); C. M. de la Gorce, *La république et son armée* (1963); R. T. Thomas, *British and Vichy: The Dilemma of Anglo-French Relations 1940–42* (1979).

AMERICAN POLICIES

C. C. Tansill, *Back Door to War: The Roosevelt Foreign Policy 1933–41* (1952); D. Drummond, *The Passing of American Neutrality* (1955); W. A. Williams, *The Tragedy of American Diplomacy* (1966); W. L. Langer and S. E. Gleason, *The Challenge to Isolation* (1952), *The Undeclared War* (1953); S. Friedlander, *Prelude to Disaster: Hitler and the United States* (1967); W. S. Cole, *Roosevelt and the Isolationists 1932–45* (1983); C. A. Beard, *President Roosevelt and the Coming of War* (1946); R. Dallek, *Franklin D. Roosevelt and American Foreign Policy 1932–45* (1979); G. C. Smith, *American Diplomacy during World War II* (1965); G. Kolko, *The Politics of War: Allied Diplomacy and the World Crisis of 1943–45* (1969); W. L. Langer, *Our Vichy Gamble* (1966); K. S. Davis, *The American Experience of War* (1970); B. J. Bernstein (ed.), *Towards a New Past* (1968); J. L. Gaddis, *The United States and the Origins of the Cold War 1941–47* (1972); R. A. Divine, *The Reluctant Belligerent: American Entry into World War II* (1965).

RUSSIAN RESISTANCE

N. A. Voznesensky, *The Economy of the USSR in the Period of the Patriotic War* (1948); V. Conolly, *Beyond the Urals* (1967); N. Jasny, *Soviet Industrialization 1928–52* (1961); A. G. Mazour, *Soviet Economic Development* (1968); M. Fainsod, *Smolensk under Soviet Rule* (1959); D. J. Dallin, *Soviet Foreign Policy 1939–42* (1945); E. H. Carr, *German–Soviet Relations between the Two World Wars* (1952); J. Erickson, *The Soviet High Command: A Military–Political History 1918–1941* (1962); R. Kolkowicz, *The Soviet Military and the Communist Party* (1967); A. Dallin, *German Rule in Russia 1941–45* (revd edn 1981); V. M. Mastny, *Russia's Road to the Cold War: Diplomacy, Warfare and the Politics of Communism 1941–45* (1979). And *see under* The Fighting.

GREAT BRITAIN AT WAR

There are numerous excellent volumes in the Civil series of the official History of the Second World War. In addition:

A. Bullock, *The Life and Times of Ernest Bevin*, vol. 2: *Minister of Labour 1940–45* (1967); A. Marwick, *Britain in the Century of Total War* (1968); A. S. Milward, *War, Economy and Society 1939–45* (1977); H. Pelling, *Britain and the Second World War* (1970); A. Calder, *The People's War: Britain 1939–45* (1971); P. Addison, *The Road to 1945: British Politics and the Second World War* (1975); A. J. Youngson, *The British Economy 1920–57* (1960); M. Bruce, *The Coming of the Welfare State* (1968).

THE FIGHTING

The campaigns are covered in detail in the various official histories. In addition:

(i) *General Surveys and Strategy*

B. H. Liddell Hart, *History of the Second World War* (1970); G. Wright, *The Ordeal of Total War 1939–45* (1968); H. Michel, *La seconde guerre mondiale*, 2 vols. (1968–9); S. E. Morison, *American Contributions to the Strategy of World War II* (1958), *Strategy and Compromise* (1968); A. J. Marder, *From the Dardanelles to Oran* (1974); M. Howard, *The Mediterranean in the Second World War* (1968); F. H. Hinsley, *Hitler's Strategy* (1951); K. R. Greenfield, *American Strategy in World War II: A Reconsideration* (1963); A. Bryant (ed.), *The Turn of the Tide* (1957), *Triumph in the West* (1958), extracts with commentary from Lord Alanbrooke's papers; C. Bekker, *The Luftwaffe War Diaries* (1967); General F. Halder, *Kriegstagebüch* (ed. H. A. Jacobsen, 1962–6); General W. Warlimont, *Im Hauptquartier der deutschen Wehrmacht 1939–45* (1962), English translation: *Inside the Führer's Headquarters* (1964).

(ii) *The First Year*

V. Tanner, *The Winter War* (1975, Finland); Maj.-Gen. J. L. Moulton, *The Norwegian Campaign of 1940* (1966); N. Harman, *Dunkirk, the Necessary Myth* (1980); W. Lord, *The Miracle of Dunkirk* (1983); Telford Taylor, *The March of Conquest* (1958), *The Breaking Wave* (1967); H. R. Allen, *Who Won the Battle of Britain?* (1974); R. Wright, *Dowding and the Battle of Britain* (1964); R. Wheatley, *Operation Sea Lion* (1958).

(iii) *The Mediterranean and North Africa*

D. Macintyre, *The Battle for the Mediterranean* (1964); B. Pitt, *The Crucible of War: The Western Desert* (1980); Maj.-Gen. J. M. Strawson, *The Battle for North Africa* (1965), *El Alamein: Desert Victory* (1981); Field-Marshal Lord Carver, *Tobruk* (1964), *El Alamein* (2nd edn 1979); Corelli Barnett, *The Desert Generals* (2nd edn 1983); I. M. G. Stewart, *The Struggle for Crete* (1966).

(iv) *The Atlantic*

P. Beesly, *Very Special Intelligence* (1977); Vice-Admiral Sir P. Gretton, *Convoy Escort Commander* (1964), *Crisis Convoy: The Story of HX231* (1974); Vice-Admiral B. B. Schofield, *The Arctic Convoys* (1977); J. Rohwer, *Geleitzug Schlachten in März 1943* (1975), English translation: *The Critical Convoy Battles of March 1943* (1977).

(v) *The Russian Fronts*

J. Erickson, *Stalin's War with Germany*, vol. 1: *The Road to Stalingrad* (1975), vol. 2: *The Road to Berlin* (1983); Col. A. Seaton, *The Battle for Moscow* (1971), *The Russo-German War* (1971); A. Werth, *Russia at War 1941–45* (1964); D. Irving, *Hitler's War* (1977); S. Bialer (ed.), *Stalin and His Generals: Soviet Military Memoirs of World War II* (1970); A. Clark, *Barbarossa* (1964); H. E. Salisbury, *The Siege of Leningrad* (1969); L. Goure, *The Siege of Leningrad* (1962); G. Jukes, *Kursk: The Clash of Armour* (1968); Marshal V. I. Chuikov, *The Beginning of the Road* (English translation 1963), *The End of the Third Reich* (English translation 1967); J. Thorwald, *Es begann an der Weichsel* and *Das Ende an der Elbe* (combined and abbreviated English translation: *Flight into the Winter*, 1953); F. W. Deakin and R. Storry, *The Case of Richard Sorge* (1966); R. Cecil, *Hitler's Decision to Invade Russia* (1975); B. A. Leach, *German Strategy against Russia 1939–41* (1973); G. C. Herring, *Aid to Russia 1941–46* (1973).

(vi) *Italy*

W. G. F. Jackson, *The War in Italy* (1967); G. A. Shepherd, *The Italian Campaign 1943–45* (1968); Janusz Piekalkiewicz, *Cassino* (1980); R. Trevelyan, *The Fortress: A Diary of Anzio and After* (1956); P. Verney, *Anzio: An Unexpected Fury* (1978); D. W. Orgill, *The Gothic Line* (1967); D. W. Elwood, *Italy 1943–45* (1985).

(vii) *The Last Year*

J. Keegan, *Six Armies in Normandy: From D-day to the Liberation of Paris* (1982); S. Westphal, *The German Army in the West* (1951); Forrest C. Pogue, *The Supreme Command* (1954); R. Lamb, *Montgomery in Europe* (1983); Carlo d'Este, *Decision in Normandy: The Unwritten Story of Montgomery and the Allied Campaign* (1983); C. Bauer, *The Battle of Arnhem* (1966); C. Hibbert, *The Battle of Arnhem* (1962); C. Ryan, *A Bridge Too Far* (1974); Maj.-Gen. J. M. Strawson, *The Battle for the Ardennes* (1972); C. B. McDonagh, *The Battle of the Bulge: The Definitive Account* (1984); H. Essame, *The Battle for Germany* (1969).

(viii) *Bombing and Countermeasures*

A. Verrier, *The Bomber Offensive* (1968); N. Frankland, *The Bombing Offensive against Germany* (1965); H. Rumpf, *The Bombing of Germany* (1963); R. V. Jones, *Most Secret War* (1978); M. Middlebrook, *The Peenemünde Raid* (1982), *The Nuremberg Raid of 30–31 March 1944* (1973); D. Irving, *The Destruction of Dresden* (2nd edn 1966); A. S. Milward, *The German Economy at War* (1965); M. Kaldor, 'The German War Economy' in *Essays in Economic Policy*, vol. 2 (1964); B. Klein, *Germany's Economic Preparations for War* (1959); A. Milward, *The German Economy at War* (1964).

OCCUPATION, COLLABORATION, RESISTANCE, REVOLUTION

A. M. Meerloo, *Total War and the Human Mind* (1944); M. R. D. Foot, *Resistance: An Analysis of European Resistance to Nazism 1940–45* (1976); E. H. Cookridge, *Inside SOE* (1967); Bradley F. Smith, *The Shadow Warriors: OSS and the Origins of the CIA* (1982); David Stafford, *Britain and the European Resistance 1940–45* (1980); P. Auty and R. Clogg (eds.), *British Policy towards the Wartime Resistance in Greece and Yugoslavia* (1975); Werner Rings, *Leben mit dem Feind* (1979), English translation: *Life with the Enemy* (1982); Henri Michel, *La guerre de l'ombre* (1970), English translation: *The Shadow War: Resistance in Europe 1939–45* (1972), *Paris allemand* (1981), *Les courants de la pensée dans la Résistance* (1962); Pierre Lorain, *Armement clandestin: SOE 1941–44 France* (1972), expanded English translation: *Secret Warfare: The Arms and the Techniques of the Resistance* (1984); C. Bellanger, *Presse clandestine 1940–44* (1961); P. Arnoult, *La France sous l'occupation* (1959); J. Kruuse, *Madness at Oradour* (1969); P. Novick, *The Resistance versus Vichy: The Purge of Collaborators in Liberated France* (1968); H. R. Lottmann, *The People's Anger: Justice and Revenge in Post-Liberation France* (1986); W. Warmbrunn, *The Dutch under German Occupation* (1963); W. B. Maass, *The Netherlands at War 1940–45* (1970); T. Bor-Komorowski, *The Secret Army* (1950); J. Gorlinski, *Poland, SOE and the Allies* (1969); V. M. Mastny, *The Czechs under Nazi Rule* (1971); Tore Gjelsvik, *Hjemmefronten* (1977), English translation: *Norwegian Resistance 1940–45* (1979); J. O. Thomas, *The Giant Killers: The Story of the Danish Resistance Movement 1940–45* (1975); J. Bennett, *British Broadcasting and the Danish Resistance Movement 1940–45* (1966); J. K. M. Hanson, *The Civilian Population and the Warsaw Uprising of 1944* (1982); Mark C. Wheeler, *Britain and the War for Yugoslavia* (1980); Jozo Tomasevich, *War and Revolution in Yugoslavia 1941–45* (1975); V. Dedijer, *Tito Speaks* (1953); E. W. Deakin, *The Embattled Mountain* (1971); C. F. Delzell, *Mussolini's Enemies: The Anti-Fascist Resistance* (1961); Roberto Battaglia, *Storia della Resistenza Italiana* (1953), abbreviated English translation: *The Story of the Italian Resistance* (1957); G. Bocca, *Storia dell'Italia partigiana* (1964); C. Amè, *La guerra segreta in Italia 1940–43* (1954); E. Schramm von Thadden, *Griechenland und die Grossmachte im zweiten Weltkrieg* (1955); C. M. Woodhouse, *Apple of Discord* (1948); D. G. Kousoulas, *Revolution and Defeat* (1965); D. Eudes, *Les Kapetianos* (1970), English translation: *The Kapetianos: Partisans and Civil War in Greece 1943–49* (1972); J. C. Loulis, *The Greek Communist Party* (1982); N. Hammond, *Venture into Greece: With the Guerrillas 1943–44* (1983); E. C. W. Myers, *Greek Entanglement* (1955); A. Dallin, *German Rule in Russia 1941–45* (revd edn 1981); J. A. Armstrong (ed.), *Soviet Partisans in World War II* (1964); A. Oras, *Baltic Eclipse* (1948); C. G. Cruickshank, *The German Occupation of the Channel Islands* (1975); A. Roberts (ed.), *The Strategy of Civilian Defence* (1967). Also the periodicals *Revue d'histoire de la deuxième guerre mondiale* and *Esprit de la Résistance*; *European Resistance Movements, 1939–45* (proceedings of the International Conferences on the History of the Resistance, Milan 1961 and Oxford 1962).

ANTI-NAZI GERMANS

H. Rothfels, *Die deutsche Opposition gegen Hitler* (1958), English translation: *The Secret Opposition to Hitler* (1962); C. Sykes, *Troubled Loyalty* (1968); G. Ritter, *Carl Goerdeler und die deutsche Widerstandsbewegung* (1954), English translation: *The German Resistance* (1958); F. von Schlabrendorff, *The Secret War against Hitler* (1966); W. Hoettl, *The Secret Front* (1954); M. Mourin, *Les complots contre Hitler* (1948); H. Höhne, *Canaris* (1976), English translation: *Canaris* (1979); T. Prittie, *Germans against Hitler* (1964); G. C. Zahn, *German Catholics and Hitler's War* (1963), *In Solitary Witness* (1964); G. Lewy, *The Catholic Church and Nazi Germany* (1964); A. Leber, *Das Gewissen steht auf* (1954); E. Kordt, *Nicht aus den Akten* (1950); V. von Hassell, *Vom anderen Deutschland: aus den nachgelassenen Tagebüchern 1938–44* (1946), abbreviated English translation: *The von Hassell Diaries 1938–44* (1948).

PSYCHOLOGICAL WARFARE, PROPAGANDA

E. K. Bramstedt, *Goebbels and National Socialist Propaganda 1925–45* (1965); Z. A. B. Zeman, *Nazi Propaganda* (1964), *Selling the War: Art and Propaganda in World War II* (1978); L. Fraser, *Propaganda* (1957); M. Mégret, *La guerre psychologique* (1963); D. Lerner (ed.), *Sykewar: Psychological War against Germany* (1949).

ANTI-SEMITISM, THE CAMPS, THE HOLOCAUST

M. A. Meyer, *The Origins of the Modern Jew* (1967); Gerald Fleming, *Hitler und die Endlösung* (1982); G. Reitlinger, *The Final Solution* (1953); N. Cohn, *Warrant for Genocide* (1967); L. Poliakoff, *Harvest of Hate* (1956); Reuben Ainsztein, *Jewish Resistance in Nazi-Occupied Eastern Europe* (1974); Lucy S. Davidowicz, *The War against the Jews 1933–45* (1975); Yisrael Gutman, *The Jews of Warsaw*

1939–43: Ghetto, Underground and Revolt (English translation from Hebrew, 1983); D. S. Wyman, *The Abandonment of the Jews: America and the Holocaust 1941–1945* (1984); Martin Gilbert, *Auschwitz and the Allies* (1981); A. D. Morse, *Why Six Million Died* (1968); S. Friedländer, *Pius XII and the Third Reich* (1968); P. E. Lapide, *The Last Three Popes and the Jews* (1967); C. Falconi, *The Silence of Pius XII* (1970); B. Wasserstein, *Britain and the Jews of Europe* (1975). Also: the series of Records and Documents of the Holy See relating to the Second World War in the course of publication.

AT THE TOP

H. Feis, *Churchill, Roosevelt and Stalin: The War They Waged and the Peace They Sought* (1967); W. H. MacNeill, *America, Britain and Russia: Their Co-operation and Conflict 1941–46* (1963); D. S. Clemens, *Yalta* (1971); A. Theoharis, *The Yalta Myths* (1971); J. M. Burns, *Roosevelt, the Soldier of Fortune 1940–45* (1971); R. A. Divine, *Roosevelt and World War II* (1970); R. Sherwood (ed.), *The White House Papers of Harry Hopkins* (1948); H. L. Stimson and McGeorge Bundy, *On Active Service in Peace and War* (1947); C. Hull, *The Memoirs of Cordell Hull* (1948); A. B. Ulam, *Stalin, the Man and His Era* (1973); Guy Hentsch, *Stalin négociateur: une diplomatie de guerre* (1967); Martin Gilbert, *Winston S. Churchill* (1979); E. Barker, *Churchill and Eden at War* (1978); C. de Gaulle, *Mémoires de guerre*, vol. 1: *1940–42*, vol. 2: *1942–44*, vol. 3: *1944–46* (1954–59), English translation: *War Memoirs* (1955–60); Stephen E. Ambrose, *Eisenhower: Soldier, General of the Army, President-Elect 1890–1952* (1984); N. Hamilton, *Monty*, vol. 1: *The Making of a General 1887–1942* (1981), vol. 2: *Master of the Battlefield 1943–44* (1983); R. Lewin, *The Chief: Field Marshal Lord Wavell, Commander-in-Chief and Viceroy 1939–47* (1980); K. Sainsbury, *The Turning Point: Roosevelt, Stalin and Churchill 1943* (1985); E. Barker, *British Policy in South-East Europe in the Second World War* (1976); F. Kersaudy, *Churchill and de Gaulle* (1981); M. Kitchen, *British Policy towards the Soviet Union during the Second World War* (1986); A. M. de Zayas, *Nemesis at Potsdam: The Anglo-Americans and the Expulsion of the Germans* (1979).

ON THE FRINGES

Urs Schwarz, *The Eye of the Hurricane: Switzerland in World War II* (1980); F. G. Weber, *The Evasive Neutral: Germany, Britain and the Quest for a Turkish Alliance* (1979); R. A. Humphreys, *Latin America in the Second World War*, vol. 1: *1939–42* (1981), vol. 2: *1942–45* (1982); C. Falconi, *Il silenzio di Pio XII* (1965), English translation: *The Silence of Pius XII* (1970); S. Friedländer, *Pius XII and the Third Reich* (1966); Geoffrey Warner, *Syria and Iraq 1941* (1974); Jean Stengers, *Léopold III et le gouvernement: les deux politiques belges de 1940* (1980); D. G. Anglin, *The St Pierre and Miquelon Affair of 1941* (1966).

ULTRA INTELLIGENCE

Peter Calvocoressi, *Top Secret Ultra* (1980); Patrick Beesly, *Very Special Intelligence: The Story of the Admiralty's Operational Intelligence Centre 1939–1945* (1977); J. Garlinski, *Intercept: The Enigma War* (1979); Gordon Welchman, *The Hut 6 Story* (1982); Ralph Bennett, *Ultra in the West* (1979); Aileen Clayton, *The Enemy is Listening: The Story of the Y Service* (1980); Andrew P. Hodges, *Alan Turing: The Enigma* (1983).

DECEPTION

C. G. Cruickshank, *Deception in World War II* (1979); David Mure, *Master of Deception* (1980); J. C. Masterman, *The Double-Cross System* (1971); E. Howe, *The Black Game* (1982).

NUREMBERG

Bradley F. Smith, *The Road to Nuremberg* (1980), *Reaching Judgement at Nuremberg* (1977); Anne and John Tusa, *The Nuremberg Trial* (1984); Robert E. Conot, *Justice at Nuremberg* (1983); Werner Maser, *Nuremberg: Tribunal der Sieger* (1977), English translation: *A Nation on Trial* (1979); Peter Calvocoressi, *Nuremberg: The Facts, the Law and the Consequences* (1947).

PERSONAL ANGLES

Christabel Bielenberg, *The Past is Myself* (1968); Ninetta Jucker, *Curfew in Paris* (1960); Gustav Herling, *A World Apart* (English translation from Polish 1951); Christopher Burney, *Solitary Confinement* (2nd edn 1984); Primo Levi, *La tregua* (1963), English translation: *The Truce* (1963), *The Periodic Table* (1984); Norman Lewis, *Naples '44* (1978); Curzio Malaparte, *La pelle* (1950), English translation: *The Skin* (1952); Goronwy Rees, *A Bundle of Sensations* (1960); M. Picard, *Hitler in uns selbst* (1946); S. Terkel, *'The Good War': An Oral History of World War II* (1984); E. Newby, *Life and War in the Apennines* (1983).

LIMITS OF GERMAN, JAPANESE AND ITALIAN
DOMINANCE 1934 - 1944

~ARTHUR BANKS~

WORLD POWER 1949

U S S R

I. MONGOLIA

TIBET

CHINA
(Communist)

INDIA

Singapore

Philippine
Is

INDONESIA

Hong Kong

TAIWAN (Nationalist)

JAPAN

Tokyo

Aleutian Is

ALASKA

C A

Pacific

Midway I

Hawaiian Is

Marshall Is

Caroline Is
NEW GUINEA

Ocean

Indian
Ocean

AUSTRALIA

Sydney

NEW ZEALAND

USA and allies (NATO and Japan).	
USSR and dependencies.	

~ARTHUR BANKS~

INDEX:
The Western Hemisphere

Battle of Britain 157, 516, 517; Battle of Atlantic 468, 478; Mediterranean war 178, 314, 375, 379, 382, 390, 391; North European war 548, 550, 557, 561
Umberto II of Italy, King: accession 408
United Nations 369, 575
United States of America, *see also* Roosevelt; inter-war period 5, 43, 45–7, 63, 102, 209–11; pre-war attitude to China 211–12; pre-war attitude to Germany 49, 61, 66, 76, 209–11, 213, 224–5; pre-war attitude to Japan 211–12, 225; neutrality 76, 206–9, 212, 216–21, 223–4, 582–3; French affairs 216, 328, 336–7; aid to Britain 219–21, 447–9, 462–3, 584; aid to Russia 221, 354, 475–6, 584; aid to Resistance 298–9, 307–8, 310, 315, 340–41; war on Germany 159–60, 206, 224–9, 351; Jewish refugees 260; Middle East 183; relations with allies 351, 354–5; war with Japan 113, 204–5, 224; North Africa 357, 372, 385–9, 393–5; Italy 396–7, 399, 400, 533–4; Op. Anvil 328, 357–8, 536; Polish question 504–7; policies for Latin America 213–15; economy 447–9, 462, 523, 584–7; war crime trials 572–3; casualties 578; post-war stance 9, 368–70, 578, 580, 582–9
United States Air Force (USAF) 160, 514; bombing of Germany 520–22, 526; North Africa 382; Italy 533, 535; Polish operations 506; invasion and after 539; losses in Europe 517
United States Army: strengths 356; Torch 385–6, 389–91; Italy 397; Overlord and After 367–8, 538–2 *passim*, 541, 562, 563–6
United States Navy (USN): destroyers supplied 219, 465, 470; Atlantic force 221, 223–4, 228, 356, 467–8; convoy system 221, 223, 224, 463, 466; Pacific commitment 477; Pearl Harbor 205

V weapons: development 453, 542, 556–9; on Britain 433, 441, 559–60
Vandenburg resolution 589
Vansittart, Lord: plan for Franco-British union 141
Vatican *see* Roman Catholic Church
Vatutin, Marshal: command of Front 501
Vemork attacks 293

Venizelos, Eleutherios: pre-war diplomacy 170; land distribution 307; succeeded by Papandreou 310
Vercors battle 342
Vercors (Jean Bruller): *Le silence de la mer* 285
Versailles, Treaty of (1919): German limitations xxv, 147; abandonment xxvi, 52, 68, 69, 72, 74, 93, 148
Vichy: in France 267–9, 317, 320–33, 338–40; Jewish purge 253, 255, 324; in Africa 143, 335–6, 387, 389, 392; Middle East 172, 179, 182–3, 335; St Pierre et Miquelon 336–7
Victor Emmanuel of Italy, King: indifference to Fascism 38, 405; dismisses Mussolini 399–400; flight and abdication 401, 404, 406, 407–8
Victorious, HMS: *Bismarck* action 222
Vienna 18–19
Vienna Awards (1938; 40) 91, 168, 271
Vietinghoff, Gen.: Western Front command 561
Vittorio Veneto: at Matapan 172
Vlasov, Gen. A. A.: ROA leader 489, 491, 492
Volk concept 30–31
Volkdeutsche policy 240–42, 305, 489
Volksstrum 523, 560
Voroshilov, Marshal K. E.: pre-war Polish question 98; replaced by Timoshenko 189; German invasion 197, 198
Voznesenski, N. A.: on allied aid 476; on Stalin's direction of labour 484

Wafd 373, 374
Wannsee conference 251–2
War crimes *see under* Germany
Warsaw: consigned to Germany 99; in New Order 240, 250–51; bombing 150; rising 369, 491, 504–7
Watson-Watt, Robert: development of radar 153
Wavell, F.-M. Sir Archibald: North African campaign 171–2, 184, 373, 375; help for Greece 172, 174, 178; concern for India 349; Viceroy of India 381
Welles, Sumner: European mission 216, 570
Wellington aircraft 515
Werewolves 560
West Wall 114